I0867413

This is the first comprehensive study of Gerhard Scharnhorst in any language. Other than the author's *The Enlightened Soldier: Scharnhorst and the Militärische Gesellschaft in Berlin, 1801-1805* (1989), there exists no other work on Scharnhorst in English. Of the major German works, *Das Leben des Generals von Scharnhorst* (1869/71), written by Hanoverian historian Georg Heinrich Klippel, was a popular biography with no critical analysis. In keeping with the political correctness of his time, Klippel failed to include a single document from Scharnhorst's voluminous papers that was disparaging toward the social, political, and military cultures in Hanover. Seventeen years later, Prussian historian Max Lehmann published his study of *Scharnhorst* (1886/87), which corrected many of the flaws in Klippel's work, but failed to provide any critical analysis of Scharnhorst's modernisation, especially as it applied to Prussia. Like Klippel, Lehmann complied with the political correctness of his time in Prussia and Germany. Rudolf Stadelmann, *Scharnhorst: Schicksal und Geistige Welt* (1952), is an incomplete fragment that offers some interesting insights.

Scharnhorst: The Formative Years uses the previous German studies as a starting point to present many unpublished discoveries about his youth, his education and training, his extensive service in Hanover, and the modernisation program Scharnhorst sought to implement in Hanover, and later realised in part in Prussia.

A follow-up volume, detailing Scharnhorst's career in Prussian service, is in preparation.

Dr Charles E. White was a historian with the United States Army for 33 years. After leaving active military duty and earning his doctorate in history from Duke University, he served as the Chief of Military History at the United States Army Infantry School, Fort Benning, Georgia; then as the Command Historian for the 21st Theater Army Area Command in Germany. Following those assignments, Dr White served as the Army's Lewis and Clark Historian during the national bicentennial commemoration of that expedition. Before retiring, he was the Command Historian for the United States Army Forces Command, Fort Bragg, North Carolina. He is the author of *The Enlightened Soldier: Scharnhorst and the Militärische Gesellschaft in Berlin, 1801-1806* (1989), *The US Army and the Lewis and Clark Expedition* (2002), as well as articles and papers on American and German military history.

Scharnhorst

The Formative Years 1755-1801

Charles Edward White

Helion & Company

For my lovely wife Mary, and our beautiful children
Catherine, Joseph, Rebecca, and Robert,
our daughter-in-law Naomi, and precious grandsons Valerius and Tiberius

Helion & Company Limited
Unit 8 Amherst Business Centre
Budbrooke Road
Warwick
CV34 5WE
England
Tel. 01926 499619
Email: info@helion.co.uk
Website: www.helion.co.uk
Twitter: @helionbooks
blog.helion.co.uk

Published by Helion & Company 2020
Designed and typeset by Mach 3 Solutions Ltd (www.mach3solutions.co.uk)
Cover designed by Paul Hewitt, Battlefield Design (www.battlefield-design.co.uk)

Cover: Portrait of General Gerhard Johann David von Scharnhorst, circle of Friedrich Bury c.1810. (Public Domain)

ISBN 978-1-913118-99-0

British Library Cataloguing-in-Publication Data.
A catalogue record for this book is available from the British Library.

For details of other military history titles published by Helion & Company Limited, contact the above address, or visit our website: http://www.helion.co.uk

We always welcome receiving book proposals from prospective authors.

Contents

List of Maps

Preface

Thirty years have passed since the publication of *The Enlightened Soldier: Scharnhorst and the Militärische Gesellschaft in Berlin, 1801-1805* (1989). That study focused primarily on Scharnhorst's pivotal role as the intellectual father and educator of the Prussian army, whose amazing recovery following its catastrophic defeat in 1806 remains one of the most remarkable feats in military history.

Following the publication of *The Enlightened Soldier,* I embarked on the research and writing of this book. So much is known about Scharnhorst and his activities in Prussian service. So little is known or has been written about his formative years in Hanover, where he carefully crafted and endeavoured to implement the modernization program he later realized in part in Prussia. This point is significant. When Scharnhorst arrived in Berlin in 1801, he already had his master plan in mind and continually looked for ways to bring the Prussian army and its leadership in step with the transformation of war shaped by the wars of the French Revolution and Napoleon.

This study of Scharnhorst presents unpublished discoveries about his youth, his education, and his extensive time in Hanoverian service. Scholarship in the field of German history during the late 18th and early 19th Centuries has increased dramatically over the past 30 years; the most significant for this study was the publication of Scharnhorst's Papers [*Nachlaβ Scharnhorst*] in eight massive volumes, with over 3,000 documents. These papers formed the foundation upon which I built my story of this enlightened soldier. I used primarily the first two volumes that deal with his long career in Hanover. Selected documents from other volumes are also included.

With the Internet came access to so many key sources that I might not otherwise have been able to obtain and research. Nearly all the rare books and journals I had studied in Germany in the early 1980s are now available on the worldwide web, especially the irreplaceable journals of the University of Bielefeld digital collection. Through the Internet I was also able to connect with other scholars who led me to addition resources and websites.

Over the past 30 years I have received considerable assistance and encouragement in the research and writing of this book. I would especially like to thank Dr Stephen Summerfield, Oliver Schmidt, and Paul Demet for sending me links to many valuable sources used in this study. Likewise, Sylvia Rose assisted with her knowledge of documents housed in the Geheimes Staatsarchiv Preuβischer Kulturbesitz. The wonderful ladies at the John L. Throckmorton Library on Fort Bragg, North Carolina, graciously obtained for me many key works through inter-library loan. My heartfelt thanks to all the delightful people and institutions who assisted my research.

I have many colleagues and friends to whom I am so grateful. At the Consortium on the Revolutionary Era, 1750-1850, I met many of the leading scholars in the field. They include: Professors of History Michael M. Leggiere, Frederick C. Schneid, Lee W. Eysturlid, Llewellyn Cook, and Alexander Mikaberidze, as well as independent scholars Colonel John Gill and Peter Hofschröer. The Consortium has provided a wonderful platform for the exchange of ideas. Some of my colleagues from the Consortium have provided critical commentary on portions of this book, making vital suggestions for its improvement.

Additionally, a number of colleagues and friends from the United States Army historical community have also provided encouragement and guidance throughout my many years in public service. Fellow Duke University alumni Doctor David W. Hogan, Jr. never failed to ask, 'How is Scharnhorst doing?' whenever we met at various Army historical functions. Doctor Arthur Coumbe, Jeffrey W. Miller, Russell Rodgers, and Robert Seals also shared their time and insights on Scharnhorst and how current he is to the military. My thanks to the Army historians who helped shape this study of Gerhard Scharnhorst.

I would be remiss if I failed to thank two wonderful friends and colleagues: Bruce Gudmundsson from the United States Marine Corps University, and retired Army officer, former student, and independent scholar Donald Vandergriff. For the past 30 years, ever since the publication of *The Enlightened Soldier*, both have endeavoured to educate Marines and soldiers using the sound methods of Gerhard Scharnhorst. Bruce recently published a wonderful article on the impact of my first book on the Marine Corps, entitled, 'The Education of the Enlightened Soldier,' *Marine Corps University Journal* 9:1 (Spring 2018), pp.33-44. I am grateful for their steadfast encouragement and friendship.

A special debt goes to Professor of History Dennis Showalter of the Colorado College for his enthusiastic support for this project for nearly 40 years. We first met in 1980 at the Militärgeschichtliche Forschungsamt, then located in Freiburg am Breisgau. Since then Professor Showalter has been a wonderful mentor and friend. After reading Chapter 2, he encouraged me to publish it. Following some revision, major portions of Chapters 2 and 3 first appeared as 'Scharnhorst's Mentor: Count Wilhelm zu Schaumburg-Lippe and the Origins of the Modern National Army,' *War in History* 24:3 (July 2017), pp.258-85. Professor Showalter then advised me to publish Scharnhorst's thoughts on the General Staff, which I had originally drafted in 2003. They are scheduled to appear as 'Setting the Record Straight: Scharnhorst and the Origins of the Nineteenth-Century Prussia General Staff,' *War in History* (forthcoming). The contents of both articles are used in this work with the kind permission of SAGE Publishing. I would also like to thank Professor Showalter for reading the entire manuscript and graciously providing his valuable commentary for improvement.

My deepest thanks go to my wife of over 30 years – Mary Lynne, and our four lovely children – Catherine, Joseph, Rebecca, and Robert. They represent all that family should be. They encouraged me to write this book and supported me wholeheartedly throughout its development, offering sound advice and encouragement without stint. Joseph also provided some critical commentary on several chapters. What merits this book may possess are due in large part to their love. May it represent some small measure of my heartfelt gratitude to them. Only the errors are my sole responsibility.

Finally, I would like to thank Andrew Bamford, the series editor, whose patience, guidance, and support brought this book to publication.

Note on Translations

Unless otherwise stated, all translations in this book are my own. They are derived from the context of Scharnhorst's writings, from 18th and 19th century German, French, and English dictionaries, and from other contemporary texts, in order to obtain the most accurate understanding of the author's intent. One of the challenges of 18th-century German is the variety of vocabularies and dialects then in use. German words and phrases often do not translate exactly into modern English. Moreover, 18th-century German spelling and punctuation were far from regular or consistent. For clarity I have sometimes modernised the spelling and punctuation Scharnhorst used in his writings. Scharnhorst's own spelling and grammar remained constant challenges throughout his life. Any revisions I made always maintained the original meaning Scharnhorst sought to convey to his reader. Oliver Schmidt and Hans-Karl Weiss from the Napoleon Series Forum offered their assistance with the translation of some archaic and difficult German terms and phrases. I am most grateful and thankful to them.

Introduction

Scharnhorst regarded the process of *Bildung* as central to the professional growth of the military leader. A fruit of Germany's classical age, *Bildung* was the perfectibility of the individual's character and intellect through the process of education and training. It was rooted in the 16th Century, when Martin Luther used the term *Bild* (meaning 'image') to describe how the devout Christian continually seeks to cultivate his God-given talents and abilities according to the image and likeness of the Eternal God. In keeping with this scriptural foundation, *Bildung* implied a well-balanced relationship between mind, body, and soul.[1]

Originally, *Bildung* had a strictly religious character. Over the next two centuries after Luther, German intellectuals secularised it without losing its original meaning of formation.[2] By the middle of the 18th Century, *Bildung* was fundamental not only to the progress of the individual, but to the perfection of society as well. It had become 'an important attribute of social repute' and 'the battle cry of rising intellectual and artistic elites struggling for social recognition'.[3] For Scharnhorst, *Bildung* was the mental fitness that empowered the military leader. It enabled him to assimilate knowledge from a variety of sources and then to synthesise and fashion that data into an appropriate response to the challenge at hand. It was a recurrent process rather than mere training to accomplish a certain skill.

To achieve this perfectibility of man, German *philosophes* turned to the study of man in classical antiquity [*Alterstumwissenschaft*] as their guide for the contemporary world. They respected the Greeks and Romans for their 'world view' [*Weltanschauung*], their tranquil yet intrepid nature, and especially their consummate and progressive concept of knowledge and learning.[4] German 'intellectuals' [*Aufklärer*] believed that both the physical

1 There is no exact equivalent of *Bildung* in English. It refers to a lifelong process of human spiritual and cultural development. Thus, education, training, formation, structure, culture, self-cultivation, and growth are all part of it. Matthew Levinger, *Enlightened Nationalism: The Transformation of Prussian Political Culture, 1806-1848* (Oxford: Oxford University Press, 2000), p.xiv, offers one of the better descriptions of *Bildung*.

2 See '*Bildung* and the Inborn Drive toward Perfection', Chapter Two of Peter Watson, *The German Genius: Europe's Third Renaissance, the Second Scientific Revolution, and the Twentieth Century* (New York: Harper Perennial, 2010), pp.65-88. Of some interest is Ute Frevert, 'Die bürgerlichen Meisterdenker und das Geschlechterverhältnis: Konzepte, Erfahrungen, Visionen an der Wende vom 18. zum 19. Jahrhuntert', in Ute Frevert (ed.), *Bürgerinnen und Bürger* (Göttingen: Vandenhoeck & Ruprecht, 1988), pp.17-48.

3 Hans Rosenberg, *Bureaucracy, Aristocracy, and Autocracy: The Prussian Experience, 1660-1815* (Boston: Beacon Press, 1968), pp.182-88; the quoted passages are from p.182. Also see Peter Lundgreen, 'Bildung und Bürgertum', *Sozial-und Kulturgeschichte des Bürgertums* (Göttingen: Vandenhoeck & Ruprecht, 2000), pp.173-94.

4 Eliza Marian Butler analyses this in her classic study, *The Tyranny of Greece Over Germany: A Study of the Influence Exercised by Greek Art and Poetry over the Great German Writers of the Eighteenth, Nineteenth and Twentieth Centuries* (Cambridge: Cambridge University Press, 1935).

and spiritual realms were characterized by constant change. Understanding earlier times enabled the enlightened person to deal with the present. Scharnhorst agreed wholly with this function of history. Studying the past, especially military history, was for him fundamental for the intellectual growth of the military leader. History would provide the soldier with the vicarious combat experience he could not obtain in peacetime, an understanding that would prepare him for success in war.

Among the first German *Aufklärer* to express this progressive notion of history was Gotthold Ephraim Lessing (1729-81), a critic, dramatist, and philosopher. Lessing wanted to develop in the German people a sense of reflection and critical analysis that would hone their world view. He felt German literature was in a deplorable state. Like Immanuel Kant (1724-1804), Moses Mendelssohn (1729-86), and Johann Gottfried von Herder (1744-1803), Lessing endeavoured to teach the German people how to think critically and objectively. The thoughts of these thinkers (especially their emotional appeal) echo throughout the writings of Scharnhorst, as he sought to educate his fellow soldiers in the art of war.

Lessing's *Letters Concerning the Latest Literature* (1759-65) are splendid examples of this enlightened approach to *Bildung* and its importance to literary criticism.[5] Significantly, he wrote these *Letters* in response to the wishes of a Prussian officer recovering from wounds he had received during the Battle of Zorndorf (1758). This 'deserving officer, and at the same time a man of taste and learning', wanted a German publication that would keep him abreast of the latest developments in the world of literature.[6] Another German critic, friend, and founder of the famous *Nicolaische Buchhandlung* in Berlin, Christoph Friedrich Nicolai (1733-1811), along with Moses Mendelssohn, collaborated with Lessing in this literary endeavour.

Lessing set the tone with his dialogical approach to literary criticism. His *Letters* inspired men such as theologian, mathematician, and writer Thomas Abbt (1738-66), who continued in Lessing's footsteps as writer and editor of *Letters* upon the latter's departure in 1765. Herder also acknowledged the noteworthy influence of Lessing's *Letters* on his own *Bildung*, stating that Lessing was both 'Creator and Father', while his lively and stimulating *Letters* ushered in a new era of German literary criticism – in marked contrast to the 'lack of passion and exuberance' that had heretofore plagued German letters.[7]

Like so many of his German colleagues, Lessing was constantly annoyed and offended by the French tendency of stereotyping Germans as 'backward'. Writing from Göttingen for the *Berlin Privileged Newspaper*, Lessing was fed-up with arrogant French writers always characterising Germans as either 'drunks' or 'empty-headed pedants'.[8]

5 Gotthold Ephraim Lessing, *Briefe, die Neueste Literatur betreffend* (Berlin: Friedrich Nicolai, 1759-65).

6 See Lessing, 'Einleitung' (1759); in Lessing, *Briefe*, p.3.

7 For Herder's perceptive commentary on Lessing's life, see 'Gotthold Ephraim Lessing', in Berhard Suphan (ed.), *Herders Sämmtliche Werke* (Berlin: Weidmann, 1877-1913), Vol.15, pp.486-512. The influence of Lessing's *Briefe* on German *Aufklärer* can be found in Vol.15, pp.494-96; the quoted passages are from Vol.15, pp.494 and 495, respectively.

8 Lessing's piece for the *Berlinische Privilegierte Zeitung* (25 September 1751) can be found in Lachmann and Muncker (eds), *Lessings Sämtliche Schriften* (Leipzig: G. J. Göschen'sche Verlagshandlung, 1886-1924), Vol.4, pp.358-59; the quoted passages are from p.359.

> Can't a couple of French wits have an argument without letting it slip at least once or twice that Germans lack wit and taste? Do we always accuse them of lacking sound and sober understanding [*gesunden und gesetzten Verstande*]?[9]

In his first play, *The Young Scholar* (1747), Lessing addressed this issue to his fellow Germans. This comedy featured the main character, a young scholar named Damis, ridiculed for preferring the 'dead society' of books to a life of lust and pleasure. At the end of the play, Damis decides to leave Germany for enlightenment elsewhere, since only 'rudeness and stupidity' [*Grobheit und Dummheit*] rein in the Fatherland. The necessity of leaving Germany and travelling abroad for the social polish required of an educated person clearly disgusted Lessing. He concluded his play by having Damis castigate his fellow Germans for not nurturing their minds to think for themselves.[10]

According to Herder, Lessing spent virtually his entire life 'with eyes for the truth'. Herder believed Lessing finally found the truth, expressing it in his most celebrated and influential study, *The Education of the Human Race* (1780).[11] In *The Education of the Human Race*, Lessing maintained religion and education are inseparable, and only *Bildung* can integrate the spiritual and physical natures of man. Religion is the divine formation of humanity throughout history, since God is love, and love is patience over time. Accordingly, God directs the perfectibility of man through the process of *Bildung*. In time, and through empirical discovery, Divine Providence informs the individual's will in an orderly and coherent fashion, teaching the individual how to reason for himself.[12] Scharnhorst would later acknowledge Lessing's approach in his defence of *Bildung* for the military.

In sharp contrast to French critics of this philosophy (especially the importance of religion), Johann Heinrich Gottlob von Justi (1717-1771) agreed wholeheartedly with Lessing. One of the leading German political economists of the 18th Century, Justi wrote that 'Divine Revelation in no way limits human reason'.[13] For Justi, *Bildung* was essential for the formation of morally mature and reasoning adults, whether accomplished individually or in a community setting. In this context Justi believed Lessing gave the concept of *Bildung* a genuine historical and religious sense. Significantly, this confident belief on the benefits of religion was one of the distinguishing characteristics of the German Enlightenment. Even though Kant, Mendelssohn, and others worried that religious authorities might try to squash individual freedom of thought and constructive criticism, German intellectuals

9 Lessing's piece for the *Berlinische Privilegierte Zeitung* (3 August 1754) can be found in Lachmann and Muncker (eds), *Lessings Sämtliche Schriften.*, Vol.5, pp.421-22; the quoted passage is from p.422.

10 Gotthold Ephraim Lessing, *Der junge Gelehrte: Ein Lustspiel in drey Aufzügen*; in Lachmann and Muncker (eds), *Lessings Sämtliche Schriften*, Vol.1, pp.279-372; the quoted passages are from pp.292 and 369, respectively.

11 Herder, 'Gotthold Ephraim Lessing', Vol.15, pp.486-512; the quoted passage is from p.510.

12 Gotthold Ephraim Lessing, *Die Erziehung des Menschengeschlects*; in Lachmann and Muncker (eds), *Lessings Sämtliche Schriften* Vol.13, pp.414-36. For a good English translation, see Gotthold Ephraim Lessing (trans. F.W. Robertson), *The Education of the Human Race* (London: Anthroposophical Publishing Company, 1927). A recent English edition is H.B. Nisbet (trans. and ed.), *Lessing: Philosophical and Theological Writings* (Cambridge: Cambridge University Press, 2005). Chapter 17, pp.217-40, contains his study on *The Education of the Human Race.*

13 See Johann Heinrich Gottlob von Justi, 'Ueber die von den Deisten vorgegebene Unnötigkeit der christlichen Offenbarungslehre', *Hessische Beiträge zur Gelehrsamkeit und Kunst* 2/1 (1785), pp.5-11; the quoted passage is from p.11.

were never as anti-religious, especially anti-Christian, as were their French counterparts. In Germany, 'enlightenment and piety went hand in hand'.[14]

In his essay, 'On the Question: What is Enlightenment?' Mendelssohn continued this trend. He defined 'enlightenment' [*Aufklärung*] as 'culture' [*Kultur*] and 'formation' [*Bildung*] working harmoniously together to achieve 'the destiny of man' [*Bestimmung des Menschen*].[15] Along with Kant and Herder, Mendelssohn viewed *Bildung* as the means of breaking the fetters of dogma, formulas, and the simplistic answers religious and state authorities provided. He felt that through *Bildung* the individual could throw off the yoke of immaturity and be recognised as a thinking adult. Scharnhorst clearly approved of this supreme importance of the individual and his ability to think freely for himself. Indeed, it formed the very foundation of German classical humanism and Scharnhorst's approach to life. Each individual would mature through training and education. Each personality would develop through the harmonious cultivation of all its potential.[16] All of this was predicated upon a free society which would continuously evolve for the better.

Another renown thinker, Johann Gottfried von Herder (1744-1803) took the concept of *Bildung* to its logical conclusion. Herder viewed *Bildung* as central to the formation of a free society. *Bildung* was the means the German *Volk* (a classless, egalitarian society) could liberate themselves from their oppressive political and cultural structures. Like Lessing and Kant, Herder was troubled by the cultural backwardness of the German people, caused mainly by the particularism of Germany's petty princes, who purposely kept their subjects illiterate. He argued that every person has the natural capacity for 'self-realisation' [*Bildung*], and that it was the obligation of the prince to create an environment in which his people could fulfil their destinies.[17] The key was the appropriate use of language and literature.[18] Like Lessing, Herder was convinced that a German language and a German literature (instead of French) were fundamental to a German culture, and would eventually lead to the development of 'a national self-consciousness and emancipation'.[19] Those imbued

14 Joachim Whaley, 'The Protestant Enlightenment in Germany', in Roy Porter and Mikulas Teich (eds), *The Enlightenment in the National Context* (Cambridge: Cambridge University Press, 1981), pp.106-17; the quoted passage is from p.112. Also see Klaus Epstein, *The Genesis of German Conservatism* (Princeton: Princeton University Press, 1955), especially Chapter 3, pp.112-75.

15 See Moses Mendelssohn's perceptive essay, 'Ueber die Frage: Was heiβt Aufklärung?' *Berlinische Monatschrift* 4 (September 1784), pp.193-200; and later incorporated in G. B. Mendelssohn (ed.), *Moses Mendelssohn's Gesammelte Schriften* (Leipzig: F. A. Brockhaus, 1843-45), Vol.3, pp.399-403. An English translation can be found in James Schmidt (ed.), *What is Enlightenment? Eighteenth-Century Answers and Twentieth-Century Questions* (Berkeley: University of California Press, 1996), pp.53-57.

16 This is the central theme of the collected essays on *Bildung* by German philosophers. See Ehrhard Bohr (ed.), *Was ist Aufklärung? Thesen und Definitionen* (Stuttgart: Philipp Reclam, 1974).

17 On Herder, see Michael N. Forster (trans. and ed.), *Herder: Philosophical Writings* (Cambridge: Cambridge University Press, 2002). Also see Hans Adler and Wulf Koepke (eds), *A Companion to the Works of Johann Gottfried Herder* (Studies in German Literature Linguistics and Culture) (New York: Camden House, 2009). For a detailed, intellectual study of Herder, see Rudolf Haym, *Herder nach seinem Leben und seinen Werken* (Berlin: Rudolph Gaertner, 1880). A good English analysis can be found in Robert T. Clark, Jr., *Herder: His Life and Thought* (Berkeley: University of California Press, 1969).

18 See Benjamin W. Redekop, *Enlightenment and Community: Lessing, Abbt, Herder, and the Quest for a German Public* (Montreal: McGill-Queens University Press, 2000), especially Chapter 4, pp.198-212.

19 See Otto Dann, 'Herder und die Deutsche Bewegung', in Gerhard Sauder (ed.), *Johann Gottfried Herder, 1774-1803* (Hamburg: Meiner, 1987), pp.308-40; the quoted passage is from p.332.

with *Bildung* would continually challenge the socio-political status quo, seeking to engage society, especially the ruling elites, to achieve its highest ideals.[20] Scharnhorst embodied Herder's idea of *Bildung.*

Bildung was one of the most significant concepts to emerge from the German Enlightenment. For nearly a decade, in letters, pamphlets, and journals, German philosophers, scholars, soldiers, and officials carried on an unending exchange with each other on this important concept.[21] By the time Scharnhorst reached adulthood, *Bildung* had become the centrepiece of his professional military growth. When the Wars of the French Revolution clearly placed a new urgency on the *Bildung* of military leaders, only an enlightened soldier like Scharnhorst was able to grasp this reality.

'Dare to Know!' [*Sapere aude*!], Kant exhorted his readers in his famous essay, 'An Answer to the Question: What is Enlightenment?'[22] Cast off the yoke of tutelage! Reject dogmas and formula – those 'mechanical tools designed for reasonable use', but transformed by princes into 'the fetters of an everlasting nonage'.[23] 'Have the courage to use your own reason! This is the motto of the Enlightenment'.[24] In a small farming village near Hanover, the son of a free peasant farmer took this advice to heart, exemplifying the concept of *Bildung* throughout his life.

20 An interesting study of how *Bildung* manifested itself in German society throughout the 19th and early 20th Centuries can be found in Walter Horace Bruford, *The German Tradition of Self-cultivation: Bildung from Humboldt to Thomas Mann* (London: Cambridge University Press, 1975). Also see Margret Kraul, 'Bildung und Bürgerlichkeit', in Jurgen Kocka (ed.), *Bürgertum im 19. Jahrhundert: Deutschland im europäishcen Vergleich* (Munich: Deutscher Taschenbuch Verlag, 1988), Vol.3, pp.45-73.

21 These essays, originally published in the *Berlinische Monatschrift*, have been collected in a single volume; in Norbert Hinske (ed.), *Was ist Aufklärung? Beiträge aus der Berlinischen Monatschrift* (Darmstadt: Wissenschaftliche Buchgesellschaft, 1981). English translations of several of these essays can be found in Schmidt (ed.), *What is Enlightenment?*

22 Immanuel Kant, 'Beantwortung der Frage: Was ist Aufklärung?' *Berlinische Monatschrift* 4 (December 1784), pp.481-95; later incorporated as part of Ernst Cassirer (ed.), *Immanuel Kants Werke* (Berlin: Bruno Cassirer, 1922/23), Vol. 4: *Schriften von 1783-1788*, pp.167-76; the quoted passages are from p.169. For an informative discussion that seeks to place Kant's stimulating essay in its original context, see James Schmidt, 'The Question of Enlightenment: Kant, Mendelssohn, and the *Mittwochgesellschaft*', *Journal of the History of Ideas* 50:2 (Apr-Jun 1989), pp.269-91.

23 Cassirer (ed.), *Immanuel Kants Werke*, Vol.4, p.170.

24 Cassirer (ed.), *Immanuel Kants Werke*, Vol.4, p.169.

1

The Call to Arms

Gerhard Johann David von Scharnhorst was born of humble origins on Wednesday, 12 November 1755, in Bordenau, a small village in Lower Saxony, located a short distance northwest of Hanover on the Leine River plain, near the Steinhuder Meer.[1] Bordenau lay in the region known as Calenberg, the heartland of the Electorate of Hanover and the ancestral home of the royal family of Great Britain. At the time of Scharnhorst's birth, Lessing and Kant were established scholars, while Mendelssohn was still seeking recognition. Herder was 11, Goethe only six. Schiller, Hegel, Fichte, and Humboldt were yet to be born.

In Lower Saxony, people were enjoying an uneasy period of peace. Behind this tranquil façade, Austria and France, along with Russia, Saxony, and Sweden, were secretly conspiring to cripple or destroy Prussia. They were alarmed by its growing power and territorial expansion. Austria, in particular, was seeking revenge for the loss of Silesia a decade earlier.[2] After learning of his neighbours' intentions, Frederick II of Prussia launched a pre-emptive strike on 29 August 1756, crossing the Saxon frontier, shattering the fragile peace of Europe, and initiating what became known in Europe as the Seven Years War (1756-63). Significantly, hostilities between England and France had already begun along the Virginia frontier and Ohio Valley in North America, where this conflict was called the French and Indian War. In Europe the Seven Years War raised small Prussia to 'great power' status and made Frederick 'the Great'. A brilliant organiser and prudent administrator, an intrepid leader and superb battle captain, Frederick the Great would become one of Scharnhorst's favourite examples whenever he endeavoured to educate his German colleagues on the changing art of war.

Scharnhorst was the second child and eldest son of Ernst Wilhelm Scharnhorst (1723-82) and Friederike Wilhelmine Tegtmeyer (1728-96). The name Scharnhorst belonged almost exclusively to commoners in Lower Saxony during the 18th Century, although there were at least two noblemen with that name in 1775. One was a colonel [*Oberst*] and regimental commander (later promoted to *General-Major*); the other a captain [*Hauptmann*] serving

1 Scharnhorst's birth certificate can be found in *Nachlaβ Scharnhorst*, Nr.2; deposited at the Geheimes Staatsarchiv Preuβischer Kulturbesitz, 196/VI. HA Familienarchive und Nachlässe, Berlin (Dahlem).

2 See the interesting discussions in Dennis E. Showalter, *The Wars of Frederick the Great* (London: Longman Group Limited, 1996), pp.116-34; and H.M. Scott, 'Prussia's Emergence as a European Great Power, 1740-1763', in Philip G. Dwyer (ed.), *The Rise of Prussia, 1700-1830* (London: Pearson Education Limited, 2000), pp.153-76.

at Gibraltar.[3] Originally, both the Scharnhorst and Tegtmeyer families were tenant farmers, 'far down on the corporate, feudal pyramid of the time'.[4] In the aftermath of the Thirty Years War (1618-48), the Scharnhorst family remained tenant farmers in Bordenau.

Seeking a better life, the enterprising and ambitious Johann Otto Tegtmeyer (1647-1702) moved to nearby Poggenhagen and took up tenant farming there. It was not long before he became the steward of a large noble estate. Although it took time for agriculture to return to its pre-war productivity, Tegtmeyer managed the estate with such skill and fiscal responsibility that he was able to turn a profit for his noble master.[5] More good fortune favoured the financially frugal Tegtmeyer, who in 1700 was able to purchase the noble 'free estate' [*Freigut*] in Bordenau, which made him a 'free peasant' [*Freisass*] and member of the local association [*Landschaft*] of noble and free landowners. Later he bought two other farms; one in Bordenau, the other in nearby Otternhagen.[6] Upon his death in 1702, his son, Johann David Tegtmeyer (1687-1759), inherited his property and title.

Also aspiring to be more than a poor tenant farmer in some small, rural German village, Ernst Wilhelm Scharnhorst left Bordenau in 1743 and enlisted in the 8. Dragoner Regiment du Pontpietin, serving honourably during the War of the Austrian Succession (1740-48). His talents and abilities set him apart and enabled him to rise to the rank of sergeant [*Quartiermeister*], then senior sergeant [*Wachtmeister*].[7] Seeing little future in the army, Scharnhorst returned home to Bordenau after the war, but had difficulty adjusting to the customs, social order, and prejudices of village life.[8] At a local dance he met his future wife – Friederike Tegtmeyer – the youngest daughter of the wealthiest and most influential man in the village. In the carefully stratified German society of the time, the social

3 See Georg Heinrich Klippel, *Das Leben des Generals von Scharnhorst* (Leipzig: F.A. Brockhaus, 1869/71), Vol.1, p.9 (Note 2).

4 The quoted passage is from Klaus Hornung, *Scharnhorst: Soldat-Reformer-Staatsmann. Ein Lebens- und Zeitbild* (Gilching: Driffel-Vowinckel Verlag, 2013), p.13. Information on the Scharnhorst and Tegtmeyer families comes from the first two chapters of Klippel, *Scharnhorst*, Vol.1, pp.9-33, who used the often-neglected parish registers of births, deaths, and marriages. These parish registers have greatly increased our knowledge about the details of family life in rural German villages before the 19th Century. The town archives of Bordenau also contain extensive genealogical data on the Scharnhorst family. See the study by Claus-Dieter Gelbke and Jens Th. Kaufmann, 'Genealogische Übersichten über den Preußischen General und Heeresreformer Gerhard von Scharnhorst' (27. Juni 2010).

5 Although dated, the controversy surrounding the state of the German economy before the Thirty Years War, as well as the economic effects of that war, is nicely summarised in Theodore R. Rabb, 'The Effects of the Thirty Years' War on the German Economy', *The Journal of Modern History* 34:1 (March 1962), pp.40-51. For another view that seeks to equate the consumption of alcoholic beverages in Upper Bavaria with economic prosperity, see F.L. Carsten, 'Was There an Economic Decline in Germany before the Thirty Years' War?' *The English Historical Review* 71:279 (April 1956), pp.240-47. In his masterful study of this conflict, Peter H. Wilson, *The Thirty Years War: Europe's Tragedy* (Cambridge: Harvard University Press, 2009), provides a good synthesis of 'The Human and Material Cost', in Chapter 22, pp.779-821. On how this fits into the larger historical picture, see David Hackett Fischer, *The Great Wave: Price Revolutions and the Rhythm of History* (Oxford: Oxford University Press, 1996).

6 Information on the Bordenau estate can be found in Part 2 of the Kuntze Family Papers; see Hann 91: *Gutakten Kuntze* (Nr.16-29); deposited at the Niedersächsisches Landesarchiv, Hanover.

7 On Ernst Wilhelm Scharnhorst's military career, see Klippel, *Scharnhorst*, Vol.1, p.10; and Ludwig von Estorff, *Scharnhorst und Wir* (Berlin and Leipzig: R. F. Koehler, 1926), pp.11 and 14.

8 Rudolf Stadelmann, *Scharnhorst: Schicksal und Geistige Welt* (Wiesbaden: Limes Verlag, 1952), p.36. For an excellent study of village life in Germany, see John Thiebault, *German Villages in Crisis: Rural Life in Hesse-Kassel and the Thirty Years' War, 1580-1720* (New Jersey: Humanities Press International, 1995).

difference between the two was considerable. The Tegtmeyer family was at the top of the social order; Ernst Wilhelm Scharnhorst ranked among those third from the bottom of the village hierarchy.[9]

Social barriers did not dissuade the young couple, who began seeing each other regularly. Their impassioned relationship and blithe indifference to local custom and politics in Bordenau soon scandalized the Tegtmeyer family. When they approached her father to ask his permission to marry, the haughty Tegtmeyer staunchly refused to permit his daughter to marry or even to continue to see the lowly 'tenant farmer' [*Brinksitzer*] Scharnhorst.[10] Tegtmeyer wanted his daughter to marry a man of wealth and position, neither of which Scharnhorst could provide at the time, even though the marriages Tegtmeyer had arranged for his two other daughters had ended miserably for both of them. The eldest (Margarethe Elisabeth) was 18 in 1729 when her father gave her in marriage to the son of the mayor of Rodenberg (in Hesse). His name was Wolff and was often drunk and abusive to his wife. In the end he lost his job and left Margarethe, who returned to Bordenau with their children to live with her parents. Similarly, the second daughter (Catharina Justina Lucia) had just turned 17 in 1742 when Tegtmeyer married her to Friedrich Christian Bierdemann, the pastor of the tiny village of Hoyerhagen. Her life was one of extreme poverty and hard physical work – experiences she had never known nor liked. When her husband died in 1756, she too returned to Bordenau with their two young sons to live with her parents.

Watching the lives of her two older sisters ruined by their proud father's designs most likely convinced Friederike Tegtmeyer that she was better off with Ernst Wilhelm Scharnhorst – a man she knew and liked very much – than with some total stranger her father thought best for her. It appears that Friederike, who was in her late teens or early twenties when she met Scharnhorst, had for several years been successfully fending-off her father's plans to marry her.[11] Despite the various obstacles her father placed in her path, young Friederike continued to see Scharnhorst, and their 'passionate courtship' soon became the talk of the town.[12] By all accounts she was an enchanting young woman, strong-willed and fiercely independent; he was a handsome and strong young man, energetic and hard-working. His military bearing and cheerful demeanour clearly set Scharnhorst apart from other eligible men.

Friederike and Ernst Wilhelm seemed meant for each other, and it seems that many of the villagers supported their relationship. They were weary of the way in which the ingrate Tegtmeyer asserted his free peasant status, a status he had inherited and not earned himself. When Friederike became pregnant (a practice commonly used by many young couples to obtain consent for their marriage), her changing appearance became a source of

9 Klippel, *Scharnhorst*, Vol.1, p.11 (Note 1), lists the intricate, eight-tier caste system that existed even among the peasantry in Bordenau.

10 See the important study of rural village life in Saxony (a treatise produced from a University of Strassburg seminar in 1892); in F.J. Haun, *Bauer und Gutsherr in Kursachsen, Schilderung der ländlichen Wirtschaft und Verfassung im 16., 17. und 18. Jahrhundert* (Strassburg: Karl J, Trübner, 1892). Haun discusses marriage arrangements among village social classes on pp.6-7.

11 See the documents contained in the later 'Legal Proceeding' [*Proceß*] and cited in Klippel, *Scharnhorst*, Vol.1, p.12 (Note 2).

12 Hornung, *Scharnhorst*, p.13.

embarrassment for her family.[13] So, Tegtmeyer sent her away to Deckbergen, a tiny, isolated village in Prussia, southwest of Bordenau, and a fair distance from any populated area. The nearest town was Bückeburg, some seven miles northwest across the border in Schaumburg-Lippe.[14] In Deckbergen on 6 September 1750, Friederike gave birth to a daughter (Elisabeth Sophia Wilhelmina). Still, her parents refused to permit her to return home and marry Scharnhorst, the child's father. He lacked property and had no social standing. It was only after Friederike returned to Bordenau with her baby (in defiance of her father) that her parents reluctantly consented to her marriage to Ernst Wilhelm. The wedding took place in the church of Bordenau on 31 August 1752.

For the next three years Scharnhorst laboured under the harsh dictates of his father-in-law. The bitterness Tegtmeyer felt toward his son-in-law seemed to know no bounds, as he used his wealth and influence in Bordenau and in the outlying villages to make sure Scharnhorst found no work except under his tutelage.[15] While they provided living quarters to the Scharnhorst family, the Tegtmeyers ostracised their youngest daughter and her family. This included Friederike's sisters, who viewed Scharnhorst as a charming, very intelligent, but cunning intruder.[16] When their first son was born in 1755, Ernst Wilhelm and Friederike sought a rapprochement with her parents by baptising the boy with the name of his two grandfathers – Gerhard Johann David. This thrilled the Tegtmeyers, who agreed to a reconciliation and welcomed the Scharnhorst family into the old manor house. Over the next two years, Scharnhorst endeared himself to his in-laws by his careful co-management of the estate during the harsh French occupation of Lower Saxony during the Seven Years War.

All seemed well until Tegtmeyer died in September 1759, a month after the French had withdrawn from Hanover. In his will, he left his entire estate and its management to his wife. Most likely on the counsel of her two oldest daughters, the widow Tegtmeyer (who knew nothing about farming) declined to let Scharnhorst run the estate, so he moved his family to nearby Hämelsee in October 1759 and leased the large noble estate belonging to the Hoya family of Busch-Münchhausen. Scharnhorst soon transformed the moor and meadows of the estate into an efficient farm.[17] He also contracted with his mother-in-law and her three daughters to secure the Bordenau estate upon her death.[18]

13 See the discussion of this practice in Haun, *Bauer und Gutsherr in Kursachsen*, pp.6-7.

14 While seven miles may seem short by 21st Century standards, in the 18th Century it was a considerable distance, since most villagers rarely travelled far from their local environment, and certainly not across country borders. There was also an absence of proper roads throughout much of Germany at this time; most were 'dirt paths' [*Naturwege*]. These and other interesting facts about village life can be found in Mack Walker, *German Home Towns: Community, State, and General Estate, 1648-1871* (Ithaca: Cornell University Press, 1998).

15 See the fascinating article by Jerome Blum, 'The Internal Structure and Polity of the European Village Community from the Fifteenth to the Nineteenth Century', *The Journal of Modern History* 43:4 (December 1971), pp.541-76, in which Blum analyses the central role of the rural village in controlling virtually every aspect of village life. Years later Blum followed this with his massive study, *The End of the Old Order in Rural Europe* (Princeton: Princeton University Press, 1978).

16 Siegfried Fiedler, *Scharnhorst: Geist und Tat* (Herford and Bonn: Maximilian-Verlag, 1963), pp.56-58.

17 The farming life of the Scharnhorst family is described in Klippel, *Scharnhorst*, Vol.1, pp.10-15.

18 See 'Aus dem Theilungsvertrage der Tegtmeyer'schen Erben', in Klippel, *Scharnhorst*, Vol.1, pp.181-83 (Appendix I).

This detailed agreement took nearly three months to finalize. It provided each of the three sisters an equal monetary share of the value of the livestock, field inventories, and moveable goods. It also guaranteed generous stipends for Margarethe and Catharina, an annual income for both from the farm profits, and a lifetime guarantee for Margarethe that she could live on the smaller farm in Bordenau. A final and important stipulation stated that if Ernst Wilhelm outlived Friederike and remarried, he could not bring another wife onto the estate. All parties signed the contract in the district legal office in Hanover on 8 January 1760, where it was then legally notarised and affirmed by oath.

Two years later the Scharnhorst family became embroiled in a bitter, 12-year legal battle over the Tegtmeyer estate.[19] When his mother-in-law died in October 1761, Ernst Wilhelm endeavoured to take possession of the Bordenau estate according to the terms of the contract. Unbeknownst to him, his sisters-in-law appear never to have had any intention of abiding by the terms of that agreement.[20] During the contract negotiations, Margarethe and Catharina agreed to its terms only on the condition that Scharnhorst pay their stipends in instalments in advance. Over the next two years, they travelled regularly to Hämelsee to collect their money, which totalled over 100 thalers. When their mother died, the unmarried sisters asked their uncle in Neustadt (am Rübenberge) to supervise the settlement of the estate. Before the parties met, Margarethe had travelled to Munstorf on 8 December to seek an injunction that would allow both sisters and their families to retain custody of the estate. Then she and Catharina met with Ernst Wilhelm and Friederike a week before Christmas. After dividing the livestock, field inventory, and moveable goods equally among the sisters, Scharnhorst paid Margarethe and Catharina cash for their shares and arranged to move his family into the Bordenau estate. Meanwhile, the two sisters and their families remained on the property.

To his astonishment, Ernst Wilhelm and his family were not permitted to move onto their property in January 1762. Under the sway of the village pastor, his brother, and some officials in Neustadt, Scharnhorst's sisters-in-law had petitioned the county seat in Neustadt to remain on the estate while they repudiated the contract they and their mother had made with Scharnhorst and his wife. They accused Scharnhorst of taking advantage of them following their father's death, manipulating them and their grieving mother, and trying to steal their inheritance. Scharnhorst appealed to the district court in Hanover. He stated that the contract was legally binding, that he had not acted in any devious manner, and that his family had the legal right of possession. In his affidavit, Scharnhorst also noted that he had already paid well over 1,000 thalers in cash to both sisters for their shares of the estate goods, and that it was Margarethe who was acting deceptively.[21] Significantly, the district

19 Kronanwalt Huschke summarised this legal battle in '*Acta in causa* des *Conductoris* Scharnhorst *proprio et uxoris nomine* Implorantan wider die Tegtmeyer'schen Vormünder, Imploranten'. The actual *Proceß* is 235 pages long and is entitled: '*Designatio actorum* Sachen des *Conductoris* zu Hämelsee Ernst Wilhelm Scharnhorst *proprio et uxoris nomine* Implorantan wider Margarethe Elisabeth Wolffen und Katharine Lucie Bierdemann geborene Tegtmeyer *modo* deren bestellte Vormünder, Imploranten'. Both are cited in Klippel, *Scharnhorst*, Vol.1, p.25 (Note).

20 See the interesting commentary in Max Lehmann, *Scharnhorst* (Leipzig: S. Hirzel, 1886/87), Vol.1, p.5. Lehmann suggests that the 'clever' Ernst Wilhelm nearly met his match in the even more cunning Margarethe.

21 Scharnhorst's affidavit of 4 February 1762 can be found in Klippel, *Scharnhorst*, Vol.2, pp.28-29. Determining the value of money in the 18th Century can be a daunting task. Nevertheless, using as a benchmark the most recent data from Michael V. Leggiere, *Blücher: Scourge of Napoleon* (Norman, OK: University of Oklahoma Press, 2014), p.454

court ruled that until the dispute could be settled, Scharnhorst and his family had the legal right of joint possession of the Bordenau estate, and that all parties were to appear before the court on 15 March 1762 to present their cases.

Realising they would likely lose, Margarethe and Catharina refused to abide by the district court's ruling. They enlisted the Calenberg *Landschaft* and officials from Neustadt to make sure Scharnhorst and his family could not take joint possession of the estate. Margarethe also had her two daughters and their families occupy the two smaller farms. Then Margarethe and Catharina failed to appear before the district court in Hanover on 15 March. Instead, they filed a brief challenging the court's ruling. They claimed the court had failed to consider adequately their extenuating circumstances and began inundating the court with malicious briefs. The dispute really became acrimonious when the two sisters asserted that the only reason Scharnhorst had married their sister was that he coveted the Tegtmeyer estate.[22] Margarethe and Catharina noted that it was only to restore the honour of the family that their father had agreed to the marriage in the first place. The fact that Scharnhorst had carried on an illicit affair with their young and impressionable sister 'for over six years' (in direct violation of their father's wishes) and had impregnated Friederike, who bore his child out of wedlock, was proof enough.[23]

The testimony, 'for over six years', is questionable. Friederike gave birth to her first child in September 1750, which means that if the statement of Margarethe and Catharina was true, Ernst Wilhelm and Friederike would have had to have been dating each other from 1744 or earlier. In 1744, Friederike was 16 years old, while Ernst Wilhelm was serving in the Hanoverian cavalry during the War of the Austrian Succession. He did not return to Bordenau until sometime in 1748 or even later. Perhaps the two had met before Ernst Wilhelm had enlisted in the army, but no evidence appears to support such a claim. The evidence indicates Ernst Wilhlem and Friederike met after Scharnhorst had returned to Bordenau after the war, sometime after 1748.

Meanwhile, the Bordenau estate was in financial trouble. With their eyes focused almost exclusively on keeping the Scharnhorst family from acquiring their inheritance, Margarethe and Catharina had failed miserably to manage the farms and their tenants. They had no knowledge of farming, nor any desire to administer the estate. Scharnhorst noted this in his petition to the court, seeking to obtain administration over and management of the Bordenau estate while the court heard his case. Again, the sisters pleaded for help from their local supporters and officials from Neustadt prevented Scharnhorst from running the estate. These 'profit-seeking solicitors' had set up trustees for the two sisters and a joint management of the estate, leasing the three farms and collecting very generous fees for themselves and taxes from the tenants.[24] They clearly did not want Scharnhorst to interfere

(Footnote 2 of Chapter One), 250 years ago, Scharnhorst paid his two sisters-in-law in thaler worth nearly 10,000 US dollars at that time, which was three times the later annual salary of Goethe in Weimar. For information on Goethe's wage, see the detailed income charts of the various classes of society in Weimar in the late 18th and early 19th Centuries in Appendix I, p.428, of Walter Horace Bruford, *Culture and Society in Classical Weimar, 1775-1806* (Cambridge: Cambridge University Press, 1962).

22 See the statement from the judicial proceedings; in Klippel, *Scharnhorst*, Vol.1, p.12 (Note 2).

23 Klippel, *Scharnhorst*, Vol.1, p.12 (Note 2); see also see Haun, *Bauer und Gutsherr in Kursachsen*, pp.6-7.

24 Klippel, *Scharnhorst*, Vol.1, p.30. The quoted passage comes from Lehmann, *Scharnhorst*, Vol.1, p.5.

with their fruitful endeavours. Three years after the district court in Hanover had rendered its initial verdict, the court issued its decision on 5 March 1765, ruling again in favour of the Scharnhorst family.

Unwilling to accept this decision, Margarethe and Catharina filed yet another brief on 3 April 1765. This time they requested the appellate court in Celle review the entire case. The appellate court agreed to exam the case, setting 11 and 17 July 1767 as dates for the hearing. After listening to the testimony from all of the witnesses, the appellate court ordered the court physician to examine and determine the physical and mental well-being of Margarethe.[25] While the court tended to agree with Scharnhorst about the character and motivation of Margarethe, it would take another four years for the process to be completed. Meanwhile, Margarethe used this opportunity to delay any ruling while she gathered numerous character witnesses on her behalf and flooded the court with their statements. Despite Margarethe's best efforts (as well as those who had financial interests in the estate), the appellate court in Celle rendered its final decision on 24 June 1771: the free estate in Bordenau (along with the other two farms) rightfully belonged to Ernst Wilhelm Scharnhorst and his wife Friederike.[26]

What a triumph for the Scharnhorst family! Not only did the appellate court confirm the district court ruling six years earlier, it also reprimanded the lawyers representing Margarethe and Catharina for their misconduct, ordered all parties who had conspired against Scharnhorst (Pastor Toll, his brother, the Neustadt officials, and the lawyers for the two sisters) to pay full restitution to Scharnhorst, and then sentenced Margarethe to 14 days in jail for her misconduct.[27] In the end, Margarethe, Catharina, and their families lost everything. Scharnhorst had them evicted from the estate, to include the two smaller farms. Still, even after all that his family had endured, Ernst Wilhelm and Friederike did not formally gain possession of the estate until 5 August 1772, over a year after the court ruling.

Once again, those dissatisfied with the court verdict sought to delay its implementation. When a higher court rejected their appeal, they invoked an old Lower Saxony custom that called for a complete inventory of the estate, as well as the repair of any defects, before the Scharnhorst family could move in. Ostensibly, this was to ensure that the estate was fit for occupation.[28] Then there was the matter of negotiating fair settlements with the tenants who had leased the farmlands under agreements with those 'profit-seeking solicitors', two of whom were the Toll brothers, whose four-year lease expired in 1774. Over their objections, the court permitted Scharnhorst to buy out their leases. Then he went back to court to recover his money.[29] After all rites of this ritual were complete, the Scharnhorst family was finally able to settle into their home. With the acquisition of the Bordenau estate, the

25 Klippel, *Scharnhorst*, Vol.1, p.31.

26 The decision of the *Oberappellationsgericht zu Celle* (24 June 1771) can be found in Klippel, *Scharnhorst*, Vol.1, pp.31-32.

27 Klippel, *Scharnhorst*, Vol.1, p.32.

28 Klippel, *Scharnhorst*, Vol.1, pp.32-33. Also see Blum, 'The Internal Structure and Polity of the European Village', pp.545-46.

29 Klippel, *Scharnhorst*, Vol.1, p.33. This *Proceß* would take decades to resolve, but Ernst Wihlelm was determined to prevail. Indeed, his son Gerhard was still seeking restitution from the estate of Pastor Toll as late as 1811. See the Legal Brief [*Mandat*] from the Westphalian Appellate Court; in 'Prozeß des kgl. preuss. Generalmajors Gerhard v. Scharnhorst gegen die Erben des Pastors Tolle – Mandat des Westfälischen Appellationshofes zu Celle, 27 März

social, political, and economic situation of the Scharnhorst family changed fundamentally. The elder Scharnhorst was now a free peasant, the owner of a former noble estate, and a voting member of the Calenberg *Landschaft*.[30] He was also exempt from paying taxes. Now he could focus on a career for his eldest son Gerhard.

Throughout the lengthy legal process, Gerhard Scharnhorst spent all of his childhood and most of his adolescence farming with his father. By all accounts, he was 'a lively and cheerful boy', and clearly 'the favourite of his simple and gentle mother'.[31] Nonetheless, these were difficult times for young Scharnhorst. His family was poor and barely surviving. Every time the family won a legal decision, his aunts would appeal that ruling and the process would continue with no end in sight. All too often these suits dragged on, sometimes for decades, while the costs of litigation piled up to the serious detriment of the Scharnhorst family.[32] Indeed, the legal manoeuvres of Scharnhorst's aunts caused the process to take over 10 years to resolve and consumed most of the earnings and savings of the family. In later years, Scharnhorst never spoke positively about this time of his life.[33] As one friend from this time later recalled, the constant legal battles with Margarethe and Catharina controlled virtually every aspect of Scharnhorst's family life and cast a dark shadow on his youth.[34] On the other hand, this experience affected young Scharnhorst in many positive ways.

Gerhard Scharnhorst grew up accustomed to privation. Watching his father's forbearance in the face of all the malicious assaults on his character taught him how to swallow offenses in silence. He also learned the value of genuine friendship, as he witnessed the many families coming to the aid of his own family in times of trouble. When the Scharnhorst family returned to Bordenau in the fall of 1772 to claim their estate, 17-year-old Gerhard saw how his aunts and their families still refused to abide by the court's decision. The district magistrate had to use physical force to evict them from the estate. Then the brother of Pastor Toll used his influence as a clerk in the government office in Neustadt to keep the elder Scharnhorst from becoming a member of the 'provincial parliament' [*Landtag*], claiming that there was no official documentation to prove his free peasant status. So, Ernst Wilhelm had to file yet another brief in the district court to obtain his rights. Finally fed up with the conduct of certain officials in Neustadt, the district court in Hanover provided Ernst Wilhelm Scharnhorst with an official certificate legitimising his free peasant standing, and issued an order to those Neustadt officials that they were to abide by the all of the court's rulings, and were to cease all further actions against the Scharnhorst family.[35] The district magistrate personally delivered this decree to officials in Neustadt. So, when his father finally triumphed and achieved justice, Gerhard Scharnhorst recognised the value of

1811', *Nachlaß Scharnhorst*, Nr.3; deposited at the Geheimes Staatsarchiv Preuβischer Kulturbesitz, 196/VI. HA Familienarchive und Nachlässe, Berlin (Dahlem).

30 On the local *Landschaft*, see Carl-Hans Hauptmeyer, *Calenberg: Geschichte und Gesellschaft einer niedersächsischen Landschaft* (Hanover: Fackelträger, 1983).

31 Hornung, *Scharnhorst*, p.14.

32 See the discussion of legal redress in village life; in Blum, 'The Internal Structure and Polity of the European Village', p.545.

33 Stadelmann, *Scharnhorst*, p.37.

34 See Friedrich Wilhelm von Benicken, *Scharnhorst*, which is Band 1 of *Preuβens Helden* (Weimer: Wilhelm Hoffmann, 1830), p.29.

35 See the court's official transcript of 5 December 1775; in Klippel, *Scharnhorst*, Vol.1, p.37 (Note 1).

patience, forbearance, and temperance, as well as modesty and undaunted diligence. These character traits would later serve him well.

Looking back over the previous decade reveals that these were difficult times not only for the Scharnhorst family, but also for the German people of Lower Saxony. War had come in July 1757, when a French army numbering 100,000 men invaded the Electorate of Hanover and won a decisive victory at the Battle of Hastenbeck on 26 July. In accordance with the Convention of Kloster-Zeven (8 September 1757), an uneasy peace came to Lower Saxony. French troops occupied most of the Electorate and exacted a heavy burden from the population. It would take another two years before the great field commander Ferdinand, Sovereign Prince of the Holy Roman Empire and Duke of Braunschweig-Lüneburg (1721-92), defeated the French at the Battle of Minden on 1 August 1759, ending their occupation. Interestingly, Duke Ferdinand was another of Scharnhorst's favourite military leaders.

Meanwhile, the people of Lower Saxony suffered greatly under the yoke of the French. The French 'laid waste' to the Electorate of Hanover. They ransacked the countryside, raped women and young girls, quartered their soldiers in local towns, villages, and the capital Hanover, and exacted a heavy tax burden from the local inhabitants. All of this came with Austrian consent.[36] Young Scharnhorst was not even a year old when the Seven Years War began. He was barely four when the family left Bordenau for Hämelsee following the death of the elder Tegtmeyer. Two days before his fifth birthday, his mother gave birth to her second son, Ernst Wilhelm. Four months after the Treaty of Hubertusberg had ended the Seven Years War, Friederike gave birth to a third son (Friedrich Heinrich Christoph), who joined the Scharnhorst family on 5 June 1763.

While living in Hämelsee, young Gerhard performed work around the house and in the fields, guarded the livestock, and served as a messenger for his father, who now administered a sizeable noble estate. At seven he began attending school in the neighbouring village of Anderten, since Hämelsee had neither school nor church. There he learned the rudiments of reading, writing, and arithmetic, along with the Christian catechism. Spelling was a constant nightmare for him, as his numerous papers reveal. To conquer this challenge, Scharnhorst employed a simple technique. As he later wrote:

> Here is my method. I almost never had any formal instruction. In order to learn how to spell, each day I asked my siblings to dictate a page from my reader. I then corrected what I had written and marked any word that I had spelled incorrectly. The next day, I reviewed the words that I had marked. If I failed to remember the mistakes that I had made, I marked the word a second time. This was an indication that I should go back to that word before I went any further. In this way, I made steady progress. By the time I reached the fifth page of the book, I was able to spell all of the words correctly the first time that they were dictated to me, with the only exception being terms of art that were new to me.[37]

36 See the discussion of the French occupation in Johann Wilhelm von Archenholz, *Geschichte des Siebenjähren Krieges in Deutschland von 1756-1763* (Berlin: Haude & Spener, 1793), pp.86, 103, 124, and 207; the quoted passage is from p.103.

37 See Gerhard Scharnhorst, 'Anleitung zur Lecture und zu den Feld-Uebungen der Officiere', *Militair-Bibliothek* (Hanover: Gebrüdern Helwing, 1782-84), Vol.1, pp.1-38; the quoted passage is from pp.30-31.

Because of his lack of a formal education, Scharnhorst also had difficulties with spoken German, having learned only the local dialect in daily conversation and never being formally taught any 'standard' German.[38]

A fire destroyed nearly all of the Hämelsee estate in August 1765, and along with it most of the family possessions. So, the elder Scharnhorst moved his family to nearby Bothmer, where he assumed the tenancy of the noble estate there.[39] Life in Bothmer was characteristic of many outlying German settlements of this period. Bothmer had no school, so the children rotated from one farmhouse to another, learning from the village sexton (Christian Heinrich Beckmann) what little knowledge he and the other adults possessed. The only formal structure came from studying the catechism. A fourth brother (Johann Heinrich) joined the family in 1768, but sadly he died two years later. A fifth brother (Heinrich Dietrich Christian) was born in 1770, just two weeks after Gerhard's 15th birthday. Unable to support his growing family on just his stewardship of the Bothmer estate, Ernst Wilhelm took on another tenancy in neighbouring Schwarmstedt, where teenage Gerhard now spent nearly all of his time in the fields with his father. There was little time for reading and study. After years of this hard life, the elder Scharnhorst learned of the appellate court's decision and moved his family back to Bordenau.

Over the course of 10 years, Ernst Wilhelm Scharnhorst had served as the steward of two large noble estates – the first in Hämelsee; the second in Bothmer. He had earned a solid reputation as an administrator, farmer, and breeder of livestock. Influential noble families in the area often turned to him for advice on agricultural matters. In Schwarmstedt lived many of his former comrades from the army, as well as many wealthy families. As more and more people learned of his legal battle with his sisters-in-law, many came to his aid, including the von Bothmer family, his former army comrades, and Pastor Wilhelm Johann Friedrich Marburg of Schwarmstedt. The fellowship with these families provided great joy for the Scharnhorst family. Gerhard loved to listen to the veterans speak of their adventures with the Hanoverian contingent in the army of Frederick the Great and tell their war stories. He also borrowed books from Pastor Marburg's small library. Most were studies in military history or pamphlets on the Seven Years War and the War of the Austrian Succession.

Under the tutelage of Pastor Marburg, Gerhard Scharnhorst found the time and inclination to read, cultivating his interest in history and storing up in his highly retentive memory the material from which he would later leaven many a lecture, historical study, and modernisation treatise. Listening intently to the veterans and learning how to question their accounts, he acquired not just factual knowledge, but also a keen interest in critical historical analysis and synthesis. Often, during these years, he expressed his desire to become a soldier. With the legal fight still raging, the elder Scharnhorst did not want his son to go into the army as a common soldier and end up as he had. He was well aware of the prejudices against the common-born in the feudal environment of Germany and desired a better career for Gerhard. At first, he planned for his son to follow him in agriculture, where

38 For a brief discussion of the conflict Scharnhorst faced with the standard spoken German of his day, see Andreas Broicher, *Gerhard von Scharnhorst: Soldat-Reformer-Wegbereiter* (Aachen: Hedios, 2005), p.26.

39 The leasing agreement between Johann Heinrich Böschen zu Eickeloh and Ernst Wilhelm Scharnhorst regarding the Bothmer estate can be found in the Kuntze Family Papers. See Hann.91: *Gutakten Kuntze*, Nr.24; deposited at the Niedersächsisches Landesarchiv, Hanover.

his worthiness and competitiveness would prevail. Over time he realised that Gerhard possessed the call to arms.

With the acquisition of the 'free estate' [*Freigut*] in Bordenau, the social advancement of Ernst Wilhelm Scharnhorst now made it 'socially acceptable' for him to think about a career as an officer for his eldest son.[40] When the Scharnhorst family moved into the Bordenau estate in 1772, they found it in wretched shape. Drawing from all of his previous experience, Ernst Wilhelm soon enhanced agricultural productivity, most likely by revitalising the soil with crop diversity and rotation, better irrigation, and fallow periods. He also increased his livestock with better food and breeding. Within a year, productivity had risen dramatically. It soon became apparent that Ernst Wilhelm Scharnhorst was one of the better farmers in the area. He also acquired a solid reputation for his managerial skills.

In achieving his success, Ernst Wilhelm Scharnhorst (as well as Johann Otto Tegtmeyer before him) had both managed noble estates. This was significant. These 'knightly estates' [*Rittergüter*] were largely immune from the strict control of the village leadership, which often regulated who farmed what fields, what crops they would plant, and how the produce would be distributed.[41] This autonomy to farm as they chose enabled the enterprising Tegtmeyer and Scharnhorst to circumvent the feudal village structure and obtain much better use of the resources at hand.[42] As his reputation in agrarian matters spread, Ernst Wilhelm Scharnhorst became a leading member of the Calenberg *Landschaft*, and was often sought out for his expertise.

News of the elder Scharnhorst's innovative endeavours soon reached the ears of 'Imperial Count' [*Reichsgraf*] and sovereign ruler Friedrich Wilhelm Ernst zu Schaumburg-Lippe (1724-77), one of the few enlightened rulers in Europe at that time. His state of Schaumburg-Lippe neighboured Hanover and was one of those German lands that had suffered greatly from the ongoing territorial disputes among the more powerful princes of the Holy Roman Empire. Originally formed in the 12th Century as the Lordship of Lippe of the Holy Roman Empire, Lippe was located between the Weser River and the south-eastern part of the Teutoburg Forest. From 1613 onwards, Lippe was continuously divided, with each major division retaining the status of a county, while the secondary divisions rarely possessed any territory of note other than the odd castle or town.[43] With the death of the childless Count Otto V of Holstein-Schaumburg in 1640, the older and larger principality of Schaumburg went to the only legal heir, Countess Elisabeth, Otto's mother. In 1643, she transferred her sovereign rights to her brother, Philipp zur Lippe-Alverdissen, with whom she ruled as co-regent until her death in 1646. Further partitions followed with the Peace of Westphalia that formally ended the Thirty Years War (1618-48). Holstein-Pinneberg was

40 Hornung, *Scharnhorst*, p.14.

41 See the recent study on this by Alex Flügel, *Bürgerliche Rittergüter: sozialer Wandel und politische Reform in Kursachsen (1680 - 1844)*; in *Bürgertum: Beiträge zur europäische Gesellschaftgeschichte*, Band 16 (Göttingen: Vandenhoeck & Ruprecht, 2000).

42 Walter Goerlitz, *Scharnhorst. Bedeutende Niedersächsische Lebensbilder* 1 (Hanover: Niedersächsische Landeszentrale für Heimatdienst, 1955), p.9.

43 Information on the evolution of Schaumburg-Lippe comes from Matthias Blazek, *Die Grafschaft Schaumburg 1647–1977: Episoden und Quellensynthese* (Stuttgart: Ibidem, 2011); Walter Maack, *Die Geschichte der Grafschaft Schaumburg* (Rinteln: Bösendahl, 1986); and Stefan Brüdermann (ed.), *Schaumburg im Mittelalter* (Bielefeld: Verlag für Regionalgeschichte, 2014).

transferred to the King of Denmark, while the Lordship of Bergen (in Holland) was sold. The Lordship of Gehmen (in Westphalia) was given to the Count of Limburg, while the State of Sternberg went to Lippe. Braunschweig-Lüneburg and Hessen also received considerable concessions.[44] What remained formed the diminutive country of Schaumburg-Lippe, with its capital at Bückeburg. At the time of Scharnhorst's birth in 1755, Schaumburg-Lippe was among the smallest (if not the tiniest) of the German states of the Holy Roman Empire.

While on one of his journeys, Count Wilhelm took time away from his official duties to travel to Bordenau to meet and speak with Scharnhorst on agriculture, farming techniques, and horse-breeding.[45] It was during these discussions that Scharnhorst sensed an opportunity for his son and requested an appointment for him to Wilhelmstein, the military academy of Schaumburg-Lippe. After interviewing Gerhard, Count Wilhelm acknowledged the very favourable impression he had of the teenager but noted the substantial gaps in his education. As Wilhelm told the elder Scharnhorst, all applicants had to pass an entrance examination before admission. For the next few months, young Scharnhorst dedicated himself almost exclusively to an intensive self-study program, which he later described his methodology in his first publication, *Military Library*.[46]

In *Military Library*, Gerhard Scharnhorst elaborated on his self-study program. It covered spelling, grammar, and sentence structure (areas that remained challenges throughout his life), mathematics, French and English, and the military sciences. It was a systematic approach that required constant repetition and dealt with both known and unknown quantities. Scharnhorst acquired written French by translating literary works like *Les Aventures de Télémaque* (The Adventures of Telemachus, Son of Ulysses), published from 1693–94 by French Roman Catholic Archbishop, poet, theologian, and writer François de Salignac de La Mothe-Fénelon (1651-1715). He also translated the play *Le Père de famille* (Father of the Family) by Denis Diderot (1713-84). Scharnhorst would then compare his translations with known German sources. A retired captain in Schwarmstedt tutored him in mathematics, since it was the primary focus of the entrance examination. Years later, as a teacher and educator in Hanover, he would remember fondly this period of his life and the enjoyment it provided him, and would endeavour to pass on to his colleagues and friends the value of self-instruction, independent thinking, and discovery, which were far more valuable than just the rote memorization fashionable at the time. He also travelled to Bückeburg for discussions with Count Wilhelm, who was truly impressed by the enthusiasm and desire of young Scharnhorst to improve himself.[47]

44 These 'concessions' or 'Feudal Rights' placed a severe financial and security yoke on the rulers of Schaumburg-Lippe for the next 150 years.

45 Count Wilhelm's keen interest in agriculture appears in several of his early biographies. See T[heodor]. Schmalz, 'Beschreibung der Vestung Wilhelmstein im Steinhuder Meer', *Journal von und für Deutschland* 5 (1788), pp.90-92; especially p.92 (Column 1); and Herman Tiemann, *Geschichte der Festung Wilhelmstein im Steinhuder Meer* (Stadthagen: Verlag von Heinrich Heine, 1907), pp.36-37.

46 See Gerhard Scharnhorst, 'Vom dem Studieren selbst, und den Auszügen', *Militair-Bibliothek*, Vol.1, pp.28-33.

47 See the Letter of 27 April 1773 from *Major* Franzose Jean d'Etienne (1725-98), Commandant of Wilhelmstein, to Count Wilhelm, notifying him that Scharnhorst was traveling to Bückeburg for his interview with the Count; cited in Lehmann, *Scharnhorst*, Vol.1, p.10. The letter also indicates that this was not the first time Scharnhorst had visited Wilhelmstein and had spoken with Count Wilhelm.

Gerhard Scharnhorst passed the entrance examination for Wilhelmstein in the spring of 1773. On 29 April, he formally entered the Schaumburg-Lippe engineer and artillery corps as a cadet.[48] For an ambitious young man with a delicate sense of justice, admittance to the military academy at Wilhelmstein was a major step for Scharnhorst. Although only 17, his life experiences had matured him beyond his age. For the next four years, Count Wilhelm would use the process of *Bildung* to stimulate, guide, and cultivate young Scharnhorst's character, intellect, and world view.

48 See the letter from Ernst Wilhelm Scharnhorst to Count Wilhelm (27 April 1773), stating that his son had passed the entrance examination and requesting admission for Gerhard to Wilhelmstein; in Johannes Kunisch (ed.; arranged by Michael Sikora and Tilman Stieve), *Gerhard von Scharnhorst: Privat und dienstliche Schriften* [hereafter cited as Kunisch (ed.), *Scharnhorst: Privat und dienstliche Schriften*] (Köln/Weimar/Wien: Veroffenlichungen aus dem Archiven Preuβischer Kulturbesitz, 2002-15), Vol.1: *Schüler, Lehrer, Kriegsteilnehmer (Kurhannover bis 1795)*, p.1. Scharnhorst's oath upon admittance to the academy is the next page.

2

Scharnhorst's Mentor

Revered as an 'enlightened' [*Gebildeter*] soldier, Friedrich Wilhelm Ernst zu Schaumburg-Lippe devoted his adult life to the profession of arms. Born in London on 9 January 1724, he was the second son of Albrecht Wolfgang (1699-1748), *Reichsgraf* and sovereign ruler of Schaumburg-Lippe (1728-48) and his first wife, Countess Margarete Gertrud of Oeynhausen (1701-26). He was two when his mother died in Mannheim on 8 April 1726, while she and her husband were on a diplomatic mission for King George I. Wilhelm and his older brother Georg were subsequently raised in England by their pious and well-educated fraternal grandmother, Countess Johanna Sophie of Hohenlohe-Langenburg (1673-1743), who was Maid of Honour and Mistress of the Robes to Princess Caroline Elizabeth of Great Britain (1713-57).[1] Johanna Sophie had a very profound influence on both Wilhelm and Georg. They were educated in the classics and trained in the social etiquette of English court life. Wilhelm cherished the English lifestyle and liked to be called 'William'. Indeed, English social, political, and military thought would later have a guiding influence on the young count.[2] It was not until he was nearly five that Wilhelm (along with Georg) travelled for the first time to Germany and to their ancestral home in Bückeburg. There, under the mentorship of their father, Georg and Wilhelm learned continental ways.

As Lessing lamented, learning European ways often meant studying abroad. Due mainly to the fragmentation of and disunity within the German states, its universities had not yet achieved the renown of those in neighbouring countries. From 1735 to 1740, Georg and

1 A good overview of Count Wilhelm's life can be found in Curd Ochwadt (ed.), *Wilhelm Graf zu Schaumburg-Lippe: Schriften und Briefe* (Frankfurt am Main: Vittorio Klostermann, 1977-83), Vol.1: *Philosophische und politische Schriften*, pp.463-88. Three contemporary accounts of Count Wilhelm include: Theodor Schmalz, *Denkwürdigkeiten des Grafen Wilhelms zu Schaumburg-Lippe* (Hanover: Helwingisches Hofbuchhandlung, 1783); Christian August Stützer, 'Charakteristik des Grafen Wilhelm von Lippe-Bückeburg', *Militärischer Kalender auf das Gemein-Jahr 1805* (Berlin: Johann Friedrich Unger, 1805), pp.2-70; and Karl August Varnhagen von Ense, 'Graf Wilhelm zur Lippe', *Biographische Denkmale* (Leipzig: F.A. Brockhaus, 1872), Vol.1, pp.1-79. The Foreword by Varnhagen von Ense to the first edition is dated, 'Berlin, in January 1824'. The brief account by Rudolf Falkmann, 'Wilhelm, Graf von Schaumburg-Lippe', *Allgemeine Deutsche Biographie* (1898), Vol.43, pp.202-03, summarises Schmalz and Varnhagen.

2 A sophisticated study of Count Wilhelm, his social, political, and military thought, does not exist. Fortunately, retired *Generalleutnant* Hans Heinrich Klein has written a fine study that covers the critical aspects of Wilhelm's formation and life as an enlightened sovereign and soldier. See *Wilhelm zu Schaumburg-Lippe: Klassiker der Abschreckungstheorie und Lehrer Scharnhorsts. Studien zur Militärgeschichte, Militärwissenschaft und Konfliksforschung*, Band 28 (Osnabrück: Biblio Verlag, 1982).

Wilhelm were in Geneva, Switzerland (at that time an independent republic), where they studied the arts, sciences, religion, horsemanship, fencing, and sketching, as well as seamanship. They obtained first-hand experience in business and finance from observing the local merchant and banking communities. They also enjoyed the theatre and watched the Swiss political system. Wilhelm was very partial to the study of languages, and soon became fluent in five languages: English and French, and later German, Italian, and Portuguese. He 'spoke four European languages except German, was interested in scientific endeavours, and read in Latin the classical authors'.[3] In the autumn of 1740, the two young men travelled to Holland, where they furthered their education in the university town of Leiden, known for its many publishing houses and fine cheese. There they studied music, agriculture, and natural law. Wilhelm also employed a private tutor so he could continue his mathematical studies. Georg and Wilhelm later journeyed to the Prussian residence near The Hague, where they met Voltaire, who was promoting *Anti-Machiavelli*, an essay Frederick II of Prussia had published a few months after he becoming king.[4] The next spring Georg and Wilhelm completed their formal education with a trip to Italy, by way of Strasbourg, Lyon, and Montpellier.

As the second son, Wilhelm was destined for a military career. In 1742 he was back in England, where he was assigned to the Horse Guards, the senior regiment in the British Army. As a young officer he was particularly fascinated with gunnery, but had real difficulties adjusting to military life. He often found himself in financial trouble or under house arrest for disciplinary infractions. Whatever challenges Wilhelm faced becoming a soldier seem to have vanished completely following the tragic death of Georg, who died in a duel on 6 August 1742. Seeking to keep his remaining son (and now the heir) out of harm's way, Count Albrecht had Wilhelm transferred from British service to his command in the Dutch army. He also had Wilhelm politely decline an invitation from Frederick of Prussia to enter his service.[5] At 19, Wilhelm accompanied his father on campaign during the War of the Austrian Succession. He saw his first combat action with the English-Hanoverian army (under the personal command of King George II of England, who was also the Elector of Hanover) at the Battle of Dettingen (am Main), between Hanau and Aschaffenburg, on 27 June 1743. Following this action, and with his father's prompting, Wilhelm left the army and travelled to England, Saxony, Austria, and Italy to relax and enjoy the life of a young nobleman and heir. In Italy he studied music and learned to play the piano very well.

Ever restless, Wilhelm yearned for excitement and danger. In April 1744 he may have joined the Royal Navy. If so, chronic seasickness forced the young heir to abandon any idea of a naval career.[6] Against his father's wishes, he left England for northern Italy, where in

3 Hornung, *Scharnhorst*, p.15.

4 On the relationship between Voltaire and Wilhelm, see Curd Ochwadt, *Voltaire und die Grafen zu Schaumburg-Lippe* (Bremen and Wolfenbüttel: Jacobi Verlag, 1977).

5 See Wilhelm's Letter of 14 January 1743 to Frederick II; in Ochwadt (ed.), *Wilhelm Graf zu Schaumburg-Lippe*, Vol.3: *Briefe*, p.30.

6 Varnhagen, 'Graf Wilhelm zur Lippe', p.5. On p.15 of his study, *Wilhelm zu Schaumburg-Lippe*, Klein questions Varnhagen's assertion, stating that Wilhelm 'allegedly' joined the Royal Navy, since he could find no credible evidence to support Varnhagen's findings. Interestingly, among Count Wilhelm's papers are notes relating to the development of a means to counter seasickness. See 'Notizen zum Modell einer Einrichtung gegen Seekrankiheit', in Ochwadt (ed.), *Wilhelm Graf zu Schaumburg-Lippe*, Vol.1, p.221.

April 1745 he entered the Austrian army (as a volunteer colonel), commanded by Bohemian Prince (and Austrian *Generalfeldmarschall*) Johann Georg Christian von Lobkowitz (1686-1755). A year earlier, Lobkowitz had driven the main Spanish army out of northern Italy. Anxious for some action, Wilhelm soon became dismayed with Lobkowitz. He observed how the Spanish forces (now allied with France, Naples, and Genoa) continually outmanoeuvred the Austrians. From Bassignano on 16 August 1745, Wilhelm wrote to his father to ask 'forgiveness' for his rash behaviour, and to describe the conditions that would soon lead to Lobkowitz's defeat.[7] Unwilling to wait for the inevitable defeat he saw coming, he 'left the army' in disgust in early September, 'tired of so many retreats, without experiencing any hope'. On 27 September, Spain and her allies defeated the Austrians at Bassignano. At that moment Wilhelm was on his way home to Bückeburg, where he arrived a month later. At home he composed his first military study: a campaign analysis of the recent debacle in northern Italy.[8]

With his father's permission, Wilhelm left that autumn for Saxony, Austria, Italy, and England. His goal was to introduce himself abroad and to secure a commission, and hopefully with it an alliance for Schaumburg-Lippe. He was in Vienna on 7 September 1746, where he requested a colonelcy in the Imperial Austrian army. Three days later he met with Empress Maria Theresa (1717-80) to discuss his candidacy. Shortly afterwards, he left Austria for Verona to visit his renowned uncle, *Reichsgraf* and Venetian *Feldmarschall* Johann Matthais von der Schulenburg (1661-1747). He was hoping to learn as much as he could about the art and science of war.[9] While in Verona he learned Maria Theresa had declined his application, citing his changing religious affiliations and his illicit affair with Italian 'Theater Princess' Elena Barbanti.[10]

Schulenburg had had an illustrious military career. He initially fought with the Austrian army in Hungary against the Ottomans in the Great Turkish War (1687-91), then with the Saxon army in the Great Northern War (1700-21) against Charles XII of Sweden. He was severely wounded in 1701 but returned to fight in three major battles – Kliszow (1702), Poniec (1704), and Fraustadt (1706). Schulenburg defeated Charles XII at Poniec but was double enveloped at Fraustadt. During the War of Spanish Succession (1701-14), he served under Prince Eugene of Savoy-Carignan and saw action in the battles of Oudenarde (1708) and Malplaquet (1709). Schulenburg finished his military career defending Corfu against the Turks in 1716. In retirement he became a collector of Italian art, amassing over 88 pieces. In Verona, he related his exploits to Wilhelm, who listened intently to his uncle's analysis of military operations. The detailed discussions the two had on the Venetian militia may have been the inspiration for a similar system Wilhelm later implemented in Schaumburg-Lippe.[11]

7 Letter of 16 August 1745 to Albrecht Wolfgang; in Ochwadt (ed.), *Wilhelm Graf zu Schaumburg-Lippe*, Vol.1, pp.41-42.

8 See Wilhelm zu Schaumburg-Lippe, 'Mémoires militaires de tout ce qui s'est passé à l'armée autrichienne en Italie, depuis le 9 avril 1745 jusqu'à l'onze de septembre de la même année', Ochwadt (ed.), *Wilhelm Graf zu Schaumburg-Lippe*, Vol.2: *Militärische Schriften*, pp.1-8; the quoted passages are from the last paragraph on p.8.

9 On Schulenburg, see Karl August Varnhagen von Ense, 'Graf Matthais von der Schulenburg', *Biographische Denkmale* (Leipzig: F.A. Brockhaus, 1872), Vol.1, pp.80-172.

10 This application process took nearly two months and can be followed in Ochwadt (ed.), *Wilhelm Graf zu Schaumburg-Lippe*, Vol.1, pp.50-57. Also see the commentary by Ochwadt on p.467.

11 Klein, *Wilhelm zu Schaumburg-Lippe*, p.16.

On 14 March 1747, Johann von der Schulenburg died, and Wilhelm left for London, where he was again unsuccessful in securing a commission, this time in the British service. More disappointment came when Wilhelm's request for a commission in the Russian army had also been denied. Although no written evidence for these rejections has been found, it appears that they most likely resulted from the carefree and wasteful life Wilhelm had spent as a young nobleman.[12] Leaving London, he arrived home in the spring of 1748. That autumn, on 24 September 1748, Albrecht Wolfgang died. On 25 October 1748, Wilhelm succeeded his father as *Reichsgraf* and sovereign ruler of Schaumburg-Lippe. He was three months shy of his 25th birthday.

At Bückeburg, Wilhelm found his small state in despair. Notwithstanding the best efforts of his father to provide for his people, Schaumburg-Lippe was deeply in debt, with unemployment high and emigration on the rise.[13] Wilhelm took immediate steps to raise the morale of his people. Captivated by the spirit of enlightened absolutism, he rooted out every vestige of frivolous and wasteful spending and began selling and mortgaging state property to reduce the debt with Hanover. He sealed the borders of Schaumburg-Lippe to stop emigration and foreign agents from impressing his subjects. Interestingly, neighbouring Hanover offered a 50 thaler bounty for the killing of any Prussian or other foreign recruiters on Hanoverian soil.[14]

In Schaumburg-Lippe, Wilhelm began establishing industry by building a silk factory, an iron mill, foundries, and brickyards. He promoted commerce and agriculture by creating farming communities in which he recruited settlers and provided them with housing, seed, and tax incentives. He reformed the school system by setting common standards throughout the land. He built an orphanage, provided care for widows, gave jobs to the poor, and compelled beggars to work [*Frondienst*]. He also introduced fire and health insurance for his people.[15] Although he was opposed by his own subjects in much of this innovative work, Wilhelm's programs later became models for public education and social welfare in 19th Century Germany and later spread internationally. In 1756, he built one of the first chocolate factories in Germany, then recruited experts from Portugal to teach his subjects the trade. The heavy 'burden of debt' was the only factor that 'greatly restricted Wilhelm's freedom of action'.[16]

12 Hornung, *Scharnhorst*, p.15. Also see the commentary in Ochwadt (ed.), *Wilhelm Graf zu Schaumburg-Lippe*, Vol.1, p.469.

13 Albrecht Wolfgang had shown considerable charity toward widows and orphans, had built hospitals and schools, and even a water storage system for Bückeburg.

14 See George II, 'Edict, gegen die Preussischen und fremden Werber, vom 3./14. Decembr. 1731', *Chur-Braunschweig-Lüneburgische Landes-Ordnungen und Gesetze* (Lüneburg: Sternischen Buchdruckerei, 1742), Vol.2 (Cap. III. Sectio I), pp.117-118.

15 Wilhelm's reform efforts are summarised in Ochwadt's overview of the Count's writings. See Ochwadt (ed.), *Wilhelm Graf zu Schaumburg-Lippe*, Vol.1, pp.478-79. Ochwadt includes in his text excerpts from key documents, with references to the source material that is published in Volume 1. Also see the discussions in Stadelmann, *Scharnhorst*, pp.134-35; and in Klein, *Wilhelm zu Schaumburg-Lippe*, pp.212-14. For a general survey of growing state power and its associated rise in welfare programs, see Peter H. Wilson, *Absolutism in Central Europe* (London: Routledge, 2000), pp.99-103.

16 Klein, *Wilhelm zu Schaumburg-Lippe*, p.26.

Hoping to transform Bückeburg into a centre of education, science and culture, and to raise the *Weltanschauung* of his people, Wilhelm sought out scholars, scientists, and artists. Only after the French were driven out of Schaumburg-Lippe could he secure the services of Johann Christoph Friedrich Bach (1732-95), the ninth son of Johann Sebastian Bach. A harpsichordist, Bach became 'Concert Master' [*Konzertmeister*] in 1759. In charge of the 'court band' [*Hofkapelle*], Bach was responsible for the composition of music and its recital. Concerts were given twice a week, with Wilhelm often playing the flute or piano. Since Wilhelm was partial to Italian vocal music, Bach adjusted his choices to the tastes of the count. In 1765, Thomas Abbt accepted the position as 'Councillor of the Court' [*Hofrat*]. Wilhelm was particularly interested in Abbt's political and historical writings and enjoyed many gratifying conversations with his court councillor.[17]

In 1771, Bach's Protestant music lured Herder to Bückeburg. Wilhelm appointed him to the prominent and influential posts of 'Ecclesiastic Councilor' [*Konsistorialrat*] and 'Court Preacher' [*Hofprediger*]. While at Bückeburg, Herder completed his *Treatise on the Origin of Language* (1772), which won first prize from the Berlin Academy of Sciences, and made him one of the prominent figures of the later German *Sturm und Drang* literary movement.[18] For his part, Wilhelm 'was a typical representative of enlightened absolutism', noted for his love of chamber music, mathematics, science, philosophy, history, languages, horse-breeding, archaeology, and military affairs.[19] He was also an avid tennis player, which he had learned in England.

To the classical humanists, Wilhelm was a man of refined culture and dignity. 'Oh, how remote is his way of thinking from the general way of reigning monarchs!' wrote Mendelssohn.[20] Given the political fragmentation and particularism of Germany and the Holy Roman Empire, Wilhelm could not arrogate reasoning to himself. He was just a minor prince who was not even an elector, let alone the kind of 'prince' Machiavelli had in mind. Any thinking would have to be collective. Wilhelm understood this reality and sought to develop a societal leadership in Schaumburg-Lippe by creating representative councils among the merchants, artisans, and farmers to advise him on their needs.[21]

Wilhelm's dynamic approach and progressive domestic initiatives certainly inspired men like Goethe and Mendelssohn, who viewed him as 'truly a great friend of humanity'.[22] Scharnhorst agreed, later writing:

17 See the intriguing articles on Abbt by Benjamin W. Redekop, 'Thomas Abbt and the Formation of an Enlightened German 'Public'', *Journal of the History of Ideas* 58:1 (1997), pp.81-103; and Eva Piirimäe, 'Dying for the Fatherland: Thomas Abbt's Theory of Aesthetic Patriotism', *History of European Ideas* 35:2 (2009), pp.194-208. Count Wilhelm was especially interested in Abbt's views on dying for the Fatherland.

18 A brief description of Herder's life at Bückeburg can be found in Clark, *Herder*, pp.138-42, 156, 180-81, and 233-34.

19 Hornung, *Scharnhorst*, p.15.

20 Letter of 22 July 1766 to Thomas Abbt; in Mendelssohn (ed.), *Mendelssohn's Gesammelte Schriften*, Vol.5, pp.365-69; the quoted passage is from p.367.

21 For a discussion of Wilhelm's domestic programs, see Schmalz, *Denkwürdigkeiten des Grafen Wilhelms zu Schaumburg-Lippe*, pp.73-113. Also see Stadelmann, *Scharnhorst*, pp.138-39.

22 Moses Mendelssohn to Thomas Abbt (22 July 1766); in Mendelssohn (ed.), *Mendelssohn's Gesammelte Schriften*, Vol.5, pp.365-69; the quoted passage is from p.367.

> Seldom has there been a man like him, one who combined such unconditional goodness of the heart with so many great qualities of the mind. His affability, the goodness of his heart, and his charity made him the universal father and provider of his state. He never left people living in poverty without help; he never left widows and orphans without care. Every expense of his small court was reduced so that he might enjoy the one happiness of making others happy.[23]

At a time when the lavishness and indulgence of the European aristocracy were reaching yet another whimsical height, Wilhelm zu Schaumburg-Lippe was the pious opposite. His love of chivalry, coupled with his now strict moral code, his longing for adventure and danger, his courage and daring, his sense of honour and contempt of luxury, all made him 'a unique character of the Rococo period in Germany'.[24]

In 1774, the Jewish philosopher met the man who once invited him to settle in Bückeburg. It was an exhilarating experience for both. Mendelssohn recalled how Count Wilhelm 'loved hard and dangerous physical exercises, the sciences, and great deeds. *Dévoucement à la mort* was his watchword'.[25] Indeed, Wilhelm's 'devotion to death', as well as his concept of military honour, can also be found in one of his 'Instructions' on the character formation [*Bildung*] of the soldier, in which he praises a *Wachtmeister* Hirsch, who found himself surrounded by 18 enemy Hussars and chose death and thus honour rather than surrender.[26]

> Death for the sake of freedom and justice, the future of life, and Providence were the topics of his ordinary conversation. I never heard a man talk with more warmth about the truths of natural religion. Free from all prejudice that leads to discord and hatred of men, he was permeated to the degree of enthusiasm with the pure, beneficial teachings of religion.

To Moses Mendelssohn, Wilhelm was 'the finest Greek soul in a rough Westphalian body'.[27] Other men of letters agreed. Goethe wrote that Wilhelm endeavoured to bring to Bückeburg not just professional people, but also artists, musicians, philosophers; in short, 'men of

23 Scharnhorst's testimony can be found in his first published article, 'Von den Militär-Anstalten des verstorbenen regierenden Grafen von Schaumburg-Lippe Königl. Portugisischen Generalissimi &c'., in August Ludwig Schlözer (ed.), *Briefwechsel meist historischen und politischen Inhalts* (Göttingen: Vandenhoekschen Buchhandung, 1776-82), 10:56 (1782), pp.93-101; later incorporated as Appendix II of Klippel, *Scharnhorst*, Vol.1, pp.183-88; the quoted passages are from pp.95-96 (Schlözer) and Vol.1, p.185 (Klippel).

24 Stadelmann, *Scharnhorst*, p.132. Also see Falkmann, 'Wilhelm, Graf von Schaumburg-Lippe', p.202.

25 Wilhelm's frequent discussions on '*Dévoucement à la mort*' ('Devotion to Death' or 'Self-Sacrifice') can be found throughout his thoughts on life and death. See, for example, Ochwadt (ed.), *Wilhelm Graf zu Schaumburg-Lippe*, Vol.1, pp.47, 71, 99, 120, 125, 176, 188-91, and 483. The quoted passages in the text come from the notes Mendelssohn made to his correspondence in Mendelssohn (ed.), *Mendelssohn's Gesammelte Schriften*., Vol.5, pp.405-08; the quoted passages are from p.406.

26 See 'Beytrag zur Ersten Abtheilung der Beyspiele zur Bildung eines Soldatens' (25 November 1768); in Ochwadt (ed.), *Wilhelm Graf zu Schaumburg-Lippe*, Vol.2, p.386.

27 See the notes Mendelssohn made to his correspondence in Mendelssohn (ed.), *Mendelssohn's Gesammelte Schriften*, Vol.5, pp.405-08; the quoted passages are from p.406.

great promise'.[28] Voltaire, Herder, Mendelssohn, and Swiss philosopher and later famous Hanoverian court physician, Johann Georg Ritter von Zimmermann (1728-95), were four such men.

Perhaps the most noteworthy aspect of Wilhelm's reign was the magnitude of the standing army he maintained to deter aggression against his small state. 'The peace of the state is an essential condition for the happiness of the people', he proclaimed.[29] Unfortunately, the geographical location of Schaumburg-Lippe was 'latent with danger'.[30] Surrounded by Hanover to the north and east, Hesse-Kassel in the south, and Prussia in the west, Albrecht Wolfgang had carefully cultivated vital relationships with England, Hanover, and Prussia. Wilhelm endeavoured to solidify these unwritten alliances. He was prompted by fears that Hesse-Kassel might seize the rich Bückeburg mines.[31] He was also eager to stop Hesse-Kassel, Prussia, and Hanover from using his country as a source of recruitment and replenishment. His solution was to mobilise the entire population and material resources of Schaumburg-Lippe in defence of the state.[32] In doing so, Wilhelm became one of the first sovereigns in modern European history to champion the nation-in-arms as a deterrent against foreign encroachment and invasion, and as a school of the nation.

To the delight of the classical humanists, the Count practiced what he believed. He revived the 'medieval levy' [*Heerbahn*] and introduced universal military service, 'because every citizen is a soldier, every soldier a citizen, and every nobleman a soldier and citizen'.[33] All able-bodied men were 'enrolled' in this militia and liable for service in defence of Schaumburg-Lippe. Wilhelm authorized few exceptions.[34] The sovereign's right to compel his subjects to serve in the military was nothing new in European history. The Swedish 'Classification System' [*Indelningsverk*] was one such innovation by Charles XI (1672-97).[35]

In Schaumburg-Lippe, Wilhelm organised his state into military districts that provided both men and material for the defence of the state. Following the completion of the citizen's initial military training and service, Wilhelm reduced his time of active service, placed him in the militia, and established an annual training program designed to maintain readiness

28 See Ernst Beutler (ed.), *Johann Wolfgang von Goethe: Gedenkausgabe der Werke, Briefe und Gespräche* (Zürick: Artemis-Verlag, 1950-71), Vol.10: *Dichtung und Wehrheit*, p.365.

29 The quoted passage is from Wilhelm's thoughts on war. See Number 84 of the Section 'Über den Krieg', in Ochwadt (ed.), *Wilhelm Graf zu Schaumburg-Lippe*, Vol.2, p.142.

30 Klein, *Wilhelm zu Schaumburg-Lippe*, p.33.

31 On the threat from Hesse-Kassel, see Wilhelm zu Schaumburg-Lippe, 'Memoranda pour le cas d'invasion de la part des Hessois' and 'Contre l'invasion de la Hesse', in Ochwadt (ed.), *Wilhelm Graf zu Schaumburg-Lippe*, Vol.1, pp.273-74 and 274-75; respectively.

32 Ochwadt has grouped the various and extensive contingency plans Count Wilhelm wrote on the security of his country under the title, 'Zur Verteidigung Schaumburg-Lippes'. See Ochwadt (ed.), *Wilhelm Graf zu Schaumburg-Lippe*, Vol.1, pp.273-387. The key documents 'for land defence' [*Zur Landesverteidigung*] are: 'Quelques réflexions sur les arrangements de la défense de ce pays' (p.276); 'Über die Verteidigungs-Einrichtungen Schaumburg-Lippe 1777' (p.276); and 'Quelques réflexions sur la manière de défendre ce pays-ci' (pp.276-77).

33 Wilhelm is cited by Lehmann, *Scharnhorst*, Vol.1, p.13. Before the absolutist state, the *Heerbahn* was the obligation of the native inhabitant to the general defence of his homeland.

34 See Wilhelm zu Schaumburg-Lippe, *Reglement für den Land-Ausschuss* (Bückeburg, 1751); in Ochwadt (ed.), *Wilhelm Graf zu Schaumburg-Lippe*, Vol.2, pp.376-85.

35 See Chapter 5 (pp.71-89) of Anthony F. Upton, *Charles XI and Swedish Absolutism* (Cambridge: Cambridge University Press, 1998).

and to develop leaders for the regular army.[36] Militiamen were drilled in uniform on Sundays during the spring and autumn months. Good pay, decent treatment, and adequate pensions did much to make service in the militia tolerable. Wilhelm also rewarded bravery, initiative, leadership, and faithful service with honours and medals, gold and other distinctions. 'Such revolutionary thinking' is what distinguished Count Wilhelm and Schaumburg-Lippe from other German princes and their principalities.[37]

Contrary to much of the historiography on the subject, Schaumburg-Lippe was not part of the German 'Soldier Trade' [*Soldatenhandel*] of the eighteenth century.[38] Unlike Hesse-Kassel, Württemberg, Brunswick, and a number of other smaller German principalities, Wilhelm did not raise his military forces to be sold or hired out to other German princes, and certainly never to any foreign power, especially France. Instead, he sought to establish a national people's army to protect his own people, so that they could develop their God-given talents and abilities according to the German concept of *Bildung*. And while his peacetime army was 8.8 percent of the population of Schaumburg-Lippe ('the most extreme case' among German states), Wilhelm created it solely for the defence of his tiny country.[39] Undeniably, decades before the famous revolutions in America and France, a sovereign German prince had endeavoured to instil in his subjects an ideal of service, self-sacrifice, and love of country, by creating a national people's army based on popular support.[40]

'Imagine the kind of man he must have been', wrote August Wilhelm Neithardt von Gneisenau (1760-1831) to an early biographer of Count Wilhelm. Gneisenau, one of Scharnhorst's close personal associates during the years of reform and modernisation in Prussia, believed that Count Wilhelm was one 'whose mind so early on developed the most important ideas about war; ideals whose subsequent realisation were to cause the collapse of Napoleon's power'.

> Our whole program of mobilising the people in 1813, *Landwehr* and *Landsturm*, all of modern warfare from broadest principle to the most minute detail was exhaustively treated by this man; everything was already understood, taught, and implemented by him.[41]

36 Lehmann, *Scharnhorst*, Vol.1, p.25, describes these field exercises.

37 Lehmann, *Scharnhorst*, Vol.1, pp.18-21; the quoted passage is from p.18.

38 On the German 'Soldier Trade', see the excellent articles by Peter H. Wilson, 'The German 'Soldier Trade' of the Seventeenth and Eighteenth Centuries: A Reassessment', *The International History Review*, 18:4 (November 1996), pp.757-92; and 'The Politics of Military Recruitment in Eighteenth-Century Germany', *The English Historical Review*, 117:472 (June 2002), pp.536-68.

39 According to Peter H. Wilson, 'Most German states maintained peacetime armies equivalent to 0.5-2 per cent of their population in the mid-eighteenth century'. See Peter H. Wilson, *War, State and Society in Württemberg, 1677-1793* (Cambridge: Cambridge University Press, 1995); the quoted passage is from p.78.

40 See the discussion in Peter Paret, *Clausewitz and the State* (Oxford: Clarendon Press, 1976), pp.61-62.

41 August von Gneisenau to Varnhagen von Ense, 'Graf Wilhelm zur Lippe', p.52. While agreeing with Varnhagen's overall assessment of Count Wilhelm, Gneisenau believed Varnhagen had not gone far enough, proclaiming: 'He was even greater than you suggest'.

Count Wilhelm zu Schaumburg-Lippe was truly 'one of the first champions of the idea of a national army'.[42]

Wilhelm used the time between the War of the Austrian Succession and the Seven Years War to build his armed forces. From 1748 to 1755, he regularly travelled to Potsdam to confer with Frederick II on military affairs, and then on to Berlin and the fellowship of the Berlin Academy of Sciences. He established his regular army in 1749, forming an infantry regiment of eight companies that eventually totalled nearly 800 men, including a company of light infantry.[43] A year later he organised an artillery corps that grew to around 200 men, including its train. The militia was officially reorganised in 1751 to secure the national defence.[44] Engineers, miners, sappers, and staff personnel completed the force in the years 1753-55. No costs were spared in training and equipping these units. All were modelled after Prussian organisations, but manned almost entirely by residents of Schaumburg-Lippe.[45] With this armed force, and with the help of England, Wilhelm hoped to become an equal partner in any alliance with Prussia and Hanover, which would then deter Hesse-Kassel.

From his academic studies in Geneva and Leiden, Wilhelm had developed a passion for all aspects of artillery gunnery. His mathematics tutor in Leiden may have been Henri Claude du Frainoy of Luxemburg, who later became chief of the Schaumburg-Lippe engineer and artillery corps.[46] If so, Frainoy quickly discovered Wilhelm's taste for 'pyrotechnics and gunnery', as well as his fondness for invention and experimentation.[47] Wilhelm was essentially a pioneer who built a weapons foundry in Bückeburg in 1754 to satisfy his scientific curiosity, and as part of his ongoing program to make Schaumburg-Lippe self-sufficient. At Bückeburg, he conducted experiments in metallurgy and hydraulics, ballistics and powder mixtures, the construction of gun carriages and siege equipment, and the manufacture of projectiles, breech-loading weapons, cannons, and armour plating.

Artillery became an obsession with Count Wilhelm. He investigated nearly every aspect of gunnery and wrote extensively about it, so much so that his passion earned him the title, 'The Cannon Count'. He also experimented with various tactical formations and technical changes.[48] More than a decade before the revolutionary innovations of the French artillery officer and engineer Jean-Baptiste Vaquette de Gribeauval (1715-89), Wilhelm was casting

42 Theodore Ropp, *War in the Modern World*, new rev. ed., with an Introduction by Alex Roland (Baltimore: The Johns Hopkins University Press, 2000), p.132.

43 On the light infantry formations, see G.W. von Düring, *Geschichte des Schaumburg-Lippe-Bückeburgischen Karbiner-und Jäger-Korps* (Berlin, Posen, und Bromberg: Ernst Siegfried Mittler, 1828).

44 According to Klein, *Wilhelm zu Schaumburg-Lippe*, pp.34-36, the beginnings of an organised militia in Schaumburg-Lippe date from 11 April 1665. However, not every citizen served until Wilhelm ended all exemptions with his 'Enrollment System' of 28 October 1749. He then formalized the process on 19 April 1751. See Wilhelm zu Schaumburg-Lippe, *Reglement für den Land-Ausschuss*; in Curd Ochwadt (ed.), *Wilhelm Graf zu Schaumburg-Lippe*, Vol.2, pp.376-85. Lehmann, *Scharnhorst*, Vol 1, p.19 and Note 1, writes that while the *Reglement für den Land-Ausschuss* states that eligibility began at 16 years, documents from 1756 show that the obligation to serve actually started at 14 years.

45 Klein, *Wilhelm zu Schaumburg-Lippe*, pp.42-50.

46 Klein, *Wilhelm zu Schaumburg-Lippe*, p.8. Based on written correspondence from Ochwadt, dated 5 April 1979, Klein claims no conclusive evidence exists to say with certainty that du Frainoy was Wilhelm's teacher in Leiden. See p.294 (Note 20).

47 Klein, *Wilhelm zu Schaumburg-Lippe*, p.8.

48 See the discussion in Klein, *Wilhelm zu Schaumburg-Lippe*, pp.51-52.

smoothbore cannon of iron and bronze, using a hollow-core drill that he had invented. He was also creating mobile field artillery to support his infantry, engineers, and militia on the battlefield. He was producing lighter guns, while strengthening their carriages. He was harnessing horses in pairs instead of in tandem and was using soldiers as teamsters and not hired civilians, who were often very unreliable on the battlefield. He was also equipping his artillery batteries with caissons and limbers.[49] Over the next 20 years, the foundry at Bückeburg became one of the most technologically advanced but relatively unknown in Europe, supplying weapons, powder, and military equipment to many of the German armies of Europe.[50] Wilhelm Ernst zu Schaumburg-Lippe stands out as one of the great military innovators and artillerymen of his age.

During the Seven Years War, troops from Schaumburg- Lippe fought alongside those allied with Prussia and Great Britain against Austria and France. Driven from his country after the Battle of Hastenbeck (1757), Wilhelm and his troops joined other north German contingents to form the Hanoverian Army of Observation, under the command of Duke Ferdinand of Braunschweig-Wolfenbüttel.[51] Ferdinand appointed Wilhelm *Generalfeldzeugmeister* of the Electorate of Hanover and commander of the allied artillery.[52] He was instrumental in achieving 'the impossible victory' of Britain, Hanover, and other German contingents over the French at the Battle of Minden (1759).[53] Wilhelm's troops also fought at Marburg Castle

49 See Strack von Weissenbach, *Regierender Graf Wilhelm zu Schaumburg-Lippe, bezüglich seiner Leistungen als Artillerist, insbesondere im siebenjährigen Kriege: Als Erinnerungsgabe in Kurzen Umrissen zusammengestellt von Strack von Weissenbach* (Ludwigsburg: Greiner & Ungeheuer, 1884). Also note the discussion by Scharnhorst in 'Von den Militär-Anstalten des verstorbenen regierenden Grafen von Schaumburg-Lippe', pp.97-101 (Schlözer) and Vol.1, pp.186-88 (Klippel).

50 A good summary of Count Wilhelm's endeavours here can be found in Klein, *Wilhelm zu Schaumburg-Lippe*, Chapter 7, pp.51-56.

51 In his *Armies and Warfare in Euorpe, 1648-1789* (Manchester: Manchester University Press, 1982), pp.48-49, John Childs erroneously writes that Count Wilhelm 'raised and sold' his soldiers to the Hanoverian army in 1756 'simply to provide revenue' for his coffers. Childs provides no source to substantiate his assertion. In contrast, Klein, *Wilhelm zu Schaumburg-Lippe*, pp.59-63, supports his assertion that Schaumburg-Lippe joined England and Prussia against Austria and France on 28 August 1756, a day before Prussia crossed the Saxon frontier. Klein bases his conclusion on Wilhelm's own wartime reports and concluded that Wilhelm commanded his own troops during the Seven Years War. See Wilhelm's two wartime reports, 'Nachrichten von dem Schaumburg-Lippischen Grenadier-Regiment' (1771) and 'Nachrichten, das Schaumburg-Lippische Artillerie-und Ingenieur-Corps betreffend', in Ochwadt (ed.), *Wilhelm Graf zu Schaumburg-Lippe*, Vol.2, pp.104-05 and pp.105-07; respectively.

52 The excellent scholarship of Mark Wishon, *German Forces and the British Army: Interactions and Perceptions, 1742-1815* (New York: Palgrave Macmillan, 2013), does an admirable service in refuting the unsupported generalisations found in Childs, *Armies and Warfare in Europe*. The term *Generalfeldzeugmeister* has no exact English translation. During the Seven Years War it was used to designate Count Wilhelm as the Commander-in-Chief of Coalition Artillery.

53 Like John Childs, Stuart Reid, *The Battle of Minden 1759: The Impossible Victory of the Seven Years War* (Croydon, England: Frontline Books, 2016), also makes several unsupported claims about Count Wilhelm. Reid notes on p.25, that Wilhelm's 'talents as a practical artillerist and administrator never lived up to his reputation'. He then writes that 'it was not until the arrival of the British contingent that the artillery improved in effectiveness'. Later on p.104, Reid states that Wilhelm was 'absent' when the battle began, which led Duke Ferdinand to deploy 'his own artillery' as it was 'arriving on the battlefield'. In both cases, Reid provides no supporting documentation. Then in Appendix IV – 'Contemporary Accounts of the Battle of Minden', Reid contradicts his previously unsupported statements by publishing part of an eyewitness account from a British officer who wrote: 'The batteries erected under the care of the Graf de la Lippe de Buckeburg, grand master of the artillery, ..., contributed greatly to decide the fortune of the

(1759), the siege of Münster (1760), the relief of Kassel (1761), and the Battle of Hamm (1761). Returning home in 1761, he found his people once again devastated by the rape, plunder, and pillage of the French occupation. Wilhelm immediately began rebuilding Schaumburg-Lippe but was called away in 1762 to command English and Portuguese troops defending Portugal against Spanish aggression.

In the so-called 'Fantastical War' [*Guerra Fantástica*] of 1762, Count Wilhelm defeated an invasion by Spanish troops, thus preserving Portuguese independence. In a series of brilliant marches, countermarches, and surprise attacks, his forces repeatedly baffled the Spanish, who possessed a three-to-one superiority, but always found themselves confronted by English and Portuguese troops in very good defensive positions. Wilhelm's most aggressive and successful subordinate commander was English Brigadier General John Burgoyne (1722-92). Burgoyne's capture of the Spanish city of Valencia de Alcántara by surprise and his defeat of the Spanish at Vila Velha, demonstrated the wisdom of the old adage that the best defence is a good offense.[54] For his services, King George II made Count Wilhelm a British field marshal and personally thanked him for his allegiance and faithful service with a gift of thoroughbred horses.[55] These horses became the basis of the Bückeburg 'Princely Riding School' [*Fürstliche Hofreitschule*], which later became a German centre of equestrian arts.

At the request of Sebastião José de Carvalho e Melo (1699-1782), the first Marquis of Pombal and first Count of Oeiras, Wilhelm remained in Portugal after the peace agreement to rebuild and train the Portuguese army to a more professional standard.[56] The Marquis of Pombal was Secretary of State and 'Prime Minister' [*Algarves*] to Joseph I of Portugal. As the most prominent minister, Pombal was the *de facto* head of Portugal. He was a competent leader and ushered in a series of economic and military reforms. Under the direction of Count Wilhelm, the Marquis established a military academy and artillery school, and completely reformed the Portuguese army. Inspired by the works of Vauban and Wilhelmstein (the island fortress Count Wilhelm was building at home), Pombel had the Fort de Nossa Senhora da Graça constructed. In honour of Portugal's great defender, the Marquis renamed it, 'Fort de Lippe'.[57]

While modernising the Portuguese army, Wilhelm implemented a combined arms doctrine. This '*New System of Tactics*' called for the battlefield integration of infantry,

day'. See Reid, *The Battle of Minden*, p.168. This English soldier (who Reid believes was Colonel Robert Byrd) goes on to state that Count Wilhelm's direction of allied artillery fire 'totally extinguished the fire of the enemy's batteries', causing 'great havock [sic] among the Swiss and grenadiers de France'. It appears from an eyewitness account that Count Wilhelm's actions mirrored his reputation.

54 For Wilhelm's report on the defence of Portugal, see Wilhelm zu Schaumburg-Lippe, 'Mémoire de la champagne de Portugal en 1762', in Ochwadt (ed.), *Wilhelm Graf zu Schaumburg-Lippe*, Vol.2, pp.33-65. A map of the Portuguese theatre of operations can be found in Klein, *Wilhelm zu Schaumburg-Lippe*, p.156.

55 For Wilhelm's service in Portugal, see the wonderful study by Christa Banaschik-Ehl, *Scharnhorsts Lehrer: Graf Wilhelm von Schaumburg-Lippe in Portugal;* in *Studien zur Militärgeschichte, Militärwissenschaft und Konfliksforschung*, Band 3 (Osnabrück: Biblio-Verlag, 1974).

56 Wilhelm's modernisation of the Portuguese army is covered in detail in Banaschik-Ehl, *Scharnhorsts Lehrer*, pp.79-170. Illustrations 2-5 and 8 at the end of the book (no page numbers) contain the various tactical formations, field encampment scheme, and manoeuvre plans Wilhelm developed for the Portuguese army.

57 Illustration 9 at the end of Banaschik-Ehl, *Scharnhorsts Lehrer* is a sketch of Fort de Lippe.

cavalry, artillery, engineers, and militia.[58] Wilhelm had experimented with these 'new' tactics during the 'Fantastic War', in which he was concerned with the all-around defence of his force. The unique formation, dubbed 'The Bückeburg Square' [*Das Bückeburger Kreuz*], combined infantry, artillery, and engineers into one manoeuvre unit, with cavalry and militia forces in close support. It was a mobile unit designed to fight independently or with other formations on the battlefield. 'The Bückeburg Square' was yet another pioneering approach that contradicted the rigid, linear tactical ideas of the eighteenth century.[59] It was also like many of the tactical ideas French theorists later espoused during their debate on tactics following the Seven Years War.[60]

Returning to Schaumburg-Lippe in late 1764, Wilhelm continued the rebuilding of his own country. Due mainly to the extreme reluctance of his subjects who did not share his dream of preserving their liberty and enhancing their prosperity, little had been accomplished during his two-year absence. So, with renewed vigour, Wilhelm drove his people to finish Wilhelmstein, a star-shaped fortress of four bastions and a citadel, located on the artificial island in the Steinhuder Meer (the largest lake in north-western Germany). On the top of the citadel he built an observatory. Wilhelm designed this fortress to be impenetrable – the last line of defence for Schaumburg-Lippe. He knew that any enemy would have to launch a waterborne assault across the lake to capture it. With its 166 guns (3-, 6-, and 12-pound cannons), its mortars and small arms fire, such an attack would be suicidal.[61]

Should his country be overrun and occupied (as it had been in the previous two wars), Wilhelm planned to garrison Fortress Wilhelmstein with sufficient troops and supplies and then, in concert with his militia, conduct 'small war' operations against the enemy's lines of communications, interdicting his supplies, harassing his garrisons and outposts, and tying down as many of his troops as possible.[62] Wilhelm based many of his 'small war' concepts on his experience in Portugal. Significantly, in 1787 (just 10 years after Wilhelm's death), Landgrave Wilhelm IX of Hesse-Kassel (1743-1821) invaded, overran, occupied, and attempted to annex Schaumburg-Lippe. Only the Fortress Wilhelmstein could not be taken. After two months, troops from Prussia and Hanover (acting on behalf of the Imperial Court

58 See Wilhelm zu Schaumburg-Lippe, 'Cinq articles pour être ajoutés au *Novo Methodo Para Dispor* etc., formant la Première Section de l'Essay d'un Noveau Sistème de Tactique' (Bückebourg 1775); in Ochwadt (ed.), *Wilhelm Graf zu Schaumburg-Lippe*, Vol.2, pp.184-225. Scharnhorst discusses this combined arms approach in 'Von den Militär-Anstalten des verstorbenen regierenden Grafen von Schaumburg-Lippe', pp.96-98 (Schlözer) and Vol.1, pp.185-86 (Klippel); and in his two-part article, 'Neue Taktik, welche der verstorbene regierende Graf Wilhelm von Schaumburg-Bückeburg bey seinem Truppen eingeführt', *Neues militärisches Journal* 1 (1788), pp.1-38; and 'Fortsetzung der neuen Tactik des verstorbenen regierende Grafen Wilhelm von Schaumburg-Lippe', *Neues militärisches Journal* 2 (1788), pp.131-61.

59 See the discussion in Banaschik-Ehl, *Scharnhorsts Lehrer*, pp.132-45. Illustrations 4 and 5 (at the end of the text) show the Bückeburg Square in a 'Movement to Contact' and 'Defence' formation; respectively.

60 See the striking similarity of Count Wilhelm's tactical thought with French theorists of the period; in Robert S. Quimby, *The Background of Napoleonic Warfare: The Theory of Military Tactics in Eighteenth-Century France* (New York: Columbia University Press, 1957).

61 Klein, *Wilhelm zu Schaumburg-Lippe*, p.255, provides a detailed placement of these guns, and how they would be employed to stop any attack.

62 Wilhelm's conceptual thoughts can be found in Wilhelm zu Schaumburg-Lippe, 'Zur Verteidigung Schaumburg-Lippes', in Ochwadt (ed.), *Wilhelm Graf zu Schaumburg-Lippe*, Vol.1, pp.273-387.

of the Holy Roman Empire) marched in and liberated Schaumburg-Lippe and forced Hesse-Kassel to withdraw its forces.

Constructing this massive fortification was one of the great engineering feats of the time.[63] Beginning in 1761, Wilhelm laid the foundation of the artificial island on which Wilhelmsten was built. The small population of Schaumburg-Lippe (around 17,000 inhabitants) hauled tons of gravel, stone, wood, and other material to the lakeshore at Steinhude, where fishermen loaded it on their boats and transported it approximately two miles due west to the south-central part of the lake, where the island was being created. As the island was nearing completion, Fortress Wilhelmstein was built during the next 19 months, from 26 August 1765 to 30 March 1767.

At the same time, Wilhelm constructed 16 smaller islands that surrounded and shielded the main fortress. On each he built bastions protecting the four cardinal directions, with four ravelins and eight curtains shielding the bastions.[64] All were linked together by interlocking fields of fire, and to the main island by draw bridges.[65] Within the outer fortifications were barracks, family housing, commissaries, small hospitals, workshops, recreational and study areas, magazines, and a library. Wilhelm also planted gardens on each, so soldiers manning the fortifications would have fresh fruit and vegetables to eat. Nearly 250 soldiers (along with their families) manned Fortress Wilhelmstein on a rotational basis throughout the year. In time of war, Wilhelm planned to garrison the fortress with only 800 soldiers.

Another essential component of Wilhelm's national defence plan was the concept of 'fortified townships' [*Contrées fortifies*]. On the moorland southwest of Steinhuder Meer, he drained the large swampy area, established 'agricultural colonies' [known as the *Wilhelmsteiner Feld*] for his soldiers and their families, and constructed a smaller fort with an echeloned belt of over 20 redoubts and numerous covered positions designed to protect these settlements.[66] Nearby he built training facilities and a small port from which a fleet of approximately 20 gunboats patrolled the waters around the fortress islands and

63 See the interesting study (complete with sketches, plans, and diagrams from the Bückeburg archives) by Curd Ochwadt, *Wilhelmstein und Wilhelmsteiner Feld. Vom Werk des Grafen Wilhelm zu Schaumburg-Lippe (1724-1777)* (Hanover: Charis Verlag, 1978). For a contemporary account, see T[heodor]. Schmalz, 'Beschreibung der Vestung Wilhelmstein im Steinhuder Meer', *Journal von und für Deutschland* 5 (1788), pp.90-92.

64 A ravelin was a triangular fortification that faced outward from the main fortress, between two curtains. The outer walls of the ravelin were configured so they would divide an assault force and permit the guns in the ravelin to fire upon the attacking troops as they approached a curtain. A curtain was a rectangular fort also facing outward and situated so as to support its flanking bastion and ravelin. This 'Fortress Plan of Wilhelmstein' [*Grundriss der Wilhelmstein*] can be found on p.256 of Klein, *Wilhelm zu Schaumburg-Lippe.* Contemporary drawings can be found in Ochwadt, *Wilhelmstein und Wilhelmsteiner Feld.* The 'Island Plan' [*Grundriss derer Wilhelms Insuln~.*] is on the back cover.

65 Following the death of Wilhelm, Scharnhorst wrote a detailed analysis of Fortress Wilhelmstein and its strong defensive capabilities. See 'Die von dem verstorbenen regierenden Graf Wilhelm von Schaumburg-Bückeburg auf dem Steinhuder Meer erbaute Festung Wilhelmstein', in Kunisch (ed.), *Scharnhorst: Privat und dienstliche Schriften*, Vol.1, pp.24-30 and 31-34; respectively. Scharnhorst planned to publish this piece but could not get permission from officials in Schaumburg-Lippe to do so.

66 Klein, *Wilhelm zu Schaumburg-Lippe*, pp.238-44, discusses this national defence plan. On p.242 is a sketch of a *Contrée fortifiée*. On the inside back cover of Ochwadt, *Wilhelmstein und Wilhelmsteiner Feld* is a foldout of the actual '*Plan des Wilhelmsteiner Feldes*'.

the Steinhuder Meer.[67] The very first German submarine was built here in 1772. Dubbed the 'Pike of Steinhude', it resembled the long-snouted teleost fish. It had a crew of eight and could operate submerged for about 12 minutes. Its deepest recorded depth was nearly 10 feet.[68] All of these elaborate measures certainly demonstrate the determination of Wilhelm zu Schaumburg-Lippe to protect his people and their homes from invasion and occupation.

Problems of homeland defence now completely absorbed Count Wilhelm. The weakness of the German frontiers filled him with prophetic dismay. From his classical education and his expensive experience during the Seven Years War (especially in Portugal), Wilhelm understood that his tiny country required full, national mobilisation of all of its resources (social, economic, and military) in order to maintain its independence.[69] In Portugal he had witnessed first-hand the powerful and desperate passions of a people defending their homeland, and the tremendous energy, capabilities, and resilience of peasant forces repulsing the superior army of the Spanish invasion. Seeking to apply this experience to Schaumburg-Lippe, he planned to garrison his borderlands, villages, and towns with militia farmers and merchants. The regular army would occupy the 'fortified townships' (or strong points) to hamper any enemy advance into his country. Then, through skilful manoeuvre and offensive operations, Wilhelm planned to rout any invader with his regular army and militia forces fighting to defend their homes and families. The island fortress of Wilhelmstein would serve as his command and control centre.[70]

Following the death of his only child Emilie in 1774, and his wife from tuberculosis two years later, Count Wilhelm died on 10 September 1777, most likely from an infection he had incurred while caring for his wife. Wilhelm had met Marie Barbara Eleonore, Countess zur Lippe-Biesterfeld (1744-76) through her brother Ferdinand, who had been on Wilhelm's staff in Portugal. Wilhelm and Marie were married on 12 November 1765, a year following his return from Portugal. Although he was 20 years older than his bride, by all accounts their marriage was a happy one; they seemed meant for each other. Because there was no heir, a collective diet ruled Schaumburg-Lippe until the Imperial Court of the Holy Roman Empire approved Wilhelm's cousin, Philipp Ernst zu Lippe-Alverdissen (1723-87), to succeed him.

The logical connection Wilhelm had made between military, economic, social, and political reform at the national level for Schaumburg-Lippe was considered out-of-touch by Philipp and his wife. They were not at all imbued with the progressive sentiments of Wilhelm. With the willing support of many sectors of society that resented the idea of national service, Philipp and his wife relocated the academy from Wilhelmstein to Bückeburg and renamed it *Ecole militaire*. Then they began dismantling the army and militia. At the same time, they acquiesced to the demands of the merchants, artisans, and political elites and revoked many of the social, political, cultural, and economic reforms that Wilhelm had implemented to

67 Klein, *Wilhelm zu Schaumburg-Lippe*, Chapter 20 (pp.249-61) provides a good discussion of Count Wilhelm's extensive fortifications.

68 Detailed sketches of the 'Pike of Steinhude' can be found in Ochwadt, *Wilhelmstein und Wilhelmsteiner Feld*, pp.8-9.

69 Heinz Stübig, *Scharnhorst: Die Reform des preußischen Heeres;* in *Persönlichkeit und Geschichte*, Band 131 (Göttingen: Muster-Schmidt Verlag, 1988), p.13.

70 Wilhelm's rationale for building Wilhelmstein can be found in the Foreword to Wilhelm zu Schaumburg-Lippe, 'Mémoire sur les Isles Guillaume (1770)', in Ochwadt (ed.), *Wilhelm Graf zu Schaumburg-Lippe*, Vol.1, pp.298-338. The six 'Articles' that follow explain the defence of Wilhelmstein and Schaumburg-Lippe, which is summarised in the text above.

create more equality and opportunity among his people. Virtually all that Count Wilhelm had built to enhance the welfare and preserve the independence of Schaumburg-Lippe was gone within a decade of his death. Then Hesse-Kassel, sensing an easy opportunity to annex its tiny neighbour, launched its invasion of defenceless Schaumburg-Lippe in 1787, and quickly overran the entire state, except for the Fortress Wilhelmstein.

In an age of dynastic states and professional armies, the character of *Reichsgraf* Friedrich Wilhelm Ernst zu Schaumburg-Lippe, his enlightened ideas on universal military service, and his continuing *Bildung* of military and civilian leaders, mark him as one of the most important military *philosophes* in history.[71] Wilhelm was a zealous propagator of service to humanity, a brave warrior, and a man of austerity and charity towards the poor and weak. The happiness of his people was his greatest motivation. Unfortunately, it took the death of their father-figure to make the people of Schaumburg-Lippe realise just how much Count Wilhelm had really cared for them. Nearly 10 years of peasant unrest characterized Schaumburg-Lippe during the reign of Count Philipp and his wife.[72]

Count Wilhelm fought against offensive war and worked to strengthen the power of his small state. This often placed him in opposition to the ruling elites, artisans, and businessmen of Schaumburg-Lippe. Indeed, many of his reforms were very unpopular and caused unrest among different sections of society. Nevertheless, he sought to return war to the people, but the people of Schaumburg-Lippe wanted no part in the defence of their own land. And while Guibert's *General Essay on Tactics* (1772) is often hailed as the landmark theoretical work that advocates a citizen army, it was actually Count Wilhelm who established the prototype of the nation-in-arms that later became the model throughout the western world. In keeping with his thoughts on the national army, Wilhelm was one of the few western military thinkers openly to condemn the immorality of war and to brand aggressive war as illegal.[73] From his perspective as the ruler of a small and vulnerable country (surrounded by larger and potentially hostile neighbours), and from his wartime experience in Germany and Portugal, Count Wilhelm maintained that the only just war was a defensive one waged by an 'armed citizenry' [*Landmiliz*] in the defence of their liberties.

All of Count Wilhelm's concepts affected young Gerhard Scharnhorst profoundly. They became paramount to his later modernisation efforts in Hanover and Prussia. Central to Scharnhorst's early formation was the military academy at Wilhelmstein, the first of its kind in European history. Based on the premise that experience and reason should stand in a close reciprocal relationship, and also in constant competition with existing doctrines, Count Wilhelm sought to create a new generation of German leaders, imbued with a military knowledge and understanding that would enable them to think critically and act independently in time of war.[74] These leaders studied all of the technical branches of war, especially science, technology, and engineering, while simultaneously receiving a broad,

71 In his chapter on 'The Military *Aufklärers*', Azar Gat, *The Origins of Military Thought: From the Enlightenment to Clausewitz* (Oxford: The Clarendon Press, 1989), p.60, writes that Count Wilhelm is perhaps 'the most interesting case' of enlightenment education in Germany.

72 See the interesting article by Carl-Hans Hauptmeyer, 'Die Bauernunruhen in Schaumburg-Lippe 1784-1793', *Niedersächsisches Jahrbuch für Langesgeschichte*, Band 49 (Hildesheim: August Lax,1977), pp.149-207.

73 It would take another 200 years before the Nuremburg Tribunal acknowledged the wisdom of Count Wilhelm.

74 Hornung, *Scharnhorst*, p.17.

liberal, and enlightened *Bildung* that focused on the higher dimensions of the art of war. Wilhelm himself taught most of the senior-level classes, firmly believing that through the moral formation of young men, he could develop competent military and civilian leaders.

Schaumburg-Lippe was 'the quintessential military state'. It was Count Wilhelm's belief in a 'people's army' and a 'people's war' that set him far apart from other German princes and mark him as a true champion of the German Enlightenment. He maintained that the nation-in-arms was 'the most rational, efficient, and practical form of military organisation to serve national policy and to facilitate pure defensive war'.[75] In numerous writings Wilhelm pioneered a new system of combined arms tactics identical in many respects to those French theorists later espoused in their debate on tactics following the Seven Years War. And yet, despite the fact he enjoyed a solid reputation as an enlightened sovereign and combat leader, Count Wilhelm was largely unknown in his lifetime, even among his own German countrymen. Nevertheless, it was into this environment that Scharnhorst came as a student in 1773, and later wrote of his experience at Wilhelmstein: 'In every respect he [Count Wilhelm] was a great man, of whom Germany can be proud'.[76]

75 Patrick J. Speelman, 'Lippe, Field Marshal Friedrich Wilhelm Ernst, Graf zu Schaumburg (1724-1777)', in Daniel Coetzee and Lee W. Eysturlid (ed.), *Philosophers of War: The Evolution of History's Greatest Military Thinkers* (Santa Barbara: Praeger, 2013), pp.92-94; the quoted passages are from p.94.

76 Scharnhorst is quoted in Hornung, *Scharnhorst*, p.18.

3

Formation at Wilhelmstein

With the island fortress nearing completion, Wilhelm turned his attention to the *Bildung* of his military. In the fall of 1766, he drafted his initial concept for a theoretical and practical school intended for the education and training of engineers and artillerymen, because 'perfection in the art of waging war leads to the prevention of war'.[1] To this end the school, the army, and the citizen militia were vital components of Wilhelm's 'testing ground for a reformation of the art of war'. As he so astutely put it, 'According to the present political and military structure of states, the principle activity of citizens and soldiers is directed toward offensive and not defensive wars'.[2] Wilhelm intended to change this mindset.

Like so many of his fellow *Aufklärer*, Wilhelm sought 'to surmount the contemporary military politics of professional armies' through the process of *Bildung*.[3] His curriculum included a broad list of subjects that were linked to his endeavours to expand the economy of Schaumburg-Lippe, to raise the prosperity of his people, and to defend Schaumburg-Lippe. Students 'were to be infused with' [*informirt werden*] the essence of religion and French.[4] For Wilhelm, religious formation was paramount for the development of leaders. As he so succinctly put it, 'The military without religion is a great danger in war'.[5] Mastery of French was vital, too, since most of the texts studied at Wilhelmstein were written in French. Pupils were then taught arithmetic, geometry, statistics, ballistics, hydraulics, hydrostatics,

1 See Wilhelm zu Schaumburg-Lippe, 'Anhang, die theoretischen und praktischen Schulen zur Unterweisung Unseres Ingenieur- und Artillerie-Coprs, betreffend' (7 November 1766); in Ochwadt (ed.), *Wilhelm Graf zu Schaumburg-Lippe*, Vol.1, pp.281-84. The quoted passage is from p.338 of the Lecture, 'Graf Wilhelm zu Schaumburg-Lippe', which Professor Walter Arnsberger presented to the Historical Association of Lower Saxony on 17 February 1902; and published in *Zeitschrift des Historischen Vereins für Niedersachsen* 3 (1902), pp.331-47.

2 See Wilhelm's thoughts in Number 85 of the Section 'Über den Krieg', in Ochwadt (ed.), *Wilhelm Graf zu Schaumburg-Lippe*, Vol.2, p.142.

3 See Ochwadt, 'Zur Biographie des Grafen Wilhelm zu Schaumburg-Lippe', in Ochwadt (ed.), *Wilhelm Graf zu Schaumburg-Lippe*, Vol.1, p.481.

4 See 'Zum Unterrichtsplan', in Ochwadt (ed.), *Wilhelm Graf zu Schaumburg-Lippe*, Vol.2, p.96. This was the initial draft, according to Ochwadt. In his Explanatory Note 20 in Vol.2, p.414, Ochwadt cites Count Wilhelm, who wrote before 1767, 'This list of possible subjects of instruction is not to be regarded as final'.

5 For Wilhelm's various thoughts on religion, see Ochwadt (ed.), *Wilhelm Graf zu Schaumburg-Lippe*, Vol.1, pp.50-53 ('Condition de l'homme'), 68-69 ('L'amour-propre est-il cause de vertu'), 110-14 ('Zu Religion und Atheismus'), and Vol.2, p.159 ('Zur Kritik des Militärberufs'). The quoted passage is from Wilhelm zu Schaumburg-Lippe, 'Nachlase zu den *Mémoires pour server à l'art militaire défensif*, in Ochwadt (ed.), *Wilhelm Graf zu Schaumburg-Lippe*, Vol.2, p.244.

mechanics, chemistry, medicine, anatomy, and surgery, 'to the extent they would have an immediate influence in building industry, agriculture, and the mechanical arts; in all kinds of factories, mines, and in the military, etc.'[6]

Significantly, theology, philosophy, history, metaphysics, geography, and rhetoric were not formally taught at Wilhelmstein, simply because Wilhelm viewed these subjects as vital components of an enlightened pedagogy and were thus to be acquired in the normal course of the student's learning activities, especially through his reading, self-study, and tutorials. Wilhelm also listed 'physical fitness' [*Phisique*] as a subject to be taught.[7] Here is yet another example of this sovereign German prince caring for the physical and mental welfare of his men.

From this initial draft Count Wilhelm proceeded to clarify his plan for 'the theoretical and practical schools' of instruction for the Schaumburg-Lippe artillery and engineer corps.[8] He made it clear that 'in the theoretical school', students would study the theory of gunnery, the attack and defence of fortified areas, military engineering, and other 'military' subjects using the various textbooks the school provided. Two artillery lieutenants under the supervision of the Chief of Artillery would tutor students each Monday and Friday for one hour in the lieutenant's quarters. Every Wednesday and Saturday mornings from nine to 12, officers, warrant officers, cadets from the artillery corps, 'and no one else', would attend mandatory study halls in the library.[9] No one was excused from these sessions unless he was sick, on duty, or on special leave.[10]

In the practical school students received hands-on training in the laboratories specifically built at Wilhelmstein for experimenting with powder mixtures and explosives, types of cannon and mortar shells, mines, grenades, and artillery equipment. They also visited local civilian industries and craft enterprises to gain an understanding of manufacturing processes. During the summer months they would apply their theoretical knowledge in practical field exercises at the training areas located at Steinhude, Hagenburg, and Grossenheidorn. These included military and civil engineering projects, and artillery

6 'Zum Unterrichtsplan', in Ochwadt (ed.), *Wilhelm Graf zu Schaumburg-Lippe*, Vol.2, p.96.

7 Ochwadt (ed.), *Wilhelm Graf zu Schaumburg-Lippe*, Vol.2, p.96, notes the term 'Physical fitness' appears smudged (or lined through) in the original document. Ochwadt concludes that 'perhaps it [physical fitness] may have been deleted' from the curriculum. Interestingly, from the perspective of medicine and anatomy, *Phisique* meant the development of the human body.

8 See Wilhelm zu Schaumburg-Lippe, 'Anhang, die theoretischen und praktischen Schulen zur Unterweisung Unseres Ingenieur- und Artillerie-Corps, betreffend' (7 November 1766); in Ochwadt (ed.), *Wilhelm Graf zu Schaumburg-Lippe*, Vol.1, pp.281-84.

9 Wilhelm zu Schaumburg-Lippe, 'Anhang, die theoretischen und praktischen Schulen zur Unterweisung Unseres Ingenieur- und Artillerie-Corps, betreffend' (7 November 1766); in Ochwadt (ed.), *Wilhelm Graf zu Schaumburg-Lippe*, Vol.1, p.281. The term 'warrant officer' is used to translate *Conducteur*, based on Wilhelm's description of his duties: 'In case of need, such as when or where there is a shortage of officers, conducteurs perform the duties of officers. Conducteurs are not non-commissioned officers'. See Ochwadt (ed.), *Wilhelm Graf zu Schaumburg-Lippe*, Vol.2, p.98 (Note 32).

10 Wilhelm zu Schaumburg-Lippe, 'Anhang, die theoretischen und praktischen Schulen zur Unterweisung unseres Ingenieur- und Artillerie-Corps, betreffend' (7 November 1766); in Ochwadt (ed.), *Wilhelm Graf zu Schaumburg-Lippe*, Vol.1, p.281.

live-fire exercises using stationary and moving targets. In September, students would participate in the annual army manoeuvres.[11]

When 'the theoretical artillery school' opened on 21 April 1767, and the 'school of practice for the artillery and engineers' two months later on 9 June, Wilhelm soon realised he may have moved too quickly. Instruction turned out to be 'more or less haphazard'. Students listened mainly to lectures presented at the discretion of their officer-instructors.[12] Wilhelmstein was little more than a technical school for the training of officers and officer candidates in science and technology. Non-commissioned officers and the common soldiers were excluded.[13] This was normal for the times, but totally unsatisfactory for Wilhelm, who decided this had to change. A more inclusive and formal approach was necessary to guarantee all of his military and civilian students received a thorough training and education in leader development. Implementing such a curriculum took another two-and-a-half years.

On 20 February 1770, Wilhelm introduced a revised and much more comprehensive program of studies. Now all soldiers, as well as civilian artisans essential to the army, were included. To avoid any future misconceptions, he prescribed in detail both the subject matter and its method of instruction.[14] He then issued subsequent 'Instructions' [*Befehle*] that updated the governance of the school, as well as 'Notes' [*Notizen*] on the curriculum and other matters.[15] At the same time he raised the character of the institution from simply an artillery and engineering school to a military academy. General subjects now included: theoretical and applied mathematics, physics and chemistry, civil engineering, mechanics, hydraulics, hydrostatics, natural history, economics, medicine, anatomy, surgery, religion, geography, and foreign languages. Military courses consisted of military history, campaign planning, tactics, gunnery, military engineering, surveying, fortifications, ballistics, and terrain sketching.[16]

Unlike other military schools that focused primarily on remedial military training, Wilhelmstein emphasised the *Bildung* of leaders, thoroughly educated and trained in the art

11 Wilhelm zu Schaumburg-Lippe, 'Anhang, die theoretischen und praktischen Schulen zur Unterweisung Unseres Ingenieur- und Artillerie-Corps, betreffend' (7 November 1766); in Ochwadt (ed.), *Wilhelm Graf zu Schaumburg-Lippe*, Vol.1, pp.281-82 and 284.

12 Klein, *Wilhelm zu Schaumburg-Lippe*, pp.262-63.

13 See the discussion in Bernard Poten, *Geschichte des Militär-Erziehungs-und Bildungswesen in den Landen deutscher Zunge 5: Sachsen, Schaumburg-Lippe, Schleswig-Holstein, Schweiz, Königreich Westfalen, Württemberg*; in *Monumenta Germaniae Paedagogica*, Band 17 (Berlin: A. Hofmann, 1897), pp.236-37.

14 See Wilhelm zu Schaumburg-Lippe, *Reglement, die Studia und Exercitia derer Schaumburg-Lippe-Bückeburgischen Ingenieurs und Artilleristen betreffend* (Stadthagen: Johann Friedrich Althans, 1770); reprinted in Ochwadt (ed.), *Wilhelm Graf zu Schaumburg-Lippe*, Vol.2, pp.78-88.

15 Wilhelm zu Schaumburg-Lippe, *Reglement, die Studia und Exercitia betreffend*; in Ochwadt (ed.), *Wilhelm Graf zu Schaumburg-Lippe*, Vol.2, pp.88-103.

16 In addition to the *Reglement, die Studia und Exercitia betreffend*, see Poten, *Geschichte des Militär-Erziehungs-und Bildungswesen: Schaumburg-Lippe*, pp.234-64, for a discussion of the syllabus and methods of instruction. A comparative analysis of contemporary military schools can be found in Oliver Schulz, 'Die Vorstellungen des Grafen Wilhelm von Schaumburg-Lippe von Rekrutierung, Ausbildung und gesellschaftlicher Rolle militärischer Eliten und ihre Umsetzung in der Militärschule auf der Festung Wilhelmstein', in Gundula Gahlen and Carmen Winkel (ed.), *Militär und Gesellschaft in der Frühen Neuzeit: Themenheft Militärische Eliten in der Frühen Neuzeit* (Potsdam: Universitätsverlag Potsdam, 2010), pp.215-28. Also see the interesting commentary in Klein, *Wilhelm zu Schaumburg-Lippe*, Chapter 21, pp.262-69.

of war. Students were taught in small groups, in which a tutorial methodology was employed. This was essential, especially later as the student body grew and was composed of young men who had begun their studies at different times and with varying degrees of understanding.[17] Wilhelm may have even grouped pupils by talent and ability, since the evidence indicates those working on the same assignments would meet together with a common tutor. Wilhelm's intent was to introduce pupils to a broad, liberal education in the arts and sciences, one similar to what he had experienced as a young man.[18] Modern languages (French and English, and later Portuguese), as well as drawing, were also included. Because he believed in the 'absolute necessity' of applying all learning 'in an actual environment', he continually monitored all theoretical classroom instruction and linked it with practical laboratory experiments and field training exercises.[19]

Wilhelm appointed his most talented and clever officers as tutors. Their mission was to teach, mentor, and inspire, not to lecture. Among those mentioned in the records are *Lieutenants* Colson, Dolle, and Döring; Murdtfeldt, Prätorius, Rauschenbusch, Sustmann, and Weissich. In keeping with the regulations governing the academic week, these officers mentored their pupils each Monday, Tuesday, Thursday, and Friday, for at least one hour in their quarters. During these small group sessions, students discussed their assigned projects, received assistance from fellow pupils and guidance from their tutor, and worked together on their completion. On Wednesday and Saturday, they, 'and no one else without our special permission', continued their education in two four-hour study halls in *Courtine* 6 (the library), located in one of the outer fortifications. Pupils spent this time in group classes and self-directed study. Afternoons were set aside specifically for individual self-study. For Count Wilhelm, this meant studying the books and manuscripts, examining the maps and charts, and operating the models and instruments in the library. In special cases, some small group study was conducted in the afternoons.[20]

The voluminous library housed many of the finest military, theological, scientific, and political classics. Manuscripts, numerous maps and charts, and some of the best scientific

17 See Wilhelm zu Schaumburg-Lippe, 'Befehle, die Eintheilung derer Unterofficiers, Cadets, Lernenden Artilleristen und Gemeinen in Classen betreffend' (15 July 1772); in Ochwadt (ed.), *Wilhelm Graf zu Schaumburg-Lippe*, Vol.2, pp.88-89.

18 Schmalz, *Denkwürdigkeiten des Grafen Wilhelms zu Schaumburg-Lippe*, pp.59-68, provides a lengthy commentary on the educational environment at Wilhelmstein at this time, especially the subjects addressed in the small groups.

19 The quoted passages are from Paragraph 4 of *Reglement, die Studia und Exercitia betreffend*; in Ochwadt (ed.), *Wilhelm Graf zu Schaumburg-Lippe*, Vol.2, p.82. Further clarification of his pedagogical approach can be found later in the two important instructions Wilhelm issued in 1774 and 1776. See Wilhelm zu Schaumburg-Lippe, 'Befehle, welche dem *Reglement, die Studia und Exercitia des Artillerie-Corps etc. betreffend*, beyzufügen; vom 10. März 1774' and 'Befehle, welche unserm *Reglement, die Studia und Exercitia* unsers *Ingenieur- und Artillerie-Corps betreffend*, beyzufügen' (30 August 1776); in Ochwadt (ed.), *Wilhelm Graf zu Schaumburg-Lippe*, Vol.2, pp.92-93 and 93-95; respectively.

20 For a good understanding of the academic life at Wilhelmstein, see Poten, *Geschichte des Militär-Erziehungs-und Bildungswesen: Schaumburg-Lippe*, pp.234-64; Klein, *Wilhelm zu Schaumburg-Lippe*, pp.262-69; Schulz, 'Die Vorstellungen des Grafen Wilhelm von Schaumburg-Lippe', pp.215-28; and Lehmann, *Scharnhorst*, Vol.1, pp.21-26. The quoted passage comes from Wilhelm zu Schaumburg-Lippe, *Reglement, die Studia und Exercitia betreffend*; in Ochwadt (ed.), *Wilhelm Graf zu Schaumburg-Lippe*, Vol.2, p.79.

instruments of the time were also contained in this library.[21] Wilhelm spared no expense to get the best for his students. Special tutorials were also part of the program of studies. One such event took place in the observatory of the fortress on the evening of 19 February 1776. It lasted three hours, from four to seven, was led by *Lieutenant* Prätorius, and dealt with astronomical observations.[22] Another took place on 2 November 1776, when *Lieutenant* Weissich presented two lectures on the *Letters of Euler on Different Subjects in Natural Philosophy: Addressed to a German Princess* (St. Petersburg, 1768-72). The morning talk was in French from 11 to noon; the afternoon session was in German from two to three.[23]

As the students progressed in the comprehension of their course work, Wilhelm added to their empirical studies. Practical field exercises now included tactical map problems without troops, terrain sketching, estimating distances, and map making, along with the handling of mines and bombs, and the employment of light, mobile artillery with infantry units. This training offered ample opportunities for students to apply their knowledge, verify their skills and techniques, and develop their leadership potential.[24] During the annual army manoeuvres, officer candidates had to prepare at least one practical exercise for implementation.[25] All of this later became fundamental to Scharnhorst's own programs in Hanover and Prussia.

Aware that nations needed educated and well-trained civilian and military leaders, Wilhelm transformed Wilhelmstein into a true formational experience.[26] Central to Wilhelm's concept of *Bildung* was his emphasis on self-study. He believed that what a leader lacked in experience he could make up through self-study. He also knew that young leaders required proper mentoring to guide their self-study. Dividing the student body into seven classes, he placed a lieutenant in charge of each.[27] Classes were then sub-divided into five sections: the first contained officer candidates; the other four were composed of *Bombardiers* (artillerymen), *Mineurs* (military miners and sappers), *Ouvriers* (craftsmen who built military carriages, riggings, and machines), and *Canoniers* (gunners). Here Wilhelm grouped pupils according to their functional duties. Non-commissioned officers were then distributed among the classes to assist the lieutenant and to provide 'hands-on' training to the

21 For an interesting study of Count Wilhelm's library, see Heike Matzke, 'Die Bibliothek des Grafen Wilhelm zu Schaumburg-Lippe (1724-1777): Annäherung an die Persönlichkeit eines Landesherren des 18. Jahrhunderts durch die Rekonstrucktion seiner Büchersammlungen' (Diplomarbeit im Studiengang Bibliothekswesen an der Fachhochschule Hannover-Wunstorf, 2003). *Lieutenant* Döring was charged with the supervision of the library and its holdings.

22 Poten, *Geschichte des Militär-Erziehungs-und Bildungswesen: Schaumburg-Lippe*, p.241.

23 See Wilhelm zu Schaumburg-Lippe, 'Notizen zur Arbeit in der Militärschule', in Ochwadt (ed.), *Wilhelm Graf zu Schaumburg-Lippe*, Vol.2, p.103 (Number 54). Interestingly, *Lieutenant* Weissich was recently commissioned, having been a former *Conducteur*.

24 See Paragraph 4 of *Reglement, die Studia und Exercitia betreffend*; in Ochwadt (ed.), *Wilhelm Graf zu Schaumburg-Lippe*, Vol.2, pp.82-85. Also see the interesting discussion in Klippel, *Scharnhorst*, Vol.1, pp.51-54.

25 Klein, *Wilhelm zu Schaumburg-Lippe*, p.264.

26 See Schulz, 'Die Vorstellungen des Grafen Wilhelm von Schaumburg-Lippe', pp.215-28. On pp.224-25, especially Note 26, Schultz contrasts Wilhelmstein with other military schools of the time and concludes that Wilhelmstein was a genuine 'academy' in the eighteenth century meaning of the term.

27 See Wilhelm zu Schaumburg-Lippe, 'Befehle, die Eintheilung derer Unterofficiers, Cadets, Lernenden Artilleristen und Gemeinen in Classen betreffend' (15 July 1772) to Commandant *Major* Franzose Jean d'Etienne; in Ochwadt (ed.), *Wilhelm Graf zu Schaumburg-Lippe*, Vol.2, pp.88-89.

students. The student body numbered over 300 pupils in the early years of the academy but fell to around 150 students annually in later years, due mainly to the success of the enlightened education and training at Wilhelmstein.[28]

Subjects for the tutorials, group classes, and guided self-study were related to the defence of Schaumburg-Lippe. Because Wilhelmstein was the centrepiece of Count Wilhelm's defensive strategy, it followed that science and technology, engineering and mathematics, and artillery gunnery techniques, were the major topics of study. This was consistent with the siege warfare and fortifications mentality of the eighteenth century. Even the translation exercises for the most part dealt with ballistics, shipbuilding, mathematics, and siegecraft. During the 1774 Easter examinations, students were also given selections to translate from Plutarch and Cato, and from Guibert's *General Essay on Tactics*.[29] Furthermore, Wilhelm directed that tutors always view the syllabus as a starting point for a broader exploration of the subjects under consideration, as well as for their own professional development.[30]

Wilhelm chose some of the best, practical textbooks for his students. Foremost was *New Course in Mathematics for Use by the Artillery and Engineers* (Paris, 1725), by Bernard Forêt de Bélidor (1698-1761). This text appeared in German editions in 1746, 1759, and 1773. Composed of 16 books (including their associated tables, charts, and formulas), *New Course in Mathematics* discussed and illustrated the theory and practical application of mathematics for artillery and engineering students. Bélidor's work proved invaluable and provided the foundation of all scientific and mathematical studies at Wilhelmstein.[31] Each book began with the introduction of a mathematical proposition, and then proceeded to its practical application. Each book was a self-contained unit of instruction that built upon material discussed in previous books. *New Course in Mathematics* was the ideal self-study text. Students could proceed at their own pace until they had achieved mastery of the subject matter. Instructors could monitor the progress of their pupils and provide mentoring and remedial instruction as necessary. Routine examinations evaluated the student's comprehension of the subject material.[32] Before leaving Wilhelmstein in 1777, Scharnhorst was able to complete the first 12 books of Bélidor's text and had solved Problem 32 of Book 13, which dealt with the application of geometry to the division of fields (or territory), and with the use of proportional compasses. Problem 32 had the pupil calculate the diameter of cylinders used to measure powder charges.[33]

In the regulation governing the academy, Wilhelm discussed the various textbooks, linking them to their specific courses and explaining how tutors were to integrate them into

28 See the discussion in Klippel, *Scharnhorst*, Vol.1, p.50; and in Klein, *Wilhelm zu Schaumburg-Lippe*, p.263.

29 See Wilhelm zu Schaumburg-Lippe, 'Memoranda, das Ostern-Examen von 1774 betreffend', in Ochwadt (ed.), *Wilhelm Graf zu Schaumburg-Lippe*, Vol.2, p.101.

30 The spirit Wilhelm encouraged his tutors to follow can be found throughout his instructions, as well as his important 'Notizen zur Arbeit in der Militärschule', in Ochwadt (ed.), *Wilhelm Graf zu Schaumburg-Lippe*, Vol.2, pp.96-103.

31 Bernard Forêt de Bélidor, *Nouveau cours de mathématique à l'usage de l'artillerie et du genie* (Paris: Charles-Antoine Jombert, 1725). In Bélidor's time, the word '*genie*' was associated with military endeavours, especially engineering.

32 An overview of Scharnhorst's examinations can be found in his 'Prüfungsprotokolle' [examination protocol]; in Kunisch (ed.), *Scharnhorst: Privat und dienstliche Schriften*, Vol.1, pp.3-23.

33 Bélidor, *Nouveau cours de mathématique*, pp.473-75. Scharnhorst was examined on 28 August 1777. See 'Prüfungsprotokolle', in Kunisch (ed.), *Scharnhorst: Privat und dienstliche Schriften*, Vol.1, p.13.

the learning process.[34] Beginning artillerymen studied Carl August Struensee's *Rudiments of the Artillery* (Leipzig, 1769) and Heinrich Johann Vogel's *Instruction in Artillery Science* (Zürich, 1739 and 1756). Students also used three more advanced works to learn artillery and the art of fortifications. These were the seminal work of Sébastien le Prestre, Marquis de Vauban, *Treatise on the Attack and Defence of Positions* (La Hare, 1737), followed by Pierre Surirey de Saint Remy's *Memoirs on the Artillery* (Paris, 1697), and Bélidor's *Engineer Science* (1729). Vauban's *Treatise* 'was the standard work for students of fortifications and siegecraft' until the second half of the 19th Century.[35] Saint-Remy was one of the leading artillery officers of the French army during the reign of Louis XIV. His *Memoirs on the Artillery* is the classic French work of the period on artillery and educated several generations of artillery officers, including young Napoleon.[36] This comprehensive and richly illustrated work described the manufacture of various sizes and types of cannons, the production of gunpowder and cannonballs, techniques for mounting cannon on carriages and on ships, the organisation of artillery batteries, and the positioning of guns within batteries, their ranging, tactics, attack, and defence. Bélidor's *Engineer Science* dealt with aspects of military engineering and was later translated into German in 1764. This book, along with his civil engineering text, *Hydraulic Architecture* (1737–39), established Bélidor as one of the leading proponents of engineering mechanics, especially hydraulics and ballistics.[37]

As part of their engineering curriculum, pupils studied *The Premier Book on Architecture* (Paris, 1567), written by the great master architect of the French Renaissance, Philibert de L'Orme. L'Orme had synthesised the secrets of the ancient master stone masons and successfully grafted their techniques onto a classic French architectural design. Jean Florent de Vallière's *Treatise on the Defence* (Paris, 1768) and Friedrich Roth-Scholtz's *Thoughts on Chemistry* (1719) were also among the fundamental works Wilhelm used. Willem Jacob s'Gravesande's *An Explanation of Newtonian Philosophy* (Leiden, 1723), along with Anton Rüdiger's *Systematic Instruction on Pure and Especially Applied or General Chemistry* (Leipzig, 1756), were used to study physics and chemistry. Required texts for learning the basics of calculus and analysis were Charles René Reyneau's *Demonstrated Analysis* (Paris, 1708), Abraham Gotthelf Kaestner's *Rudiments of Mathematics* (Göttingen, 1759), and Guillaume François Antoine, Marquis de l'Hôpital's *Analysis of the Infinitely Small* (Paris, 1696).[38] Providing meaningful perspective to these texts were the *Commentaries and Postscripts* (1726-83) of Leonhard Euler, who was arguably one of the great mathematicians of the eighteenth century, as well as a brilliant physicist. For translation practice, students

34 See Wilhelm zu Schaumburg-Lippe, *Reglement, die Studia und Exercitia betreffend*; in Ochwadt (ed.), *Wilhelm Graf zu Schaumburg-Lippe*, Vol.2, pp.78-88; especially, pp.80-82.

35 Gat, *The Origins of Military Thought*, p.37. On the influence of Vauban, see Henry Guerlau, 'Vauban: The Impact of Science on War', in Peter Paret (ed.; with the collaboration of Gordan A. Craig and Felix Gilbert), *Makers of Modern Strategy: From Machiavelli to the Nuclear Age* (Princeton: Princeton University Press, 1986), pp.64-90.

36 *Memoirs on the Artillery* went through several French editions (1702, 1741, and 1745) and was translated into Russian (1732-33). Portions were later translated into English in 1756.

37 See the nice biographical sketch of 'Bernard Forêt de Bélidor' by Charles C. Gillispie; in Charles C. Gillispie (ed.), *Dictionary of Scientific Biography* (New York: Charles Scribner's Sons, 1970–80), Vol.1, pp.581-82.

38 For a comparative study of several of the textbooks used at Wilhelmstein, see Mónica Blanco Abellán, 'Textbooks on Different Calculus in Eighteenth Century Europe: A Comparative Stylistic Analysis', *Journal of Data Science* 5 (2007), pp.597-612.

often used Denis Diderot's and Jean Le Rond d'Alembert's *Encyclopedia, or a Systematic Dictionary of the Sciences, the Arts, and the Trades* (Paris, 1751-72).[39]

Annual examinations provided important milestone checks on the progress of each student. This was crucial. Wilhelm believed not only in a broad, general education for his future leaders, but also in the objective and critical evaluation of their understanding and future potential. Exams were held on the third day after Easter and Pentecost, and on 29 September (the feast of Saint Michael the Archangel).[40] Only tactics, mathematics, physics, geography, civil engineering, and French were initially tested. Economics and English were later added. During one of his English exams, Scharnhorst had to discuss portions of Benjamin Robins, *New Principles of Gunnery* (London, 1742).[41] On other exams he was to address: the production of a hygrometer, drafting a concept by which an army near the Steinhuder Meer could entrench, measuring the height of a tower, discussing various means for reinforcing a trench with palisades, leading a sapping operation, answering questions of geography, translating texts from French and English, writing an essay on ambition and another on chaos, discussing portions from Mungo Murray's *A Treatise on Ship-Building and Navigation* (London, 1765), measuring distances, and drawing a map of the Leyne region near Bordenau.[42] Wilhelm often appeared without notice at the examinations and was known to post both successful and flawed solutions in the fortress atrium.[43] He also reserved the right to hold special evaluations at his discretion. After he posted the results of the Easter exams of 19-21 April 1775, Gunnery Sergeant [*Feuerwerker*] Scharnhorst received a gold medallion for his outstanding performance.[44]

Constantly seeking to upgrade and refine the quality of *Bildung* at his academy, Wilhelm further divided selected members of the student body into three specialty groups he called 'Private Information' [*Privatinformation*].[45] These 'tutorials' were in addition to the student's regular curriculum. Here again Wilhelm sought to foster an appreciation of how theory and practice are linked. Students wrote essays, drew maps and diagrams, translated texts, solved mathematical problems, and proved scientific theorems. Any chemical processes or experiments conducted during these seminars had to be approved beforehand by the Count. Scharnhorst later wrote about the many enjoyable opportunities he had to experiment with

39 John A. Lynn, 'The Treatment of Military Subjects in Diderot's *Encyclopédie*', *Journal of Military History* 65:1 (January 2001), pp.131-65, provides an interesting analysis of these topics. Reviewing Scharnhorst's translation exercises in Kunisch (ed.), *Scharnhorst: Privat und dienstliche Schriften*, Vol.1, pp.8-9, does not reveal the specific subjects he was given to translate.

40 See Paragraph 5 of *Reglement, die Studia und Exercitia betreffend;* in Ochwadt (ed.), *Wilhelm Graf zu Schaumburg-Lippe: Schriften und Briefe*, Vol.2, pp.85-86. From the 'Examination Protocol' cited in Kunisch (ed.), *Scharnhorst: Privat und dienstliche Schriften*, Vol.1, pp.3-23, yearly exams were also held in December; and monthly (February-August 1777), the last year of Count Wilhelm's life.

41 See Kunisch (ed.), *Scharnhorst: Privat und dienstliche Schriften*, Vol.3: *Lehrer, Artillerist, Webbereiter (Preußen 1801-1804)*, p.596 (Note 11). Robins was a military engineer and Professor of Mathematics at the Royal Military Academy at Woolwich.

42 See Scharnhorst's 'Prüfungsprotokolle', in Kunisch (ed.), *Scharnhorst: Privat und dienstliche Schriften*, Vol.1, pp.6-23.

43 Schmalz, 'Beschreibung der Vestung Wilhelmstein im Steinhuder Meer', p.92 (Column 2).

44 See Scharnhorst's 'Prüfungsprotokolle', in Kunisch (ed.), *Scharnhorst: Privat und dienstliche Schriften*, Vol.1, p.10.

45 See Wilhelm zu Schaumburg-Lippe, 'Befehle, die Privatinformationes und Vorlesungen in unserer Militairschule auf denen Wilhelms Inseln betreffend, vom 9. März 1773', in Ochwadt (ed.), *Wilhelm Graf zu Schaumburg-Lippe*, Vol.2, pp.91-92.

powder mixes, the effects of artillery fire on different targets, and the influence of wind and distance on gunnery techniques, to name just a few.[46]

Wilhelm chose his top three lieutenants to oversee students through their programs of study. *Lieutenant* Döring was charged with all engineering and artillery instruction (construction, mines, and pontoons), using Bélidor's *Engineer Science* and Vauban's *Treatise on the Attack and Defence of Positions.* He also monitored each student's progress through Bélidor's *New Course in Mathematics. Lieutenant* Dolle taught the military application of the mechanical arts (casting and iron works, using coal, limestone, and brick) on Wednesday and Saturday afternoons, from two until three. His group also discussed economics and pyrotechnics, and the leading ideas in mineralogy and chemistry. *Lieutenant* Prätorius taught courses on geography, field fortifications, castrametation, and the integration of military engineers when conducting reconnaissance, planning and leading marches, setting up and dismantling camps, surveying and field sketching. From 11 to noon on Wednesday and Saturday, his group solved physics problems, discussed the philosophy of Christian Wolff, and experimented with the discoveries of Pieter van Musschenbroek and Jean-Antoine Nollet.[47]

Musschenbroek and Nollet were noted eighteenth century scientists. Pieter van Musschenbroek (1692-1761) was a Dutch physician and natural scientist, who focused his research primarily on problems of electricity and capillarity, always emphasising an empirical approach. While teaching at the Universities of Duisburg and Leiden, he played an important role in the spread of Newtonian physics. He later published his lectures notes as *The Elements of Natural Philosophy: Chiefly Intended for the Use of Students in Universities* (1744). Musschenbroek is credited with the invention of the first capacitor in 1746. Fifteen years later he met another great electrician, Benjamin Franklin, who was visiting Leiden.[48]

Jean-Antoine Nollet (1700-70) was a Catholic deacon whose love of science (especially electricity) earned him one of the first French professorships of experimental physics. Nollet is credited with discovering osmosis in 1748. He also invented an electroscope. From 1753 he was a professor of physics at the Collège de Navarre in Paris, and from 1761 a professor at the engineering and artillery school in Mézières during the time Lazare Carnot was a student. Interestingly, Nollet is reputed to have given the name 'Leyden jar' to the capacitor Pieter van Musschenbroek had invented.

A year later in March 1774, Wilhelm further clarified instruction and the examination process.[49] Officers were now to teach students in the language of their textbooks (French, German, or English). As part of their self-study, officer candidates were required to keep detailed journals of their critical reading and thinking. Wilhelm attached great importance here. As he had written earlier: 'Experience without military insight is more harmful than

46 For a description of some of these experiments, see Scharnhorst, 'Von den Militär-Anstalten des verstorbenen regierenden Grafen von Schaumburg-Lippe', pp.98-99.

47 See Wilhelm zu Schaumburg-Lippe, 'Befehle, die Privatinformationes und Vorlesungen in unserer Militairschule auf denen Wilhelms Inseln betreffend, vom 9. März 1773', in Ochwadt (ed.), *Wilhelm Graf zu Schaumburg-Lippe*, Vol.2, pp.91-92.

48 Walter Isaacson, *Benjamin Franklin: An American Life* (New York: Simon & Schuster, 2003), p.200.

49 See the separate section at the end of Wilhelm zu Schaumburg-Lippe, 'Befehle, welche dem *Reglement, Die Studia und Exercitia des Artillerie-Corps, etc betreffend*, beyzufügen; vom 10. März 1774', in Ochwadt (ed.), *Wilhelm Graf zu Schaumburg-Lippe*, Vol.2, p.93.

useful. Such stupidity makes one obstinate and prideful'.[50] All experiments, particularly those dealing with gunnery, ballistics, mines, and pyrotechnics, were to be noted in the student's journal. These journals were kept secret and remained in the library, where the Count would often read them to gauge the intellectual capacity and originality of his pupils. He would then select the most promising officer candidates for his 'Private Information' seminars.

The final portion of Wilhelm's order of March 1774 contained a new examination protocol. Now the yearly exams were a three-day affair.[51] During the first day students solved various mathematical problems as a preparation for the second day. On the second day they were to apply their problem-solving techniques to questions of mathematics, mechanics, physics, siege operations, artillery, and construction. Day Three consisted of a 'pure practicum' [*die pure Praxin*] of translations from English, Portuguese, and French (in both written and oral formats), as well as sketching, drawing, and model construction.

Wilhelm issued a final set of instructions a year before his death. This important order detailed how the study of economics was to be integrated into the curriculum, focusing on both its civilian and military applications.[52] On the civilian side, Wilhelm endeavoured to improve the agriculture of Schaumburg-Lippe using the concepts Professor Johann Beckmann had developed in his work, *Principles of German Agriculture* (1775 Edition). On the military side, officers, students, and civilians studied wartime logistical operations, especially the subsistence of an army on campaign. They also updated the logistical annexes of the operational plans for the Schaumburg-Lippe army.

For their continuing professional development, civilian and military leaders attended weekly presentations at the Count's residence at Hagenburg. These were held every Sunday afternoon from four to five, or from four to six. Military personnel at Wilhelmstein also attended weekly classes every Wednesday afternoon from two to three, or from two to four. It appears no one escaped Wilhelm's developmental approach, which linked theoretical classroom instruction with practical 'on-the-job' training.

Practical military training for students (both civilian and military) took place at Wilhelmstein. When not in the classroom or study halls pursuing their academic endeavours, or on field trips observing local industry and agriculture, students engaged in the daily military operations of the fortress, where they performed the various duties of the soldier and learned the responsibilities of the rank and file. On Sunday afternoons, weather permitting, officers, non-commissioned officers, artillerymen, soldiers, and students exercised the various defensive contingency plans of the fortress. This weekly routine continued annually for 10 months. In August and September, students served in various artillery and engineer positions during the annual army manoeuvres.[53] In this way Count Wilhelm endeavoured

50 See Wilhelm zu Schaumburg-Lippe, 'Kalendernotiz 1772', in Ochwadt (ed.), *Wilhelm Graf zu Schaumburg-Lippe*, Vol.2, p.90.

51 See Wilhelm zu Schaumburg-Lippe, 'Befehle, Welche dem *Reglement, Die Studia und Exercitia*; vom 10. März 1774', in Ochwadt (ed.), *Wilhelm Graf zu Schaumburg-Lippe*, Vol.2, pp.92-93.

52 Wilhelm zu Schaumburg-Lippe, 'Befehle, welche unserm *Reglement, Die Studia und Exercitia* unsers *Ingenieur-und Artillerie-Corps betreffend*, beyzufügen' (30 August 1776); in Ochwadt (ed.), *Wilhelm Graf zu Schaumburg-Lippe*, Vol.2, pp.93-95.

53 Scharnhorst discusses the various aspects of his academic life at Wilhelmstein in 'Von den Militär-Anstalten des verstorbenen regierenden Grafen von Schaumburg-Lippe', pp.93-101 (Schlözer) and Vol.1, pp.183-88 (Klippel)..

to train, educate, and integrate both civilian and military leaders in the active defence of Schaumburg-Lippe.

Perhaps the most significant and revolutionary aspect of the Wilhelm's academy was the social composition of the student body. Nearly all pupils at Wilhelmstein were commoners. In the years Scharnhorst attended the academy, only four noblemen versus 20 commoners were students.[54] 'Each class consists of a proportionate number of non-commissioned officers, cadets, learning artillerymen, bombardiers, *mineurs*, *ouvriers*, and enlisted gunners'.[55] Scharnhorst noted how Count Wilhelm made no social distinction between non-commissioned officers, cadets, soldiers, and civilians within each class, and expected his subordinates to follow his example.[56] A second lieutenant led each class as its mentor.[57] His task was to assist the primary instructors (tutors) and facilitate the theoretical and practical instruction of his class. Pupils lived alternately in Steinhude, Wilhelmstein, and at the Bückeburg castle, rotating monthly between the town, fortress, and castle. In 1772, the academy had seven classes; in 1777 (the year Wilhelm died) only four.[58]

Each new officer candidate class consisted of 12 cadets, who ranged in age from 13 to 17 years. Count Wilhelm personally interviewed and selected each of these cadets, and each 'carried out the usual duties of the non-commissioned officer' as part of his daily routine. Cadets were distributed among the classes to hone their leadership skills. No one enjoyed preferential treatment and every student stood guard.[59] The Count accepted just 44 officer candidates at Wilhelmstein during the 10 years of its existence. The moral character and diligence of these young men (and not how many) was most important to him. Of the 44 candidates, 35 were later commissioned officers. Eleven made it to the rank of second lieutenant, while 22 reached the ranks of first lieutenant to colonel in either the Schaumburg-Lippe or other German armies. Only Scharnhorst and his friend Heinrich Wilhelm von Zeschau (later the Saxon Minister of War) rose to general officer rank. The most well-known graduate of Wilhelmstein was Scharnhorst. Only he attempted to put into practice what he had learned at Wilhelmstein.[60]

When Scharnhorst arrived at Bückeburg on 29 April 1773, he learned the value of *Bildung*. Count Wilhelm whetted his appreciation of the art of war (particularly the art of defensive war), teaching young Scharnhorst that the profession of arms was a continuous process of development that could not be mastered by simply learning existing techniques. To understand his profession, the officer must have some idea of its

54 Hornung, *Scharnhorst*, p.17.

55 Wilhelm zu Schaumburg-Lippe, 'Befehle, die Eintheilung derer Unterofficiers, Cadets, Lernenden Artilleristen und Gemeinen in Classen betreffend' (5 July 1772); in Ochwadt (ed.), *Wilhelm Graf zu Schaumburg-Lippe*, Vol.2, pp:88-89; the quoted passage is from p.88. Also see the discussion in Schulz, 'Die Vorstellungen des Grafen Wilhelm von Schaumburg-Lippe', pp.224-25; particularly Note 26.

56 See [Gerhard Scharnhorst], 'Charakterzüge und Anecdoten von dem verstorbenen Grafen Wilhelm von Schaumburg-Bückeburg', *Neues militärisches Journal* 1 (1788), pp.123-27; especially, pp.123-24.

57 It was around this time that Wilhelm introduced the rank of *Secondelieutenant* in his artillery corps. It corresponded to the rank of *Fähnrich* or Ensign. See Ochwadt (ed.), *Wilhelm Graf zu Schaumburg-Lippe*, Vol.2, p.103 (Note 52).

58 Klein, *Wilhelm zu Schaumburg-Lippe*, p.263.

59 See Schmalz, 'Beschreibung der Vestung Wilhelmstein', p.91 (Column 2)-p.92 (Column 1); the quoted passage is from p.91 (Column 2).

60 See Klein, *Wilhelm zu Schaumburg-Lippe*, p.268.

relationship to other fields of knowledge and the ways in which they contribute to his own. This was the typical Enlightenment approach to *Bildung*. Accordingly, a military leader could not develop his analytical skills and insights, imagination and judgment, if he was merely trained in routine military duties, or given scenarios to follow. Nearly all the talents, abilities, and habits of thought and reflection which the military leader required in combat could in large part be acquired only through the broader avenues of learning outside his profession.[61] The methods of organising and equipping, educating and training, deploying and fighting a military force were intimately related to the entire political, social, and cultural pattern of society. This meant that the leader was continually dealing with people (both soldiers and civilians) and thus required him to understand these people, their beliefs, attitudes, motivations, and behaviour. Only a broad, liberal education could stimulate this appreciation.

Unlike other vocations, the profession of arms required a broad, general education for its mastery. During his brilliant military career, Wilhelm wrote numerous treatises on the art of war, the profession of arms, philosophy, and war and society.[62] He also corresponded with many prominent heads of state, philosophers, and other literary figures. Wilhelm's educational goal was to produce a selfless servant of the people, one who possessed the highest and purest of civil and military virtues, and one who could cope with the certainty of death.[63] Scharnhorst later wrote that Count Wilhelm 'sought to clarify the noblest aspects of the art of war, and to bring them to the highest perfection'.[64]

As an enlightened soldier-sovereign, Wilhelm zu Schaumburg-Lippe was an authority on the profession of arms, and exhibited an extraordinary understanding of the physical, moral, and psychological aspects of human behaviour and conflict. From his wartime experience and extensive study of history and people, Scharnhorst's mentor maintained that: 'War is one of the greatest calamities that afflict mankind … an evil inevitability'.[65] Because war is 'usually *the triumph of the most harmful passions*' (Wilhelm listed as these harmful

61 See Paragraphs 3 and 4 of *Reglement, die Studia und Exercitia betreffend;* in Ochwadt (ed.), *Wilhelm Graf zu Schaumburg-Lippe*, Vol.2, pp.80-82 and pp.82-85; respectively.

62 The clarifications Ochwadt provides in *Wilhelm Graf zu Schaumburg-Lippe* to the various documents are extremely valuable in understanding the evolution of Wilhelm's thoughts and their relationship to the French, English, and German Enlightenments. Wilhelm's commentaries on the profession of arms are scattered throughout his writings. In particular, see the four groups Ochwadt has compiled in Volume 2: 'Über den Krieg' (pp.142-44), 'Über Kriegsführung und Heerführer' (pp.145-47), 'Zu Militärpsychologie und Disziplin' (pp.148-55), and 'Über den Militärberuf' (pp.156-59).

63 See Wilhelm zu Schaumburg-Lippe, 'Reflections on Service' (Première Partie) in his *Mémoires pour server à l'art militaire défensif* (1775); in Ochwadt (ed.), *Wilhelm Graf zu Schaumburg-Lippe*, Vol.2, pp.180-84. This monograph, together with its associated drafts and sketches, can be found on pp.167-375. Also see his thoughts on selfless service and the certainty of death in 'Maximen über Schwäche, Stärke, Erhabenheit', Ochwadt (ed.), *Wilhelm Graf zu Schaumburg-Lippe*, Vol.1, pp.99-100.

64 See Scharnhorst, 'Von den Militär-Anstalten des verstorbenen regierenden Grafen von Schaumburg-Lippe', p.94 (Schlözer) and Vol.1, p.184 (Klippel).

65 See Wilhelm zu Schaumburg-Lippe, 'Quelques réflexions générals sur les devoirs de l'homme par rapport à la guerre', which is Number 112 of the Section 'Über den Militärberuf', in Ochwadt (ed.), *Wilhelm Graf zu Schaumburg-Lippe*, Vol.2, pp.156-57, and 'Nachlese zu den *Mémoires pour server à l'art militaire défensif*, Vol.2, pp.243-49; the quoted passages are from p.156 and p.243; respectively.

passions ambition, envy, avarice, cruelty, vanity, vengeance, and the thirst for power to dominate), it must not be conducted solely 'to fill the gazettes and almanacs'.[66]

It was clear to Wilhelm that neither the glorification nor admiration of war, nor the fatalistic acceptance or pacifistic denunciation of war represented the appropriate kind of thinking or enlightened approach toward war. His wartime experiences and incessant thinking about the nature of the war manifested themselves in his most memorable work, *Memoirs for Serving the Art of the Military Defence* (1775):

> The real source of wars lies in the harmful passions of the human heart. It is useless to flatter oneself in this respect. There are in men's hearts the inclination to do good, as well as passions, or at least germs of passions, that can only be satisfied at the expense of another's happiness.[67]
>
> To wage war on the offensive is to serve the evil passions, while to dedicate oneself to the defensive is to consecrate oneself to the welfare of humanity.[68]

At Wilhelmstein, Wilhelm taught his pupils that waging offensive war was evil and beneath the dignity of an honourable and enlightened man.[69] Only defensive war was justified. 'Man prevents war, or at least diminishes it, by means of the defence'.[70]

In keeping with the ideals of the German Enlightenment, Wilhelm was convinced that only through the process of *Bildung* could man overcome his evil passions. The reason to study war 'systematically' (hence the term the 'science' of war), 'is not the sad business of discovering more skilful means of murder, but rather to render a true service to humanity'.

> The more perfectly military science is studied, the more dangerous it will be to start a war, and thus will wars be conducted less frequently. And when war does occur, the more removed it will be from useless murder.
>
> Man seems by nature to have an inclination toward war, just as certain beasts have an inclination toward predatory behaviour.[71]

66 The quoted passages are from Number 89 of the Section 'Über den Krieg' and from Number 90 of the Section 'Über Kriegsführung und Heerführer', in Ochwadt (ed.), *Wilhelm Graf zu Schaumburg-Lippe*, Vol.2, p.144 and p.145; respectively.

67 See Wilhelm zu Schaumburg-Lippe, *Mémoires pour server à l'art militaire défensif*; in Ochwadt (ed.), *Wilhelm Graf zu Schaumburg-Lippe*, Vol.2, p.180 (Paragraph 3). This treatise was written in French, printed in only a few copies, and kept a state secret.

68 Wilhelm zu Schaumburg-Lippe, *Mémoires pour server à l'art militaire défensif*; in Ochwadt (ed.), *Wilhelm Graf zu Schaumburg-Lippe*, Vol.2, p.182 (Paragraph 10).

69 Scharnhorst, 'Von den Militär-Anstalten des verstorbenen regierenden Grafen von Schaumburg-Lippe, p.94 (Schlözer) and Vol.1, p.184 (Klippel). Also see the discussion in Klein, *Wilhelm zu Schaumburg-Lippe*, p.262.

70 Wilhelm zu Schaumburg-Lippe, *Mémoires pour server à l'art militaire défensif*; in Ochwadt (ed.), *Wilhelm Graf zu Schaumburg-Lippe*, Vol.2, p.180 (Paragraph 5).

71 The quoted passages are from the '*Vorrede*' (Introduction) of *Mémoires pour server à l'art militaire défensif*. They were first cited in 1783 by Schmalz, *Denkwürdigkeiten des Grafen Wilhelms zu Schaumburg-Lippe*, p.70; then in 1869 by Klippel, *Scharnhorst*, Vol.1, p.43 (who referenced Schmalz); again in 1902 by Professor Arnsberger, 'Graf Wilhelm zu Schaumburg-Lippe', p.338; and finally, in 2013 by Hornung, *Scharnhorst*, p.16. All of these citations are virtually identical; and yet, these passages appear nowhere in the original documents in Ochwadt (ed.), *Wilhelm Graf zu Schaumburg-Lippe*, Vol.2, pp.167-375, which is the source Hornung provides on p.285 (Note 5). Upon further

Count Wilhelm maintained that just as man can educate and train himself to overcome his primeval and animalistic impulses, so too can he educate and train himself about war, so that in minimising it, he can develop qualities of bravery, magnanimity, and greatness.[72]

In a world characterized by treachery and inhumanity, Wilhelm was convinced that a strong defence could mitigate and perhaps even neutralize the aggressive tendencies of his neighbours. In his study of the defensive art of war, he wrote that if the smaller states of Europe could strengthen their defensive postures through the harnessing of their potential, perhaps an alliance of such nations would eventually balance the might of their larger and stronger neighbours, and may even deter their aggressive tendencies.[73] This would mean applying the concept of *Bildung* to the entire nation. In an age of absolutism, nepotism, and despotism, Count Wilhelm's ideas were extremely rare, novel, and potentially dangerous to established authority. No parallel in Europe existed.[74] In Schaumburg-Lippe, Wilhelm sought to link his military programs to his social, political, and cultural initiatives. He also acknowledged the key to their success was educating and training civil and military leaders capable of implementing his vision.

As the academy's director, inspector, and chief instructor, Count Wilhelm used the power of his personality and military expertise to inspire and challenge his students. He was a passionate teacher who fired the imagination and cultivated the minds of many. As young Scharnhorst noted, 'Towards those around him he was ever pleasant and courteous'. The humanitarian spirit of the German Enlightenment was clearly present and understood at Wilhelmstein. This was so evident to Scharnhorst, who remembered: 'He brought happiness to many young people, and his lessons are already bearing fruit'.[75] Discipline came less through punishments; rather, Count Wilhelm continuously praised, sometimes admonished, but always led by example. He always rewarded outstanding achievement with gratuities and gold medallions.

investigation, the thoughts and even some of the exact words appear in other documents of the Count. Ochwadt states in his explanatory notes (pp.436-43) that a 'Preamble' existed, and that Wilhelm had sent it to Johann Georg Zimmerman, Countess Charlotte Sophie von Bentinck, and Brigadier James Ferrier for their review. Ochwadt then printed highlights of their responses on pp.438-39, which make clear that there was a Preamble to *Mémoires pour server à l'art militaire défensif*, but now appears to be lost. As a final piece of evidence, he cited the 'Vorrede des Verfassers' (Introduction by the Publisher) from Scharnhorst's article, 'Neue Taktik, welche der verstorbene regierende Graf Wilhelm von Schaumburg-Bückeburg bey seinem Truppen eingeführt', *Neues militärisches Journal* 1 (1788), pp.1-38, in which he concludes that Scharnhorst, as the Count's favourite pupil, knew of a *Vorrede*.

72 Once again, Wilhelm's thoughts are scattered throughout Ochwadt (ed.), *Wilhelm Graf zu Schaumburg-Lippe*. From Vol.1 see: 'Condition de l'homme' (pp.50-53), 'L'amour-propre est-il cause de vertu' (pp.68-69), and 'Zu Religion und Atheismus' (pp.110-14). From Vol.2 see: 'Über den Krieg' (pp.142-44), 'Über Kriegsführung und Heerführer' (pp.145-47), 'Zu Militärpsychologie und Disziplin' (pp.148-55), and 'Über den Militärberuf' (pp.156-59).

73 Wilhelm's thoughts on collective security can be found in the five groups Ochwadt has compiled in Volume 2 of *Wilhelm Graf zu Schaumburg-Lippe*. See 'Nachlese zu den *Mémoires pour server à l'art militaire défensif*' (pp.243-49), 'Zur bisherigen Diskussion über kleine und grosse Staate' (pp.282-85), 'Frühe Niederschriften zum Vergleich kleiner und grosser Staaten' (pp.286-98), 'Kleine und grosse Staaten in ihrem Verhältnis zum Kriege' (pp.299-311), and 'Über Regierungsgrundsätze, Politik, Öffenlichkeit und Staatengrösse' (pp.312-41).

74 See Franz Schnabel, *Deutsche Geschichte im 19. Jahrhundert* (Freiburg am Breisgau: Herder & Co., 1947), Vol.1, p.336; and Hermann von Boyen, *Beiträge zur Kenntnis des Generals von Scharnhorst und seiner amtlichen Thätigkeit in den Jahre 1808-1813* (Berlin: Ferdinand Dümmler, 1833), p.32. Also see Lehmann, *Scharnhorst*, Vol.1, pp.18-21.

75 The quoted passages are from Scharnhorst, 'Von den Militär-Anstalten des verstorbenen regierenden Grafen von Schaumburg-Lippe', p.96 (Schlözer) and Vol.1, p.185 (Klippel).

Like everyone else, Scharnhorst entered Wilhelmstein as an apprentice artilleryman [*Lernender Artillerist*]. He was promoted to corporal of artillery [*Unteroffizier bei den Bombardiers*] in 1775, and then to gunnery sergeant [*Feuerwerker*]. A year later he was raised to senior non-commissioned officer [*Stückjunker*], and then to warrant officer [*Conducteur*] that same year. From 1775 onward, Gerhard Scharnhorst stood at the head of his class.[76] Thanks largely to the personal interest Count Wilhelm took in him, Scharnhorst was able to close the significant gaps in his education through study, self-discipline, intellectual curiosity, and lots of hard work. Concurrently, he laid a firm foundation to his own professional development.[77]

To stimulate Scharnhorst's intellectual curiosity and broaden his horizons, Wilhelm introduced his apprentice to the military and cultural currents of the time. Wilhelm understood that a careful grounding in history develops useful theories, ideas, and interpretations that could assist the leader in the practical application of his profession. The study of history develops broad powers of observation and analysis and compensates for any deficiencies in the soldier's own experience. Wilhelm's 'Essay on the Exercise of Military Meditation' made it clear that the study of history matters.

> The practical science of war, or the art of making the most suitable use of troops in the occasion, embraces objects so numerous, so complicated, and so variable, that it is impossible to establish laws of conduct sufficiently circumstantial only for officers in the regiments.[78]
>
> It is therefore fitting that the officer should have a sufficiently trained mind and a sufficiently ample memory of good military ideas, so that on occasions when all circumstances of his conduct cannot be prescribed to him by the regulations or the orders from his immediate superiors, he can find in himself the necessary lights to take a proper course.[79]

Broad, intellectual, and critical reading was essential here.

Wilhelm understood that reading develops and trains the mind to think in a special way. From critical reading comes well-organised sentence structure that feeds logical thought, while correct grammar disciplines the brain and organises the flow of ideas.

> Reading serves to train the military spirit and to provide it with ideas. By it one is enriched by the lights and experience of others, and officers could do no better, nor could it be more agreeable for those who love their profession, especially during

76 Scharnhorst's progression through the ranks is detailed in Lehmann, *Scharnhorst*, Vol.1, pp.26-27. It can also be followed in 'Prüfungsprotokolle', Kunisch (ed.), *Scharnhorst: Privat und dienstliche Schriften*, Vol.1, pp.3-23.

77 Lehmann, *Scharnhorst*, Vol.1, pp.28-29.

78 Wilhelm zu Schaumburg-Lippe, 'Mémoire sur les Exercices de Meditation Militaire, pour être Envoyé (en cas que sa Majesté très fidèle l'approuve,) à Mrs. les Généraux et Gouverneurs des Provinces, afin détre distribué à Mrs. les Chefs des Regiments des Armées de S.M. – 1773' (21 September 1773); in Ochwadt (ed.), *Wilhelm Graf zu Schaumburg-Lippe*, Vol.2, pp.119-25; the quoted passage is from Section 2 (p.119).

79 Wilhelm zu Schaumburg-Lippe, 'Mémoire sur les Exercices de Meditation Militaire', in Ochwadt (ed.), *Wilhelm Graf zu Schaumburg-Lippe*, Vol.2, Section 3 (pp.119-20).

> the functions of daily service in times of peace, than to employ the hours of leisure which remain with military reading.[80]

Influenced by the teachings of Herder, perhaps no other sovereign of his time understood better than Count Wilhelm that the welfare and progress of society depended on a literate population, both military and civilian. Both clearly understood that the written word facilitates the transfer of ideas and culture, thereby providing the continuity of any civilization.

Wilhelm believed that the accumulated wisdom expressed in literature is what makes soldiers human. Accordingly, he included a variety of non-military works in his curriculum. Among those Scharnhorst read were: Plutarch and Cato (most likely their moral teachings), Edward Gibbon (1737-94), *The History of the Decline and Fall of the Roman Empire* (London, 1776-88); Guillaume-Thomas-François (1713-96), also known as Abbê Raynal, *A Philosophical and Political History of the Settlements and Trade of the Europeans in the East and West Indies* (Amsterdam, 1770-74); André Guillaume Contant d'Orville (1730-1800), *History of the Different Peoples of the World, Containing the Religious and Civil Ceremonies, the Origin of Religions, their Sects and Superstitions, and the Manners and Customs of each Nation* (Paris, 1770); Christian August Schultze, *The Study and Art of Farming and Commerce, or Other Writings dealing with Agriculture, Trade Crafts, and Manufacturing, etc.* (Leipzig, 1764-69); and the philosophical works of Adam Ferguson (1723-1816), probably his critically acclaimed *An Essay of the History of Civil Society* (London, 1767).[81]

Count Wilhelm understood the necessity for forward thinking leaders and clarified the purpose of reading the military classics. For Wilhelm, a military classic was not a work to be read lightly and then tossed aside. He understood that this happens when leaders, too consumed by their immediate pressures, are unwilling to take time to meditate on the past. The professional soldier must read a military classic repeatedly, to obtain wisdom from the author, and then using that understanding as a reference at those critical junctures of his career when necessity or leisure steers him to the contemplation of the past.[82] If a leader has no understanding of the past, how can he cope with the present? If the leader cannot deal with the present, how can he help shape the future for his people?

Wilhelm recognised that the essence of war never really changes; and while a knowledge of military history is certainly no panacea for success, it clearly provides a firm foundation for solving the challenges military leaders face.

> It is not a question here of training scholars or making a parade of erudition. The purpose of this institution is only to exercise the talents of the readers and to provide them, either by reading themselves or by the meditation they occasion,

80 Wilhelm zu Schaumburg-Lippe, 'Mémoire sur les Exercices de Meditation Militaire', in Ochwadt (ed.), *Wilhelm Graf zu Schaumburg-Lippe*, Vol.2, Section 4 (p.120).

81 What Scharnhorst read comes from Kunisch (ed.), *Scharnhorst: Privat und dienstliche Schriften*; Ochwadt (ed.), *Wilhelm Graf zu Schaumburg-Lippe*; Stadelmann, *Scharnhorst*; and Hornung, *Scharnhorst*. On p.19 of Hornung, *Scharnhorst*, he incorrectly writes that Scharnhorst read Ferguson's *History of the Roman Republic* while at Wilhemstein. This cannot be, since this work first appeared in 1783, six years after Scharnhorst had left Wilhelmstein.

82 In particular, see Section 9 of Wilhelm zu Schaumburg-Lippe, 'Mémoire sur les Exercices de Meditation Militaire', in Ochwadt (ed.), *Wilhelm Graf zu Schaumburg-Lippe*, Vol.2, p.121.

with ideas which they can, if necessary, make immediate use of in practice. The feelings of the authors being not authorized in such a way as to oblige obedience, we may use their maxims with choice, reflect on the diversity of opinions, and be enlightened even by their errors.[83]

'As the talents of the mind are perfected by meditation', Wilhelm continued, 'the germ of the virtues of the heart is developed by the admiration excited by beautiful examples... It would be desirable' to reads books 'which present examples of those sublime virtues' the soldier seeks to emulate; in particular, to obtain:

... a special opportunity to practice, such as the heroic devotion to death, confidence in danger and suffering, disinterestedness and resigned obedience, magnanimity towards the vanquished, etc., etc. It will be necessary to choose these historical features with discernment, to admit only those which are well proven and without any mixture of any circumstance which can tarnish the brightness.[84]

Heading the list of the examples Wilhelm cited are those from 'The Fantastical War' in Portugal. He praised the Portuguese people, 'whose heroic virtues' triumphed over the Spanish and French invaders and delivered their homeland from the clutches of evil men.

Foremost among the military literature Scharnhorst studied at Wilhelmstein were the *Memoirs* of Raimondo Montecuccoli (Köln, 1704), 'arguably the most-read, most-cited theorist of war during this period'.[85] Other notable works included: *The Art of War* by Jacques-François de Puységur (Paris, 1749); the *Memoirs* of Antoine de Feuquières (Paris, 1741); Frederick the Great's *Military Instructions to His Generals* (Frankfort and Leipzig, 1761) and his *Treatise on the Duties of Light Cavalry*; the Comte de Turpin's *Essay on the Art of War* (Paris, 1754); *The Art of Making War* by Ray de Saint Génies (Paris, 1754); *Military and Political Reflections* by Santa Cruz de Marcenado (Madrid, 1724-30); Thomas Auguste Le Roy Grandmaison's *The Small War* and *A Treatise on the Service of Light Troops on Campaign* (Paris, 1756); *Treatise on the Column* by Jean-Charles de Folard (Paris, 1724); *Treatise on the Small War* by Armand Francois de La Croix (Paris, 1752); and *The Engineer on Campaign* by Louis André, the Chevalier de Clairac (Paris, 1757).[86] Interestingly, many of these works were the companions of George Washington, Frederick the Great, James Wolfe, and other distinguished military leaders of the eighteenth century.[87] Scharnhorst would later cite many of these works in his analysis of the French Revolutionary Wars.

83 Wilhelm zu Schaumburg-Lippe, 'Mémoire sur les Exercices de Meditation Militaire' (Section 6); in Ochwadt (ed.), *Wilhelm Graf zu Schaumburg-Lippe*, Vol.2, p.120. Scharnhorst would later reiterate these thoughts in his 'Anleitung zur Lecture', *Militair-Bibliothek* (Hanover: Gebrüdern Helwing, 1782-84), Vol.1, pp.1-38.

84 Wilhelm zu Schaumburg-Lippe, 'Mémoire sur les Exercices de Meditation Militaire' (Section 9); in Ochwadt (ed.), *Wilhelm Graf zu Schaumburg-Lippe*, Vol.2, p.121.

85 Wilhelm zu Schaumburg-Lippe, 'Über die eigene Taktik' (1765); in Ochwadt (ed.), *Wilhelm Graf zu Schaumburg-Lippe*, Vol.2, pp.164-66. The quoted passage is from Showalter, *The Wars of Frederick the Great*, p.43.

86 These sources are listed in Wilhelm zu Schaumburg-Lippe, 'Mémoire sur les Exercices de Meditation Militaire', in Ochwadt (ed.), *Wilhelm Graf zu Schaumburg-Lippe*, Vol.2, Section 7 (pp.120-21).

87 On Washington, see *A Catalogue of the Washington Collection in the Boston Athenaeum*, compiled and edited by Appleton P.C. Griffin (Boston: The Boston Athenaeum, 1897); on Wolfe, see Childs, *Armies and Warfare in Europe*,

Among the German cultural literature Scharnhorst studied with at Wilhelmstein were the philosophical writing of Lessing and several works of young Goethe, especially his 1773 drama, *Götz von Berlichingen*, as well as his 1774 novel, *The Sorrows of Young Werther*. Scharnhorst also read the poetry of Christian Friedrich Daniel Schubart, the ode *My Fatherland* by poet Friedrich Gottlieb Klopstock, *The Wandsbeck Messenger*, a popular newspaper by poet Matthias Claudius, and the long, brilliant, and intriguing 'Night Thoughts' (published between 1742 and 1745) by English poet Edward Young.[88] Moreover, 'there can be no doubt' that Scharnhorst heard the weekly sermons of Johann Gottfried von Herder, the Court Preacher at Bückeburg from 1771-76. He may have also listened to Moses Mendelssohn when he visited Bückeburg in 1774 and was familiar with the works of some of the other guests of Count Wilhelm. These included the renowned publicist, historian, social analyst, and Chief Justice [*Justiciarius*] of the criminal court in Osnabrück, Justus Möser (1720-94), as well as the Swiss physician, philosophical writer, and naturalist Johann von Zimmermann.[89]

Gerhard Scharnhorst was nearly 22 years old when he finished his studies at Wilhelmstein. When he took the entrance examination in April 1773, his scores were passing, but below average. Two years later he received a gold medallion for his success in the April exams. Then he was advanced to *Stückjunker* following the December 1775 assessments; then to *Conducteur* after the October 1776 tests.[90] On 28 August 1777, he attained the highest mark of 'Good' on all subjects tested: theoretical and applied mathematics, military and civil engineering, campaign planning (both offensive and defensive operations), economics, geography, physics, and a question on a topic of his choice. Only his translations of French and English were scored 'Pretty Good'.[91] For his notable achievement, Count Wilhelm honoured Gerhard Scharnhorst with a gold medallion.[92]

Scharnhorst was truly thankful to the man who believed in him, gave him an opportunity, and nurtured his intellectual growth. 'I am filled with enthusiasm whenever I remember the ways of this man', he later wrote.[93] Wilhelm zu Schaumburg-Lippe was 'the first great experience of his youth', and the most significant educational influence in Scharnhorst's life. Without question, Count Wilhelm was 'probably the only superiority he [Scharnhorst] ever acknowledged'.[94] The *Bildung* Scharnhorst obtained during his four years at Wilhelmstein 'led him directly into a career of military education, and thirty years later still exerted an influence on his reform programs and policies'.[95]

pp.91-92; and on Frederick, see Jay Luvaas (ed. and trans.), *Frederick the Great on the Art of War* (New York: The Free Press, 1966), pp.35-56. Like Count Wilhelm, Dettingen was Wolfe's first battle and where they may have met.

88 See the analysis of Scharnhorst's intellectual and cultural life at Bückeburg in Stadelmann, *Scharnhorst*, pp.99-103.

89 Klippel, *Scharnhorst*, Vol.1, pp.58-59; the quoted passage is from p.59.

90 See 'Prüfungsprotokolle', in Kunisch (ed.), *Scharnhorst: Privat und dienstliche Schriften*, Vol.1, p.10.

91 Stübig, *Scharnhorst*, pp.17-18.

92 Scharnhorst's test records can be found in 'Aus Scharnhorsts erster militärischer Dienstzeit', *Militär-Wochenblatt*, 101 (3 December 1887), pp.2202-2209; especially pp.2205-2208, which discusses Scharnhorst's examination results during his time at Wilhelmstein.

93 Scharnhorst, 'Von den Militär-Anstalten des verstorbenen regierenden Grafen von Schaumburg-Lippe, p.96 (Schlözer) and Vol.1, p.185 (Klippel).

94 Stadelmann, *Scharnhorst*, p.132.

95 Paret, *Clausewitz and the State*, p.60.

4

Apprenticeship in Northeim

With the death of Count Wilhelm, Scharnhorst returned home. From Bordenau he sought admission to the Hanoverian army. This process took over a year. After he had submitted his application, he met with his future regimental commander. Once his regimental commander had received him into the regiment, a formal 'Letter of Acceptance' was forwarded from Hanover through the Hanoverian Chancery in London to the Court of St James for approval. King George III of England approved Scharnhorst's application on 28 July 1778 and appointed him *Fähndrich* ['officer candidate'] in the 8. Dragoner Regiment von Estorff, the unit in which his father had served, now under different commander.[1] Unfortunately, Scharnhorst could not report for duty in Hanover until he obtained his release from Schaumburg-Lippe. Count Philipp initially denied his request, not wanting to lose a valuable officer. Even the courteous letters from Scharnhorst's future regimental commander failed to persuade him. Only the intervention of *Feldmarschall* and Governor-General of the Electorate of Hanover, Christian Ludwig von Hardenberg (1700-81), convinced Count Philipp to acquiesce. On 9 October 1778, he reluctantly approved Scharnhorst's discharge from Schaumburg-Lippe service.[2] *Fähndrich* Scharnhorst was now free to enter Hanoverian military service.

The Electorate of Hanover in 1778 was lost in time, 'a moribund state, frozen in a post-medieval, pre-absolutist' world.[3] Much like the history of Schaumburg-Lippe, the House of Hanover began more than a century earlier with Georg, Duke of Brunswick-Lüneburg (1582-1641), who inherited the Principality of Calenberg in 1635 and moved his residence to Hanover. Merged with the Principality of Lüneburg (its capital was Celle), this newly created state of Brunswick-Lüneburg-Hanover (more commonly referred to as Hanover) had much in common with other German states of the Holy Roman Empire. Its population

1 A photograph of Scharnhorst's listing on the regimental roster can be found in Fiedler, *Scharnhorst*, on the third page following p.152. Scharnhorst is listed fourth from the bottom. Today the rank of *Fähndrich* is spelled *Fähnrich*, which is usually translated as 'officer candidate' or 'ensign'.

2 The correspondence relating to Scharnhorst's *Entlassung* (discharge) from Schaumburg-Lippe service can be followed in Kunisch (ed.), *Scharnhorst: Privat und dienstliche Schriften*, Vol.1, pp.34-37; and in Klippel, *Scharnhorst*, Vol.1, pp.62-64.

3 Richard W. Fox, 'Conservative Accommodation to Revolution: Friedrich von der Decken and the Hanoverian Military Reform, 1789-1820. An Inquiry into the Role of the Military in State and Society' (Ph.D. Thesis, Yale University, 1972). Chapters 1 (pp.11-37) and 2 (pp.38-94) provide an excellent assessment of Hanover at this time. The quoted passage is from p.11.

was around 700,000 at the time of Scharnhorst's birth. It was one of the largest states of the Holy Roman Empire; yet, it was predominately agricultural with a small middle class.[4] Like Schaumburg-Lippe, Hanover had retained its feudal social structure, with 'the corporate elites' [*Ständestaat*], dominated by the landed nobility. This 'ancient nobility' [*Uradel*] controlled agricultural production, while an intricate guild system governed the artisan and merchant classes.

As Prince of Calenberg, Georg ruled this loose association of *Ständestaat*, situated between the western and central parts of Prussia. It became an Electorate of the Holy Roman Empire in 1708, known officially as the Electorate of Brunswick-Lüneburg, unofficially as the Electorate of Hanover, after its capital city. When Georg's grandson became King George I of Great Britain in 1714 and left the Electorate, the corporate elites moved quickly to seize control of the central government, monopolising both state and local power, wealth and privilege. In the following decades the *Uradel* managed to insulate and isolate itself almost completely from any influence from the minor nobility and the middle class.[5] The union of Hanover with Great Britain made England a continental state in many respects. It also placed Hanover 'at the mercy of the major European powers'.[6]

Fähndrich Gerhard Scharnhorst was fortunate that his new regimental commander, *General-Major* Emmerich Otto August von Estorff (1722-96), was genuinely imbued with the pedagogic ideals of the German Enlightenment. Estorff knew Count Wilhelm well, having served with him during the Seven Years War, when he was *Adjudant* and *General-Quartiermeister* to Duke Ferdinand of Braunschweig-Wolfenbüttel.[7] A cultured officer, Estorff was familiar with Wilhelm's educational methodology.[8] He loved reading, especially contemporary literature, military and scientific studies. He also enjoyed associating with the many learned men at nearby Göttingen. He was extremely proud of his extensive private library and made it available to his officers. Later he established a regimental library and obtained regular donations from a variety of patrons.[9] Estorff also possessed a keen interest

4 See the interesting series of lectures collected under the title, *Great Britain and Hanover: Some Aspects of the Personal Union*, presented by Adolphus William Ward (Oxford: Clarendon Press, 1899). A more recent collection of essays addressing this relationship can be found in Brenden Simms and Torsten Riotte (ed.), *The Hanoverian Dimension in British History, 1714-1837* (Cambridge: Cambridge University Press, 2007).

5 Friedrich Ludewig von Berlepsch, *Pragmatische Geschichte des landschaftlichen Finanz-und Steuerwesens der Fürstentümer Galenberg und Göttingen* (Frankfurt und Leipzig: Unknown Publisher, 1799), is an important contemporary account of the social and economic conditions in Hanover at this time. Also see the discussion in Lehmann, *Scharnhorst*, Vol.1, pp.81-86.

6 Fox, 'Conservative Accommodation', p.11. As proof of Hanover's precarious position and the political naivety of the English and Hanoverian elites in the face of French republican values, Ward in his introductory lecture in *Great Britain and Hanover*, p.18, cites the 1794 declaration by King George III, that even though Great Britain was at war with France, the 'Calenberg nation' was neutral in any war with the French Republic. Also see Torsten Riotte, 'George III and Hanover', *The Hanoverian Dimension in British History*, pp.72-73.

7 Bernhard Poten wrote a brief outline of Estorff's cosmopolitan life and military career entitled, 'Estorff, Emmerich Otto August von', *Allgemeine Deutsche Biographie* (1904), Vol. 48, pp.434-35.

8 See the excellent study that compares and contrasts the pedagogical philosophies of Wilhelm and Estorff and how they helped shape Scharnhorst's own thinking on military education and the art of war; in Bruce Gudmundsson, 'The Education of the Enlightened Soldier', *Marine Corps University Journal* 9:1 (2018), pp.33-44.

9 On these libraries, see HansJoachim Kiefert, 'Zur Geschichte der Militärbibliotheken in Hannover', *Hannoversche Geschichtsblätter* Neue Folge 17:4 (1963), p.294 (Note 45).

in agriculture. In 1764 he became a founding member of the Agricultural Society of Celle, one of the first associations for farmers in Germany.[10]

Unlike most of his fellow regimental commanders, Estorff was very passionate about the *Bildung* of his officers and non-commissioned officers. Like Wilhelm he firmly believed military leaders required both a general and professional education. He published a 'sensible, very well written work', *Fragments of Military Observations on the Institution of Warfare Established in the Intermediary States during Time of Peace* in 1780. This was the culmination of his philosophy on military *Bildung*, and challenged the traditional notion dating back centuries that the conduct of war was simply a craft mastered only though apprentice and experience.[11]

Upon assuming command of the 8. Dragoner Regiment in the spring of 1766, *General-Major* Estorff began training and educating the junior officers and cadets on his staff.[12] Two years later he published his pedagogical thoughts in a memorandum entitled, 'Instructions for Officers of the Regiment Estorff'.[13] During the winter months they read and studied the theory of their profession. Estorff supplemented his lectures with reading lists that provided his troopers with a survey of important military literature for their continued self-study. Included with these lists were instructions on 'how the officer must read, which books he has to select, and how to make the best application from the readings'.[14] Like Count Wilhelm, *General-Major* Estorff placed great emphasis on self-study.

Estorff ranked historical studies first on his reading lists. As he stated, 'The study of history is of the highest importance for the warrior [*Krieger*], if he is to think comprehensively'.[15] In Article 4 of his 'Instructions for Officers of the Regiment Estorff', he elaborated on the 'benefits' that come 'from reading, and how theory may be combined with practice' to obtain 'a perfect military science'.[16] He argued that this was especially true for developing what the French called the 'strike of the eye' or *coup d'oeil*, which was the ability to discern at a single glance the salient features of a given piece of ground or man-made structure, quickly determining its advantages and disadvantages, and then making accurate, spilt-second tactical decisions regarding the utility of that terrain or structure.

10 See Ludwig Deike, 'Die Celler Sozietät und Landwirtschaftsgesellschaft von 1764', in Rudolf Vierhaus (ed.), *Deutsche patriotische und gemeinnützige Gesellschaften* (Munich: Klaus International Publications, 1980), pp.161-194.

11 Emmerich Otto August von Estorff, *Fragmente militairischer Betrachtungen über die Einrichtung des Kriegswesens in mittlern Staaten, in der Muße des Friedens angestellt* (Frankfurt und Leipzig: Unknown Publisher, 1780). Estorff's thoughts on the formation [*Bildung*] of leaders can be found throughout the second part, pp.99-170. The quoted passage is from the insightful analysis of Paret, *Clausewitz and the State*, p.62n.

12 Estorff's educational endeavours are discussed in Bernard Poten, *Geschichte des Militär-Erziehungs-und Bildungswesen in den Landen deutscher Zunge 2: Hannover, Hessen-Cassel, Hessen-Darmstadt, Hessen-Hanau, Mecklenburg-Schwerin, Münster, Nassau, Oldenburg. Monumenta Germaniae Paedagogica*, Band 17 (Berlin: A. Hofmann, 1891), Vol.2, pp.16-19.

13 See Emmerick Otto August D'Estorff, 'Anweisung für die Officiers des Kurbraunschweig-Lüneburgischen Regiments von Estorff, Cavallerie oder Dragoner, wie selbige zur Lecture und zu welcher Sie sich zu appliciren haben; von Ihrem Regiments-Chef dem Kurbraunschweig-Lüneburgischen Herrn General-Major von Estorff erteilet 1768' (8 August 1768); printed in part under the title, 'Anweisung für Officiere aus dem Jahre 1768', *Militär-Wochenblatt* 84:44 (20 May 1899), pp.1173-80.

14 Segments of Estorff's instructions are quoted in Klippel, *Scharnhorst*, Vol.1, p.68.

15 Estorff, *Fragmente militairischer Betrachtungen*, p.103.

16 Estorff, 'Anweisung für Officiere aus dem Jahre 1768', p.1173.

To develop their *coup d'oeil*, Estorff encouraged his troopers to link their critical reading and thinking with what he called 'supposing' [*supponieren*], a type of mental fitness in which the soldier visualized various combinations of forces (infantry, cavalry, and artillery) on whatever piece of terrain about which he happened to be reading or analysing.

> An officer who has, out of true passion, dedicated himself in this way to the honourable study of war, each time he goes for a walk or a ride, instead of looking at things casually, will view them with a military eye, ... Each village will provide him with a new subject for study, how he will attack it if it is occupied by the enemy, or, if he is using it to quarter his troops, how he will defend it.[17]

As a cavalryman, Estorff understood the critical importance of this quality in a trooper whenever he executed his wartime missions.

To ascertain the progress of his pupils, Estorff held periodic examinations like those Wilhelm gave at Wilhelmstein. In the spring he took his troopers to the field, where they translated their theoretical studies with practical drills, polishing their troop-leading skills with map exercises, terrain walks, field sketching, and tactical problems without troops. Here the cavalry leader trained his *coup d'oeil* and 'supposing' using the various types of ground Estorff had listed in his 'Instructions'. This extensive listed included practically every category of terrain: 'defiles, rivers, ravines, plains, intersecting regions, scattered heights or chains of mountains, large forests or wooded thickets, and swamps or areas intersected with canals'.[18] Most of these exercises dealt with the wartime missions of the cavalry: reconnaissance and security, planning routes of march, foraging, establishing and conducting outpost operations, conducting raids and ambushes, mapping the area of operations, and quartering troops.[19]

Estorff clearly understood the value of a broad, liberal education for his officers. He wanted officers of culture and bearing in his regiment. In the 'Conclusion' of his 1768 'Instructions' he strongly encouraged his officers to expand their reading to include works on religion, politics, philosophy, natural history, commerce, international trade, and manufacturing, as well as the shorter encyclopaedias of the day.[20] Such an intensive self-study program would expand their horizons significantly and 'distinguish' them from those 'boring military people who, in the company of ladies and other notable people, brag about nothing but battles and skirmishes'. Estorff wanted his officers to be genuinely sophisticated enough to be able to converse intelligently with learned people from other occupations during both official functions or social occasions, 'entertaining them according to their state, genius, and position, especially when on important missions in other countries'.[21]

Estorff also placed an emphasis on the study of natural history. This was especially useful for the cavalry trooper. Indeed, as he noted, the search for specimens often provide an ideal 'pretext' for reconnoitring 'the environs of a fortress and its adjoining heights'.

17 Estorff, 'Anweisung für Officiere aus dem Jahre 1768', p.1174.
18 Estorff, 'Anweisung für Officiere aus dem Jahre 1768', p.1174.
19 Klippel, *Scharnhorst*, Vol.1, pp.68-69. Also see the commentary in Lehmann, *Scharnhorst*, Vol.1, pp.31-32.
20 Estorff, 'Anweisung für Officiere aus dem Jahre 1768', pp.1179-80.
21 Estorff, 'Anweisung für Officiere aus dem Jahre 1768', p.1180.

An enterprising cavalryman might also act as 'a lover of hunting, forestry, and economics' while he is out riding, and this may give him 'sufficient pretext to infiltrate whole regions … of the interior of a country'. When conducting such critical and often secretive missions, Estorff advised his men to be particularly prudent, since the astute soldier 'does well to proclaim much ignorance of the military, so as to attract less attention to himself'.[22]

Like Count Wilhelm and other German *Aufklärer*, *General-Major* Estorff placed a premium on the religious formation of the military. Indeed, his words are remarkably similar to those of Count Wilhelm.

> For a soldier without religion is a miserable creature; and the officer, who does not base his heartiness on it, is, at the outset of danger, an uncertain brute; his actions are accompanied side-by-side with indecision, and he ends his career with aggravation in the most disgraceful way. I am aware of many examples of it; and you, gentlemen, cannot be stupid.[23]

Among the religious works he recommended were the writings of Lutheran church historian and Chancellor of the University of Göttingen, Johann Lorenz von Mosheim (1693-1755). Like many other German philosophers, Estorff cautioned his officers about the 'hidden poison' contained in the religious criticism of Voltaire and Jean-Baptiste de Boyer, Marquis d'Argens (1703-71).

Turning to the other subjects on his list, Estorff endorsed a number of prominent works of the Enlightenment. Those mentioned included *Universal Business Dictionary: Natural History, and the Arts and Crafts* (1723-30), by Jacques Savary des Brûlons (1657-1716). A leading expert in business and commerce, Savary des Brûlons had served as Inspector General of Manufacturing under Louis XIV. The political and economic writings of Justi, as well as *Political Institutions* (1760-1832) by Prussian writer, statesman, and advisor to Frederick the Great, Jakob Friedrich von Bielefeld (1717-79) were also cited. Two interesting encyclopaedias were recommended. The first was *Philosophical and Political History of European Settlements and Trade in the Two Indies* (better known as *History of the Two Indies*), an anthology on trade between Europe and the Far East, published anonymously in Amsterdam in 1770 and attributed to Abbot William Thomas Raynal (1713-96). Another was *Encyclopaedic Journal* (1756-93). Estorff told his officers all of these works could be obtained through the Berlin bookdealer Nicolai. He also suggested his officers occasionally pursue Nicolai's catalogue, *New Literature*, to keep current with available titles.[24]

When the regimental headquarters moved to Northeim in 1770, Estorff formally established a regimental school there. Its goal was to develop an 'esprit de corps' [*Innungsgeist*] within the 8. Dragoner Regiment by educating and training officers, staff officers, junior officers, cadets, non-commissioned officers, and promising cavalrymen. Officers from the regimental staff were the primary instructors, assisted by able non-commissioned officers. They taught the rudiments of mathematics, geometry, field sketching, the use of the compass, horsemanship, military subsistence, administrative duties, and field reporting

22 Estorff, 'Anweisung für Officiere aus dem Jahre 1768', p.1180.
23 Estorff, 'Anweisung für Officiere aus dem Jahre 1768', p.1179.
24 Estorff, 'Anweisung für Officiere aus dem Jahre 1768', pp.1179-80.

procedures.[25] During inclement weather, his men remained indoors and used 'sand table exercises' [*Sandkastenspiel*] to re-enact historic battles, but more importantly, to demonstrate and practice the manoeuvres of the cavalry.[26] This innovative methodology was 'one of the earliest recorded uses of a sand table in military training'.[27] Estorff also employed two non-commissioned officers from the artillery to teach his men basic gunnery techniques. Those not achieving the very elementary standards he set were dismissed from the regiment.[28]

A reading knowledge of French (and later of English) was essential at Northeim. Most of the important military works of the day and especially those on Estorff's list were written in French.[29] *General-Major* Estorff required his officers not only to be able to read, but also to be conversant in French. To this end, they met several evenings a week, for a total of 12 hours. To stress the importance of these sessions toward the *Bildung* of his officers, Estorff charged the director of the school, *Major* Jakob Konrad Niemeyer (ca. 1730-1808), to lead these gatherings, known as the 'French Assembly'. Discussions on a variety of topics of interest to this group were held only in French.[30]

One of the more impressive examples of Estorff's zeal for the *Bildung* of his soldiers came in 1776 and 1777, when Great Britain purchased the services of several German contingents during the American Revolution. Not one to let a great opportunity pass, Estorff used those occasions to train his men in the movement and quartering of Hessians and other German soldiers as they travelled through Hanover to their ports of embarkation.[31] These missions included a variety of critical tasks, such as planning routes of march (including shipping men and material up the Weser River), extensive liaison activities with local officials, escort duty along the way, and billeting considerations.[32]

25 In his first periodical, Scharnhorst mentions the 'unsurpassed' excellence of the Hanoverian cavalry. See Scharnhorst, *Militair-Bibliothek*, Vol.2, p.129.

26 See Gerhard Scharnhorst, 'Nachricht von der Einrichtung, dem Fortgang, und sich zeigenden Nutzen der, beim 8ten Hannoverischen Cavallerie Reglment von Estorff Dragoner, etablirten KriegsSchule', *Stats-Anzeigen* 8:32 (1785), pp.465-75. A discussion on this 'maneuver table' can be found on p.469.

27 Peter Hofschroer, *The Hanoverian Army of the Napoleonic Wars* (London: Osprey, 1989), p.5. Also see the discussion in Joachim Niemeyer and Georg Ortenburg (ed.), *Die Hannoversche Armee 1780-1803* (Beckum: Deutschen Gesellschaft für Heereskunde, 1976/81), Vol 2: *Das 'Gmundener Prachtwerk'*, pp.12-14.

28 Citing the records of the Hanoverian *General-Adjudant*, Klippel, *Scharnhorst*, Vol.1, p.70, provides an interesting anecdote in which Estorff wrote to *Feldmarschall* Hardenberg on 1 July 1778, that he (Estorff) had to discharge an ensign because of his inability to write properly. With a touch of humor, Estorff concluded by telling Hardenberg, 'Even the royal Prussian troops would be better off without this recruit'.

29 Klippel, *Scharnhorst*, Vol.1, p.71.

30 See Scharnhorst's passing mention of this 'French Assembly' in his letter to Uncle Heinrich (between November 1778 and 22 February 1779); in Kunisch (ed.), *Scharnhorst: Privat und dienstliche Schriften*, Vol.1, p.40.

31 Klippel, *Scharnhorst*, Vol.1, p.72. Also see Scharnhorst, 'Nachricht von der 8ten Hannoverischen Cavallerie Reglment von Estorff Dragoner KriegsSchule', p.470.

32 The extensive documentation from these operations can be found in Hann 41: *Durchmärsche*; deposited at the Niedersächsisches Landesarchiv, Hanover; and listed individually in the bibliography below. See for example, Hann 41, V, Nr.15: *Korrespondenz des Generalquartiermeisters von Estorff mit den hessischen Generalleutnants von Gohr und von Heister nebst einem Gesamtetat (Gesamthaushalt) der hessischen an England überlassenen Truppen, 01.1776-03.1776*; and Nr.13: *Rapporte (Berichte) des Hauptmanns Niemeyer über die Durchführung der ersten Kolonne hessischer Truppen, bestehend aus dem Grenadieerbataillon von Block, dem Regiment von Mirbach, dem Regiment von Donop und dem Regiment Erbprinz, 03.1776.*

When Scharnhorst reported for duty, Estorff recognised his potential and posted him to the school's faculty. The challenge Estorff faced at that time was obtaining competent instructors.[33] Most of the faculty simply familiarized their pupils with the details of their own daily duties, much like the instructors at Wilhelmstein had initially done before Count Wilhelm stepped in and modified the curriculum. With the arrival of Scharnhorst, Estorff now hoped to educate, and not merely train, his officers and men.[34]

Sensing the high expectations of his commander, Scharnhorst began studying the educational methods of the Württemberg military college, 'Hohe Carls-Schule', which *Oberst* Ferdinand Friedrich von Nicolai (1730-1814) had established.[35] One of the leading military *Aufklärer* of his time, Nicolai had originally studied law at the University of Tübingen, earning his doctorate in 1751. He then travelled to Berlin and Vienna seeking answers to some questions of military law remaining from his dissertation research.[36] Upon his return he began writing on military themes. In 1756 he entered Württemberg service as a *Fähnrich* in the artillery. Pressed into Austrian service during the Seven Years War, the Württemberg contingent was nearly annihilated at the Battle of Leuthen in December 1757. This had a profound effect on Nicolai and other Württemberg officers, who were contemptuous of Austrian fondness toward leadership of the Holy Roman Empire and its *Reichsarmee*, without the least concern for the welfare of the other German states.

Austrian contempt for the German states was widespread in the eighteenth century. For example, when Austria had notified Count Wilhelm on 28 August 1756 that Schaumburg-Lippe was obligated to serve under the banner of the Holy Roman Empire against Prussia, Wilhelm replied to Maria Theresa 'in spacious language and a vicious tone' that she, without ever consulting him or his neighbouring German sovereigns, had given France 'the legal right' to cross German territory to aid Saxony against Prussia. Wilhelm pointed out to Maria Theresa that France had overrun and was still occupying his country, and that England, Hanover, and Prussia – not Austria, were coming to liberate Schaumburg-Lippe from the hated French. He also questioned the loyalty of Austria toward the Germanic states and wondered why his troops should be part of a *Reichsarmee* fighting Prussia and not France. Wilhelm made it clear to Maria Theresa that France was the enemy of Germany, implying that perhaps Austria was as well.[37] Nicolai may have agreed with Count Wilhelm.

Because of his exceptional abilities, Nicolai was able to rise very quickly, attaining the rank of *Hauptmann* and 'royal adjutant' [*Flügal-Adjudant*]. When the Seven Years War ended, he was 32 years old, a 'lieutenant colonel' [*Oberstlieutenant*] and member of the general

33 See Stübig, *Scharnhorst*, p.20.

34 Stübig, *Scharnhorst*, p.20. Also see Klippel, *Scharnhorst*, Vol.1, p.73.

35 Rudolf Stadelmann explored this association in an unpublished manuscript entitled, 'Scharnhorst und die Hohe Karlsschule', *Nachlaß Stadelmann*, Nr.3; deposited at the Bundesarchiv, Koblenz.

36 Nicolai's dissertation was entitled, 'De Munere et Immunitate Metatorum Militarium Electa Quaedam Capita' [On the Obligation and Exemption from Payment for the Quartering of the Military]. A photo of the title page of Nicolai's Tübingen Dissertation can be found in Daniel Hohrath, 'Ferdinand Friedrich von Nicolai: Bemerkungen zur Biographie eines gelehrten Offiziers', in Daniel Hohrath (ed.), *Die Bildung des Offiziers in der Aufklärung: Ferdinand Friedrich von Nicolai (1730-1814) und seine Enzyklopädischen Sammlungen* (Stuttgart: Württembergische Landesbibliothek, 1990), p.9.

37 See the interesting discussion in Klein, *Wilhelm zu Schaumburg-Lippe*, pp.86-89. The quoted passages are from Varnhagen von Ense, 'Graf Wilhelm zur Lippe', pp.13-14.

staff.[38] Four years later in 1767, with the approval of Carl Eugen, Duke of Württemberg (1728-93), and in collaboration with the University of Tübingen, Nicolai began designing an 'Officer's Academy and School of Artillery' that would become a college of the university.[39] By 1771, Nicolai had his 'Primary Military School' [*Militärpflanzschule*] ready to begin instruction the following spring. The high quality of education was such that it was soon renamed 'Military Academy' in 1773. Under Nicolai's direction it became renowned throughout Europe, and 1781 Holy Roman Emperor Joseph II raised it to university status and renamed it 'Hohe Carls-Schule'.[40] Next to Wilhelmstein, the Hohe Carls-Schule 'was the first institution of its kind established on the concept of a military enlightenment'.[41] Its curriculum and methods of instruction were similar to those at Wilhelmstein. One of the more illustrious students who attended the Hohe Carls-Schule was the later philosopher and poet, historian and playwright, Johann Christoph Friedrich von Schiller (1759-1805). Meanwhile, Nicolai had been promoted to *Oberst* in 1774 and given command of a newly formed artillery regiment.

Like Estorff, Nicolai was profoundly concerned about the *Bildung* of soldiers. What is significant here is that in the aftermath of the Seven Years War, most military schools in Germany had been established, not by princes or sovereigns, but 'on the independent initiative of regimental commanders' to provide a systematic (or 'scientific' as it was called) education and training for their soldiers.[42] Because of aristocratic scorn for *Bildung*, far too many officer candidates were entering their regiments with little formal schooling. Estorff and Nicolai had recognised this and began exchanging ideas and techniques, in the hope of learning from each other's experiences.[43] In 1775, Nicolai published his innovative study, *An Attempt at a Blueprint for the Formation of Officers*, which outlined his pedagogical concepts.[44] They were strikingly similar to those of Count Wilhelm and *General-Major* Estorff.

38 Bernhard Poten wrote a brief outline of Nicolai's life and career, entitled, 'Nicolai, Ferdinand Friedrich von', *Allgemeine Deutsche Biographie* (1886), Vol. 23, pp.579-80. Perhaps the best study of Nicolai to date is Hohrath, 'Ferdinand Friedrich von Nicolai', pp.7-27. Testifying to Nicolai's remarkable achievements, Hohrath notes on p.15 that Nicolai had achieved in just six years - rank, honours, and position, which usually took an officer of the *Ancien Régime* decades to attain.

39 Stadelmann, 'Scharnhorst und die Hohe Karlsschule', p.14, notes that this idea originated with a *Hauptmann* Bilfinger.

40 On the Hohe Carls-Schule, see the exhaustive study by Heinrich Wagner, *Geschichte der Hohen Carls-Schule* (Würzburg: C. Etlinger, 1856-58). For a contemporary account, see August Friedrich Batz, *Beschreibung der Hohen Karls-Schule zu Stuttgart* (Self-Published, 1783). A more recent study is Franz Quarthal, 'Die Hohe Carlsschule: *O Fürstin der Heimath! Glükliches Stutgard*', in Christoph Jamme and Otto Pöggeler (ed.), *Politik, Kultur und Gesellschaft im deutschen Südwesten um 1800* (Stuttgart: Klett-Cotta, 1988), pp.35-54.

41 See Daniel Hohrath, 'Die 'Bildung des Officiers' im 18. Jahrhundert', in Hohrath (ed.), *Die Bildung des Offiziers in der Aufklärung*, pp.28-63; the quoted passage is from p.56.

42 In Chapter 3: 'The Military Thinkers of the German *Aufklärung*', Gat, *The Origins of Military Thought*, pp.54-66, does a fine job discussing the military proponents of the German Enlightenment. The quoted passage is from p.60. Also see the excellent article by Daniel Hohrath, 'Spätbarocke Kriegspraxis und aufgeklärte Kriegswissenschaften: Neue Forschungen und Perspektiven zu Krieg und Militär im "Zeitalter der Aufklärung"', *Aufklärung* 12:1: 'Die Kriegskunst im Lichte der Vernunft: Militär und Aufklärung im 18. Jahrhundert' 2 (2000), pp.5-47.

43 Hohrath, 'Ferdinand Friedrich von Nicolai', pp.22-23; especially Footnote 146.

44 Ferdinand Friedrich von Nicolai, *Versuch eines Grundrisses zur Bildung des Officiers* (Ulm: August Lebrecht Stettin, 1775). The German word *Grundrisses* in this context has an architectural design meaning; hence my translation as 'Blueprint'. *Bildung* in this context means 'formation'. Nicolai's discussion in his book validates these translations.

Nicolai questioned the widely held view that only a man of genius is capable of success in war. Such an assumption negated all that the Enlightenment held dear: that man could and should transform himself and society through the process of *Bildung*. While nature may 'create the general', Nicolai wrote, war was not the province of genius alone. The ancients understood this and had developed a methodical approach to the study and conduct of war which, as Nicolai maintained, 'all of the experiences of the past 1,500 years' substantiate. Even the 'invention of gunpowder', he continued, as well as other technological achievements over the centuries had not altered 'the basic principles upon which the ancient art of war had been built'. Nicolai pointed to Maurice of Nassau and Gustavus Adolphus as proof, and was grateful to Raimondo Montecuccoli for re-introducing 'the scientific nature of war'.[45]

From this theoretical foundation Nicolai then proceeded to explain his curriculum. In language similar to Count Wilhelm, Nicolai maintained that military leaders must acquire a broad general education in the arts and sciences before they ever embark on a military education. And like Wilhelm, Nicolai's program provided for a basic education in religion, foreign languages, the arts, sciences, and the classics. Upon his successful completion of these fundamental courses, the officer would then proceed to more advanced studies in the pure and applied sciences, history, geography, logic, statistics, ethics, civil and military law, the military sciences (gunnery, the art of fortifications, and tactics), and the art of war. For each subject Nicolai produced a detailed study guide, along with an extensive bibliography.

Perusing Nicolai's work must have delighted Scharnhorst. He had just completed such a program of study at Wilhelmstein and probably recognised many of the texts Nicolai recommended. With the blessing of Estorff, he began corresponding with Nicolai, seeking his advice on how to improve the current program of instruction at his regimental school.[46] Based largely on Nicolai's suggestions, and with the approval of Estorff, Scharnhorst expanded his course load to include field sketching, gunnery techniques, the art of fortifications, geography, and history.[47]

Despite his best efforts, Scharnhorst was not happy with his first assignment. In letters to his family and relatives he often complained about being an instructor. 'I lecture six hours a week', he wrote to his uncle in 1778, 'two on mathematics, two on tactics, and two on the engineering sciences'.[48] With all of the time and effort he put into his preparing and teaching his classes, Scharnhorst noted his endeavours caused him 'nothing but trouble'.[49]

45 See Nicolai's remarks in the Preface and Introduction of *Versuch eines Grundrisses zur Bildung des Offiziers*. The quoted passages are from pp.1, 11, 10, and 11-12; respectively. It is probably no coincidence that an excellent study of these three enlightened soldiers Nicolai mentions can be found in Gunther Rothenberg, 'Maurice of Nassau, Gustavus Adolphus, Raimondo Montecuccoli, and the "Military Revolution" of the Seventeenth Century', in Paret (ed.), *Makers of Modern Strategy*, pp.32-63.

46 Klippel, *Scharnhorst*, Vol.1, p.73.

47 Scharnhorst noted his correspondence with Nicolai in 'Nachricht von der 8ten Hannoverischen Cavallerie Reglment von Estorff Dragoner KriegsSchule', p.471. Also see Poten, *Geschichte des Militär-Erziehungs-und Bildungswesen: Hannover*, Vol.2, p.19.

48 See Scharnhorst's Letter of 'around' November 1778 to Uncle Heinrich; in Kunisch (ed.), *Scharnhorst: Privat und dienstliche Schriften*, Vol.1, pp.38-39; the quoted passage is from p.38.

49 Letter to Uncle Heinrich (between November 1778 and 22 February 1779); in Kunisch (ed.), *Scharnhorst: Privat und dienstliche Schriften*, Vol.1, pp.39-40; the quoted passage is from p.40.

He was disappointed with the ignorance of his fellow officers and wondered what they had learned over the previous years. As he told his uncle: 'No one here knows anything about war'.[50] Nevertheless, his patience and perseverance paid off. Within a year Scharnhorst was the chief instructor at Northeim. Still, on 23 February 1779, he grumbled to his parents about his differences with Estorff, which have 'caused a lot of trouble'.

> Generally speaking, all is going very well here, although the General has to deal with my contrary [*contrair*] method. The General rushes and brushes over things lightly. I prefer to work in such a way that no one should miss the essentials, according to the deliberate method of the exalted Count. Of course, I always finish up late; that's not right, but then we're all good when we're finished.[51]

It seems that Estorff was a 'fast thinker', while Scharnhorst a 'slow thinker'.[52] The difference here is significant.

Estorff understood the critical importance to be able to think automatically and quickly in combat. By developing his own *coup d'oeil* and 'supposing', he had conditioned himself over time to think fast until it had become second nature to him, but not to his men. Scharnhorst, who was learning to develop his *coup d'oeil* and 'supposing' was moving slowly using the methodical approach he had learned at Wilhelmstein, until he had grasped the intricacies of fast thinking. His slow method was ideal for the classroom. Scharnhorst would take an idea, ask the class to reflect on it, question it, and consider it from various points of view. In this way he would engage his class in a lively discussion on that idea, seeking to get each student to develop his 'supposing' by performing a similar set of operations on the idea under consideration. This play of minds was the technique he was teaching his fellow cavalrymen.

Over time, the deliberate method Scharnhorst employed earned the admiration and appreciation of Estorff. It did not take Estorff long to recognise that Scharnhorst's approach involved the systematic investigation of all circumstances from various viewpoints in order to achieve a workable solution. Not only was it modelled after the method he had learned at Wilhelmstein, it also incorporated the *coup d'oeil* and 'supposing' practices Estorff sought to develop in his troopers. Scharnhorst had thus combined both ways of thinking into a logical study of the art of war. It also appears that this is just what the students at Northeim required to grasp the material taught to them. As Scharnhorst told his uncle on 4 March, 'The General [Estorff] is very pleased with me'. 'I am also very well accredited with all of

50 Letter of 'around' November 1778 to Uncle Heinrich; in Kunisch (ed.), *Scharnhorst: Privat und dienstliche Schriften*, Vol.1, p.39.

51 See Scharnhorst's Letter of 23 February 1779 to his parents; in Kunisch (ed.), *Scharnhorst: Privat und dienstliche Schriften*, Vol.1, pp.40-42; the quoted passages are from p.42.

52 See the interesting and important discussion of this difference in Gudmundsson, 'The Education of the Enlightened Soldier', pp.40-41. For a fascinating, in depth study of these two techniques, see Daniel Kahneman, *Thinking, Fast and Slow* (New York: Farrar, Straus, and Giroux, 2011). Gudmundsson stated that this is the source upon which he based his conclusions.

the officers'.[53] In the eyes of his regimental commander, Scharnhorst personified the ideal soldier, one 'who combines the academician and officer inseparably in his person'.[54]

Always seeking to improve himself, Scharnhorst sought out other educational pursuits. Northeim was a small town that provided little intellectual stimulus outside of his own teaching, research, and Niemeyer's French class. Following the example of his regimental commander, Scharnhorst ventured south to the university town of Göttingen, seeking enlightenment there.[55] He could not have selected a better place.

Founded in 1734 by 'Imperial Knight' [*Reichsfreiherr*] and Privy Councilor Gerlach Adolph von Münchausen (1688-1770) to educate and train statesmen, administrators, lawyers, and scholars, 'Georg-August Universität Göttingen' was named in honour of King George II of England. Like Wilhelm and other German noblemen, Münchausen had been forced to study abroad in order to obtain the social polish required to enter court life. Like Lessing and other German intellectuals, Münchausen wanted German universities to provide this education. When he became a member of the Hanover Privy Council in 1728, Münchausen campaigned incessantly for a state university in the Electorate of Hanover. So successful was he that he was appointed its first 'Trustee' [*Kurator*].

Münchausen would govern the University of Göttingen for over 30 years. He was determined to avoid the critical mistakes of other German universities, while still attracting the best students and finest faculty from across Europe.[56] To obtain quality professors, Münchausen and his advisors selected only those scholars with good reputations and granted them (as well as their students) freedom of expression both in the classroom and in their publications. This was a major component of any *Bildung*. Göttingen also paid its professors higher salaries than most other German universities, included moving expenses, as well as arranging suitable housing for its faculty. By placing a premium on recruiting and retaining quality faculty who were first and foremost motivating teachers (not so much erudite scholars and publicists), Gerlach Münchausen made the University of Göttingen the most attractive educational institution in Germany.[57] In the eyes of many intellectuals, Göttingen was '*the* university of the age of Enlightenment'.[58]

53 Letter of 4 March 1779 to Uncle Heinrich; in Kunisch (ed.), *Scharnhorst: Privat und dienstliche Schriften*, Vol.1, pp.43-44; the quoted passage is from p.43.

54 Paret, *Clausewitz and the State*, p.62n. The quoted passage is from Estorff, *Fragmente militairischer Betrachtungen*, p.108.

55 Scharnhorst first mentions this to his Uncle Heinrich in his Letter of 24 May 1779; in Kunisch (ed.), *Scharnhorst: Privat und dienstliche Schriften*, Vol.1, p.46.

56 On Münchhausen, see Walter Buff, *Gerlach Adolph Freiherr von Münchhausen als Gründer der Universität Göttingen* (Göttingen: Dieterichschen Universitäts-Buchdruckerei, 1937).

57 For documents relating to the establishment of the University of Göttingen, see Emil F. Rössler, *Die Gründung der Universität Göttingen: Eine Sammlung Bisher Ungedruckter Entwürfe, Berichte und Briefe* (Göttingen: Verlag von Vandenhoeck und Ruprecht, 1855). A nice collection of essays reflecting the spirit of the times can be found in Jürgen von Stackelberg (ed.), *Zur geistigen Situation der Zeit der Göttinger Universitätsgründung 1737: Eine Vortragsreihe* (Göttingen: Vandenhoeck and Ruprecht, 1988). For a standard history of the university, one that is especially good on the eighteenth century, see Götz von Selle, *Die Georg-August Universität zu Göttingen 1737-1937* (Göttingen: Vandenhoeck and Ruprecht, 1937).

58 Thomas Biskup, 'The university of Göttingen and the Personal Union, 1737-1837', in Simms and Riotte (ed.), *The Hanoverian Dimension in British History*, pp.128-60; the quoted passage is from p.159.

Thanks largely to the leadership of Münchausen, Göttingen chartered a new course in education, becoming the atypical German university.[59] Working closely with his distinguished colleague Johann Matthais Gesner (1691-1761), Münchausen established the university library and appointed Gesner the first librarian. Gesner organised the library to meet the academic needs of the four instructional departments (theology, medicine, law, and philosophy). He also published catalogues of the library's holdings.[60] The Hanoverian Estates provided generous funding so Gesner could acquire quality books, manuscripts, maps, instruments, and other resources. Soon this prestigious and voluminous library attracted many serious scholars and students, since both professors and students had borrowing privileges, the only university in Europe to grant this.[61] A classical scholar and former schoolmaster, Gesner became the first Professor of Rhetoric and Classics at the University of Göttingen, where he established his renowned philological seminar.[62]

Gesner was instrumental in reviving the study of Greek and the teaching of classical languages. Mastering Greek and Latin was considered fundamental for enlightenment. To Gesner, the classics served to form the mind and to cultivate the intellect. His vision attracted a great deal of attention and became a guiding principle for other German *Aufklärer*, such as art historian and archaeologist Johann Joachim Winckelmann (1717-68), whose *History of Ancient Art* (1764) was one of the first books in German to become a classic of European literature.[63] Gesner also served as Professor of Eloquence and Poetry.[64] In 1738, he founded the 'German Society' [*Deutsche Gesellschaft*] for the study and writing of German literature. So renowned was Gesner that his old friend and colleague Johann Sebastian Bach dedicated his *Canon a 2 perpetuus* (from *Musical Offering*) to the professor.[65]

To provide professors a means of showcasing their work, Münchausen and physician Albrecht von Haller (1708-77) founded the *Göttingen Scholarly Reports* in 1739. With Haller its editor, the *Göttingen Scholarly Reports* soon became a leading publication in the literary

59 Rössler, *Die Gründung der Universität Göttingen*, pp.iv-v. For a good understanding of the University of Göttingen and its place in the history of German *Bildung*, see Charles E. McClelland, *State, Society, and University in Germany, 1700-1914* (Cambridge: Cambridge University Press, 1980), pp.35-57.

60 Before coming to Göttingen, Gesner was Rector at the prestigious St Thomas School in Leipzig from 1730-34. There he became a close friend of the Cantor, Johann Sebastian Bach, whom Gesner admired and had known previously in Weimar.

61 See the contemporary account by the prominent Professor of Law, Johann Stephan Pütter, *Versuch einer akademischen Gelehrtengeschichte von der Georg-Augustus-Universität zu Göttingen* (Göttingen: Wittwe Vandenhoeck, 1765/88). On Vol.1, p.219, Professor Pütter points out the university's borrowing privileges are 'an advantage that hardly any other library in Germany, and perhaps in other areas, can challenge'. On pp.222-23, he provides the layout of the library.

62 On Johann Matthias Gesner, see Reinhold Friedrich, *Johann Matthias Gesner: Sein Leben und sein Werk* (Roth: Genniges, 1991).

63 See Ulrich Schindel, 'Die Anfänge der Klassischen Philologie in Göttingen', in Reinhard Lauer (ed.), *Philologie in Göttingen: Sprach- und Literaturwissenschaft an der Georgia Augusta* (Göttingen: Vandenhoeck und Ruprecht, 2001), pp.9-17.

64 See Thomas Haye, 'Göttingens Ruhm in der Dictung des Johann Matthias Gesner (1691-1761)', in Klaus Grubmüller (ed.), *1050 Jahre Göttingen: Streiflicher auf die Göttinger Stadtgeschichte* (Göttingen: Wallstein Verlag, 2004), pp.48-77.

65 See Rens Bod, *A New History of the Humanities: The Search for Principles and Patterns from Antiquity to the Present* (Oxford: Oxford University Press, 2013), pp.156-57.

and scientific life of Germany.[66] His reviews led German readers to new authors, such as Rousseau.[67] Hailing from Switzerland, Haller is an example of the lengths Münchausen took to secure quality professors. A naturalist and poet, Haller was also one of the great anatomists and physiologists of the eighteenth century and is often referred to as 'the father of modern physiology'.[68] His research and writings on botany and anatomy gained for Haller a European reputation. He received a personal invitation from King George II (which Münchausen no doubt arranged) in 1736 to chair the Department of Medicine (which included anatomy, botany, and surgery).

At Göttingen, Haller became a principal figure of the German Enlightenment. His studies focused primarily on human physiology, and in 1747 he published the subject's first textbook, *First Lines of Physiology*. A physician by training, Haller sought to apply his scientific studies to practical medicine. His findings were first published in the *Göttingen Scholarly Reports* and later in his massive study, *Physiological Elements of the Human Body* (1757–66), which became a landmark in medical history and encouraged others throughout Europe to follow his lead. Apart from his classroom work, Haller established one of the first surgical amphitheatres in Germany for instruction, a medical museum, an obstetrics school, and the university's botanical gardens. The quantity of his work was immense. In 1751, Münchausen and Haller established 'The Royal Society of Sciences', with Haller its first president. Göttingen now became one of the few cities in Europe to possess both a university and an academy of science.

Not only was Haller a great scientist, he was also an important literary figure of the German Enlightenment. Throughout his scientific career, Haller continued to write and publish reflective poetry, one of his earliest and livelong passions. He published his most famous poem, *The Alps* (1729), after his first journey through the Alps. It describes the life of the Swiss Alpine people, and was soon acknowledged as one of the first poems to examine mountains and their flora as objects of natural beauty and fascination – 'a whole new poetic landscape'.[69] What made *The Alps* an immediate success was the way in which

66 This journal first appeared under the title, *Göttingische Zeitungen von Gelehrten Sachen*. It became *Göttingische Anzeigen von Gelehrten Sachen* when the Royal Society of Sciences assumed control in 1753. See Heinrich Albert Oppermann, *Die Göttinger gelehrten Anzeigen während einer hundertjährigen Wirksamkeit für Philosophie, schöne Literatur, Politik und Geschichte* (Hanover: C.F. Kius, 1844). Also see Friedrich Ekkard, *Allgemeines Register über die Göttingischen gelehrten Anzeigen von 1753 bis 1782* (Göttingen: Johann Christian Dieterich, 1784).

67 For Haller's published reviews in the *Göttingen Scholarly Reports*, see Karl S. Guthke (ed.), *Hallers Literaturkritik* (Tübingen: Max Niemeyer, 1970), pp.48-194.

68 On Haller, see Christoph Siegrist, *Albrecht von Haller* (Stuttgart: J.B. Metzler and Carl Ernst Poeschel, 1967) and Richard Toellner, *Albrecht von Haller: Über die Einheit im Denken des letzten Universalgelehrten* (Wiesbaden: F. Steiner, 1971). Also see Otto Sonntag, 'Albrecht von Haller on Academics and the Advancement of Science: The Case of Göttingen', *Annals of Science* 32 (1975), pp.379-91; and Erich Hintzsche, 'Einige kritische Bemerkungen zur Bio- und Ergographie Albrecht von Hallers', *Gesnerus* 16 (1959), pp.1-15. Additionally, Shirley A. Roe provides a good biographical sketch of Haller in *The Natural Philosophy of Albrecht von Haller* (New York: Arno Press, 1981), while Dorothy R. Wiswall, *A Companion of Selected Poetic and Scientific Works of Albrecht von Haller* (Bern: Lang, 1981), analyses the best of Haller's works. The quoted passage is from Stefano Sandrone, *Brain Renaissance: From Vesalius to Contemporary Neuroscience* (Oxford: Oxford University Press, 2015), p.135.

69 See Caroline Schaumann, 'From Meadows to Mountaintops: Albrecht von Haller's *Die Alpen*', in Sean Ireton and Caroline Schaumann (ed.), *Heights of Reflection: Mountains in the German Imagination from the Middle Ages to the Twenty-First Century* (New York: Camden House, 2012), pp.57-76. The quoted passage is from Peter Skrine, 'Albrecht

Haller endowed 'the mountains with moral qualities, exuberantly celebrating the simple, rural life in preference to the decadence and turmoil that prevailed in courtly society'. *The Alps* was also the first German literary piece to associate high mountains with 'a mixture of fear and awe typical of later definitions of the sublime'.[70] Albrecht von Haller was clearly the type of 'Renaissance Man' Münchausen sought for the University of Göttingen.

Foremost among the many innovations Münchausen introduced was the 'relatively quiet role' theology and religion played at a university. He was determined that the campus of Göttingen would not become a battleground of religious intolerance that had been raging among various Protestant sects in Germany for over half a century. Göttingen became the first university in Germany to end the traditional right of censorship the theological faculty enjoyed.[71] While Münchausen never intended to lessen the authority of the church, it is difficult 'to overstate the historical importance of this measure'.[72] Catholics were encouraged to enrol at Göttingen, and Münchausen took great risks to guarantee their freedom to practice their faith openly. With the assistance of noted theologian Johann Lorenz von Mosheim, as well as several prominent officials in Hanover, Münchausen crafted the statues that governed faculty and students; statues which emphasised the Enlightenment ideals of *Bildung* and sought to create a healthy learning environment by focusing the energies of professors and students toward productive avenues of learning, and not dissension and factionalism.[73]

A church historian and preacher, Mosheim is generally considered 'the father of modern homiletics'.[74] Like many of the professors Münchausen recruited, Mosheim saw in coming to a new university an opportunity to renew both himself and his profession. At Göttingen he was able to achieve both.[75] Under his leadership, Göttingen theologians enjoyed a degree of intellectual liberty unimaginable in other parts of Europe.[76] In 1747, Mosheim was appointed the first chancellor of the university. So great was his influence that even after his death, Mosheim's lecture notes were published as standard texts in the field of theology.

With Münchausen's organisational measures and selection of faculty in place by 1737, the University of Göttingen officially began to reinvigorate higher education in Germany.[77]

von Haller 1708-1777', in Matthais Konzett (ed.), *Encyclopedia of German Literature* (Chicago: Fitzroy Dearborn Publishers, 2000), p.401.

70 Schaumann, 'Albrecht von Haller's *Die Alpen*', p.57.

71 See Watson, *The German Genius*, pp.50-55; the quoted passage is from p.51.

72 See the masterful study by Thomas Albert Howard, *Protestant Theology and the Making of the Modern German University* (Oxford: Oxford University Press, 2006); the quoted passage is from p.110.

73 The extensive correspondence between Münchausen and Mosheim, from 20 November 1734 to 22 September 1735, can be found Rössler, *Die Gründung der Universität Göttingen*, pp.163-220. The various drafts, discussions, and recommendations concerning academic statues can be found on pp.257-304.

74 A good study of Mosheim and his involvement in the establishment of the University of Göttingen can be found in Bernd Moeller, 'Johann Lorenz von Mosheim und die Gründung der Göttinger Universität', in Bernd Moeller (ed.), *Theologie in Göttingen: Eine Vorlesungsreihe* (Göttingen: Vandenhoeck & Ruprecht, 1987), pp.9-40.

75 Alexander Bitzel, 'Theology of the Sermon in the 18th Century', in Joris van Eijnatten (ed.), *Preaching, Sermon and Cultural Change in the Long Eighteenth Century* (Leiden: Koninklijke Brill, 2009), pp.73-74.

76 See 'Johann Lorenz von Mosheim, Organiser of the First Clerical Defence', which is part of Chapter 2 of John Stroup, *The Struggle for Identity in the Clerical Estate: Northwest German Protestant Opposition to Absolutist Policy in the Eighteenth Century* (Leiden: E.J. Brill, 1984), pp.50-81.

77 Although founded in 1734, classes did not begin until 1737, when Münchausen had completed his plans.

Epitomising the ideals of the German Enlightenment with its progressive concept of *Bildung*, Göttingen soon attained a 'remarkable degree of academic freedom'. This engendered an 'intellectual liveliness' and transformed Göttingen into 'one of the chief seats of scholarship and science in Central Europe'.[78] 'From the very beginning', wrote Professor of Oriental Languages Johann David Michaelis (1717-91) in his *Observations on the Protestant Universities in Germany* (1768), 'Göttingen has been an entirely different university'.[79] So, when Scharnhorst endeavoured to further his own professional development and embarked on an educational journey at the University of Göttingen, he could not have picked a finer institution. Its 'freedom to think, write, and publish was unsurpassed in Germany', and Scharnhorst was clearly imbued with this optimism.[80]

Like many German universities in the aftermath of the Seven Years War, the University of Göttingen offered weekly lectures on the art of war.[81] Mostly likely at the prompting of Estorff, Scharnhorst attended the addresses of the renowned Professor of Mathematics Albrecht Friedrich Ludwig Meister (1724-88). In his later journal, *Library for Officers* (1785), Scharnhorst wrote how Meister's 'thorough knowledge of the military sciences' was known throughout Hanover. Meister's 'Collegium on Tactics', along with his 'subject expertise' [*Sachkunig*], were 'held in high esteem'. Scharnhorst also admired the extensive collection of books on military history and theory in the University of Göttingen library.[82]

Because of his mathematical background, Meister's favourite topic was 'military engineering' [*Kriegsbaukunst*]. In 1765, he had journeyed to the Netherlands and France on a paid sabbatical to study their fortifications and to observe and analyse the French military school system. Upon his return he published his *Treatise on Military Instruction and Information on the French Royal Military Schools* (1766), which he subsequently used as a primer for his own instruction on the art of war.[83] Over the next 20 years Professor Meister taught the art of war, always reminding his students that 'the conduct of war alone is not sufficient'.[84] Soldiers must also have a practical knowledge of their profession.

Scharnhorst was certainly fond of Professor Meister and learned much from him.[85] Like Count Wilhelm, Meister understood the relationship between civil and military societies. In his book, *On the Study of the Military-Mathematical Sciences at Universities* (1788), Meister stressed the necessity for military personnel to study not only the sciences, both also the new humanitarian ideas of pedagogy and psychology. Civil societies must be a part of

78 See the interesting discussion in Klaus Epstein, *The Genesis of German Conservatism* (Princeton: Princeton University Press, 1966), pp.32-35. The first quoted passage is from Epstein's analysis of the University of Göttingen on p.547. The second and third quoted passages reinforce Epstein's conclusion, and are from McClelland, *State, Society, and University in Germany*, p.41.

79 See the commentary in Johann David Michaelis, *Raisonnement über die protestantischen Universitäten in Deutschland* (Frankfurt und Leipzig: Unknown Publisher, 1768-76), Vol.1, p.127.

80 McClelland, *State, Society, and University in Germany*, p.39.

81 See Poten, *Geschichte des Militär-Erziehungs-und Bildungswesen: Hannover*, Vol.2, pp.23-24; and Friedrich Hossbach, *Scharnhorst*; in *Der Göttinger Arbeitskreis Schriftenreihe*, Heft 55 (Würzburg: Holzner-Verlag, 1955), pp.10-11.

82 Gerhard Scharnhorst, *Bibliothek für Officiere* (Göttingen: Johann Christian Dieterich, 1785), Vol.3, pp.286-87.

83 Albrecht Friedrich Ludwig Meister, *Abhandlung von dem Kriegsunterricht und Nachricht von den königlich französischen Kriegsschulen* (Göttingen: Bossiegel, 1766).

84 Professor Meister is quoted in Max Jähns, *Geschichte der Kriegswissenschaften vornehmlich in Deutschland.* (Munich and Leipzig: R. Oldenbourg, 1889-91; reprint ed, Hildesheim: Georg Olms, 1966), Vol.3, p.2448.

85 Fiedler, *Scharnhorst*, pp.92-93.

this effort as well. University curriculums must include the military sciences. Scharnhorst wholeheartedly agreed, writing in his review of Meister's work that universities should not be just for teachers, physicians, lawyers, theologians, and other professionals, but for military officers, too. Here is an early indication that Scharnhorst considered soldiering a profession requiring continuous study. 'It is essential', he concluded, 'to see officers learning at the university'.[86]

While at Göttingen, Scharnhorst also came under the influence of three other renowned scholars, teachers, and publicists: Professors of History August Ludwig Schlözer (1735-1809) and Johann Christoph Gatterer (1727-99), and Professor of Law Johann Stephan Pütter (1725-1807). All three were deeply imbued with the ideals of the German Enlightenment and the concept of *Bildung*. Pütter was one of the most prestigious scholars of 'public law' [*jus publicum*] of his time, and taught at Göttingen for half a century.[87] Pütter had been teaching 'Imperial Trial Law' [*Reichsprozess*] since 1747, and his classes attracted a wide variety of students, two of which were Klemens Wenzel Lothar von Metternich (later a diplomat and Austrian Foreign Minister) and Wilhelm von Humboldt (philosopher and later founder of the University of Berlin). One of his most famous visitors was Benjamin Franklin, who spent two weeks with Pütter in July 1766, discussing the constitutional basis of the federation of German states known as the Holy Roman Empire.[88] In addition to public law, Pütter taught 'intellectual history' [*Gelehrtengeschichte*]. In 1786, he sought to demonstrate that the imperial law which governed the Holy Roman Empire was not established from some abstract principle, but unfolded over time with the development of society, a notion in line with Lessing's *Education of the Human Race*. Pütter's massive, three-volume study of the German Reich was his finest literary achievement and soon became a classic.[89]

Professor Johann Christoph Gatterer had been teaching all areas of history since 1759, with a specialisation in ancient and medieval history. He was primarily interested in making history more precise through an in depth and critical analysis of events.[90] When Schlözer joined the faculty in 1769, he and Gatterer were instrumental in developing a modern, scientific, and interpretive approach to the study of history, which later became known as

86 See Gerhard Scharnhorst's Review of Friedrich Meister, *Ueber das Studium der militärisch-mathematischen Wissenschaften auf Universitäten* (1788); in *Allgemeine Literatur-Zeitung* (Jena), 198 (1788), pp.460-64; the quoted passage is from p.464. This review is also published in Klippel, *Scharnhorst*, Vol.1 (Appendix 9), pp.217-19.

87 On Pütter, see Wilhelm Ebel, *Der Göttinger Professor Johann Stephan Pütter aus Iserlohn* (Göttingen: O. Schwartz, 1975); and Patrick Ernst Sensberg, 'Johann Stephan Pütter aus Iserlohn', *Die grossen Juristen des Sauerlandes: 22 Biographien herausragender Rechtsgelehrter* (Arnsberg: F.W. Becker, 2002), pp.31-46.

88 See the interesting discussion by Jürgen Overhoff, 'Benjamin Franklin, Student of the Holy Roman Empire: His Summer Journey to Germany in 1766 and His Interest in the Empire's Federal Constitution', in Paul E. Kerry and Matthew S. Holland (ed.), *Benjamin Franklin's Intellectual World* (Madison, NJ: Fairleigh Dickinson University Press, 2012), pp.77-88.

89 Johann Stephan Pütter, *Historische Entwickelung der heutigen Staatsverfassung des Teutschen Reichs* (Göttingen: Wittwe Vandenhoeck, 1786-87).

90 For an excellent introduction to Gatterer, see Peter Hanns Reill, 'Johann Christoph Gatterer', in Hans-Ulrich Wehler (ed.), *Deutscher Historiker* (Göttingen: Vandenhoeck & Ruprecht, 1971-82), 6 (1980), pp.7-22. For the most recent scholarly study, see Martin Gierl, *Geschichte als präzisierte Wissenschaft: Johann Christoph Gatterer und die Historiographie des 18. Jahrhunderts im ganzen Umfang* (Stuttgart: Frommann Holzboob Verlag, 2012).

the 'Göttingen School'.[91] Here is yet another example of the decisive influence of Gerlach von Münchausen. As one of the 'philosophical' subjects, history held a traditionally low ranking at most German universities, relative to more 'practical' studies, such as theology, law, and medicine. And while Münchausen considered the study of law as 'the backbone of the Göttingen curriculum', he elevated the professional status of philosophical studies considerably.[92] History, mathematics, and the courtly arts (dancing, fencing, music appreciation, drawing, riding, foreign language conversation, manners, and etiquette) 'gained lavish promotion' compared to other German universities.[93] When Michaelis discussed the courtly arts in his *Observations*, he called the courtly arts 'Eloquence' [*Eloquentia*].[94] Eloquence fulfilled that long-standing desire of Münchausen, Lessing, and other German *Aufklärer* for German universities to provide this social polish. Münchausen also encouraged the introduction of new fields of study, such as 'statistics' [*Staatenkunde*].

At the University of Göttingen, the study of history became 'the favourite field of knowledge of our time'. In his examination of Protestant universities in Germany, Michaelis applauded the importance Münchausen placed on the study of history, particularly its significance to the fields of theology, law, and medicine.[95] He also noted Professor Meister's course on the art of war, and discussed why officers needed to attend similar university lectures to obtain – through an in depth study of history – a theoretical understanding of the art of war and a practical knowledge of their profession. Language study was also crucial for the *Bildung* of officers.[96] In a remarkable statement for his time, Michaelis concluded that the health of any university was directly linked to the well-being of its philosophical faculty.[97]

An eloquent theologian, biblical scholar, and teacher, Johann David Michaelis was the foremost student of Semitic languages in Europe during the eighteenth century. He is another example of the quality professor Münchausen brought tó Göttingen. Shortly after his appointment as Professor of Oriental Languages in 1746, Michaelis published the first textbook that focused on a historical and critical approach to the New Testament. He also popularized the use of scholarly notes in his Bible translations and sought to turn his beloved Old Testament into a historical document.[98] In 1761, he convinced Frederick V of Denmark to fund an expedition to Egypt, the Arabian Peninsula, and Yemen to collect manuscripts

91 Hermann Wesendonck, *Die Begründung der neueren deutschen Geschichtsschreibung durch Gatterer und Schlözer* (Leipzig: Johann Wilhelm Krüger, 1876). For a broader and more recent interpretation, see Peter Hanns Reill, *The German Enlightenment and the Rise of Historicism* (Berkeley: University of California Press, 1975).

92 See Gerlach Adolph von Münchausen, 'Nachträgliches Votum' [Intended for the Geheimes Ratskollegium (16 April 1733)]; in Rössler, *Die Gründung der Universität Göttingen*, pp.33-38. His thoughts on the legal faculty are on p.36. The quoted passage is from McClelland, *State, Society, and University in Germany*, p.43.

93 McClelland, *State, Society, and University in Germany*, p.42.

94 See Michaelis, *Raisonnement über die protestantischen Universitäten in Deutschland*, Vol.1, p.196.

95 Michaelis, *Raisonnement über die protestantischen Universitäten in Deutschland*, Vol.1, pp.193-234; the quoted passage is from p.183.

96 Michaelis, *Raisonnement über die protestantischen Universitäten in Deutschland*, Vol.1, Section 31 (pp.165-71).

97 See the commentary in McClelland, *State, Society, and University in Germany*, p.343 (Note 15).

98 On Michaelis and the impact of his work, see the fascinating study of Michael C. Legaspi, *The Death of Scripture and the Rise of Biblical Studies* (Oxford: Oxford University Press, 2010).

and other material essential to his research pursuits.[99] Michaelis was also a major source of inspiration for Herder's biblical studies.[100] His extensive and diverse academic activities earned for Michaelis a worldwide reputation, and when Benjamin Franklin visited Göttingen in 1766, he chose to stay in the home of Professor Johann Michaelis. Because he enjoyed history and geography, antiquity and languages, anthropology and natural science, Johann David Michaelis had a far-reaching influence on German theological studies and biblical criticism.

Fulfilling Münchausen's vision, professors used history as a means of obtaining a realistic or 'pragmatic' view of contemporary conditions. In the words of Gatterer, pragmatic history is that which 'unearths the causes and effects of important events'.[101] Göttingen historians looked at the world from a fresh point of view. Instead of merely narrating events, they examined in detail the political, legal, and financial systems of a society, as well as other cultural influences to gain new interpretations.[102] With their newly appointed colleague, Ludwig Timotheus Spittler (1752-1810), Gatterer and Schlözer endeavoured to write scholarly, analytical, and critical history, and were deeply sceptical of popular history.[103]

Gatterer, Schlözer, and Spittler synthesised 'German erudition, English empiricism, and French rationalism' into a coherent whole, and launched an intellectual revolution that culminated 'in the creation of the nineteenth-century historical science'.[104] Along the way Gatterer vehemently denounced what he called '... the pretentious little Humes or Robertsons, the little German Voltaires. We must hunt down these insects without mercy, wherever they may be. They can be dangerous, like all insects'.[105] While Gatterer's prodigious literary output won for him considerable acclaim during his lifetime, he was soon eclipsed by his more talented (but no less outspoken) colleague, August Schlözer.[106]

99 On the Danish-German Arabia Expedition, see Han F. Vermeulen, *Before Boas: The Genesis of Ethnography and Ethnology in the German Enlightenment* (Omaha: University of Nebraska Press, 2015), Chapter 5 (pp.219-68).

100 See Christoph Bultmann, 'Herder's Biblical Studies', in Hans Adler and Wulf Koepke (ed.), *A Companion to the Works of Johann Gottfried Herder* (New York: Camden House, 2009), p.234.

101 Johann Christoph Gatterer, *Historisches Journal, von Mitgliedern des königlichen historischen Instituts zu Göttingen* (Göttingen: Witwe Vandenhoeck 1772–81), 6 (1776), pp.165-66.

102 See 'The Rise of the German Historical School', which is Chapter 2 of Herbert Butterfield, *Man on His Past* (Cambridge: Cambridge University Press, 1969), pp.32-61. Rudolf Vierhaus, 'Die Universität Göttingen und die Anfänge der modernen Geschichtswissenschaft im 18. Jahrhundert', in Hartmut Boochmann and Hermann Vellenreuter (ed.), *Geschichtswissenschaft in Göttingen: eine Vorlesungsreihe* (Göttingen: Vandenhoeck & Ruprecht, 1987), pp.9-29, writes on p.13 that Göttingen was the first university to make history an 'independent' and 'institutionally established field of knowledge [*Wissenschaft*]'.

103 Appointed Professor of History in 1778, Spittler collaborated with Gatterer, Schlözer, and Pütter on several important projects. In 1786 Spittler published a history of the Electorate of Hanover, and in 1796 a history of the Danish Revolution of 1660. On Spittler, see Peter Hanns Reill, 'Ludwig Timotheus Spittler', *Deutscher Historiker*, Vol.9, pp.42-60. On p.24 of his *Germany and the French Revolution* (New York: Longmans, Green, and Company, 1920), George P. Gooch claims Spittler was 'the most brilliant historical teacher of his time'.

104 See the penetrating analysis of Frederick C. Beiser, *The German Historicist Tradition* (Oxford: Oxford University Press, 2011). The quoted passages come from p.200 of Ernst Breisach, *Historiography: Ancient, Medieval, and Modern* (Chicago: University of Chicago Press, 1994). See especially Chapter 13 (pp.199-214). Also see Friedrich Meinecke, *Historicism: The Rise of a New Historical Outlook* (New York: Herder and Herder, 1972).

105 Gatterer, *Historisches Journal*, 1 (1772), p.2.

106 Gatterer's literary accomplishments are analysed and placed within the context of his time by Martin Gierl, 'Kommunikation, Institution und Fach: die *Allgemeine historische Bibliothek* und das *Historisches Journal* Johann

As an *Aufklärer*, Schlözer focused much of his endeavours on changing the social injustice he saw in Germany. He brought historical study and criticism into the public realm.[107] His main target was the character of the state, and he was often referred to as the 'Imperial Publicity Councilor' [*Reichs-Publicitäts-Rath*]. Schlözer had a keen interest in historical analysis, statistics, political systems, and journalism.[108] He believed in change and improvement and hoped to use *Bildung* and publicity to awaken the minds of the German people, hoping they would develop an independent political consciousness that would alter the behavior of the aristocracy. From 1776 to 1793, he published two important periodicals: *Exchange of Letters Containing Mostly Historical and Political Content* (1776-82) and its continuation, *State Reports* (1782-93).[109] Using these journals to spread his thoughts, Schlözer had 'an undreamt-of success'.[110]

Like Thomas Jefferson, Schlözer believed only 'cultivated' [*Gebildete*] people were truly competent to participate fully in public discourse. Unlike Jefferson, Schlözer included women. He felt that the intellect of a woman was as good as that of any man. No doubt he was thinking of his own daughter Dorothea, one of the most beautiful and erudite women of her time. By 16 she had mastered nine foreign languages: French, English, Dutch, Swedish, Italian, Latin, Spanish, Hebrew and Greek. Fellow colleague, Professor of Mathematics Abraham Gotthelf Kästner (1717-1800), was simply amazed at her ability to analyse and solve complex mathematical problems. Under her father's tutelage Dorothea studied botany, zoology, optics, religion, mining, and mineralogy. As a woman, she also learned the female arts, such as playing the piano, singing, sewing, knitting, and cooking. In 1787, Dorothea became the first woman in Germany to earn her doctorate. She was only 17 years old. When Dorothea married, she became the first woman in Germany to use a double surname. Although denied academic accreditation, her home in Lübeck became a centre of social and intellectual life.[111]

Even though he was highly critical of the ruling elites (he deplored royal absolutism and despotism, aristocratic privilege, and clerical intolerance), Schlözer always remained faithful to the precepts of the Enlightenment. He abhorred violence and especially revolution as a means of change. His articles made a strong impression on his nearly 4,400 subscribers, and certainly within the German nobility. Schlözer's biting commentaries and those of others published in *State Reports* belong to the most important political and social

Christoph Gatterers und die Entwicklung von Fachzeitschriften in der Geschichteswissenschaft', in Steffen Hölscher and Sune Erik Schlitte (ed.), *Kommunikation im Zeitalter der Personalunion (1714-1837): Prozesse, Praktiken, Akteure* (Göttingen: V&R Unipress, 2014), pp.155-82.

107 See James Van Horn Melton, 'From Enlightenment to Revolution: Hertzberg, Schlözer, and the Problem of Despotism in the late Aufklärung', *Central European History* 12:2 (June 1979), pp.103-23.

108 On Schlözer, see Martin Peters, *Altes Reich und Europa: Der Historiker, Statistiker und Publizist August Ludwig (v.) Schlözer (1735-1809)* (Münster: LIT Verlag, 2005); the quoted passage is from p.29.

109 August Ludwig Schlözer (ed.), *Briefwechsel meist historischen und politischen Inhalts* and *Stats-Anzeigen* (Göttingen: Vandenhoekschen Buchhandlung, 1776-93). Scharnhorst had his first two articles published in these journals.

110 On Schlözer's fascinating life and career, see the collection of essays in honour of the 200th Anniversary of his death. See Heinz Duchhardt and Martin Espenhorst (ed.), *August Ludwig (von) Schlözer in Europa* (Göttingen: Vandenhoeck & Ruprecht, 2012). The quoted passage is from Stübig, *Scharnhorst*, p.21.

111 See Londa Schiebinger, *The Mind Has No Sex? Women in the Origins of Modern Science* (Harvard: Harvard University Press, 1989), pp.257-60.

discussions of eighteenth-century Germany.[112] He sought to uncover and publish state and local abuses in law and administration, and to fight unlawful torture, imprisonment, 'judicial murder' [*Justizmord*], and other violations of basic human rights. Schlözer provided his readers with current information on important economic, political, and social developments in the numerous German principalities.[113] *State Reports* was the first German periodical to publish the French 'Declaration of Human Rights' (promulgated in 1789).[114] Unfortunately, Schlözer's unabated criticism of many tyrannical German princes led to the official suppression of *State Reports* in 1793. In bidding farewell to his readership, Schlözer proclaimed, 'We Germans need reforms'. Then he closed with, 'But preserve us, dear God, from revolutions!'[115]

At Göttingen, Schlözer nurtured Scharnhorst's intellectual and professional growth, building upon the firm foundation Count Wilhelm had laid at Wilhelmstein. Germany's foremost political analyst introduced Scharnhorst to the intellectual world of Göttingen and to many of its prominent figures. On 10 March 1779, Scharnhorst was accepted as an apprentice in the masonic lodge, 'The Golden Compass' [*Zum goldenen Zirkel*].[116] The Golden Compass had been officially established on 23 June 1777 by 15 students and recent graduates of the University of Göttingen, nine military officers, one master craftsman, and one civil servant.[117] The majority of its members also belonged to an informal literary group founded in 1772 and known as 'The Göttingen Grove' [*Göttinger Hain*].[118] Among the noted *Aufklärer* who presented talks at both The Göttingen Grove and The Golden Compass was Gottfried August Bürger (1747-94), a poet whose romantic ballads were very popular in Germany at the time. Bürger had studied theology at the University of Halle, law and literature at the University of Göttingen. He served as district magistrate at Altengleichen, not far from Göttingen. His famous ballad, *Lenore*, captivated readers throughout Europe, and was translated into English and French.[119] During its 19 years of existence, The Golden Compass reached a membership of 285, with students and young doctors of philosophy composing

112 The depth and breadth of Schözer's ideas are covered well in Werner Hennies, *Die politische Theorie August Ludwig von Schlözers zwischen Aufklärung und Liberalismus* (Munich: Tuduv Studien, 1985). A concise summary can be found in Stübig, *Scharnhorst*, pp.21-22.

113 See Han Erich Bödeker, 'The Concept of the Republic in Eighteenth-Century German Thought', in Jürgen Hiedeking and James A. Henretta (ed.; with the assistance of Peter Becker), *Republicanism and Liberalism in America and the German State, 1750-1850* (Cambridge: Cambridge University Press, 2004), pp.35-52. Schlözer coined the word *Justizmord* in his response to the execution of Zurich Pastor Johann Heinrich Waser by the Swiss republican government for Waser's opposition to policies of the city government. See Epstein, *The Genesis of German Conservatism*, pp.270-71. For a fascinating study that exposes this long-forgotten crime, see Jeffrey Freedman, *A Poisoned Chalice* (Princeton: Princeton University Press, 2002).

114 'Déclaration des Droits de l'Homme et du Citoyen', *Stats-Anzeigen* 16 (1791), pp.85-89.

115 See Schlözer's closing remarks, 'Detmold, im Decemb. 1793', *Stats-Anzeigen* 18 (1793), pp.559-60; the quoted passages are from p.560.

116 Karl Demeter, *Scharnhorst und die Freimaurerei* (Hamburg: Akazien-Verlag, 1961), p.8. On the previous page (Note 2), Demeter points out that of all of the biographies of Scharnhorst written since his death in 1813, only Friedrich Hossbach's 1955 study mentions Scharnhorst's association with the Freemasons, both in Göttingen and later in Berlin. What is even more telling is the fact that Scharnhorst's intellectual life in Göttingen is not even mentioned by either Klippel or Lehmann.

117 Stübig, *Scharnhorst*, pp.22-23.

118 On the *Göttinger Hain*, see Alfred Kelletat, *Der Göttinger Hain* (Stuttgart: Reclam, 1967).

119 On Bürger, see Gunter E. Grimm (ed.), *Gottfried August Bürger: Gedichte* (Ditzingen: Reclam, 1997).

the largest group, followed by military officers, merchants, members of free occupations, and public officials.[120]

Joining The Golden Compass offered Scharnhorst a sense of community, opening his mind to the popular culture of his time, and often to the social and political challenges facing Germany. Freemasonry was the association that linked Scharnhorst with Schlözer, Gatterer, Pütter, and other *Aufklärer* in Göttingen. During the second half of the eighteenth century, educated men with strong egalitarian beliefs began organising (apart from the state) into masonic lodges throughout Germany. Dedicated to the cultivation and propagation of secular ideals, freemasonry penetrated virtually every level of educated society, and included princes, high government officials, wealthy bourgeoisie, as well as many of the scholarly and literary elites. Freemasons discussed the political and philosophical questions of the time in a spirit of academic freedom, away from princely arbitrariness and aristocratic encroachment. Often these gatherings were evening dinner parties, where Estorff's concept of *Bildung* paid enormous dividends for Scharnhorst.

Without question, 'freemasonry symbolized an emerging civil society that was increasingly coming to view itself as autonomous from the state'.[121] Masonic lodges chose secrecy to protect the identities their members and their ideology from control and censorship by the absolutist state. With its focus on the *Bildung* of man – not as a subject of the state, but as a citizen and autonomous human being – German freemasonry captured the central ideals of the Enlightenment, and thus presented a highly political, social, and cultural, as well as perhaps even a revolutionary attack on the absolutist regime. Paradoxically, by its very nature, absolutism 'necessitated the genesis of the Enlightenment'.[122] The fellowship of freemasonry, with its lively exchange of ideas (especially political opinions), clearly influenced Scharnhorst.

Scharnhorst also participated in the Gauss Reading Society, another educated group that discussed scientific and economic questions. In 1799 it transformed into one of the emerging 'Museum Societies' that were springing up at that time. Here Scharnhorst became acquainted with the newest books and other literature being published. He also enjoyed the exchange of ideas between the various middle-class sectors of society, the merchants and tradesmen, privy councillors, physicians, soldiers, and other professionals. In the Gauss Reading Society, he most likely became acquainted with two later Hanoverian officials,

120 On the Masonic Lodge *Zum goldenen Zirkel*, see Arndt Wolf, *Zur Geschichte der Freimaurerei: Die Freimaurerlogen in Göttingen* (Göttingen: Bürger-Archiv, 1997); and Paul Ssymank, *Die Geschichte der Freimaurerei in Göttingen: 1744 bis 1935* (Göttingen: Unknown Publisher, 1935). Ssymank's paper was printed privately for lodge members.

121 See the important discussion on freemasonry in Chapter 8 (pp.252-72) of James Van Horn Melton, *The Rise of the Public in Enlightenment Europe* (Cambridge: Cambridge University Press, 2001); the quoted passage is from p.273. As state employees, Klippel and Lehmann may have chosen not to discuss Scharnhorst's association with freemasonry, since freemasons were perceived by the ruling elites as a possible threat to the state. This was certainly the case following the Carlsbad Decrees of 1819. Also see the provocative study by Gerhard Krüger, *... gründeten aus unsere Freiheit: Spätaufklärung, Freimaurerei, preussisch-deutsche Reform, der Kampf Theodor von Schöns gegen die Reaktion* (Hamburg: Bauhütten Verlag, 1978).

122 Reinhard Koselleck, *Critique and Crises: Enlightenment and the Pathogenesis of Modern Society* (Cambridge, MA: MIT Press, 1988), p.8.

August Wilhelm Rehberg (1757-1836) and Ernst Brandes (1758-1810), who at the time were students at the University of Göttingen.[123]

In the years following the Seven Years War, the German Enlightenment renewed itself with an 'extraordinarily rapid diffusion of new and progressive ideas' that originated from universities such as Göttingen, scholarly journals and newspapers like those of Schlözer and Matthias Claudius (*The Wandsbeck Messenger*), as well as the individual studies of renowned historians, philosophers, poets, jurists, and theologians. The audience for these ideas was 'a wider and rapidly increasing public composed of all educated elites', including those 'citizens' [*Bürger*] who were 'genuinely literate'.[124] On a person note, it was during his initiation into The Golden Compass that Scharnhorst met fellow novice Theodor Anton Heinrich Schmalz (1760-1831), who was studying law under Professor Pütter. Schmalz was the son of a Hanoverian official and later become a renowned jurist and the first rector of the University of Berlin in 1810. With the help of Scharnhorst, he wrote the first biography of Count Wilhelm.[125] It was through this acquaintance that Scharnhorst met his wife, Klara Christiana Johanna Schmalz (1762-1803).

Scharnhorst's own pragmatic thinking was clearly influenced by the discussions he participated in at the lodge meetings, the reading circles, and other social gatherings. The *Bildung* he received at Göttingen began to open Scharnhorst's eyes to the tremendous possibilities of a free and open society, including the fundamental conviction that a modernisation of the absolutist state was becoming increasing necessary.[126] At this time Scharnhorst remained cautious and deliberate, listening to and observing the actions of others around him. He continued his veracious reading habits and developed the methodical thoroughness that became a hallmark of his activities. In the coming years, as he sensed his own worth as a soldier, educator, and writer (and later as a combat leader), Scharnhorst realised he would never be able to achieve his aspirations without a thorough reform of the political and social structure of the absolutist state. It was at this point that he became part of the growing discourse and debate on reforming German society.

Meanwhile, in addition to attending the military science lectures and the art of war colloquium of Professor Meister, Scharnhorst listened to the political science lectures of Professor Schlözer. It is also probable that he attended the lectures of Professors Gatterer, Pütter, and Spittler. On 8 March 1780, he achieved full membership in The Golden Compass, which he attended regularly during this time. In 1780, as part of the research for his courses at Northeim, Scharnhorst perfected a micrometre telescope that possessed a unique mechanism for estimating distances and ranging to targets.[127] According to one contemporary account, his invention was ideal for the military and a substantial improvement over other

123 Hornung, *Scharnhorst*, p.25.

124 See the important discussion on this topic in John G. Gagliardo, *Germany Under the Old Regime, 1600-1790* (London: Taylor and Francis, 1991), especially Chapter 23 (pp.375-95); the quoted passages are from p.375.

125 On Schmalz, see the massive study by Hans-Christof Kraus, *Theodor Anton Heinrich Schmalz (1760-1831): Jurisprudenz, Universitätspolitik und Publizistik im Spannungsfeld von Revolution und Restauration* (Frankfurt am Main: Vittorio Klostermann Verlag, 1999).

126 Stübig, *Scharnhorst*, p.22.

127 Klippel, *Scharnhorst*, Vol.1, p.74. Also see Gerhard Scharnhorst, 'Nachricht von der Einrichtung eines Micrometers zum militärischen Gebrauch' (before 20 June 1789); in Kunisch (ed.), *Scharnhorst: Privat und dienstliche Schriften*, Vol.1, pp.89-90 [12.].

micrometre telescopes.[128] Scharnhorst used the statistical data he had collected while experimenting with this device and assembled it in a set of tables that were later published in the second volume of his *Handbook for Officers* (1788).[129] Scharnhorst most likely learned how to use statistical analysis from August Schlözer.

Reflecting on the four years he spent at his regimental school in Northeim reveals the firm foundation Scharnhorst built for his future as an educator, writer, and combat leader. He used these years wisely to read broadly and in depth (especially in the military sciences), acquiring a comprehensive knowledge in numerous fields of study. More importantly, he was able to cultivate his *coup d'oeil* and 'supposing', learning from Estorff an essential method for solving tactical problems. The historical, cultural, and political education he received at Göttingen also expanded his intellectual horizon, as did his association with freemasonry. Both served him well. Scharnhorst's wide-ranging understanding of the art of war through reading, self-study, and practical field training (but without actual combat experience) soon earned him the label of a military *Aufklärer*, 'a judgment which was clearly strengthened by his poor military; indeed, his nearly careless appearance'.[130] Interestingly, Scharnhorst participated in his first field training exercise with the 8. Dragoner Regiment near Herzberg in the spring of 1779. He came totally unprepared, and in a letter to his Uncle Heinrich, related how his company commander had to counsel him about this. He then asked his uncle for money to pay for the many items he required while in the field.[131]

128 A *Colonel* Alent of the French Engineers wrote an article entitled, 'On Reconnoitring', which was originally published in Paris in 1806 and highlights Scharnhorst's key invention. Alent's piece was later incorporated in *Essays on the Theory and Practice of the Art of War* [Chiefly Translated from the Best French and German Writers by the Editor of *The Military Mentor*] (London: T. Gillet, 1809). See Vol.1, p.66, for Alent's commentary on Scharnhorst's micrometre.

129 In his *Handbuch für Officiere in den anwendbaren Theilen der Kriegs-Wissenschaften* (Hanover: Gebrüdern Helwing, 1787-90), Vol.2, pp.3-38, Scharnhorst devoted the first section to explaining in detail the use of his micrometre.

130 Stübig, *Scharnhorst*, pp.24-25.

131 See his Letter of 24 May 1779; in Kunisch (ed.), *Scharnhorst: Privat und dienstliche Schriften*, Vol.1, pp.44-46.

5

An Artillery School for Hanover

Like most European armies at the time, the Hanoverian military sought to capitalize on recent developments in warfare. The devastating power of artillery fire had improved dramatically during the Seven Years War, thanks largely to the efforts of Count Wilhelm and others. Artillery had also become more mobile and standardised. Even more significant was the link between the artillery, the Enlightenment, and the German classical tradition. Unlike the infantry and cavalry (where the patent of nobility was normally required), the artillery and engineers were the two branches of the service most associated with the concept of *Bildung*, and where most commoners found opportunity.

From the time of the ancient Greeks, Persians, and Romans, as well as the Japanese and Chinese, the aristocracy had traditionally looked upon itself as the divinely ordained leaders of society. As the self-proclaimed guardians of the people, the nobility relieved itself of any obligation to perform manual labour, so noblemen could stand watch and protect the lower classes, and by doing so, become honourable men. Over the centuries there emerged among these self-appointed guardians of the masses a deeply rooted prejudice against physical labour and *Bildung*. This mentality reached its zenith in Western society during the Middle Ages, when this form of chivalry was firmly entrenched and sanctioned by royal decree and by religious authority as divinely ordained by God.[1] These feudal values still prevailed in an age when discovery and advances in science and technology, along with the questioning of religious and political authority, had altered the art of war, the face of battle, and the feudal concept of chivalry. Because of their scientific and technical nature, the artillery and engineers came to symbolize the Enlightenment and its notions of *Bildung*, and thus threatened much that the nobility held sacred.[2]

At Harburg (now a suburb of Hamburg) in October 1799, *Major* Victor Lebrecht von Trew (1736-1804) established a 'primary school' for the education of his artillerymen. A quiet man, Trew was a good field soldier, 'rich in military knowledge', but with a tendency

1 See the important discussion of this mentality in William H. Maehl, *Germany in Western Civilization* (University, AL: Alabama University Press, 1981), Chapter 8 (pp.94-105); and in John Desmond Bernal, *Science in History* (Cambridge, MA: MIT Press, 1971), Vol.1, pp.65-77, 91-109, 128-39, 234-37, and 287-301.

2 See Alfred Vagts, *A History of Militarism: Civilian and Military* (New York: The Free Press, 1959), p. 109; and John U. Nef, *War and Human Progress: An Essay on the Rise of Industrial Civilization* (New York: W.W. Norton & Company, 1963), pp.318-19.

toward being a stubborn, 'rather crude and strict' martinet.[3] During the Seven Years War he had served under Count Wilhelm and admired his techniques. After the war he began replicating the cannon tests Wilhelm was conducting at Wilhelmstein, experimenting with gun tube length and finding a way to reduce the weight of cannon. Under his aegis the foundry and school at Harburg soon earned for Trew a reputation as an innovator. At the request of Hardenberg, he sent the commanding general his 'Memorandum on Providing Instruction', which detailed his program.[4] Hardenberg was impressed, and when Hanover began modernising its artillery, he turned to Trew, promoted him to *Oberstlieutenant* on 9 March 1781, relocated him to the capital, and directed him to draw up plans for an artillery school.

As the senior artillery officer, Trew received a free hand under the sponsorship of Hardenberg. On 10 May he submitted a plan that was remarkedly similar to his program at Harburg. Ideally, artillerymen seeking to become non-commissioned officers, non-commissioned officers, cadets, and junior officers would be admitted to the artillery school. They would learn mathematics, the artillery sciences (ballistics, mechanics, hydraulics, etc.), military sciences, French, drawing, and the composition of military essays. Students would be divided into three classes: the first was composed of non-commissioned officer aspirants and non-commissioned officers; the second contained cadets seeking to become artillery officers; the third comprised young officers from the artillery, and those from infantry and cavalry desiring to learn how to employ the cannon assigned to support their units. Classes would be held four days a week, four hours each day. On designated afternoons pupils would perfect their gunnery skills in live-fire exercises. On other afternoons they would spend two hours learning French and drawing. Staff officers from the artillery regiment would preside over the periodic and final examinations to insure impartiality. Discretionary funds from all of the regimental accounts would cover the costs of the school.[5] Not surprisingly, Trew's concept drew immediate criticism.

Many officers in Hanover were adamantly opposed to the establishment of an artillery school, convinced that formal 'academic learning' [*Schulpedanterie*] was totally unnecessary.[6] They remained content with the informal customs and traditions (meaning mostly mentoring) for the education, training, and socialization of cadets, pages, and young officers.[7] An artillery school meant standardisation of instruction and publicly educating

3 This characterization of Trew comes from Klippel, *Scharnhorst*, Vol.1, p.81; and Lehmann, *Scharnhorst*, Vol.1, p.33.

4 Trew's pioneering endeavours in Harburg can be followed in Hann 41, III, Nr.66: *Die Unterweisung der Bombardiere (Artillerieunteroffizier) und Kadetten. Die Verteilung der Bombardierungskompanien und ihrer Offiziere. Promemorien des Generalleutnants Braun und des Majors von Trew zu Harburg, 1779-1781*; deposited at the Niedersächsisches Landesarchiv, Hanover; and discussed briefly in Poten, *Geschichte des Militär-Erziehungs-und Bildungswesen: Hannover*, Vol.2, pp.26-28.

5 On the establishment and operation of the artillery school, see the source documents in Hann 41, VIII, Nr.33/1 and Nr.33/2: *Entwürfe und Pläne zur Einrichtung einer Artillerieschule und Ingenieurschule Vakanthaltung der Chefstelle beim Artillerieregiment , 1781-1793*; deposited at the Niedersächsisches Landesarchiv, Hanover; and cited in Klippel, *Scharnhorst*, Vol.1, pp.81-120; Lehmann, *Scharnhorst*, Vol., pp.33-34 and 39-44; Poten, *Geschichte des Militär-Erziehungs-und Bildungswesen: Hannover*, Vol.2, pp.26-44; and Kunisch (ed.), *Scharnhorst: Privat und dienstliche Schriften*, Vol.1, pp.57-198.

6 Scharnhorst later discussed this resistance in Gerhard von Scharnhorst, *Handbuch der Artillerie* (Hanover: Helwing, 1804-14), Vol.2, p.536.

7 Hornung, *Scharnhorst*, p.28.

not just the middle and lower classes, but also the aristocracy. It entailed book-learning, the exchange of ideas, competition among students, periodic examinations to measure progress, and public recognition, all of which the ruling elites viewed as a dangerous precedent. Because of aristocratic meddling, it would take Trew nearly a decade for all the issues of curriculum content, examination protocol, student selection, and costs to be resolved in a way that maintained the social conditions within the Hanoverian army.[8]

Despite resistance to his program, Trew was unrelenting as he sparred with opponents of the school. When his main supporter Hardenberg died on 26 November 1781, plans for opening an artillery school were deferred, pending the appointment of a new commanding general.[9] Five months later on 26 April 1782, Trew sent Hardenberg's successor, *General der Infanterie* Johann Wilhelm von Reden (1717-1801), his 'Concept for the Establishment of the Artillery School', requesting it be forwarded to King George for his approval. Reden complied, and the king gave his endorsement on 17 May 1782. Trew then addressed faculty concerns in memorandum of 22 June, in which he told Reden he had selected *Lieutenanten* Ludwig von Wissel and Ludwig Martens as instructors. Both had taught at the school in Harburg. When Martens left the service, Trew informed Reden he knew of 'no other officer who possessed more skill and ability for this work' than *Fähndrich* Scharnhorst of the cavalry.[10] Trew then wrote to Estorff requesting Scharnhorst, whose reputation had made him the obvious choice.[11]

'I am so convinced', Commandant Trew told *General-Major* Estorff, 'that the acquisition of *Fähndrich* Scharnhorst will be an essential; indeed, an increasingly necessary advantage for the mentioned institute'. Repeating what he had told Reden, Trew said he knew of 'no officer who possesses more aptitude and ability for this work' than Scharnhorst.[12] Although Estorff was reluctant to lose his best teacher, 'whom he loved like a son', he understood Trew's situation.[13] In July 1782, Scharnhorst transferred from his regimental school to the artillery school. Before reporting for duty in Hanover he travelled home to Bordenau, where his father passed away on 5 August after a long illness. As the oldest son, Gerhard inherited the Bordenau estate and with it a seat and voice in the Calenberg *Landschaft*. Following his father's funeral and arranging for the management and maintenance of the estate, Scharnhorst departed for his new duty assignment in Hanover.[14]

8 See the discussion in Louis von Sichart, *Geschichte der Königlich-Hannoverischen Armee* (Hanover: Hahn Hofbuchhandlung, 1866-98), Vol.4, pp.132-34. 'Instruction für die Artillerie-Schule' (5 June 1789) follows on pp.138-45.

9 On this transition of authority, see Hann 41, III, Nr.179: *Ableben des Feldmarschalls von Hardenberg und Übertragung des Armeekommandos an den General der Infanterie von Reden, 1781*; deposited at the Niedersächsisches Landesarchiv, Hanover.

10 Trew's memorandum of 22 June 1782 to Reden is cited in Klippel, *Scharnhorst*, Vol.1, p.83; and in Lehmann, Scharnhorst, Vol.1, p.34; the quoted passage is from Lehmann.

11 O.F. Schweder, *Scharnhorsts Leben* (Berlin: E.S. Mittler und Sohn, 1865), p.15.

12 See Trew's Letter of 28 June 1782 to Estorff; printed in Klippel, *Scharnhorst*, Vol.1, pp.78-79; the quoted passages are from p.78.

13 Klippel, *Scharnhorst*, Vol.1, p.79.

14 The settlement of the Bordenau estate following the death of Ernst Wilhelm Scharnhorst can be found in Appendix X of Klippel, *Scharnhorst*, Vol.1, pp.240-41.

When Scharnhorst arrived in Hanover, he found conditions at the artillery school in flux. While Trew understood the need for a military *Bildung*, he also realised that most artillerymen lacked the basic knowledge they required to perform their duties adequately. Therefore, he focused more on the technical training of artillerymen in the practical application of their craft than on the *Bildung* of leaders. This also pleased the *Ständestaat*. When classes began in September, Wissel and Scharnhorst taught the entire curriculum, rotating between classes. They were to receive monthly instructor honorariums, but because of conflicts with commanders who were reluctant to pay the costs of educating their soldiers, or to release their men to attend classes (fearing other soldiers would have to perform the duties of these students), it took Trew nearly two years to achieve this goal.[15] The main textbook was *Rudiments of Arithmetic, Algebra, Geometry, and Trigonometry* (1776-90) by Johann Friedrich Ludwig Häseler (1732-97). The other work, *Beginnings of Practical Artillery Instruction for Senior Non-Commissioned Officers, Gunnery Sergeants, and Artillerymen in the First Class of the Artillery School* (1782), was mostly likely written by Trew and Wissel.[16]

Trew filed his first report on 24 October 1782. In it he stated that 15 *Bombardiers* were attending the first class, while five *Feuerwerkers* and 10 cadets were being taught in the second class. No officers were enrolled, so there was no third class. He also noted that two distinguished visitors, *General-Major* Count Jakob Johann Taube von Kudding (1727-99), *Chef* of the 11. Infanterie Regiment, and *Oberst* Count Georg Ludwig von Oeynhausen (1734-1811) from the *Leibgarde* Regiment, had toured the school, perhaps to ascertain its potential for training their officers.[17] Oeynhausen was a nephew of the late Count Wilhelm. Both he and Taube had served as *Ober-Adjudanten* to Duke Ferdinand during the Seven Years War. While this appeared not to be a promising beginning, Scharnhorst sensed an opportunity to further his cause for the *Bildung* of leaders. To accomplish this, he did not limit his teaching solely to his assigned subjects but sought to broaden the horizons of not only his students but the army as well. Characteristic of this endeavour was his first publication, *Military Library*.

Shortly after his arrival in Hanover, Scharnhorst published *Military Library* (1782-84). This was a periodical of around 150-170 pages, intended to acquaint officers of all arms of the service with important military literature, and to provide information on the 'internal spirit' or condition of different armies (their discipline, means of supply, training, and artillery). *Military Library* was designed primarily for infantry and cavalry officers, 'who are able to procure few books for themselves'. Scharnhorst told his readers that in no other journal 'can one learn the details of newly published military books', especially the announcements and reviews from Vienna, which were not available in northern Germany.[18] The idea for *Military Library* originated at Northeim and was patterned off the works of Estorff and

15 Trew's efforts can be followed in Klippel, *Scharnhorst*, Vol.1, pp.80-87. Also see the discussion in Sichart, *Geschichte der Königlich-Hannoverischen Armee*, Vol.4, p.132.

16 See the notes in Poten, *Geschichte des Militär-Erziehungs-und Bildungswesen: Hannover*, Vol.2, pp.33 and 34. Also see the discussion in Jähns, *Geschichte der Kriegswissenschaften vormehrlich in Deutschland*, Vol.3, p.2367.

17 Poten, *Geschichte des Militär-Erziehungs-und Bildungswesen: Hannover*, Vol.2, p.31. The duty positions of Taube and Oeynhausen are listed in Sichart, *Geschichte der Königlich-Hannoverischen Armee*, Vol.3, pp.93 and 88; respectively.

18 See Scharnhorst, 'Vorbericht', *Militair-Bibliothek*, Vol.1, pp.i-iv; the quoted passages are from pp.iii and ii; respectively.

Nicolai.[19] Judging by its format and contents, it was ideally suited for the curriculum at the artillery school.

Scharnhorst understood the critical importance of reading and study for the *Bildung* of military leaders. Moreover, he felt this formation was best accomplished within a community of learning, as he had experienced at Wilhelmstein, Northeim, and Göttingen. Soldiers learned best how to read and interpret their studies under the guidance of enlightened leaders. This was the main purpose of the *Military Library*. Indeed, when Scharnhorst recommended two foundational works, he cautioned his readers not to study these books outside of a learned community. The first was *An Attempt at a Blueprint for the Formation of Officers* (1775) by Nicolai; the second *An Attempt to Study the Art of War* (1775) by Zanthier. Scharnhorst felt these superbly written works made 'far too many demands' on the 'beginner' [*Anfänger*] to be useful at the early stage of the officer's development. While Scharnhorst applauded both Nicolai and Zanthier and highly recommended their books, he worried that without the requisite knowledge and experience of more informed soldiers, the mental discipline Nicolai and Zanthier required would 'scare off' many young officers.[20]

Scharnhorst provided a self-study reading program for officers, using his own experience as his guide. It was entitled, 'Introduction to Reading and Field Exercises for Officers', and was similar to the 'Instructions' Estorff had provided his regiment.[21] Focusing on the study of mathematics, the military sciences, tactics, weaponry and gunnery, fortifications, and the operations of a corps and army, this comprehensive self-study program contained bibliographies that offered a variety of renowned military authors. Among those Scharnhorst listed were: Montecuccoli, Maurice de Saxe, Guibert, Turpin, Folard, Puységur, Feuquières, Maizeroy, Turenne, Frederick the Great, and Santa-Cruz. Much of the content contained in these classics was part of the lively and at times acrimonious debate taking place within the French army following its humiliating defeats during the Seven Years War.[22] Judging by the vigour and clarity of his language, there is no doubt Scharnhorst sought to stir up a similar and passionate discussion on the military art and sciences within the armies of the German states.

In addition to these books, Scharnhorst recommended basic works to provide the officer with a broad and well-rounded military formation. Works on mathematics and the military sciences highlighted this list, and included gunnery, weaponry, fortifications, tactics, and large-scale operations that he believed would be helpful for students of the first and second classes at the artillery school. Many of these titles he had studied under Count Wilhelm and *General-Major* Estorff. To familiarize officers with the fundamentals of higher

19 In the 'Contents' of his journal, Scharnhorst stated his program was based largely on the unpublished manuscript *General-Major* Estorff had written on professional education for the officers of his regiment. See 'Inhalt', *Militair-Bibliothek*, Vol.1, p.ix.

20 Gerhard Scharnhorst, 'Inhalt', *Militair-Bibliothek*, Vol.1, pp.vii-xii; the quoted passages are from p.viii. This commentary is also among the 'Notizen' in Kunisch (ed.), *Scharnhorst: Privat und dienstliche Schriften*, Vol.1, p.189 [1.].

21 See Gerhard Scharnhorst, 'Anleitung zur Lecture und zu den Feld-Uebungen der Officiere', *Militair-Bibliothek*, Vol.1, pp.1-38. This was the first half of his program. Unfortunately, the second part on field exercises was never forthcoming. In the forward to the second edition, Scharnhorst stated that the lack of space forced him to move the field exercises portion to the third edition. See 'Vorbericht', *Militair-Bibliothek*, Vol.2, p.4. Unfortunately, no explanation of its absence was forthcoming in either the third or fourth editions.

22 For a study of this intellectual activity, see Quimby, *The Background of Napoleonic Warfare*.

command, Scharnhorst created a special section using the keyword 'On Strategy', which included the memoirs and writings of great battle captains. Not surprisingly, two of these were Montecuccoli and Frederick the Great.

In the second edition of *Military Library* (1783), Scharnhorst supplemented his initial listings with another bibliography of 'the most distinguished practical books on the science of war'.[23] Titles on cavalry, infantry, and artillery stood at the top of his list, followed by reference books on the art of fortifications and siege warfare, large-scale operations and small wars. Under each section he listed works 'Indispensable' [*Unentbehrliche*] and those for 'Light Reading' [*Zur Nachlese*]. Scharnhorst considered as essential reading such familiar names as Guibert, Folard, Frederick the Great, Bélidor, Maizeroy, and Grandmaison. Light reading included works by Turpin, Montalembert, and Zanthier. Later editions followed this format.

Military Library was an impressive survey of contemporary military literature and provides an interesting commentary on the state of *Bildung* within the armies of Germany during the last quarter of the eighteenth century.[24] Clearly evident in the format and content of this periodical was the mentoring Scharnhorst had received from Wilhelm, Estorff, Nicolai, Meister, and Schlözer. Each new edition featured an increasing number of articles on the latest weapons technology and selected sections and translations from recently published German and foreign military works. In the first edition Scharnhorst listed 14 annotated titles in his bibliography; a year later 48 studies. Rounding out the contents of *Military Library* were critical book reviews. It is a testimony to his enthusiasm for military *Bildung* that Scharnhorst's first literary venture soon became one of the most widely read and popular journals in Europe, with 668 subscribers – a truly remarkable achievement for that time. Subscribers ranged from Copenhagen to Vienna, and from Lisbon to Graudenz in West Prussia. Berlin, Hanover, and Leipzig accounted for nearly two-thirds of the subscriptions.[25] Scharnhorst's endeavour to encourage officers to participate in the intellectual and scientific life of the time attracted a receptive audience, especially among junior officers.

In his 'Instruction for Reading', Scharnhorst argued the case for military *Bildung*. Continuing in the footsteps of his mentors and referring particularly to the uneducated infantry and cavalry officer, Scharnhorst asked:

> What kind of confidence and respect can soldiers have in a leader who must frequently betray [*verraten*] to them that he leads them blindly – one who exposes them to danger in a reckless manner, and one who is unable to assess the work of those who are under his command?[26]

23 Scharnhorst, *Militair-Bibliothek*, Vol.2, pp.1-6.

24 See the prefatory remarks of Colmar von der Goltz on *Military Library*; in Colmar von der Goltz (ed.), *Militärische Schriften von Scharnhorst* (Berlin: F. Schneider, 1881), p.61.

25 See 'Verzeichniβ der Herren Subscribenten der Militair-Bibliothek', and 'Verzeichniβ der nachgekommenen Herren Subscribenten', *Militair-Bibliothek*, Vol.2, pp.xi-xii and Vol.4, pp.v-vi; respectively.

26 For Scharnhorst's discussion on the importance of military *Bildung*, see 'Anleitung zur Lecture', *Militair-Bibliothek*, Vol.1, pp.1-38; particularly pp.5-13; the quoted passage is from pp.5-6.

With that question he launched his attack against connection and nepotism, ignorance and pedantry. 'Ignorance', he warned his readers, 'humiliates and dishonours the military and often the entire state'. On the other hand, 'the *Bildung* of officers refines the military little by little'.[27]

Scharnhorst understood the educated officer manifested a sense of enlightenment to 'the man of the land' and to civil society as a whole. The ignorant officer created 'a dormant military that is a plague to the land, and introduces idleness, the corruption of traditions, weakness, etc'.[28] In a later discussion on this topic, he cited Lessing's *Education of the Human Race* as it applied to the steady 'progress' in the art of war.[29] Because the conduct of war demands 'a spirit accustomed to activity, training, and skill in the estimation and performance of its affairs', he noted that the competent leader must combine an endless amount of knowledge and wisdom, talent and ability. To achieve this level of proficiency would not be easily. From his own limited experience, Scharnhorst recognised this and told his readers that there were many prejudices against *Bildung*.[30]

Garrison life was clearly the greatest enemy of *Bildung*. As Scharnhorst wrote:

> The daily monotonous duty, which is often more irksome than necessary, and the constant drilling, which contributes nothing to the improvement of essential duties, can develop neither the officer nor the soldier. This constant repetition of an action enervates the spirit and exhausts its activity, engendering antipathy and dissatisfaction.

Only through much hard work and study could the officer overcome apathy and routine and master his profession. In this respect, Scharnhorst (like Wilhelm and Nicolai) held the Roman military to be 'the model of a wise nation', because Roman soldiers were educated and trained for service in both war and peace.[31]

Having established his rational for military *Bildung*, Scharnhorst then discussed its specifics. 'How does the officer educate himself?'[32] Unlike most of his contemporaries, Scharnhorst did not believe experience was the ultimate teacher. While many thought that experience was the best teacher, he pointed out that rarely does the officer have the luxury of choosing the time, manner, or place of his experience. Moreover, he noted that no regulation or command directive could prescribe every possible scenario found in combat. In fact, military regulations train only 'the mechanical tasks'.

27 Scharnhorst, 'Anleitung zur Lecture', *Militair-Bibliothek*, Vol.1, p.9.

28 Scharnhorst, 'Anleitung zur Lecture', *Militair-Bibliothek*, Vol.1, p.8.

29 See Gerhard Scharnhorst, 'Ueber die Vor-und Nachtheile der stehenden Armeen', *Neues militärisches Journal* 6 (1792), p.369.

30 Scharnhorst, 'Anleitung zur Lecture', *Militair-Bibliothek*, Vol.1, p.8.

31 Scharnhorst, 'Anleitung zur Lecture', *Militair-Bibliothek*, Vol.1, p.6. As a source for this conclusion, Scharnhorst cited *Théorie de la guerre* (1777) by Paul Gideon Joly de Maizeroy (1719-80).

32 Scharnhorst, 'Anleitung zur Lecture', *Militair-Bibliothek*, Vol.1, p.9.

> The officer must therefore know how to take the necessary measures in uncertain circumstances. In all circumstances he must understand how to choose the best means appropriate to the situation.

In order to master military leadership, 'a scientific culture is demanded of all great field commanders' [*Feld-Herrn*].[33]

Scharnhorst maintained that in the absence of actual combat experience, a careful study of military history provides the officer with a repository of ideas and methods for use in battle. To support his case, he cited excerpts from the writings of Count Wilhelm, Jean Charles, the Chevalier de Folard (1669-1752), Frederick the Great, and Benjamin Robins (1707-51).[34]

Military history also gives the officer a sense of comradeship with the heroes of every age. With the study of military literature (especially military history), 'one disciplines the spirit to martial tasks, enriching oneself with the insights and experiences of others'. Since book learning alone would not suffice, officers would also have to practice their profession. Echoing his experience at Northeim, Scharnhorst wrote:

> In the field the officer must almost always discover, compare, and select the most appropriate means. The more he trains himself in this, the more rapidly and correctly can he determine the situation and its true nature, by placing possible courses of action side by side and ascertaining their outcomes.[35]

By continuously integrating classroom instruction and self-study with practical field exercises, leaders could maintain that careful balance between theory and practice.

'Practical intelligence rests upon theory and from the simplest of combinations', Scharnhorst told his readership. 'All elements of military knowledge are closely related'.[36] Formation was thus essential for all soldiers, not just leaders. 'Without *Bildung*', he noted, 'many a corporal, who has participated in many campaigns, remains, with all his abilities, just a corporal'. Not surprisingly, Scharnhorst's corporal is reminiscent of the tale Frederick the Great told about Prince Eugene's mule.[37] 'Even the duties of subordinate officers demand constant evaluation, examination, and practice'. In closing, he noted how junior leaders learn little of value from their garrison routines, especially those officers serving in aristocratic units such as the 'Corps de Garde'.[38]

For Scharnhorst, the profession of arms was not just a guild with its unique craft or techniques (which are primarily mechanical), or solely an art (which requires unique talent and ability). It was instead an extraordinarily complex intellectual and practical occupation that

33 Scharnhorst, 'Anleitung zur Lecture', *Militair-Bibliothek*, Vol.1, p.7-8; the quoted passages are from p.8.

34 A Newtonian mathematician, Benjamin Robins wrote a renowned treatise on artillery entitled, *New Principles in Gunnery* (1742), which Scharnhorst had studied at Wilhelmstein. In his *A Military History of the Western World* (New York: Funk & Wagnalls Company, 1954-56), Vol.2, p.350, John Frederick Charles Fuller called Robins 'the father of modern gunnery'.

35 Scharnhorst, 'Anleitung zur Lecture', *Militair-Bibliothek*, Vol.1, p.7.

36 Scharnhorst, 'Anleitung zur Lecture', *Militair-Bibliothek*, Vol.1, p.7.

37 See Jay Luvaas (trans. and ed.), *Frederick the Great on the Art of War* (New York: The Free Press, 1966), p.47.

38 Scharnhorst, 'Anleitung zur Lecture', *Militair-Bibliothek*, Vol.1, p.7.

demanded continual study and training. He constantly reminded his readers what both Frederick the Great and the Chevalier de Folard had written about the importance of studying the art of war. Quoting Frederick, he noted: 'In every age war is first among the arts'. Then he cited Folard's profound truism: 'War is a science for the educated man, a craft for the ignorant'.[39] Regrettably, in the minds of many of Hanover's ruling elites, while artillerymen and engineers may require a sound technical education, *Bildung* was not important for aristocratic infantry and cavalry officers.

In Hanover, social status and connection was the reality. Although Scharnhorst believed *Bildung* would enhance the fighting abilities of leaders, he was in the minority. As long as many senior military officials felt that the primary role of the officer in combat was to maintain unit cohesion, fire discipline, and movement – all of which they thought could be trained on the parade ground, what need was there for additional knowledge that might transform an officer from a parade-ground puppet into a thinking soldier? On the other hand, as Meister (and now Scharnhorst) had pointed out, no parade-ground exercise can adequately simulate actual wartime conditions, with its uncertainly, anxiety, fatigue, and death, not to mention the horrific sensory stimuli associated with battle. Every combat veteran understood this, and while he had no combat experience, Scharnhorst had the collected memory of the great captains and those who understood war. *Bildung*, as he concluded, would certainly expand the officer's *Weltanschauung* and develop his independent judgment.

Among the authors who influenced Scharnhorst's earliest writings was Henry Humphrey Evans Lloyd (c.1729-83).[40] The son of a Welsh clergyman, Lloyd had studied theology and law for service with the church before accepting a position as a military instructor in geography and field fortifications. His detailed sketches of the village around Fontenoy (11 May 1745) attracted the attention of the French. *Marshal de France* Maurice de Saxe offered him a commission, and for the next 30 years Lloyd served with nearly every European army, often changing sides in the middle of a campaign. During the War of the Austrian Succession (1740-48) he served with the French. In 1745 he was with 'Bonnie' Prince Charles Edward Stuart (1720-88) during the Young Pretender's invasion of Great Britain. During the Seven Years War (1756-63), Lloyd served with the armies of Austria and Brunswick. A few years later he commanded a Russian division fighting the Turks in the Russo-Turkish War of 1768-74. Lloyd's conduct was not unusual in eighteenth century Europe, since there was common bond among European officers, such that they considered themselves part of an international calling or brotherhood and could thus offer their services to whatever country or prince they pleased.[41]

In his *History of the Late War in Germany* (1766), and its *Continuation* (1781), Lloyd demonstrated he was 'a man of great natural sagacity and insight, decidedly luminous and

39 Scharnhorst, 'Anleitung zur Lecture', *Militair-Bibliothek*, Vol.1, pp.8-9.

40 The actual date of Lloyd's birth is unknown. The brief biographical sketch of Lloyd by H. Manners Chichester, found in Sir Leslie Stephen and Sir Sidney Lee (ed.), *Dictionary of National Biography* (Oxford: Oxford University Press, 1921-22), Vol.11, pp.1301-02, lists the year '1720?' The finest study of Henry Lloyd to date is Patrick J. Speelman, *Henry Lloyd and the Military Enlightenment of Eighteenth-Century Europe* (Wesport, CT: Greenwood Press, 2002). Speelman dates Lloyd's birth c.1729.

41 See the interesting commentary on this subject in Schulz, 'Die Vorstellungen des Grafen Wilhelm von Schaumburg-Lippe', in Gahlen and Winkel (ed.), *Militär und Gesellschaft in der Frühen Neuzei*, pp.222-23.

original'.[42] His expensive operational experience, coupled with his theories on the nature and conduct of war, certainly inspired Scharnhorst.[43]

> It is universally agreed upon, that no art or science is more difficult than that of war; yet, by an unaccountable contradiction of the human mind, those who embrace this profession take little or no pains to study it. They seem to think that the knowledge of a few insignificant and useless trifles constitute a great officer.
>
> This opinion is so general, that little or nothing else is taught at present in any army whatsoever. The continual changes and variety of motions, evolutions, etc. which the soldiers are taught, prove evidently, they are founded on mere caprice.
>
> This art, like all others, is founded on certain and fixed principles, which are by their nature invariable, the application of them only can be varied; but they are in themselves constant.[44]

Typical of many military *Aufklärer*, Lloyd sought to deduce 'principles' from the vast history of warfare that might guide commanders and free them from the constraints of linear warfare. He believed that this 'most difficult science' could be divided into two distinct domains: 'one mechanical and may be taught by precepts; the other has no name, nor can it be defined or taught'.

> It consists in a just application of the principles and precepts of war, in all the numberless circumstances and situations which occur; no rule, no study, or application, however assiduous, no experience, however long, can teach this part; it is the effect of genius alone.
>
> As to the first, it may be reduced to mathematical principles; its object is to prepare the materials which forms an army, for all the different operations which may occur; genius must apply them according to the ground, number, species, and quality of the troops, which admit of infinite combinations.
>
> In this art, as in poetry and eloquence, there are many who can trace the rules by which a poem or an oration should be composed, and even compose, according to the exactest [sic] rules; but for want of that enthusiastic and divine fire, their productions are languid and insipid: so in our profession, many are to be found who know every precept of it by heart; but, alas! when called upon to apply them, are immediately at a stand.

42 This was the conclusion of Thomas Carlyle, *History of Friedrich II of Prussia, called Frederick the Great* (London: Chapman and Hall, 1897/98), 6:72n. For Lloyd's impact on the history of military thought, see Michael Howard, 'Jomini and the Classical Tradition', in Michael Howard (ed.), *The Theory and Practice of War* (New York: Praeger, 1966), pp.5-8. A recent, more in-depth analysis of Lloyd by one of Sir Michael's graduate students can be found in Gat, *The Origins of Military Thought*, pp.67-78.

43 Scharnhorst's announcement of the first German edition of Lloyd's *Continuation of the History of the Late War in Germany* (1781) can be found in *Militair-Bibliothek*, Vol.1, pp.105-06. His review essay, 'Der Herrn General von Lloyds Abhandlung über die allegemeinen Grundsätze der Kriegskunst', can be found in *Militair-Bibliothek*, Vol.4, pp.99-116.

44 Henry Humphrey Evans Lloyd, *Continuation of the History of the Late War in Germany between the King of Prussia and the Empress of Germany and Her Allies* (London: S. Hooper, 1781), pp.vi-vii.

> These form the great book of war; and he who cannot read it, must for ever [sic] be content with the title of a brave soldier, and never aspire to that of a great general.[45]

Judging from his review of Lloyd's *Continuation of the History of the Late War in Germany* (1781), Scharnhorst accepted Lloyd's general line of argument, but remained sceptical of the latter's position on genius. Scharnhorst titled his essay, 'Lloyd's Discussion on the General Principles of the Art of War', to alert his readers that Lloyd was attempting to prescribe rules or principles governing military relationships. 'The present work is no history of the war; rather, it contains the general principles of it and constitutes them perfectly'.[46]

The historical and empirical foundation that Lloyd had established as the basis for his philosophy of war clearly stimulated Scharnhorst's thinking on military affairs. On the other hand, he disagreed completely with Lloyd that only a man of genius is capable of success in war. He then noted the considerable attention Lloyd had devoted to the important human dimension of war, the 'national character' of the combatants, and how these and other unquantifiable forces affect military theory and practice.[47] Reading this portion of Lloyd's book may have reminded Scharnhorst of his preferred military writer.

Raimondo Montecuccoli (1609-80) was Scharnhorst's 'favourite author'.[48] Born into a noble family near Modena in northern Italy, Montecuccoli entered the Imperial Army at 16 and served the Hapsburgs throughout his long and distinguished military career. He fought in nearly all of the battles of the Thirty Years War (1618-48) – Breitenfeld (1631), Lützen (1632), Nördlingen (1634), Kaiserlautern (1635), Wittstock (1636), Chemnitz (1639), and Melnik (1639), becoming a dashing cavalry leader and rising to the rank of general.[49] After the Peace of Westphalia in 1648, he represented Holy Roman Emperor Leopold I (1658-1705) and Pope Innocent X (1644-55) on several diplomatic missions to Flanders, England, and Sweden. He then commanded the Austrian corps sent to aid Poland against Sweden in the Nordic War (1656-60). When the Turks invaded southern Europe in 1663, Montecuccoli was again in command, this time of a combined European army that decisively defeated a superior Turkish force at St Gotthard Abbey on the Raab River, on 1 August 1664. Hailed as the saviour of Europe, a grateful Leopold appointed him to *Feldmarschall-Lieutenant* of the Empire, one of the highest ranks in the army and second only to the emperor himself. In 1668, Leopold added another accolade to Montecuccoli's impressive resume, making him president of the Austrian Imperial War Council [*Hofkriegsrat*].

Montecuccoli now held the two highest military offices of the Hapsburg Empire. For the next 10 years, he focused on his military studies and writings, while improving the professionalism of the Imperial army. When war broke out against France in 1673, he received command of the Imperial forces. During the campaign of 1673, he completely outmanoeuvred his rival Henri de La Tour d'Auvergne, Vicomte de Turenne (1611-75) along the Neckar and the Rhine, then captured Bonn and advanced to the lower Rhine, where he linked up

45 Lloyd, *Continuation of the History of the Late War in Germany*, pp.vii-viii.

46 Scharnhorst, 'Lloyds Abhandlung über die allgemeinen Grundsätze der Kriegskunst', *Militair-Bibliothek*, Vol.4, p.99.

47 *Militair-Bibliothek*, Vol.4, pp.99-109.

48 Stadelmann, *Scharnhorst*, p.93.

49 On Montecuccoli, see Thomas M. Barker, *The Intellectual and Battle: Raimondo Montecuccoli and the Thirty Years War* (Albany: The State University of New York Press, 1975).

with the army of the Dutch Stadtholder William III, Prince of Orange, to block any eastward expansion of the French.

Returning home from the war, the weary Montecuccoli retired from active military service, but was recalled in 1675 to face Turenne again. After weeks of indecisive manoeuvre, Turenne was killed on the eve of battle, and Montecuccoli invaded Alsace to face Louis de Bourbon, Prince of Condé (1621-86), who had taken command of Turenne's forces. Now Montecuccoli found himself 'in yet another duel between two virtuosos of maneuver warfare', as he endeavoured to outgeneral 'the Great Condé' [*le Grand Condé*], as Louis de Bourbon was called.[50] Failing to defeat the French, Montecuccoli re-crossed the Rhine into Germany. There in 1676 he achieved his last success in war, with the siege and capture of Philippsburg in Baden.[51]

Following this campaign against France, William of Orange 'invaded' England in 1688 in what became known as the Glorious Revolution. William and Protestant leaders feared a Catholic monarchy in England, one which might unite with France against the Dutch United Provinces. With the overthrow of King James II, William and his wife Mary became joint sovereigns, and their reign began the transition of Great Britain from the personal rule of the Stuarts to the more parliamentary rule of the House of Hanover. The Electorate of Hanover was gradually united with Great Britain, and from 1714 onward, London governed her German territory.[52]

The career of Montecuccoli provided Scharnhorst with a wealth of military, diplomatic, political, and social experience. Montecuccoli's military writings were deeply rooted in his vast experience, and in Scharnhorst's opinion, offered a firm *Bildung* for the military professional. What captivated Scharnhorst was the way in which Montecuccoli endeavoured to understand the complexity of war and its relationship with society, through a rational and systematic (or scientific) approach.[53] Years later Scharnhorst wrote to *General-Lieutenant* Heinrich Wilhelm von Zeschau (1760-1832), 'my oldest friend' (and classmate at Wilhelmstein), to recommend the *Memoirs of Montecuccoli* (1759). He told Zeschau that Montecuccoli's classic was his 'constant companion'.[54] Indeed, the spirit of Montecuccoli remained with Scharnhorst throughout his life, and the knowledge and concepts he drew from reading Montecuccoli over and over again, gave him many profound insights into war

50 The quoted passage is from Russell F. Weigley, *The Age of Battles: The Quest for Decisive Warfare from Breitenfeld to Waterloo* (Bloomington: Indiana University Press, 1991), p.117.

51 Other good English accounts of Montecuccoli's military service can be found in John A. Mears, 'Count Raimondo Montecuccoli: Servant of a Dynasty', *The Historian* 32 (1970), pp.392-409; in Gat, *The Origins of Military Thought*, pp.13-24; and in Rothenberg, 'Maurice of Nassau, Gustavus Adolphus, Raimondo Montecuccoli, and the "Military Revolution" of the Seventeenth Century', in Paret (ed.), *Makers of Modern Strategy*, pp.55-63.

52 See the excellent study by Simms and Riotte (ed.), *The Hanoverian Dimension in British History, 1714-1837*.

53 The Vienna War Archives compiled Montecuccoli's extensive writings in four volumes; in Alois Veltzé (ed.), *Ausgewaehlte Schriften des Raimund Fürsten Montecuccoli* (Vienna: Wilhelm Braumüller, 1899-1900). In Vol.1, the editor describes Montecuccoli's literary work, which spanned 30 years. The first two volumes contain his military writings, while the third his historical works, and the fourth his correspondence and miscellaneous thoughts.

54 See Scharnhorst's Letter of 30 August 1810 to Saxon *General-Lieutenant* Heinrich Wilhelm von Zeschau; in Kunisch (ed.), *Scharnhorst: Privat und dienstliche Schriften*, Vol.6: *Geschäftsführender Kriegsminister und Ratgeber im Hintergrund (Preußen 1809-1811)*, pp.600-02; the quoted passages are from pp.600 and 602. On p.602 (Note 4), the editors are 'pretty certain' Scharnhorst recommended to Zeschau the *Commentaires sur le mémoires de Montecuccoli*, published by le Comte Turpin de Crissé (Paris, 1759).

and society, which he incorporated into his own evolving ideas and observations on the changing art of war.[55]

Scharnhorst found a kindred spirit in Montecuccoli. His writings offered Scharnhorst a complete course on the art and science of war. What certainly must have impressed Scharnhorst was the way in which Montecuccoli approached the study of war, the breadth and depth of his knowledge and understanding, how he sought to apply meaning to his experience, and how remarkably consistent Montecuccoli remained throughout all of his works. Scharnhorst would endeavour to imitate Montecuccoli, and his writings bear a striking resemblance to the format, style, and technique of Raimondo Montecuccoli.

In his 'Instruction for Reading', Scharnhorst echoed the preface Montecuccoli had written in his first work, *Treatise on War* (1641). In that address – 'To the Reader' – Montecuccoli laid the foundation of his methodology:

> Many ancients and moderns have written on war. Most of them, however, have not transcended the limits of theory. Even if some, … have combined theory with its application, they have undertaken to cultivate only one part of this vast field, or they have restricted themselves to generalities without immersing themselves in the details of the supporting sciences, knowledge of which in general include those which make the perfect military leader. After all, it is impossible to understand the whole, if one does not comprehend the parts which constitute it.[56]

'I can swear' [*Ich kann schwören*], Montecuccoli proclaimed to his readers, that it took him years of careful reading and study to achieve this mastery. Like Montecuccoli, Scharnhorst endeavoured to convince his audience to devote time and effort to professional reading so that they would become better soldiers and understand the changing art of war.

To his reading and study, Montecuccoli combined his personal experience. This enabled him to fashion his thoughts on the art of war in a more practical and comprehensive manner than any of his predecessors.

> I have read attentively the most important histories of the Ancients and the best [of the modern] authors, who have provided instructions on war. To these I have added examples from what the experience of fifteen successive years has been able to teach me.[57]

55 The Index to Scharnhorst's Papers lists 20 documents in which Montecuccoli is mentioned. See Kunisch (ed.), *Scharnhorst: Privat und dienstliche Schriften*, Vol.8: *Der tragische Vollender (Preußen 1813; Nachträge)*, p.863. Montecuccoli is also cited in virtually all of Scharnhorst's published works.

56 See Raimondo Montecuccoli 'An den Leser', *Abhandlung über den Krieg* [*Trattato Della Guerra*]; in Alois Veltzé (ed.), *Ausgewaehlte Schriften des Raimund Fürsten Montecuccoli*, Vol.1, pp.5-9; the quoted passages are from pp.5-6. Compare the last sentence of Montecuccoli quoted passage here with a remarkably similar sentence in Scharnhorst, 'Anleitung zur Lecture', *Militair-Bibliothek*, Vol.1, p.10.

57 Montecuccoli 'An den Leser', p.6. Montecuccoli provided no list of the authors he read; however, Rothenberg, 'Montecuccoli and the "Military Revolution" of the Seventeenth Century', p.60, writes that Montecuccoli 'carefully footnoted' his last work, and 'his sources included 15 ancient, five late-medieval and Renaissance, and 22 contemporary and near-contemporary authors'.

Montecuccoli continued his address by explaining that war is always part of a larger historical picture, and in order to understand war, the professional soldier must study its component parts, recognising the unique characteristics of each historical period, its particular social, military, political, cultural, and economic systems.[58] For Montecuccoli, a detailed study of history was essential to the development of his own theory of war, and the process he used to achieve this was clearly evident in the self-education of Scharnhorst, who also read the key historians and writers of the past and present and placed great weight on the study of history.

Scharnhorst admired how Montecuccoli continually refined his ideas. As new experience and information became available to him, Montecuccoli took the time to reflect on this knowledge before assimilating it into his own thoughts on war. In the introduction of his second, more polished work, *On the Art of War* (1653), he explained:

> I have attempted within this limited framework, to summarise methodically the exceedingly vast territory of this science, seeking to discover that singular art [*die einzige Kunst*] which is of the upmost importance to the monarchy.

Here Montecuccoli cited Cicero and Justus Lipsius, suggesting a relationship between religion, politics, and the art of war. He then discussed his quest to find 'that singular art'.

> From here I have done my upmost to discover those general rules upon which each science is created, and the innumerable branches and fruits flowing from their roots.
>
> Having considered the whole of world history from the beginning of things, I dare to say that I have not found a single notable military deed that would not fit within these rules.[59]

Not only did Scharnhorst adopt this approach in his endeavours, but also taught it to others in his own lectures and writings.

Typical of many intellectuals of his age, Montecuccoli believed scientific discovery emanated from human experience that was then captured, collated, studied, and translated into universal or fundamental truths.[60] He also maintained that while science seeks to place human experience in its proper perspective, 'that singular art' is the correct application of these universal or fundamental truths at any given time and place, through skilful judgment and leadership.[61] 'The art of war is the ability to fight well and to win'.[62] Here

58 Montecuccoli 'An den Leser', pp.7-9.

59 See Raimondo Montecuccoli, *Von der Kriegskunst* [*Del Arte Militare*]; in Alois Veltzé (ed.), *Ausgewaehlte Schriften des Raimund Fürsten Montecuccoli*, Vol.2, pp.29-30; the quoted passages are from p.29.

60 Montecuccoli, *Von der Kriegskunst*, pp.29-30. Also see Montecuccoli, *Abhandlung über den Krieg*, Vol.1, pp.7-8.

61 Montecuccoli, *Abhandlung über den Krieg*, Vol.1, pp.7-8; and *Von der Kriegskunst*, Vol.2, pp.29-30.

62 Montecuccoli, *Abhandlung über den Krieg*, Vol.1, p.21. A similar passage can be found in *Von der Kriegskunst*, Vol.1, p.31.

Montecuccoli named Julius Caesar (as Emperor and General) 'the greatest military leader [*Feldherr*] in the world'.[63]

After years of reflection, in his celebrated classic, *On the War against the Turks in Hungary* (1670), Montecuccoli offered the culmination of his thinking on the art of war.

> The innate forces of reason, while comprehending the objects, also turns them into concepts, which it stores in the memory. From several combined recollections experience emerges, and from many experiences there springs general understanding, which is the beginning of all sciences and arts.[64]

Using this approach he produced his sophisticated study of war. In the first part of his book, he presented, 'as the mathematician is in the habit of doing', those fundamental concepts or truths which, in the second part, he applied – 'like derivatives' [*Aphorismen*] – to his study of the war against the Turks in Hungary.[65] This was why his *War against the Turks* was so popular in Scharnhorst's time. Here was the scientific method applied to the study of war.

Montecuccoli selected examples from actual combat experience, analysed them, and then offered universal principles of war to guide the action of military leaders (in almost the same way Lloyd would do a century later). The mutual dependence of theory and practice was clearly evident to Montecuccoli, and he sought to demonstrate this truth to his readers. For Montecuccoli, the art of war was the creative and intuitive application of a theory of war to specific situations. As he concluded, 'Disregarding the invention of artillery, which has somewhat changed the forms of war, the rest of the rules remain correct and valid'.[66]

Raimondo Montecuccoli clearly captivated Scharnhorst by his unending quest to find a universal paradigm of war. This journey led Scharnhorst to Montecuccoli's extensive and systematic treatment of politics and war. It marks him as a leading theorist of the seventeenth century. It was no wonder that he was so widely read in the eighteenth century. His works encompassed not only the military, but also the political, social, and cultural aspects of war and society. Furthermore, he wrote from the viewpoint of a seasoned soldier. All of this influenced Scharnhorst, who by his late twenties had assimilated Montecuccoli's scientific and historical approach (as well as his humanistic and conceptual framework) into his own literary process. In Scharnhorst's mind, Montecuccoli 'had superseded Livy and Tacitus, Xenophon and Vegetius'.[67] Virtually all of Scharnhorst's writings reveal the debt he owed to Raimondo Montecuccoli.

Opportunities for intellectual growth in Hanover were beginning to develop when Scharnhorst arrived in 1782. At that time the population of the city was scarcely 17,000 inhabitants. Like the university town of Göttingen, the capital city of the Electorate sought

63 Montecuccoli, *Abhandlung über den Krieg*, Vol.1, p.7.

64 Raimondo Montecuccoli, *Vom Kriege mit dem Türken* [*Delle Guerra col Turco in Ungheria*]; in Alois Veltzé (ed.), *Ausgewaehlte Schriften des Raimund Fürsten Montecuccoli*, Vol. 2, p.199.

65 Montecuccoli, *Vom Kriege mit dem Türken*, Vol.2, p.200.

66 Montecuccoli, *Vom Kriege mit dem Türken*, Vol.2, pp.199-200.

67 Stadelmann, *Scharnhorst*, p.94.

to benefit from the cultural and literary life of the German Enlightenment.[68] Thanks largely to the efforts of Münchausen, a significant association between the capital city Hanover and the intellectual centre Göttingen had developed by the last quarter of the eighteenth century.[69] Most of the Hanoverian civil service now received their education, training, and initial court indoctrination at Göttingen. In the capital a Natural History and Economic Society was founded in 1779, to which Trew belonged.[70] It was Trew who introduced Scharnhorst to this society and to the renowned political economist Johann Beckmann (1739-1811).[71] Beckmann was educated at Göttingen and had published a number of analytical works on technology. He was the first to use the word 'technology' in his writings and in his classroom. A renowned scholar, he was a member of the scientific societies in Celle, Halle, Munich, Erfurt, Amsterdam, Stockholm, and St Petersburg. He was appointed a councillor to the Hanoverian court in 1784. Scharnhorst may have remembered him, since Count Wilhelm had implemented Beckmann's *Principles of German Agriculture* (1775) in Schaumburg-Lippe.[72] Significantly, the Natural History and Economic Society possessed an extensive library of natural science and economic works, which provided Scharnhorst with a wide variety of reading material.

From the Natural History and Economic Society came the Gans Reading Society, established in 1781. Scientific endeavours were the main emphasis of its activities, but soon the club embraced contemporary literature and plays.[73] The most important critical newspapers and magazines were also discussed. Around the same time another association called 'Museum' was founded. Its goal was to improve the general education and welfare of the population as a whole, which included the teaching of German literature.[74] Scharnhorst participated in all of these forums. Besides the existing libraries, the local book trade was also important for the intellectual life of the city. There were some letterpress printing houses, as well as the court publishing house of Helwing, which published most of Scharnhorst's works. These activities became an integral part of social, cultural, and intellectual life of Scharnhorst in Hanover.

That spring, on 19 April 1783, Commandant Trew sent his report to King George on the first year of instruction. He discussed the progress of the school, noting the outstanding

68 See the discussions in Stübig, *Scharnhorst*, pp.27-28; and in Klippel, *Scharnhorst*, Vol.1, pp.138-147. It is sad that Klippel spends nearly 10 pages discussing Scharnhorst's intellectual life in Hanover and yet not one word on his earlier formation in Göttingen.

69 R. Hartmann begins to develop this association in his *Geschichte der Residenzstadt Hannover von den ältesten Zeiten bis auf die Gegenwart* (Hanover: Ernst Kniep, 1880), starting on p.366. Another interesting source is Thomas Biskup, 'The university of Göttingen and the Personal Union, 1737-1837', in Simms and Riotte (ed.), *The Hanoverian Dimension in British History*, pp.128-60.

70 Trew was also a member of the St John Grand Masonic Lodge in Hamburg. See Wilhelm Graupenstein, *Geschichte der St Johannis-Loge zur goldenen Kugel in Hamburg* (Hamburg: F. W. Wulff, 1870). Trew is first mentioned on p.39, when he established a 'daughter' lodge in nearby Harburg, called 'Crocodile' [*Krokodill*].

71 Stadelmann, *Scharnhorst*, p. 122. Also see R. Hartmann, *Geschichte der Residenzstadt Hannover von den ältesten Zeiten bis auf die Gegenwart* (Hanover: Ernst Kniep, 1880), pp.366, 387-88, and 403.

72 On Beckmann, see Thorsten Mohr, 'Johann Beckmann. Leben, Werk, Wirkung' (M.A. Thesis, Universität Karisruhe (TH): Institut für neuere und neueste Geschichte, 2004).

73 Stadelmann, *Scharnhorst*, p.130.

74 See the interesting study by Georg Friedrich Grotefeld, *Geschichte des Lyceums der Königlichen Residenz-Stadt Hannover während des Zeitraums von 1773 bis 1833* (Hanover: Brüder Jänecke, 1833).

performance of the instructors, especially Wissel, and recommended he be promoted. The king responded on 27 May, expressing his 'special satisfaction' with the 'glorious endeavours of the teachers' at the school. He then sent his military aide, *General-Lieutenant* Heinrich Wilhelm von Freytag (1720-98), to inspect the school and provide a detail report. After receiving Freytag's glowing account, King George sent a letter to Reden on 8 July, writing:

> We are especially delighted to hear that the non-commissioned officers of the artillery regiment garrisoned there attend the instruction. On the other hand, it is very displeasing to hear that none of the officers took advantage of this opportunity, as was intended.

Reden answered the king on 15 August. He told him he had arranged for six pages to attend classes in the coming year. Addressing the lack of officer participation, Reden indicated that because Wissel conducted his classes in his quarters (like the tutors at Wilhelmstein), there was insufficient space for officers to attend. Realising this was a poor excuse, he informed King George that 'since the Pavilion (at the Calenberger Gate) intended for the artillery school has now been set up, I have ordered officers to attend the instruction'.[75]

Later that spring Scharnhorst requested extended leave to visit the artillery schools of several German states. This was highly unusual, since such a journey was usually reserved 'only for young nobles and the sons of upper-class citizens'.[76] Scharnhorst noted that such a lengthy trip was necessary if he was to be properly prepared for his duties as an artilleryman, which in turn would benefit the school.[77] Perhaps as a hidden agenda, Scharnhorst also wanted sufficient time along the way to study the battlefields of the Seven Years War and to gather material for his literary endeavours.[78] Altogether, he tramped at least seven battlefields, taking copious notes, making detailed sketches, and reliving the course of the fighting in detail.[79] Scharnhorst would later use this information in his lectures and in his publications.

With his travel plans approved, Scharnhorst began his trip across central Europe, stopping in Hesse, Württemberg, Austria, Saxony, and Prussia.[80] Arriving in Hesse, he visited Kassel and Darmstadt. He then rode to Stuttgart, where he met with Nicolai, who had recently published another work, *Arrangement of a General School of War for all Branches* (1781),

75 See the exchange of letters and discussion on these issues in Hann 41, VIII, Nr.19: *Verlegung der Stückgießerei von Celle nach Hannover. Erbauung der Artillerie-Schuppen vor dem Calenberger Tore und des Gießhauses am Steintore, 1775-1796*; and Nr.21: *Verhandlungen zwischen dem König Georg III. und der Kriegskanzlei wegen Artilleriesachen, 1775-1802*; deposited at the Niedersächsisches Landesarchiv, Hanover; and cited in part in Klippel, *Scharnhorst,* Vol.1, pp.87-88.

76 Hornung, *Scharnhorst*, pp.28-29; the quoted passage is from p.29.

77 Lehmann, *Scharnhorst*, Vol.1, p.34; and Klippel, *Scharnhorst*, Vol.1, p.135.

78 Klippel, *Scharnhorst*, Vol.1, p.135.

79 Some of Scharnhorst's notes and sketches from his battlefield studies can be found in Kunisch (ed.), *Scharnhorst: Privat und dienstliche Schriften*, Vol.1, pp.48-52 (Olm), 52-54 (Bergen), and 54-57 (Dettingen). Lehmann, *Scharnhorst*, Vol.1, p.39, adds that Scharnhorst also visited the battlefields of Kolin, Lowositz, Freiberg, and Rossbach.

80 None of the sources agree on the exact route Scharnhorst took; however, logic, geography, and time suggests the route stated above. Scharnhorst's reports from his visits to Austria, Saxony, and Prussia can be found in Kunisch (ed.), *Scharnhorst: Privat und dienstliche Schriften*, Vol.8, pp.445-48, 449-60, and 461-81; respectively.

which clearly inspired Scharnhorst when he later advanced similar ideas in Hanover.[81] He was delighted and fortunate to spend three profitable days with Nicolai, discussing a variety of subjects and pursuing the vast collection of military maps ('around 13,000') and sketches ('6305 pieces' of which '3400 are tactical') Nicolai possessed.[82]

From Stuttgart Scharnhorst travelled to Munich, where he found the Bavarian military 'in every respect in wretched shape'.[83] Leaving Munich, he ventured to Vienna and Prague, where his impressions of the Austrian army were more favourable. He was deeply moved by the Austrian military welfare service that often gave soldiers the choice of living in monasteries instead of barracks.[84] From Vienna he continued on to Saxony, stopping at Dresden and Freiberg. At Freiberg he met fellow artilleryman, *Hauptmann* Johann Gottlieb Tielke (1731-87), who had published two well-known and very popular works, *Instruction for Field Engineers* (1769) and *Contributions to the Art of War and a History of the War from 1756-1763* (1775-87).[85] Later that December he thanked Tielke for his hospitality and their discussions on the training of engineers. He included a copy of his study of Fortress Wilhelmstein, which officials in Schaumburg-Lippe had not permitted him to publish.[86]

Leaving Saxony, Scharnhorst journeyed to Berlin, Spandau, and Potsdam, where he spent considerable time with another artilleryman, *Major* Georg Friedrich Ludwig Tempelhof (1737-1807). A noted *Aufklärer*, Tempelhof was a mathematician and astronomer, music composer, and military scholar. He was a graduate of the Brandenburg University of Frankfurt (am Oder) and the Friedrich University of Halle. He had joined the Prussian army in 1756 as an infantryman, then served as an artillery gunner, participated in some of the major battles of the Seven Years War, and was commissioned in 1759, following his achievement during the Battle of Kunersdorf.[87]

Tempelhof was an accomplished writer when Scharnhorst arrived in Berlin. Interestingly, none of his early works were on military subjects. He had completed his first book, *Principles of Finite Analysis* (1768), followed by its companion volume, *Principles of Infinite Analysis*

81 Ferdinand Friedrich von Nicolai, *Anordnung einer allgemeinen Kriegsschule für alle Waffen* (Stuttgart: Johann Benedikt Mezler, 1781). There are many similarities between the content of Nicolai's work and the central points contained in the later memoranda Scharnhorst submitted to his Hanoverian superiors.

82 See Scharnhorst's Letter of 7 December 1784 to *Hauptmann* Johann Gottlieb Tielke; printed in Kunisch (ed.), *Scharnhorst: Privat und dienstliche Schriften*, Vol.1, pp.59-60; the quoted passages are from p.60. This letter confirms that Scharnhorst was in Stuttgart and met with Nicolai; something Klippel, *Scharnhorst*, Vol.1, p.135, states 'probably' took place.

83 Gerhard Scharnhorst, 'Bayrisches Militair', *Militair-Bibliothek*, Vol.4, p.134. Also see Lehmann, *Scharnhorst*, Vol.1, p.34. It is sad that Lehmann spends nearly six pages discussing Scharnhorst's journey of 1783, but not one word on his earlier and clearly more profound educational experience in Göttingen.

84 Lehmann, *Scharnhorst*, Vol.1, p.35.

85 Johann Gottlieb Tielke, *Unterricht für die Officiers, die sich zu Feld-Ingenieurs bilden, oder doch den Feldzügen mit Nutzen beywohnen wollen* (Dresden and Leipzig: Johann Nicholaus Gerlach W. und Sohn, 1769); translated into English as *The Field Engineer* (London, 1789); and *Beyträge zur Kriegs-Kunst und Geschichte des Krieges von 1756-1763* (Freiberg: Samuel Friedrich Barthel, 1775-87).

86 See Scharnhorst's Letter of 7 December 1784 to *Hauptmann* Tielke; printed in Kunisch (ed.), *Scharnhorst: Privat und dienstliche Schriften*, Vol.1, pp.59-60. Scharnhorst's study of Fortress Wilhelmstein can be found on pp.23-30.

87 For a nice biographical sketch of Tempelhof and his works, see Bernhard Poten, 'Tempelhof: Georg Friedrich von', *Allgemeine Deutsche Biographie*, Vol.37, pp.561-62. Also see Jähns, *Geschichte der Kriegswissenschaften*, Vol.3, pp.1873-74. Frederick ennobled Tempelhof in 1784.

(1769). Four years later he published *Complete Introduction to Algebra* (1773). His *Thoughts on the Tuning of Pianos* appeared in 1775, followed six years later by his first military work, *The Prussian Bombardier or Projectile Movement* (1781). Then came *Geometry for Soldiers and Those who are not* (1790). When Scharnhorst visited Berlin, Tempelhof was teaching mathematics, ballistics, and fortress theory to officers of the Berlin garrison, and was set to publish the first volume of his massive and influential work, *History of the Seven Years War* (1783-94), which was a detailed analysis of that war, a spirited defence of Frederick the Great, and (more importantly) a nice rebuttal of Henry Lloyd's study of the same conflict. Perhaps Lloyd was a topic of discussion between Scharnhorst and Tempelhof.

From this initial encounter developed a relationship between Tempelhof and Scharnhorst that 18 years later would play a key role in the latter's appointment to Prussian service in Berlin. In his assessment of the Prussian artillery, Scharnhorst found its horse harnesses in poor condition, attributing this to the practice of allowing farmers to use artillery horses to plough their fields in times of peace. He also wondered about the salaries of Prussian officers, how they distinguished the funds they received from their private, entrepreneurial interests, and those from their official duties.[88] Of course, his major reason for visiting Berlin was to observe the training exercises of the Prussian artillery, and to inspect the weapons factories in Spandau and Potsdam. After accomplishing those tasks, he left Potsdam and returned to Hanover via Magdeburg. In every place he visited, Scharnhorst was keenly interested in the health and welfare of the soldier, his quarters and mess, his clothing and equipment, his weapons and ammunition, his methods of training and education, his wage or salary, his duty hours, and his leisure time.

Looking back on his first year in Hanover must have pleased Scharnhorst. His reputation as an instructor at his regimental school at Northeim had inspired the newly selected commandant of the Hanoverian Artillery School to request his appointment to its faculty. Trew placed great faith in the teaching abilities of Scharnhorst, who did not disappoint. In keeping with the best of the classical traditions, Scharnhorst was also able to further his own intellectual growth through his participation in three academic societies in Hanover. He also published his first major work, *Military Library*, which achieved remarkable success. Scharnhorst then capped his first year with an extended trip across central Europe, where he visited the most notable military schools in Germany and Austria. Returning to Hanover in the late summer of 1783, he was set to resume his teaching duties at the artillery school.

88 Scharnhorst's commentary can be found in his report on the Prussian artillery; printed in Kunisch (ed.), *Scharnhorst: Privat und dienstliche Schriften*, Vol.8, pp.470-72.

6

Educator in Hanover

Back in Hanover Scharnhorst prepared for the coming school year. After a fruitful summer he was getting ready for his teaching assignments. In a letter to Trew he requested the honorarium for the previous year to which he was entitled but had not yet received. He reminded Trew this was a 'condition' of his transfer to the artillery school. He hinted that without this allowance 'my teaching could not be done with the pleasure and zeal that such work requires'. He also promised to forward 'this week' his report on the Austrian artillery.[1]

Scharnhorst continued by advising Trew that now was the time to put caution aside and begin educating (not just training) students attending the artillery school. It was apparent to him that there were still those contemptuous of *Bildung*. He also knew Trew was anxious about being replaced, even stating 'the school could come under someone who would hire his own officers, if only for the politics'. He then reminded Trew of the positive aspects of their situation, referring to the points Freytag had told the king. He also noted how officials supportive of the school had approved the new curriculum with its clearly defined tasks and measurable standards. They had agreed to 'a certain methodology' that ensured standardisation of instruction and had provided 'the most appropriate materials and resources'. Most importantly, King George had blessed their efforts.[2]

After urging Trew to forge ahead with the *Bildung* of leaders, Scharnhorst repeated his request for funding so he could teach all three classes 'practical field work', which he described as the 'art of field fortifications, tactics, the defence and attack of entrenchments and fortresses, etc'. He also included writing 'military reports'. He noted that 'no adequate textbooks on these subjects and no method' for conducting this training currently exist. Nevertheless, he said he would be willing to assemble this material, even though it would be 'somewhat cumbersome', requiring a fairly extensive reading program as well as developing the appropriate lesson plans. As he told Trew:

> I do not fancy that I do more than my duty, only that maybe something more appropriate for the whole thing may be done by others in the same proportion, and that

1 See Scharnhorst's undated letter to Trew (1783/1784); printed in Klippel, *Scharnhorst*, Vol.1, pp.97-99. This correspondence is also published in Kunisch (ed.), *Scharnhorst: Privat und dienstliche Schriften*, Vol.1, pp.57-58.

2 Scharnhorst to Trew; printed in Klippel, *Scharnhorst*, Vol., p.98, and in Kunisch (ed.), *Scharnhorst: Privat und dienstliche Schriften*, Vol.1, pp.57-58.

my contribution is to the formation of people who can be useful in every situation, those who produce and who honour the school.[3]

In closing his letter, he had asked Trew to intercede for him with Reden to have him officially assigned to the artillery regiment, which was also part of the agreement when he transferred from the cavalry.

With the blessings of King George and the backing of Reden, Commandant Trew submitted his program for the 1783/84 academic year on 1 August 1783. This ambitious syllabus endeavoured to correct the major deficiencies of the previous year. Thanks largely to the encouragement of Scharnhorst, the curriculum focused on leader development.[4] Students were again divided into three classes. The first was designed solely for non-commissioned officers and those seeking to become non-commissioned officers. The second class was a mixture of cadets possessing the qualifications to become officers, pages who desired to become artillery officers, and officers who lacked the 'necessary detailed knowledge' for their 'continued success' as leaders. Qualified officers of all arms who wanted to improve their professional *Bildung* and learn how to employ artillery in battle made up the third class. Instruction was to begin in late September (on or near the Christian feast of St Michael the Archangel) and to end around Easter of the following year.

The curriculum fitted the needs of each class. Those assigned to the first class received instruction in applied arithmetic and geometry, mechanics, field sketching, and gunnery techniques. This would enable them to be competent non-commissioned officers. Periodic exams ascertained their progress. The second class was essentially a remedial or preparatory course for those requiring additional teaching in basic mathematics (arithmetic, algebra, geometry, and trigonometry) and the applied components of the military sciences. Included in this class were 'designated school children' (young noblemen) requiring 'special instruction' to prepare them to become cadets or pages.[5] Successful completion of this instruction was required before advancing to the third class. Both the first and second classes lasted just one year.

Instruction for the third class took place over two years and endeavoured to synthesise what the cadet, page, and young officer had learned to date and to provide advanced teaching in mathematics and the applied military sciences, such as gunnery techniques, mechanics (mainly ballistics), aerometry, hydrostatics, weaponry, tactics, siege craft, field fortifications, and large-scale operations. Infantry and cavalry officers stationed in and around Hanover were encouraged to attend this course to further their education and to learn how to integrate

3 Scharnhorst to Trew (1783/1784); printed in Klippel, *Scharnhorst*, Vol., p.98, and in Kunisch (ed.), *Scharnhorst: Privat und dienstliche Schriften*, Vol.1, pp.57-58.

4 See 'Einrichtung der neu anzulegenden Artillerie-Schule in Hanover' (1783); Appendix III of Klippel, *Scharnhorst*, Vol.1, pp,188-93. Comparing this document with the ones Trew had previously submitted reveals a substantial shift of the curriculum from just a technical knowledge of the artillery to a broader study of the art of war, as is evident in Scharnhorst's writings at the time.

5 See Paragraph 2 of 'Einrichtung der Artillerie Schule', Appendix III of Klippel, *Scharnhorst*, Vol.1, pp.189. A special set of instructions was published to regulate the education of these school children. It was entitled, 'Gesetze der Ecoliers der Artillerie-Schule' (1 August 1783); and cited in Bernard Poten, *Geschichte des Militär-Erziehungs-und Bildungswesen: Hannover*, Vol.2, p.35; and in Klippel, *Scharnhorst*, Vol.1, p.91.

artillery into their manoeuvre schemes. Regardless of class, all students were taught mathematics, French, drawing, the military sciences, and other subjects as necessary.[6]

Afternoons were reserved for drawing and design, French language training, and composition. 'Laboratories' [*Laboratorio*] or practical field exercises were held on Wednesday.[7] 'Cannon craft' was the central focus of these exercises. Here the sergeants, pages, cadets, and officers learned how a gun crew and battery operated. They were taught how to evaluate an area for its offensive and defensive capabilities, how to occupy firing positions, how to lay cannon and batteries, how to estimate firing distances, and how to fire various cannon and howitzers in different offensive and defensive modes.[8] During the spring months Scharnhorst taught field craft to all three classes. These exercises were pretty demanding and tested the ability of the student to put into practical what he had learned in the classroom.[9] Pupils manoeuvred artillery in support of infantry and cavalry units, prepared maps and sketches, completed staff problems, and briefed their solutions to their regimental commanders. Emphasis was placed on teamwork among pupils, regardless of rank or class.[10]

The selection of textbooks emphasised a military *Bildung*. The goal here coincides with the ideas of Scharnhorst to introduce students not just to the theory and practice of the artillery, but also to its tactical employment in support of the infantry and cavalry.[11] The main texts for the first class were *Rudiments of Arithmetic, Algebra, Geometry, and Trigonometry*, and the newly published *Practical Artillery Instruction for Non-Commissioned Officers of the Artillery Regiment* (1783), which was an updated version of the 1782 text. The first two parts of *Rudiments of Mathematics* (1774-81), by Austrian *Major* Leopold Freiherr von Unterberger, were used to teach the second class, while the third and fourth parts were studied in the third class. Other books Scharnhorst listed include: *Elements of Tactics and an Introduction to Military Evolutions for the Infantry* (1784) by Prussian *General-Lieutenant* Friedrich Christoph von Saldern, and *Treatise on Cavalry* (1776) by French *Lieutenant Général* Louis Hector Drummond de Melfort. The inclusion of *Rudiments of Military Engineering* (1772) by Danish *Capitain* Karl August von Struensee, and *A Study of the Marches of the Army, its Depots, Battles, and Operational Plans* (1778) by Schaumburg-Lippe *Major* Friedrich

6 Class schedules are printed in Paragraph 4 of 'Einrichtung der Artillerie Schule', Appendix III of Klippel, *Scharnhorst*, Vol.1, pp.189-90. Also see the discussion on the curriculum in Poten, *Geschichte des Militär-Erziehungs-und Bildungswesen: Hannover*, Vol.2, pp.33-35. Scharnhorst's commentary at the time can be found in 'Nachricht von einer in Hannover errichteten Kriegsschule', *Militair-Bibliothek*, Vol.3, pp.173-91. Also see his discussion in his *Handbuch der Artillerie*, Vol.2, p.536. Later he wrote a much more detailed pedagogical report entitled, *Nachricht von der Militair-Schule in Hannover* (not before 1791); in Kunisch (ed.), *Scharnhorst: Privat und dienstliche Schriften*, Vol.1, pp.167-78.

7 Laboratories are discussed in Paragraphs 5 and 8 of 'Einrichtung der Artillerie Schule', Appendix III of Klippel, *Scharnhorst*, Vol.1, pp.190 and 191.

8 Scharnhorst, 'Nachricht von einer in Hannover errichteten Kriegsschule', *Militair-Bibliothek*, Vol.3, pp.180-88.

9 Some idea of how these drills were conducted can be found in Hann 41, IV, Nr.50: *Artillerieexerzierreglement vom Jahre 1782. Enthält u.a.: 3 Tabellen mit 14 Aufstellungsplänen am Geschütz und Lafette*; and in Hann 41, III, Nr.67: *Unterhaltung und Ordonnanz der Regimentsartillerie im Frieden und im Felde. Aufwand für die jährlichen Übungen, 1780-1784*; deposited at the Niedersächsisches Landesarchiv, Hanover.

10 Stübig, *Scharnhorst*, p.28.

11 See the discussion in Lehmann, *Scharnhorst*, Vol.1, pp.33-34.

Wilhelm Christian von Zanthier, also suggests a curriculum that sought to provide a understanding of the army on campaign.[12]

The goal of the artillery school was to make the student not just a well-rounded artilleryman, but also an important member of a combined arms team. Classes were taught much like those at a German university. The major difference was at the artillery school the instructor might have to repeat his main points '3 to 4 times' before his pupils fully grasped 'the fundamental principles' of the lesson. After each lecture, presentation, or discussion, selected pupils were called forward to demonstrate their comprehension of the material in front of their classmates. At other times, depending on the content of the lesson, students were placed in competition with each other. Periodic tests ascertained the progress of the pupil, while annual, final examinations determined whether the student successfully completed his course of instruction. During their practical field exercises, students were grouped into sections and given tactical problems to solve. Sometimes groups were pitted against each other. Pupils then presented their solutions in front of their peers, their instructor and Commandant Trew, or other military officials.[13]

When classes began in late September 1783, newly promoted *Capitain* Wissel and *Fähndrich* Scharnhorst began their instruction. Joining them were two outstanding *Feuerwerker* – Heinrich Ludolph Hugo and Cuno Josua Rehwinkel – who Trew had selected to assist them. He described Hugo 'as a coach of the first rank, who even before this assignment had established a respectable foundational knowledge and possessed very good skill'. Trew also appointed Rehwinkel to serve as the school's adjutant, since he had 'a lot of skill and a steady nature'.[14] In addition to his artillery and military science courses, Scharnhorst taught arithmetic and analysis to the second class on Monday and Thursday mornings from eight to 10, geometry and trigonometry and a basic introduction to field warfare to the third class, every Tuesday and Friday morning from 10 to 12. He also offered remedial instruction in arithmetic, algebra, geometry, and trigonometry to the second class on Tuesday and Thursday afternoons, from two to four. Hugo taught geometry to the first class.[15]

As in the previous year, Scharnhorst continued collecting material for the school library. Thanks to the generous donation of 489 books from the estate of the late *General-Lieutenant* Henning Anton Ulrich Braun (1704-80), Scharnhorst had begun with a solid foundation.[16] With funding from the War Chancery, he zealously developed the holdings, often traveling to local book fairs and regularly to Göttingen to bookseller Johann Christian Dieterich (1722-1800) in search of quality books, manuscripts, maps, instruments, and other material

12 Scharnhorst, 'Nachricht von einer in Hannover errichteten Kriegsschule', *Militair-Bibliothek,* Vol.3, pp.175-77. Also see Jähns, *Geschichte der Kriegswissenschaften vormehrlich in Deutschland,* Vol.3, p.2367.

13 Scharnhorst, 'Nachricht von einer in Hannover errichteten Kriegsschule', *Militair-Bibliothek,* Vol.3, p.178-80; the quoted passage is from p.178.

14 See the excerpts from Trew's Report of 9 June 1783; cited in Klippel, *Scharnhorst,* Vol.1, pp.84 (Note 2).

15 Poten, *Geschichte des Militär-Erziehungs-und Bildungswesen: Hannover,* Vol.2, pp.34-35; and Klippel, Scharnhorst, Vol.1 pp.86-87.

16 On the artillery school library, see Kiefert, 'Zur Geschichte der Militärbibliotheken in Hannover', pp.281-324; especially pp.294-296. Also see the source documents in Hann 41, VIII, Nr.22: *Ableben des Generalleutnants Braun, dessen Testament in Bezug auf seine Verlassenschaft an Büchern, Instrumenten und so weiter*; deposited at the Niedersächsisches Landesarchiv, Hanover.

for the library.[17] Trew soon entrusted him with the management of the library, which was for the use of anyone attending the artillery school.[18] Library material could be borrowed for a maximum of three weeks, depending on the difficulty of the book or the needs of the pupil. In a novel move, Scharnhorst received permission of open the library to the public on Saturday afternoons. By the end of the first six months (September 1782 to Easter 1783), he had collected another 179 volumes. In the summer of 1783, he published the library's first catalogue, which listed over 668 volumes.[19]

On 4 October 1783, Professor Meister submitted his assessment of the new curriculum. 'I find nothing to complaint about', he began. On the whole he felt the curriculum would 'undoubtedly be of great benefit, if strictly observed'. As a true academic he believed the syllabus was still not challenging enough. 'Perhaps the following remarks about some minor matters', he continued, would 'serve to show my good will and at least confirm the plan which they did not improve'. Meister felt subjects essential for the artilleryman were not being taught. Among those he listed were higher mathematics, chemistry, physics, mechanics, and modelling.[20] Meister wanted a university-level education at the artillery school. Whether he knew of the extent of the illiteracy of the student body is not clear. Trew, Wissel, and Scharnhorst certainly understood that soldiers attending the artillery school simply did not have the basic educational foundation to grasp these subjects and to achieve success in the kind of truly academic environment Meister sought. That the curriculum was divided into tiers of learning also indicated the difficulty of teaching soldiers with vastly different levels of knowledge. Remedial instruction was introduced to raise the level of learning among students. Another factor may have been the objections of those who felt such subjects were far too academic and not critically important for artillerymen.

Albrecht Meister was advocating a more enlightened approach to military education. He wanted Hanover 'to commit to new ways'. In the last sentence of his memorandum he proposed using the spring months to correlate classroom theory with field practice, and to make sure students had mastered their studies. A native Württemberger, Meister wanted Hanover to follow the lead of the Hohe Carls-Schule and transform the entire Hainberg area near Göttingen into a military training facility, like what Nicolai was attempting in Stuttgart. Nicolai was endeavouring 'to do away with the dusty books and the drawing board' and take the student to the field, where he would be trained and educated through

17 Statistics on the artillery school library can be found in Appendix II of Commandant Trew's report on the school and published as 'Nachricht von einer zu Hannover errichteten KriegsSchule', August Ludwig Schlözer (ed.), *Stats-Anzeigen* (Göttingen: Vandenhoekschen Buchhandlung, 1782-93), 8 (1785), pp.316-17. On Dieterich, see Elisabeth Willnat, *Johann Christian Dieterich: ein Verlagsbuchhändler und Drucker in der Zeit der Aufklärung* (Frankfurt am Main: Buchhändler-Vereinigung, 1993).

18 On Scharnhorst's management of the library, see Stübig, *Scharnhorst*, pp.30-31.

19 *Verzeichniß von größenteils in die mathematische und Militär-Wissenschaften einschlagenden Bücher der Artillerie-Bibliothek* (Hanover, 1783). Also see the source documents in Hann 41, XXVI, Nr.15: *Verzeichnis sämtlicher Bücher, mathematischen Instrumente, Modelle und Armaturstücke (Bewaffnung) der Artillerie-Schule Hannover, 1789*; and Nr.14: *Die Bibliothek der Schule und ihre Ausgaben. Bergung der Bücher und Instrumente im Jahre 1795*; deposited at the Niedersächsisches Landesarchiv, Hanover. According to Thomas Fuchs and Ulrich Kandolf, 'Die Wehrbereichsbibliothek II und ihre Vorgängerinstitutionen', in *Die Wehrbereichsbibliothek II (Hannover)* (Hameln: Niedersächsischen Landesbibliothek, 2004), p.171, of the original Braun collection of 489 volumes, only 60 remain.

20 Professor Meister's Pro Memoria of 4 October 1783 is printed in Klippel, *Scharnhorst*, Vol.1, pp.101-03.

real-world exercises that tested current military doctrine. Nicolai believed this methodology was a far more beneficial pedagogy than 'learning rules and explaining classical writings'.[21]

Meister agreed completely with Nicolai's methodology. Ever since his return from Paris in 1765, where he had travelled officially and specifically to study first-hand French war schools, Meister had been advocating to Hanoverian officials to reject the fragmentation he had found in France, with its specialised military schools, and instead create one, general school of war.[22] Hanover should educate its leaders 'through perception and experience, not just from abstract theories'. This would enable them to synthesise and use what they had learned.[23] Scharnhorst liked what Nicolai and Meister were seeking to do, and even convinced Trew to permit him to implement such a program at the artillery school. It is a testament of Trew's faith in Scharnhorst that he gave him a free hand in conducting these field exercises.

The character of military education was a hotly debated topic throughout many of the German states, not just in Hanover.[24] Scharnhorst had entered this conversation with *Military Library*. Given his character and growing knowledge of the artillery, it was only a matter of time before he began advocating improvement to the syllabus and examination process at the artillery school. In his mind the educational experience at the artillery school fell far short of the *Bildung* he had received at Wilhelmstein and that which Estorff had provided at Northeim.[25] Following the lead of Nicolai, Scharnhorst began presenting 'concept papers' [*Entwürfe*] to his superiors.[26] This soon became a trait that characterized his behaviour throughout his career, as he continually strove to place enlightened and progressive ideas before his superiors for their consideration and endorsement. Trew certainly appreciated his support and encouragement, recommending him for promotion. In recognition of his significant contributions, King George promoted Scharnhorst on 2 April 1784 to *Titular-Lieutenant* ['lieutenant, in title only'].[27]

The examinations held from 15 to 19 June 1784 validated the efforts of Commandant Trew and his four instructions: Wissel and Scharnhorst, Hugo and Rehwinkel. In his report of 19 June, Trew informed Reden of the examination results:

> In the first class, of the 32 pupils tested: 1 bad [*schlecht*], 6 mediocre [*mittelmässig*], 16 pretty good [*recht gut*], and 9 superb [*ganz vorzüglich*]. The second class consisted of 24 men, including 5 royal pages; 4 of them tested bad, 15 pretty good, and 5 most notably good [*ganz besonders gut*]. On the following day this class tested again:

21 See Meister's Pro Memoria; in Klippel, *Scharnhorst*, Vol.1, p.103. Also see the interesting discussion about this in Stadelmann, *Scharnhorst*, pp.146-49; the quoted passages are from p.148.

22 Klippel, *Scharnhorst*, Vol.1, pp.80-120, provides a pretty good discussion (citing numerous source documents) on the pedagogical debate over the character and curriculum of the artillery school in Hanover.

23 Stadelmann, *Scharnhorst*, pp.148.

24 Stadelmann, *Scharnhorst*, pp.146-49.

25 See the discussion on this in Lehmann, *Scharnhorst*, Vol.1, pp.40-41.

26 Interestingly, in his memoranda, Scharnhorst used the term 'Military School' or 'School of War' when writing about the artillery school.

27 The term 'titular' meant Scharnhorst held the rank of *Lieutenant* in title only, without the corresponding income. He was still paid the rank of *Fähndrich*. Hence my translation 'lieutenant, in title only'. See the discussion of this in Appendix II of Kunisch (ed.), *Scharnhorst: Privat und dienstliche Schriften*, Vol.1, p.813 (*Titularrang*).

> 4 mediocre, 14 pretty good, and 6 exceptionally good [*ausserordentlich gut*]. The third class, which tested alone on the 19th, consisted of 12 students: 3 received very good [*sehr gut*] and 9 excellent [*vorzüglich*].[28]

Reden forwarded Trew's report to the king on 25 June, informing him that, "as far as I am concerned', the artillery school was 'a very useful institute', thanks 'to the two teachers, *Kapitian* von Wissel and *Lieutenant* Scharnhorst, who demonstrated continual diligence', and also to the students who confirmed their 'improved knowledge' by their examination results.[29] As a consequence of these achievements, the king promoted Trew to *Oberst* on 13 July 1784 and appointed him *Chef* of the Artillerie Regiment.[30]

When Hanover promoted Scharnhorst, he was six months shy of his 29th birthday. Later that year he unexpectedly stopped publishing *Military Library*, in spite of a wide-ranging reading audience. He gave no reason until the appearance the next year of a second journal, *Library for Officers* (1785). It appears the editor of the rival *Bellona: A Military Journal* (Dresden, 1781-85) was exceptionally upset with Scharnhorst's review of his journal. In that evaluation, Scharnhorst had listed the contents the *Bellona* purported to contain, then followed with a section entitled, 'The Actual Contents'.[31] He noted that some of the material in the *Bellona* had already been published in other journals, while the reviews were generally uncritical. When Scharnhorst discovered an incomplete, but to him a valuable treatise entitled, *On the Duty of Light Cavalry in the Field, Particularly for the Junior Officer*, he asked: 'Why is this very interesting study not completely published?' He suggested the *Bellona* 'not consider lightly such essays, since they are the ones to be read'.[32]

Constructive criticism was characteristic of the German Enlightenment. While his commentary about the *Bellona* was consistent with his other reviews, Scharnhorst clearly did not endear himself to the editor of the *Bellona*.[33] Later, when he reviewed a book written by a colonel, the editorial staff of the *Bellona* took the concept of 'peer review' literally, seizing the opportunity to criticise and even ridicule the '*Lieutenant*' Scharnhorst for his presumption in reviewing a book written by a senior officer. Such indiscretion on Scharnhorst's part was unforgiveable.[34] When the editor of the *Bellona* refused to cease his malicious and slanderous attacks, even endeavouring to gain support from other journal editors, Scharnhorst decided to change the title, publisher, and place of publication of his periodical, hoping to

28 Trew's report of 19 June 1784 on the success of the students on their examinations can be found in Klippel, *Scharnhorst*, Vol.1, p.88. Also see Poten, *Geschichte des Militär-Erziehungs-und Bildungswesen: Hannover*, Vol.2, p.35.

29 See Reden's report to King George on 25 June 1784; in Klippel, *Scharnhorst*, Vol.1, pp.88-89.

30 See Hann 41, VIII, Nr.22: *Verleihung des Artillerieregiments an den Obersten von Trew, 1784*; deposited at the Niedersächsisches Landesarchiv, Hanover.

31 Scharnhorst reviews of *Bellona, ein militairisches Journal* can be found in *Mililtair Bibliothek*, Vol.2, pp.54-59 and 71-75; the quoted passage is from p.55.

32 See Scharnhorst's commentary on this book in *Mililtair Bibliothek*, Vol.2, p.56.

33 According to Jähns, *Geschichte der Kriegswissenschaften*, Vol.3, pp.1789 and 1815, Conrad Walters was the editor and publisher the *Bellona*.

34 See the discussion in Jähns, *Geschichte der Kriegswissenschaften*, Vol.3, pp.1817-18; Lehmann, *Scharnhorst*, Vol.1, pp.47-50; and Klippel, *Scharnhorst*, Vol.1, pp.122-24. For Scharnhorst's account, see 'Nachrichten, welche bei Bibliothek für Officiere betreffen', *Bibliothek für Officiere* (Göttingen: Johann Christian Dieterich, 1785), Vol.3, pp.294-96.

avoid further controversy.[35] Bookseller Johann Christian Dieterich in Göttingen agreed to publish this new journal, *Library for Officers*.

Literary commentary was the source of this controversy. Objective criticism was a hallmark of the German Enlightenment and pivotal to the process of *Bildung*. This was one of Scharnhorst's expressed goals when he had published *Military Library* and continued with *Library for Officers*. The very purpose of these journals necessitated the critical review of sources, and Scharnhorst endeavoured in his reviews to teach his readers how 'to compare the worth of a book to others'.[36] Decades later, when a voracious reader and avid student of war such as Napoleon reflected on his own reading experience, he confessed:

> Something is lacking in a great state where the young studious man has no way of receiving good direction in what he wishes to study and is forced to grope his way and waste months and years of searching through useless readings for the real meat of instruction.
>
> I have studied a great deal of history, and often, for want of a guide, have been forced to lose considerable time in useless reading.[37]

As the editor of *Military Library* and *Library for Officers*, Scharnhorst felt obligated to provide his readers with a guide to reading worthwhile military literature.

'My reviews', Scharnhorst pointed out in his introduction to *Library for Officers*, 'are nothing more than an exact compilation of the facts, and a comparison of the opinions of the author with those of other respected writers'.[38] He also reserved a section in *Library for Officers* for authors to respond to any criticism of their works. In a brief but biting commentary on current military reviews, Scharnhorst stated that for the most part, they are 'governed more by connection than by impartial judgment'. He urged a return to the objective criticism and passionate debate that once existed among 'the greatest of men'. 'One knows what transpired between Schlözer and Herder, between Nicolai and Wieland, between Kästner and Zimmerman'.[39] From his critical readings Scharnhorst certainly knew what had happened between Schlözer and Herder, between Nicolai and Wieland, and between Kästner and Zimmerman. Unfortunately, his largely ignorant audience probably had little idea of what he was implying. Thus, when his explanation failed to stop the attacks against him, Scharnhorst decided to end publication of *Library for Officers*. It seems that

35 Stübig, *Scharnhorst*, p.32, suggests that business reasons may have also played a role in Scharnhorst's decision to publish in Göttingen.

36 See Gerhard Scharnhorst, 'Antwort auf eine Recension über die Bibliothek für Officiere, welche in May dieses Jahrs dem Herausgeber derselben eingeschicht ist', *Bibliothek für Officiere*, Vol.4, pp.157-61; the quoted passage is from p.158.

37 Napoleon Bonaparte, 'Observations sur un project d'établissement d'une école spéciale de littérature et d'histoire au collège de France' (19 April 1807); in J.B.P. Vaillant (ed.), *Correspondance de Napoleon Ier* (Paris: Henri Pion and J. Dumaine, 1858-70), Vol.15 (12416), pp.102-10; the quoted passages are from pp.108 and 109. Napoleon's observations in 1807 bear a remarkable resemblance to Scharnhorst's writings on military education in 1782.

38 Scharnhorst, 'Vorrede', *Bibliothek für Officiere*, Vol.1, p.iii.

39 See Scharnhorst, 'Recensionen', *Bibliothek für Officiere*, Vol.4, p.153. This commentary is also among the 'Notizen' in Kunisch (ed.), *Scharnhorst: Privat und dienstliche Schriften*, Vol.1, p.193 [16.].

objectivity had no place in German military circles, as connection and pettiness, arrogance and vindictiveness, triumphed over enlightened reason and *Bildung*.

This incident failed to diminish Scharnhorst's stature. In the three years since his arrival in Hanover he had established a wide reputation as an erudite educator, scholar, and writer. He had helped develop and refine the curriculum at the artillery school. During the summer of 1783 he had made a research journey to a number of the German-speaking armies to study their military institutions. Along the way he tramped many of the significant battlefields of the Seven Years War. On a personal note, in late 1784, he requested permission to marry Klara Christiane Johanna Schmalz. In accordance with army regulations, company-grade officers had to obtain permission from the commanding general to marry. This was to insure that they had 'sufficient means' to provide for their families, especially while 'on campaign in time of war'.[40] In his letter to Trew, which was forwarded on 4 January 1785 to newly promoted *Feldmarschall* von Reden, Scharnhorst informed Hanoverian officials that his officer salary, the honorarium he received from teaching at the artillery school, 'the several hundred thaler annually' he obtained from the Bordenau estate, plus additional money from his publishing endeavours, all combined to provide him with sufficient means of supporting a wife and family.[41]

Once he had received approval to marry, Scharnhorst wrote a lengthy 13-page dialog on love and marriage to his bride-to-be. Using the painting, 'The Marriage of Amaryllis and Myrtillo' (1635) by Abraham Bloemaert (1564-1651), he poured out his love and affection for Klara, comparing the radiant beauty of Amaryllis to his future bride and spoke of the happiness that awaited them in marriage. He spoke to Klara about the harmony of their emotions and bodily attraction; of intimate love and purity of heart. He told her how he disliked extravagance and pretence. His enduring interest was only to her and their future family.[42] They were wed on 24 April 1785. Throughout their 18 years as husband and wife, which produced five children (three of whom reached adulthood), the love between Gerhard and Klara Scharnhorst was so strong that he freely and frequently confided to her his innermost thoughts.

Three months before Scharnhorst's marriage, Trew published his comprehensive report on the Hanoverian artillery school in Schlözer's *State Reports*.[43] Most of this account came from the description Scharnhorst had published in *Military Library*.[44] With the notoriety resulting from a positive publication in *State Reports* came further recognition from King George and Hanoverian officials. Improvements soon followed. Trew was at last able to implement many of the concepts he, Wissel, and Scharnhorst had developed over the previous three years. To assist Trew, King George established a 'Commission' headed by

40 Sichart, *Geschichte der Königlich-Hannoverischen Armee*, Vol.3, pp.123-24; the quoted passage is from p.123.

41 Scharnhorst's request to Trew (before 4 January 1785) is printed in Kunisch (ed.), *Scharnhorst: Privat und dienstliche Schriften*, Vol.1, p.70. On Reden's promotion, see Hann 41, III, Nr.180: *Ernennung des Generals von Reden zum Feldmarschall*; deposited at the Niedersächsisches Landesarchiv, Hanover.

42 See Scharnhorst's Letter to Klara (written sometime before 24 April 1785); in Kunisch (ed.), *Scharnhorst: Privat und dienstliche Schriften*, Vol.1, pp.70-76.

43 See Victor Lebrecht von Trew, 'Nachricht von einer zu Hannover errichteten KriegsSchule' (27 January 1785), in Schlözer (ed.), *Stats-Anzeigen*, 8 (1785), pp.305-19; and incorporated as Appendix IV of Klippel, *Scharnhorst*, Vol.1, pp.193-201.

44 See Scharnhorst, 'Nachricht von einer in Hannover errichteten Kriegsschule', *Militair-Bibliothek*, Vol.3, pp.173-91.

Freytag and Secret War Councillor Ernst Franz Carl von Hake to determine how the artillery and engineer schools could be used for the training of officers and cadets of the infantry and infantry.[45] Scharnhorst now began teaching three, two-hour courses (each two days a week) on fortification, geometry, and drawing. He also continued his practice of introducing military history into his instruction.

Seeking to raise the level of military *Bildung* in Hanover, Scharnhorst sent Trew a concept paper in 1785 entitled, 'On the Establishment of a Military School for our Corps'. In this memorandum he proposed to transform the artillery school into a general school of war as Meister sought. His commentary was indicative of the low level of education most soldiers possessed. It was time, he stated in his first sentence, that 'every young officer ... spend three years at the school'. Each infantry battalion should send at least one to two officers, and every cavalry regiment at least two to three officers, for an annual total of 70 to 80 'eager-to-learn school children' [*Ecoliers*].[46] Only motivated and quality instructors would teach at this school. To avoid any connection or nepotism, students would be examined quarterly by the director of the school and annually by a board of staff officers and captains, chaired by a general officer. Upon completion of this three-year program, students would undergo 'a double examination'. One would be in front of a board of officers chaired by a general officer; the other before the director of the school and the commanding general of the corps.

Examination results would be issued to the student according to a three-tier scheme. At the bottom would be those achieving a 'low' or 'inferior' [*ordinär*] score. The middle level would be students with a score of 'diligent' or 'hardworking' [*fleißig*]. Ranking at the top would be pupils with 'special ability' or 'genius' [*besonders Genie*]. Scharnhorst also wanted a censure given to those who failed to take their examinations seriously. This statement would read: 'To those who have produced nothing, nothing is given'.[47] Officers conducting the exams 'must swear an oath that they will not act according to connection [*Connexion*] and will sign all testimonials and protocols'. Clearly thinking of the useless officers in the Hanoverian army, Scharnhorst also suggested that it might be wise to examine the lieutenants and captains in each regiment in order to weed out those no longer fit for service, instead of allowing them to linger on active duty while younger and more capable officers are denied advancement because they lack 'seniority' [*Ancienneté*].[48]

Judging from the language and tone of this memorandum, it was clear to Scharnhorst that there were some in Hanover who viewed the artillery school as a breeding ground for succeeding generations of pages, cadets, and noble officers, imbued with a certain formal

45 Sichart, *Geschichte der Königlich-Hannoverischen Armee*, Vol.4, pp.132-33.

46 Gerhard Scharnhorst, 'Einrichtung einer Militair-Schuhle [sic] für unsere Corps', in Kunisch (ed.), *Scharnhorst: Privat und dienstliche Schriften*, Vol.1, pp.115-17; excerpted in Klippel, *Scharnhorst*, Vol.1, pp.95-97; and also discussed in Lehmann, *Scharnhorst*, Vol.1, pp.41-44. The quoted passages are from Kunisch (ed.), *Scharnhorst: Privat und dienstliche Schriften*, Vol.1, p.115; and Klippel, *Scharnhorst*, Vol.1, p.95.

47 Scharnhorst, 'Einrichtung einer Militair-Schuhle [sic] für unsere Corps', in Kunisch (ed.), *Scharnhorst: Privat und dienstliche Schriften*, Vol.1, p.116; and Klippel, *Scharnhorst*, Vol.1, p.96.

48 Scharnhorst, 'Einrichtung einer Militair-Schuhle [sic] für unsere Corps', in Kunisch (ed.), *Scharnhorst: Privat und dienstliche Schriften*, Vol.1, p.117; and Klippel, *Scharnhorst*, Vol.1, pp.96 and 97. Source documents relating to advancement in the artillery can be found in Hann 41, VIII, Nr.22: *Berücksichtigung junger Edelleute und anderer Männer von gutem Herkommen bei den Avancementsvorschlägen (Beförderungsvorschlägen)*; deposited at the Niedersächsisches Landesarchiv, Hanover.

culture that would prepare them for court but not military life.[49] This knightly culture was a throwback to the age of chivalry and included riding, fencing, dancing, French, and just enough formal schooling to make the young nobleman appear educated. Scharnhorst, on the other hand, believed that military leaders must prove themselves through study and practical work, just as they would have to do on the battlefield. This 'dichotomy of educational goals' was evident in many of his memoranda and acknowledged the substantial gap that existed in most armies of the late eighteenth century between the educated and technically trained commoner, and the ignorant and 'courtly irreproachable nobleman'.[50]

In another memorandum written around 1785, Scharnhorst recommended royal pages not be excluded from the artillery school. Realising that their exclusion was unrealistic, he suggested instead that they receive additional 'private instruction' so that they would be able to meet the academic standards and not suffer embarrassment by their failure to do so. He recommended they learn as he had at Wilhelmstein, using the sound and proven 'Private Information' sessions of Count Wilhelm.[51] Scharnhorst also wanted to present intensive foreign language instruction, as well as the formal teaching of history, since he believed both were essential for the formation of leaders. He finished this memorandum with the following thoughts on military education, which clearly echoed the mindset of his mentors:

> All formation [*Bildung*] of officers, which does not have as its main focus the sharpening of the intellect and the evaluation of military events, misses the actual purpose.[52]

Scharnhorst clearly rejected the anxiety of many Hanoverian officials that such *Bildung* would hinder the proper development of leaders.

Scharnhorst stressed how important it is for junior leaders to obtain a foundational knowledge of the art of war and its associated sciences at an early age, even if this learning is not used until much later when the officer reaches the senior ranks.

> If a young man, who is destined for the military, does not learn to use his mind right, to discern correctly and conclusively mathematics and the theory of war, then no experience will help him. One has to give young people destined to become officers the early opportunity to think about their profession, to use the insights and experiences of others. To do that they must first have the right fundamental concepts. Without these they will find no interest in reading and will gradually become idle and inactive.

49 See the interesting reports in Hann 41, XXVI, Nr.7: *Regimentsberichte über die seit dem Jahre 1780 als Offiziere angestellten Hofpagen, 1788*; deposited at the Niedersächsisches Landesarchiv, Hanover.

50 See the discussion in Stadelmann, *Scharnhorst*, p.147.

51 Scharnhorst's untitled memorandum (around 1785) can be found in Klippel, *Scharnhorst*, Vol.1, pp.105-08; and in Kunisch (ed.), *Scharnhorst: Privat und dienstliche Schriften*, Vol.1, pp.118-20; the quoted passages are from p.105 of the former and p.118 of the latter.

52 Scharnhorst's untitled memorandum (around 1785); in Klippel, *Scharnhorst*, Vol.1, p.108; and in Kunisch (ed.), *Scharnhorst: Privat und dienstliche Schriften*, Vol.1, p.120.

> The lessons at our institute aim to stimulate the ambition. The students become, due to the circumstances they live in, interested in things they would not have otherwise been interested in. They judge among themselves, dispute, ask, read further, and in doing so learn gradually to examine a topic thoroughly, rather than only to repeat it in private instruction.[53]

Scharnhorst also noted how history demonstrated time and again that there is never sufficient time for an intensive and comprehensive study of war while the leader is young, and even less desire for such a study with senior rank and advanced age.

> If Frederick, Gustavus Adolphus, Condé, Caesar and Alexander had had no theory, and had not studied war according to principles, how could they have commanded armies, won battles and made conquests in their young age, in which none of them could have had practical experiences in warfare?
>
> If many years of service would be sufficient to create generals, one could give old corporals or privates these opportunities.[54]

These observations must have dismayed some Hanoverian officials. Not only was Scharnhorst advocating the development of independent, thinking leaders, he was also telling senior military officers this was already underway at the artillery school, at least in the courses he taught, which mirrored the 'contrary method' he had employed at Northeim.

Scharnhorst followed this brief with 'Several Proposals Pertaining to the Artillery School'. For the coming academic year, he recommended six crucial modifications to the syllabus. First, he sought monthly (instead of quarterly) examinations for all three classes, in order to ascertain better the progress of each student and help those having difficulties. Second, he felt that even those not attending the school regularly should be subject to the monthly exams. Third, students performing well on their exams should be recognised publicly with certificates of achievement presented to them by Commandant Trew.[55]

While the first three recommendations seemed logical, the progressive nature of Scharnhorst's last three ideas may have engendered an air of disquiet among those of the aristocracy not used to having to earn their way in life. In his fourth proposal Scharnhorst stated it was 'fundamental' to learning that advancement within the school must be earned through proven performance and the successful completion of examinations. 'Those who wish to advance must demonstrate the appropriate knowledge'. To create competition among students, Scharnhorst's fifth proposal was to rank-order pupils according to their examination performance.

> This was the method of the late sovereign Count from Bükeburg [sic], and I noticed how advancement and rewards worked well for those who had ambition.

53 The quoted passages are from Scharnhorst's untitled memorandum (around 1785); in Klippel, *Scharnhorst*, Vol.1, p.107; and from Kunisch (ed.), *Scharnhorst: Privat und dienstliche Schriften*, Vol.1, p.119.

54 Scharnhorst is quoted here by Lehmann, *Scharnhorst*, Vol.1, p.43.

55 Gerhard Scharnhorst, 'Einige Vorschläge, die Artillerie Ecole betreffend' (1786?); printed in Klippel, *Scharnhorst*, Vol.1, pp.93-96; and in Kunisch (ed.), *Scharnhorst: Privat und dienstliche Schriften*, Vol.1, pp.120-21.

As a final recommendation, Scharnhorst wanted to publish examination results in the popular *Hanover Magazine* and the professional journal, *Göttingen Scholarly Reports*. He felt this would 'inspire young people to useful work'.[56] These last three proposals may have horrified some of the *Ständestaat*.

Scharnhorst then submitted a 50-page treatise entitled, 'On the Use and Establishment of a Military School for Young Officers in General, but Particularly for Those from the Artillery'.[57] This lengthy paper clearly demonstrated the erudition of the 35-year-old lieutenant who had conceived it. Scharnhorst started by noting that while current military and cadet schools give their students 'some idea of the different components of the art of war', they do not 'train their judgment', nor 'give any opportunity to work diligently in the field and accustom their eyes to the nature of things'.[58] Once again he desired a more intensified program of instruction that would hone the *coup d'oeil* and 'supposing' of the leader. As a student of war, Scharnhorst clearly grasped the fundamental components of a 'military *Bildung*', which should, as he wrote:

> [F]orm the young officer in general, but in particular one from the artillery and infantry, through a scientific program of instruction and practical field exercises, so that on campaign he is immediately ready to perform the duties of an experienced leader.

Scharnhorst then explained that the 'instruction' required to develop military leaders 'is entirely different from that at universities'. Whereas 'the jurist, theologian, and artist' can acquire immediate benefit from the knowledge they gain in their studies, the military leader cannot. With military leaders, learning must focus primarily on three pivotal areas: 'on self-motivation' [*auf Antriebsmittel*]; 'on the formation of judgment' [*auf Bildung der Beurtheilung*]; and 'on practice in the field' [*auf die Uebung auf dem Felde*].

> Without judgment, all knowledge is of no use to the officer, since he must never act according to a certain standard, but rather according to the circumstances of his profession. Without the development of judgment and practice in conceptualising and implementing military operations in the field, the officer may acquire the correct concepts, but he does not know how to apply them. He has not accustomed his eye to the terrain. He has not learned to take into consideration the particular circumstances, and thus would be of no use in the execution of the operation.

56 The quoted passages are from Scharnhorst, 'Einige Vorschläge, die Artillerie Ecole betreffend', in Klippel, *Scharnhorst*, Vol.1, pp.94 and 95; and from Kunisch (ed.), *Scharnhorst: Privat und dienstliche Schriften*, Vol.1, p.121. Examination results were never published.

57 Gerhard Scharnhorst, 'Ueber den Nutzen und die Etablirung einer Militärschule für die jungen Officiere ueberhaupt, insbesondere aber für die von der Artillerie' (1786?); printed in Kunisch (ed.), *Scharnhorst: Privat und dienstliche Schriften*, Vol.1, pp.122-39. Lehmann, Scharnhorst, Vol.1, p.42 (Note 1) states that this 'Unpublished Memorandum' is 'Without date, written around 1790'.

58 Scharnhorst, 'Ueber den Nutzen und die Etablirung einer Militärschule für die jungen Officiere', in Kunisch (ed.), *Scharnhorst: Privat und dienstliche Schriften*, Vol.1, p.123.

In perhaps the most significant statement of this treatise Scharnhorst wrote, 'In the art of war, it is more difficult to apply the rules of operation than to deduce them from the nature of the circumstances'.[59]

Citing examples from the campaigns and writings of Montecuccoli, the Marquis de Feuquières, the Marquis de Puységur, and Frederick the Great, Scharnhorst wrote that war is not a matter of chance. History demonstrates that a great deal of knowledge, study, and meditation is required to conduct it well. The skilful military leader must combine endless knowledge and wisdom, talent and ability. He must have a thorough understanding of tactical operations: how to manoeuvre infantry, cavalry, and artillery on the battlefield; how to conduct marches, reconnaissance and security operations; how to lay out camps and quarter troops; how to command outposts and lead detachments and convoys; how to attack and defend positions (to include villages and towns); in short, all of the dispositions that war demands.

Echoing the 'Instructions' Estorff provided his regiment, Scharnhorst listed skills necessary for the military leader. First, he must be capable of taking full advantage of the terrain, correctly estimating distances, positioning his troops with skill, and fighting with superiority. He must also be able to write well, so that he can communicate his intent clearly, make good, comprehensive reports, and keep detailed combat journals. He must also have full knowledge of the country in which he wages war. For the infantry officer, he can never ignore matters concerning the attack and defence of fortresses.[60] Periodic testing would make sure the officer met the standards of what was expected of an experienced combat leader.

From this line of thought Scharnhorst never wavered. The concepts he expressed would appear over and over again in various memoranda in Hanover and later in Prussia, and in his published works. The practical wisdom of his recommendations may have been viewed as revolutionary by some in the Hanoverian aristocracy, who questioned the need for a military *Bildung* outside of their own archaic institutions. Thus, in order to assist officers achieve a basic level of military proficiency, and hopefully to circumvent the efforts of some Hanoverian officials, Scharnhorst went public with his first textbook.

Scharnhorst published his first book in 1787. Because there was no suitable textbook for all three classes at the artillery school, Scharnhorst had requested and Trew had approved his desire to prepare such a manual. The Helwing Brothers agreed to publish his *Handbook for Officers on the Practical Components of the Military Sciences*, which appeared in three parts from 1787-90. This *Handbook* explained the various arms of the service, clarified their relationships in war, and provided the inexperienced and uneducated officer with sufficient practical knowledge required to become a successful combat leader.[61] As Scharnhorst told his readers:

59 Scharnhorst, 'Ueber den Nutzen und die Etablirung einer Militärschule für die jungen Officiere', in Kunisch (ed.), *Scharnhorst: Privat und dienstliche Schriften*, Vol.1, p.124.

60 Scharnhorst lists these requirements in 'Ueber den Nutzen und die Etablirung einer Militärschule für die jungen Officiere', in Kunisch (ed.), *Scharnhorst: Privat und dienstliche Schriften*, Vol.1, pp.127-28; and goes into some detail in the following pages to examine each, offering techniques that correlated classroom theory with practice in the field.

61 Gerhard Scharnhorst, *Handbuch für Officiere in den anwendbaren Theilen der Kriegswissenschaften* (Hanover: Gebrüdern Helwing, 1787-90).

> My intent is to provide a short course in all aspects of the military sciences, in general for the junior officer.
>
> I was motivated toward this enterprise by the lectures which I presented for four years on these sciences in the above-mentioned military school.
>
> I did not find a book that made me feel comfortable, and for which my pupils could read, and which could serve them repeatedly, and at the same time would be indispensable for them, since the public exams required that they should know this scholarly knowledge.[62]

Scharnhorst's *Handbook* was essentially a compilation of his research and teaching to date and presents an interesting portrayal of his own professional development during the first decade of his military service.

In his opening remarks, Scharnhorst reiterated with greater lucidity his earlier argument for military *Bildung*. Using language similar to that expressed in the many papers he had submitted to his superiors, Scharnhorst noted the conditions in most armies of his time and concluded that 'many officers attain positions of authority without the slightest idea of what to do'.[63] Because the vast majority of officers believed that only senior leaders influenced events, they consequently viewed with contempt the duties and responsibilities of the junior leader. That the subaltern should think this way was not at all surprising to Scharnhorst, given the triviality of the junior officer's peacetime existence, which led to laziness and depravity.

Scharnhorst sought to convince the junior officer to study his profession conscientiously as he had been taught. By doing so the junior leader would understand the theory and practice of his profession and would realise that every leader is vitally important in battle, regardless of his position, rank, or authority. Indeed, as Scharnhorst pointed out, it is the subaltern who, through his sound leadership, creates the conditions for success at the higher levels of command. Only when the officer understood the theory and practice of his profession would he be able to determine what is essential in war, 'and then to know with certainty what he must do'. 'Officers must study war in order to have some idea of what to do in every situation'.[64]

Handbook for Officers was a very elementary military text designed to provide junior officers with some understanding of what to do in various situations during wartime. Like Bélidor's *New Course in Mathematics*, Scharnhorst divided each volume into small sections designed to teach foundational knowledge. Each section began with a simple discussion of theory and then proceeded to its practical application. Each section was a self-contained unit of instruction that built upon material discussed in previous sections. *Handbook for Officers* was thus an ideal self-study text. It also provided an interesting and historical benchmark on military developments of the eighteenth century.[65]

62 Scharnhorst, 'Vorbericht', *Handbuch für Officiere*, Vol.1, pp.iii-iv.

63 Scharnhorst, 'Vorbericht', *Handbuch für Officiere*, Vol.1, p.viii.

64 Scharnhorst, 'Vorbericht', *Handbuch für Officiere*, Vol.1, pp.vii-viii; the quoted passages are from pp.viii and vii; respectively.

65 Source documents related to this handbook can be found in Hann 41, XXVI, Nr.8: *Das für Offiziere von dem Artillerieleutnant Scharnhorst entworfene Handbuch zum Unterricht der Kanoniere und Unteroffiziere: 'Einleitung*

The first volume of *Handbook for Officers* treated the basic theory and practice of the artillery. It included a discussion of cannons, howitzers, mortars, and rockets; their carriages, powders, and projectiles; their operation during war; their effect on various targets; and the care and maintenance of their horses and equipment. Scharnhorst wrote extensively on the duties of the artilleryman in the field, during sieges, and while defending fortresses. He always used historical examples, figures, charts, and drawings to illustrate his points. In his introduction, 'On Studying and Reading', Scharnhorst reiterated his message about the vital importance of reading and study and suggested two essential works: Tempelhof's *History of the Seven Years War* and Tielke's *Contributions to the Art of War and a History of the War.* Anyone studying the first volume of *Handbook for Officers* would come away with a good idea of the organisation and operation of artillery in the latter half of the eighteenth century.[66]

The other two volumes followed this format. The second instalment of *Handbook for Officers* (1788) covered the 'Art of Entrenchment', which was receiving a good deal of attention at that time.[67] In this volume Scharnhorst examined field fortifications and their construction, as well as the attack and defence of fortified areas. After further thought he planned to write a fourth volume, 'On Fortress Warfare' [*Von dem Festungskrieg*], to accompany this second volume, but never completed it.[68] Scharnhorst also planned a fifth book dealing with the attack of small cities and fortresses, as well as a sixth volume on field warfare (establishing camps, marches, battle formations, and winter quartering), using historical campaigns to clarify their use in war.[69] Neither volume came into print.

Volume Three of *Handbook for Officers* (1790) focused on tactics and was essentially a 'how-to-fight' manual for junior leaders. Beginning with the musket and socket bayonet, Scharnhorst described the basic small arms of the soldier (musket, carbine, and pistol), various firing methods and drills for each, and ballistics theory. He then devoted a whole chapter on the bayonet and its use. From here he examined in detail infantry tactics. Not only did he discuss the tactical movements of smaller formations, but also those of larger units, so that the junior officer would see how leadership at his level contributed to the success of his battalion. While most of these drills were practiced on the parade ground and during annual field exercises, far too many officers had little understanding of the theory behind these tactical movements or how they supported the battalion or regimental mission. Scharnhorst sought to explain this to his readers, hoping all leaders would participate with more zeal. He then concluded with an examination of cavalry tactics.

in die Kriegs-Wissenschaft' mit Zeichnung: Kugelbahn und Visierlinie, 1788; deposited at the Niedersächsisches Landesarchiv, Hanover.

66 Two of the leading journals of Germany published favourable reviews of Vol.1. See *Allgemeine Literatur-Zeitung* (Jena), 152a (1788), pp.665-67; and *Oberdeutsche Allgemeine Literatur-Zeitung* (Salzburg), 4 (1789), pp.51-52. Both of these reviews, as well as the reviews of the second and third volumes, were incorporated as Appendices VII and VIII of Klippel, *Scharnhorst*, Vol.1, pp.209-12 and 213-16; respectively.

67 Hornung, *Scharnhorst*, p.32.

68 See Jähns, *Geschichte der Kriegswissenschaften*, Vol.3, p.1807. This treatise, 'Manuscript zum 4. Teile des Handbuch für Officiere von Scharnhorst', can be found in *Nachlaß Scharnhorst*, Nr. 142; deposited at the Geheimes Staatsarchiv Preußischer Kulturbesitz, 196/VI. HA Familienarchive und Nachlässe, Berlin (Dahlem); and is published in Kunisch (ed.), *Scharnhorst: Privat und dienstliche Schriften*, Vol.8, pp.487-513.

69 Scharnhorst, 'Vorbericht', *Handbuch für Officiere*, Vol.1, p.v.

One of the most interesting and noteworthy features of *Handbook for Officers* is Scharnhorst's broad understanding of military affairs and detailed knowledge of the artillery, infantry, and cavalry, which came from reading and study, and limited field operations, rather than from actual combat experience. As he informed his readers:

> Those who expect to learn everything from experience are like the proud men who believe they already know everything. Theory is based upon and learned from the experience and judgment of the greatest warriors.[70]

Among the greatest warriors Scharnhorst cited as examples throughout the *Handbook* are Alexander the Great, Caesar, Turenne, Montecucoli, Feuquieres, Luxemburg, Prince Eugene, Count Wilhelm, Maurice de Saxe, Duke Ferdinand, and Frederick the Great.

Scharnhorst also studied and included many contemporary writers (particularly those in France) in his *Handbook*. He kept in close touch with the intellectual climate of the times and wanted his German colleagues to do so as well. The writings of Puységur, Folard, Saxe, Mesnil-Durand, Guibert, Du Teil, Grandmaison, and Maizeroy (along with their various tactical concepts and gunnery experiments) were discussed and analysed in the three volumes of *Handbook*.[71] Scharnhorst himself was very impressed with the Gribeauval artillery reforms, because they were both practical and affected nearly every aspect of gunnery.[72] It is interesting to note that virtually all the theory the French later transformed into reality during the Wars of the French Revolution can be found in Scharnhorst's *Handbook for Officers*.

In October 1787, Scharnhorst laid out his 'Manual in Folio', a loose-leaf folder in which he registered his many intellectual activities. This Manual was like the one Nicolai maintained, and contained Scharnhorst's book and map collections, preliminary notes and draft material for his publications (including the initial draft of *Handbook for Officers*), regular entries of his thoughts from his readings, titles from the newest trade catalogues, the bookstores he visited, business letters to bookstores and publishers, letters to subscribers, professional correspondence with other *Aufklärer* and writers (such as Estorff, Nicolai, Mauvillon, Tempelhof, and Tielke), and a host of various miscellaneous material.[73] Scharnhorst continually conceived new ideas for publication, such as a 'Hanover Pocket Diary', which was

70 Written in 1787, Scharnhorst's words here were later published in 'Militärische Gedankensplitter aus vergangener Zeit', *Österreichische Militärische Zeitschrift* 44 (1903:), pp.25-26; the quoted passage is from p.26.

71 In an interesting display of nationalism, the reviewer for the Jena *General Literary Gazette* wondered why Scharnhorst spent so much time discussing French sources when Germany had her own notable writers, such as Thielke and Tempelhof. See *Allgemeine Literatur-Zeitung* (Jena), 152a (1788), pp.665-66.

72 For a discussion of these reforms, see Ropp, *War in the Modern World*, pp.100-101.

73 See the discussions in Klippel, *Scharnhorst*, Vol.1, p.151; and Stadelmann, *Scharnhorst*, pp.105-06. Klippel, pp.152-59, provides a sampling of material contained in this Manual. On p.105, Stadelmann asserts this Manual 'was lost through carelessness', but this may not be the case. According to several archivists I spoke with at the Geheimes Staatsarchiv Preuβischer Kulturbesitz, the folder itself may have been lost or destroyed, but its contents appear to have been sorted by subject matter and placed in other folders when Scharnhorst's Papers were reorganised following the Second World War. The arrangement of documents in Kunisch (ed.), *Scharnhorst: Privat und dienstliche Schriften* confirms this, with many of the items from the original 'Manual in Folio' that Klippel and Stadelmann list in their studies published in the eight volumes of Kunisch (ed.), *Scharnhorst: Privat und dienstliche Schriften*.

to be a guide to the geographical, scientific, and cultural life of the Electorate. Because he had a habit of reading important military, political, scientific, and cultural literature of the day, and taking copious notes, this 'Manual in Folio' provides a singularly important key to Scharnhorst's intellectual development. Carl Philipp Gottlieb von Clausewitz (1780-1831), his favourite pupil in Berlin and one of his closest personal associates, reviewed it and believed the essential elements of Scharnhorst's military and political genius were laid down here.[74]

With the popularity of his *Military Library, Library for Officers*, and *Handbook for Officers*, came some notoriety for *Lieutenant* Gerhard Scharnhorst. Beginning in 1787, he had received Trew's permission to present public lectures on various military topics. Among the topics listed in his papers are: military mathematics, field instruments, gunnery techniques of various armies, light artillery, field fortifications, and infantry weapons. Most of this material came from his lectures at the artillery school. Other themes included: 'On the Prejudice against Scientific Knowledge', 'Obtaining the Skills of the Officer', and 'The Errors of Exercise Regulations'.[75] Virtually all of this material can be found in his *Handbook for Officers.*

As an enlightened soldier, Scharnhorst wanted to educate the public by sharing the results of his research and writing with others. The importance of this civic awareness about military affairs was essential for the *Bildung* of society, as Lessing and Herder had emphasised. Significantly, while on one of his journeys through north-western Germany, German writer, freemason, and leading member of the Order of the Illuminati, Adolph Ludwig Freiherr von Knigge (1752-96), visited the Hanoverian artillery school. 'Among the skilful teachers at this military school', he wrote in 1792, 'I must mention to you *Hauptmann* Scharnhorst, whom I hold with high regard for his thorough knowledge, his noble humility, and his gentle character'.[76]

During his time at the artillery school, Scharnhorst published a third periodical, *New Military Journal* (Hanover, 1788-1805). This was his most ambitious literary undertaking and clearly showed the maturation of his thoughts on war and society.[77] The first seven volumes (1788-93) were a continuation of *Military Library* and *Library for Officers*, and reflected the traditional view of warfare as a state action conducted by princes, fought by standing professional armies, and won or lost by the education and skill of the officers, the training and discipline of the soldiers, the financial and material resources of the state, and the success of any alliance system. The last six volumes (1797-1805) appeared after his combat experience in the War of the First Coalition (1792-97) and focused on the French Revolutionary Wars.

Beginning in 1797, *New Military Journal* carried the subtitle, *Military Commentaries of our Time, in Particular the French Revolutionary War in the Year 1792 and its Continuation.*

74 Hornung, *Scharnhorst*, p.40.

75 See the listing in Kunisch (ed.), *Scharnhorst: Privat und dienstliche Schriften*, Vol.1, pp.178-80; and in Klippel, *Scharnhorst*, Vol.1, pp.116-18.

76 See the commentary by Knigge in *Reisen, Literatur*; in Wolfgang Fenner (ed.), *Adolph Ludwig Freiherr von Knigge Ausgewählte Werke* (Hanover: Fackelträger Verlag, 1991-96), Vol.4, pp.77-78.

77 See the interesting reviews of *New Military Journal* in the *Allgemeine Literatur-Zeitung* (Jena), 365 (1799), pp.417-24 and 366 (1799), pp.425-32.

Scharnhorst's attitude about war and society had by this time changed considerably. Before the War of the First Coalition he had put his faith in the professional standing army, even though at that time he had expressed significant doubts about its recruitment, discipline, training, and leadership. Having witnessed how the French had put into practice, with phenomenal success, the teachings of his mentor Count Wilhelm, Scharnhorst now emphasised the people and their willingness to sacrifice for a cause. He believed these factors were far more significant than the physical size and strength of the army. He also recognised that war was now united with the politics of the people (not just the prince and the ruling elites) and had to be unified into a consistent whole. Social, moral, cultural, political, religious, and military forces now influenced and often determined the course of a conflict. Moreover, the political and social order of society played a key role in the effective utilization of the state's military potential. All of these factors Count Wilhelm had laboured so long and diligently to achieve in Schaumburg-Lippe.[78]

As the currents of revolution began to sweep across Europe during the last decade of the eighteenth century, Scharnhorst began to clarify his political beliefs. After listening to Professor Schlözer's lecture on 'The Theory of Constitutions' (10 February 1790), Scharnhorst wrote in his journal:

> Each form of government has its good and its bad. What is to be said about this is that ... not from theory does one draw the balance, but from history. That should be done with cold blood.[79]

Coming less than a year after the outbreak of revolution in France, it appears Scharnhorst disagreed with Schlözer regarding the use of violence to affect change. Indeed, he was growing increasingly weary of the way Hanoverian military officials treated him. While Trew and others regarded him as 'a highly industrious officer', they also felt his calling was that of an educator and writer, not as a field soldier. There was thus no reason to promote him further or give him any command assignments.[80]

Around this time Scharnhorst wrote an interesting essay on the evolution of the artillery school. It was entitled, 'Information on the Military School in Hanover', and provided some subtle but fascinating facts on the pedagogical debates regarding curriculum content and development. While Trew originally designed the school to train only artillerymen, Scharnhorst stated:

78 See Gerhard Scharnhorst, 'Entwickelung der allgemeinen Ursachen des Glücks der Franzosen in dem Revolutions-Kriege, und insbesondere in dem Feldzuge von 1794. Als Einleitung zur Geschichte dieses Feldzuges', *Neues militärisches Journal* 8 (1797), pp.1-154. This study was later incorporated as part of Colmar von der Goltz (ed.), *Militärische Schriften von Scharnhorst* (Berlin: F. Schneider, 1881), pp.192-242; and then in Ursula von Gersdorff (ed.), *Gerhard von Scharnhorst: Ausgewählte Schriften* (Osnabrück: Biblio Verlag, 1983), pp.45-110; and in Hansjürgen Usczeck and Christa Gudzent (ed.), *Gerhard von Scharnhorst: Ausgewählte militärische Schriften* (Berlin: Militärverlag der deutschen demokratischen Republik, 1986), pp.97-150.

79 See 'Nachschrift aus Schlözers Vorlessung', cited in Stadelmann, *Scharnhorst*, p.123.

80 Hornung, *Scharnhorst*, p.40.

> As early as the second year after the establishment of this school, there were several officers, non-commissioned officers, and cadets of the infantry and cavalry who sought permission to go there.

This must have thrilled Scharnhorst, who noted that many of those seeking to attend the school came 'from garrisons outside Hanover', despite the fact that 'to stay here' meant 'economic' hardship. 'This prompted an extension of the institute', he continued.

> In order to give these pupils the benefit of the school which their situation permitted, a separate instruction was established in 1789 for the cavalry and infantry officers, non-commissioned officers, and cadets, which lasted only half a year, and provided the most indispensable knowledge to these types of troops.[81]

The Commission King George had established under the direction of Freytag and Hake had arrived at this solution following consultation with Trew and the Chief of the Engineer Corps, *General-Lieutenant* Georg Josua du Plat.

Turning to pedagogical issues, Scharnhorst pointed out the significance and sequence of the curriculum content. He noted how it progressed in a logical and coherent manner, based largely on the ability of the student to retain and use the knowledge he had learned. Scharnhorst then focused on the importance of studying mathematics, because it provides the mental discipline and firm foundation upon which all other subjects build. Mathematics deals with the use of reason in an orderly, cogent manner, or as Scharnhorst wrote, it provides 'a correct sequence of proofs and application to the practicing parts'. He praised the format and content of Häseler's *Rudiments* for its 'detail and clarity', and concluded that once the student had truly mastered mathematics, he would be able 'to learn the rest of the sciences through books', while 'anyone who frequents the school for only one year will be able to help themselves to some degree afterwards'. Then, in one of his detailed explanatory notes, Scharnhorst countered the argument 'perceived in this institute' that the study of 'pure mathematics stifles the mind and restrains one's own judgment'. Instead, he wrote, it permits 'deeper penetration and more rigorous investigation', while heightening 'judgment' and creating 'a certain sense of correctness'.[82] After examining the content of each course in meticulous detail, and analysing the various texts used for each subject, he turned his attention to the military sciences.

Scharnhorst stated that there is a direct link between the study of mathematics and the art of war. Both had to be learned following a scientific or systematic approach. Here he discussed the details of his *Handbook for Officers*, which offered a useful text for understating the linkage between mathematics and the study of war. Scharnhorst spent more than half of this essay addressing the military sciences, using historical examples (battles and leaders) to illustrate his points. In one of his lengthy clarifications, he again emphasised the

81 Gerhard Scharnhorst, *Nachricht von der Militair-Schule in Hannover* (not before 1791); in Kunisch (ed.), *Scharnhorst: Privat und dienstliche Schriften*, Vol.1, pp.167-78; the quoted passages are from pp.167 and 168.

82 Scharnhorst, *Nachricht von der Militair-Schule in Hannover* (not before 1791); in Kunisch (ed.), *Scharnhorst: Privat und dienstliche Schriften*, Vol.1, pp.169-70 and 171.

need for young leaders to study the higher components of the art of war in order to understand their role in the larger scheme of manoeuvre.

> Suppose, however, that these lessons were omitted, and that the officer occupied himself only with what he needed in the lower grades; could one then expect that in his older years he would devote himself to this new study? The art of war generally constitutes a coherent science, and as such must be learned according to systematic development. If they are learned only according to the sequence of needs, then the scientific connection is torn apart, and piecemeal results. The worst thing about this science is that it is not possible to conduct the lower parts quite expediently unless one has an overview of the higher one.
>
> If the officer has the most basic general knowledge and loves his position, then he begins to study for himself and to accept his ideas in every experience. For the time being, if he had no knowledge of the higher parts, he would no longer expand his knowledge as a common soldier does during wartime.

Repeating what he had stated in *Military Library*, Scharnhorst concluded this essay by stating how the pupil who 'wishes to learn more about this later, can help himself through the books recommended to him'.[83]

In 1792, one of the more enlightened soldiers of his day, *General-Lieutenant* Martin Ernst von Schlieffen (1732-1825), founded in Wesel the Patriotic Society for Students of the Art of War. As a subaltern, Schlieffen had been discharged from Prussian service because of sickness. He then joined the Hessian army and served with great distinction, first as *Adjudant* to Duke Ferdinand during the Seven Years War, then as *1. General-Adjudant* to Counts Friedrich II and Wilhelm IX of Hesse-Kassel. Schlieffen was the Hessian military envoy to the Court of St James during the American Revolution, where he coordinated the operational and logistical support of the Hessians in America. From London he returned to Hesse-Kassel to become Minister of War. Following the death of Frederick the Great in 1786, Friedrich Wilhelm II (1786-97) recalled Schlieffen to Prussian service as governor of Wessel.[84]

Not long after the founding of the Patriotic Society, Scharnhorst advocated the establishment of similar military societies throughout Germany. He suggested the military society could be an excellent means of promoting professional military *Bildung* by encouraging officers to study the art of war in a learned community.[85] His argument was familiar. At their best, military schools provided only a foundation upon which to build. Without further study and education, the officer would stagnate and be of little use in war. During times of peace, nothing could develop his 'situational judgment in war' better than realistic field exercises. The only problem was getting officers to the field and away from the lazy

83 Scharnhorst, *Nachricht von der Militair-Schule in Hannover*, in Kunisch (ed.), *Scharnhorst: Privat und dienstliche Schriften*, Vol.1, pp.177-78 and 176.

84 For service data on Schlieffen, see Kurt von Priesdorff, *Soldatisches Führertum* (Hamburg: Hanseat, 1936-42), Vol.2 (776), pp.281-85.

85 See Gerhard Scharnhorst, 'Ein Mittel, wodurch man die Officiere zu militärischen Arbeiten aufmuntern und ihre weiter Ausbildung bewirken kann', *Neues militärisches Journal* 6 (1792), pp.199-203.

routine of garrison life. Scharnhorst felt this 'could be accomplished through a kind of military society' under the direction of general officers and general staff personnel, men who he believed possessed a varied knowledge of military affairs. Every three months these leaders could pose tactical problems to the membership. Any officer who wished to submit his solution, would have to travel to the field location where the problem had to be solved. After completing his answer, he could send it to the secretary of the club, who would then mark it with only a number to ensure anonymity and impartiality. Winners would be selected every quarter and would receive personal recognition from their prince. Their names would be published in the local newspaper and they would also be given a substantial monetary prize. Scharnhorst recommended 75 Reichsthaler. He hoped this would encourage participation among the officer corps while simultaneously developing good regimental libraries.[86]

This article reveals several noteworthy aspects of Scharnhorst's own professional growth. The most important feature was his apprehension about impartiality. From his experience editing *Military Library* and *Library for Officers*, Scharnhorst had developed a 'deeply rooted fear of prejudice and suppression of the truth' and wanted military societies to possess the same freedom from censorship enjoyed by other learned societies.[87] Another key point was the link between the military society and general staff. Scharnhorst mentioned this association and suggested that the general staff was ideally suited to play a leading role in the professional development of officers.

Hanover promoted Scharnhorst to *Titulair-Capitain* ['captain, in title only'], on 19 October 1792. This was probably the highest rank for his calling as an instructor.[88] His second and most popular work, *Military Pocket Book, for Use on Campaign* also appeared that year. Published in three subsequent German editions and translated into English in 1811 as *Military Field Pocket Book*, this book was 'one of the most widely used practical guides' of its time.[89] Typical of his style, Scharnhorst's *Military Field Pocket Book* was another 'how-to-fight' manual written to help junior leaders in the execution of independent missions in war, especially reconnaissance and security operations. It was essentially a condensed version of his very popular *Handbook for Officers*. The *Military Field Pocket Book* was divided into four sections and designed to be carried in the officer's saddlebag. The first part covered 'the little war' [*der kleine Krieg*], and included reconnaissance and security operations, marches, patrolling, and ambushes. The second section treated gunnery; the third fortifications.[90] The fourth section examined the attack and defence of fortified areas. All four were illustrated with historical examples.[91] Appendices supplemented the text with mathematical tables, monetary conversion rates, weights and measures, and other statistical data that the leader

86 Scharnhorst, 'Ein Mittel, wodurch man die Officiere zu militärischen Arbeiten aufmuntern'. The quoted passages are from pp.199 and 200.

87 Stadelmann, *Scharnhorst*, p.179 (Note 60/61).

88 Hornung, *Scharnhorst*, p.40.

89 Peter Paret, *Yorck and the Era of Prussian Reform, 1807-1815* (Princeton: Princeton University Press, 1966), p.42. The second and third editions were published in 1793 and 1794; respectively.

90 The English translators deleted those sections dealing with permanent fortifications, since they felt such material was of no use in the Peninsular Campaign. See Hofmann and Haverfield (trans.), Gerhard Scharnhorst, *Military Field Pocket Book* (London: Vogel and Schulze, 1811), p.ii.

91 Among the examples Scharnhorst cited, four were taken from the American Revolution, compared to over 60 from the Seven Years War. See Paret, *Yorck*, p.42 and Note 109.

would need on campaign. In his classic treatise *On War*, Clausewitz considered *Military Field Pocket Book* 'the best that had ever been written about actual war'.[92]

Once again, much of the material in *Military Field Pocket Book* came from Scharnhorst's teachings and public lectures. What made this book so welcomed was the practical guidance its author provided infantry and cavalry officers unaccustomed to acting on their own. Scharnhorst took his reader by the hand and led him step-by-step through the process of conducting marches, patrols, assaults, field security, and a host of other missions that junior officers undertake in combat. He also addressed specific questions, such as how to get a cannon up a steep mountain, and how to assault and seize a house or tower. Like the reviews of his previous publications, commentary on *Military Field Pocket Book* praised Scharnhorst and his innovative teaching style.[93]

In 1792 Scharnhorst entered the debate on standing armies. His contribution came in two parts in *New Military Journal* and was entitled, 'On the Advantages and Disadvantages of Standing Armies'.[94] He stated that it was necessary for him to join this discussion to counter the false public picture of professional standing armies presented in Schlözer's *State Reports* and other German periodicals.[95] These journals portrayed the professional standing army as the cause of all human misfortune, producing depravity and spreading vice everywhere. Based mainly on economic and moral concerns, these attacks listed the usual complaints about the costs of the army, the loss of manpower to less productive uses in society, and the lack of morality associated with the misconduct of soldiers. The anonymous author in *State Reports* devoted most of his discussion to the miserable living conditions of the soldier and their social consequences.

Two years earlier, Scharnhorst had begun outlining his thoughts in a paper titled, 'Standing Armies'.[96] The preliminary ideas he discussed in this fragment were based on his reading of *The Citizen Soldier*, published anonymously 'ten years earlier'.[97] He was intrigued with the 'Frenchman' who:

> ... first sought in detail to persuade the world of the advantages of a militia and to show the expendability of a standing army. Many mediocre minds repeated these ideas with some modification.

92 Michael Howard and Peter Paret (trans. and ed.), Carl von Clausewitz, *On War* (Princeton: Princeton University Press, 1976), Book II, Chap.6 (p.170).

93 See, for example, the review in *Allgemeine Literatur-Zeitung* (Jena), 138 (1794), pp.227-29.

94 See Gerhard Scharnhorst, 'Ueber die Vor-und Nachtheile der stehended Armeen', *Neues militärisches Journal* 6 (1792), pp.234-54 and 345-80. Max Lehmann discusses these beliefs in 'Scharnhorst's Kampf für die stehenden Heere', *Historische Zeitschrift* 53 (1885), pp.276-99.

95 The anonymous article Scharnhorst referred to was 'Versuch über die nachteiligen Folgen der jetzigen Verfassung des Kriegs Standes überhaupt, und der, der InfanterieCorps insbesondere', in Schlözer (ed.), *Stats Anzeigen* 17 (1791), pp.56-67.

96 Gerhard Scharnhorst, 'Stehende Armeen'(1790/1791?); in Kunisch (ed.), *Scharnhorst: Privat und dienstliche Schriften*, Vol.1, pp.96-98.

97 *Le soldat citoyen, ou Vues patriotiques sur la manière. La plus avantageuse de pourvoir à la defence du royaume. Dans le pays de la liberté* (Neufchatel, 1780). According to the catalogue of the *Bibliotheque Nationale*, the author was most likely Guibert. See Note 3 of Scharnhorst, 'Stehende Armeen', Kunisch (ed.), *Scharnhorst: Privat und dienstliche Schriften*, Vol.1, p.97; the quoted passage is from p.96.

Significantly, this Frenchman cleverly used the word 'citizen' to describe only those living in a democratic republic. 'Subjects' were those under monarchical rule. Scharnhorst tacitly noted this distinction and wrote that while this Frenchman was 'a witty and scholarly military writer', he nevertheless 'contradicted the actual events of war more than a hundred times'. Scharnhorst continued his critique, stating, 'A writer who undermines the standing army of his nation may always, with few exceptions, erect a monument to his heart, but for his brothers he prepares shackles, or else history lies'.[98] Interestingly, as Scharnhorst pointed out, 'While war was more frequent in monarchical forms of government, it was less devastating, less in duration'.

Scharnhorst followed these statements with a noteworthy commentary about the author of *The Citizen Soldier* and his misuse of history: 'Unable to deduce results from experience, individual events have been torn out of history and established as evidence of generality'. Scharnhorst then ended his discourse with another significant conclusion. He explained the Frenchman's evidence was 'derived from the history of small republics, which were favoured by special circumstances, geographical location, etc'.[99] Scharnhorst doubted they applied to larger states.

When Scharnhorst joined the lively discussion on standing armies, it had been an ongoing debate for nearly a century, having begun in England with blistering attacks against the absolutist Tudor monarchy.[100] At that time the Bill of Rights (1688) declared that a standing army in peacetime can only exist with the agreement of Parliament, and that only protestant subjects may possess arms suitable for their defence. A century later Scottish philosopher, historian, economist, and essayist David Hume (1711-76) wrote in his *Essays, Moral, Political, and Literary* (1754) that the royal army was a clear sign the country was at war with itself. In his *Commentaries on the Laws of England* (1765), English judge and Tory politician Sir William Blackstone (1723-80) referred to the soldier's condition as a kind of the slavery. Historian and Member of Parliament Edward Gibbon (1737-94) described compulsory military service in peacetime as idleness. These influential Englishmen viewed high taxes, military conquest, and political corruption as a direct consequence of the professional standing army. They also saw the standing army as a significant threat to individual liberty.

On the continent, French philosophers agreed with their English counterparts. Political thinker Charles-Louis de Secondat, Baron de La Brède et de Montesquieu (1689-1755) argued persuasively in his *Considerations on the Causes of the Grandeur and Decadence of the Romans* (1734) that the military expansion of Rome led to its inevitable decline by introducing corruption and a professional standing army, in which the loyalty of its citizen soldiers was transferred from the people of Rome to their generals. In his story of *Candide* (1759), François-Marie Arouet, known by his *nom de plume* as Voltaire (1694-1778), called professional soldiers hired murderers. Another French philosopher, Claude Adrien Helvétius (1715-71), demanded the abolishment of standing armies in his famous book, *The Mind* (1758). For Helvétius, this was the precondition for the abolishment of kings, who he called the 'butchers of their citizens'. Ironically, Helvétius was one of a few French

98 Scharnhorst, 'Stehende Armeen', in Kunisch (ed.), *Scharnhorst: Privat und dienstliche Schriften*, Vol.1, p.97.

99 Scharnhorst, 'Stehende Armeen', in Kunisch (ed.), *Scharnhorst: Privat und dienstliche Schriften*, Vol.1, pp.97-98.

100 The basic outline for this paragraph and the next comes from Lehmann, 'Scharnhorst's Kampf für die stehenden Heere', pp.276-82; which Hornung summarised in *Scharnhorst*, pp.45-51.

philosophers who spent time with Frederick the Great. In his *Émile, or Treatise on Education* (1762), Genevan philosopher and writer, Jean-Jacques Rousseau (1712-78) called standing armies the 'plague of Europe'. Echoing the author of *The Citizen Soldier*, Rousseau praised the citizen militias of Switzerland as a viable alternative.

Most German *Aufklärer* tended to agree with their French and English contemporaries. In his often quoted *Kriegslied* (1778), poet and journalist Matthias Claudius lamented war, describing it as cruel and painful. Indeed, German scholars argued that professional standing armies led to war, because they satisfied the marital ambitions of arrogant despots. While the common people did all of the fighting and suffered the most, the aristocrats reaped whatever fame and glory that followed.[101] Even conservative German jurist and social theorist Justus Möser wanted to see the professional standing army replaced by the old Germanic *Herrbahn*. Significantly, this had been Count Wilhelm's solution.

Typical of his approach, Scharnhorst went into excruciating detail as he systematically demolished the popular arguments against standing armies. He first focused on economics, since most economists of the time ranked standing armies among the least productive elements of society and demanded their replacement by citizen militias. Contrary to this erroneous belief, Scharnhorst noted the very positive economic influence the standing army had on society. The standing army was very good for the local economy and provided meaningful work for many, especially the middle and poor classes. Clearly the livelihood of many inhabitants depended on the standing army. The soldier's clothing and equipment, his armaments, his housing, and his sustenance, all came from the so-called 'productive' members of society – weavers, bakers, butchers, artisans, farmers, and merchants – all of whom, Scharnhorst pointed out, earned their living from the standing army. He wondered how these people would survive without the professional standing army.[102]

While many believed the soldier to be the least productive member of society, Scharnhorst stated that the soldier clearly provided the most important service. As he pointed out, the standing army 'preserves the internal order'. It also protects 'each inhabitant of the country from the enemy', who is intent on stealing his property, enslaving his family, abusing his women, and forcing him to pay tribune.[103] For smaller states, the professional standing army may also deter the aggression of larger nations. Decades later, Clausewitz restated this truism in his study *On War*.

> The aggressor is always peace-loving (as Bonaparte always claimed to be); he would prefer to take over our country unopposed. To prevent his doing so one must be willing to make war and be prepared for it. In other words it is the weak, those likely to need defence, who should always be armed in order not to be overwhelmed. Thus decrees the art of war.[104]

101 See the discussion on this point in Epstein, *The Genesis of German Conservatism*, pp.289-93.
102 Scharnhorst, 'Ueber die Vor-und Nachtheile der stehenden Armeen', pp.244-49 and 249-50.
103 Scharnhorst, 'Ueber die Vor-und Nachtheile der stehenden Armeen', p.350.
104 Howard and Paret (trans. and ed.), Clausewitz, *On War*, Book VI, Chap.5 (p.370).

Scharnhorst concluded that those nations with the largest standing armies with respect to their size – 'Prussia, Hanover, Saxony, and Austria' – 'are the safest countries in the entire world'.[105] For what more could any citizen ask?

Echoing the shallow arguments Rousseau presented in his *Social Contract*, Scharnhorst turned to a discussion of these fundamental political questions using Rousseau's line of reasoning to refute him and others, and to justify the professional standing army. Like Rousseau, Scharnhorst spoke of 'commitments'.

> Whoever wants to enjoy the advantages of society must sacrifice some natural human rights.
>
> Everyone who steps into an association with others or into a society, which constitutes the state, is received to a certain extent by it with a contract. Both parts now have mutual obligations, and the more exact and the more diverse the associations are, the more the natural freedoms are weakened by them. This is undeniable.

With the professional standing army, Scharnhorst concluded: 'The innate rights of men are exchanged here for other advantages'. People surrender some of their sovereignty in return for the protection of the state, so that they could go about their endeavours in peace. The standing army ensures that protection.[106]

Scharnhorst also spent considerable ink countering the common argument of the times. This fallacy stated that in the American War of Independence, it was the American militiaman who had gained victory for the Colonies. Most uninformed people believed the colonial militias were far superior to the professional standing armies of England and her auxiliary troops. Scharnhorst disagreed, pointing out that the British had to overcome 'many disadvantages' to fight on the North American continent. The most significant was logistics. He explained how the 'great transportation distances' across the Atlantic Ocean severely hampered British operations. The vast territory of colonial America also proved extremely difficult to control. The colonial population was initially neutral during the early years of the conflict but turned hostile and joined the fight against the English as British frustration and brutalities increased. The leadership of George Washington, Henry Lee, and others surprised many, and these generals proved to be very capable professional soldiers who, as Scharnhorst emphasised, led regular (not militia) forces. The assistance of a French professional army was also significant. 'These and many other circumstances' led to the defeat of the British, not the American militiamen.[107] Interestingly, Scharnhorst did not mention the vital contribution of the French navy.

For Scharnhorst, the most intriguing aspect of the American and French Revolutions was 'the spirit of the people'. Since he felt the standing army was essential for most states, he doubted whether the American and French spirit could be transferred as a model elsewhere. In America he noted 'a people who had only the common purpose before them and were able to protect themselves'. Then he wondered if the French people, whose violent passions, 'without state authority; that is, without disciplined armies', could be restrained. 'Whether

105 Scharnhorst, 'Ueber die Vor-und Nachtheile der stehenden Armeen', p.357.
106 Scharnhorst, 'Ueber die Vor-und Nachtheile der stehenden Armeen', pp.361, 362, and 364; respectively
107 Scharnhorst, 'Ueber die Vor-und Nachtheile der stehenden Armeen', pp.368-69.

the North American States can exist without standing armies is not yet established', he noted.[108] In Scharnhorst's mind, the 'new North American State' was still too young for an impartial answer here. In the meantime, the professional standing army was, in his mind, the guardian of the state against external and internal threats. Nevertheless, in his brief discussion of the American and French Revolutions, Scharnhorst sensed the moral forces at play in war, even though he clearly had not yet fully comprehended this phenomenon.

Scharnhorst was certainly in favour of standing armies. He was tired of the 'half-truths' used by so many idealistic men of letters, and decidedly rejected their one-sided arguments in favour of more realistic ones. His cunning rebuttal of Rousseau was perhaps the highlight of this endeavour. For Scharnhorst, the naïve concepts of these so-called 'enlightened' men would only lead to war, revolution, and anarchy. The constant readiness of the standing professional army was thus indispensable for the defence of the land. 'Eternal peace is a chimera', he concluded. 'As long as people have passions they will show them; and from ambition, revenge, etc., they will become involved in war with each other'. On the other hand, 'Our princes are generally speaking not inhuman despots; their formation [*Bildung*] has progressed with the formation [*Bildung*] of the people'.[109]

Can the same be said of democratic societies, Scharnhorst asked? If individual liberty is restricted in absolutist states, is it not also restricted in so-called democratic societies? He certainly appreciated the service to society that the professional standing army provided. He also acknowledged its vital contributions to the *Bildung* of the common soldier: its discipline, its sense of honour, and its esprit de corps. For Scharnhorst, military service must be the prerogative of a state-sponsored, professional organisation.

Reflecting on recent events in France, Scharnhorst wrote to now-*Oberst* Tempelhof in Berlin in late January 1793, telling him, 'I have an extraordinary enthusiasm for truth and justice, and I love them both, just as if they were my brothers'. At the same time, he informed Tempelhof that he was becoming increasingly dissatisfied with the stubborn resistance of the arrogant and recalcitrant Hanoverian nobility, in which 'most members of the ruling elites are too wicked and stupid' to realise what was happening – 'thus, a revolution is inevitable if the lower classes are to improve themselves'.

> In twenty years, I hope the ruling elite classes will be better educated and able to think more reasonably. The universities, and especially Göttingen, can contribute much to this. On the other hand, I regard it as an obligation, where one can, to reproach the ruling elites in societies for their arrogant way of thinking, their unjust ways, and to show them in such a way that this can no longer continue.
>
> It is self-evident, that one can make a great difference here among the individual members of the ruling elites, because many among them think reasonably and fairly.[110]

108 Scharnhorst, 'Ueber die Vor-und Nachtheile der stehenden Armeen', pp.235-36.

109 Scharnhorst, 'Ueber die Vor-und Nachtheile der stehenden Armeen', pp.244 and 365; respectively.

110 Gerhard Scharnhorst to Georg Friedrich von Tempelhof (27 January 1793); in Kunisch (ed.), *Scharnhorst: Privat und dienstliche Schriften*, Vol.1, pp.102-04; the quoted passages are from pp.103 and 104.

Written less than two months before Hanover joined the dynastic crusade against revolutionary France, Scharnhorst still believed the weapons to fight the wickedness and stupidity of societies were history, science, and literature. Like other *Aufklärer* (especially August Schlözer), he abhorred the violence, havoc, and instability revolution and war left in every area of life. On the other hand, his sense of history told him that if reforms and justice were not enacted in Hanover, sooner than later they would come through revolution.

The significance of Gerhard Scharnhorst's teaching and literary endeavours in Hanover from 1778 to 1793 can best be seen in the light of the French Revolutionary Wars (1792-99) and the subsequent Napoleonic Wars (1800-15). When Hanover joined the coalition against France in March 1793, Scharnhorst was nearly 40 years old. His entire military career had been spent in a peacetime academic environment, with neither troop command nor extensive field experience. Nevertheless, these had been highly formative years for him. Fifteen years of peace had given him the opportunity to read broadly and to develop and refine his ideas on the profession of arms and the art of war. From this detailed understanding and reflection, Scharnhorst concluded that *Bildung* was the sole means of preparing the soldier for war. Few agreed with this bold assertion, but the test of combat would prove the validity of his argument.

7

Baptism of Fire

Like so many uprisings, the French Revolution generated violence and destruction. Between 20 and 26 March 1793, seven weeks after the French Republic had declared war on Great Britain, the Hanoverian Auxiliary Corps marched off to war as part of the British expeditionary force.[1] Scharnhorst left his faculty post and reported for duty as a supernumerary with the horse (or mobile) artillery.[2] During the campaign in Flanders he fought in the Battle of Famars (23 May), where the Hanoverians made their combat debut.[3] From there he participated in the siege of Valenciennes (13 June-28 July). Then the Hanoverians formed 'a covering army' to protect the flank of British Prince Frederick Augustus (1763-1827), Duke of York and Albany, as he besieged Dunkirk.[4]

1 For the Hanoverian perspective, see Vol.4 of Sichart, *Geschichte der Königlich-Hannoverischen Armee*. The organisation of the 13,000 soldiers of the Hanoverian Auxiliary Corps can be found on pp.30-42. An abbreviated version of this organisation can be found in Appendix II of Klippel, *Scharnhorst*, Vol.2, pp.354-59. Source documents on this organisation come from Hann 38 E, Nr.20: *Etat, Formation und Abmarsch eines kurhannoverschen Auxiliar-Korps von 12.000 Mann*; and Nr.30: *Verzeichnis des gesamten Generalstabes und Besetzung der Offiziersstellen bei den Regimentern; Etats der Kavallerie und Infanterie; Instruktionen für den Generalstabsquartiermeister und Generalwagenmeister; Adjutanten der königlichen Prinzen; Besetzung der Feldhospital-Stellen, 02.1793-03.1793*; deposited at the Niedersächsisches Landesarchiv, Hanover. For an excellent, modern English study that incorporates extensive archival research and collates data found in various German sources, see Paul Demet, *'We are Accustomed to do our Duty': German Auxiliaries with the British Army 1793-95* (Warwick: Helion & Company, 2018); the organisation, strength, and assessment of the Hanoverian Auxiliary Corps can be found in Chapter 9 (pp.125-55).

2 Hanover's 'mobile' [*geschwinde*] artillery had four 3-pound guns and two 7-pound howitzers, was commanded by *Capitain* Georg Gustav Braun, and contained three additional officers, two sergeants, 12 corporals, three blacksmiths, two drummers, 48 gunners and bombardiers, two armorers, and one surgeon. See Sichart, *Geschichte der Königlich-Hannoverischen Armee*, Vol.4, pp.35-39. Source documents relating to the organisation of artillery companies can be found in Hann 41, VIII, Nr.42: *Dienstsachen der im Felde gestandenen Artilleriekompanien, 1793-1802*; deposited at the Niedersächsisches Landesarchiv, Hanover.

3 See the account of Christian von Ompteda; in John Hill (trans.), *A Hanoverian-English Officer: A Hundred Years Ago: Memoirs of Baron von Ompteda* (London: H. Grevel and Company, 1892), pp.43-54; the artillery action is discussed on p.49. Another good narrative can be found in Sichart, *Geschichte der Königlich-Hannoverischen Armee*, Vol.4, pp.209-23. Also see the report of the Duke of York to King George III (24 May 1793); in Arthur Aspinall (ed), *The Later Correspondence of George III* (Cambridge: Cambridge University Press, 1962-70), Vol.2, pp.41-44. Freytag's report to the king can be found in Hann 38 E, Nr.78: *Schlacht bei Famars am 23. Mai 1793: Bericht des Feldmarschalls von Freytag an den König*; deposited at the Niedersächsisches Landesarchiv, Hanover.

4 Highlights of the 1793 campaign are taken from the anonymous writer of *Uebersicht der Campagne, der Königlich Chur-Hannöverschen Truppen in Flandern, vom Jahre 1793* (Hanover: Gebrüdern Hahn, 1794); from Sichart, *Geschichte der Königlich-Hannoverischen Armee*, Vol.4, pp.187-327; from Vol.1 of Maximilian von Ditfurth, *Die*

Map 1 Theatre of War in the Austrian Netherlands and Northern France, 1793-94.

Hessen in den Feldzügen 1793, 1794 und 1795 in Flandern, Brabant, Holland und Westphalen (Kassel: J. Bohné, 1839-40); and from Sir John W. Fortescue, *British Campaigns in Flanders, 1690-1794. Being Extracts From 'A History of the British Army'* (London: Macmillan and Company, 1918), pp.177-264. The quoted passage is from p.227 of Fortescue's work. The term 'covering army' was also used to describe the Hanoverian force in the anonymous work, *A Concise Narrative of all the Actions, in which the British Forces were engaged during the Present War on the Continent of Europe. Extracted from Private Letters of Officers on Service There* (Manchester: Sowler and Russell, 1797), p.29. A recent study of British operations in the Low Countries that seeks 'to redress' the imbalance of earlier ones is Andrew Robert

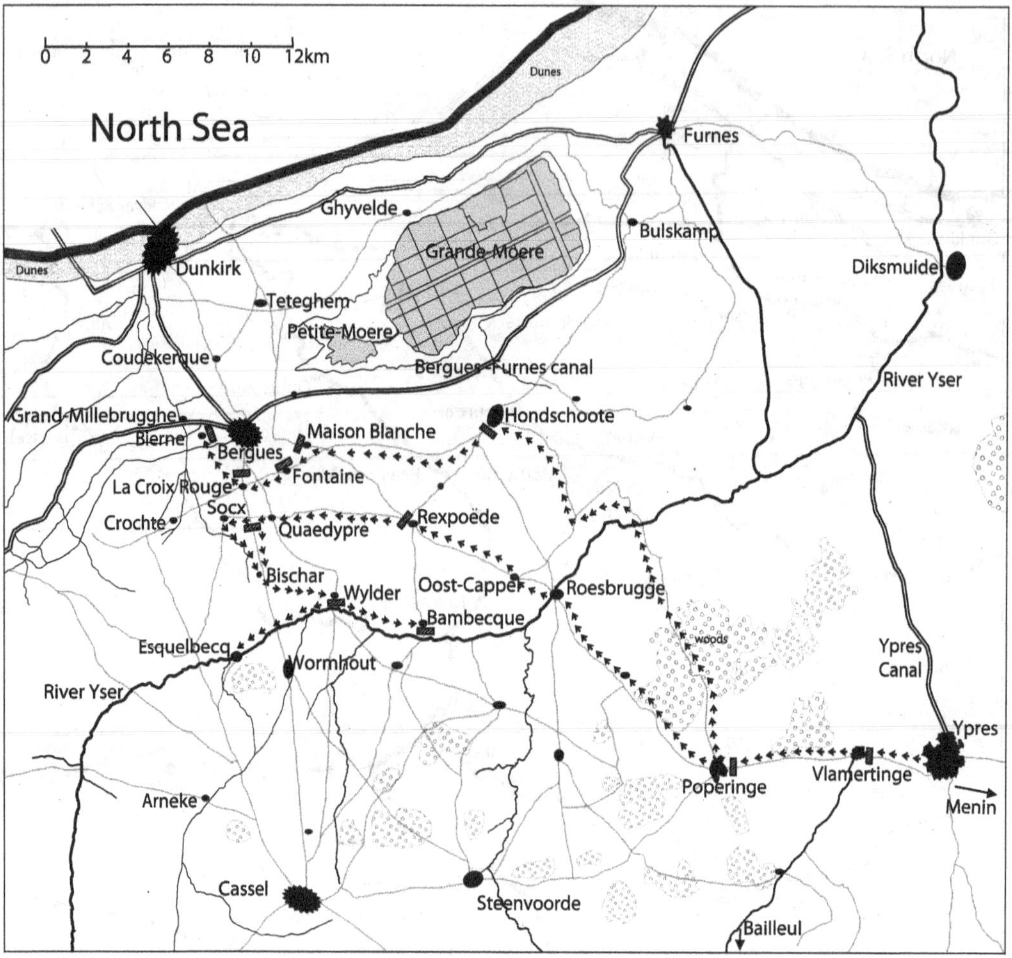

Map 2 Freytag's Advance, 19-25 August 1793.

As the British and Hanoverians pushed westward toward Dunkirk, they encountered increasing French resistance. A considerable amount came from the local inhabitants.[5] Following nearly three weeks of almost continual marching and seeking to bring the French to battle, including the engagement at Caesar's Camp on 7/8 August, the Hanoverians began establishing their cordon defence east of Dunkirk, but may have dangerously overextended

Limm, 'Fairly Out-Generaled and Disgracefully Beaten: The British Army in the Low Countries, 1793-1814' (Ph.D Thesis, University of Birmingham, 2015); later published as *Walcheren to Waterloo: The British Army in the Low Countries during the French Revolutionary and Napoleonic Wars 1793-1815* (South Yorkshire: Pen & Sword Military, 2018). Also see Chapter 3 (pp.33-51) of Demet, *'We are Accustomed to do our Duty'*.

5 See the comments of the Duke of York and his brothers, Prince Ernest and Prince Adolphus, to their father King George III, in their Letters of 26 August 1793; in Aspinall (ed), *The Later Correspondence of George III*, Vol.2, pp.78-82.

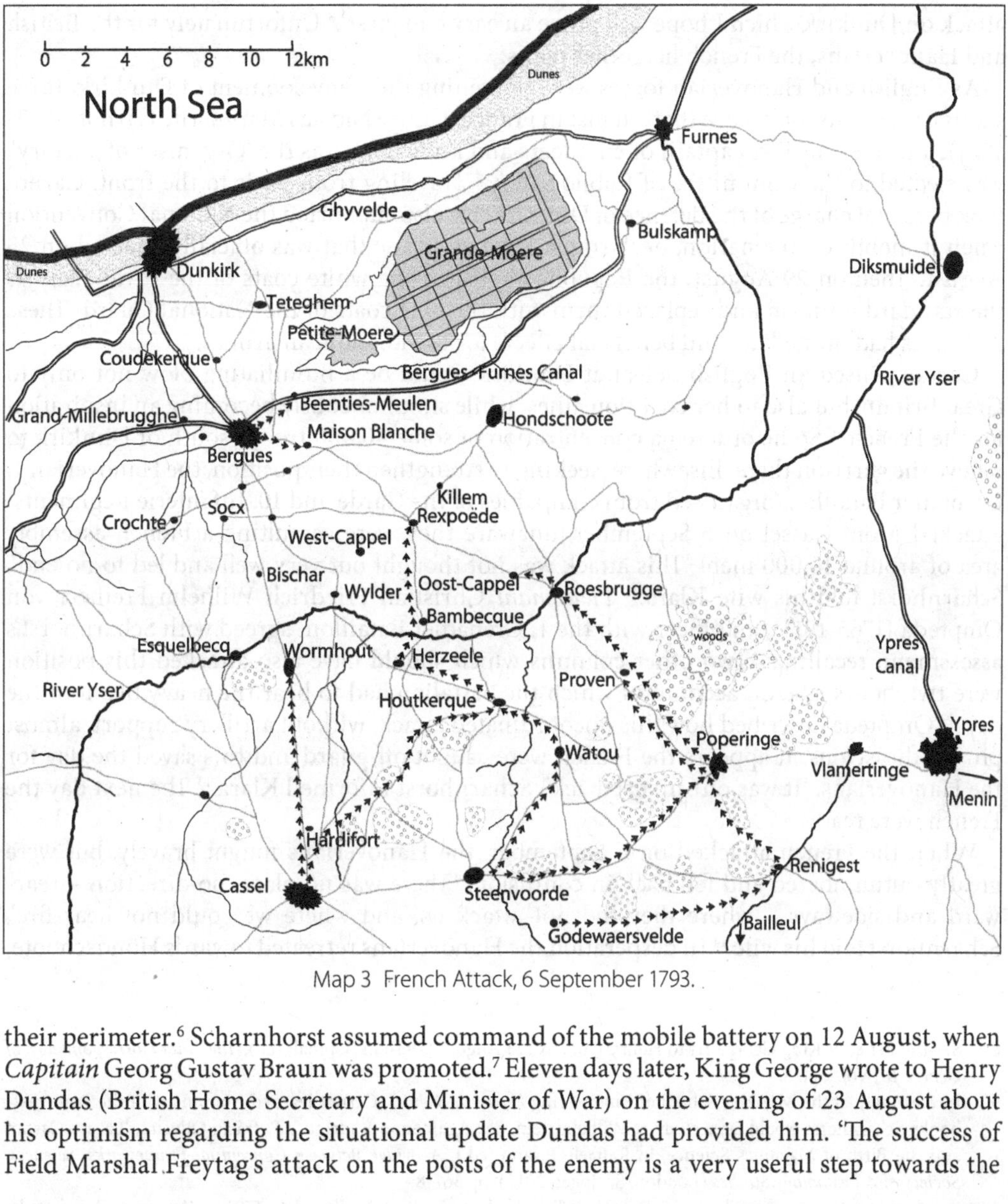

Map 3 French Attack, 6 September 1793.

their perimeter.[6] Scharnhorst assumed command of the mobile battery on 12 August, when *Capitain* Georg Gustav Braun was promoted.[7] Eleven days later, King George wrote to Henry Dundas (British Home Secretary and Minister of War) on the evening of 23 August about his optimism regarding the situational update Dundas had provided him. 'The success of Field Marshal Freytag's attack on the posts of the enemy is a very useful step towards the

6 This was the situational assessment of the Hanoverian commander, *Feldmarschall* Wilhelm von Freytag. See Demet, *'We are Accustomed to do our Duty'*, p.37. On p.34, Demet lists the organisation of the Hanoverian forces at this juncture, while on the next page he provides a map of the situation. Fortescue, *British Campaigns in Flanders*, p.236, agreed with Freytag, as he analysed the situation the Hanoverians faced. For a detailed account of these actions from a French perspective, see the superb study of Arthur Chuquet, *Hondschoote*, Vol.11 of *Les Guerres de la Révolution* (Paris: Léon Chailley, 1887-96), pp.141-49.

7 Klippel, *Scharnhorst*, Vol.2, p.20.

attack on Dunkirk which I hope will prove an easy conquest'.[8] Unfortunately for the British and Hanoverians, the French had other plans.

As English and Hanoverian forces were tightening their envelopment of Dunkirk, three significant events took place that August in France. Lazare Nicolas Marguerite Carnot (1753-1823), a former royalist captain of engineers and known later as the 'Organiser of Victory', was elected to the Committee of Public Safety.[9] Traveling from Paris to the front, Carnot took personal charge of the defence of Dunkirk. He also supported the National Convention when it mobilised the nation, declaring a *levée en masse* that was officially enacted on 23 August. Then on 29 August, the Republic abolished the white coats of the royal army as the standard uniform and replaced them with the blue coats of the National Guard. These measures had immediate and beneficial effects for the Republican armies.

Carnot sensed an English defeat at Dunkirk would be a humiliating blow not only to Great Britain, but also to her coalition allies, while simultaneously becoming an inspiration for the French.[10] So he ordered a concentration of some 40,000 troops south of Dunkirk to relieve the garrison there. Elsewhere, seeking to strengthen their position, the Hanoverian 1. Grenadier Bataillon (organised from companies of the Garde and 10. Infanterie Regiments) attacked Mont Cassel on 5 September, unaware they were assaulting a French assembly area of around 16,000 men. 'This attack was not thought out very well and led to no end', Scharnhorst told his wife Klara.[11] *Lieutenant* Christian Friedrich Wilhelm Freiherr von Ompteda (1765-1815), an officer with the 1. Grenadier Bataillon, agreed with Scharnhorst's assessment, recalling: 'Two other columns which should have also attacked this position were two hours late, on account of which the battalion had to bear the heavy brunt of the day'.[12] Ompteda described how this uncoordinated attack, without artillery support, almost proved disastrous. It appears the French were caught off-guard and this saved the day for the Hanoverians. 'It was our first setback', Scharnhorst informed Klara.[13] The next day the French were ready.

When the French attacked on 6 September, the Hanoverians fought bravely, but were greatly outnumbered and fell back in confusion. 'There was no place, no direction – rearward and sideways – where they did not attack us, and where we could not hear fire', Scharnhorst told his wife.[14] In desperation the Hanoverians retreated towards Hondschoote,

8 See the Letter of King George III to Henry Dundas (23 August 1793); in Aspinall (ed), *The Later Correspondence of George III*, Vol.2, p.78.

9 Interestingly, at the Mézières School of Engineering (*École du Génie*), Carnot learned from many of the same textbooks Scharnhorst would later study at Wilhelmstein. See Agamenon Rodrigues Eufrásio Oliveira, 'Lazare Carnot and the Birth of Machines Science', in Raffaele Pisano (ed.), *A Bridge Between Conceptual Frameworks: Sciences, Society and Technology Studies* (London: Springer, 2015), pp.367-84.

10 See the introductory remarks in Victor César Eugène Dupuis, *La champagne de 1793 à l'Armee du Nord et des Ardennes, de Valenciennes à Hondschoote* (Paris: Librairie Militaire R. Chapelot et Ce, 1906), pp.1-4.

11 See Gerhard Scharnhorst's Letter to Klara Scharnhorst (after 8 September 1793); in Kunisch (ed.), *Scharnhorst: Privat und dienstliche Schriften*, Vol.1, pp.257-60; the quoted passage is from pp.257-58.

12 Ompteda, *A Hanoverian-English Officer*, p.69. Ompteda was wounded in this action.

13 Letter of 'after' 8 September 1793; in Kunisch (ed.), *Scharnhorst: Privat und dienstliche Schriften*, Vol.1, p.258. For a nice account of this action see Demet, *'We are Accustomed to do our Duty'*, pp.38-39.

14 Letter of 'after' 8 September 1793; in Kunisch (ed.), *Scharnhorst: Privat und dienstliche Schriften*, Vol.1, p.258. On p.29 of the British account, *A Concise Narrative of all the Actions*, the anonymous author wrote how the French 'attacked the Hanoverians' with manic violence, 'pouring upon them superior numbers which became irresistible'.

via Rexpoëde, unaware Rexpoëde had fallen to the French.[15] While the French relief forces attacked the Hanoverians, Carnot ordered the Dunkirk defenders to sally forth, assault the British aggressively, and pin down the Duke of York's troops so they could not support the Hanoverians.[16]

At Rexpoëde, the Hanoverians marched straight into an ambush. At the head of their column was their commanding general, *Feldmarschall* Freytag, accompanied by the British Prince Adolphus Friedrich (1774-1850), commander the Hanoverian Garde Infanterie Regiment, *General-Major* Trew, their aides, and a sizeable escort of dragoons and guard infantrymen. Freytag and Adolphus were wounded and taken prisoner, but the prince (assisted by his aide *Lieutenant* Wangenheim) managed to escape.[17] It was 'a confusing fight', Scharnhorst told his wife.[18] Assuming command of the Hanoverian Auxiliary Corps was *General der Cavallerie* Johann Ludwig, *Reichsgraf* von Wallmoden-Gimborn (1736-1811), who quickly ordered a counterattack that rescued Freytag. Suffering from a head wound (as well as a back injury after being knocked off his horse) and in need of medical care, Freytag was taken to Furnes.[19]

Meanwhile, Wallmoden tried urgently to reorganise his scattered forces into a coherent defence at Hondschoote. Militarily, Hondschoote was a very weak position, much too narrow in width and lacking in depth. Wallmoden realised the danger and wanted to withdrawal, but coalition leaders ordered him to defend Hondshoote and protect the flank of the Duke of York.[20] To reinforce Wallmoden they sent two battalions of the Hesse Cassel Regiment Erb-Prinz, led by *General-Major* Johann Friedrich von Cochenhausen (1728-1793).[21] Wallmoden organised his defence with his right flank commanded by *General-Major* Rudolf Georg Wilhelm Freiherr von Hammerstein (1735-1811), while the left was commanded by *General-Major* August Ludwig Friedrich von Diepenbroick (1728-1805). *Titular-Capitain* Scharnhorst commanded his battery of horse artillery near the centre of the Hanoverian position.[22]

15 A good illustration of this action can be found in Sketch Map 4 'Dunkirk' (opposite p.72); in Alfred H. Burne, *The Noble Duke of York: The Military Life of Frederick Duke of York and Albany* (London: Staples Press, 1949).

16 Quoting one contemporary British minister at the time, Fortescue, *British Campaigns in Flanders*, p.249, wrote, 'Our whole enterprise is defeated and our situation embarrassing in the extreme'. For an excellent study of British operations in Flanders in 1793, see Nathaniel W. Jarrett, 'The Enemy of My Enemy is What, Exactly? The British Flanders Expedition of 1793 and Coalition Diplomacy' (M.A. Thesis, University of North Texas, 2013).

17 See the account by Prince Adolphus in his Letter of 8 September 1793 to King George III; in Aspinall (ed), *The Later Correspondence of George III*, Vol.2, pp.88-89.

18 Letter of 'after' 8 September 1793 to Klara; in Kunisch (ed.), *Scharnhorst: Privat und dienstliche Schriften*, Vol.1, pp.258-59; the quoted passage is from p.259. On p.44 of Demet, *'We are Accustomed to do our Duty'*, is a painting of this incident.

19 See the letters of concern from King George to Freytag and Prince Adolphus; in Hann E, Nr.95: *Affäre bei Hondscooten: Briefe des Königs an den Feldmarschall von Freytag über seine und des Prinzen Adolph Verwundung in der Affäre, 09.1793*; deposited at the Niedersächsisches Landesarchiv, Hanover.

20 For an interesting analysis of the Coalition plan, see Michael Duffy, '"A Particular Service": The British Government and the Dunkirk Expedition of 1793', *The English Historical Review* 91 (July 1976), pp.529-54.

21 Ditfurth, *Die Hessen in den Feldzügen 1793, 1794 und 1795*, Vol.1, p.114. Also see Demet, *'We are Accustomed to do our Duty'*, pp.45-48.

22 Source documents relating to this defence can be found in Hann 38 E, Nr.92: *Affäre bei Hondscooten: Pläne und Dislokationen*; deposited at the Niedersächsisches Landesarchiv, Hanover.

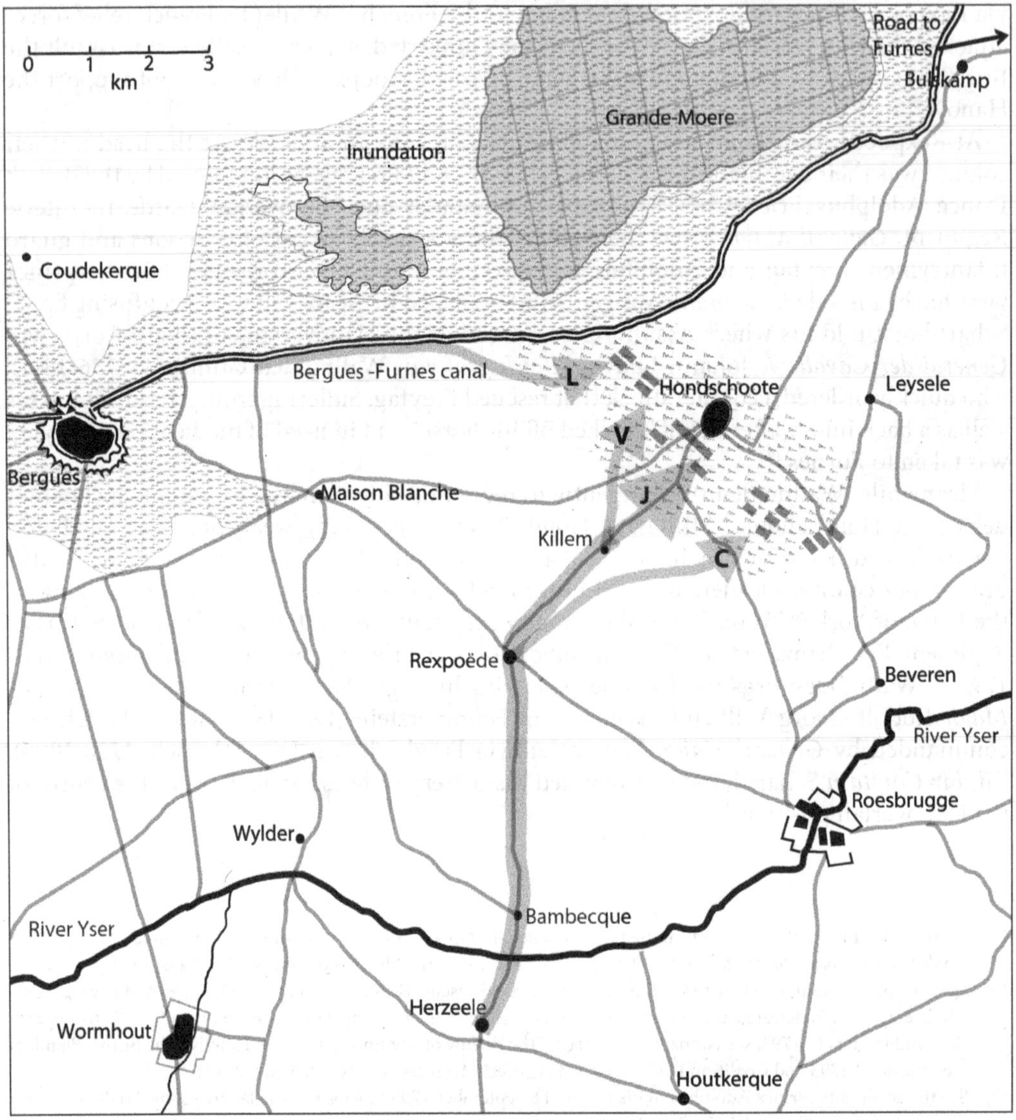

Map 4 French Attack at Hondschoote, 8 September 1793.

Fortunately, the French paused their attack to reorganise. This gave the Hanoverians and Hessians precious time to prepare their defence. Wallmoden ordered the reserve ammunition brought up from Furnes, while the defenders built abattis, erected hasty barricades, and constructed entrenchments and redoubts.[23] Meanwhile, the Hanoverian cavalry set idle on

23 See Gerhard Scharnhorst, 'Gehorsamster Bericht von den Verhalten der Artillerie in den Affären von 6ten, 7ten und 8ten Sept. 1793' (after 8 September 1793); in Kunisch (ed.), *Scharnhorst: Privat und dienstliche Schriften*, Vol.1, pp.261-62.

the difficult terrain, failing to provide adequate security and protection, as French reconnaissance troops soon discovered. Led by engineer officer Simon François Gay de Vernon (1760-1822), French scouts were able to get close enough to the Hanoverian defence to determine its strengths and weaknesses, count its batteries, the number and types of guns, and ascertain its key terrain features.[24] With this information, the French commander, *Général de Division* Jean Nicolas Houchard (1738-93), drew up his plan of attack.

When the French renewed their attack on the morning of 8 September, the broken ground and hedges before Hondschoote ideally suited their use of open-order tactics. Scharnhorst, who had already proven his ability as an educator and scholar, now demonstrated his stable leadership under fire. Fierce fighting, sometimes hand-to-hand, ebbed and flowed throughout the morning. Shortly before noon French columns moved forward in a series of massed bayonet attacks. 'All of a sudden we saw the enemy columns in front of us', Scharnhorst told Klara. In an attempt to stop the French momentum, he redirected his two guns, using canister fire. This was not enough. 'Their fire on us became stronger and stronger'. Then he told his wife, 'The French rushed at us three times shouting'. 'They took us in the flank, and now the situation demanded serenity [*Countenance*]'.[25]

According to French prisoners, Houchard attacked the Hanoverians thinking they were British, since both wore red coats. The French came at the Hanoverians in three successive waves, as Scharnhorst noted. 'This accounts for their superiority', wrote one British officer, 'and for the great carnage'. 'The dead lay in such heaps' as the French advanced. Indeed, the French 'were obliged sometimes to stop and move the bodies aside, to let the columns pass'.[26] As more than 20,000 shouting French troops overwhelmed the Hanoverian defence of around 13,000 men (including the Hessians), Scharnhorst sensed his moment. Without orders, he took command of several shattered infantry units fleeing the battlefield and halted their impending rout. By noon the Hanoverians were exhausted and running out of ammunition. Fearing the French would cut his line of retreat, Wallmoden ordered a withdrawal to Furnes.[27] Taking charge, Scharnhorst organised an effective rearguard action and began conducting an orderly withdrawal until Hammerstein assumed overall command. Scharnhorst's actions helped preserve the entire Hanoverian corps.[28]

24 See the account of Simon François Gay de Vernon, *Mémoire sur les Opérations Militaire des Généraux en Chef Custine et Houchard, pendant les Années 1792 et 1793* (Paris: Librairie de Firmin Didot Frères, 1844), pp.264-65.

25 Letter of 'after' 8 September 1793; in Kunisch (ed.), *Scharnhorst: Privat und dienstliche Schriften*, Vol.1, p.259. For a nice account of this action, including a map, see Demet, *'We are Accustomed to do our Duty'*, pp.45-51. In his brief report, the Duke of York told his father, 'at break of day the enemy made a general attack upon all the Field Marshal Freytag's posts'. See the Letter of the Duke of York to King George III (7 September 1793); in Aspinall (ed), *The Later Correspondence of George III*, Vol.2, p.88.

26 See the anonymous account, *The Present State of the British Army in Flanders, With an Authentic Account of their Retreat from before Dunkirk by a British Officer of that Army, Who was living on the 24th of September* (London: H.D. Symonds, 1793), pp.4-5.

27 In his Report of 18 September 1793, the Duke of York told King George 'that after doing everything that troops could do Count Wallmoden had been overpowered through numbers' and forced 'to retreat close to Furnes'. See Aspinall (ed), *The Later Correspondence of George III*, Vol.2, pp.91-101; the quoted passage is from p.100.

28 This action can be followed in Lehmann, *Scharnhorst*, Vol.1, pp.119-24. A good map of this battle can be found in Fortescue, *British Campaigns in Flanders*, p.237. Also see Sichart, *Geschichte der Königlich-Hannoverischen Armee*, Vol.4, pp.267-81; Scharnhorst's performance is cited on p.280. The Hessian account can be found in Ditfurth, *Die*

The alert and courageous actions of Scharnhorst and other junior officers with him, coupled with an exhausted and disorganised French force, permitted the Hanoverians and Hessians to fall back unmolested, first to Bulskamp and later to Furnes, covered by their cavalry that finally sprang into action. Most of the sick and wounded were Hanoverians, who 'bore the blunt of all the battles' and 'perished on the road for want of attendance'. The wagon train containing the wounded 'formed a line of at least two miles'.[29] Fortunately, the French did not vigorously pursue the two intermingled columns of Hanoverians and Hessians. Instead, Carnot ordered Houchard to march toward Tournai. In the midst of this disaster Scharnhorst told his wife, 'General von Wallmoden behaved like a clever, brave general'.[30]

Apart from some outpost actions later that fall and winter, Hondschoote effectively ended Hanoverian participation in the Flanders campaign of 1793. Their losses were high. Nearly 18 percent were killed, wounded, missing, or taken prisoner in just three days.[31] Although the Hanoverians were badly shaken after nearly a week of endless fighting, Scharnhorst believed their composure remained unbroken.[32] Challenging this view was Major General Sir James Murray, Adjutant General to the Duke of York. In his report of 9 September 1793, Murray wrote: 'The Hanoverians who really behaved with the greatest Gallantry are now entirely dispirited & by the confession of their own officers can be no longer depended upon'.[33] Written a day after the action at Hondschoote and during the retreat to Furnes, Murray's report clearly captured the moment well, but his conclusion about the long-term condition of the Hanoverians proved incorrect. In this case Scharnhorst was right. The Duke of York agreed, telling his father on 21 September: 'The troops have quite recovered the very severe fatigue they have undergone, and are in the highest spirits'.[34]

Over the next few months Wallmoden was able to refit and reorganise the Hanoverian Auxiliary Corps. Meanwhile, York was quick to blame the defeat of the Hanoverians for 'my having in consequence been obliged to retire from before Dunkirk, …' 'The only consolidation I have is that I do not think that I can impute any blame to myself', he told King George.[35]

Hessen in den Feldzügen 1793, 1794 und 1795, Vol.1, pp.110-28; followed by a good analysis on pp.129-33. For the French perspective, see Chuquet, *Hondschoote*, pp.186-229.

29 See Anon., *The Present State of the British Army in Flanders*, p.4.

30 Letter of 'after' 8 September 1793; in Kunisch (ed.), *Scharnhorst: Privat und dienstliche Schriften*, Vol.1, p.260.

31 Hanoverian casualties are listed in Sichart, *Geschichte der Königlich-Hannoverischen Armee*, Vol.4, pp.281-87; an analysis can be found on pp.287-92. Demet, *'We are Accustomed to do our Duty'*, pp.50-51, provides a nice summary of all German casualties from both English and German sources. Source documents relating to artillery casualties can be found in Hann 41, VIII, Nr.41: *Verlustlisten der Regimentsartillerie, 1793-1795*; deposited at the Niedersächsisches Landesarchiv, Hanover.

32 Scharnhorst's brief analysis and estimate of the situation can be found in his Letters of 5 and 6 October 1793 to his wife; in Kunisch (ed.), *Scharnhorst: Privat und dienstliche Schriften*, Vol.1, pp.265-67.

33 Murray is quoted in Demet, *'We are Accustomed to do our Duty'*, p.50.

34 Letter of 21 September 1793 from the Duke of York to King George III; in Aspinall (ed), *The Later Correspondence of George III*, Vol.2, p.102.

35 Letter of 9 September 1793 from the Duke of York to King George III; in Aspinall (ed), *The Later Correspondence of George III*, Vol.2, p.89. Also see his later elaboration of 18 September 1793; on pp.97-101. In defence of the Hanoverians, Sichart, *Geschichte der Königlich-Hannoverischen Armee*, Vol.4, p.290, wrote: 'the Hanoverians were indisputably made the victims of a mistaken plan of campaign, in which the Duke of York separated himself from

On the other hand, Prince Ernest (who had fought with the rear guard at Hondschoote) told his father about 'the goodness of Providence & the bravery of your Hanoverian Infantry'.

> One thing, however sorrowful this event has been, is that the Hanoverians have render'd [sic] themselves immortal through their amazing bravery, for nothing but that has saved us.[36]

Regardless of what many coalition leaders felt, from a social, political, and military perspective, the French triumph was a direct result of its 'revolutionary *élan*', and demonstrated the awesome power of the *levée en masse*. This marked the true beginning of French military domination in Europe.[37]

In his report to Wallmoden on the action at Hondschoote, Trew, 'who had long disliked the independent attitude of Scharnhorst', gave credit for what Scharnhorst had achieved to his nephew, *Lieutenant* Wilhelm von Bonnivet.[38] 'He [Trew] reported it to General Wallmoden in my presence. I was silent', a stunned and angry Scharnhorst later told his wife.[39] This truly despicable act by Trew was one of the many examples of nepotism and preferential treatment Scharnhorst had witnessed throughout the campaign, and which appeared to be 'the good old Hanoverian way'.[40] Fortunately for Scharnhorst, Wallmoden did not believe Trew's report. He was there and witnessed the events, as did other senior Hanoverian leaders.

Even as the truth reached the troops, Trew continued to credit Bonnivet. While connection may certainly have played a role in Trew's decision to recognise his nephew, another possibility was the fact that Scharnhorst had mentioned leaving Bonnivet in charge of the two cannon while he gathered infantry support for the protection of the guns and their crews.[41] Diepenbroick clarified this conversation when he praised Scharnhorst for rallying and steadying his infantrymen, while Scharnhorst and *Fähndrich* Röttiger (who led the artillery in support of Diepenbroick's 10. Infanterie Regiment) 'greatly distinguished themselves in this action'. Diepenbroick 'never even mentioned' Bonnivet in his report.[42] Hammerstein

Prince Coburg [Frederick Josias of Saxe-Coburg-Saalfeld (1737-1815)] to besiege Dunkirk with resources wholly insufficient for that purpose'.

36 Letter of 10 September 1793 from Prince Ernest to King George III; in Aspinall (ed), *The Later Correspondence of George III*, Vol.2, pp.90-91; the quoted passages are from pp.90 and 91; respectively.

37 This was the conclusion of Hans Delbrück, *Geschichte der Kriegskunst im Rahman der politischen Geschichte* (Berlin: Georg Stilke, 1900-20), Vol.4, p.458. The quoted passage is from Paul W. Schroeder, *The Transformation of European Politics, 1763-1848* (Clarendon: Oxford University Press, 1994), p.136.

38 See the insightful commentary by Lehmann, *Scharnhorst*, Vol.1, p.123. Unfortunately, Lehmann fails to explain the disharmony between Trew and Scharnhorst.

39 See Scharnhorst's Letter of 14 April 1794 to Klara; in Kunisch (ed.), *Scharnhorst: Privat und dienstliche Schriften*, Vol.1, pp.369-70; the quoted passages are from p.369. Scharnhorst told his wife he was singled-out for his actions at Hondschoote in 'a small brochure' entitled, *Overview of the 1793 Campaign in Flanders*. See Anon., *Overview of the 1793 Campaign in Flanders*, p.33.

40 Lehmann, *Scharnhorst*, Vol.1, p.123.

41 For Scharnhorst's Report to Trew, see 'Gehorsamster Bericht von den Verhalten der Artillerie in den Affären von 6ten, 7ten und 8ten Sept. 1793' (after 8 September 1793); in Kunisch (ed.), *Scharnhorst: Privat und dienstliche Schriften*, Vol.1, pp.261-62.

42 See Scharnhorst's commentary to Klara in his Letter of 14 April 1794; in Kunisch (ed.), *Scharnhorst: Privat und dienstliche Schriften*, Vol.1, pp.369-70; the quoted passages are from p.369.

then added his praise of Scharnhorst's outstanding leadership. It was Hammerstein who (after assuming command of the rearguard during the retreat from Hondschoote) had observed how Scharnhorst and *Lieutenant* von Behr, 'senior adjutant' [*Oberadjudant*] to Wallmoden, had 'voluntarily remained' with the artillery of the 2. Grenadier Bataillon that was covering the withdrawal. 'Their combined efforts', he told to Wallmoden, 'contributed immensely to the order with which the retreat was conducted, despite the intense passion with which the enemy pursued us from the start'.[43] In his letter to Klara, Scharnhorst was thankful for the support he had received from the 150 infantrymen of the Garde Regiment under *Capitain* Georg Carl Löw von und zu Steinfurt (1750-1811) and from *Capitain* Hugo's company of the 10. Infanterie Regiment.[44] While Scharnhorst was certainly gratified by the glowing praise he had received from many of his fellow officers, he simply could not shake the yoke Trew was trying to place around his neck.

Later that winter Hanover decided to raise another company of horse artillery. Scharnhorst (as the senior *Titular-Capitain*) assumed he would receive this command. Trew thought otherwise, and created an 'enhanced company' with *Major* Braun in command.[45] When Scharnhorst appealed to Wallmoden, citing his seniority and army regulations to support his case, the acting Commanding General supported him.[46] It appears Trew then went around Wallmoden directly to Freytag, citing the original instructions from the Hanoverian Chancery in London that 'any promotion or individual advancement' must have 'the recommendation of the regimental commander and the approval of our field marshal' [Freytag].[47] In the end Scharnhorst did not get promoted nor receive this company command.

Sensing Trew's animosity toward Scharnhorst, Wallmoden reassigned his battery to the fortress town of Menin (in southern Belgium). Wallmoden was grateful for Scharnhorst's leadership at Hondschoote and sought to protect him against the wrath of Trew. Upon learning this, Trew ordered *Major* Georg Wilhelm Ritter, Commander of the 2. Division Artillerie (already in Menin) to present 'credentials' [*Certificat*] to the Austrian general in

43 See the Report of C. Meissner, Auditor of the Hanoverian General Staff; cited in Sichart, *Geschichte der Königlich-Hannoverischen Armee*, Vol.4, p.280. After-action reports on this engagement can be found in Hann 38 E, Nr.94: *Affäre bei Hondscooten: Meldungen nach der Affäre vom 8. bis 16. September 1793*; deposited at the Niedersächsisches Landesarchiv, Hanover. The Hanoverian list of casualties, dated 13 September 1793, has Behr wounded and taken prisoner. A *Lieutenant* Rehwinkel, mostly likely Scharnhorst's colleague at the Artillery School, was killed in action. See Hann 38 E, Nr.93: *Affäre bei Hondscooten: Listen der von 5. bis 8. September 1793 Gefallenen, Verwundeten und Gefangenen (unvollständig)*; deposited at the Niedersächsisches Landesarchiv, Hanover. Also see Appendix VII of Klippel, *Scharnhorst*, Vol.2, pp.370 and 371, for a summary of Hanoverian casualties.

44 See Scharnhorst's Letter of 'after' 8 September 1793 to Klara; in Kunisch (ed.), *Scharnhorst: Privat und dienstliche Schriften*, Vol.1, p.259.

45 See Scharnhorst's Letter of 1 and 5 January 1794 to Klara; in Kunisch (ed.), *Scharnhorst: Privat und dienstliche Schriften*, Vol.1, p.307. Source documents relating to this new organisation can be found in Hann 41, VIII, Nr.43: *Formation der Artillerie zum Ausmarsch. Bewaffnung und Verstärkung derselben. Gehaltsverbesserungen der reitenden Artillerie, 1794-1796*; deposted at the Niedersächsisches Landesarchiv, Hanover.

46 See the discussion in Klippel, *Scharnhorst*, Vol.2, pp.33-35. Scharnhorst's Letter of 30 December 1793 to Wallmoden is also published in Kunisch (ed.), *Scharnhorst: Privat und dienstliche Schriften*, Vol.1, pp.296-97. His attached Memorandum, 'Gründe für die Creirung eines wirklichen Capitäns bey der jetzt zu errichtenden Batteerie geschwinder Artillerie' (30 December 1793), follows on pp.297-98.

47 See 'Instruction für den Commandirenden General des Auxiliar-Corps' (2 April 1793); printed in Sichart, *Geschichte der Königlich-Hannoverischen Armee*, Vol.4, pp.194-96; the quoted passages are from Paragraph 5 (p.196).

command that placed all artillery under Ritter's control. When the Austrian commandant requested clarification, Ritter acted like 'a blundering idiot', Scharnhorst told Klara. 'He was just so outrageous'. The Austrian commander was clearly unaware of Trew's scheme, but 'the clever Wallmoden' was, and stepped in to remedy the situation. For the time being, Scharnhorst was free of Trew's influence. As he told his wife, 'The General [Trew] is beside himself that I act as a free man and do not bow like a slave before him'.[48]

Scharnhorst described these situations in lengthy, detailed, candid, and affectionate letters to his beloved wife Klara, providing a copious record of the routine and daily activities of his life on campaign.[49] His letters reveal the lack of respect he had for so many officers, especially the ignorant, the lazy, and those who failed to perform their duties with honour, virtue, and diligence. Scharnhorst understood that leaders are shaped by the values they embrace, and often wondered about the motives of commanders who willingly sacrificed the lives of their soldiers in worthless actions, without any sense of remorse. He also distrusted and looked with distain at the vengeful French *émigrés*, who he said were 'self-absorbed, ignorant, and superstitious'. Most 'deserved their fate'.[50]

As the campaign dragged on with no resolution in sight, Scharnhorst became increasingly frustrated by its lack of purpose. 'Every operation must have an objective', he maintained, referring to the lessons of history. 'What was the objective of this operation?' he wondered. At the time his wrote these thoughts Scharnhorst was trying to ascertain why the Duke of York had separated his force from Prince Coburg, leaving the Hanoverians strung-out across the front supporting the British, while simultaneously trying to maintain contact with the Austrians.[51] He had no way of knowing the political or military objectives of the British expeditionary force, and that London had altered York's mission, ordering him to take Dunkirk.[52]

48 See Scharnhorst's Letter of 17 and 18 November 1793 to Klara; in Kunisch (ed.), *Scharnhorst: Privat und dienstliche Schriften*, Vol.1, pp.287-90; the quoted passages are from p.288. From what he told his wife, Scharnhorst sensed in his heart that he would not be promoted and given command of a company. Two months later he told Klara that his worse fears about his future in the artillery were coming true. See his Letter of 1 and 5 January 1794 (p.307). Doubts about his future career possibilities also appear in several of his earlier letters to his wife. For example, see his Letters of 5 and 6 October 1793 (pp.265-67) and 12 and 13 October 1793 (pp.274-76).

49 For reasons unknown, none of Scharnhorst's letters to his wife during this campaign are published in Klippel, *Scharnhorst*; and only a few (mostly those critical of Hanoverian ways) can be found in Lehmann, *Scharnhorst*.

50 See Scharnhorst's Letter of 21-29 April 1793 to Klara: in Kunisch (ed.), *Scharnhorst: Privat und dienstliche Schriften*, Vol.1, pp.205-08; the quoted passages are from p.206 (21 April). Similar comments about the French *émigrés* can be found in Ompteda, *A Hanoverian-English Officer*, p.73, who noted that they 'crawl everywhere at some distance in the rear of our armies, like noxious vermin, and largely quench any feelings of sympathy one might have for their condition by their own despicable conduct'. Likewise, Johann Wolfgang von Goethe stated his lack of empathy for the French *émigrés* in his 'Kampagne in Frankreich 1792', *Goethe Werke*, Herausgegeben im Auftrage der Groβherzogin Sophie von Sachen, Band 33 (Weimar: Hermann Böhlaus, 1898), p.10.

51 Gerhard Scharnhorst, 'Relation von den Angrif des Caesarschen Lagers bey Cambray, mit einigen Bemerkungen über die weitern Operationen und der Disposition zu den Angrif des obigen Lagers von Prinz von Coburg' (September/October 1793); in Kunisch (ed.), *Scharnhorst: Privat und dienstliche Schriften*, Vol.1, pp.262-64; the quoted passages are from p.264. A good illustration of this action can be found in Sketch Map 3 'Caesar's Camp' (opposite p. 64); in Burne, *The Noble Duke of York*.

52 According to Jarrett, 'The British Flanders Expedition of 1793 and Coalition Diplomacy', p.88: 'The British government refused to allow its army to fight for the German powers as long as their war remained distinct from the

The misery of war also disturbed Scharnhorst. The plight of the elderly and so many innocent women and children really upset him, as did the tremendous waste of lives and property that this war was producing.[53] Reflecting on his Enlightenment ideals of peace, progress, and service to humanity, he told his wife in late April 1793, 'Leibnitz proved that this world is the best. That may be true, but I cannot understand why'.[54] A year later he told Klara how he dreamed he was a pure and noble knight, riding endlessly 'through a desert of completely savage animals'.[55] After witnessing the beautiful and majestic church tower of the ancient city of Valenciennes set ablaze and needlessly destroyed by coalition artillery fire, he wrote to his wife, 'I wish that this war, just this one, would end, even if another one follows right away'.[56] Often thinking of his own family in these situations, Scharnhorst prayed that nothing like what he observed would ever become their fate.

Scharnhorst's intimate letters to his wife and family paint a picture of a kind, warm-hearted, and sensitive man, who was often volatile and insecure. They also highlight many of the issues military families historically encounter during a long separation. Scharnhorst yearned to be home with his wife and their two young children. Often pensive and introspective, he longed to be engaged in productive activities, such as research, study, teaching, and pursuing his literary endeavours. Like many soldiers in time of war, he wanted his surrounding to conform to his home lifestyle, as if he had never left home, even though he was far from familiar surroundings.

To this end Scharnhorst asked Klara to write detailed letters to him, describing her daily life at home and the activities of their children, just like she would tell him when he would arrive home from work. 'Don't write such short letters to me, my darling wife', he implored Klara during the siege of Valenciennes.[57] He confessed his loneliness to her, how much he loved and missed her and their children, and even suggested that if she could not write more detailed letters to him, perhaps it would be better if she not write at all. Of course, he clearly did not mean this, and immediately apologised to her with humility and sadness. He simply missed his family so much and was anxious to hear from them.

Anglo-Dutch war with France'. For an incisive analysis of the intricate and duplicitous British and Austrian diplomatic maneuverings during this time, see Schroeder, *The Transformation of European Politics*, pp.111-36.

53 English Corporal Robert Brown, *An Impartial Journal of a Detachment from the Brigade of Foot Guards, commencing 25th February, 1793, and ending 9th May, 1795* (London: John Stockdale, 1795), pp.24-25, was also troubled by the plight of the innocent and the cruelty they suffered.

54 Letter of 21-29 April 1793 to Klara; in Kunisch (ed.), *Scharnhorst: Privat und dienstliche Schriften*, Vol.1, pp.205-08; the quoted passage is from p.206 (21 April).

55 Letter of 13 April 1794 to Klara; in Kunisch (ed.), *Scharnhorst: Privat und dienstliche Schriften*, Vol.1, pp.368-69; the quoted passage is from p.368.

56 Letter of 7 and 8 July 1793 to Klara; in Kunisch (ed.), *Scharnhorst: Privat und dienstliche Schriften*, Vol.1, pp.236-37; the quoted passage is from p.237 (8 July). Scharnhorst's account of this incident can be found in his letter of 30 June 1793 (p.235). Ompteda, *A Hanoverian-English Officer*, p.57, described this event in more detail. Also see Anon., *An Accurate and Impartial Narrative of the War by an Officer of the Guards* (London: Cadell and Davies, 1796), Vol.1, p.63. For a French perspective, see Chapter 9 (pp.261-72) of Arthur Chuquet, *Valenciennes (1793)*, Vol.10 of *Les Guerres de la Révolution* (Paris: Léon Chailley, 1887-96). A nice map of the siege can be found on the page just after the preface.

57 Letter of 14 July 1793 to Klara; in Kunisch (ed.), *Scharnhorst: Privat und dienstliche Schriften*, Vol.1, pp.239-41; the quoted passage is from p.239.

By this time in the deployment, Scharnhorst had calculated just how long it will take for Klara's letters to reach him (even when the army was on the move), and how long it will take for his letters to arrive at home. Sometimes he would stop writing in the middle of a sentence or thought, telling Klara that if he did not give his letter to the courier in a few minutes, it would not be mailed on time, and would not arrive on schedule to her. While waiting to hear from her, he often told her what great delight he took in reading her letters over and over again, and what joy he felt in his heart whenever their five-year-old daughter Julia sent him a gift she had made especially for her father. Full of nostalgia and concern for his family's well-being, Scharnhorst thought of his wife and their children all the time, and usually read their letters (as he often confessed) with tears in his eyes.[58]

As a child of the Enlightenment, Scharnhorst was determined to use this war and his potential to excel in his profession. Even though he had no command role in the beginning, he understood that war offered him the only hope of advancement. And while he was frustrated and angry being just a supernumerary, he realised he would have to be patient and wait for the right opportunity, and asked his wife to be at peace, too. 'I suppress all of my views here, which often attack me in a terrible way', he confessed to Klara.[59] At the same time, he was mortified by the savagery of war.

Scharnhorst frequently spoke of his disgust with war and killing, a loathing he maintained throughout his military career. 'I am not made to be a soldier', he confessed to Klara after his baptism of fire at Famars.

> I can face danger without difficulty, but I am enraged and thrown into an insupportable mood by the sight of innocent people moaning in their blood at my feet, by the flames of burning villages, which men have put to the torch for their own pleasure, by the other horrors of this universal devastation.[60]

Interestingly, Robert Thomas Wilson (1777-1849), a 16-year-old cornet with the British 15th Light Dragoons, remembered a similar vision that spring.

> The night was a memorable one, and I have never forgotten the awful and meditative sight of thirteen villages in flames. The horizon seemed to be indeed on fire; and, inexperienced as I then was in the horrors of war, nature and education combined to make me feel unhappy at so much calamity.[61]

While not expressly stating the obvious, Wilson's insightful observations during this campaign make it clear the discipline that had once characterized British regiments was

58 In his Letter of 21-29 April 1793 to Klara; Kunisch (ed.), *Scharnhorst: Privat und dienstliche Schriften*, Vol.1, pp.205-09, Scharnhorst first mentioned how difficult it was to write to his family without tears in his eyes.

59 Letter of 21 April 1793 to Klara; in Kunisch (ed.), *Scharnhorst: Privat und dienstliche Schriften*, Vol.1, pp.205. Scharnhorst rarely suppressed his views to Klara, as his letters reveal.

60 Letter of 21-24 May 1793 to Klara; in Kunisch (ed.), *Scharnhorst: Privat und dienstliche Schriften*, Vol.1, pp.214-16; the quoted passage is from p.215 (24 May).

61 See Herbert Randolph (ed.), *Life of General Sir Robert Wilson* (London: John Murray, 1862), Vol.1, p.63.

seriously lacking during the 1793 Flanders campaign. As he wrote just before joining his regiment, 'Drinking and gaming were then very general habits'.[62]

'We seldom had success', Scharnhorst informed his wife about the missed opportunities at Famars and how the quest for decisive victory kept eluding the coalition during the early months of the campaign.[63] 'Everywhere, officers clearly failed to know what they must do at every opportunity', he told Jakob Mauvillon, a professor of politics in Brunswick.[64] Interestingly, several British officers agreed with Scharnhorst's assessment. One member of York's staff (at the time a young civilian secretary from the Foreign Office) recalled how Freytag 'had been a famous partisan in the Seven Years War, but had not served since. He was, of course, not young, and had become slow and inactive'.[65] Another officer, a lieutenant colonel with the 2nd Dragoon Guards, described Freytag as 'an old woman'.[66] Wallmoden did not fare much better. Although 'a clever and well-informed man', Wallmoden was characterized as 'slow and undecided, and a bad horseman'. Indeed, according to British observers, the senior leaders in the Hanoverian Auxiliary Corps 'were mostly old men, though some of them did good service, particularly General Hammerstein'.[67]

In his report on the fight at Famars, Scharnhorst softened his harsh criticism. After presenting a very detailed account of the action, he simply stated the obvious – 'in every battle errors of some kind are inevitable'.[68] A lack of good intelligence and communications between senior leaders during the battle was the main source of these mistakes and missed opportunities.[69] Too many essential details (such as coordination between infantry

62 Randolph (ed.), *Life of General Sir Robert Wilson* Vol.1, p.59. In his analysis of coalition forces, Fortescue, *British Campaigns in Flanders*, pp.179-81, 185-88, 197-98, and 200, spoke of the 'undisciplined and raw recruits' England had sent to the continent, as well as the 'hard drinking' and overall lack of discipline 'especially among the officers'. The quoted passages are from pp.185 and 200. Interestingly, Corporal Brown, *An Impartial Journal of a Detachment from the Brigade of Foot Guards*, never mentions any drinking or lack of discipline among British troops in 1793.

63 Letter of 21-24 May 1793 to Klara; in Kunisch (ed.), *Scharnhorst: Privat und dienstliche Schriften*, Vol.1, p.215. Ompteda, *A Hanoverian-English Officer*, pp.51-53, arrived at a similar conclusion regarding the fight at Famars. A good illustration of this action can be found in Sketch Map 2 'Camp at Famars' (opposite p. 49); in Burne, *The Noble Duke of York*.

64 For Scharnhorst's critical analysis of the fight at Famars, see his Letter of 5 June 1793 (most likely to Jakob Mauvillon in Brunswick); in Kunisch (ed.), *Scharnhorst: Privat und dienstliche Schriften*, Vol.1, pp.220-25; the quoted passage is from p.223. Those who compiled Scharnhorst's papers believe this letter was addressed to Mauvillon, since a copy of it was found in Mauvillon's papers in 1823. See Note 2 (p.220). On the upper right-hand corner of this letter is written, 'Tell no one about the contents of this letter'.

65 See the interesting commentary in Ernest Taylor (ed.), *The Taylor Papers, Being a Record of Certain Reminiscences, Letters, and Journals in the Life of Lieut-Gen Sir Herbert Taylor* (London: Longmans, Green and Co., 1913), p.29.

66 See James Harris, *Diaries and Correspondence of James Harris, First Earl of Malmesbury* (London: Richard Bentley, 1844), Vol.3, p.19.

67 Taylor (ed.), *The Taylor Papers*, pp.29-30. For a contrary view, see Bernard Poten, 'Die Generale der Königlich Hannoverischen Armee und ihrer Stammtruppen', *Beihefte zum Militär-Wochenblatt* (1903), pp.243-334.

68 Gerhard Scharnhorst, 'Relation der Schlacht bey Famars, den 23ten May 1793, zwischen der verbundenen Armee unter Anführung des Prinzen von Colburg und der französischen unter den Befehl des General La Marck' (after 23 May 1793); in Kunisch (ed.), *Scharnhorst: Privat und dienstliche Schriften*, Vol.1, pp.225-31; the quoted passage is from p.230. A nice map of this engagement can be found in Ludwig von Estorff, 'Von der hannoverschen Armee in den Revolutionskriegen 1793-1795', *Zeitschrift des historischen Vereins für Niedersachsen* (1906), p.50.

69 Ompteda, *A Hanoverian-English Officer*, pp.44-54, agreed completely with Scharnhorst's assessment. Also see Anon., *A Narrative of the War by an Officer of the Guards*, Vol.1, pp.46-54.

and cavalry units, and especially with their artillery support) were not clearly specified. On the other hand, the French conducted their defence 'in a clever way'.[70]

Scharnhorst praised the bravery and performance of the junior leaders and soldiers during the fight at Famars. 'Overall, the attack was executed without disorder, following a well-designed plan'.[71] Even though he clearly understood the need for discretion here, Scharnhorst just had to tell Klara of an incident 'carefully concealed' in the official Hanoverian report on the battle.[72] 'No one must know this', he warned her sternly.[73] While engaged in an artillery duel with French gunners, 15 crews from the 2. Division Artillerie, together with their cannon and ammunition trains, suddenly panicked and fled the battlefield. They had to be brought back to the fight by the cavalry they were supporting.[74] Scharnhorst told his wife he was thankful he was not part of the 2. Division.[75]

Scharnhorst refused to condone the murderous acts of Coalition soldiers. What really angered him was the callous attitude and conduct of some senior officers who excused and even inspired such atrocities. One English prince thought war was sport. In his letter of 3 May 1793, Prince Ernest Augustus (1771-1851), the eighth child of George III and later the Duke of Cumberland and King of Hanover (1837-51), told his father about a brief action against the French, and how 'I embraced with the greatest eagerness ye opportunity of sharing in the sport'.[76] As Scharnhorst told Klara, 'Prince Ernest is very angry with the French. Several times he has rebuked the troops for taking prisoners; they should have massacred them. It is dreadful to see murdered people everywhere'.[77] At the end of the

70 Scharnhorst, 'Relation der Schlacht bey Famars, den 23ten May 1793'; in Kunisch (ed.), *Scharnhorst: Privat und dienstliche Schriften*, Vol.1, p.231.

71 Scharnhorst, 'Relation der Schlacht bey Famars, den 23ten May 1793'; in Kunisch (ed.), *Scharnhorst: Privat und dienstliche Schriften*, Vol.1, p.230. Also see the recollections of Brown, *An Impartial Journal of a Detachment from the Brigade of Foot Guards*, who wrote on p.20 that 'the Hanoverian flying artillery' were among the troops which displayed the most valor and activity. 'It was a glorious fight', Brown concluded on p.21.

72 See Explanatory Note 3 to Scharnhorst's Letter of 1-3 June 1793 to Klara; in Kunisch (ed.), *Scharnhorst: Privat und dienstliche Schriften*, Vol.1, pp.216-19; the quoted passage can be found on p.217.

73 Scharnhorst's Letter of 1-3 June 1793 to Klara; in Kunisch (ed.), *Scharnhorst: Privat und dienstliche Schriften*, Vol.1, pp.216-19; the quoted passage is from p.217 (1 June).

74 Prussian *Major* August von Witzleben discussed this event in his study, *Prinz Friedrich Josias von Coburg-Saalfeld, Herzog zu Sachsen* (Berlin: R. Decker, 1859), Vol.2, p.202. He noted that Prussian *Oberstlieutenant* Bogislav Friedrich Emanuel Graf von Tauentzien (1760-1824) had reported this incident in his letter to the Prussian king; however, Witzleben also stated neither Prince Coburg nor the Duke of York cited it in their official accounts. While never mentioning this occurrence, Sichart, *Geschichte der Königlich-Hannoverischen Armee*, Vol.4, p.222, stated that after the battle the Duke of York singled-out 'the officers and men of the Artillery Regiment with special praise'. Interestingly, John Hill noted on p. 53 of *A Hanoverian-English Officer*, that Ompteda's account of the action 'corrects' the commentary by Witzleben, 'especially the incorrect statement about the Hanoverian artillery, p.202'.

75 Letter of 1-3 June 1793 to Klara; in Kunisch (ed.), *Scharnhorst: Privat und dienstliche Schriften*, Vol.1, p.217 (1 June).

76 Letter of 3 May 1793 from Prince Ernest Augustus to King George III; in Aspinall (ed), *The Later Correspondence of George III*, Vol.2, pp.35-36; the quoted passage is from p.35. Prince Ernest commanded the Hanoverian 9. Leichte Dragoner Regiment.

77 Letter of 25 July 1793 to Klara; in Kunisch (ed.), *Scharnhorst: Privat und dienstliche Schriften*, Vol.1, pp.244-45; the quoted passage is from p.244. Writing to his father six months earlier on 7 February 1793, Ernest wished 'we were already in Holland, and that those murderers had received a complete drubbing'. See Aspinall (ed), *The Later Correspondence of George III*, Vol.2, p.3. In his memoirs, Randolph (ed.), *Life of General Sir Robert Wilson*, Vol.1, pp.87-88, Cornet Wilson recalled the 'disgusting slaughter of prisoners' at Roubaix.

day, following the carnage he witnessed, and with foreboding in his heart, he told Klara, 'God, give us peace soon'.[78]

Cornet Wilson was also horrified by the plundering and rape perpetrated 'by battalions of barbarians'.[79] He recalled an inspiration by Austrian *General-Major* Rudolph Ritter von Otto (1735-1811), a cavalry commander who reminded his troops, 'Gentlemen! remember, your numbers do not permit prisoners'. Wilson then described how English and Austrian squadrons responded to Otto's speech with 'enthusiastic cheers', as they galloped forward with sabres 'pointed to the sky, as if appealing to Heaven as witness of their plighted faith'.[80]

'God, what a life this is!' Scharnhorst exclaimed to his wife during the endless bombardment of Valenciennes. 'Everything with the military is just devastation!'[81] As he watched the wanton destruction of Valenciennes, Scharnhorst was convinced of the importance of *Bildung*.[82] 'The man without *Bildung*', he wrote to Mauvillon, referring to the plundering of villages in Flanders, 'is surely a genuine beast, an inhuman animal … In general, I have found that only well-educated people sought to alleviate the horrors of war, and that uneducated officers were just as bestial as the rank and file'.[83]

A day earlier he had told his wife the same thing: 'The man without *Bildung* is surely an inhuman animal'.[84] The ignorance and depravity that plagued Coalition troops was just so appalling to Scharnhorst. 'Most of the time the English gave no quarter to prisoners. Likewise, the Austrian hussars rarely pardoned prisoners'.[85] 'Instances of cruelty committed

78 Letter of 21-24 May 1793 to Klara; in Kunisch (ed.), *Scharnhorst: Privat und dienstliche Schriften*, Vol.1, pp.214-16; the quoted passage is from p.216 (24 May).

79 See Randolph (ed.), *Life of General Sir Robert Wilson*, Vol.1, pp.63-64; the quoted passage is from p.63. Also see a similar recollection in the Note on p.53 of Vol.1 of Anon., *A Narrative of the War by an Officer of the Guards*. Corporal Brown, *An Impartial Journal from the Brigade of Foot Guards*, p.22, claimed 'foreign troops' were those who plundered 'without hinderance' [sic], because British soldiers 'were always strictly forbidden to plunder'. He added on p.24, 'Every house was plundered in a most unfeeling manner, by the Austrians and others of the foreign troops'. Foreign Office Secretary Taylor, *The Taylor Papers*, p.30, remembered how: 'The Hanoverian Infantry were great plunderers also, and indeed so were the British'.

80 Randolph (ed.), *Life of General Sir Robert Wilson*, Vol.1, p.66..

81 Letter of 25 July 1793 to Klara; in Kunisch (ed.), *Scharnhorst: Privat und dienstliche Schriften*, Vol.1, pp.244-45; the quoted passages are from p.244. A similar conclusion can be found in Ompteda, *A Hanoverian-English Officer*, pp.57-59, 62, and 65. Ompteda blamed the French Minister of Police, Charles Cochen de Lapparent (1750-1825), for the unnecessary hardship he caused both sides by not surrendering Valenciennes earlier, when all hope of relief had vanished.

82 Scharnhorst's thoughts on the importance of *Bildung* are apparent in the perspective of Austrian *Chef der Artillerie*, Leopold Freiherr von Unterberger, *Tagebuch der Belagerung und Bombardirung der französischen Festung Valenciennes, durch die Kaiserlichen Königlichen, Königlichen Englischen und Chur-Hannöverischen Truppen, im Monat Junius und Julius, des Jahres 1793* (Vienna: Carl Ferdinand Beck, 1815). Unterberger's diary provides not only an excellent account of this siege, but also reveals the callous disregard for lives and property that possessed Unterberger and other coalition leaders who ordered the destructive bombardment.

83 Letter of 5 June 1793 (most likely to Jacob Mauvillon); in Kunisch (ed.), *Scharnhorst: Privat und dienstliche Schriften*, Vol.1, pp.220-26; the quoted passage is from p.224.

84 Letter of 4 and 5 June 1793 to Klara; in Kunisch (ed.), *Scharnhorst: Privat und dienstliche Schriften*, Vol.1, pp.219-20; the quoted passage is from p.219 (4 June). On the back of this letter Scharnhorst told his wife to guard it with care.

85 Letter of 5 June 1793 (most likely to Jacob Mauvillon); in Kunisch (ed.), *Scharnhorst: Privat und dienstliche Schriften*, Vol.1, p.224. For an English rebuttal, see Anon., *A Narrative of the War by an Officer of the Guards*, Vol.1, pp.58-80. On pp.72-73, this Officer of the Guards noted 'Englishmen are brave and generous', while 'those savages, who always form part of every German army', are 'so shockingly depraved' and 'capable of every wanton and atrocious act of cruelty'.

by the Austrian hussars on disabled prisoners were frequent in the campaign of 1793', wrote one Englishman who agreed with Scharnhorst.[86]

Earlier, Scharnhorst had told Klara, 'I can well pride myself that nobody knows the connection here better than I do. Here are such awfully stupid and cowardly people', referring to the 2. Division of Hanoverian Heavy Artillery.[87] At the same time he did not hesitate to admit to his wife that he was 'ashamed to say that I almost find pleasure in this infamous occupation. But my reason punishes me, and my longing for honour is satisfied even less then in times of peace'.[88] This inner conflict between primal delight in malicious violence and destruction, and Enlightenment notions of reason and conscience, was a constant theme in Scharnhorst's correspondence.

Doubts about his Enlightenment beliefs in reason and virtue gnawed at Scharnhorst's conscience. On one occasion he arrived at Gierle, a small village not far from Antwerp, late in the evening of 25 April. After a march of nearly 10 hours, he was tired and sought a place to rest. A Catholic priest was kind enough to offer him a room. As he prepared for sleep, the peaceful tranquillity of the local inhabitants did not escape his keen observation. He was intrigued by the charity they showed toward strangers.[89] The pleasant, joyful, and detached life of these priests and people of the Catholic Brabant was vastly different from his Protestant experience in Hanover.[90]

'It is a wonderful thing about religion', Scharnhorst told Klara, 'One is always ready, without feeling for what is right and wrong, to abandon oneself to the loving God!' Then, reflecting on his own miserable condition, he lamented, 'It makes me sad to see that the events of the world do not harmonize at all with reason'. Scharnhorst was most likely questioning whether the educated person was truly the master of his own destiny, as Leibnitz and so many other philosophers of the Enlightenment alleged.[91] Perhaps faith, as the Catholic Church taught, was much more than just a private matter confined to the individual heart and mind. What Scharnhorst observed in the ordinary and pious people of Gierle, even in the face of danger, was an inner joy and peace that radiated from them to others around them.[92] Their outward charity and humility towards others clearly impressed Scharnhorst. Faith was no private matter for the Catholic citizens of Gierle. This made Scharnhorst wonder if some 'divine forces' were at work here.[93]

86 See Anon., *A Concise Narrative of all the Actions*, p.37.

87 Letter of 1-3 June 1793 to Klara; in Kunisch (ed.), *Scharnhorst: Privat und dienstliche Schriften*, Vol.1, pp.216-19; the quoted passage is from p.217 (1 June 1793).

88 Letter of 28 August 1793 to Klara; in Kunisch (ed.), *Scharnhorst: Privat und dienstliche Schriften*, Vol.1, pp.252-53; the quoted passage is from p.252.

89 Letter of 21-29 April 1793 to Klara; in Kunisch (ed.), *Scharnhorst: Privat und dienstliche Schriften*, Vol.1, pp.205-08.

90 See the commentary on this in Hornung, *Scharnhorst*, p.43. In 1793, the Duchy of Brabant was an independent state of the Holy Roman Empire.

91 Letter of 21-29 April 1793 to Klara; in Kunisch (ed.), *Scharnhorst: Privat und dienstliche Schriften*, Vol.1, pp.205-08; the quoted passages are from p.207 (25 April).

92 'Priests and religious communities were the marked objects of their [the French] ravage, and exposed to frequent butchery', wrote the anonymous author of *A Concise Narrative of all the Actions*, p.49. Scharnhorst made a similar comment to Klara on 25 April; in Kunisch (ed.), *Scharnhorst: Privat und dienstliche Schriften*, Vol.1, p.207.

93 Letter of 25 April 1793 to Klara; in Kunisch (ed.), *Scharnhorst: Privat und dienstliche Schriften*, Vol.1, p.207.

As he continued to ponder his situation, Scharnhorst was so delighted that the soldier's life on campaign was not the regimented drudgery of garrison life. 'I love our way of life each day more than I otherwise did', he told Klara on 25 April.[94] In the field he felt an independence that truly delighted and inspired him. He wondered if perhaps it was those 'divine forces' at work within him. When describing his daily activities to his family, he told them about the wonderful people he met, the interesting sights he saw, and his impressions about both. He also discussed his convictions about war, and how this conflict affected the behaviour of people. He observed how Braun 'provides only for himself', while Trew 'never visits us'.[95] Scharnhorst understood military leadership demanded much more.

At Hondschoote, Scharnhorst had set a fine example of leadership rarely seen in the standing professional army of the absolutist state. As he was directing artillery fire, he noticed several frightened infantrymen wandering aimlessly without effective leadership. Instead of ignoring these frightened men, he placed Bonnivet in charge of the two cannon while he rode over to the infantrymen, dismounted, and placed one of their wounded on his horse. It was his first time on foot under fire, and Scharnhorst seemed to cherish the moment, especially as he reassured the men around him. As he did this, he was at eye level with these soldiers – an essential leadership trait seldom seen in the professional standing army of the absolutist state. 'I told the troops to pay attention to me, and to follow me', he told Klara. His kindness toward one of their wounded must have been a sight to behold. When did any officer in the Hanoverian army ever dismount, place a wounded soldier on his horse, and then lead on foot? Scharnhorst did, and as he informed his wife, 'Everything went well'. The infantrymen remained with him. As the situation deteriorated, he acted to save these men. 'I had no order to stay, so I led only the infantry out'.[96]

In nearly every occasion, Scharnhorst was polite and hospitable, and his behaviour attracted the attention of others. Because he was an 'extra' with no specific duties, he was able to mingle freely with not only Hanoverians, but also with Englishmen, Austrians, Hessians, and Prussians. Interestingly, Scharnhorst seldom associated with any of his peers in the other artillery divisions. In fact, it appears he endeavoured to avoid them as much as possible, since he had little in common with these men. Instead, he regularly visited the artillery subalterns who commanded the guns assigned to the various infantry and cavalry units, many of whom he had taught at the artillery school. He wanted to see how they were doing, to assist them wherever possible, and to learn first-hand the importance artillery played in combined arms operations, which reinforced his pre-war views. Because of their low rank and position, Trew and other officers of the artillery regiment routinely ignored them.

While on these journeys he made friends easily with his fellow officers from the infantry and cavalry, and often told Klara of these contacts: 'Yesterday [4 May] five officers from the Guards wanted me to come by and visit them. I was unable to speak with them, as I was

94 Letter of 25 April 1793 to Klara; in Kunisch (ed.), *Scharnhorst: Privat und dienstliche Schriften*, Vol.1, p.207.

95 For his comment on Braun, see his Letter of 30 March 1793 to Klara; in Kunisch (ed.), *Scharnhorst: Privat und dienstliche Schriften*, Vol.1, p.201. For his comment on Trew, see his Letter of 17-19 July 1793 to his wife; in Kunisch (ed.), *Scharnhorst: Privat und dienstliche Schriften*, Vol.1, p.240 (17 July).

96 Letter of 'after' 8 September 1793 to Klara; in Kunisch (ed.), *Scharnhorst: Privat und dienstliche Schriften*, Vol.1, p.259.

on my way to Mechelen, a large town 1.5 miles from here'.[97] So, a couple of days later, those officers came looking for Scharnhorst. As he told Klara:

> Yesterday morning [8 May], shortly after I had eaten, a party of guard officers whom I had passed on the way to Mechelen came by. Together we visited the local churches and monasteries and saw the eleven guns captured from the French on the 2nd of May.[98]

Scharnhorst often visited the forward outposts to check on the soldiers there. With the exception of *General-Major* Hammerstein, most officers in the Hanoverian Auxiliary Corps ignored their men on outpost duty. On one occasion, Scharnhorst was '300 paces from enemy sharpshooters' and seemed to enjoy this dangerous experience, as he told his wife.[99]

Later that summer Scharnhorst wrote to Klara's aunt, thanking her for the gifts she had sent and relating another interesting incident that certainly thrilled him.

> Once [late July] I came upon a battery where the Austrian captain had asked about me. He knew of me because he had read my books. He was also a professor, as was the battery commander next to him. Together we laughed and drank some wine.[100]

Imagine, Scharnhorst told his aunt, three professors meeting on a battlefield, reminiscing, and drinking some wine together.

His fluency in French was also noticed. Scharnhorst devoted at least an hour a day to his French studies and hoped this knowledge would be useful to the army.[101] Neither German nor English was spoken in Belgium. When Prince Adolphus travelled to various locations in Flanders on sensitive missions, and needed someone who understood French, Scharnhorst accompanied him. They spoke freely on a variety of issues, and Scharnhorst remembered how the Prince was 'exceedingly kind to me'.[102] Years later, when Prince Adolphus was being groomed to command the Hanoverian army, he asked Scharnhorst to mentor him as he pursued more advanced military studies. Following the capitulation of Valenciennes, Scharnhorst also had the opportunity to use his knowledge of French when his fellow officers were questioning French prisoners of war. The calm demeanour of these

97 Letter of 5-12 May 1793 to Klara; in Kunisch (ed.), *Scharnhorst: Privat und dienstliche Schriften*, Vol.1, p.209-14; the quoted passage is from p.210 (5 May). 'Here' was the small village of Duffel, where the Hanoverians camped in early May 1793.

98 Letter of 5-12 May 1793 to Klara; in Kunisch (ed.), *Scharnhorst: Privat und dienstliche Schriften*, Vol.1, p.209-14; the quoted passage is from p.211 (9 May). These guns were most likely captured during the outpost fight at Rumes. See Sichart, *Geschichte der Königlich-Hannoverischen Armee*, Vol.4, pp.207-08.

99 Letter of 30 June 1793 to Klara; in Kunisch (ed.), *Scharnhorst: Privat und dienstliche Schriften*, Vol.1, p p.235-36; the quoted passage is from p.235.

100 Letter of 'after' 1 August 1793 (most likely to Klara's aunt); in Kunisch (ed.), *Scharnhorst: Privat und dienstliche Schriften*, Vol.1, pp.247-49; the quoted passage is from p.248.

101 See his Letter of 21-29 April 1793; in Kunisch (ed.), *Scharnhorst: Privat und dienstliche Schriften*, Vol.1, p.206 (21 April), in which he told Klara about his French studies.

102 Letter of 5-12 May 1793; in Kunisch (ed.), *Scharnhorst: Privat und dienstliche Schriften*, Vol.1, pp.209-10; the quoted passage is from p.210 (5 May).

Frenchmen, especially their forthright answers to questions about the Revolution and their republican government, convinced Scharnhorst and others that not everyone in France was a Jacobin.[103]

From the beginning of the deployment he described to Klara the many hardships of the march. It is 'the worst ordeal for an artillery officer'. A typical day's movement commenced shortly after sunrise and ended just before sunset. Whenever difficulties arose along the way, it was almost always *Titular-Capitain* Gerhard Scharnhorst who ended up taking charge, because the 'lazy major' (*Major* Johann August Bonsack, Commander of the 1. Division Artillerie) and 'the totally worthless captain' [Braun], 'who fashions himself a God', did nothing. Most of the challenges arose from the poor roads, sometimes bad weather, the lack of food and forage, but mostly from the excessive baggage train, which included two unmarried women who accompanied Bonsack's division. 'I am totally exhausted', Scharnhorst told his wife just a week into the deployment.[104]

In late April 1793, infantrymen from the grenadier companies of the Garde and 10. Infanterie Regiment refused to move until they were paid. These were the soldiers selected from each battalion to man and operate the three-pound cannons that supported their battalion. For this additional duty they received extra pay.[105] When they failed to receive their money as promised, they refused to move, and the column came to a halt.[106] *Lieutenant* Ompteda was sent to report this incident to the Duke of York, who promptly left his headquarters at Tournai and rode over 50 miles to the scene. His unexpected arrival clearly surprised officers and men alike. Using a translator, York spoke graciously to the disgruntled troops, promised them they would be paid, and requested they 'conduct themselves like good soldiers and brave fellows'.[107] The next day – 25 April, Ompteda was delighted when the 'Articles of War' were read aloud to the assembled grenadiers 'with the utmost military solemnity', and this (according to Ompteda) 'brought everything back into its previous order'.[108] In a general order dated 26 April, York awarded these men their entitlements.

Upon learning of this incident, Scharnhorst was beside himself. He told Klara it was all about officers upholding 'their authority' and not about caring for the health and welfare of their men. He prayed that God would prevent 'the spirit of unrest' from afflicting his artillerymen, since there was disquiet amongst the artillery and train as well. He also implored the Almighty 'that in the future those in senior leadership positions would

103 Letter of 29 July 1793 to Klara; in Kunisch (ed.), *Scharnhorst: Privat und dienstliche Schriften*, Vol.1, pp.245-47. Ompteda, *A Hanoverian-English Officer*, pp.62 and 65-66, was also relieved to find Frenchmen opposed to the revolutionary government in Paris.

104 Letter of 30 March 1793 to Klara; in Kunisch (ed.), *Scharnhorst: Privat und dienstliche Schriften*, Vol.1, pp.201-03; the quoted passages are from pp.201 and 203; respectively.

105 See the explanation of this practice in Hofschroer, *The Hanoverian Army of the Napoleonic Wars*, p.6.

106 See Scharnhorst's Letter of 21-29 April 1793 to Klara; in Kunisch (ed.), *Scharnhorst: Privat und dienstliche Schriften*, Vol.1, p.208 (29 April). On pp.32-33 of his memoirs, Ompteda, *A Hanoverian-English Officer*, recalled this 'spirit of insubordination' among the grenadiers of the 10. Infanterie Regiment.

107 The quoted passage is from Ompteda, *A Hanoverian-English Officer*, p.33. Also see the explanation by the Duke of York in his Letter of 26 April 1793 to King George III; in Aspinall (ed), *The Later Correspondence of George III*, Vol.2, pp.31-32.

108 Ompteda, *A Hanoverian-English Officer*, p.34.

prevent this misfortune from happening again, by treating their men with dignity and respect'.[109]

In his report, York agreed with Scharnhorst. The Duke of York told to his father that before he addressed the soldiers, he had met with their officers, 'who seemed more vexed and affected than be described'. He informed King George 'that even before they left Hanover', the men knew they 'were to receive English pay'. When one soldier mentioned this aloud to his comrades, 'one of the Officers was obliged to order him to be silent, and threatened him with a very severe punishment if he uttered another word upon the subject'. When they received Hanoverian instead of English pay, the men initially accepted it. Later, after being 'very ill treated' [sic] and not fed on two occasions', they revolted. York attributed this to 'the smallness of their pay', which had prevented the grenadiers from purchasing adequate food for themselves.[110] Why soldiers had to purchase their own food was never clarified in the Duke's letter. Nevertheless, it was clear that the leadership of the Hanoverian Auxiliary Corps failed to feed its own troops and then sought to quiet them when they complained.

This incident provides an ideal opportunity to assess military leadership within Coalition forces. The attitude and conduct of aristocratic officers like *Lieutenant* von Ompteda really infuriated Scharnhorst. As he told his wife, these noblemen should have acted as leaders and should have been concerned for the welfare of their soldiers. Had they cared about their men this unpleasant situation could have been avoided. It was obvious to Scharnhorst that regard for the welfare of the common soldier was not a responsibility of leadership taught to young aristocrats, nor was it part of their social upbringing.[111] The idea that the nobleman was a gentleman who served humanity (which is the original meaning of the word 'noble'), and which Scharnhorst had experienced under Count Wilhelm, was nowhere to be found in the world view of Ompteda.[112] Judging by his memoirs, Ompteda's accident of birth clearly did not make him a gentleman. Indeed, he applauded the stern measures taken to bring 'everything back into its previous order'. Upholding rigid class distinctions, while maintaining strict order and discipline among the troops, seemed to be the Hanoverian way.

Significantly, throughout the campaign the Duke of York tried sincerely to demonstrate sound leadership. In this case he believed 'the affair was so pressing' that he ordered Freytag to halt the Hanoverian column at Mechelen 'for a few days' so he could have them resupplied from Bruges.[113] The Duke told his father that the lack of bread and forage had caused severe hardship for the Hanoverians and made it difficult to maintain good order and

109 Letter of 21-29 April 1793 to Klara; in Kunisch (ed.), *Scharnhorst: Privat und dienstliche Schriften*, Vol.1, pp.205-08; the quoted passages are from p.208 (29 April).

110 See the fascinating commentary of York to his father on 26 April 1793; in Aspinall (ed), *The Later Correspondence of George III*, Vol.2, pp.31-32; the quoted passages are from p.31. Significantly, the extremely poor leadership of the Hanoverians is not mentioned in any of the German sources.

111 See the discussion on this topic in Fox, 'Conservative Accommodation to Revolution', pp.71-77.

112 Ompteda, *A Hanoverian-English Officer*, pp.4-9, wrote about his upbringing and education, which included attending Göttingen, 'indisputably the dearest University in Germany'. From what he stated, there was no rigor in his studies at Göttingen; he attended whatever classes he wished (and whenever he wished), without any responsibility to perform. His later apprenticeship at court focused solely on the social polish required of a young debutant. Throughout his memoirs Ompteda never mentioned any ideal of service except that owed to his own class and to his prince.

113 See the commentary of the Duke of York on 26 April 1793 to his father; in Aspinall (ed), *The Later Correspondence of George III*, Vol.2, pp.31-32; the quoted passages are from p.32.

discipline. Later on 30 April, when the Hanoverians reached Tournai, the Duke again had them rest for a few days, 'to let them recover a little from the long march which they have had'.[114] He had them paid and resupplied, and on 3 May, he told King George: 'I am very happy to inform your Majesty that everything appears now perfectly quiet'.[115]

What is remarkable and truly significant about this 'mutiny' is the fine example of leadership the Duke of York exhibited. Upon learning of the discontent among his Hanoverian soldiers, York rode directly to them and personally assessed the situation. He spoke politely but firmly with the unhappy troops and then took the necessary steps to ensure they were promptly paid, fed, and resupplied. When they reached his location, he again had them fed, rested, and resupplied. Threatening the men by reading them the articles of war may have been Freytag's solution. If so, this certainly increased the strain that already existed between the Duke of York and Freytag.[116]

The Duke of York was trying his best to be a good leader. As the second son of George III, the prince was formally educated and trained for military leadership. Before 1793 he had served with both the British and Hanoverian armies and had spent more than six years in Hanover (from 1781 to 1787), traveling throughout the land, attending lectures at Göttingen, visiting neighbouring states and introducing himself, and attending the annual manoeuvres of the Hanoverian, Prussian, and Austrian armies. The Duke knew first-hand how these armies operated. Under the expert tutelage of his famous uncle, Duke Karl Wilhelm Ferdinand of Brunswick-Wolfenbüttel (1735-1806), young Frederick had learned the strategy and tactics of eighteenth-century warfare. His uncle also gave him a personal tour of the battlefield at Minden. Additionally, it was Duke Karl who introduced his nephew to Frederick the Great, who was impressed with the young prince. The pinnacle of his military training came in 1785, when Frederick the Great invited him to attend the grand manoeuvres of the Prussian army in Silesia.

The Duke of York was an active soldier who brought a great deal of personal energy and diligence to his work. Even though the king's ministers objected to York's appointment as commander of the British and Hanoverian troops (due mainly to his youth and lack of combat experience), King George knew his son's royal standing as a British prince (as well as the son-in-law of Britain's ally, King Friedrich Wilhelm II of Prussia) was essential when working with other Coalition leaders. Undeniably, 'high social rank counted for a great deal' within the Coalition.[117] During the Flanders campaign, York endeavoured to do his best under very trying conditions, and to make life more tolerable for the newly-recruited soldiers under his command.[118]

114 Letter of 30 April 1793 from the Duke of York to King George III; in Aspinall (ed), *The Later Correspondence of George III*, Vol.2, p.34.

115 Letter of 3 May 1793 from the Duke of York to King George III; in Aspinall (ed), *The Later Correspondence of George III*, Vol.2, p.34-35; the quoted passage is from p.34.

116 Sichart, *Geschichte der Königlich-Hannoverischen Armee*, Vol.4, pp.204-09, provides a wonderful summary of the cool relationship between Freytag and York throughout the campaign.

117 See the important discussion on this topic in Derek Winterbottom, *The Grand Old Duke of York: A Life of Prince Frederick, Duke of York and Albany, 1763-1827* (South Yorkshire: Pen & Sword Military, 2016), p.51.

118 See the discussion in Limm, 'Fairly Out-Generaled and Disgracefully Beaten, pp.8-10. Few good biographies of York exist. For a nice, although clearly biased study (complete with beautiful sketch maps) that seeks to re-examine

On the other hand, after serving admirably under Frederick the Great during the Seven Years War, the 73-year-old Freytag spent the next 30 years as 'aide de camp and close confidant' of the Duke's father.[119] He travelled regularly to Hanover to update King George on his German dominions. Freytag was the ultimate courtier, and for his reward King George placed him in command of the Hanoverian army on 6 December 1792, and then promoted him on 22 February 1793 to field marshal.[120] Ironically, Freytag had become the king's military aide the year that York was born, had seen the prince grow up, and clearly resented taking orders from someone so young and without any wartime experience.[121] So, as the Hanoverian Auxiliary Corps marched to war in March 1793, Freytag had not soldiered in 30 years.[122]

Here is also an opportune time to pause and assess the character of *Titular-Capitain* Gerhard Scharnhorst. In so many of his letters home, Scharnhorst complained about virtually everything, giving the impression that he had little practical field experience. The fact that he was totally exhausted after just one week in the field is ample proof. In many of his letters home he appeared self-centred, blaming others (including his wife Klara) for the unpleasant circumstances around him. His obsession with promotion and obtaining a company command constantly occupied his thoughts. Yet while Scharnhorst was quick to find fault in others, he seldom applied the same scrutiny to himself. This attitude clearly did not endear him to Trew and other artillery officers.

For more than a decade before Hanover deployed to fight in the War of the First Coalition, Scharnhorst was an instructor at the artillery school, while Bonsack, Ritter, and Braun, as well as most of the other officers of the artillery regiment, had spent the same time practicing their craft. They understood the needs and daily battle rhythm of the artilleryman in the field far better than did Scharnhorst. They also had years of practical gunnery experience, whereas whatever field experience and training Scharnhorst had most likely come from the academic 'laboratories' of the artillery school, together with the annual manoeuvres of the army. Yet, despite these shortcomings, it was *Titular-Capitain* Gerhard Scharnhorst who demonstrated the qualities of leadership required of an officer on campaign and in combat. These attributes he had learned at Wilhelmstein, at Northeim, and from studying books and imitating the examples of the great battle captains of the past he had read about in those books.

the Duke's tarnished reputation, see Burne, *The Noble Duke of York*. A more balanced narrative, yet still bias, is Winterbottom, *The Grand Old Duke of York*.

119 See Torsten Riotte, 'George III and Hanover', in Simms and Riotte (ed.), *The Hanoverian Dimension in British History*, pp.58-85: the quoted passage is from p.68.

120 See the biographical sketch of Freytag by Bernhard Poten, 'Freytag: Heinrich Wilhelm von Freytag', *Allgemeine Deutsche Biographie*, Vol.7, pp.374-76. In his Letter of 7 February 1793 to King George, Prince Ernest told his father: 'The whole army is rejoiced that your Majesty has given us General de Freytag to command us on this expedition'. See Aspinall (ed), *The Later Correspondence of George III*, Vol.2, p.3. Also see the source documents on Freytag in Hann 41, III, Nr.192: *Enthebung des Feldmarschalls von Reden vom Armeekommando und Übertragung desselben an den General von Freytag (1792), Avancement (Beförderung) des letzteren zum Feldmarschall (1793)*; deposited at the Niedersächsisches Landesarchiv, Hanover.

121 Demet, *'We are Accustomed to do our Duty'*, pp.26-27.

122 Interestingly, his Letter of 7 February 1793 to King George, Prince Ernest hoped that Freytag's health 'may not be injured by the excessive work' of commanding the Hanoverian Auxiliary Corps; in Aspinall (ed), *The Later Correspondence of George III*, Vol.2, p.3.

Unlike his fellow officers in the artillery, Scharnhorst refused to accept that appearance and personal loyalty (and not *Bildung*) meant everything to the hypocritical martinet Trew. This was the 'spit and polish' ethos that had moulded most European armies after the Seven Years War, following the example of Prussia and Frederick the Great. Most artillery officers were not the least impressed with the intellectual prowess or academic credentials of Scharnhorst. They looked for an officer of leisure like themselves. One would think Scharnhorst, with all his mental acumen, and who clearly understood this reality, would have taken the necessary steps to look sharp in uniform and to behave like a soldier on parade. He should have been more circumspect in his actions and should have known how to adapt himself to the dispositions of others. If this meant at times playing the role of 'slave' to Trew, then he should have learned how to grovel with dignity and style, without compromising his integrity or independence. Scharnhorst seems to have forgotten his first field experience with the 8. Dragoner Regiment, how he arrived in camp wholly unprepared and had to be counselled by his company commander.[123] Indeed, at that time *Fähndrich* Scharnhorst had been so embarrassed that he had turned to his uncle (and not to his father) for comfort and financial assistance.[124]

Scharnhorst certainly understood that troop duty was the legitimate path of advancement in the Hanoverian army. This is evident from his letters to his wife and his endless quest for a company command. Yet, his emphasis was clearly elsewhere. All too often he felt others should adopt his standards of behaviour and leadership. His unwillingness to conform to the traditional norms of the professional standing army (even if in appearance only), along with his avoidance of other artillery officers, definitely contributed to the isolation, anger, frustration, and disappointment *Titular-Capitain* Gerhard Scharnhorst experienced on campaign.

These observations about the character and behaviour of Scharnhorst are not meant to dismiss his keen analysis of Coalition leadership. In nearly every case he was correct in his assessment. Count Wilhelm represented to Gerhard Scharnhorst the supreme model of military leadership. Regrettably, few of his fellow officers ever heard of Count Wilhelm, and even fewer had any desire to follow his example. Therefore, while Scharnhorst sought to emulate Count Wilhelm, most Hanoverian officers willingly followed the ethos of their superiors and remained ignorant, unprofessional, and truly conceited.

Returning to the campaign, in many of his earliest letters Scharnhorst mentioned how well the officers, non-commissioned officers, and gun crews under his immediate charge were fed. 'We had chicken soup and a chicken, rice pudding, and smoked meat', he told Klara shortly after leaving Hanover.[125] Good German foods and drink filled their stomachs. This appears to contrast the plight of the Hanoverian infantrymen, whose leaders failed miserably to take care of their needs. After supper, Scharnhorst usually inspected the troops, checked the mail schedule, and then retired to his quarters to drink coffee and

123 See the important discussion on this mentality in Stübig, *Scharnhorst*, pp.24-25.

124 See his Letter of 24 May 1779 to Uncle Heinrich; in Kunisch (ed.), *Scharnhorst: Privat und dienstliche Schriften*, Vol.1, pp.44-46.

125 Letter of 30 March 1793 to Klara; in Kunisch (ed.), *Scharnhorst: Privat und dienstliche Schriften*, Vol.1, pp.201-03; the quoted passage is from p.201.

write home, often 'with tears' in his eyes.[126] On several occasions he described in detail the homes in which he was quartered, their exterior and interior designs, the various kinds of furniture, glassware, linen, interesting fixtures, and other items he thought would interest her and their children.

Once in Holland, the English commissary system failed to function well. Even though the English had told the Dutch the route the Hanoverians would take, the Dutch marched before schedule and took all of the supplies meant for the Hanoverians, thus causing great hardship for them.[127] Nourishment soon became a major concern, as Scharnhorst told his wife: 'I have already seen here in Holland that one must take care of one's own provisions. These past few days I have had to pay 1 Gulden every night, regardless of what food and beverages were served'. To remedy this situation, he bought a 21-pound ham, along with bacon and butter, and vowed that as soon as he returned to Holland, he would buy 'an entire [wheel of] cheese'.[128] As if to reassure his wife, he told Klara: 'I have not been sick at all, because a good diet is most often the best defence against illness, and I maintain a good diet. I drink no wine or brandy'.[129] If thirsty, Scharnhorst preferred coffee or tea, or a mixture of water with lime or lemon. On a special occasion – when he met some fellow professors – he would indulge himself with a glass of wine.

The lack of essential food and supplies became a major problem for the Hanoverians as they advanced through Holland into Belgium. From London, the British government insisted on presenting a veil of civility toward the Belgian people, as did the Austrian Emperor. Indeed, the Austrian government had even forbidden the construction of field fortifications, so as not to destroy the farmlands, orchards, meadows, and canals in Flanders.[130] Foraging was carefully monitored, and British officials paid Belgian citizens for any food and other essentials.

Regrettably, the English commissariat had not distributed funds to the Hanoverians so they could purchase what they required.[131] On several occasions York complained about this to his father. The Duke of York felt his Commissary General, Brook Watson (1735-1807), was far too cautious and deliberate, unwilling to adjust to the current situation.[132]

126 Letter of 21-29 April 1793 to Klara; in Kunisch (ed.), *Scharnhorst: Privat und dienstliche Schriften*, Vol.1, pp.205-09; the quoted passage is from p.207 (25 April).

127 See the Letter of 23 April 1793 from the Duke of York to King George III; in Aspinall (ed), *The Later Correspondence of George III*, Vol.2, p.30.

128 Letter of 'before' 21 April 1793 to Klara; in Kunisch (ed.), *Scharnhorst: Privat und dienstliche Schriften*, Vol.1, pp.204-05; the quoted passage is from p.204.

129 Letter of 5-12 May 1793 to Klara; in Kunisch (ed.), *Scharnhorst: Privat und dienstliche Schriften*, Vol.1, pp.209-14; the quoted passage is from p.211 (10 May).

130 See Ditfurth, *Die Hessen in den Feldzügen 1793, 1794 und 1795*, Vol.1, p.147.

131 See the fascinating account by the British Deputy Commissary General Havilland le Mesurier, *The British Commissary* (London: C. Roworth, 1801). This source reveals the practical experience of supplying an army in difficult circumstances. According to le Mesurier, Wallmoden and Dundas asked him to provide them details on how the Commissary should function in the field, so that lessons could be applied in future operations. The first draft of this book was completed in 1796 but kept confidential until its release in 1801. See the documentation in Hann 38 E, Nr.291/1 and 291/2: *Korrespondenz des Generals von Wallmoden mit dem englischen Generalkommissar Mr. le Mesurier über Verpflegungssachen der hannoverschen und der übrigen englischen Subsidientruppen*; deposited at the Niedersächsisches Landesarchiv, Hanover.

132 See the Letters of 17, 27, and 31 May 1793 from the Duke of York to King George III; in Aspinall (ed), *The Later Correspondence of George III*, Vol.2, pp.39, 43, and 45. Also see the documentation in Hann 38 E, Nr.297:

To Herbert Taylor (the young Foreign Office Secretary on the Duke's staff), Watson was 'a good methodical man of business', who worked chiefly through contractors. Herein lay the problem. As Taylor wrote: 'The principal contractor was Mr. Eckhardt, a Hanoverian Jew, a clever man who did his best for the army and *himself*, for he made a large fortune and became Baron von Eckhardstein'.[133] York felt that Watson was relying too much on his experience from the American War of Independence, when supplies to the army had come directly from England. To remedy this, the Duke had requested the Hanoverians make their state-of-the-art bakery available to Watson, and to upgrade it so it could serve 20,000 troops.[134] This proved unfortunate for the Hanoverians.

The English coveted the Hanoverian bakery. In his recollections, York's aide-de-camp, Captain Harry Calvert, described how 'His Majesty's Hanoverian kitchen joined us some time before we left Tournay, with an amazing retinue of cooks and laced footmen'. Clearly envying the Hanoverians, Calvert lamented how little the English had done to provision their expedition, expecting the host countries to provide food, shelter, and other necessities.[135] When York decided to keep the Hanoverian kitchen situated with his headquarters, he left the Hanoverians to fend for themselves.[136] Ironically, he told his father that it was the lack of cooked meat, food stuffs, and supplies – all of the items the kitchen provided – along with English money, that had caused the mutiny of the Hanoverian grenadiers. Interesting, he failed to mention that he had appropriated the Hanoverian kitchen.[137]

In early June, while encamped at Famars, Scharnhorst exclaimed to Klara, 'Everything here is so outrageously expensive!' His daily ration consisted of barley or rice with white fish for his noon meal, cheese and ham, with butter at suppertime. What he had for breakfast was never mentioned in his letters, nor were fruits and vegetables. 'We have coffee, but without milk; all of the cows have been slaughtered'. Wine and beer could be expensive, while bread was cheap. A wagon loaded with rice, salt, and other necessities arrived from Brussels on 1 June, and he made sure 'everything was sold immediately' to his men.[138]

Meanwhile, Austrian and Prussian soldiers were out gathering food and supplies at will. Following an exchange of some frank messages with British leaders, *Oberstlieutenant* Adolph Ludwig von Spörcken, the *General-Adjudant* to *Feldmarschall* Freytag, was able to proclaim in late May, 'Thank God! After two days, bread arrived yesterday evening'.[139] It seems that

Korrespondenz des Generals von Wallmoden mit dem englischen Commission General Brook Watson, 1794; deposited at the Niedersächsisches Landesarchiv, Hanover.

133 Taylor, *The Taylor Papers*, p.29. Scharnhorst would later have difficulties dealing with Eckhardt.

134 See the Letters of 22, 25, and 30 March 1793 from the Duke of York to King George III; in Aspinall (ed), *The Later Correspondence of George III*, Vol.2, pp.23-25.

135 See Sir Harry Verney (ed.), *The Journals and Correspondence of General Sir Harry Calvert, Comprising the Campaigns in Flanders and Holland in 1793-94* (London: Hurst and Blackett, 1853), p.80.

136 See the interesting documents that shed light on the plight of the Hanoverians; in Hann 38 E, Nr.295: *Berichte des Generals von Wallmoden an den Herzog von York über die vom englischen Kommissariat beschafften Rationen und Portionen im Feldzuge von 1793*; deposited at the Niedersächsisches Landesarchiv, Hanover.

137 See the Letter of 26 April 1793 from York to King George III; in Aspinall (ed), *The Later Correspondence of George III*, Vol.2, pp.31-32.

138 Letter of 1-3 June 1793 to Klara; in Kunisch (ed.), *Scharnhorst: Privat und dienstliche Schriften*, Vol.1, pp.216-19; the quoted passages are from p.216 (1 June).

139 This situation and the exchange of messages about the lack of food and money to pay for supplies can be found in Sichart, *Geschichte der Königlich-Hannoverischen Armee*, Vol.4, pp.227-28 (Note 1); the quoted passage is from

by the end of May, Watson had finally figured a way to keep the Hanoverians supplied with food from their own kitchen. Once foraging was approved, Scharnhorst wrote to Klara that he had spoken with 'a pair of regimental quartermasters' who were out gathering food and supplies. He wanted to make sure that the artillerymen supporting the various infantry and cavalry units received their fair share of sustenance.[140] Like many soldiers on campaign, Scharnhorst learned to adapt to whatever food was available. After the first few months, he seldom spoke of food, as other more pressing issues occupied his thoughts.

Scharnhorst's frustration with the caste-ridden Hanoverian military was a major recurring theme in his letters. During the two-month bombardment of Valenciennes, he poured out his wrath at the gross stupidity, ignorance, and injustice he saw happening all around him: 'Since prejudice governs us here, gallantry is no longer a virtue, while reason – this truly divine inspiration – is considered foolishness'.[141] These words provide additional proof Scharnhorst understood the world view and priorities of the Hanoverian army but refused to conform to these norms. They clearly contradicted his conscious and what he had learned at Wilhelmstein. Citing the blatant hypocrisy around him, he told Klara how soldiers were given 'a greater freedom of speech here' (in the face of the enemy); but this was mere pretence, he noted. Soldiers were not permitted to speak candidly or critically about anything, especially military operations. 'I see the inexpediency of many orders', he told Klara in early June, 'but dare not say a word'.[142]

Two officers of the Garde Regiment were not so discreet. After speaking their minds about the campaign, the siege of Valenciennes, and what they considered the fruitless operations of 'the Duke', *Capitains* G.C.U. von Mecklenburg and Georg Christoph Ludwig von Bülow had permitted their soldiers on two occasions to desert their posts in the trenches and return to their camps in the rear. Once in camp, these men encouraged others to do the same. When news of these incidents reached Wallmoden, he immediately informed Freytag and the Duke of York, noting the disparaging remarks and conduct of these two noblemen bordered on mutiny and treason. After discussing the situation with Freytag, York ordered both officers arrested and sent home, since 'Hanoverian Courts Martial are so exceedingly slow', and he did not want those officers in camp, nor did he want to usurp the prerogatives of the king.[143] Again, this prompt action by the Duke of York restored order in the regiment. Mecklenburg and Bülow remained under arrest in Hanover until 20 June 1794,

p.228. Interestingly, the day before the Battle of Famars, several Hanoverian generals had met with the Duke of York 'and had used the opportunity to complain about the lack of soldiers out foraging and gathering food'. See Sichart, *Geschichte der Königlich-Hannoverischen Armee*, Vol.4, p.221.

140 See his Letter of 5-12 May 1793 to Klara; in Kunisch (ed.), *Scharnhorst: Privat und dienstliche Schriften*, Vol.1, pp.209-14; the quoted passage is from p.210 (5 May).

141 Letter of 1-3 June 1793 to Klara; in Kunisch (ed.), *Scharnhorst: Privat und dienstliche Schriften*, Vol.1, pp.216-19; the quote passages is from p.217 (1 June).

142 Letter of 1-3 June 1793 to Klara; in Kunisch (ed.), *Scharnhorst: Privat und dienstliche Schriften*, Vol.1, pp.216-19; the quoted passages are from pp.217 (1 June) and 218 (3 June); respectively.

143 See the Letters of 5 and 19 July 1793 from the Duke of York to King George III; in Aspinall (ed.), *The Later Correspondence of George III*, Vol., pp.57-58 and 61; the quoted passage is from p.58 (5 July). King George's Letter of 12 July 1793 to Freytag acknowledging receipt of Freytag's report on this incident can be found in Wilhelm L.A. von Hassell, *Das Kurfürstentum Hannover vom Basler Frieden bis zur preussischen Occupation im Jahre 1806* (Hanover: Carl Meyer, 1894), p.138 (Note 1).

when they were dismissed from the service.[144] Significantly, Ompteda makes no mention of this flagrant misconduct by two fellow noblemen in his memoirs. Afterwards, *General-Major* Joachim Friedrich von dem Bussche-Ippenburg (1732-96), who led one of the wings of the Hanoverian Auxiliary Corps, visited Scharnhorst and other officers to remind them to guard their opinions and words carefully.[145]

After this episode King George wanted to relieve Prince Adolphus of his command of the Garde Regiment. In a letter of 23 July to the king, Adolphus convinced his father not to remove him, since such a move would only further hurt the morale 'of one of the finest Regiments of Infantry in your service'. He was afraid other officers would simply 'quit' the regiment out of shame that their commander was relieved.[146] Prince Adolphus explained to his father that his soldiers were not cowards nor malingerers, but recently inducted peasants without proper military training and discipline.[147] They were following the orders of their officers and non-commissioned officers, many of whom were themselves newly appointed and did not fully understand their duties and responsibilities. As the prince told his king, 'the number of young officers ... are almost children', while 'we were forced to make' non-commissioned officers 'who do not yet know their duty'. Of course, this was certainly not true of *Capitains* Mecklenburg and Bülow, who were not freshly-minted officers.

Prince Adolphus alleged the hasty recruitment and lack of proper training and discipline among the Hanoverians led to the current crisis of morale, as well as challenges to legitimate authority. He noted 'the second time [his soldiers left the trenches] all the detachments of the other Regiments also quitted'. As he told King George, 'we had not time enough to drill before we marched', and since then had 'such a hard service that we have not had a moment's time for exercising'.[148] 'I can venture to assure you that the Captains Mecklenbourg and Bulow are certainly not the immediate cause of this misbehaviour', Prince Adolphus told King George in closing his letter.[149]

Prince Adolphus was certainly correct in his assessment of the situation. Here is another fine example of what Scharnhorst had advocated time and again about the importance of a sound military *Bildung* for officers, non-commissioned officers, and soldiers alike; advice

144 See Scharnhorst's Letter of 8-12 July 1793 to Klara; in Kunisch (ed.), *Scharnhorst: Privat und dienstliche Schriften*, Vol.1, pp.237-39; especially p.238 (Note 3).

145 Letter of 8-12 July 1793 to Klara; in Kunisch (ed.), *Scharnhorst: Privat und dienstliche Schriften*, Vol.1, p.238. Documents relating to this incident are printed in Sichart, *Geschichte der Königlich-Hannoverischen Armee*, Vol.4, pp.119-26.

146 See the Letter of 23 July 1793 from Prince Adolphus to King George III; in Aspinall (ed.), *The Later Correspondence of George III*, Vol.2, pp.64-65; the quoted passages are from p.64.

147 Ompteda agreed with Prince Adolphus. Writing on p. 29 of *A Hanoverian-English Officer*, Ompteda noted 'the majority' of troops were 'freshly recruited peasant lads'. Interestingly, in his pre-war Letter of 7 February 1793 to his father, Prince Ernest had also mentioned the very poor quality 'of the vast number of recruits that fail'. See Aspinall (ed.), *The Later Correspondence of George III*, Vol.2, p.3. Also see the source documents relating to the recruitment and training of these soldiers in Hann 38 E, Nr.35: *Aushebung der Rekruten im Lande und Abgabe derselben an die marschierdenden Regimenter*; deposited at the Niedersächsisches Landesarchiv, Hanover.

148 Letter of 23 July 1793 from Prince Adolphus to King George III; in Aspinall (ed.), *The Later Correspondence of George III*, Vol.2, pp.64-65; the quoted passages are from p.64. Sichart, *Geschichte der Königlich-Hannoverischen Armee*, Vol. 4, pp.112-47, discusses the pre-war recruitment and training of the Hanoverians.

149 Letter of 23 July 1793 from Prince Adolphus to King George III; in Aspinall (ed.), *The Later Correspondence of George III*, Vol.2, pp.64-65; the quoted passage is from p.65.

that was largely ignored in the Hanoverian army and which had led to this unnecessary misfortune. The leadership of the Hanoverian Auxiliary Corps never took sufficient time and effort to mould their subordinate leaders and soldiers into a coherent and combat effective unit before marching off to war and while on campaign. Interestingly (and significantly), the French suffered from the same challenges of leadership with their *levée en masse*.[150] The major difference was the command climate in which coalition and French leaders operated. The French were not burdened by a policy of grooming aristocratic children as officers in their army, and ruthlessly removed and executed incompetent or unsuccessful leaders. The French also trained their recruits on the march, while the Hanoverians did not.

What also infuriated Scharnhorst during the siege of Valenciennes was the nonchalant attitude of officers who took no steps to stop the rape and murder of innocent locals, and the unwarranted pillage and destruction of their property. Interestingly, it was just a year earlier in his spirited defence of the professional standing army that Scharnhorst had stated one of its significant functions was the protection of people and their property. Now he watched helplessly as this very institution was responsible for the rape and murder, pillage and plunder, of people and their property. 'You know well my feelings', he told his wife as he watched in dismay the destruction of village after village in Flanders. 'It is not easy to view this war with impartial eyes'.[151]

Scharnhorst believed that the largely uneducated coalition officer corps was following what he described as 'the blind path of honour'. Honour to these mostly noble officers meant following orders instinctively, without question or applying any moral or ethical standard, or without considering the consequences of their actions.[152] Indeed, in nearly every case, there was no consequence for immoral or criminal behaviour. No system of military justice punished these perpetrators. Perhaps a proper military *Bildung* might have prevented this needless barbarism. Is it any wonder that during the Enlightenment there was a direct correlation between the educated middle class, its desire for rationality, its demand for education and reform, and its utter contempt for the uneducated nobleman? Ignorance was truly bliss within the leadership of the coalition army.

Following the Seven Years War, every European army had sought to learn from that conflict. Sadly, few coalition officers had studied their profession with any formality or conscientiousness during those 30 years of peace. Despite years of field exercises, few leaders on both sides had any idea how to conduct a campaign or fight a battle. Scharnhorst made this clear in his critical analysis of coalition operations after the fall of Valenciennes. He concluded that had British and Austrian leaders in 1793 'followed the example of Prince Eugene during the Campaign of 1708', when Eugene had besieged Lille (and not Valenciennes), they might have been able to reconquer Flanders and drive the French out, just as the Austrians and

150 In his intriguing study, *Bayonets of the Republic: Motivations and Tactics in the Army of Revolutionary France, 1791-94* (Chicago and Urbana: University of Illinois Press, 1984), John A. Lynn provides a fascinating account of how the French moulded their Armée du Nord into an effective military unit. This was the army that faced the Hanoverians in 1793.

151 Letter of 5-12 May 1793 to Klara; in Kunisch (ed.), *Scharnhorst: Privat und dienstliche Schriften*, Vol.1, pp.209-14; the quoted passages are from p.211 (9 May).

152 Letter of 5-12 May 1793 to Klara; in Kunisch (ed.), *Scharnhorst: Privat und dienstliche Schriften*, Vol.1, p.211 (9 May). The insight Scharnhorst made here about noblemen is often commonplace in the memoirs of Ompteda. Wilson also recognised this aristocratic tendency, but only years later after much reflection.

British had done under Eugene and Marlborough 85 years earlier.[153] Instead, it was the coalition that was now on the run.

After the disappointing end to the 1793 campaign in Flanders, Scharnhorst reflected a great deal on what had transpired. For him, history provided the answer.

> Anyone who has studied the art of war properly can learn a lot from this war. Everywhere I see mistakes, and I believe this is a reason why very good armies like ours, even against similar opposing ones, have not taken advantage of unforeseen opportunities as they should have done.[154]

It was clear to Scharnhorst that coalition leaders had no sense of the past, and this was why they failed miserably to take advantage of unforeseen opportunities. In all of his analyses, reports, and publications on the operations in Flanders, Scharnhorst cited historical examples to support his conclusions.[155]

The most valuable lesson Scharnhorst learned from the Flanders campaign was the importance of a sound, formal military education. In sharp contrast to previous ideas that all an army required to fight was the proper amount of discipline, training and drill, and esprit de corps, Scharnhorst recognised that disciplined intellect was the essential ingredient to the profession of arms. As a true empiricist he never succumbed to the lofty, pre-war ideas that demanded the abolition of the standing army in favour of a so-called people's militia. He had to see the worth of these new forces demonstrated in combat before he would accept them. The War of the First Coalition offered this undeniable proof, revealing the inherent weaknesses of traditional military establishments with their institutional inbreeding, and the promising future of national citizen armies. Interestingly, Scharnhorst also used historical analogies to reassure his wife and family. Writing to Klara in early May 1793 about his frustrations with the Hanoverian ruling elites, he predicted 'the prejudice necessitated by the present age cannot continue much longer'. Just as he had told Tempelhof in late January 1793, the violent revolution of the French people against their aristocratic masters clearly demonstrated this reality. He then informed Klara the present age was slipping away.[156]

153 See Gerhard Scharnhorst, 'Relation von den Angrif des Caesarschen Lagers bey Cambray, mit einigen Bemerkungen über die weitern Operationen und der Disposition zu den Angrif des obigen Lagers von Prinz von Coburg' (September/ October 1793); in Kunisch (ed.), *Scharnhorst: Privat und dienstliche Schriften*, Vol.1, pp.262-64; the quoted passage is from p.264. Why no unity of effort existed within coalition forces in 1793 is a major theme of Jarrett, 'The British Flanders Expedition of 1793 and Coalition Diplomacy'.

154 Letter of 20-22 July 1793 to Klara; in Kunisch (ed.), *Scharnhorst: Privat und dienstliche Schriften*, Vol.1, pp.242-43 (21 July).

155 For one of these articles, see Gerhard Scharnhorst, 'Ueber den jetzigen Krieg und das jetzigen Kriegstheater', *Neues militärisches Journal* 7 (1793), pp.52-78.

156 Letter of 5-12 May 1793 to Klara; in Kunisch (ed.), *Scharnhorst: Privat und dienstliche Schriften*, Vol.1, pp.209-14; the quoted passage is from p.211 (9 May).

8

A Frustrating Situation

Titular-Capitain Gerhard Scharnhorst longed for his own company. Command was an essential prerequisite for advancement. It also served to legitimise the standing of officers in the army.[1] The administration of a company was basically a small business enterprise. Known as 'Company Business' [*Kompaniewirtschaft*], a frugal and resourceful commander who knew how to manage his company profitably could earn a lucrative income for himself.[2] Regrettably for Scharnhorst, in the carefully stratified society of his time, command was reserved for the 'high-born estate', or for the privileged middle-class in the artillery and engineers, whose sense of honour and concept of professionalism 'could not be shared with inferiors'.[3] Scharnhorst's social status was clearly inferior to that of his well-connected comrades. Indeed, in the Electorate of Hanover, 'this most exclusively aristocratic of all German principalities', Scharnhorst found his social origins a severe handicap that neither his solid reputation as a teacher and scholar, nor his outstanding combat leadership could effectively surmount.[4] Although rigid exclusion of bourgeois officers had proven impossible, they were usually assigned to the technical branches, such as the artillery or engineers. As Scharnhorst told his wife, 'hereditary title' [*aus dem Lande eingesetzt*] was what truly mattered in the Hanoverian army.[5]

Most Hanoverian officers held office by hereditary claims and connection, not because of any intellectual or professional standards.[6] A typical example of this occurred in early June 1793. 'Once again', Scharnhorst explained to Klara, 'a twelve-year-old aristocrat' will be inducted into the 10. Infanterie Regiment (Diepenbroick), while her half-brother *Fähndrich*

1 See the interesting documentation in Hann 38 E, Nr.49: *Grundsätze über Avancement der Offiziere im Felde und bei den im Lande sich befindenden Regimentern, 1793-1794*; deposited at the Niedersächsisches Landesarchiv, Hanover.

2 See the exhaustive examination of this culture in Fritz Redlich, *The German Military Enterpriser and His Work Force: A Study of European Economic and Social History, Vierteljahrschrift für Sozial- und Wirtschaftsgeschichte*, Beihefte, 47-48 (Wiesbaden: Franz Steiner Verlag, 1964/65); especially Vol.2 (Beiheft 48).

3 See the important discussion on this topic in Alfred Vagts, *A History of Militarism: Civilian and Military* (New York: The Free Press, 1959), p.67.

4 The quoted passage comes from the discussion in Herbert Rosinski, *The German Army* (Washington, D.C.: The Infantry Journal, 1944), p.37.

5 Gerhard Scharnhorst to Klara Scharnhorst (1-3 June 1793); in Kunisch (ed.), *Scharnhorst: Privat und dienstliche Schriften*, Vol.1, pp.216-19; the quoted passage is from p.218 (3 June).

6 See the interesting sources documents relating to the appointments of Princes Edward, Ernst, and Adolphus in Hann 41, I, Nr.6: *Dienstverpflichtungen der königlichen Hoheiten, der Prinzen Eduard, Ernst, Adolph als Obersten in der Armee, 1787-1793*; deposited at the Niedersächsisches Landesarchiv, Hanover.

August Scharlock, 'who is equally qualified, is being set back only because he has no title'. Here is a fine example of one of those 'children' officers Prince Adolphus had mentioned to his father, in which he suggested that the appointment of such young aristocrats without any formal military *Bildung* was hindering the development of sound leadership in the army. Formal initiation into a regiment was a great honour, but middle-class officers had to earn this distinction while it was simply a rite of passage for noblemen. Recognising this significant difference, Scharnhorst asked Trew to intervene on Scharlock's behalf to prevent an injustice. Unfortunately, 'he [Trew] pushed me away', Scharnhorst told Klara. Scharlock would have 'to earn this high distinction through merit promotion', Trew informed Scharnhorst.[7]

In respond to Trew's stance, Scharnhorst told Klara, 'The dumbest ass succeeds here almost as well as the most intelligent'.[8] Clearly frustrated with the rigid class distinctions in the army, Scharnhorst informed his wife, 'The young man [Scharlock] is despondent. He wants to go over to the French, but I will do everything possible to look after him here'. He then reassured Klara, 'Nothing helps more here than good patience'.[9] Thinking of Scharlock, he then turned to his own situation and revealed the emotional maelstrom in which he found himself.

Scharnhorst explained to Klara the empty notion of 'merit promotion'. Advancement was based almost always on connection and preference. 'I would be happy if only I could achieve some purpose', he lamented.[10] He related how he had the duties and responsibilities of an 'actual [*wirklicher*] captain', but was paid the salary and ration allowance of a lieutenant. He observed how noblemen with no apparent talent, ability, or record of outstanding achievement were being promoted while he remained a titular captain. Interestingly, in one of his notes Scharnhorst had listed and compared promotion rates among the various branches of the service, and it appears Trew was making sure he spent the maximum time in grade before being promoted.[11] 'And so, my ambition is not satisfied', he told Klara.[12]

Later in the campaign, even after he had distinguished himself at Hondschoote, he was still not promoted. Scharnhorst again complained to Klara: 'There is nothing I like about this entire war. And what infuriates me more than anything else is that I will not profit through advancement because of it'. 'If only I was an actual captain', he continued, thinking about his pension and how he would provide for Klara and their family should anything happen to him.[13] Returning to the plight of Scharlock, Scharnhorst concluded his letter of 3 June 1793 with a statement that clearly captured the spirit of the times for most enlightened

7 Letter of 1-3 June 1794 to Klara; in Kunisch (ed.), *Scharnhorst: Privat und dienstliche Schriften*, Vol.1, pp.216-19; the quoted passages are from p.218 (3 June).

8 Letter of 1-3 June 1794 to Klara; in Kunisch (ed.), *Scharnhorst: Privat und dienstliche Schriften*, Vol.1, p.218. Scharnhorst repeated this comment to his wife two months later in his letter of 28 August 1793 (p.252).

9 Letter of 1-3 June 1794 to Klara; in Kunisch (ed.), *Scharnhorst: Privat und dienstliche Schriften*, Vol.1, p.218 (3 June). Interestingly, when France occupied Hanover in 1803, Scharlock did go over to the French, becoming a major in a newly-created French cavalry regiment.

10 Letter of 1-3 June 1793 to Klara; in Kunisch (ed.), *Scharnhorst: Privat und dienstliche Schriften*, Vol.1, p.218 (3 June).

11 See Gerhard Scharnhorst, '*Avancement*' (Hanoverian Period); in Kunisch (ed.), *Scharnhorst: Privat und dienstliche Schriften*, Vol.1, pp.197-98.

12 Letter of 1-3 June 1793 to Klara; in Kunisch (ed.), *Scharnhorst: Privat und dienstliche Schriften*, Vol.1, p.218 (3 June).

13 Letter of 5 and 6 October 1793 to Klara; in Kunisch (ed.), *Scharnhorst: Privat und dienstliche Schriften*, Vol.1, pp.265-67; the quoted passages are from p.267 (6 October).

soldiers of humble origins: 'We are being set back in favour of the aristocrats, and yet we fight for them'.[14]

Scharnhorst again expressed his bitterness when he realised that he would not be promoted no matter how well he performed. So much for the notion of merit promotion. What really angered him, as he told Klara after discussing his career prospects with Trew on 5 October 1793, was the fact that 'the widow's pension [of an actual captain] is so much more than that of the most senior *titular* captain'.[15] By regulations he should be an actual captain. Thanks to Trew, he was neither promoted nor given a company command. This was the legacy of feudalism; the continuing efforts of the *Ständestaat* to maintain their hierarchy of legally defined classes of society.[16] What he could not understand was why Trew refused to acknowledge his loyalty and devotion to the artillery and its chief during the past 11 years. Interestingly, just after the incident with Scharlock, Scharnhorst remembered his conclusion about the Hanoverian elites before the war and told Klara, 'I see more and more that my first inclinations about this war were correct'.[17]

As the Hanoverians refitted and reorganised their forces in the late fall of 1793, Scharnhorst suddenly (overnight it seems) changed his pessimistic mood and informed his wife on 12 October, 'I feel newly born'. He had been out walking instead of riding and had dreamed about a visit from his family. In great spirits, he was anxious to see them and even prescribed a detailed route for them to travel. From their home in Bordenau, Klara and their children were to proceed to Hanover, then to Lippstadt, and on to Düsseldorf, where his brother Heinrich would meet them. *Lieutenant* Heinrich Scharnhorst was serving with the Hessians. Following some rest and obtaining fresh horses, they would travel to his location at Tournai, in southwest Belgium.[18]

The next day Scharnhorst related a sad incident to Klara. As he was gathering the personal effects of the late *Capitain* Friedrich Georg August Sympher (who had been mortally wounded at Hondschoote), Sympher's father arrived at headquarters, unaware his son had passed away. 'He wept bitterly' when told of his son's death. Scharnhorst then thanked Klara for all her love, and for the shirts and other items she had sent him. He also told her he had received the latest issue of *New Military Journal*. In his closing remarks he wondered when the army would move into winter cantonments. 'God knows, in other wars one went into winter quarters in October'.[19] It would be another month before the Hanoverians 'marched into their cantonments'.[20]

14 Letter of 1-3 June 1793 to Klara; in Kunisch (ed.), *Scharnhorst: Privat und dienstliche Schriften*, Vol.1, p.218 (3 June).

15 Letter of 12 and 13 October 1793 to Klara; in Kunisch (ed.), *Scharnhorst: Privat und dienstliche Schriften*, Vol.1, pp.274-76; the quoted passage is from p.274 (12 October). Scharnhorst's discussion with Trew is mentioned on p.265 (5 October).

16 See the discussion in Fox, 'Conservative Accommodation to Revolution', pp.43-48.

17 Letter of 8-12 July 1793 to Klara; in Kunisch (ed.), *Scharnhorst: Privat und dienstliche Schriften*, Vol.1, pp.237-39; the quoted passage is from p.238 (8 July). Scharnhorst's pre-war thoughts on the Hanoverian elites can be found in his letter of 27 January 1793 to Tempelhof on pp.102-04.

18 Letter of 12 and 13 October 1793 to Klara; in Kunisch (ed.), *Scharnhorst: Privat und dienstliche Schriften*, Vol.1, pp.274-76; the quoted passage is from p.274 (12 October).

19 Letter of 12 and 13 October 1793 to Klara; in Kunisch (ed.), *Scharnhorst: Privat und dienstliche Schriften*, Vol.1, pp.274-76; the quoted passage is from p.275 (13 October).

20 On 12 November 1793, York reported to his father that the Hanoverians went into winter quarters that Sunday, 10 November 1793; in Aspinall (ed), *The Later Correspondence of George III*, Vol.2, pp.119-20; the quoted passage is from p.119.

A week later, on 18 October, Scharnhorst wrote about another incident that really upset him. One of the artillery train's captains suddenly passed away and Scharnhorst 'had to take care of his belongings. It struck me so hard. He had a wife and ten children and had not answered any of the fourteen letters they had sent him'. Deeply moved, Scharnhorst confided to Klara that no matter what happens, his 'entire happiness' depended solely on their love for one another and their love for their children, and he promised her he would always answer her letters.[21] As he awaited news about winter quarters, he began writing down more of his thoughts on the recent campaign.

Over the winter of 1793-1794, Scharnhorst summarised his ideas on coalition operations in Flanders and submitted two interesting memoranda, most likely to Trew. The first was titled, 'Some Observations on the Use of Artillery during the Campaign of 1793'. He began by noting the lack of adequate artillery in the coalition armies compared to what the French had fielded. He concluded that the French had larger calibre guns in every category, and nearly a 2:1 advantage in total guns over coalition forces. The French distribution of guns among their infantry and cavalry units was also superior to the allies. 'We will not have enough guns if we continue with the present system', he told Trew, 'even if we remain in a purely defensive posture'.[22] He then ventured into a potentially politically and socially sensitive area.

Stating that Hanover had far too much cavalry and not enough artillery, Scharnhorst indicated that the cavalry was practically useless during the recent campaign, while the artillery was much more effective. Comparing the cost-ratio benefits of having more artillery with the current state of the cavalry, he showed that a squadron of cavalry cost far more than a battery of artillery. While Scharnhorst clearly understood the creation of more horse artillery might be a difficult undertaking, he cited one example after another from the recent campaign to prove that artillery was essential for battlefield success, while the Hanoverian cavalry had proven ineffective. Summarising his analysis, he emphasised that horse artillery was offensively much more flexible than cavalry and even heavy artillery, and 'can definitely be more useful in every situation'. 'We must therefore increase the artillery at the expense of the cavalry'.[23]

Scharnhorst continued this line of thought in his second memorandum, focusing solely on horse artillery. 'The need for increasing our horse artillery is already known', he began. 'So is its outstanding performance'. He followed these opening lines with an evaluation of Hanover's artillery force. The howitzers assigned to the horse artillery 'are too heavy', he maintained. 'For the most part they are effective only against the enemy at a great distance'. The number of howitzers must therefore be decreased by 30 percent, from 54 to 36 pieces. Scharnhorst also suggested that there was an urgent need for 'lighter gun carriages', for 'every artilleryman to be riding', and for increasing the number of

21 Letter of 18 October 1793 to Klara; in Kunisch (ed.), *Scharnhorst: Privat und dienstliche Schriften*, Vol.1, pp.276-77; the quoted passage is from p.277.

22 Gerhard Scharnhorst, 'Einige Bemerkungen über den Gebrauch der Artillerie in der Campagne von 1793' (Winter 1793/94?); in Kunisch (ed.), *Scharnhorst: Privat und dienstliche Schriften*, Vol.1, pp.298-303.

23 The quoted passages are from Scharnhorst, 'Einige Bemerkungen über den Gebrauch der Artillerie in der Campagne von 1793', in Kunisch (ed.), *Scharnhorst: Privat und dienstliche Schriften*, Vol.1, pp.299, 302, and 299; respectively.

crewmen per gun.[24] After providing some general observations on how coalition forces could make more effective use of their artillery, he focused on six crucial points, three of which stand out.

Scharnhorst first maintained that the horses hauling the guns were 'far too restless' under fire. 'It was a big mistake to think horses are accustomed to this fire'. Instead of providing a solution, he cited an incident in which one poor artilleryman was dragged away by the horses he was holding.[25] Scharnhorst most likely assumed this example would prove his point. What seems to be missing from his analysis is the question of peacetime training and whether artillery horses were adequately conditioned to withstand the sights, sounds, and smell of combat. Perhaps he knew the answer to this question, or maybe he assumed others in the chain of command did.

Scharnhorst next noted that there was 'too much unnecessary and wasteful firing', which gained nothing, but expended precious ammunition. Citing Trew to support his case, he wrote, 'Our General is totally against such cannonades'. Then he closed his report by noting the third critical point, in which coalition artillerymen wasted too much of their canister rounds where they had little effect. 'Canister fire [*Cartätschen*] would often be beneficial if one wants to drive the enemy from broken [*durchschnitten*] terrain, or if he attacks us over the same ground'. Here he was most likely referring to the large seven-pounder howitzers assigned to the mobile artillery. These guns had a longer optimum range than did the smaller, lighter cannon, and Scharnhorst felt they could clear terrain of enemy troops at 1,200 paces, especially if the fire of these cannon was massed together.[26] Such concentrated fire would keep the enemy at a distance and provide more security for friendly batteries. Scharnhorst may have been referring to the broken terrain around Hondschoote, which had negated the effect of the standard artillery round shot and had allowed French infantrymen to close (relatively unimpeded) with the Hanoverians before launching their bayonet charge.

The straightforward nature of Scharnhorst's memoranda clearly reveals what he had learned from coalition operations in Flanders in 1793. Judging from the fact that Hanover decided to raise another division of horse artillery for the upcoming campaign suggests that others agreed with his assessment, even if they may never have read his reports.[27] It is also difficult to ascertain whether Scharnhorst's other recommendations were ever implemented, since most of the surviving records do not contain much (if any) of the detailed

24 Gerhard Scharnhorst, '*Reitende Artillerie*' (Winter 1793/94?); in Kunisch (ed.), *Scharnhorst: Privat und dienstliche Schriften*, Vol.1, pp.303-06. This document appears to be the last two chapters of 'Einige Bemerkungen über den Gebrauch der Artillerie in der Campagne von 1793'. See p.303 (Note a). While the title of this paper is lined through in the original document, the subject of this memorandum is clearly horse artillery. The quoted passages are from pp.303 and 304.

25 See the last part entitled, 'Section VI. *Ordinäre Artillerie*', in Kunisch (ed.), *Scharnhorst: Privat und dienstliche Schriften*, Vol.1, pp.305-06; the quoted passage is from p.305.

26 Scharnhorst, 'Section VI. *Ordinäre Artillerie*', in Kunisch (ed.), *Scharnhorst: Privat und dienstliche Schriften*, Vol.1, p.306.

27 Sichart, *Geschichte der Königlich-Hannoverischen Armee*, Vol.4, pp.47-53, discusses the strengthening of the Hanoverian Auxiliary Corps for the 1794 campaign. The addition of another division of horse artillery is mentioned on p.48. The equipment modifications and other changes Scharnhorst recommended are not discussed. Source documents relating to this 1794 organisation can be found in Hann 41, VIII, Nr.48: *Formation der Artillerie zum Ausmarsch. Bewaffnung und Verstärkung derselben. Gehaltsverbesserungen der reitenden Artillerie, 1794-1796*; deposited at the Niedersächsisches Landesarchiv, Hanover.

data about lighter carriages, restless horses, and unnecessary firing. Sadly, such documentation is all-too-often relegated to the dustbin of history, when in fact it is precisely this kind of data that is critically important when assessing the battlefield performance of a military organisation. This is exactly why Scharnhorst focused so much of his report on such information and other non-tactical topics. Significantly, the operations in Flanders in 1794 would demonstrate the validity of many of his observations and suggestions.

Without question, the most remarkable essay Scharnhorst penned around this time was one addressing light infantry. It was written during the winter of 1793-1794, around the time the Austrians and Prussians were evacuating Alsace and the Palatinate.[28] It was likely intended for publication, as portions appear in his later articles in *New Military Journal*. In Scharnhorst's mind, the advent of increasingly large numbers of light infantrymen fighting 'in open-order' [*à la débandade*] as 'skirmishers' [*tirailleurs*] was the most significant tactical innovation of the War of the First Coalition.

In his brief essay, 'On the Need to Have Light Troops, and Their Uses', Scharnhorst highlighted the significant difference between regular units using close-order tactics (rigid line formations, ordered volley fire, and massive attack columns) and irregular units employing new open-order tactics (swarms of light infantry, skirmishers, and sharpshooters using their own initiative and individually-aimed fire). The former fought with a driving force under strict control; the latter sought to become one with the land, stalking and hunting (hence the German derivative *Jäger*, or hunter). While both regular and irregular troops had been employed in battle before the War of the First Coalition, Scharnhorst noted that in earlier wars German light troops often fought as separate, specialised units, and usually performed auxiliary functions.[29]

> The proportion of these troops to line formations, however, always remained extremely small, until the present war against the French Republic came to remind us of the principle that one should always endeavour to regulate one's dispositions according to the methods of the enemy.
>
> Probably never before has a greater number of light troops appeared on the battlefield than among the ranks of the present French army, nor has military history ever been given more irrefutable examples of the essential value of such troops than during this war.
>
> If the campaigns are studied, one may be tempted to hold that at least on the French side this is entirely a war of light troops; the Republic certainly owes most of her victories to her light infantry.

'Incidentally', Scharnhorst continued, it was 'easy' for the French to raise, train, and organise good light infantry. It was the spirit of the Revolution that provided the impetus here, he

28 For the timing of this essay, see the discussion in Paret, *Yorck and the Era of Prussian Reform*, p.249.

29 Gerhard Scharnhorst, 'Von der Nothwendigkeit, leichte Truppen zu haben und deren Nutzen', *Nachlaß Scharnhorst*, Nr.271, Sheets 9-13; deposited at the Geheimes Staatsarchiv Preussischer Kulturbesitz, 196/VI. HA Familienarchive und Nachlässe, Berlin (Dahlem). This essay was incorporated into Werner Hahlweg, *Preußische Reformzeit und revolutionärer Krieg*, *Wehrwissenschaftlichen Rundschau*, Beiheft 18 (September 1962), pp.58-60. An English translation can be found in Paret, *Yorck and the Era of Prussian Reform*, pp.253-54.

said, 'the main characteristics of which are *temperament*, *enthusiasm*, and hatred of all coercion'. Light infantry came to embody this spirit. Interestingly, Scharnhorst noted that 'it was equally difficult for her [France] to achieve this goal with her cavalry'. The French 'demonstrate little inclination for the care and upkeep of horses'.[30]

Scharnhorst maintained that light infantrymen are indispensable for the army. This was in sharp contrast to what most eighteenth-century tacticians and theorists believed; they alleged light infantry performed just auxiliary functions. For Scharnhorst, light infantry executed the most essential missions in war, such as advance and rearguard missions, patrolling, convoy escort, foraging, security operations, and outpost missions. Without the successful completion of these less-glamorous tasks, no army would ever be able to manoeuvre securely so it could close with and destroy an enemy. Indeed, these were the principal topics Scharnhorst had discussed in his *Military Field Pocket Book*, and the French had proven this in one engagement after other during the recent campaign.

Scharnhorst believed that the patrolling operations of light infantrymen offer the commanding general the most reliable intelligence on the enemy and his potential operations. This was certainly the case with the French at Hondschoote: 'Without a sufficient number of light troops, a commanding general can never acquire speedy news of enemy movements, not even if he sends out masses of spies'. Remembering all the false reports and incorrect evaluation of intelligence by paid spies, he wrote:

> Yes, I dare assert that a great proportion of the pay expended on these people [spies] is wasted, and it takes a trained officer, whom experience has made cautious, not to be led into the worst labyrinth by their exaggerated reports. Intelligence gained from patrols is in any case always more precise, since professional soldiers can judge matters more correctly, and their honour is involved.[31]

During combat operations, light troops offer a distinct advantage over heavy infantry, simply because 'by constant skirmishing they weaken and slow the enemy'. Light troops can also 'mask the main effort' with diversionary, feint, or even 'false attacks'. Moreover, they can 'harass the enemy by raiding his rear and his flanks'. Scharnhorst quickly dismissed the argument 'that today heavy cavalry and line infantry are used for these duties', noting that the 'usefulness and profit from heavy troops' comes 'only in battle'.[32]

For Scharnhorst, light infantry personified the concept of *Bildung*, and he was quick to establish this rationale. 'It is also worth some consideration that light troops offer the greatest opportunity for the training of good and useful officers'.

> Through daily actions they become accustomed to danger, and by being left to rely more on their own judgment, they are taught how to tear themselves from the

30 Scharnhorst, 'Von der Nothwendigkeit, leichte Truppen zu haben und deren Nutzen', Sheets 9-10.

31 Scharnhorst, 'Von der Nothwendigkeit, leichte Truppen zu haben und deren Nutzen', Sheets 10-11. Some interesting reports from coalition spies can be found in Hann 38 E, Nr. 180: *Berichte von Spionen und Kundschaftern über die feindliche Armee, 05.1794-06.1794*; deposited at the Niedersächsisches Landesarchiv, Hanover.

32 Scharnhorst, 'Von der Nothwendigkeit, leichte Truppen zu haben und deren Nutzen', Sheets 11-12.

> machine-like process of their profession [*sich aus dem maschinemässigen Gange ihres Metiers rausreissen*].
>
> All previous teaching is as useless as it is applicable, and therefore the officers' boldness, judgment, and independence grow almost daily. Turn back to history and my statement will be supported by the honourable examples of a Laudon, a Trenck, Zieten, Seydlitz, Kleist, and Lafayette. The military talents of all of these men were developed in the light service.[33]

Scharnhorst ended this important essay with 'To be continued'. If he wrote a continuation, it has yet to be discovered.[34]

Meanwhile, the long separation from his wife and family, along with the uncertainly about his future in the artillery, were beginning to affect Scharnhorst's emotional well-being. In several of his letters over the summer and fall of 1793 he had planned for his family and brother Wilhelm to visit him while he was in winter quarters. Where these winter quarters were to be located, he did not say because he did not know. His other brother Heinrich, who was nearby with the Hessians, would join them. Scharnhorst was really looking forward to seeing his family again.[35] Whenever the situation changed, he adjusted his plans accordingly. Unfortunately, coalition leaders were hesitant to move into winter quarters. The armies of revolutionary France had initiated probing attacks at various points along the coalition front, seeking to continue the fight throughout the winter months. Although the coalition had contained French aggression by the end of 1793, a sense of uneasiness had overcome allied forces.

On 10 January 1794, Scharnhorst (now in temporary winter quarters) informed his wife of his uncertainty about a family visit.

> Until now, my dearly beloved Klara, I have been in a state of terrible uncertainty, whether we actually have winter quarters or not. Now it is certain that we do not have them, since we must be prepared to abandon them at the first attack on this side. So now what is one to do?

He still wanted to see his family and suggested they come. 'Here in Meulebeke [a village in west Flanders] you can live as cheaply as in Hanover'. Although the townsfolk were difficult to understand (because they did not speak German), Scharnhorst told his wife that Meulebeke was a pleasant place with a beautiful market. The only drawback was that this village 'is only three miles from our outposts'. Then he asked his wife's opinion: 'After many battles, after so much unrest, after all of your suffering for me, my beloved wife, and you, my beloved children, I do not know what to do'.[36]

33 Scharnhorst, 'Von der Nothwendigkeit, leichte Truppen zu haben und deren Nutzen', Sheets 12-13. Interesting, Freytag had organised and commanded the Freytag Jägers during the Seven Years War, performing admirably at the Battle of Bergen, 17 April 1759.

34 See the commentary by Paret in *Yorck and the Era of Prussian Reform*, p.249.

35 For example, see Scharnhorst's Letters of 17-19 July, 28 August, 4 and 5 September, 5 and 6 October, and 12 and 13 October 1793 to his wife; in Kunisch (ed.), *Scharnhorst: Privat und dienstliche Schriften*, Vol.1, pp.239-41, 252-53, 255-57, 265-67, and 274-76; respectively.

36 Letter of 10 January 1794 to Klara; in Kunisch (ed.), *Scharnhorst: Privat und dienstliche Schriften*, Vol.1, pp.308-09; the quoted passage is from p.308.

Scharnhorst told Klara of his 'anxious longing' to be with her and their children, and how 'an unbearable sadness afflicts me'.[37] Clearly, he was thinking only of himself here. Wanting his family to risk traveling in difficult winter weather to visit him was reckless enough. To ask his wife to make this choice (abrogating his own decision-making responsibility), especially when it might endanger their family during the journey and with the French so close to their destination, seems to be the height of selfishness on Scharnhorst's part.

Scharnhorst then tried unsuccessfully to defect attention away from his growing anxiety by mentioning 'the many projects' that have kept him busy. 'Linen and fine hats are cheap here', he told Klara. So were horses and other items. He was wondering if he and his brother might be able set up a small business and make a profit, since the exchange rate was good. No longer able to restrain the betrayal he felt toward Trew (who seems to have given Scharnhorst the impression that he would be promoted and given a company command), he informed Klara: 'I know nothing of my captain's salary and company. Soon I hope to be an actual captain'. These hopes were shortly dashed.

Scharnhorst then related the recent 'notoriety' he had received from the 'scandal' in Menin. Ritter (acting under Trew's orders) had made a spectacle of himself in front of the Austrian commander. News of this occurrence had reached the Court of St James and King George, and this kind of unwanted attention must have upset Trew, since he was the one responsible.[38] This certainly did not endear Scharnhorst to his regimental commander. In biding 'Adieu' to his wife, he told Klara that he was enclosing a copy of his after-action report on the action at Hondschoote and noted that while Diepenbroick had praised his leadership and courage during the battle and subsequent retreat, Trew had accused him of abandoning his post under fire and leaving two guns behind.[39]

On 6 February 1794, Scharnhorst rode to Brugge, in northwest Belgium, to speak with 'the generals' about his situation: Brugge was where most of the senior leaders of the Hanoverian Auxiliary Corps were quartered.[40] 'There is so much evil in the world', he told Klara. 'I am really curious how the General [Trew] who accuses me will behave'. It appears Scharnhorst had requested an official court of honour to clear his name. Ironically, because he chose to appear in person to present his case and to confront his accuser, he required Trew's 'permission to go'.[41]

The cabal, mistrust, and division within the artillery regiment that Trew had created by his favouritism was now on full display. 'All of our young officers are my intimate friends and are always on my side', Scharnhorst told his wife. He also informed her how Braun was

37 Letter of 10 January 1794 to Klara; in Kunisch (ed.), *Scharnhorst: Privat und dienstliche Schriften*, Vol.1, pp.308-09; the quoted passage is from p.309.

38 Letter of 10 January 1794 to Klara; in Kunisch (ed.), *Scharnhorst: Privat und dienstliche Schriften*, Vol.1, pp.308-09. See p.309 (Note 1); the quoted passages are from p.309.

39 Letter of 10 January 1794 to Klara; in Kunisch (ed.), *Scharnhorst: Privat und dienstliche Schriften*, Vol.1, pp.308-09. Interestingly, the two guns may have been the ones Scharnhorst left in Bonnivet's charge, since they are the only artillery pieces mentioned in this letter.

40 See the interesting documents about the coalition headquarters complex in Brügge; in Hann 38 E, Nr. 139: *Winterquartiere 1793/1794: Verhandlungen mit dem Magistrat zu Brügge wegen des dahin zu legenden Hauptquartiers, Hospitals usw., 11.1793-12.1793*; deposited at the Niedersächsisches Landesarchiv, Hanover.

41 Letter of 5-6 February 1794 to Klara; in Kunisch (ed.), *Scharnhorst: Privat und dienstliche Schriften*, Vol.1, pp.311-13; the quoted passages are from p.312 (5 February).

now going out of his way to make friends with him. 'Braun wants to have me on his side', he continued, but Scharnhorst remained on alert and highly suspicious of Braun's motives. 'I will simply not join any faction', he told Klara, 'because this is the best path now'.[42] As he prepared to leave for Brugge he reassured his wife, 'You are a good woman. You suffer so much for me. In your suffering realise your husband's unconditional love for you'.[43]

No published record of the meeting at Brugge seems to exist. From what Scharnhorst told his wife, Trew offered him command of a garrison company in Hamelin, provided its commander, *Oberstlieutenant* Prott, agreed to retire.[44] Here is another example of the machinations of Trew. Although Prott had not deployed, Trew had nevertheless promoted him. Now Trew attempted to bait Scharnhorst. If he accepted the general's offer of a garrison company, he would have to return home. It would also require Scharnhorst to relinquish command of his horse battery and leave behind (in time of war) the young officers and men he commanded, mentored, and enjoyed being with. As much as he desired a company command, Scharnhorst knew Trew was trying to get rid of him and so declined the offer. He also recognised Trew could not to be trusted and that there was no guarantee Prott would retire. It also appears Scharnhorst may have foreseen such an eventuality when he told Klara the day before he left for Brugge: 'Glory tortures me and ignores me even here, if one means worldly fame or common glory. I am ashamed of striving for it. All I desire is an honourable life and the happiness of my Klara and my children'.[45] Upon leaving Brugge, Scharnhorst seemed gratified at being exonerated, but clearly upset and angry that he was not given command of the newly raised company of horse artillery. As he told Klara, 'From now on, I do not want to write anything more on this'.[46]

Back in Menin, Scharnhorst sent Wallmoden two very interesting and significant concept papers. 'The seven weeks I have been in Menin', he wrote in his cover letter, 'have given me the opportunity to think about the actions and positions around this town'. He then introduced the two reports he was enclosing, telling the Commanding General, 'In the absence of other means, Your Highborn Count, Your Excellency, I am providing proof of my diligence, so you can see how my endeavours are worthy of your continued support. I am enclosing the paper I wrote during this time'.[47] This paper was his treatise on the 1793 fight for Menin.[48] Scharnhorst then introduced his second study concerning 'the expansion of our General and General-Quartermaster Staff'. Realising this assessment was beyond the

42 Letter of 5-6 February 1794 to Klara; in Kunisch (ed.), *Scharnhorst: Privat und dienstliche Schriften*, Vol.1, pp.311-13; the quoted passages are from p.313 (6 February).

43 Letter of 5-6 February 1794 to Klara; in Kunisch (ed.), *Scharnhorst: Privat und dienstliche Schriften*, Vol.1, pp.311-13; the quoted passages are from p.312 (5 February).

44 Sichart, *Geschichte der Königlich-Hannoverischen Armee*, Vol.4, p.18, lists Prott as a *Major* and part of the *Artillerie Regiment*.

45 Letter of 5-6 February 1794 to Klara; in Kunisch (ed.), *Scharnhorst: Privat und dienstliche Schriften*, Vol.1, pp.311-313; the quoted passages are from p.312 (5 February).

46 Letter of 5-6 February 1794 to Klara; in Kunisch (ed.), *Scharnhorst: Privat und dienstliche Schriften*, Vol.1, pp.311-13; the quoted passages is from p.313 (6 February).

47 See Gerhard Scharnhorst's Cover Letter of 18 February 1794 to Wallmoden; in Kunisch (ed.), *Scharnhorst: Privat und dienstliche Schriften*, Vol.1, p.326. Scharnhorst's words, 'worthy of your continued support', indicate he was aware the Commanding General was looking after him.

48 See Gerhard Scharnhorst, 'Über die Positionen der Corps bey Menin im Jahr 1793' (18 February 1794); in Kunisch (ed.), *Scharnhorst: Privat und dienstliche Schriften*, Vol.1, pp.327-31.

scope of his responsibility, position, and rank, Scharnhorst nevertheless believed it was his duty and obligation as a loyal subordinate to recommend the need for an expansion of the general staff. He apologised for taking the liberty to do so but hoped his suggestions might be helpful to Wallmoden.[49]

In his first essay, 'On the Positions of the Corps at Menin in the Year 1793', Scharnhorst reflected on the battle for Menin that had taken place on 12 and 13 September 1793. While not specifically mentioning the Hanoverian defensive perimeter southwest of Dunkirk around the same time, he suggested that the concept of the cordon defence (used in both actions) was simply unrealistic and extremely dangerous: 'The corps at Menin was always spread out trying to defend a great number of positions, and therefore could never conduct a good defence against the enemy attacks'.[50] This was precisely what had happened to the Hanoverians south of Dunkirk. Indeed, in his earlier report on the operations around Hondschoote, he had criticised the way in which the coalition had tried to hold every position, while the French were free to mass their forces and then manoeuvre them and attack wherever and whenever they pleased. The outcome was obvious to him. 'By moving quickly, the French often gained great advantages in this war'. Although he had not participated in the actions around Menin, Scharnhorst told Wallmoden: 'I know the terrain. In the six weeks I have been here, I have ridden around the area and have followed the analysis of the engagement published in the *Leidener Zeitung* of 27 September'.[51] Having a good sense of the previous fight, he concluded by telling the Commanding General that relying on a cordon defence had clearly doomed the coalition in Flanders in 1793.

Seeking to learn from the mistakes made in 1793, and to enhance leadership in the Hanoverian Auxiliary Corps, Scharnhorst presented his recommendations for expanding the Hanoverian General Staff. His intent here was to show Wallmoden that more officers and non-commissioned officers were needed on the General Staff to assist the Commanding General in the vital areas of reconnaissance and security, and with the operational and tactical disposition of the army, in a way similar to how Frederick the Great had used selected officers to aid him during the Seven Years War.[52]

As the art of war expanded in scope and complexity during the French Revolutionary Wars (1792-1802), battle command became increasingly more complex. Scharnhorst was among the first in any army to recognise that the War of the First Coalition had no parallel in earlier wars. The challenge coalition forces faced was fighting French armies far larger than their small professional armies. The French *levée en masse* had unleashed powerful forces, produced the nation-in-arms, and completely altered warfare.[53]

49 Scharnhorst's Cover Letter of 18 February 1794 to Wallmoden; in Kunisch (ed.), *Scharnhorst: Privat und dienstliche Schriften*, Vol.1, p.326.

50 Scharnhorst, 'Über die Positionen der Corps bey Menin im Jahr 1793', in Kunisch (ed.), *Scharnhorst: Privat und dienstliche Schriften*, Vol.1, pp.327-31; the quoted passage is from p.327.

51 See Gerhard Scharnhorst, 'Operationen der allirten Armee nach der Affaire bey Hondschot, den 8ten Sept. 1793, bis zum Dec.' (after 4 December 1793, before 18 February 1794); in Kunisch (ed.), *Scharnhorst: Privat und dienstliche Schriften*, Vol.1, pp.316-26; the quoted passages are from pp.325 and 326; respectively.

52 Gerhard Scharnhorst, 'Nutzen einer Erweiterung unsers General-Staabs' (not after 18 February 1794); in Kunisch (ed.), *Scharnhorst: Privat und dienstliche Schriften*, Vol.1, pp.331-34.

53 See Scharnhorst, 'Entwickelung der allgemeinen Ursachen des Glücks der Franzosen in dem Revolutions-Kriege, und insbesondere in dem Feldzuge von 1794', pp.1-154. This study was later incorporated as part of von der Goltz

Instead of a single army marching in a long column along a solitary route and manoeuvred in battle by one general, French military power was a group of separate armies, led by different generals, and often dispersed over a vast countryside, marching along parallel routes, and only united under the eye of a commander-in-chief on the field of battle. A more effective means of controlling this awesome power had to be developed, simply because the commander-in-chief could no longer manage to concentrate all the burdens of command in his person. Scharnhorst understood that military leadership had to rise to the challenge of leading armies of citizen soldiers.

There soon crystallized in Scharnhorst's mind a set of specific reforms designed to meet the challenge of leading the national army.[54] He advocated augmenting the staff of the commanding general with talented officers and non-commissioned officers to assist him in the vital areas of reconnaissance, security, and the disposition of the army.[55] Here he laid the first foundations of his concept that later became known as the 'General Staff with Troops' [*Truppengeneralstab*], which he continually refined to meet the needs of a changing art of war. This treatise suggests he believed the Hanoverians (and most likely the coalition) had operated blindly in 1793, without adequate maps of the theatre of war, if they had had any maps at all. He also felt that most of the senior commanders had little knowledge of the geography of Flanders, its key terrain features, the best routes to march their troops, and the most favourable manoeuvre areas on which to conduct their operations.[56] Coalition cavalry had not conducted adequate reconnaissance to ascertain and report critical information on the topography or on the French. Nor had cavalry provided reliable security during the campaign.[57]

Scharnhorst then pointed out another glaring deficiency. He told Wallmoden how Hanoverian outposts had not been properly established, adequately manned, or linked together to provide all-around security for the army and early warning of any French attack. Wallmoden must have recognised this, since he had neglected to establish forward outposts at Handschoote and then had to order Cochenhausen to move forward with his Hessians and drive off French skirmishers and reconnaissance troops. Scharnhorst concluded this portion of his paper by stating that with the addition of a few good officers and non-commissioned

(ed.), *Militärische Schriften von Scharnhorst*, pp.192-242; and then in Gersdorff (ed.), *Gerhard von Scharnhorst: Ausgewählte Schriften*, pp.45-110; and also in Usczeck and Gudzent (ed.), *Gerhard von Scharnhorst: Ausgewählte militärische Schriften*, pp.97-150.

54 See the documentation in 'Die Reorganisation der Hannoverschen Armee 1794-1800 und Scharnhorsts Anteil daran', *Nachlaß Scharnhorst*, No.73; deposited at the Geheimes Staatsarchiv Preussischer Kulturbesitz, 196/VI. HA Familienarchive und Nachlässe, Berlin (Dahlem). Most of these documents are published in Kunisch (ed.), *Scharnhorst: Privat und dienstliche Schriften*, Vol.1 and Vol.2: *Stabschef und Reformer (Kurhannover 1795-1801)*, and cited individually below.

55 See Gerhard Scharnhorst, 'Nutzen einer Erweiterung unsers General-Staabs', in Kunisch (ed.), *Scharnhorst: Privat und dienstliche Schriften*, Vol.1, pp.331-34. This treatise can also be found in Hann 41: *Akten des Generalkommandos mit den Militär-Akten der Londoner Kanzlei. 18.-19. Jahrhundert*, Nr.191, Sheets 31-34; deposited at the Niedersächsisches Landesarchiv, Hanover.

56 Gerhard Scharnhorst, '§ I. Geographische Berichte und militairische Situations-Risse', *Von dem Dienst der Officiere des Generalquartiermeister-Staabes im Kriege* (between April 1795 and October 1797); in Kunisch (ed.), *Scharnhorst: Privat und dienstliche Schriften*, Vol.1, pp.698-700.

57 On the failure of coalition cavalry, see Scharnhorst, 'Einige Bemerkungen über den Gebrauch der Artillerie in der Campagne von 1793', in Kunisch (ed.), *Scharnhorst: Privat und dienstliche Schriften*, Vol.1, p.299.

officers on the General Staff, these deficiencies could be corrected, and the commanding general would have at his disposal a much clearer picture of the theatre of war and his tactical situation, so he could operate as Frederick the Great had campaigned during the Seven Years War.

As Scharnhorst pointed out the shortcomings of the previous campaign, he provided his solutions. He first addressed the necessity for two to three additional officers responsible for reconnoitring the area of operations and providing the commanding general with a detailed analysis of the countryside, complete with maps and sketches showing the salient features of the terrain. He suggested that this type of work is extremely valuable in wartime. Security measures came next. The addition of two talented officers to oversee the establishment of good outposts and the overall security arrangements of the army 'would be of great use'. These officers would operate initially with the advance guard and monitor the security of the army on the march. After establishing the outpost system and rendering a complete report to the commanding general, they would then be responsible for maintaining liaison between the field units and for gathering intelligence on enemy dispositions and intentions. Scharnhorst also stated that it may also be necessary for these officers to lead patrols. During combat actions they would serve 'as senior assistants to the commanding general, as commanders of the flank and other columns, etc'.[58]

In the last section of his paper Scharnhorst addressed his major point. 'Indispensable to the commanding general are a few officers he can use to strengthen his control of the overall situation'.[59] This crucial concept would become the central theme of all of his later concept papers on the duties of the General Staff with Troops. These officers would assist the commanding general with the operational control and tactical disposition of the army, would develop detailed contingency plans, and would advise the individual field commanders as responsible and authoritative spokesmen of the commanding general. As always, Scharnhorst used history to support his case. This time he cited Frederick the Great's victory over the Austrians at Liegnitz (1760) to illustrate the critical importance of general staff officers capable of assisting the commanding general as needed on campaign and of adapting quickly to the ever-changing situations on the battlefield.

What is truly revealing about Scharnhorst's suggestions for expanding the General Staff is the way in which he addressed the deficiencies he noted. So as not to point the finger of blame at any person or institution, he never directly mentioned any specific failure of the Hanoverian army. Instead, he maintained a positive approach throughout, politely inferring how much more at ease the commanding general would feel if he had better knowledge of the theatre of war, if he knew the terrain on which he manoeuvred his force, and if his security measures provided adequate protection for the army. All of this and much more, the commanding general could have if he just added a few good officers to his general staff. They could perform these vital tasks for him, just as Frederick's selected officers had done for him. This would leave him free to lead the army. What is also interesting is the fact that Scharnhorst had already published (anonymously) months earlier many of his concerns

58 Scharnhorst, 'Nutzen einer Erweiterung unsers General-Staabs', in Kunisch (ed.), *Scharnhorst: Privat und dienstliche Schriften*, Vol.1, pp.331-34; the quoted passages are from p.332.

59 Scharnhorst, 'Nutzen einer Erweiterung unsers General-Staabs', in Kunisch (ed.), *Scharnhorst: Privat und dienstliche Schriften*, Vol.1, pp.332-34; the quoted passage is from p.332.

and recommendations in *New Military Journal*.[60] Although no authors are listed for these articles, they contain many of his usual phrases and choice of words.

Citing Frederick the Great was one of Scharnhorst's favourite techniques, whenever he sought to affect modernisation of the army (both in Hanover and later in Prussia). He knew nearly all the senior leaders in Hanover, Hesse, Brunswick, and Prussia had fought under the Prussian king during the Seven Years War. They certainly admired Frederick and were immensely proud to have served with him during that conflict. Scharnhorst knew the mere mention of Frederick's name would catch their attention. He was also a student and great admirer of Frederick and, from his studies of the great king, knew Frederick had the best interests of his army in mind whenever he chose to modify its tactical doctrine, organisation, or administration.

Using examples from the wars of Frederick the Great to introduce his concepts became second nature for Scharnhorst. Interestingly, while in Menin that winter of 1793-1794, he put the final touches on the 'Introduction' to his edition of *Frederick's Instructions to His Generals*, which he had tried to complete and publish prior to marching off to war in 1793. His idea at that time was to present copies to Hanover's senior military leadership, hoping that Frederick's instructions to his generals might aid Hanover's generals on campaign (just as Frederick had hoped they would with his generals).[61]

With these subtle recommendations to the Wallmoden, Scharnhorst laid the first foundations of his evolving General Staff with Troops concept. He may also have intended to demonstrate his insight and analytical ability to Wallmoden, who was probably more receptive to his ideas than was Trew. At this point in his career, Scharnhorst knew he would never be promoted nor given command of a company as long as Trew was his commanding officer.[62] Even though he was truly unhappy with this situation, he again reassured his wife, telling Klara, 'The future is so uncertain that you must settle for anything you can get'.[63] He most likely hoped that from this uncertainty would come that opportunity which would enable him to excel.

Even at Menin Scharnhorst had to deal with the continuing efforts of Trew to bring him under effective control. From what Scharnhorst told his wife in late February 1794, during the weeks after he had returned to Menin following the 6 February meeting at Brugge, Braun kept seeking him out to require him to acknowledge Braun's authority over him. This was the same Braun who had tried to solicit Scharnhorst's favour a few weeks earlier. While he obviously knew what Braun was trying to accomplish, Scharnhorst chose to recognise Braun's command role only in the spirit of army regulations. 'This is not good', he freely

60 For example, see Gerhard Scharnhorst, 'Nachricht von den Landkarten des jetzigen Kriegestheater', *Neues militärisches Journal* 7 (1793), pp.101-08; and 'Verhalten eines Officiers, welcher im Felde mit 30 bis 40 Pferden von dem Corps oder Regimente, bey welchem er dienet, auf 1 bis 2 oder wol mehrere Stunden entfernt voraus commandirt wird', *Neues militärisches Journal* 7 (1793), pp.231-76. A closer inspection of the second article reveals it contains a good deal of information from wartime operations and appears to be lessons learned from the 1793 campaign. Much of this information can also be found in the third edition of Scharnhorst's *Military Field Pocket Book* (1794).

61 See the Postscript of Scharnhorst's Letter of 29/30 March 1793 to the Helwing Bookstore; in Kunisch (ed.), *Scharnhorst: Privat und dienstliche Schriften*, Vol.1, p.200.

62 Scharnhorst told Klara this in his Letter of 12 April 1794; in Kunisch (ed.), *Scharnhorst: Privat und dienstliche Schriften*, Vol.1, p.365.

63 Letter of 1 and 5 January 1794 to Klara; in Kunisch (ed.), *Scharnhorst: Privat und dienstliche Schriften*, Vol.1, p.307.

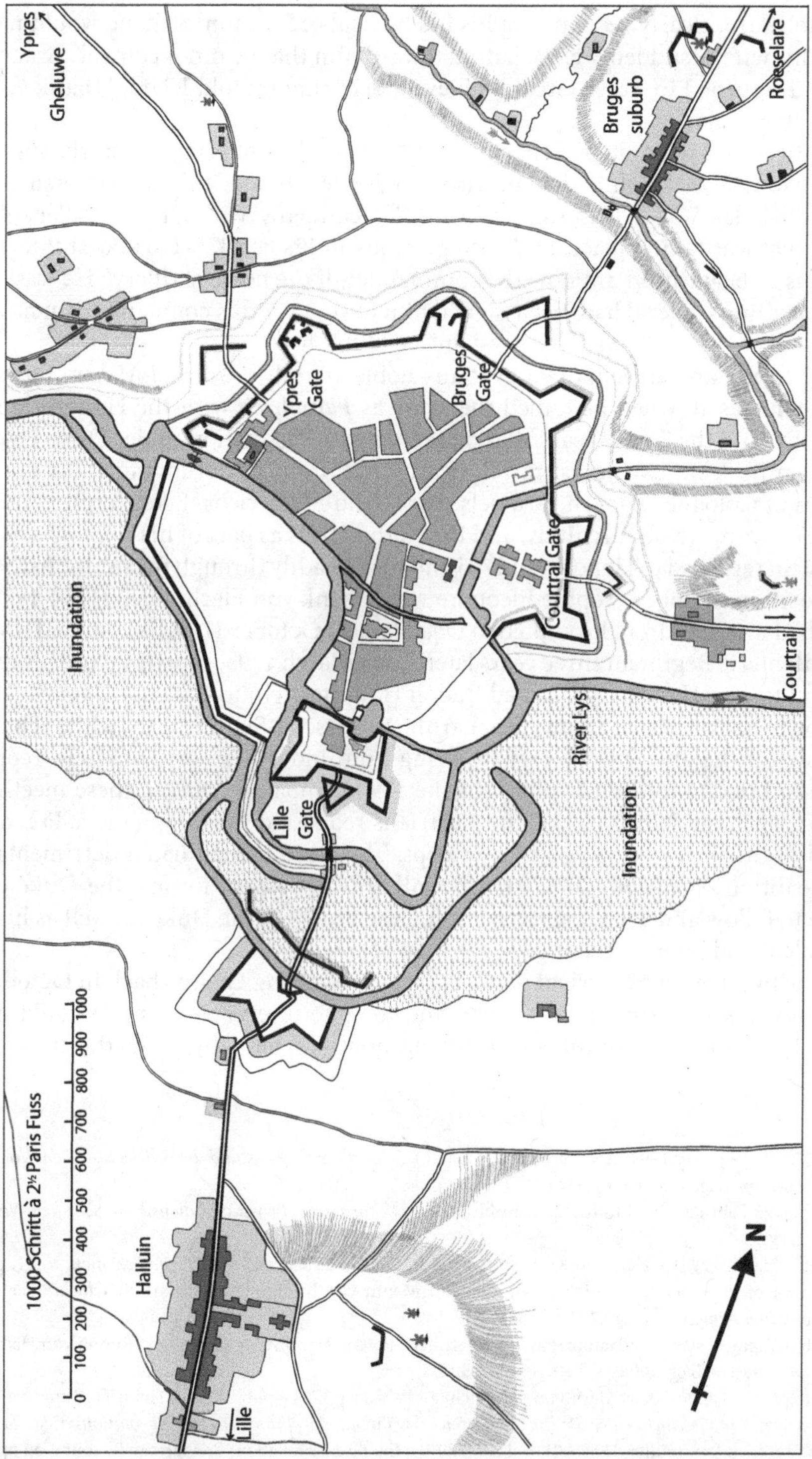

Map 5 Menin, April 1794.

admitted to Klara, clearly recognising his likely insubordination. Still, he would not yield. As he told his wife, 'I suddenly feel a hatred toward him that I cannot control'. Braun finally gave up and returned to Trew. Greatly relieved, Scharnhorst told Klara, 'Thank God I am away from that Major'.[64]

'I am so tired and frustrated', Scharnhorst told Klara in late February, as the intrigues of Trew began to take their toll.[65] Then on 1 March, his spirits suddenly skyrocketed. Arriving in Menin that day was a Hanoverian grenadier company without its artillery support. Realising what was taking place, and with great joy in his heart, Scharnhorst informed his wife, 'This is so beautiful! I am now the commander of the horse artillery'. He was ecstatic! The Commanding General had just assigned him to support this company. 'I am now under the command of General von Hammerstein', he told Klara.[66]

Hailing from an ancient Hanoverian noble family, *General-Major* Rudolf von Hammerstein was 16 when he joined the army as *Fähndrich* with the Hanoverian Garde Regiment. During the Seven Years War he served with distinction under Duke Ferdinand. After the war he spent two years travelling around Europe and studying at the prestigious universities of Cologne, Aachen, Brussels, Paris, and Maastricht. Like Count Wilhelm, he journeyed to Lyon, Strasbourg, Italy, and the Netherlands as part of his *Bildung* experience. Hammerstein returned to Hanover in 1765 and rose steadily through the ranks. In the spring of 1772, he married Louise Sophie Eleonore von Schenk von Flechtingen (1754-1835), with whom he had nine children. Promoted to *Oberst* on 22 October 1789, he assumed command of the 6. Infanterie Regiment three years later. On 3 March 1793, shortly before his regiment marched off to war, Hanover promoted Rudolf Hammerstein to *General-Major*.[67]

Wallmoden had once again come to Scharnhorst's rescue. Significantly, while Scharnhorst was fending-off the attempts of Trew to bring him under his sway, Austrian representatives were in London to discuss plans for the 1794 campaign. During these meeting with British ministers and King George, the Austrians requested the king remove Freytag from command of the Hanoverian Auxiliary Corps. They said he had had a detrimental influence on coalition operations in 1793, especially his disrespect toward the Duke of York, his failure to follow and even countermanding the orders of the Duke, as well as his lack of military talent and poor leadership.[68]

'From the moment of his arrival here', York had told King George back in October 1793, 'he [Freytag] was exceedingly shy of me, and in spite of every advance I could make to him'. The Duke of York continued by noting how Freytag 'always in the most marked

64 Letter of 21-23 February 1794 to Klara; in Kunisch (ed.), *Scharnhorst: Privat und dienstliche Schriften*, Vol.1, pp.339-40; the quoted passages are from p.339 (23 February).

65 Letter of 21-23 February 1794 to Klara; in Kunisch (ed.), *Scharnhorst: Privat und dienstliche Schriften*, Vol.1, p. 340 (23 February).

66 Letter of 1 March 1794 to Klara; in Kunisch (ed.), *Scharnhorst: Privat und dienstliche Schriften*, Vol.1, p.341. The organisation of Hammerstein's force in and around Menin can be found in Sichart, *Geschichte der Königlich-Hannoverischen Armee*, Vol.4, pp.262 and 381.

67 See the biographical sketch of Hammerstein by Bernhard Poten, 'Hammerstein: Freiherr Rudolf von Hammerstein', *Allgemeine Deutsche Biographie*, Vol.10, pp.492-93.

68 See the Report of Colonel Karl Mack von Leiberich (18 February 1794); published in Heinrich Ritter von Zeissberg (ed.), *Quellen zur Geschichte der Politik Oesterreichs während der Französiscgen Revolutionskriege (1793-1797)* (Vienna: Wilhelm Braumüller, 1882-90), Vol.2, pp.89-96; the discussion about Freytag can be found on pp.91-92.

manner avoided me and took every opportunity of finding fault with everything'. York also mentioned how Freytag would talk 'publickly [sic] here to everybody' about him behind his back.[69] Even Scharnhorst had noticed Freytag's insubordinate behaviour. In May 1793 he had told Klara how 'Freytag issues all orders without consulting the Duke'.[70] Freytag's health may have also been an issue.

After a private discussion with the senior Austrian representative, King George gave his consent. York then informed the field marshal on 8 March. 'He [Freytag] seemed a good deal affected, and I confess that though we have not always agreed yet I sincerely felt for him', York told his father.[71] Interestingly, a month after Hondschoote, York had told the king, 'I have ordered General Walmoden [sic], in whose talents, courage and prudence I have the fullest reliance, to take command of the corps'. At that time the Duke informed King George that Freytag was on his way to England, where 'he will now have the opportunity of seeing your Majesty and of explaining as well as he can his conduct'.[72] After meeting with York, Freytag left for London and King George placed Wallmoden in command of the Hanoverian Auxiliary Corps.[73] It appears Trew had lost his benefactor.

'General Wallmoden is so good to me', Scharnhorst told Klara in his letter of 12 April 1794, explaining how the Commanding General was aware of Trew's schemes. A few days earlier the artillery chief had come to Menin, ostensibly to inspect the artillery arrangements there, but most likely to quiet the negative reports about the behaviour of Ritter and Braun, who had acted on his orders. At lunch with Hammerstein, Trew clearly became agitated when Hammerstein informed him of the 'great confidence' he had in Scharnhorst, who 'prefers to be with me rather than with the horse artillery'. Infuriated by this remark, Trew lashed back at Hammerstein, declaring, 'Without me he [Scharnhorst] can do nothing!' Trew then informed Hammerstein, 'If you are so pleased with Scharnhorst, you can support him, and I will tell this to him'.[74] Trew must have told Scharnhorst; for on 13 April, Scharnhorst wrote a letter of apology to him that referred to his visit to Menin and asked the general's forgiveness for any misunderstanding.[75] Although this commentary is Scharnhorst's recollection of events, it is consistent with other evidence regarding Trew's behaviour and his displeasure with Scharnhorst, and is thus worthy of consideration.

69 See the Letter of 25 October 1793 from the Duke of York to King George III; in Aspinall (ed.), *The Later Correspondence of George III*, Vol.2, pp.112-13; the quoted passages are from p.112.

70 Letter of 5-12 May 1793 to Klara; in Kunisch (ed.), *Scharnhorst: Privat und dienstliche Schriften*, Vol.1, pp.209-14; the quoted passage is from p.210 (5 May).

71 Letter of 8 March 1794 from the Duke of York to King George III; in Aspinall (ed.), *The Later Correspondence of George III*, Vol.2, pp.183-84; the quoted passage is from p.184.

72 See the Letter of 25 October 1793 from the Duke of York to King George III; in Aspinall (ed.), *The Later Correspondence of George III*, Vol.2, pp.112-13; the quoted passages are from p.112.

73 The source documents for this action can be found in Hann 41, III, Nr.188: *Ableben des Feldmarschalls von Freytag und dessen stille Beerdigung. Übertragung seines Kommandos an den General der Kavallerie von Wallmoden-Gimborn*; deposited at the Niedersächsisches Landesarchiv, Hanover.

74 Letter of 12 April 1794 to Klara; in Kunisch (ed.), *Scharnhorst: Privat und dienstliche Schriften*, Vol.1, pp.365-66; the quoted passages are from pp.366 and 365; respectively.

75 Letter of 13 April 1794 to General Trew; in Kunisch (ed.), *Scharnhorst: Privat und dienstliche Schriften*, Vol.1, pp.367-68.

Prince Adolphus also admired *General-Major* Hammerstein and had sought to learn from him. Writing to King George during the early months of the 1793 campaign, Adolphus explained how Hammerstein was mentoring him.

> Last Saturday [1 June] I have had the inspection of the right wing, as Field Officer of the day. I was employed the greatest part of the night with General Hammerstein in placing the piquetes [sic] which were very much advanced, and in the morning at three o'clock I went with him to Briquet, a village where there is a battalion always on duty and which is relieved every night, which is only 800 yards from Valenciennes. I was very happy of doing this duty for by that a very clear idea how our chain of posts is placed.[76]

Now, a year later, the prince informed his king how Hammerstein 'is a most excellent worthy man; a person to whom I am under great obligations, as he gave me lessons in tacticks [sic] in Hannover'.[77] Significantly, in a number of his later memoranda and studies on the war and Hanoverian operations, Scharnhorst often cited Hammerstein's superb combat leadership and field craft as examples of excellence and worthy of emulation.

In late March 1794, Hammerstein informed Wallmoden of his confidence in Scharnhorst and the ability of coalition forces now assembling in and around Menin to hold the town.[78] He also reported that Austrian, Hessian, and Hanoverian soldiers, supported by a French *émigré* battalion of engineers (under the command of French *émigré Capitaine* St Paul), were working tirelessly to establish an impenetrable defensive position of earthworks and palisades.[79] In his earlier report to the Commanding General, Scharnhorst had also expressed his confidence in the ability of coalition forces to defend Menin. He cited several historical examples that illustrated how similar strongpoints in the past had successfully withstood long sieges.[80] In late March, he submitted his overall assessment of the situation, first to Hammerstein (who had requested it), and then to the Commanding

76 Letter of 4 June 1793 from Prince Adolphus to King George; in Aspinall (ed.), *The Later Correspondence of George III*, Vol.2, pp.46-47; the quoted passage is from p.47.

77 Letter of 18 June 1794 from Prince Adolphus to King George; in Aspinall (ed.), *The Later Correspondence of George III*, Vol.2, p.219.

78 Hammerstein's Report of 25 March 1794 to Wallmoden can be found in Klippel, *Scharnhorst*, Vol.2, pp.52-53. This report and a number of other reports from Hammerstein can be found in Hann 38 E, Nr.164: *Menin: Rapporte des Generals von Hammerstein aus Menin an den General von Wallmoden zu Courtray vom 27.3 und 30.4.1794 über verschiedene die Festung und deren Außenwerke betreffende Angelegenheiten, 03.1794-04.1794*; deposited at the Niedersächsisches Landesarchiv, Hanover. Demet, *'We are Accustomed to do our Duty'*, p.76, provides a listing of these forces.

79 See Hammerstein's Report of 25 March 1794 to Wallmoden; in Klippel, *Scharnhorst*, Vol.2, pp.52-53. Also see the discussion in Lehmann, *Scharnhorst*, Vol.1, pp.140-41. St Paul's reports can be found in Hann 38 E, Nr.168: *Menin: Rapporte des in englischem Sold stehenden französischen Ingenieur-Capitains Chevalier de St.Paul über die Armierung und Befestigung von Menin*; deposited at the Niedersächsisches Landesarchiv, Hanover.

80 See Gerhard Scharnhorst, 'Über die Befestigung der Stadt Menin' (11 March 1794); in Kunisch (ed.), *Scharnhorst: Privat und dienstliche Schriften*, Vol.1, pp.342-44. Also see the source documents in Hann 38 E, Nr.168: *Menin: Rapporte des Capitains Scharnhorst für einen etwaigen feindlichen Angriff. Pläne von Menin und Werwicq*; deposited at the Niedersächsisches Landesarchiv, Hanover.

General.[81] The next day Scharnhorst provided another report that summarised the work the troops had accomplished to date to fortify Menin.[82]

Despite the optimistic reports from Hammerstein and Scharnhorst, Wallmoden was concerned and he did not like the defensive posture of coalition forces.[83] In his report to King George, the Commanding General also questioned the stationing of Ritter's division in Menin. He told the king that such large calibre 'siege guns' have no place and little utility in a forward position such as Menin.[84] In doing so, Wallmoden challenged the judgment of his artillery chief, who was willing to expose his artillerymen and their siege guns to unnecessary danger. Then in early April he diverted Prince Adolphus and the Garde Regiment from Menin, unwilling to expose the prince to the dangers there.[85]

'I am really upset with our General', Scharnhorst informed Klara in mid-April.[86] While in Menin Trew had promoted Ritter to *Oberstlieutenant*, since Scharnhorst now addressed him as such.[87] Along with one of his battery commanders, *Capitain* Gottlieb Schüßler, Ritter seemed to enjoy Scharnhorst's predicament. 'It is shameful', Scharnhorst continued, 'that the General makes no distinction between capable and useless officers'. He was clearly upset both Braun and Ritter had been promoted, since both were 'useless officers' in his mind.[88] What really enraged him was the fact that it was Ritter's division that had panicked under fire at Famars and had fled the battlefield. Now Ritter was an *Oberstlieutenant* while Scharnhorst, who had distinguished himself under fire at Hondschoote and during the retreat to Furnes, remained a *Titular-Capitain*. As Scharnhorst poured out his wrath and frustration on Klara, he suddenly realised it was not her fault and apologised to her for being 'so egotistical'. In closing he told her, 'There is no security in this world, no lasting happiness, only endless catfights [*Katzbalgerey*], and I have it all'.[89]

Scharnhorst worried about the future. From Menin in late March he had told Klara, 'War is so dreadful'. While his knowledge of history was somewhat reassuring, he informed his wife that though the French were 'pretty quiet' at the moment, he believed they would

81 See Gerhard Scharnhorst, 'Aufrage und Meldung, welche ich auf Befehl des Herrn General Major von Hammerstein den Herrn General der Cavalerie Graf von Wallmoden Gimborn Excellenz gethan, nebst den Antworten desselben' (27 March 1794); in Kunisch (ed.), *Scharnhorst: Privat und dienstliche Schriften*, Vol.1, pp.353-54.

82 Report of 28 March 1794 to Wallmoden; in Kunisch (ed.), *Scharnhorst: Privat und dienstliche Schriften*, Vol.1, pp.354-55. Scharnhorst may have also attached his memorandum, 'Verstärkung des Postens von Wervik' [Editor's Title] (March/April 1794); in Kunisch (ed.), *Scharnhorst: Privat und dienstliche Schriften*, Vol.1, pp.355-56.

83 See the discussion in Gerhard Scharnhorst, 'Stärke innerer Zustand und Kriegstheater der verbundenen Armeen in den Niederlanden, im Jahre 1794', *Neues militärisches Journal* 8 (1797), pp.274-326.

84 Excerpts from Wallmoden's report (no date) are printed in Klippel, *Scharnhorst*, Vol.2, pp.62-63; the quoted passage is from p.63. Klippel notes that Wallmoden sent his report through Freytag, who was back at the Court of St James.

85 See the Letter of 8 April 1794 from Prince Adolphus to King George; in Aspinall (ed.), *The Later Correspondence of George III*, Vol.2, p.192-93.

86 Letter of 14 April 1794 to Klara; in Kunisch (ed.), *Scharnhorst: Privat und dienstliche Schriften*, Vol.1, pp.369-70; the quoted passage is from p.369.

87 According to the editors of Scharnhorst's Papers, Ritter's official date of promotion was 1 January 1794. See Note 4 of Scharnhorst's Letter of 17 and 18 November 1793 to Klara; in Kunisch (ed.), *Scharnhorst: Privat und dienstliche Schriften*, Vol.1, p.288.

88 Sichart, *Geschichte der Königlich-Hannoverischen Armee*, Vol.4, p.18. cites the pre-war ranks of Braun and Ritter in 1789 as *Capitain*.

89 Letter of 14 April 1794; in Kunisch (ed.), *Scharnhorst: Privat und dienstliche Schriften*, Vol.1, pp.369-70; the quoted passages are from pp.369 and 370.

soon unleash a horrific onslaught against the coalition. 'In all probability we can expect increasingly dangerous operations', he wrote. He then told Klara that momentarily 'all is peaceful' in Menin. His brother Heinrich (who was recently promoted to *Capitain*) was one of the outpost commanders. Two former students – *Fähndrich* August Röttiger and *Fähnrich* Georg Julius von Hartmann (later General Sir Julius von Hartmann, 1774-1836) – were there as well. Scharnhorst had been particularly impressed with young Hartmann as a student, while Röttiger had served with Scharnhorst at Hondschoote.[90] Along with several infantry officers, these artillerymen were making 'a punch' to celebrate the coming of spring. Morale was high and this clearly delighted Scharnhorst. Then he remembered: 'Today is our deployment day [*Aufmarschtag*]; we have been away one year now'. Hoping to see his wife and family soon, he thanked Klara for 'all of the friendship and goodness you have shown me'. Ending his letter, he wrote, 'If only the French would remain still for a few days more'.[91]

90 See *Major* Julius von Hartmann (ed.), *Der Königlich Hannoversche General Sir Julius von Hartmann: Ein Lebensskizze* (Hanover: Helwing Hofbuchhandlung, 1858), pp.7-9.

91 Letter of 23 March 1794 to Klara; in Kunisch (ed.), *Scharnhorst: Privat und dienstliche Schriften*, Vol.1, pp.349-50; the quoted passages are from p.350.

9

Extraordinary Combat Leader

Three weeks after Scharnhorst had written to Klara on 23 March, French armies 'made their appearance in West Flanders', as the opening moves of the campaign of 1794 began.[1] Coalition forces were again dispersed in a cordon defence instead of being concentrated. This time they were stretched in small outposts along the front, from the English Channel to the River Meuse.[2] The Hanoverians were location around Menin, Nieuport, and Ypern. Looking over the strategic situation must have reminded Wallmoden what had taken place the previous September, when the Hanoverians had found themselves in a similar defensive posture.[3] He may have also acknowledged the validity of Scharnhorst's proposals. Significantly, Wallmoden had already taken steps to improve the security of his forces, first by ordering Hammerstein to occupy and strengthen the area in and around Menin, and then by adjusting the positions of his other commands to defend against an anticipated French attack. On 24 March, he sent a letter of encouragement to the officers in Menin (most likely the main point of a French attack), thanking them for their loyal and faithful service and wishing them well in the days to come.[4] It was here that Scharnhorst secured his reputation as a warrior.

Already hard at work when Hammerstein and his command arrived in early March, Scharnhorst implemented his emerging model of a General Staff with Troops, assuming the role of 'Chief of Staff' to Hammerstein, while continuing to command his battery and

1 See the interesting contemporary account by Captain Lewis Tobias Jones, *An Historical Journal of the British Campaign on the Continent, In the Year 1794* (Birmingham: Swinney and Hawkins, 1797); the quoted passage is from p.2. Also see the later publications of Scharnhorst, 'Stärke innerer Zustand und Kriegstheater der verbundenen Armeen in den Niederlanden, im Jahre 1794'; and 'Feldzug der verbundenrn Armeen in Flanders, im Jahre 1794', *Neues militärisches Journal* 9 (1798), pp.169-369.

2 Colonel James Henry Craig, the new Adjutant General to the Duke of York, wrote a scathing letter to the War Office in London criticising the defensive measures of the coalition, predicting 'nothing but misfortune' for the Allies. See Sir John W. Fortescue, *British Campaigns in Flanders,* p.289. A good recent study of German forces is Demet, '*We are Accustomed to do our Duty*', especially Chapter 5 (pp.65-85). On p.72, Demet provides a nice map of the theatre of war from March to July 1794.

3 Significantly, Wallmoden had raised doubts about the Hanoverian defence in his report to King George around March 1794; excerpted in Klippel, *Scharnhorst*, Vol.2, pp.62-63. The organisation of the Hanoverian contingent in 1794 can be found in Sichart, *Geschichte der Königlich-Hannoverischen Armee*, Vol.4, pp.331-32; their locations in Flanders are on pp.341-42.

4 *General der Cavallerie* Wallmoden to the Officers in Menin (24 March 1794); published in Kunisch (ed.), *Scharnhorst: Privat und dienstliche Schriften*, Vol.1, p.351.

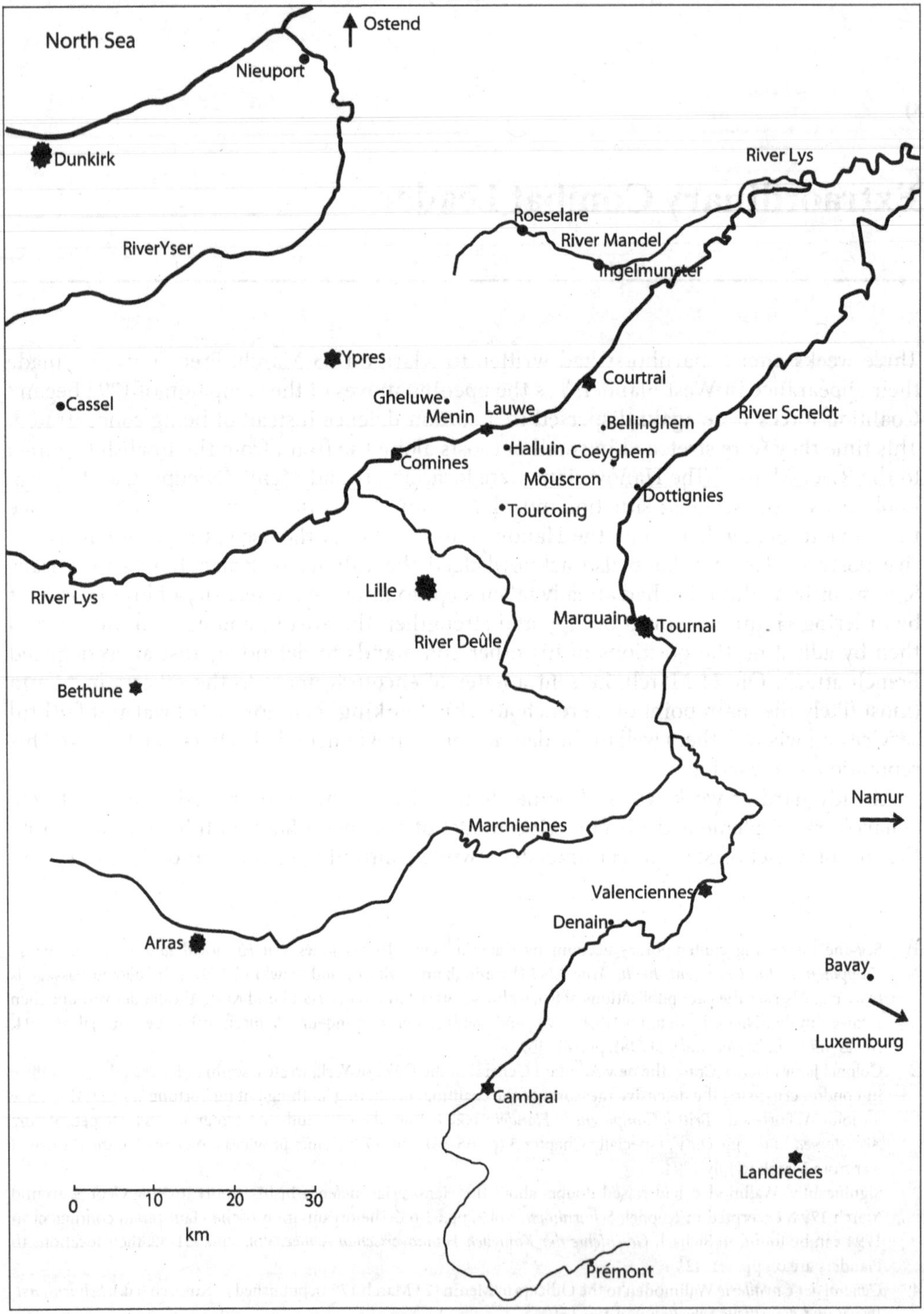

Map 6 Theatre of War in Flanders, March to July 1794.

to strengthen the town's defence. As Hammerstein's chief of staff, Scharnhorst was instrumental in coordinating all the activities of the garrison, thus relieving Hammerstein of these essential duties so he could focus his full attention on envisaging how to defend Menin. Despite a shortage of men and material, Scharnhorst was able to obtain additional help from French *émigré* engineers in British pay and set about improvising a network of strongpoints and positions, barricades and ditches, like the defensive systems he had constructed at Wilhelmstein.[5] 'A considerable body of peasants' were also employed in rebuilding Menin.[6] In a very brief message to the Wallmoden in mid-April, Hammerstein reported, 'Our troops are ready to engage the enemy'.[7]

By late April 1794, some 14,000 Frenchmen under the command of *Général de Division* Jean-Victor Moreau (1763-1813) had surrounded the small garrison of only 2,423 troops.[8] When the French failed to take Menin by storm, they began shelling the town during the night of 27 April and continued throughout the 28th. This achieved little success, even after the French brought mortars into action. The assessment Scharnhorst had made to Wallmoden that Menin would hold seemed to be coming true. Under pressure to capture Menin, Moreau offered Hammerstein generous terms of surrender on the morning of 29 April. Since French policy was to execute any *émigré* soldier, Hammerstein politely refused, informing Moreau, 'We are accustomed to doing our duty. We will not surrender'.[9] This response clearly infuriated the French, who resumed their bombardment, this time using 'red-hot shells' to burn the town to the ground. Meanwhile, coalition troops were unable to break through French lines to relieve Menin. With food, water, and ammunition running out, it was just a matter of time before Menin fell.

Scharnhorst had no trouble convincing Hammerstein during a council of war held on the evening of 29 April to save his command by launching a pre-emptive strike against the French. It was a daring, yet brilliant idea, and during the early morning hours of 30 April, coalition forces fought their way out against overwhelming odds. Even after the French had repulsed the first attempt to break through their lines, Hammerstein never wavered. He trusted implicitly in Scharnhorst's leadership and judgment. Scharnhorst had carefully studied the countryside around Menin since his arrival in November 1793; he knew the terrain well and the best way out.

At this critical juncture, Scharnhorst advised Hammerstein not to fall back into Menin. Instead he recommended Hammerstein order the rear guard forward and attack.

5 Gerhard Scharnhorst, 'Über die Befestigung der Stadt Menin' (11 March 1794); in Kunisch (ed.), *Scharnhorst: Privat und dienstliche Schriften*, Vol.1, pp.342-44. His cover letter to General Wallmoden is on p.342. Scharnhorst's detailed reports to Wallmoden throughout March and April on the various construction projects, the placement of artillery, and other defensive measures at Menin, can be found on pp.351-60 and 362-63. Several of these reports are also printed in Klippel, *Scharnhorst*, Vol.2, pp.55-60.

6 See Harry Calvert's remarks in Verney (ed.), *The Journals and Correspondence of General Sir Harry Calvert*, p.179.

7 Hammerstein's report to Wallmoden can be found in Klippel, *Scharnhorst*, Vol.2, p.64.

8 Demet, '*We are Accustomed to do our Duty*', p.76, provides the organisation of the Menin garrison. On the next page is a beautifully detailed map of Menin, based on Scharnhorst's study of the fight.

9 Hammerstein is quoted in Klippel, *Scharnhorst*, Vol.2, p.83. Moreau's request for Hammerstein to surrender, along with Hammerstein's answer, are published as Appendix XI (p.374).

Hammerstein himself led this bayonet charge.[10] Although the fighting was intense and the Hanoverian artillery failed to engage the French and cover the breakout, in the confusion of battle, Scharnhorst led coalition forces to safety. By four in the morning, Hammerstein was assembling his troops in the village of Roeselare, far beyond the reach of the French.[11] He then sent a hasty message to Wallmoden to report his successful sortie from Menin. Among those Hammerstein left behind in Menin was *Oberstlieutenant* Georg Wilhelm Ritter.[12] Because his heavy siege guns were too cumbersome to take with the breakout force, Hammerstein had ordered Ritter and his gun crews to remain in Menin and provide covering fire for the breakout, which they failed to do.[13] The Commanding General's warning to King George about the danger of placing heavy howitzers in Menin had proven correct.

In his official report to Wallmoden, Hammerstein gave sole credit for the miraculous deliverance of the garrison to *Titular-Capitain* Gerhard Scharnhorst. 'I feel obliged to mention Captain Scharnhorst before all others', Hammerstein told the Commanding General:

> This man showed, during his entire time in Menin, throughout the bombardment – and finally at the breakout – competence and talent, combined with incomparable bravery, a fervour which never fatigued, and an amazing countenance. It is to these qualities that I attribute our long tenure in Menin during the bombardment and the success of our breakout plan. He was a splendid help to me in keeping matters well organised and in progress. In all operations, he was the first and the last. Enough! It is impossible for me to list all the ways in which this officer, a paragon of military virtues, has been of help to me.

10 This action is captured in the painting found on p.80 of Demet, '*We are Accustomed to do our Duty*'. A detailed, coloured map of the breakout route can be found in Defence Ministry of the Federal Republic of Germany (ed.), *Scharnhorst: Ausgewählte Briefe und Schriften*, in *Schriftenreihe Innere Führung*, Beiheft 3:85 (1985), p.67.

11 Highlights of this action come from Gerhard Scharnhorst, '*Rapport über die Belagerung von Menin*' (3 May 1794), and his 'Bericht von den Angrif auf Menin den 26., 27., 28. und 29. und den Durchschlagen der Garnison durch das Einschließungs Corps in der Nacht von 29sten auf den 30sten May 1794' (Summer 1794); found in Kunisch (ed.), *Scharnhorst: Privat und dienstliche Schriften*, Vol.1, pp.372-75 and 375-78; respectively. In his report Scharnhorst incorrectly gave May as the month. It should be April. A decade later he published his thoughts as Gerhard Scharnhorst, 'Die Vertheidigung der Stadt Menin und die Selbstbefreiung der Garnison unter dem Königlich Großbrittannisch-Chur-Hannöverschen General-Major von Hammerstein, im April 1794', *Neues militärisches Journal* 11 (1803), pp.173-320n. According to Paret, *Clausewitz and the State*, p.64 (Note 11), Scharnhorst's account 'became a minor classic in the literature of the revolutionary wars'. It was subsequently published as *Die Vertheidigung der Stadt Menin und die Selbstbefreiung der Garnison unter dem Generalmajor v. Hammerstein* (Hanover: Helwing, 1856); then incorporated in von der Goltz (ed.), *Militärische Schriften von Scharnhorst*, pp.1-58; and republished in *Kriegsgeschichtliche Bücherei*, Band 11 (Berlin: Junker and Dunnhaupt, 1936).

12 In Trew's compilation of losses in Menin, he cites one *Oberstlieutenant* as missing. See Klippel, *Scharnhorst*, Vol.2, p.377 (Appendix XIII). Hammerstein's official casualty list from Menin can be found in Sichart, *Geschichte der Königlich-Hannoverischen Armee*, Vol.4, p.407. The artillery losses follow on p.408, then a by-name list of officers from pp.408-09, with Ritter named on p.409. The source documents for these figures can be found in Hann 41, VIII, Nr.41: *Verlustlisten der Regimentsartillerie, 1793-1795*; deposited at the Niedersächsisches Landesarchiv, Hanover.

13 Scharnhorst to his wife Klara (after 30 April 1794); in Kunisch (ed.), *Scharnhorst: Privat und dienstliche Schriften*, Vol.1, p.371 and Note 2.

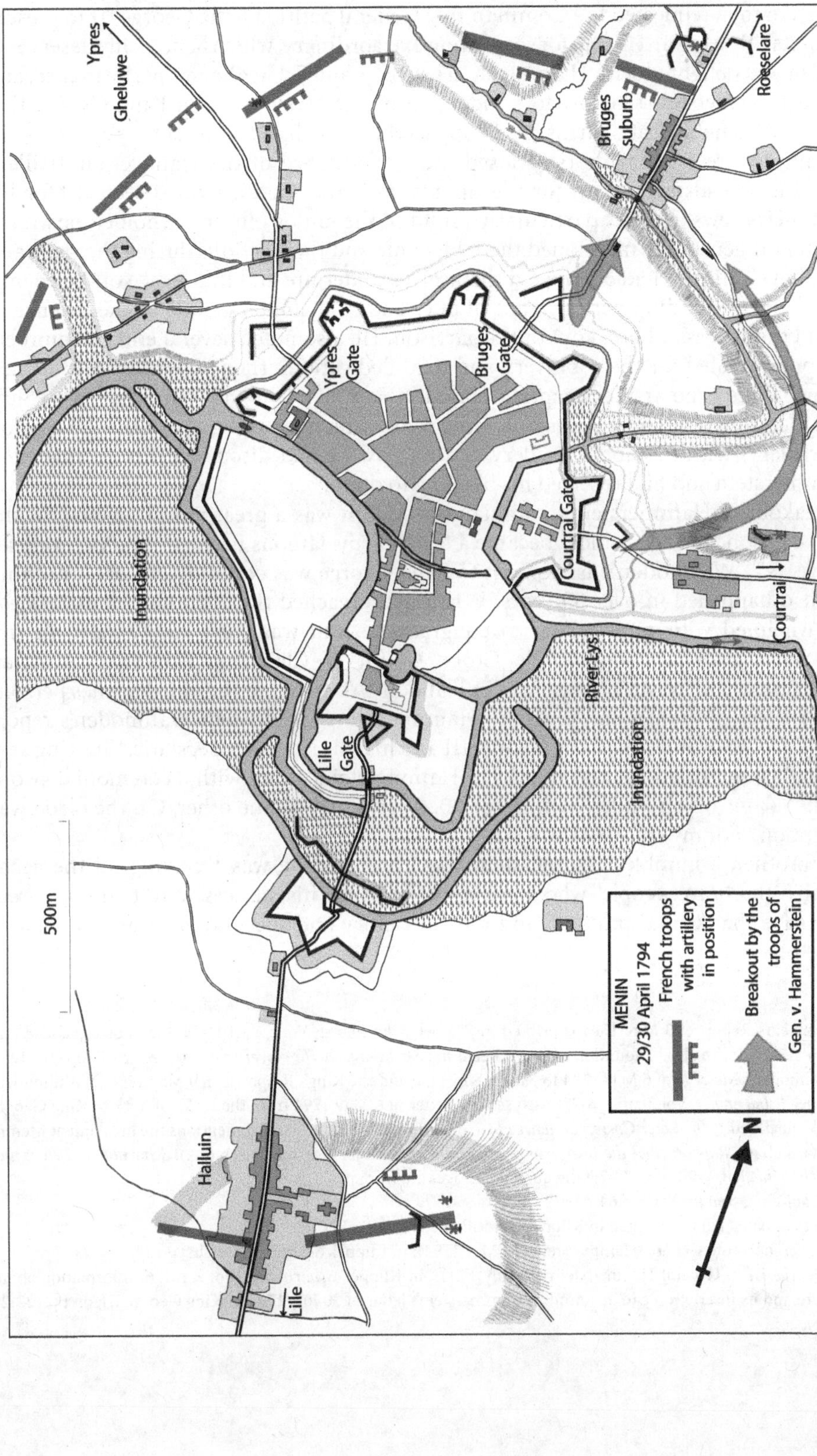

Map 7 Breakout from Menin, 29-30 April 1794.

Hammerstein then requested the Commanding General petition King George III to present Scharnhorst with 'a reward fitting for something extraordinary, which he so richly deserves'.[14] Wallmoden was delighted with Hammerstein's success and Scharnhorst's performance, and dispatched Hammerstein's report to London. In his postscript he told King George that 'nothing like this noble feat of arms has happened in more than half a century'.[15]

Reporting to Trew, Scharnhorst praised the performance of the Hanoverian artillery at Menin. He was also thankful for the infantrymen who had provided security for his guns and their crews. He was particularly proud of the junior officers, 'who demonstrated bravery and diligence'. He mentioned them by name and their actions during the siege and breakout, how well they had conducted themselves under fire and in the face of the enemy, and how their outstanding performance of duty had contributed greatly to the defence of Menin and the successful breakout of the garrison. He also noted several enlisted gunners who he congratulated for their 'bravery and total dedication'. Then Scharnhorst informed Trew, 'Since there is no artillery captain present' (Hammerstein had sent Schüßler to Sluis in the Netherlands), he had amalgamated the remaining men and guns of the 2. Division (heavy artillery) with his horse artillery, noting how he had discussed this arrangement with Hammerstein and had received his blessing to do so.[16]

The breakout of Hammerstein's command at Menin was a great moral victory for the faltering coalition, and one which 'became a feat of arms famous in the military chronicles of those years'.[17] Wallmoden's assessment to King George was certainly correct – nothing like this had happened in over 50 years. When news reached the coalition, Hammerstein was overwhelmed with praise. First to congratulate him was Austrian *Feldzeugmeister* François-Sébastien-Charles-Joseph de Croix, Count of Clairfayt (1733-98).[18] Austrian Emperor Francis II (1768-1835), who was in Flanders to command the allied armies personally, sent a letter of thanks and praise to Hammerstein.[19] And when Wallmoden's report reached the Court of St James, King George III and his ministers were ecstatic. The king sent his personal congratulations and thanks to Hammerstein, along with a ceremonial sword inscribed: 'Virtue' on one side; 'Menin, the 30. April 1794', on the other. On the blade was the inscription, 'For my country the King'.[20]

To his brother, a humble Hammerstein was upset that he was receiving all the accolades, while 'the brave people' who were responsible for his success were being ignored. While he gave thanks and praised 'God for the victory and success', he clearly wanted to

14 Hammerstein's Report of 3 May 1794 is printed in Klippel, *Scharnhorst*, Vol.2, pp.104-14; the quoted passages are from pp.113-14. It can also be found in Sichart, *Geschichte der Königlich-Hannoverischen Armee*, Vol.4, pp.409-12.

15 See Wallmoden's Message of 6 May 1794 to King George III; and the King's Response of 9 May 1794 to Wallmoden; in Klippel, *Scharnhorst*, Vol.2, pp.126-27. Also see the Letter of 6 May 1794 from the Duke of York to King George III; in Aspinall (ed.), *The Later Correspondence of George III*, Vol.2, pp.202-03, that mentions the breakout at Menin.

16 See Scharnhorst's '*Rapport über die Belagerung von Menin*' of 3 May 1794; in Kunisch (ed.), *Scharnhorst: Privat und dienstliche Schriften*, Vol.1, pp.372-75; the quoted passages are from p.374.

17 Paret, *Clausewitz and the State*, p.64.

18 Clairfayt's undated letter is printed in Klippel, *Scharnhorst*, Vol.2, pp.121-22.

19 Emperor Francis II to General Hammerstein (12 May 1794); in Klippel, *Scharnhorst*, Vol.2, p.122.

20 King George III to General Hammerstein (18 July 1794); in Klippel, *Scharnhorst*, Vol.2, p.126. Information about the sword and its inscription can be found in Hammerstein's letter of 30 July 1794 to King George III; on pp.127-28 (Note 1).

reward Scharnhorst.[21] By sending Schüßler to Holland prior to the commencement of the campaign, and by leaving Ritter behind in Menin during the breakout, Hammerstein had greatly assisted Scharnhorst by removing his closest antagonists. Reorganising all of the remaining artillery under Scharnhorst's command after the breakout sent a clear message to Trew. While no written account records Trew's reaction to these events, he may not have been very pleased with Scharnhorst's success or Hammerstein's assumption of his command prerogatives.

Elsewhere along the front, as Scharnhorst had predicted, French revolutionary fervour began sweeping coalition forces before it.[22] Despite initial coalition successes at Le Cateau, Fremont, and Vaux in April, the Duke of York worried about Austrian indecisiveness, which he believed might cause future problems for the coalition. As he told his father:

> No man on earth has more personal courage then General Clerfait [sic], but unfortunately his want of resolution and decision as a General is beyond all description, and was the real cause of the check which he received on the 29th, …[23]

In actions at Courtrai (11/12 May) and Tourcoing (17/18 May), French forces soundly defeated a combined Austro-British-Hanoverian army.[24] Following the fight at Courtrai, the Duke of York again wrote to his father, this time complaining about the bankruptcy of a cordon defence and essentially agreeing with Scharnhorst's earlier assessment to Wallmoden.

> I humbly agree with your Majesty that the system of cordons into which the Austrians have fallen ever since the beginning of this war, is exceedingly pernicious as well as dangerous, and has been the real origin of all the misfortune to which they have been subject.[25]

York then told his father that placing British, Hanoverian, and Hessian troops under Austrian command had been a big mistake, since the Austrians think only of themselves and have a 'sovereign contempt' for others.[26] By mid-May, the Duke of York had lost all confidence in Austrian leadership.

Echoing his commander's thoughts, Aide-de-Camp and now Lieutenant Colonel Harry Calvert wrote to his sister on 20 May 1794: 'The future prospects of the war are not very

21 Hammerstein's letter of 26 May 1794 to his brother can be found in Appendix XV of Klippel, *Scharnhorst*, Vol.2, p.378. Also see the summary of Hammerstein's career, which attests to his charity and humility; on pp.53-54.

22 See Scharnhorst, 'Geschichte des Feldzugs der verbundenen Armeen in Flandern, im Jahre 1794', pp.134-383.

23 Letter of 6 May 1794 from York to King George III; in Aspinall (ed.), *The Later Correspondence of George III*, Vol.2, pp.202-04; the quoted passage is from p.203.

24 See the beautiful Sketch Maps 5 'Vaux and Beaumont' and 6 'Tourcoing' (opposite pp.112 and 160; respectively); in Burne, *The Noble Duke of York*. From the Battle of Tourcoing came the English nursery rhyme, 'The Grand Old Duke of York', sometimes performed as a song. For the most recent theory regarding this rhyme, see Winterbottom, *The Grand Old Duke of York*, pp.68 and 164-69.

25 Letter of 13 May 1794 from York to King George III; in Aspinall (ed.), *The Later Correspondence of George III*, Vol.2, pp.205-06; the quoted passage is from p.205.

26 Letter of 13 May 1794 from York to King George III; in Aspinall (ed.), *The Later Correspondence of George III*, Vol.2, p.205. Interestingly, Wallmoden and Scharnhorst said the same of the British.

bright; and if the system of acting adopted by our Allies is not changed, it must, in the common course of things, become darker and darker'.[27] One of York's 'most trusted staff officers', Calvert lamented the fact the British had suffered so greatly.[28] 'I had, last year, an opportunity of seeking the Dutch and Hanoverian armies in the same state, but the sensation is very different when the blow falls on ourselves'. Again, repeating the standard excuse of the Duke of York, Calvert told his sister that 'no fault can be imputed to us, and that our loss was occasioned by the obstinate folly of others'.[29] Calvert's journal clearly exposed the tension among the senior leadership of the coalition.

Elsewhere, Hammerstein sought to halt the French advance and stabilize his immediate front. On 20 May, he wrote to Wallmoden, urgently requesting 'a battery of horse artillery', since such a battery 'would be far more useful to me than the heavy cannons I would be giving up'. Once again, Scharnhorst's report to Trew six months earlier about the utility of heavy artillery in fluid combat situations was correct. Hammerstein asked specifically for 'Captain Scharnhorst', not just because his battery of horse artillery was nearby, but more importantly, 'because this man accepts responsibility with extraordinary enthusiasm, is nearly indispensable, and I do not want to hold him back'.[30]

Wallmoden agreed and ordered Scharnhorst and his horse artillery to support Hammerstein. Ten days later Hammerstein thanked Wallmoden, telling him: 'I simply cannot praise Captain Scharnhorst enough. His talents, professionalism, and presence of mind, even in the midst of a hail of bullets [*Kugelregen*], were simply outstanding'.[31] In his operational report of 1-13 June 1794, Hammerstein noted, 'As always, at every occasion, the artillery performed just brilliantly'.[32] Prince Adolphus also mentioned Scharnhorst to his father, King George.

> I have seen General Hammerstein, who is also here with three Grenadier Battalions & the 14 Regiment. The modest [way] in which he talcks [sic] of his success at Menin does him still more credit; he speacks [sic] particularly in favour of Captain Scharrenhorst [sic] of the Artillery, whom he made use of as his Adjutant-General.[33]

This very positive discernment of Scharnhorst's battlefield competence by Hammerstein and Prince Adolphus was making major inroads against the malicious intrigue of Trew.

27 See Calvert's remarks in Verney (ed.), *The Journals and Correspondence of General Sir Harry Calvert*, p.220.

28 The quoted passage is from Burne, *The Noble Duke of York*, p.137.

29 See Calvert's remarks in Verney (ed.), *The Journals and Correspondence of General Sir Harry Calvert*, p.220.

30 See Hammerstein's request of 20 May 1794 to Wallmoden; in Klippel, *Scharnhorst*, Vol.2, p.129. In the last phrase Hammerstein indicated that not only was he aware of Scharnhorst's situation with Trew, he also wanted to make sure Wallmoden knew this as well.

31 See Hammerstein's Report of 30 May 1794 to Wallmoden; in Klippel, *Scharnhorst*, Vol.2, pp.129-30; the quoted passage is from p.129.

32 Hammerstein's comments are cited in Klippel, *Scharnhorst*, Vol.2, p.156 (Note 1).

33 See the Letter of 18 June 1794 from Prince Adolphus to King George III; in Aspinall (ed.), *The Later Correspondence of George III*, Vol.2, p.219. It is interesting that Prince Adolphus used the term 'General-Adjutant' to describe Scharnhorst's relationship with Hammerstein in Menin, since Scharnhorst's unique concept of the 'Chief of Staff' was not yet known in military circles of the time.

Seeking to honour Scharnhorst for his outstanding performance of duty, Wallmoden wrote to King George on 2 June, requesting he create a 'Second Aide to the Quartermaster General' [2. *Aide-General-Quartiermeister*] position on the Hanoverian General Staff, with the rank of *Major*, specifically for Scharnhorst, whose 'contributions and professionalism have been particularly impressive'.[34] Wallmoden assured the king that Scharnhorst was fully qualified for this position, and that Trew would not miss him, since the *Chef der Artillerie* had repeatedly reported to the Commanding General that he had enough 'good officers'.[35] Meanwhile, Wallmoden transferred Scharnhorst to the General Staff. Scharnhorst now worked directly for the Commanding General, not for the *Chef der Artillerie*.

King George III agreed with his Hanoverian field commander, and on 27 June 1794, promoted Scharnhorst to *Major*, had Wallmoden present him with a ceremonial sword for his outstanding performance of duty, and assigned him as the Second Aide to the Quartermaster General, who happened to be Scharnhorst's former mentor and regimental commander at Northeim, *General-Lieutenant* Emmerich von Estorff. 'It is not unreasonable to assume' that Estorff may have been a motivating force behind the creation of this special position just for Scharnhorst, his promotion to *Major*, and assignment to the General Staff.[36]

Interestingly, years earlier, Reden had recommended the creation of such assistants to aid the aging Estorff.[37] In March 1792 he established a 'General-Quartermaster-Lieutenant' [*General-Quartiermeister-Lieutenant*] post with engineer *Major* Friedrich Christoph Kuntze appointed to it. Kuntze held the temporary rank of *Oberstlieutenant* and received a special stipend that came with the position.[38] Unfortunately, chronic sickness throughout the war had made Kuntze unable to perform his duties efficiently; yet he still held the post. Wallmoden had been trying for months to have Kuntze sent home and replaced, but Freytag refused to agree.

Interestingly, when King George III acknowledged receipt of Wallmoden's request to have Scharnhorst named the 'Second Aide', the discerning king asked his commanding general in his letter of 3 June 1794: 'Let us also hear your expert opinion as to whether it would not be better to return Lieutenant Colonel and Aide to the General-Quartermaster Kuntze back home because of his feeble health'.[39] In his response to the king on 10 June, Wallmoden stated politely that while 'Kuntze has performed this function with great zeal', his lack of

34 See Wallmoden to George III (2 June 1795); in Klippel, *Scharnhorst*, Vol.2, p.130. The source documents for this appointment can be found in Hann 41, III, Nr.186: *Ernennung des Kapitäns Scharnhorst von der Artillerie zum Major und Aide-Generalquartiermeister, 1794*; deposited at the Niedersächsisches Landesarchiv, Hanover.

35 See the exchange of letters between Wallmoden and Chief of the German Chancery in London, Johann Friedrich Karl von Alvensleben (the Hanoverian minister to the Court of St James from 1771-95); in Klippel, *Scharnhorst*, Vol.2, p.130-33; the quoted passages are from pp.130 and 131; respectively.

36 See the analysis in Klippel, *Scharnhorst*, Vol.2, p.130.

37 See the commentary in Klippel, *Scharnhorst*, Vol.2, p.130. Significantly, Reden never suggested retiring Estorff and replacing him with a younger, more energetic man. Scharnhorst would later condemn this seniority system, which clearly had very detrimental outcomes for the army.

38 Documents relating to the creation of these positions can be found in Hann 41, III, Nr.182: *Aide-General-Quartiermeister. Rittmeister Vogelstand, Rittmeister von Estorff, Oberstleutnant Kuntze, 1787-1792*; deposited at the Niedersächsisches Landesarchiv, Hanover.

39 King George III to General Wallmoden (3 June 1794); in Klippel, *Scharnhorst*, Vol.2, pp.130-31. The contents of this letter, as well as numerous others to his sons and ministers, reveal the keen perceptiveness of King George, who kept his finger firmly on the pulse of events.

physical strength, particularly his legs, have 'hampered at times' his ability to carry out 'the necessary activity required of this highly fatiguing post'. Appreciating that Freytag did not want one of his favourites returned home (thereby forfeiting his temporary rank and special pay), Wallmoden recommended creating a second assistantship to support the physically handicapped Kuntze.[40] Scharnhorst became that 'Second Aide'. In reality, he was Wallmoden's General-Quartermaster-Lieutenant, as the official records suggest.[41]

Three days after Scharnhorst's appointment, Wallmoden wrote to Trew, informing him, 'His Majesty has raised Captain Scharnhorst of the Artillery Regiment to the rank of major'. The Commanding General also told his chief of artillery that *Major* Scharnhorst would receive full 'compensation for his previous salary' (the substantial amount Trew had denied him), and that King George has 'deigned to assign him as Second Aide to the General-Quartermaster'. And just in case Trew had any doubts, Wallmoden sent him copies of *Major* Scharnhorst's certificates of promotion and appointment. Judging by the formality and terse contents of this notification, Wallmoden may have been admonishing his chief of artillery, warning Trew about his future dealings with Scharnhorst.[42] This message contained no addressee and none of the usual polite greetings or pleasantries. Moreover, the Commanding General never mentioned Trew by name. Instead, Wallmoden used the very impersonal and (most likely in this case) disciplining term 'the Major General' [*der Herrn General-Major*] when addressing Trew. Wallmoden also notified Kuntze on 30 June of Scharnhorst's appointment.[43]

The significance of Scharnhorst's promotion to *Major* and assignment to the General Staff cannot be overstated. Wallmoden had asked King George to create a special position specifically for Scharnhorst, to promote him to major, even though at the time Scharnhorst was still a *titular- capitain*. A promotion to *Major* meant he would bypass the rank of 'actual' captain, which he should have attained (based on his seniority) the previous December, when Trew had denied him promotion and command of the newly-formed company. With this promotion and assignment to the General Staff, the Commanding General put an end to the malicious influence of Trew and had Scharnhorst fully compensated for the great injustice Trew had caused him. At long last, Scharnhorst had achieved a reward truly worthy of his endeavours – an honour virtually unheard of for a commoner.

40 *General der Cavallerie* Wallmoden to King George III (10 June 1794); in Klippel, *Scharnhorst*, Vol.2, pp.131-32; the quoted passages are from p.131. Klippel incorrectly gives the date as 11 June, while the original letter, Sheet 14 of Nr.186: *Ernennung des Kapitäns Scharnhorst von der Artillerie zum Major und Aide-Generalquartiermeister, 1794*, has the date as 10 June.

41 King George III to *General der Cavallerie* Wallmoden (27 June 1794); in Klippel, *Scharnhorst*, Vol.2, p.232. The 1793 organisation of the Hanoverian General Staff is printed in Sichart, *Geschichte der Königlich-Hannoverischen Armee*, Vol.4, p.31; the 1794 augmented organisation is on p.47. *Major* Scharnhorst appears as a 'General-Quartiermeister-Lieutenant' on p.56.

42 See Wallmoden's 'Notice' of 30 June 1794 to Trew; in Klippel, *Scharnhorst*, Vol.2, p.132. In his Letter of 1 and 5 January 1794 to Klara, Scharnhorst had tallied the income loss he was suffering under Trew. Using a six-week period, Scharnhorst had told his wife that his income as an actual captain would have been 66% higher than what he was earning as a provisional captain. His ration allowance during the same six weeks would have been 60% higher. See Kunisch (ed.), *Scharnhorst: Privat und dienstliche Schriften*, Vol.1, p.307.

43 Wallmoden's Letter of 30 June 1794 to Kuntze is Sheet 28 of Nr.186: *Ernennung des Kapitäns Scharnhorst von der Artillerie zum Major und Aide-Generalquartiermeister, 1794*; deposited at the Niedersächsisches Landesarchiv, Hanover.

Two and a half years later, on 11 November 1796, Wallmoden assigned him permanently to the General Staff, effectively ending his duties and association with the artillery regiment and Trew. As he had foreseen and had promised his beloved Klara, *Major* Gerhard Scharnhorst had accomplished something truly extraordinary, and the highest honours of the service seemed within his grasp.

Returning to operations in Flanders, Scharnhorst was very thankful to be alive and well after the fight for Menin. 'The French attacked with an indescribable anger', he told Klara, just as he had predicted in his earlier letter of 23 March. He then described the violence of the fight at Menin: how he had a horse shot from under him; how one young soldier near him had been shot twice through his hat but was miraculously not wounded; how a wagon of wounded had fallen into the hands of the French during the breakout; and how he had lost some of his clothing and other personal effects. He also worried about his brother Heinrich, who was commanding one of the outposts the French had overrun. While seeking information about Heinrich, he told Klara not to worry, since the Hessians 'are the best troops in the army'. He also told her, 'I have quite a lot of childlike love for our young officers'. He was clearly proud of their performance and that of the young soldiers around him. 'Let us therefore be satisfied and thankful', he concluded. Then he asked Klara to 'hug our lovely children for me'.[44]

With his appointment to the General Staff, Scharnhorst filled one of those additional positions he had suggested months earlier in his paper on the expansion of the Hanoverian General Staff. As the Commanding General's most trustworthy assistant, Scharnhorst soon discovered he was constantly 'on-the-move', travelling from one command to another, assessing the situation, and reporting directly to the Commanding General.[45] He had little time for his literary affairs. Fortunately, he had been collecting material throughout 1793, which he planned to use to write 'something on the organisations of the armies and this campaign'.[46] Some of this was published before he became a general staff officer; most of it appeared after his return home from the war.

Before departing Hanover Scharnhorst had instructed the Helwing Bookstore to keep publishing his journal, *New Military Journal*, giving authority to his former assistant at the artillery school, *Fähndrich* (later *Lieutenant*) Heinrich Hugo, to act on his behalf.[47] A week after deploying he had completed his study of Frederick's 'Entrenched Camp at Bunzelwitz' (1761).[48] Two months later he had sent Klara his article, 'A Map of Mainz and a Description

44 Letter of 30 April 1794 to Klara; in Kunisch (ed.), *Scharnhorst: Privat und dienstliche Schriften*, Vol.1, pp.370-72; the quoted passages are from p.371.

45 See the extensive source documents contained in Section Five: 'On Wallmoden's Staff (1794/95)' and published in Kunisch (ed.), *Scharnhorst: Privat und dienstliche Schriften*, Vol.1, pp.395-785. Also see Klippel, *Scharnhorst*, Vol.2, p.191, for a general summary of Scharnhorst's new duties.

46 Scharnhorst first told Klara he was collecting material for future writings in his Letter of 4 and 5 June 1793; in Kunisch (ed.), *Scharnhorst: Privat und dienstliche Schriften*, Vol.1, pp.219-20; the quoted passage is from 4 June (pp.219-20).

47 Gerhard Scharnhorst to the Helwing Bookstore (beginning 1793? and 29 April 1793); in Kunisch (ed.), *Scharnhorst: Privat und dienstliche Schriften*, Vol.1, pp.199 and 208-09; respectively.

48 Letter of 30 March 1793 to Klara; in Kunisch (ed.), *Scharnhorst: Privat und dienstliche Schriften*, Vol.1, p.203. For a good analysis of the action at Bunzelwitz, see Luvaas (ed. and trans), *Frederick the Great on the Art of War*), pp.251-57.

of its Fortress', asking her to have Helwing publish it in *New Military Journal*.[49] In that same issue there also appeared three other pieces: his assessment, 'On the Present War and the Present Theater of Operations', his 'Information on the Maps of the Present Theater of War', and a lengthy piece on how an officer should conduct himself on basic security missions.[50] When time permitted he tramped local battlefields and sketched local fortresses for his military studies.[51] During the long siege of Valenciennes he had begun organising the material he had collected to date, telling Klara, 'This war abounds with opportunities to make observations of some kind'.[52]

Determined to contribute to the literature being published on this war, Scharnhorst finished the second edition of his *Military Field Pocket Book*, which appeared in the fall of 1793. He also spent time updating his *Handbook for Officers* and his *Military Field Pocket Book* with the most current insights he had learned. One such piece, intended for inclusion in the third edition of his *Military Field Pocket Book* (1794), was his 'Instructions for the Officer Detached to the Infantry and Cavalry'.[53] In his letter of 5 October 1793, he discussed finances with Klara, explaining to her that the Helwing Bookstore owed them royalties for copies of *Military Field Pocket Book* (1792) sold that year, for the two articles published in *New Military Journal*, and for the initial royalties from the second edition of *Military Field Pocket Book* (1793).[54] On 17 November he finished the 'Introduction' of his edition of Frederick the Great's *Instructions to His Generals*.[55] On 1 December, he gave Helwing permission to publish it as *Instructions of the King of Prussia to the Generals of His Army* (1794). He also asked Helwing to place announcements in the newspapers and trade journals.[56]

Once on the General Staff, Wallmoden kept Scharnhorst so busy that it was difficult for him to pursue any personal agenda. While he continued to plan for his family and brother to visit him, he sensed that it may be some time before that became a reality. Spring had proven disastrous for the coalition, which was beginning to fall apart. French strength was increasing daily, while the Austrians were losing heart, especially after suffering a

49 Letter of 17-19 July 1793 to his wife; in Kunisch (ed.), *Scharnhorst: Privat und dienstliche Schriften*, Vol.1, pp.239-41; the quoted passage is from p.241. This article appeared anonymously as 'Beschreibung der Vestungswerke der Stadt Maynz, und die Belagerung derselben im Jahre 1689', *Neues militärisches Journal* 7 (1793), pp.222-30.

50 For these articles, see Scharnhorst, 'Ueber den jetzigen Krieg und das Jetzige Kriegestheater', pp.52-78; 'Nachricht von den Landkarten des jetzigen Kriegestheater', pp.101-08; and 'Verhalten eines Officiers, welcher im Felde mit 30 bis 40 Pferden von dem Corps oder Regimente, bey welchem er dienet, auf 1 bis 2 oder wol mehrere Stunden entfernt voraus commandirt wird', pp.231-76.

51 Early in the campaign Scharnhorst told his wife of his trips to 'every battlefield and fortress' in the area that might serve to enhance his writing endeavours. See his Letter of 21-29 April 1793 to Klara; in Kunisch (ed.), *Scharnhorst: Privat und dienstliche Schriften*, Vol.1, pp.205-08; the quoted passage is from p.207 (25 April).

52 Letter of 20-22 July 1793 to Klara; in Kunisch (ed.), *Scharnhorst: Privat und dienstliche Schriften*, Vol.1, pp.242-43; the quoted passage is from p.242 (21 July).

53 See Gerhard Scharnhorst, '*Zusatz zur ersten Abtheilung zu den Unterricht für den mit Infanterie und Cavalerie detashirten Officier*' (not before 1794); in Kunisch (ed.), *Scharnhorst: Privat und dienstliche Schriften*, Vol.1, pp.310-11.

54 Letter of 5 and 6 October 1793 to Klara; in Kunisch (ed.), *Scharnhorst: Privat und dienstliche Schriften*, Vol.1, pp.265 (5 October).

55 Letter of 17 and 18 November 1793 to Klara; in Kunisch (ed.), *Scharnhorst: Privat und dienstliche Schriften*, Vol.1, p.289.

56 Letter of 1 December 1793 to Christian Dietrich Helwing; in Kunisch (ed.), *Scharnhorst: Privat und dienstliche Schriften*, Vol.1, pp.293-94.

major defeat at Tourcoing. In that fight the Hanoverian 1. Infanterie Regiment was nearly destroyed. York himself barely escaped capture. A month later French forces launched a fierce counterattack at Hooglege on 17 June 1794, in which they turned an impending defeat into a stunning victory and caused coalition forces to fall back northward toward Ghent.[57] With Austrian eyes on the potentially rich gains to be made from another partition of Poland, the war against France seemed less advantageous to Emperor Francis, who soon left for Vienna, abandoning the theatre of war and command of coalition forces.[58]

From Ghent on 26 June, Scharnhorst wrote to Klara, updating his wife on the situation. He told her he was well, even though he had not slept much in the past week. He then informed her that August Scharlock 'will most likely be taken prisoner' when Nieuport falls, since the British had abandoned the 10. Infanterie Regiment and left it surrounded in Nieuport.[59] He also told her that his brother Heinrich was 'under fire again', but was in good health. Heinrich had eluded the French at Menin. 'I spoke with him yesterday, which I enjoyed very much', he told Klara.[60]

Over the next 10 days the French Armée du Nord kept the coalition off balance.[61] They invested Charleroi and compelled Prince Coburg to race south to its relief. At Fleurus on 26 June 1794, they inflicted another crushing defeat on the coalition. By 7 July, Prince Coburg was retreating eastward, creating a sizeable gap between the Austrians, the British and their German auxiliaries, and the Dutch. French troops entered Brussels on 10 July. Quickly sensing the danger to British interests, the Duke of York tried in vain to gain Austrian support for a continued defence of Flanders. When that failed, he chose on 24 July

57 See Gerhard Scharnhorst, 'Angrif des Clärfaytschen und Walmodenschen Corps auf die feindliche, bey Hochlege stehende Armee am 13. Junie 1794' (between 13 and 17 June 1794), along with his subsequent 'Notes' (14-28 June 1794) on the same subject; in Kunisch (ed.), *Scharnhorst: Privat und dienstliche Schriften*, Vol.1, pp.398 and 399-402; respectively.

58 A scathing indictment of Emperor Francis and Austrian foreign policy during this period can be found in Verney (ed.), *The Journals and Correspondence of General Sir Harry Calvert*, p.260.

59 Scharlock was wounded and taken prisoner when Nieuport fell. See Sichart, *Geschichte der Königlich-Hannoverischen Armee*, Vol.4, p.495. Fortescue, *British Campaigns in Flanders*, p.360, wrote that the English government 'attached great importance to the retention of the place' [Nieuport]. Yet, they left a weak garrison of recovering Hanoverian (not British) troops to hold the town. When the English retreated, they waited too long to evacuate the Hanoverians. Source documents relating to the coalition defence of Nieuport can be found in Hann 38 E, Nr.189: *Besetzung und Verteidigung der Festung Nieuport unter General von Diepenbroick*; deposited at the Niedersächsisches Landesarchiv, Hanover.

60 Letter of 26 and 27 June 1794 to Klara; in Kunisch (ed.), *Scharnhorst: Privat und dienstliche Schriften*, Vol.1, pp.409-10; the quoted passages are from p.410 (27 June).

61 Highlights of the 1794 Campaign in Flanders come from Weigley, *The Age of Battles*, pp.292-98; and from Thomas Charles William Blanning, *The French Revolutionary Wars, 1787-1802* (London: Arnold, 1996), pp.112-16. For Hanover's part, see Sichart, *Geschichte der Königlich-Hannoverischen Armee*, Vol.4, pp.328-551; and Demet, *'We are Accustomed to do our Duty'*, Chapter 5 (pp.65-85). English participation can be found in Fortescue, *British Campaigns in Flanders*, pp.264-395, along with the account of Jones, *Historical Journal of the British Campaign on the Continent*. For the Hessians, see Ditfurth, *Die Hessen in den Feldzügen 1793, 1794 und 1795* and Heinrich Philipp Reinhard von Porbeck, *Kritische Geschichte der Operationen welche der Englisch-combinirte Armee zur Vertheidigung Holland in den Jahren 1794 und 1795 ausgehürt hat.* (Braunschweig: Friedrich Bernhard Culemann, 1802/04). Also see the recent study of British operations in the Low Countries; in Limm, 'Fairly Out-Generaled and Disgracefully Beaten'; later published as *Walcheren to Waterloo*. For the French perspective, see Michel Henri Marie Coutanceau, Henri Leplus, and Clément Étienne Lucien Marie de Taffanel de la Jonquière, *La campagne de 1794 à l'armée du Nord*, Parts 1 and 2 (Paris: R. Chapelot et ce, 1903-08).

to withdraw into the United Provinces, falling back to the River Aa. Three days later on 27 July, the French took Antwerp. Throughout this period the Hanoverian Auxiliary Corps continued to support allied operations. On 29 July, Prince Adolphus wrote to King George, 'quite ashamed of recapitulating our retreat'. The prince told his father that his regiment was situated on left of the Hanoverian line.

> We are encamped upon a very large heath, so that we have quite a different country than we had formerly. Instead of hedges and fields we are now in an open country where the ennemy [sic] cannot advance without our being a long time before informed of it.
>
> My Regiment is at present the strongest in number of any of the Hannoverians [sic]: I have very near 700 men, which is certainly a great number, ...

Adolphus continued explaining that at long last they could make good use of their cavalry, 'which is our greatest advantage over our ennemy [sic], so that if they come here they will find it a difficult thing to force us back'. He lamented the lack of supplies and clean water, as well as the loss at Nieuport of *General-Major* Diepenbroick and the 10. Infanterie Regiment, 'by far the finest of any, as it was quite compleat [sic] and well exercised'. Prince Adolphus also informed King George that Hammerstein 'was very happy at the gracious letter your Majesty had wrote to him, and at the beautyful [sic] sword you had given him'.[62]

After a brief pause to regroup, the French renewed their advance in late August, focusing their attention on the Belgian channel ports. From Bois-le-Duc, York believed he could protect the route into Holland and aid the Dutch in the defence of their county. Captain Jones noted in his journal that the English now occupied the same camp as Prince William Augustus, the Duke of Cumberland (1721-65) had in 1747, during the War of the Austrian Succession (1740-48). Jones added: 'There was much judgment, and generalship in that timely retirement to Bois-le-Duc, without the loss of a man, as there might have been in any action'.[63] Eight miles forward of the British and Dutch positions was a line of Hanoverian and Hessian outposts on the River Dommel, where the village of Boxtel was central to its defence.[64]

In the Hanoverian camp at Berlikum (a village in the Netherlands), a thankful Prince Adolphus informed his father on 2 September about the 'very fatiguing march' they had conducted while retreating from the French, 'who were in great force before us'. Like his troops, the prince was disappointed with the current state of affairs. Again, he spoke of the diligence and energy of Hammerstein, 'who commands the advanced posts' and did not 'retire till eight in the morning', having spent the previous evening, night, and early morning hours establishing 'his chain of posts'.[65]

62 See the Letter of 29 July 1794 from Prince Adolphus to King George III; in Aspinall (ed.), *The Later Correspondence of George III*, Vol.2, p.227.

63 See the recollections of Jones, *Historical Journal of the British Campaign on the Continent*, p.119.

64 See the beautiful Sketch Map 8 'Boxtel' (opposite p.176); in Burne, *The Noble Duke of York*.

65 Letter of 2 September 1794 from Prince Adolphus to King George III; in Aspinall (ed.), *The Later Correspondence of George III*, Vol.2, p.237. Also see Scharnhorst's situational brief to Wallmoden, 'Ueber unsere jetzigen Stellungen'

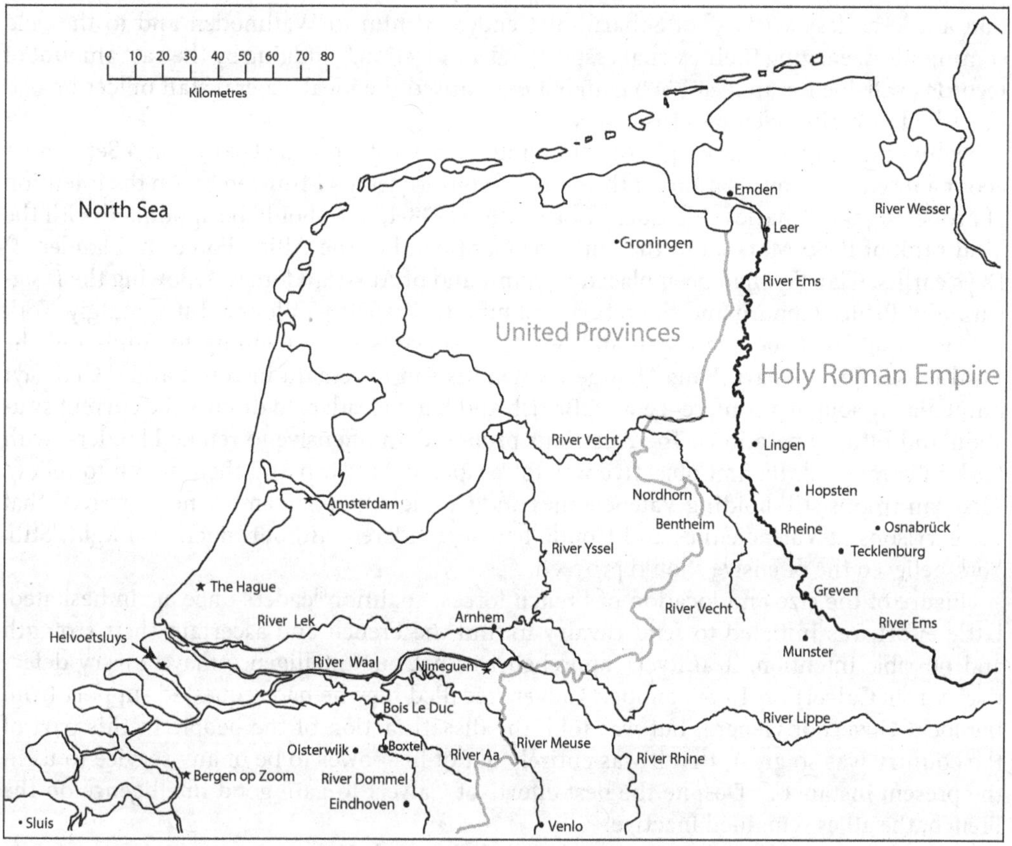

Map 8 Theatre of War in the United Provinces and Northern Germany, 1794-1795.

Throughout the late summer and into the fall, and especially during the retreat to the River Aa, Scharnhorst had assisted Wallmoden as the Hanoverians fought a series of rearguard actions protecting the British, seeking to regain contact with the Austrians, and trying to stop or delay the pursuing French. 'The exertions of General Wallmoden', noted Captain Jones, 'cannot be too gratefully acknowledged, as he was not, in any manner, pledged to give the assistance he furnished'.[66] Scharnhorst spent nearly all his time in the saddle, riding from one command to another, updating the field commanders and coordinating their actions with each other and always in accordance with the intent of the Commanding General. Most of the time he was with Hammerstein's corps, which Wallmoden utilized as the rearguard and a kind of 'fire brigade' that manoeuvred quickly from one crisis or threatened sector to another and 'shored-up' the defence as the troops fell back. The 'circumspec-

(between 30 August and 14 September 1794); in Kunisch (ed.), *Scharnhorst: Privat und dienstliche Schriften*, Vol.1, pp.429-31.

66 See the recollections of Jones, *Historical Journal of the British Campaign on the Continent*, pp.98-99; the quoted passage is from p.99.

tion and ceaseless activity' of Scharnhorst endeared him to Wallmoden and to the field commanders, earning their eternal respect and admiration.[67] Judging by the vast amount of records available for analysis, Scharnhorst epitomised the ideal general staff officer he had described to Wallmoden months before.[68]

Feeling the tremendous weight of command, York wrote to King George on 4 September about a recent communication 'in the name of your Majesty's Ministers', with the intention of proposing that Charles, Marquess Cornwallis (1738-1805) 'should be appointed with the local rank of Field Marshal to the Supreme Command of the Allied Forces in Flanders'.[69] Days earlier, Clairfayt had been placed in command of Austrian forces, following the resignation of Prince Coburg and the return of Emperor Francis to Vienna. Interestingly, York did not want to relinquish command, while Cornwallis was unwilling to command the royal Duke. For his part, King George wanted his son to remain in command.[70] Clairfayt immediately sought a conference with British and Dutch leaders to discuss the current situation and future operations. The Austrians proposed an offensive to retake Flanders, with York in command. Its first objective was to recapture Antwerp and then march to relieve Austrian troops still holding Valenciennes and Condé. On 6 September news arrived that the garrisons at Valenciennes and Condé had surrendered without much of a fight. Still, York believed the offensive should proceed.

Unsure of the size and location of French forces, coalition leaders once again hesitated. Little effort was initiated to send cavalry to find the French and ascertain their strength and possible intention. 'I am very apprehensive that our intelligence may be very defective', wrote Calvert on 13 September. Calvert recalled how he had requested support from the local Governor General but was told 'the dissatisfaction of the people in this part of the country was so great, that it was entirely out of his power to be of any service to us in the present instance'.[71] Despite the best efforts of Calvert to gain good intelligence on the French, the allies remained inactive.

Meanwhile, French reconnaissance revealed the weak Hanoverian and Hessian forces holding the River Dommel. *Général de Division* Jean-Charles Pichegru (1761-1804) decided to attack. On 14 September the French drove Hammerstein's outposts back and assaulted the Hessians at Boxtel.[72] After four hours of intense combat, the French enveloped the Hessians

67 See the summary of Scharnhorst's activities during this period in Klippel, *Scharnhorst*, Vol.2, p.159.

68 A nice sample of these reports can be found in Hann 38 E, Nr.190: *Englisch-hannoversche Armee während der Monate Juli und August, Rapporte und Berichte des Generals von Hammerstein als Kommandant sämtlicher Vorposten, Recogniscierungsberichte des Hauptmanns Scharnhorst, Marschdispositionen*; deposited at the Niedersächsisches Landesarchiv, Hanover. This folder contains some beautifully drawn situational sketches of coalition positions. The detail is simply striking.

69 See the Letter of 4 September 1794 from York to King George III; in Aspinall (ed.), *The Later Correspondence of George III*, Vol.2, pp.239-40; the quoted passages are from pp.239 and 240; respectively.

70 Curiously, there is no mention of the Duke's letter in Burne's discussion of this matter. See *The Noble Duke of York*, pp.172-76. In fact, Burne writes on p.173, that it was the Austrian Minister Florimond Claude, Comte de Mercy-Argenteau (1727-94) who suggested the idea of Cornwallis to Pitt.

71 See the recollections in Verney (ed.), *The Journals and Correspondence of General Sir Harry Calvert*, p.324.

72 See Scharnhorst's Report of 14 September 1794, notifying Wallmoden of the French attack and the withdrawal of the outposts; in Kunisch (ed.), *Scharnhorst: Privat und dienstliche Schriften*, Vol.1, p.434.

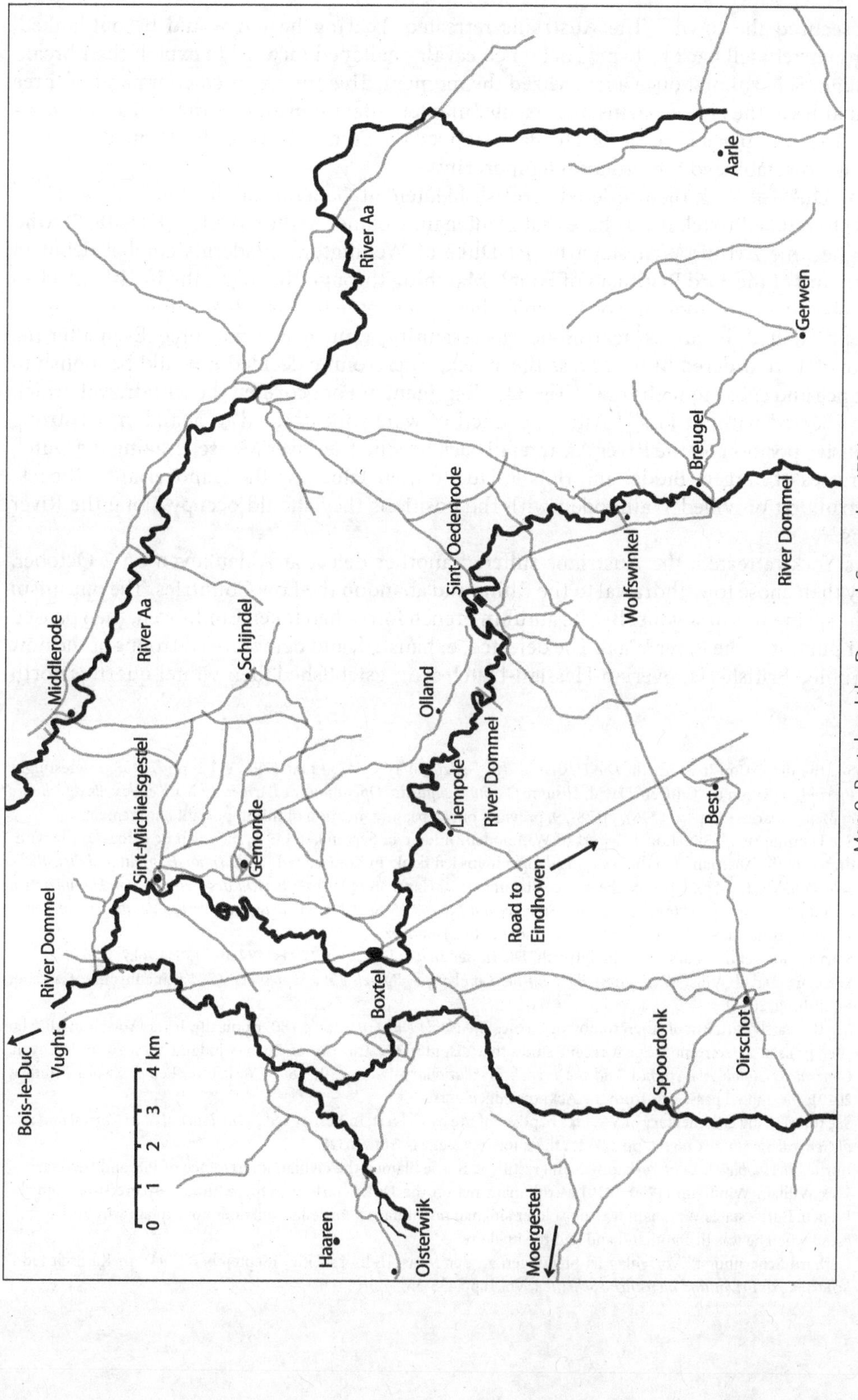

Map 9 Boxtel and the Dommel, September 1794.

and secured the town.[73] The Austrians retreated. Fearing he too would be outflanked, Hammerstein fell back to Erp.[74] As French cavalry galloped forward to exploit their breakthrough, Scharnhorst once again seized the moment. This time he took command of three companies of the Hesse Darmstadt Leichte Infanterie Bataillon and led them in a counterattack. The 'well-placed fire' of the Hessians stopped the French, who 'fell back into disarray'.[75] This action stabilized the situation temporarily.

The Duke of York then ordered Scottish Lieutenant General Ralph Abercromby (1734-1801) to retake Boxtel. It was here that Lieutenant Colonel Arthur Wesley (1769-1855), who later became Arthur Wellesley (the 1st Duke of Wellington), made his combat debut in command of the 33rd Regiment of Foot.[76] Marching through the night, the British attacked Boxtel early on the morning of 15 September. After some minor skirmishing, Abercromby abruptly halted the attack, fearing he was assaulting a much superior force. Even after the Duke of York ordered him to press the attack, Abercromby decided it would be foolish to advance and chose to withdraw.[77] The 33rd Regiment of Foot covered the withdrawal, which 'was effected without loss'.[78] After a council of war, York decided to abandon his strong defensive position on the River Aa and fall back beyond the River Meuse, 'leaving the Dutch fortresses of Bergen, Breda, and Bois-le-Duc to their fate'.[79] As the Hanoverians fell back, Scharnhorst provided Wallmoden with the positions they should occupy along the River Maas.[80]

As York retreated, the Austrians suffered another defeat at Aldenhoven on 2 October. They then chose to withdrawal to the Rhine and abandon the Low Countries. The optimism of the spring was now gone. By late autumn French forces had taken Eindhoven, then paused their pursuit at the River Waal. The defeated, exhausted, and demoralized troops of the now combined British-Hanoverian-Hessian-Dutch army established their winter quarters north

73 See the discussion in Ditfurth, *Die Hessen in den Feldzügen 1793, 1794 und 1795*, Vol.2, pp.252-55. Interestingly, Pierre Drapeyron de 'Citoyen' David, *Histoire Chronologique des Opérations de l'Armée du Nord et de celle de Sambre et Meuse* (Paris: T. Baylis, 1796), pp.78-79, provides only a passing mention of this important engagement.

74 See Hammerstein's Situational Report to Wallmoden (middle of September 1794), in which he discusses the withdrawal of the Austrians and the resulting danger to his left flank; in Kunisch (ed.), *Scharnhorst: Privat und dienstliche Schriften*, Vol.1, p.435. Also see the source documents in Hann 38 E, Nr.193: *Bericht des Generals von Hammerstein über die Vorpostengefechte bei Boxtel und Strybeck am 14. und 15. Sept.1794. Bedeutender Verlust des hessischen Korps, 1794*; deposited at the Niedersächsisches Landesarchiv, Hanover.

75 Scharnhorst's effort is described in Ditfurth, *Die Hessen in den Feldzügen 1793, 1794 und 1795*, Vol.2, p.256.

76 See Gary David Wills, *Wellington's First Battle: Combat for Boxtel, 15th September 1794* (Lincolnshire: Caseshot Publishing, 2011).

77 See the harsh criticism of Abercromby in Burne, *The Noble Duke of York*, p.180. Ironically, it was York himself who later praised Abercromby. For a recent study that disputes 'the travesty of Burne's judgment', see Carole Divall, *General Sir Ralph Abercromby and the French Revolutionary Wars, 1792-1801* (Yorkshire: Pen & Sword Military, 2019); the quoted passage is from the Acknowledgements.

78 See the glowing commentary of Wesley's baptism of fire by Calvert; in Verney (ed.), *The Journals and Correspondence of General Sir Harry Calvert*, pp.327-28; the quoted passage is from p.328.

79 Burne, *The Noble Duke of York*, p.182. Interestingly, Burne blamed the civilian interference of Pitt and Secretary of War William Windham (1750-1810) as the main reason the Duke chose to retire without any pressure from the French. Burne states Windham was 'no soldier and had no military knowledge', but does not explain why York acquiesced when he was in command and had the final say.

80 Gerhard Scharnhorst, 'Vorschlag zu Stellungen an der Maas' [Editor's Title] (September 1794); in Kunisch (ed.), *Scharnhorst: Privat und dienstliche Schriften*, Vol.1, pp.435-36.

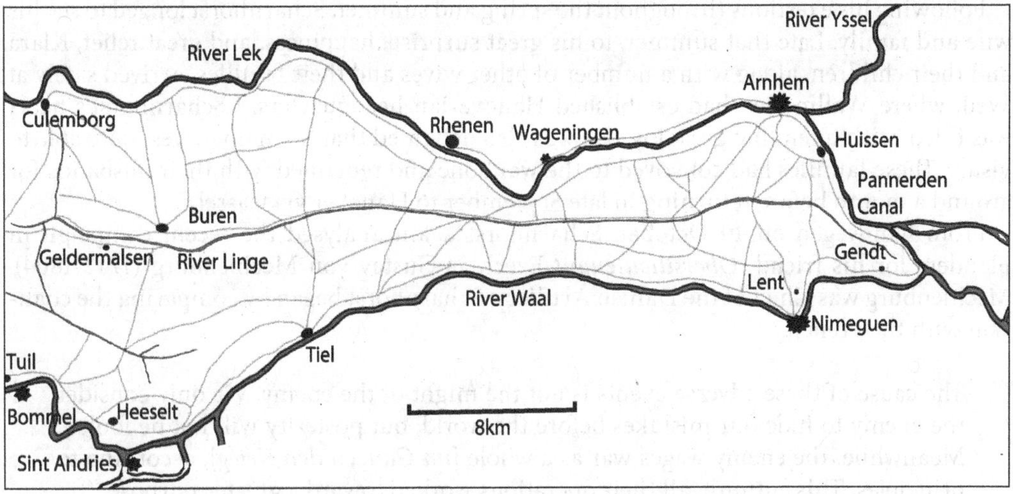

Map 10 The Waal, November 1794 to January 1795.

of the Waal, between Arnheim and Nimwegen. The Hanoverians camped at Nimwegen, where the Waal parted with the Leck.[81] They retained the mission of maintaining contact with Austrian forces at Emmerick.[82]

From camp at Well (a small town near Nimwegen), Prince Adolphus updated his father on 4 October. He began by relating that 'nothing has happened to us except the continual retreats we have made; and which, though I am persuaded they are not our fault, are very disagreeable for him who is forced to make them'. 'The Hannoverians' [sic], he continued, 'are at present divided into several little Corps for the defence of this river from Bergen down to Venloo'. Even though the soldiers had built 'a great number of worcks' [sic], and the artillery 'is almost all posted', Adolphus felt all of these measures 'will avail us very little', because 'the day before yesterday' the French had forced the Austrians out of their positions, which might cause the Hanoverians to retreat. The French cannonade was unbearable, he wrote; 'we could hear it very well, it begun at daybreack [sic] and lasted till twelve at noon'. Fortunately for the Hanoverians, French troops 'are certainly not in any force before Well'. They had focused their attention on the Austrians. Prince Adolphus concluded by telling his father: 'I am convinced that if they were to attack us here, they would meet with a very hot reception'.[83]

81 Sichart, *Geschichte der Königlich-Hannoverischen Armee*, Vol.4, pp.539-42, provides a detailed composition of each location, to include the number of batteries and the types of guns. For a nice view of the overall situation, see Sketch Map 7 'Dutch Fortresses' (opposite p. 161); in Burne, *The Noble Duke of York*.

82 Source documents relating to these defensive lines can be found in Hann 38 E, Nr.203: *Verteidigungslinie an der Maas und Waal: Verschiedene auf die obige Stellung der Truppen sich beziehende, unwichtige Meldungen, 12.1794*; deposited at the Niedersächsisches Landesarchiv, Hanover.

83 Letter of 4 October 1794 from Prince Adolphus to King George III; in Aspinall (ed.), *The Later Correspondence of George III*, Vol.2, pp.249-50.

Following his exertions throughout the spring and summer, Scharnhorst longed to see his wife and family. Late that summer, to his great surprise, happiness, and great relief, Klara and their children, along with a number of other wives and their families, arrived safely at Well, where Wallmoden had established Hanoverian headquarters.[84] Scharnhorst's heart was filled 'with unending great joy'. He was also delighted that 'so many wives' were able to visit.[85] These families had convoyed to the war zone and remained with their husbands for around a month before returning in late September to Hanover via Cassel.

From Nimwegen on 10 October, Scharnhorst again analysed the recent campaign in Flanders for his friend, *Oberstlieutenant* Ezechias Gustav von Mechlenburg (1742-1804). Mechlenburg was Chief of the Danish Artillery. Scharnhorst began by comparing the coalition with the French.

> The cause of these adverse events is not the might of the enemy. We only consider the enemy to hide our mistakes before the world, but posterity will not be fooled. Meanwhile, the enemy wages war as a whole [*im Ganzen den Krieg*], according to principles. This autumn, all their operations worked toward a greater purpose.[86]

That 'greater purpose' was to liberate northern France, Belgium, and Holland from coalition control. On the coalition side 'uncertainly reigned'. The allies had no idea of French intentions or where they would strike 'with their greatest force'.

> The French enjoyed all the advantages that offensive war brings with it. On the other hand, we have not been able to break away from them. At times we did not even focus on their movements. We just stood idly by and seemed content as the enemy pushed us back one after another.

Through inertia and lethargic leadership, the allies empowered the French, who accomplished their objective 'without ever subjecting themselves to the uncertainly of a battle'.[87]

Continuing his criticism of coalition operations, Scharnhorst noted how the allies continually planned and prepared to defend 'canals, rivers, and marshes, but rarely did.

84 In his last known letter to Klara that summer, dated 26 and 27 June 1794, Scharnhorst was still looking forward to her visit. See Kunisch (ed.), *Scharnhorst: Privat und dienstliche Schriften*, Vol.1, pp.409-10. The next known letter he sent to her was dated 30 September 1794; in Kunisch (ed.), *Scharnhorst: Privat und dienstliche Schriften*, Vol.1, pp.449-50; in which he was very nostalgic about her recent visit.

85 See Scharnhorst's Letter of 2 October 1794 to Captain du Plat (General Hammerstein's adjutant), in which he told du Plat of Klara's visit; in Kunisch (ed.), *Scharnhorst: Privat und dienstliche Schriften*, Vol.1, pp.451-53; the quoted passages are from p.451.

86 See Gerhard Scharnhorst's Letter of 10 October 1794 to *Oberstlieutenant* Ezechias Gustav von Mechlenburg; in Kunisch (ed.), *Scharnhorst: Privat und dienstliche Schriften*, Vol.1, pp.459-61; the quoted passage is from pp.459-60. Also see the tribute to the French conduct of war in Verney (ed.), *The Journals and Correspondence of General Sir Harry Calvert*, pp.403-04.

87 Letter of 10 October 1794 to Mechlenburg; in Kunisch (ed.), *Scharnhorst: Privat und dienstliche Schriften*, Vol.1, p.460. Also see the critique of Calvert, which is virtually identical to the one by Scharnhorst; in Verney (ed.), *The Journals and Correspondence of General Sir Harry Calvert*, p.397.

We occupied fortresses with men and guns but did not defend them'.[88] Remembering how long it had taken coalition forces to subdue Valenciennes and Condé a year earlier (due in large part to the stubborn and at times fanatical resistance of the French, but mainly to the ineptness of the allies), Scharnhorst told Mechlenburg: 'We simply handed the enemy Valenciennes and Condé. We also gave him all of the tremendous stocks in Valenciennes'.[89]

What is interesting here is the reaction of the French to these events. According to information Scharnhorst was able to obtain from recently released allied soldiers, he told Mechlenburg the French seemed equally ignorant of coalition designs. They could not understand why the allies simply waited for them to act. In Scharnhorst's mind, what triumphed here was the offensive mindset of the French. They seized the initiative and never let go of it.[90] On the allied side he lamented: 'With us huge misunderstandings in general and cabal among the generals have prevailed. Forgive me. I just cannot suppress my anxiety over our situation. Just believe me when I say that these adverse events will not stop until a change occurs'. Change had to be made in the coalition leadership, but this was unlikely. Turning his attention to this subject Scharnhorst asked how any military organisation could support so many 'childish [*kindisch*] old men'. The coalition charged these men with 'the defence of the fortresses, but never punished any of them for their cowardice or rewarded any of them for their bravery'.[91]

Scharnhorst made it clear that the major cause of defeat was the nonchalant attitude of coalition leaders, who failed miserably to understand that this war was very different from the dynastic wars of the past. Sacrificing their troops in futile operations, losing a fortress or even a province meant little to these aristocrats. Scharnhorst felt these noblemen were just totally indifference to the suffering and destruction they had caused by their quest to destroy the revolutionary fervour of the French people. Indeed, these aristocrats spent their energy protecting their own interests and making sure things proceeded according to their established structures: 'We haul around a lot of negligent and useless people, hoping to find a place where they can be useful. How can this lethargy and physical weakness be permitted, when extreme exertion and activity is required?'[92]

This fraternal aristocratic mindset clearly blinded the leadership of the absolutist states who made up the coalition against France. Winning the hearts and minds of the local population did not concern these noblemen. As Scharnhorst suggested (not just here but in other writings as well), serving the people rarely existed in the worldview of these aristocrats.

88 Letter of 10 October 1794 to Mechlenburg; in Kunisch (ed.), *Scharnhorst: Privat und dienstliche Schriften*, Vol.1, pp.459-61. For examples to support these claims, see Scharnhorst's 'Notes' of 14-28 June (pp.399-402); his memoranda: 'Die Defencion von Ostende betreffend' (June 1794), pp.406-07; his 'Die Besetzung der holländischen Festungen' (June 1794), p.407; and his 'Die Defencion des Canals zwischen Gent und Ostende und der Stadt Brügge' (23 June 1794), p.408.

89 The content of this paragraph and the quoted passages are from Scharnhorst's Letter of 10 October 1794 to Mechlenburg; in Kunisch (ed.), *Scharnhorst: Privat und dienstliche Schriften*, Vol.1, p.460.

90 See a similar conclusion in Verney (ed.), *The Journals and Correspondence of General Sir Harry Calvert*, p.402.

91 Letter of 10 October 1794 to Mechlenburg; in Kunisch (ed.), *Scharnhorst: Privat und dienstliche Schriften*, Vol.1, p.460. Also see the scathing indictment of coalition conduct by Calvert, which mirrors the criticism of Scharnhorst; in Verney (ed.), *The Journals and Correspondence of General Sir Harry Calvert*, pp.381, 389, 391, and 395.

92 Letter of 10 October 1794 to Mechlenburg; in Kunisch (ed.), *Scharnhorst: Privat und dienstliche Schriften*, Vol.1, p.460.

What is truly significant here is the outlook of the populations of the Austrian Netherlands and the Dutch United Provinces. They viewed the French as liberators, while they held the soldiers of the coalition in contempt, seeing them as marauders, rapists, and murderers. As a result, the professional standing armies of the absolutist states failed miserably against the national people's army of France.

Assessing the leadership of the coalition, Scharnhorst pointed to 'the lack of generals who can command a corps'. 'I know of no one in the entire Allied army except General von Wallmoden who stands out'.[93] Interestingly, Calvert agreed with Scharnhorst's assessment.

> The want of general officers to command brigades has, in this army, been an evil of the most serious nature, and has been attended with the very worst consequences.
>
> In this time, the command of brigades devolved on young men newly come into the service, whose years and inexperience totally disqualified them for the situation.
>
> The want of general officers is always a great detriment to the service; but in this army particularly so, where the field-officers are many of them boys, and have attained their rank by means suggested by government at home.[94]

Significantly, while acknowledging this serious lack of leadership in the British Army, Calvert simply accepted the policy of his government that favoured class and connection without ever questioning it.

Scharnhorst also noted that although 'the Duke of York has a very good sense of judgment', a commanding general cannot do everything himself. He needs a capable general staff to assist him.[95] Such a general staff 'does not exist in the English army'. Here again, Calvert agreed, and even provided a fine example of an instance in which Major General James Henry Craig (Adjutant General to the Duke of York) was absent from his quarters when a critical message arrived that required immediate action from him. Instead of bringing the correspondence to headquarters, Craig's servant kept it until the general returned. By that time, the English had suffered a major defeat and a serious loss of life. In his analysis Calvert wrote: 'The letter not being received was an unfortunate circumstance, which, in the absence of the Adjutant-general, certainly ought to have been provided against'. Unwilling to admit the English lacked standard staff procedures, or that they should develop them to avoid such an unfortunate circumstance in the future, Calvert merely noted that the servant was held accountable and 'sent to the provost'.[96] If only the Duke of York had 'a General-Quartermaster like Lascy or Baur', Scharnhorst concluded.[97]

93 Letter of 10 October 1794 to Mechlenburg; in Kunisch (ed.), *Scharnhorst: Privat und dienstliche Schriften*, Vol.1, p.460.

94 Verney (ed.), *The Journals and Correspondence of General Sir Harry Calvert*, pp.384 -86; the quoted passages are from pp.384 and 385.

95 Letter of 10 October 1794 to Mechlenburg; in Kunisch (ed.), *Scharnhorst: Privat und dienstliche Schriften*, Vol.1, p.460. In his interesting analysis, 'Why the French Won', Blanning, *The French Revolutionary Wars*, pp.116-28, summarised most of what Scharnhorst wrote here and cited several passages from Scharnhorst's study.

96 Verney (ed.), *The Journals and Correspondence of General Sir Harry Calvert*, pp.384 -86; the quoted passages are from pp.387 and 386; respectively.

97 Letter of 10 October 1794 to Mechlenburg; in Kunisch (ed.), *Scharnhorst: Privat und dienstliche Schriften*, Vol.1, p.461. A great organiser and administrator, Franz Moritz Graf von Lacy (1725-1801) was an Austrian *Feldzeugmeister*

From his broad historical studies and combat experience during the 1793 and 1794 campaigns in Flanders, it was very apparent to Scharnhorst that the advent of mass, citizen armies demanded a much more efficient means of command and control in the theatre of operations and especially on the battlefield. To enhance operational control of the army at the theatre level and tactical command on the battlefield, Scharnhorst advocated better organisation. Because a national army possessed more men and equipment, guns, horses, supplies, and transportation than a dynastic force, he proposed the army be partitioned into smaller, more manageable units that combined infantry, cavalry, artillery, and supporting elements.[98] A General Staff with Troops would centralise and control the activities of these corps and divisions, assisting the commander-in-chief on campaign. As Scharnhorst wrote: 'I am becoming more convinced every day that without a well-organised general staff no army can be well led. A poorly organised and slightly trained army with a good general staff will accomplish more than a good army with a poor general staff'.[99]

Because the *levée en masse* had increased the size of armies dramatically, and because the scope of their operations now extended over progressively larger geographical areas, the conduct of war had become an art pursued upon the map. Commanding generals found it essential to have accurate maps of the theatre of operations and to assign talented officers from their staffs to their subordinate commands to maintain effective command and control.[100] Yet, as Scharnhorst again wrote, no army to date had established a formal organisational structure that delineated the duties and responsibilities of general staff officers.

Scharnhorst understood better than anyone else at the time that the challenge of military leadership in an age of mass armies could only be met with a General Staff with Troops, whose members had clearly defined duties and responsibilities, and who could adapt quickly to ever-changing circumstances on the battlefield. These officers had to possess considerable talent and ability, enthusiasm and determination, because they would provide the 'impulse' [*Mechanismus*], as he wrote, that set the army in motion and then animated its operations. Only the best minds could bring flexibility to size, agility to might.[101]

and veteran of the War of the Austrian Succession and the Seven Years War. Following those conflicts, Lacy was tasked with reforming the Austrian army, which he accomplished with some remarkable results. Friedrich Wilhelm Bauer (1731-83) was an engineer and cartographer and became *General-Quartiermeister* to Duke Ferdinand during the Seven Years War. As the senior advisor to Ferdinand, Bauer was instrumental in the success of the Duke during that conflict.

98 Lehmann, *Scharnhorst*, Vol.1, pp.237-40, discussed the significance of these early recommendations. Three later, more mature studies are: Gerhard Scharnhorst, 'Ueber die Organisation einer Armee', 'Von den Vorzügen der Abteilung einer Armee in Armee-Divisionen' (1801), and 'Ueber die Stärke und Vertheilung der Artillerie bey einer in Divisionen oder Corps getheilten Armee' (between 1801 and 1802); all in Kunisch (ed.), *Scharnhorst: Privat und dienstliche Schriften*, Vol.2: *Stabschef und Reformer (Kurhannover bis 1795-1801)*, pp.545-46 and 774-82, and Vol.3: *Lehrer, Artillerist, Wegbereiter (Preußen 1801-1804)*, pp.233-47; respectively.

99 See Gerhard Scharnhorst, '*Ueber die Einrichtung des Generalstaabs einer Armee*' (after 10 October 1794); in Kunisch (ed.), *Scharnhorst: Privat und dienstliche Schriften*, Vol.1, pp..681-91; the quoted passage is from p.681.

100 Scharnhorst's thoughts on the General Staff during this period are grouped as 'Entwürfe zur Einrichtung des Generalstabs', in Kunisch (ed.), *Scharnhorst: Privat und dienstliche Schriften*, Vol.1, pp.681-717.

101 Scharnhorst, '*Ueber die Einrichtung des Generalstaabs einer Armee*' (after 10 October 1794); in Kunisch (ed.), *Scharnhorst: Privat und dienstliche Schriften*, Vol.1, pp.681-91. Also see Gerhard Scharnhorst, 'Ueber die Uebung und Bildung einer Armee in Friedenszeiten, 30 Mai 1797', *Nachlaß Scharnhorst*, Nr.131, Sheets 2-10; deposited at the Geheimes Staatsarchiv Preuβischer Kulturbesitz, 196/VI. HA Familienarchive und Nachlässe, Berlin (Dahlem). Sheets

At Nimwegen, Scharnhorst built upon the earlier recommendations he had sent to Wallmoden while in Menin. He now possessed actual combat experience as the General-Quartermaster-Lieutenant and could incorporate this into his emerging model. After reiterating his insistence that general staff officers assist the commanding general with the operational planning, tactical disposition, and logistical support of the army, Scharnhorst addressed seven key areas in which the general staff required further development. What he sought here was a consolidation of the duties and responsibilities of general staff officers and, most importantly, their authority throughout the army as responsible spokesmen of the commanding general. This authority had not been clearly delineated, nor were specific qualifications of general staff officers established. In keeping with aristocratic norms, both usually depended on the personality and preference of the commanding general. This had to change. What Scharnhorst advocated was the formal establishment of his General Staff with Troops. He was not the least interested in a capital staff that advised a head of state. His sole focus was on an organisation to command and control the field army on campaign.

'With an army of 30-40,000 men', Scharnhorst began, 'the following arrangements could be made'. He then presented his vision of the General Staff with Troops. Although much of what he recommended was neither new or unique in theory, in practice the way in which he constructed his model was an entirely new form of military leadership; for the General Staff with Troops was to become the brain and nervous system of the army, energising its daily battle rhythm and providing the impulse that set and kept the army in motion.

Scharnhorst began with the commanding general's personal staff of senior assistants and advisors.

> The General Staff must consist of the Chief of Staff [*General-Adjudant*] and four to five senior assistants [*Ober-Adjudanten*], and several others attached to the Chief of Staff. The Commanding General must never issue a command that does not go through the Chief of Staff. No report, no message most come in that the Chief of Staff does not handle.[102]

The Chief of Staff and his senior assistants would be the brain of the army. Putting this in perspective, Scharnhorst's concept of the 'Chief of Staff' and his senior assistants constituted a radical change from previous theory and practice. His chief of staff was not some senior clerk or personal secretary to the commanding general; he would exercise control over all of the essential duties of the field army and advise the commanding general accordingly, much like Scharnhorst did while serving as Hammerstein's chief of staff at Menin. This would

6-10 were later published as 'Scharnhorst über Führerauswahl und Führerverantwortlichkeit', *Militärwissenschaftliche Rundschau* 2 (1944), pp.117-19. Excerpts are printed in Lehmann, *Scharnhorst*, Vol.1, pp.235-36. This concept also appears in an important memorandum Scharnhorst later sent to Prussian *Oberst* Friedrich Wilhelm von Zastrow in 1801. Scharnhorst used the term '*Mechanismus*' in the title of this memorandum. See Gerhard Scharnhorst, 'Ueber die Einführung eines gewiβen Mechanismus der Führung der Armee, den jetzigen Zustande der Kriegeskunst angemeβen' (beginning of 1801); in Kunisch (ed.), *Scharnhorst: Privat und dienstliche Schriften*, Vol.2, pp.468-74.

102 Scharnhorst, '*Ueber die Einrichtung des Generalstaabs einer Armee*', Kunisch (ed.), *Scharnhorst: Privat und dienstliche Schriften*, Vol.1, pp.681-89.

permit the commanding general to focus his attention on the higher aspects of leading the army on campaign, just as Frederick the Great had done during the Seven Years War.

Scharnhorst's senior assistants would support the chief of staff in the execution of his duties and responsibilities. The first senior assistant would be accountable solely for the logistical support of the army. 'All matters pertaining to the subsistence' of the army is the responsibility of this officer. The first senior assistant would coordinate with the commissariat, the regiments, and smaller detachments to accomplish his mission. After observing the failure of the British commissariat to supply the Hanoverians in Holland and Flanders, the logistical support of the troops was paramount to Scharnhorst.

Administrative support of the army was the duty of the second senior assistant, who keeps 'the rosters'. 'He always knows where all of the troops are and takes care of them, so when the army marches, no one is forgotten'. In a similar manner, the third senior assistant manages 'the correspondence with the hospitals and depots, and with the commanders [*Chefs*] concerning advancements, etc'. Scharnhorst then insisted on their authority throughout the army.

> These senior assistants are to a certain extent senior assistants to the army. They must be talented and energetic men; and as soon as a corps is detached, one senior assistant goes immediately with that corps and performs the duty of the corps chief of staff.

Scharnhorst concluded that the Chief of Staff 'must be a rigorous and orderly man, one who can write and speak multiple languages'.[103]

Apart from the Chief of Staff being able to write and speak multiple languages, the organisation and functions of a modern military staff are clear in Scharnhorst's vision. So are the duties and responsibilities of his senior assistants. Together they form the corporate genius of the army. As Scharnhorst stated, they must be proven combat leaders who, 'upon arriving at a location, are able to assist when necessary, and are capable of making and executing decisions'.[104]

Turning his attention to the General-Quartermaster, Scharnhorst re-designed this staff to be the nervous system that animated the various parts of the field army. He noted that the major duties of the General-Quartermaster would remain essentially unchanged; it was still responsible for the planning and execution of marches, the quartering of troops in the field, and the maintenance of the supply system. Since the General-Quartermaster 'always has much to do', he must have an additional dozen aides and two dozen guides to assist him. He then described in sufficient detail how these aides and guides would perform their duties. In

103 In his memoirs Calvert wrote: 'Languages are the *sine qua non* to an officer who wishes to rise above the common routine of regimental duty; and I have myself felt very severely the misfortune of not understanding German'. See Verney (ed.), *The Journals and Correspondence of General Sir Harry Calvert*, pp.69-70. Interestingly, Foreign Office Secretary Herbert Taylor attributed his appointment to the staff of the Duke of York in part because of his knowledge of French and German. See the commentary in Taylor (ed.), *The Taylor Papers*, p.28.

104 Scharnhorst, '*Ueber die Einrichtung des Generalstaabs einer Armee*', in Kunisch (ed.), *Scharnhorst: Privat und dienstliche Schriften*, Vol.1, p.682.

doing so he offered a snapshot of how an army marched and encamped during the closing years of the eighteenth century.

Scharnhorst was clearly not satisfied with the performance of the General-Quartermaster in Holland or Belgium. Therefore, he used this occasion to advocate for more personnel to assist the General-Quartermaster. He also recommended the establishment of a Geographical Department within the General-Quartermaster staff to provide detailed and accurate maps of the theatre and tactical area of operations, along with the locations of the various camps and their 'supporting chains' [*Soutiens-Kette*], the locations of magazines and depots and their defensive networks, and all projected future locations. Half a dozen aides and a dozen guides, along with assistance from the field engineers or the regiments, would be necessary to perform these tasks. All of these requirements should be accomplished and briefed to the commanding general within 'six hours' of the establishment of the camps. The commanding general would then have a visual picture of the logistical arrangements of his army, while 'the Geographical Department would have a repository of plans and maps, which are extremely important'.[105]

In a similar fashion, Scharnhorst advocated the addition of an 'Outpost Commander' with a small staff selected mostly from officers of the light troops to oversee the establishment and maintenance of the army's security network. Maintaining adequate security was a constant challenge for the Hanoverians in 1793 and 1794. To emphasise the importance of security, Scharnhorst recommended creating a general officer position on the commanding general's staff with 'special supervision' over all security arrangements. This general must not be 'the General Officer of the Day' [*General du Jour*], since experience showed this 'never worked'. The sole responsibility of this general was the security of the field army. Together with the Outpost Commander, the security general would make sure each regiment and detachment had adequate security during the march, and properly established and manned outposts once encamped. All outposts were to be 'linked together in mutual support' [*Soutiens-Posten-Kette*]. The security arrangements of the field army were then to be briefed to the commanding general. So important was the security of the field army to Scharnhorst that he advocated attaching 'a senior assistant of the General Staff', as well as 'an aide-de-camp from the General-Quartermaster' to the security general to assist him.[106] To make sure the regiments built quality defensive positions while encamped or on outpost duty, Scharnhorst also wanted to enlarge the Field Engineer Department with at least 'a Director and 15 to 20 officers, and twice as many engineer non-commissioned officers' to supervise the accomplishment of these tasks.[107]

Tying all of this together, Scharnhorst reiterated the supreme importance of the Chief of Staff, who 'administers all arrangements, all commands'. In the hierarchy of his concept of a General Staff with Troops, the General-Quartermaster assembles all of the reports from the regiments and detachments and presents the disposition of the army to the Chief of Staff.

105 Scharnhorst, '*Ueber die Einrichtung des Generalstaabs einer Armee*', in Kunisch (ed.), *Scharnhorst: Privat und dienstliche Schriften*, Vol.1, pp.682-84; the quoted passages are from pp.683 and 684; respectively.

106 Scharnhorst, '*Ueber die Einrichtung des Generalstaabs einer Armee*', in Kunisch (ed.), *Scharnhorst: Privat und dienstliche Schriften*, Vol.1, pp.684-85; the quoted passages are from pp.684 and 685; respectively.

107 Scharnhorst, '*Ueber die Einrichtung des Generalstaabs einer Armee*', in Kunisch (ed.), *Scharnhorst: Privat und dienstliche Schriften*, Vol.1, p.685.

The Chief of Staff then issues any 'specific orders and instructions to insure everything is in its proper order, and that no misunderstandings exist, etc'.[108] During combat operations: 'The Chief of Staff and the General-Quartermaster must stay near or with the Commanding General, to inform him of the arrangements to be made, and then to see that all commands are executed, and to keep everything in context'. Scharnhorst added that the senior assistants to the Chief of Staff, the aides and guides to the General-Quartermaster, as well as the Director of the Field Engineer Department, must be kept up to date on current operations so they can perform their duties and responsibilities proficiently. 'The most skilful general', he concluded, 'must never be without these talented people'.[109]

With the General Staff with Troops in charge, Scharnhorst maintained that the army would function automatically, like 'an engine' [*eine Maschine*], since the General Staff with Troops would establish standard operating procedures throughout the army and would then act with authority from the Commanding General to insure the smooth, effective conduct of operations. 'No mistakes can be made without them being noticed', he stated.

> With this arrangement the Commanding General can never forget what must be done, and can make sure that what needs to be done is accomplished, even when it comes to all the decisions he has to consider, when fatigue is at work and his mind is often numb, and he suffers from other health issues, etc.

Scharnhorst was convinced his concept was sound. As he so aptly put it: 'On order, the General Staff sets the engine [the army] in motion'.[110] Indeed, in no other army of the time did anyone other than *Major* Gerhard Scharnhorst conceive of such a command and control model.

Scharnhorst closed his concept paper with a section on the selection of personnel for the general staff. Choosing the right officers and non-commissioned officers would be extremely important but very difficult. Given 'the seniority system of the regiments' [*der Ancienneté des Regiments*], the nepotism and favouritism of generals 'who usually choose their sons, relatives, or flatterers' [*Schmeicherler*], the chance of obtaining really quality personnel was slim.[111] This was certainly true of the Hanoverian Auxiliary Corps, in which family connections and patronage prevailed. As Scharnhorst noted, the present system thus guaranteed the general staff would be composed of 'an old inactive man, a child, or otherwise useless people'. Wallmoden discovered this upon assuming command of the Hanoverian forces but could do little to remove these individuals. Scharnhorst wrote that Hanover did not need leaders who placed their interests 'above the state and above the blood of the children of

108 Scharnhorst, '*Ueber die Einrichtung des Generalstaabs einer Armee*', in Kunisch (ed.), *Scharnhorst: Privat und dienstliche Schriften*, Vol.1, p.685.

109 Scharnhorst, '*Ueber die Einrichtung des Generalstaabs einer Armee*', in Kunisch (ed.), *Scharnhorst: Privat und dienstliche Schriften*, Vol.1, pp.685-86; the quoted passages are from pp.685 and 686; respectively.

110 Scharnhorst, '*Ueber die Einrichtung des Generalstaabs einer Armee*', in Kunisch (ed.), *Scharnhorst: Privat und dienstliche Schriften*, Vol.1, p.687.

111 See the interesting source documents that support Scharnhorst's conclusions; in Hann 41, III, Nr.183: *Gemeraladjutanten und Flügeladjutanten, 1792*; deposited at the Niedersächsisches Landesarchiv, Hanover.

their fellow citizens'.[112] It was clear to him that Freytag and other Hanoverian aristocrats put their selfish interests above the state and its citizens. He recommended selecting general staff officers according to the road he had taken – the path of proven combat leadership.

As Scharnhorst was perfecting his General Staff with Troops, British Prime Minister William Pitt the Younger (1759-1806) told King George on 11 October that there was a serious crisis in leadership within the coalition.

> It is but too obvious that even if the Dutch can at length be roused to suitable exertions, their efforts, added to those of your Majesty's troops, can hardly afford a confident hope of resisting the enemy during the remainder of the present campaign and thro' the winter, unless all the military operations can be put under one uniform direction, the want of which may be even more fatal now than it has shewn [sic] itself already.

Pitt outlined the difficulties that the young Duke of York had encountered with the Dutch from the beginning of the war. Now that the war had reached the United Provinces, York refused to permit the Stadtholder, Prince William V (1748-1806) to lead British troops, as did the Austrians their men. This placed the Stadtholder in an equivalent command role with foreign leaders in his own country. Pitt maintained that the appointment of Cornwallis cannot 'be further thought of', and recommended the appointment of Duke Karl of Brunswick, who had rescued the Prince of Orange from the wrath of his own people in 1787. Should the Duke of Brunswick decline, 'which seems unlikely', Pitt then said, 'the only alternative' would be '… to endeavour to establish some Council of War which might direct the general operations of all the troops in Holland according to some uniform plan'. The Prime Minister closed his letter by asking the king's immediate approval of this course of action, since 'it cannot be too soon adopted'.[113]

As Pitt sought a way to revitalize coalition leadership, the Hanoverians in Holland encountered one hardship after another during the late fall and winter of 1794. Soldiers were frequently encamped in crude huts and often forced to remain outdoors in inclement weather. Even though the English commissariat had established a special 'Corps of Royal Waggoners' [sic] to provide food, clothing, and other essentials to the troops, this experiment 'failed completely in every part, and on many occasions the service suffered very materially in consequence'.[114] The lack of sustenance, together with the severe cold weather, led to sickness and disease. As now *Capitain* Christian von Ompteda remembered:

> The prevailing extremely cold weather made the line of defence [sic] of the river wholly untenable against the now superior and triumphant enemy. Disease

112 Scharnhorst, '*Ueber die Einrichtung des Generalstaabs einer Armee*', in Kunisch (ed.), *Scharnhorst: Privat und dienstliche Schriften*, Vol.1, p.689.

113 Letter of 11 October 1794 from William Pitt to King George III; in Aspinall (ed.), *The Later Correspondence of George III*, Vol.2, pp.239-40; the quoted passage is from p.254. In his journal entry of 10 November 1794, Calvert wrote: 'The Prince of Brunswick has declined the command that was offered'. See Verney (ed.), *The Journals and Correspondence of General Sir Harry Calvert*, p.388.

114 See Mesurier, *The British Commissary*, pp.25-26; the quoted passage is from p.26.

> prevailed to a shocking extent, especially among the Hanoverians. On account of the incapacity of the English for covering and outpost service, the Germans could never be relieved from the defence [sic] of the advanced posts. Whole weeks long the infantry lay out of doors, in rough weather, without wood or straw. No wonder that the serviceable state of the troops diminished fearfully from day to day.[115]

The harsh winter was clearly taking its toll on the Hanoverians.

From Nimwegen Scharnhorst updated Klara on the situation. He told her he was in good health and had been with Hammerstein throughout most of the retreat. 'We accomplished much together'.[116] During that period Hammerstein and Scharnhorst commanded the outposts of the coalition army. Just as Scharnhorst had recommended, outpost duty was the purview of the light infantry and cavalry, assisted by line infantrymen.[117] He also informed Klara that his brother Heinrich was a prisoner-of-war in Crevecoeur. With affection in his heart he remembered when their family was together that summer and hoped to see them again that winter in Lippstadt. In a postscript he related another sad incident. Artillery *Capitain* August Sympher had walked into the nearby woods and had taken his own life. 'He was buried at the front'.[118]

On 20 October, French cavalrymen, dressed 'in the exact uniforms of the French *émigré* troops in British service', attacked the British 37th Regiment of Foot at Druten and inflicted heavy casualties. Over 400 officers and men were killed, wounded, or missing in action.[119] For the next week the French continually attacked the outposts in front of Nimwegen and eventually forced them back. Then they brought up artillery to lay siege to the town.[120] Hammerstein reported the steady progress of the French to Wallmoden, while Scharnhorst began planning a withdrawal from Nimwegen.[121] At the beginning of November, Hammerstein informed the Commanding General, 'The Fortress of Nimwegen cannot be defended this winter'. 'If one leaves the garrison here much longer, one risks becoming prisoners'.[122] After inspecting the defence at Nimwegen, coalition leaders (including the

115 See the account of Ompteda; in Hill (trans.), *A Hanoverian-English Officer*, p.75.

116 Letter of 8 and 10 October 1794 to Klara; in Kunisch (ed.), *Scharnhorst: Privat und dienstliche Schriften*, Vol.1, pp.458-59; the quoted passage is from p.458 (8 October).

117 See Calvert's recollections in Verney (ed.), *The Journals and Correspondence of General Sir Harry Calvert*, p.384, who lamented the fact that the English had no general like Hammerstein.

118 Letter of 8 and 10 October 1794 to Klara; in Kunisch (ed.), *Scharnhorst: Privat und dienstliche Schriften*, Vol.1, p.459 (10 October). In his earlier letter of 30 September 1794 (p.450), Scharnhorst had told Klara that Sympher had disappeared on his way to Nimwegen. At the time he had been reported as missing in action.

119 The quoted passage is from Jones, *Historical Journal of the British Campaign on the Continent*, pp.132-33. This was 'the calamity' Calvert discussed when Craig was absent from headquarters. Scharnhorst also noted this action in a memorandum (after 20 October 1794); in Kunisch (ed.), *Scharnhorst: Privat und dienstliche Schriften*, Vol.1, pp.466-69.

120 See the Report of 28 October 1794 by *General der Infanterie* Georg Wilhelm von dem Bussche to Wallmoden; in Kunisch (ed.), *Scharnhorst: Privat und dienstliche Schriften*, Vol.1, pp.470-71.

121 Hammerstein's assessments of the evolving situation can be followed in Kunisch (ed.), *Scharnhorst: Privat und dienstliche Schriften*, Vol.1, pp.473-82.

122 See Hammerstein's report on 'The Progress of the French Siege Preparations' [Editor's Title] (beginning of November 1794), written by Scharnhorst and found in Kunisch (ed.), *Scharnhorst: Privat und dienstliche Schriften*, Vol.1,

Stadtholder) 'had an opportunity of being an eye-witness of the truth', wrote York's aide, Lieutenant Colonel Calvert.[123] Hammerstein was correct in his assessment.

Upon receiving these reports, Wallmoden decided to launch a pre-emptive strike to halt the French. On 4 November, Hanoverian, British, Hessian, and Dutch units attacked 'with the greatest gallantry', wrote Calvert.[124] 'A dreadful carnage ensued', Captain Jones recalled. The combined British-Hanoverian-Hessian-Dutch force drove the French back at the point of the bayonet. 'As soon as the enemy retired from their works they were attacked by the cavalry, who got round their left between them and the wood, and cut several of the fugitives to pieces'.[125] Unfortunately, this action did little to impede the French, who opened fire on Nimwegen two days later, destroying a key bridge and sinking several boats.[126] The next day Wallmoden put Scharnhorst's plan of withdrawal into motion, as Hanoverian, Hessian, British, and Dutch forces evacuated Nimwegen on the night of 7 November and retreated to Arnheim.[127]

Meanwhile, Prince Ernest was worried about the health and welfare of the troops. In early November he wrote to his brother George Augustus, Prince of Wales, describing the soldiers as 'wonderfully ill', and believed that the succession of retreats was having a detrimental effect on the morale of officers and men alike. He also told his brother he 'had never seen anything like the change that had come over Wallmoden'.[128] Significantly, before the campaign had ever begun, Wallmoden and his senior field commanders had assessed the combat readiness of their troops and had notified York in March about the sickness among the Hanoverians and objected to their treatment.[129] Two months earlier in January, Prince Adolphus had also informed King George about the appearance of perhaps an epidemic in the Hanoverian force:

pp.473-74. Next comes Scharnhorst's 'Withdrawal Plan' [Editor's Title] on pp.474-75. Hammerstein's report regarding the defence of Nimwegen can be found on pp.476-78; the quoted passages are from p.476.

123 See Calvert's recollections in Verney (ed.), *The Journals and Correspondence of General Sir Harry Calvert*, pp.369-70.

124 See Calvert's recollections in Verney (ed.), *The Journals and Correspondence of General Sir Harry Calvert*, p.378.

125 Jones, *Historical Journal of the British Campaign on the Continent*, pp.34-35; the quoted passages are from p.135. Lieutenant Robert Wilson also participated in this action. See Randolph (ed.), *Life of General Sir Robert Wilson*, Vol.1, p.101.

126 See Hammerstein's Report of 6 November 1794; in Kunisch (ed.), *Scharnhorst: Privat und dienstliche Schriften*, Vol.1, pp.481-82.

127 Winterbottom, *The Grand Old Duke of York*, writes on p.72, how 'the Hanoverians under Walmoden [sic] got cold feet and urged York to abandon Nymegen [sic]'. Winterbottom provides no documentation to support his claim. This is disappointing, since Harry Calvert's journal clearly shows that a council of coalition leaders decided the fate of Nimwegen. What is more disturbing is the fact that Calvert was the Duke's aide and there is no reference to him in the text or bibliography of Winterbottom's study. Moreover, Winterbottom fails to mention how York had deserted his solid defensive position on the River Aa without a fight, and perhaps even more disgracefully, without ever being threatened by the French. Scharnhorst would later discuss this in his critique of the English.

128 Letter of 6 November 1794 from Prince Ernest to Prince Edward; in Arthur Aspinall (ed.), *The Correspondence of George, Prince of Wales, 1770-1812* (London: Cassell, 1963-71), Vol.2, pp.481-82; and cited in Demet, *'We are Accustomed to do our Duty'*, p.98.

129 See the discussion in Paul Demet, *'We are Accustomed to do our Duty'*, pp.70-72.

> In general it is amazing the number of sick the different Regiments have; mine has very near five hundred. It is a kind of fever which the men get, and which pulls them immediately so down that it is a long time before they can recover their strength.[130]

Even Wallmoden became ill that May. What is truly enlightening here are the letters the Duke of York had sent to his father on 12 and 19 March 1794, explaining why the Hanoverians were so ill. York told King George 'the principal causes of their sickness' were 'their being obliged to cook and being supplied regularly with meat'.[131] This is odd, since the Hanoverians possessed the finest mess in the army, a kitchen that could cook for 20,000 troops. It seems that the Duke of York still retained possession of the Hanoverian Bakery, which he had appropriated for his headquarters staff and troops a year earlier, leaving the Hanoverians without their own field kitchen. This he never told his father.

While recognising the ability of the Hanoverian Commanding General, English Major General James Craig felt Wallmoden was too often swayed by the opinions of others. He also stated the Hessians were led by a 'J_ F_' (a *jean-foutre* or good-for-nothing) and were fed up with the war. Craig's *jean-foutre* was *General-Lieutenant* Georg Christoph Wilhelm Adam von Dallwigk (1738-1806).[132] In defence of Wallmoden, he was following Scharnhorst's General Staff with Troops model, in which he often consulted and sought the opinion of his General-Quartermaster-Lieutenant, who was much more than a secretary like Craig was to the Duke of York. Indeed, in a letter to Henry Dundas on 21 January 1794, shortly after assuming his duties as Adjutant General, Craig had told the Secretary of War how grateful he was 'for the reception which His Royal Highness received me' and hoped York would 'honour me with his entire confidence'. Craig continued with a statement that clearly revealed his how he viewed his office and his duties.

> I think it however indispensably requisite that I should observe to you, Sir, that it is impossible for me to take the liberty of questioning His Royal Highness. I am obliged to obtain my information on many points by indirect measures.[133]

By his own admission, Craig confirmed Scharnhorst's conclusion that York had no one like a Lacy or Bauer to advise and assist him. In sharp contrast to *Major* Gerhard Scharnhorst, Major General James Craig rarely left the cosy comforts of British headquarters to visit the troops in the field in order to find out for himself the situation there. Instead, he focused his efforts on making sure 'field officers and those of a higher rank' were invited to dine with the Duke of York, who preferred the company of his family and those of his own age.[134]

130 See the Letter of 26 January 1794 from Prince Adolphus to King George III; in Aspinall (ed.), *The Later Correspondence of George III*, Vol.2, pp.149-50.

131 See the Letters of 12 and 19 March 1794 from York to King George III; in Aspinall (ed.), *The Later Correspondence of George III*, Vol.2, pp.185 and 186-87; the quoted passages are from p.185 (12 March).

132 Craig's 'Confidential' correspondence of 28 October 1794 is cited in Demet, *'We are Accustomed to do our Duty'*, p.98.

133 See the Letter of 21 January 1794 from James Craig to Henry Dundas; printed in part in Burne, *The Noble Duke of York*, pp.115-116; the quoted passages are from p.115. In his analysis, Burne discussed the difference between an eighteenth-century Adjutant General and a twentieth-century Chief of Staff, agreeing with Scharnhorst's rationale.

134 Craig is cited by Burne, *The Noble Duke of York*, pp.116-117; the quoted passage is from p.116. In his analysis, Winterbottom, *The Grand Old Duke of York*, p. 63, reminded his readers: 'we are still dealing here with the practices

Scharnhorst was correct when wrote that the British had no concept of a field army general staff. Instead of assisting their commanding general in the execution of his duties and relieving him of many of the administrative and logistical burdens, the British left the heavy burdens of command to the Duke of York alone. It also appears that York's aristocratic habits created many of his problems as well. Perhaps this is why York felt so isolated and overwhelmed. Scharnhorst certainly believed the lack of a competent chief of staff, who had the authority to question the decisions of his commanding general, made command of the British-Hanoverian-Hessian army overpowering and lonely for the Duke.

Meanwhile, Scharnhorst wrote to his wife from Arnheim on 13 November. 'Thank Heaven!' he told Klara. The retreat had ended for the moment and he was finally able to get some much-needed rest, 'after all of the disagreements and confusion' he had witnessed among coalition leaders during the previous months. He told Klara about his wonderful dream of them 'quite happy together. I see you healthy and happy. I see a happy future. I see us together in a good location'. He was clearly overjoyed to hear of Klara's pregnancy, which she had told him in her letter of 6 November. He advised her to: 'Maintain a good diet. Enjoy all the rich vegetables you can eat, avoid anything that thickens the blood, and get as much fresh air as you can'. Scharnhorst longed to see his family. He was so anxious that he had decided to travel to Lippstadt to meet them there. Unfortunately, Scharnhorst was victim of his own ideas and success. The Commanding General appears to have taken his 'Chief of Staff' concept to heart, especially after learning how well Scharnhorst had performed as Hammerstein's chief of staff at Menin and during the retreat from Flanders. 'You should not count on my coming', he told his wife. 'General von Wallmoden has become accustomed to having me by his side and does not want me to leave him alone'.[135]

In other matters, Scharnhorst informed Klara that 'there is much gossip and backbiting' in the artillery regiment. Trew was now directing his displeasure at Braun. Scharnhorst also indicated that the wrath of Trew may have been the reason Sympher had taken his own life. In a truly unexpected turn of events, he told his wife, 'The General is very good to me'. He explained that Trew's daughter had written to her father about her 'steadfast friendship' with Klara Scharnhorst, which pleased Trew very much. 'I spoke with him', he continued, telling Klara that he had urged the general to permit his family to visit him, since it would be good for the Trew family. After considerable discussion with Trew, Scharnhorst was glad to report, 'He agreed to let his family come and visit him'. Despite their capricious relationship, Scharnhorst still cared for Trew, telling Klara about the misfortunes of the recent campaign (especially the long retreat), which had taken their toll on the general, who 'is very agitated and not in good health'. Scharnhorst believed that a visit from his family would significantly help Trew. He also felt that Trew was not alone, that 'the supreme effort' of the past weeks had adversely affected 'the spirit and body' of many soldiers.[136]

of eighteenth-century warfare, where royalty and aristocracy held lavish balls and dinners in the vicinity of their military headquarters'. This was precisely the kind of archaic and snobbish aristocratic behaviour Scharnhorst condemned, especially since it was inconsistent with the current art of war the French were waging against the coalition. Winterbottom never mentioned the fact the British refused to conform their conduct accordingly.

135 Letter of 13 November 1794 to his wife; in Kunisch (ed.), *Scharnhorst: Privat und dienstliche Schriften*, Vol.1, pp.485-86; the quoted passages are from p.485.

136 Letter of 13 November 1794 to Klara; in Kunisch (ed.), *Scharnhorst: Privat und dienstliche Schriften*, Vol.1, p.486.

10

Exemplary General Staff Officer

Winter was rapidly approaching in Holland and the inclement weather throughout November was largely responsible for the relative inaction on both sides. Captain Jones noted in his journal:

> The weather at this time was very severe, there was a great deal of frost, and when not freezing it was constantly raining, by which the soldiers were much harassed, and began to get very sickly, and those who were fit for duty were constantly employed, being obliged to keep up a cordon of strong pickets along the Waal.[1]

Throughout this period Scharnhorst was presenting Wallmoden with a number of important information papers detailing: 'Possible Enemy Attack Locations' (Fall 1794), 'Critical Points along the Line of Defensive' (November 1794), 'Cantonment Locations of the Army' (21 November 1794), 'Arrangement of Winter Posts on the Waal between Lent and Bilands-Insel' (November/December 1794), the 'Locations and Strengths' of Hanoverian infantry, cavalry, and artillery units (November/ December 1794), and 'Arrangement of Troops in Cantonments' (before 11 December 1794).[2] This was the type of meticulous staff work characteristic of his General Staff with Troops concept. Scharnhorst was putting into practice what he had learned from his campaign experience and from his study of history, particularly the campaigns of Raimondo Montecuccoli and Frederick the Great.

Scharnhorst also used this lull in operations to provide his continuing analysis of the war. From Arnheim on 22 November he wrote another lengthy letter to Mechlenburg in Copenhagen, describing in greater detail the catastrophic campaign of 1794. 'The military honour (and I am afraid the spirit) of the German nation has been mortally wounded by this war'.[3] Scharnhorst worried that 'unless other measures are taken', the ruling elites would seize this opportunity to rain 'terrible destructions on some respectable institutions', when

1 See the interesting contemporary account by Captain Lewis Tobias Jones, *An Historical Journal of the British Campaign on the Continent,* pp.142-43. Agreeing with Jones was Harry Calvert, in Sir Harry Verney (ed.), *The Journals and Correspondence of General Sir Harry Calvert,* p.402.

2 See the reports in Kunisch (ed.), *Scharnhorst: Privat und dienstliche Schriften,* Vol.1, pp.487-502.

3 See Gerhard Scharnhorst's Letter of 22 November 1794 to Ezechias Gustav von Mechlenburg; in Kunisch (ed.), *Scharnhorst: Privat und dienstliche Schriften,* Vol.1, pp.502-08; the quoted passage is from p.502.

the real cause of defeat was the arrogance and cowardice of the ruling elites.[4] Apologising to Mechlenburg for not writing in over six weeks, Scharnhorst told his fellow artilleryman he had been so upset over 'our current situation' he was unable to compose his thoughts clearly. 'I simply cannot speak about this without losing my temper and forgetting myself'.[5]

'Political and military inconsistencies united to weaken the martial honour of the Germans and to discourage the princes', Scharnhorst told Mechlenburg. He described how the moral cowardice of allied leadership resulted in a lack of vigour and resolve within the coalition. There was no supreme war council nor a commander-in-chief with any real authority over military operations, just constant mistrust, jealousy, disagreements, and little cooperation among the senior field commanders. Competing factions led to a dissipation of military power and an unwillingness to give battle. Confronted by an uncompromising political direction and an often unconventional military leadership in France, and a people who generally supported the cause, the dynastic elites of the coalition simply gave up, even when faced with an inept and timid French generalship.[6] Years later, when questioned about his own experience in Holland, the Duke of Wellington recalled: 'Why – I learnt what one ought not to do, and that is always something'.[7]

Once in Holland, the Duke of York (who Scharnhorst held largely responsible for the disastrous campaign in Flanders and Holland) used the pretext of being summoned home to confer with government ministers to sail to England, abandoning his men to freeze and starve to death in the icy winter.[8] Before leaving the continent, York was ordered to hand over temporary command of British troops to Lieutenant General William Harcourt (1743-1830) and German troops to Wallmoden. It seems King George was unwilling 'to subject' his British troops to a German leader, who just happened to be senior to Harcourt.[9]

4 Letter of 22 November 1794 to Mechlenburg; in Kunisch (ed.), *Scharnhorst: Privat und dienstliche Schriften*, Vol.1, p.502 (Note c).

5 Letter of 22 November 1794 to Mechlenburg; in Kunisch (ed.), *Scharnhorst: Privat und dienstliche Schriften*, Vol.1, pp.502-08; the quoted passages are from p.502 and Note b.

6 Letter of 22 November 1794 to Mechlenburg; in Kunisch (ed.), *Scharnhorst: Privat und dienstliche Schriften*, Vol.1, pp.503-04; the quoted passage is from p.504. For an excellent analysis of the French during the campaigns of 1793 and 1794, see Lynn, *Bayonets of the Republic*.

7 Philip Henry, *Notes of Conversations with the Duke of Wellington, 1831-1851* (London: John Murray, 1889), p.182. Wellington described how his regiment sat idly by from October to January and saw only one general from headquarters the entire time. He went on to say they learned more from letters from home than from their own leadership. While not agreeing with Wellington, Calvert blamed the Prussians, Austrians, and the German princes for the disaster that befell the coalition. See Verney (ed.), *The Journals and Correspondence of General Sir Harry Calvert*, pp.395 and 401-02.

8 See the last paragraph of William Pitt's Letter of 23 November 1794 to King George III; in Aspinall (ed.), *The Later Correspondence of George III*, Vol.2, pp.271-4, in which Pitt insists that the Duke of York be recalled to London, while simultaneously seeking 'with the greatest attention to His Royal Highness's wishes and feelings' a way to make 'the Duke of York's withdrawing from command' appear in the best light. For Scharnhorst's thoughts, see his Letter of 22 November 1794 to Mechlenburg; in Kunisch (ed.), *Scharnhorst: Privat und dienstliche Schriften*, Vol.1, pp.503-04. In three successive paragraphs, he detailed the notable failures of York in Flanders (where he deserted the Austrians) and throughout Holland, where he refused to fight on the Scheldt, in the Brabant, on the Maas, and on the Waal – essentially handing Flanders and Holland to the French without a fight.

9 In his analysis of the Duke of York's behaviour, Sir John W. Fortescue, *British Campaigns in Flanders*, p.392, calls it 'absolutely indefensible'. Jones, *Historical Journal of the British Campaign on the Continent*, p. 44, defends the Duke, saying, 'Here the British army lost a father and a friend, who had endeared himself to them by his humanity, justice,

Any future use of British soldiers would thus depend on Harcourt.[10] Yet, as Scharnhorst noted, the British never hesitated to sacrifice their German auxiliaries (the Hanoverians and Hessians), along with their allies (the Austrians, the French *émigré* troops, and even the Dutch), to ensure the safety of British forces.[11]

When winter arrived in Holland, the countryside became a frozen, barren wasteland without subsistence, while the water obstacles crisscrossing it often impeded the resupply of food and other shortages. Adding to the misery of the soldiers was the fact that allied forces were simply not equipped for a winter campaign. There were not enough quartermasters, teamsters, wagons, or bakeries to provide sufficient food and water, clothing, and other essentials for the soldiers.[12] As Scharnhorst witnessed this catastrophic failure, and saw the appalling sufferings of the troops, he was more determined than ever to rectify this situation by making the logistical support of the army a principal function of his General Staff with Troops.

Once again, the French kept their relentless pressure on the coalition, continuing their offensive operations instead of going into winter quarters. As Calvert wrote, 'We cannot refuse our admiration of the energy and military virtues of the French army, commencing a winter campaign after eight months of nearly ceaseless fighting, and advancing in their enemy's country when they so urgently needed repose'. Without never acknowledging that the French were fighting a different kind of war, Calvert blamed them for waging a ruthless campaign that disregarded 'the sufferings of their own armies' and deprived their own troops 'of the provisions and comforts almost necessary to existence in that inclement winter'. When analysing the current conflict, Calvert reminded his readers, 'these circumstances must be borne in mind'.[13] Like most of his contemporaries, Calvert refused to acknowledge the truth. Contrary to coalition soldiers, French troops were willing to suffer for a cause in which they believed.

Throughout November and into early December, Scharnhorst continually updated Wallmoden on the dispositions of the German, Hessian, and British forces with courses of action should the French attack. They also included recommendations for the repositioning of artillery support.[14] On 1 December he reported that of the original Hanoverian force of

and benevolence'. For a spirited defence of York throughout the War of the First Coalition, see Alfred H. Burne, *The Noble Duke of York.*

10 Lehmann, *Scharnhorst*, Vol.2, p.191.

11 See Scharnhorst's insightful analysis in his Letter of 22 November 1794 to Mechlenburg: in Kunisch (ed.), *Scharnhorst: Privat und dienstliche Schriften*, Vol.1, pp.502-06. Also see the interesting discussion of the Duke of York's lack of leadership and his unwillingness to fight during the retreat through Holland; in Maximilian von Ditfurth, *Die Hessen in den Feldzügen 1793, 1794 und 1795*, Vol.2, pp.269-79; and especially the scathing indictment of the Duke on p.313. Andrew Robert Limm summaries the historiography on this topic in his, 'Fairly Out-Generaled and Disgracefully Beaten, pp.63-66; later published as *Walcheren to Waterloo*.

12 See the interesting remarks scattered throughout the text and appendices of the fascinating contemporary account by the British Deputy Commissary General Havilland le Mesurier, *The British Commissary*. It is clear from the commentary of le Mesurier that trying to support the army in Holland was a nightmare for the supply services.

13 See Calvert interesting remarks in Verney (ed.), *The Journals and Correspondence of General Sir Harry Calvert*, pp.403-04.

14 For example, see Gerhard Scharnhorst, 'Cantonnement der Armée, den 21ten Nov. 1794', in Kunisch (ed.), *Scharnhorst: Privat und dienstliche Schriften*, Vol.1, pp.495-500. Other briefs are found on pp.501-502 and 510-524.

13,495 men and 477 officers who had marched to war in March 1793, barely 4,652 men and 211 officers remained fit for duty.[15]

At five in the morning on 11 December, the French struck and surprised nearly every coalition outpost along the Waal. Once again, Calvert complained that 'the difficulties of obtaining any information are so multiplied both by our friends and enemies that I begin to despair'.[16] On the other hand, the French execution of this assault did not surprise Scharnhorst. It reminded him of two similar crossings from the past at the same location: the French in 1672 and the allies in 1758. As he noted: 'The area around Pandern, with a multitude of islands, peninsulas, and all the outgoing branches of the Rhine and the Waal, provides a good location to cross'.[17] Crossing the Waal in boats at several points between Ghent and Pandern, French forces quickly overran Hanoverian Redoubt 4 and captured its three cannons. *General der Infanterie* Georg Wilhelm Freiherr von dem Bussche-Haddenhausen (1726-94) marched his troops to the scene, where they received 'such a warm reception with the guns' the French had captured that the Hanoverians were 'obliged to retreat'.[18] In an counterattack Bussche was killed in action and Hammerstein took command.[19] When reinforcements arrived, the Hanoverians retook the redoubt, but not before the French had spiked the guns and re-crossed the Waal, without losing a single soldier. Elsewhere, the Austrians had been more successful defencing their positions. This pre-dawn raid caused 'an unpleasant sense of insecurity' within coalition forces.[20]

Over the next two weeks, Scharnhorst re-evaluated the coalition situation and proposed future options to the Commanding General. He was concerned that the cold weather was adversely affecting the tactical disposition of coalition forces. In his first recommendation, 'A Disposition for the Defence of the Waal for the Hanoverian Position', he suggested consolidating this defence into three main posts consisting of infantry, cavalry, and artillery working together.[21] After listing the 'Location and Strengths of the Outpost Chain from the Pandern Canal to Lent', he proposed repositioning troops from their warm cantonments in the rear further forward, so they could react more quickly to any French attack and protect their outposts. It is clear from this recommendation that Scharnhorst wanted to condition coalition troops to fight as the French did. He also advised a second line of defence on the River Leck.[22] Before he presented his plan to the Commanding General, he discussed its

15 These statistics can be found in Louis von Sichart, *Geschichte der Königlich-Hannoverischen Armee*, Vol.4, pp.552-553.

16 Calvert is cited in Verney (ed.), *The Journals and Correspondence of General Sir Harry Calvert*, pp.409-410.

17 See Gerhard Scharnhorst, 'Bericht von der Affäre, so den 11ten Dec. Bei dem Dorfe Gent ohnweit Pandern, wo die Franzosen die Waal und den Rhein zu forciren die Absicht hatten, vorgefallen ist' (not before 11 December 1794); in Kunisch (ed.), *Scharnhorst: Privat und dienstliche Schriften*, Vol.1, pp.517-19; the quoted passage is from p.517.

18 See the recollections of Jones, *Historical Journal of the British Campaign on the Continent*, pp.145-46; the quoted passages are from p.145.

19 Klippel, *Scharnhorst*, Vol.2, p.188. Also see the nice tribute to Bussche by Calvert; in Verney (ed.), *The Journals and Correspondence of General Sir Harry Calvert*, pp.412-13.

20 Fortescue, *British Campaigns in Flanders*, p.393.

21 Gerhard Scharnhorst, 'Disposition zur Vertheidigung der Waal für die hannövrische Postirung' (after 11 December 1794); in Kunisch (ed.), *Scharnhorst: Privat und dienstliche Schriften*, Vol.1, pp.519-20.

22 Gerhard Scharnhorst, 'Dislocation und Stärke der Vorposten Kette von dem Panderschen Canal bis Lent' (December 1794); and its continuation (before 18 December 1794); in Kunisch (ed.), *Scharnhorst: Privat und dienstliche Schriften*, Vol.1, pp.521-23 and 523-24; respectively. Hessian *Lieutenant* Porbeck, *Kritische Geschichte der Operationen welche*

various options with Hammerstein, who was now the senior Hanoverian field commander.[23] On 27 December, he gave Wallmoden his concept plan should the French attack.[24]

As Scharnhorst was preparing options for Wallmoden, Calvert informed the Duke of York of his concern 'that the sickness of the army daily increases'.[25] Calvert believed Scharnhorst's plan to reposition British and Germans troops forward, closer to the front, had caused this condition. Calvert confirmed this on 20 December when he penned, 'this continual state of preparation harasses the troops most terribly'. Once again, this English gentleman simply refused to accept the fact that the French were prosecuting a different kind of war; one which made life equally uncomfortable for everyone, and not just for the common soldiers.

> The sickness increases; the number of invalids is lessened only but death, and I fear that the winter, which is generally supposed to afford ease and comfort to the soldier, and recruit him after the fatigues of the summer, will prove more destructive to this army than the campaign has been.[26]

In his letter of 22 December, the Duke of York tried to ease Calvert's concerns, informing him: 'Both Wallmoden and Harcourt appear alarmed'.[27]

As the Commanding General and his senior German commanders (Hammerstein and Dallwigk) were considering their General-Quartermaster-Lieutenant's proposals, Scharnhorst updated Mechlenburg on 16 December regarding the truly pathetic condition of the coalition. 'Poor provisioning, ignorance, and heaven knows what else unites all of our misfortunes', he stated. Coalition losses in materiel alone from the surrender of so many fortresses in Flanders and Holland were just astounding. The Dutch had handed the French 700 cannons and 16 ships, while the Austrians had lost nearly all of their siege artillery when Condé, Valenciennes, and Quenoy capitulated. Scharnhorst was clearly not optimistic about the future. As he told Mechlenburg, 'If the enemy crosses over the Waal this winter, it is our fault'.[28]

Meanwhile, the cold weather increased. On Christmas Eve, as he sat and wrote in his journal, Scharnhorst told his wife he was watching Braun's son Anton. 'I am observing his work with great interest, because he reminds me of our dear Wilhelm' [Scharnhorst's

der Englisch-combinirte Armee, Vol.1, pp.804-808, discusses the elaborate nature of Scharnhorst's combined arms defensive plan.

23 See the extensive correspondence between Scharnhorst and Hammerstein, and between Wallmoden and Hammerstein regarding Scharnhorst's proposals (13-23 December 1794); in Kunisch (ed.), *Scharnhorst: Privat und dienstliche Schriften*, Vol.1, pp.524-42.

24 Gerhard Scharnhorst, 'Disposition' (27 December 1794); in Kunisch (ed.), *Scharnhorst: Privat und dienstliche Schriften*, Vol.1, pp.543-46.

25 See Calvert's Letter of 15 December 1794 to York; in Verney (ed.), *The Journals and Correspondence of General Sir Harry Calvert*, pp.413-414; the quoted passage is from p.414.

26 See Calvert's Letter of 20 December 1794 to Major General Hew Dalrymple (1750-1830); in Verney (ed.), *The Journals and Correspondence of General Sir Harry Calvert*, pp.414-16; the quoted passages are from pp.414-15.

27 Letter of 22 December 1794 from York to Harry Calvert; in Verney (ed.), *The Journals and Correspondence of General Sir Harry Calvert*, pp.416-17; the quoted passage is from p.416.

28 Letter of 16 December 1794 to Mechlenburg; in Kunisch (ed.), *Scharnhorst: Privat und dienstliche Schriften*, Vol.1, pp.527-28; the quoted passages are from pp.527 and 528.

first-born]. It seems that Wilhelm and Anton were around the same age, and Scharnhorst was clearly enjoying his time with Anton. He then updated Klara, telling her: 'Our situation here is strange'. He explained that while the ice on the Waal had solidified enough to allow passage, the French 'near us' remained awfully quiet. Perhaps they were honouring the birth of the Christ child, even though any profession of a belief in God was strictly forbidden in the French camps. Scharnhorst had no logical explanation for this; he merely told his wife, 'Everything has changed'.[29] He went on to say rumours abounded that perhaps an armistice had been reached. 'The Dutch have actually sent their Peace Commissars to Paris some time ago'. Again, he had no additional information. What he did know was the weather was extremely cold, and both sides 'cannot wait until this winter has passed'. He closed his letter, bidding 'Adieu' to his wife and saying, 'I must go'. In his postscript he asked Klara to send him four bound and six unbound copies of his recently published edition of *Frederick's Instructions to His Generals*.[30]

On Christmas Day, Calvert wrote to his sister Maria, apprehensive about the future.

> The quantities of ice which come down the rivers, keep us in daily expectation of their being frozen over, and consequently render a greater degree of vigilance and alertness necessary.
>
> The hardships experienced by the infantry of the army are great; the duty, owing to the numbers of the sick, becomes very severe, the badness of the accommodations, the scarcity of fuel, and the intenseness of the cold, give us little room to hope for any amendment.

While he lamented the fate of the army, Calvert was pleased to inform his sister that King George III, 'for the first time', was finally receiving accurate news on the conditions of his army.[31] This statement certainly says a great deal about the British Army.

Two days after Christmas, French forces crossed the Meuse on the ice, surprised the Dutch outposts at Bommel and pushed on over the frozen Waal to Tuil. A few miles north of Tuil at Meteren, the Hessians checked the French advance. With few troops on hand to repel the enemy, Wallmoden doubted the Hessians could hold much longer. Therefore, he ordered allied units nearby to support them.[32] As the Hessians, British, Dutch, and French *émigré* troops were preparing to attack, Wallmoden ordered Hammerstein to reposition his

29 Letter of 24 and 25 December 1794 to Klara; in Kunisch (ed.), *Scharnhorst: Privat und dienstliche Schriften*, Vol.1, pp.542-43; the quoted passages are from p.542 (24 December).

30 Letter of 24 and 25 December 1794 to Klara; in Kunisch (ed.), *Scharnhorst: Privat und dienstliche Schriften*, Vol.1, pp.542-43; the quoted passages are from p.543 (25 December).

31 See Calvert's Letter of 25 December 1794 to Maria Calvert; in Verney (ed.), *The Journals and Correspondence of General Sir Harry Calvert*, pp.417-19; the quoted passages are from pp.417-18.

32 Scharnhorst had provided a 'Disposition of Forces' to Wallmoden on 27 December, along with some courses of action for the Commanding General should the French attack at this very location; in Kunisch (ed.), *Scharnhorst: Privat und dienstliche Schriften*, Vol.1, pp.543-46. Also see the discussion in Porbeck, *Kritische Geschichte der Operationen welche der Englisch-combinirte Armee*, Vol.2, pp.178-90; and in Ditfurth, *Die Hessen in den Feldzügen*, Vol.2, pp.318-28. Ditfurth cites Porbeck as the source of his information.

forces.[33] On 30 December, coalition forces counterattacked.[34] Fierce fighting ensued, and the Hessians, British, Dutch, and French *émigré* troops drove the French back across the Waal. The Commanding General then used Scharnhorst's plan to reinforce positions on the Waal, while the French paused their activities in this sector. 'Thus ended the military operations of the year 1794', Captain Jones recorded in his journal. He noted with great sadness and much bitterness the sacrifices of the British, who had lost some of their finest troops, 'defending a country for a worthless set of people who had not [the] courage to defend themselves'.[35]

Scharnhorst disagreed completely with the assessment of Jones. He placed the blame squarely on the British, and especially on York, for pursuing their own selfish interests and failing to support the Dutch people.[36] Significantly, Calvert agreed in part with Scharnhorst, writing that when British troops had arrived in Holland two years earlier, 'there was no great predilection for us on the part of the inhabitants'.[37] Calvert and other Britons attributed this apathy to the intense dislike of the Dutch people toward the Stadtholder, William of Orange, who the British, the Prussians, and other members of the dynastic coalition were maintaining in power against the will of the Dutch people.[38] Interestingly, Jones never mentioned this in his critique. As British troops were marching out of Holland toward Flanders in 1793, Calvert observed that it was 'rather remarkable, that the further we get from Holland (the defence of which country is the principal object of our expedition) the more we are welcomed'.[39]

By most accounts, the Stadtholder was 'a man of almost inhuman dulness [sic], apathy, and stupidity', who later abandoned his people, fleeing to England with his family shortly after the Duke of York had deserted his men. From England he refused to offer any constitutional concessions which might have stirred the Dutch people to resist the French.[40] Thus, the Dutch welcomed the French as liberators.

Throughout the military operations of 1794, Scharnhorst had secured his reputation as a combat leader. Without any sense of modesty, he told Klara on 27 December: 'I am certain that General von Wallmoden and von Hammerstein are convinced that no one is more useful as a General-Quartermaster than I am'. Even Trew acknowledged 'with sincere acclaim'

33 See Scharnhorst's concept plan, 'An der Wahl bleibt alle Cavalerie, so jetzt daran ist' (after 27 December 1794), in which he recommended how to position those forces available to defend against the French; in Kunisch (ed.), *Scharnhorst: Privat und dienstliche Schriften*, Vol.1, pp.546-47. Wallmoden's order to Hammerstein on 28 December to reposition his forces can be found on p.548.

34 Wallmoden's 'Vorbereitungen für Gegenangriff bei Tuil' [Editor's Title] (before 29 December 1794) can be found in Kunisch (ed.), *Scharnhorst: Privat und dienstliche Schriften*, Vol.1, p.549. It appears from the available correspondence that British leaders (including Harcourt) were following Wallmoden's leadership, making him the nominal commander-in-chief. Harcourt would then update the Duke of York. See the discussion and notes in Fortescue, *British Campaigns in Flanders*, pp.394-95.

35 Jones, *Historical Journal of the British Campaign on the Continent*, p.151. Also see the many disparaging remarks by the Duke of York about the Dutch in his letters to King George III; in Aspinall (ed.), *The Later Correspondence of George III*, Vol.2, pp.13-14, 16-17, 48-49, 74-75, 105, 107, and 114.

36 See Scharnhorst's Letter of 22 November 1794 to Mechlenburg; in Kunisch (ed.), *Scharnhorst: Privat und dienstliche Schriften*, Vol.1, pp.502-08; especially pp.503-06.

37 See the recollections of Calvert; in Verney (ed.), *The Journals and Correspondence of General Sir Harry Calvert*, p.24.

38 Also see the anonymous account, *An Accurate and Impartial Narrative of the War*, Vol.2, pp.107-08.

39 See Calvert's thoughts in Verney (ed.), *The Journals and Correspondence of General Sir Harry Calvert*, p.57.

40 See the interesting analysis of William V and Dutch forces in Fortescue, *British Campaigns in Flanders*, p.179.

Scharnhorst's outstanding performance of duty during the recent campaign. 'He asked me if I wished to remain with the artillery', Scharnhorst told Klara. 'Certainly, I replied, and would like to return directly to the school'. He informed his wife that he had asked Trew again about a company command. 'He promised me I shall have it as soon as I return home, and that he himself would make sure of it'.[41] He then updated Klara regarding the recent French attack in which they had routed the Dutch at Bommel and captured many guns. He also told her of the very pleasant visit by Trew's wife and daughter. He was so pleased that the Trew family had spent a happy Christmas and New Year together. Trew's physical and emotional well-being were much better. In bidding 'Adieu' to his beloved Klara, Scharnhorst said he was not looking forward to 1795. 'Day after day I think only of you and our children'. He had wanted so much to have been home with his family for Christmas. In his postscript he told Klara 'the young Braun is still with me'.[42]

As 1794 ended, Scharnhorst formulated a number of contingency plans for 1795. One outlined the regrouping of troops following a withdrawal behind the River Leck.[43] Another sketched precautions troops should take when clearing Arnheim and their subsequent displacement.[44] A third dealt with the importance of the Waal defence.[45] Meanwhile, coalition field commanders were irate that they had not received any news, instructions, or orders for the past three weeks (as Wellington had stated), ever since York had sailed to England. On 31 December they forwarded a lengthy memorandum to the Duke, expressing their fear that coalition forces would soon cease to exist, due to the recent, strenuous combat operations and the widespread sickness in the army. At the same time, they noted how French strength was increasing daily. Warning that their line of defence was already too long, Wallmoden and senior British leaders recommended implementing Scharnhorst's plan to pull the army back to more favourable positions behind the Leck, where they could observe the Waal and be ready to counterattack should the French try to cross.[46]

From his home at York House on 5 January 1795, the Duke of York agreed with the German and British field commanders. He wrote to his father that perhaps it was time to evacuate Holland: 'As in all probability it will be necessary for your Majesty's troops to cross the Issel and fall back into Germany'. York recommended the establishment of magazines sufficient enough to support the army. Since none were currently available, he told King George of the 'utmost necessity' of furnishing immediate assistance to the soldiers from

41 Letter of 27 and 30 December 1794 to Klara; in Kunisch (ed.), *Scharnhorst: Privat und dienstliche Schriften*, Vol.1, pp.550-51; the quoted passages are from p.550 (27 December).

42 Letter of 27 and 30 December 1794 to Klara; in Kunisch (ed.), *Scharnhorst: Privat und dienstliche Schriften*, Vol.1, pp.550-51; the quoted passage is from p.551 (30 December).

43 Gerhard Scharnhorst, 'Projekt für Umgruppierung der Truppen beim Rückzug hinter den Lek' [Editor's Title] (end of December 1794); in Kunisch (ed.), *Scharnhorst: Privat und dienstliche Schriften*, Vol.1, p.552.

44 See Gerhard Scharnhorst's two memoranda, 'Vorkehrungen für Räumung Arnheims und Truppenverschiebung' [Editor's Title] (end of December 1794); in Kunisch (ed.), *Scharnhorst: Privat und dienstliche Schriften*, Vol.1, pp.553 and 554.

45 Gerhard Scharnhorst, 'Notwendige Aufgabe der Waal' [Editor's Title] (end of December 1794); in Kunisch (ed.), *Scharnhorst: Privat und dienstliche Schriften*, Vol.1, pp.554-55.

46 See the Memorandum of 31 December 1794 (signed by Wallmoden and senior British generals); deposited at The National Archives, London, and listed as War Office (WO) Record 1/172, pp.1-16; and cited in Paul Demet, *'We are Accustomed to do our Duty'*, p.101.

'the magazine which is constantly kept in the Electorate for the supply of the inhabitants in case of a bad harvest'.[47] He told his father he had already discussed this course of action with Hanoverian officials in London and they had agreed to it. Meanwhile, Wallmoden was having difficulty convincing Freytag that the Hanoverian position on the Issel was untenable.[48] As coalition commanders anxiously awaited news from England, the French renewed their offensive.

On 4 January 1795, French forces under Pichegru crossed the Waal, attacked British forces, retook Tuil, and 'created much uneasiness'.[49] The next day the British drove them back. Thaw came on 6 January and coalition forces felt they could continue to maintain their extended line on the Waal. Around 8 January, Scharnhorst listed the 'Location' of allied forces, noting: 'Each of these corps still lacks cavalry and heavy artillery'.[50] When the French renewed their assault on 10 January 1795, they struck several coalition positions simultaneously, forcing the combined British-Hanoverian-Hessian-Dutch army to retreat. The Austrians were also driven back. Wallmoden sensed trouble and ordered the entire coalition to implement Scharnhorst's plan and to fall back behind the Leck.[51] In anticipation of this withdrawal, English Corporal Robert Brown noted on 2 January, 'Every arrangement is made for a retreat across the Leck'. During the week prior to the French attack, Brown recalled the extensive measures the British had taken in anticipation of implementing Scharnhorst's plan.[52]

Interestingly, King George wrote to the Foreign Secretary, Lord Grenville (1759-1834), the day after the French attack, noting on 11 January:

> The Dutch at Breda and Gertrudenberg have kept up their shameful former conduct. I am therefore glad Genl. Walmoden and Lieut. Genl. Harcourt think of giving up the defence [sic] of the Waal and of retiring behind the Leck, as the safety of the troops under their command must otherwise be very precarious by the shameful conduct of the Dutch.[53]

47 See the Letter from York to King George III (4 January 1795); in Aspinall (ed.), *The Later Correspondence of George III*, Vol.2, p.287.

48 See the correspondence between Freytag and Wallmoden in Hann 38 E, Nr.230: *Verhandlungen zwischen General von Wallmoden und Feldmarschall von Freytag in Hannover über die kritische und unhaltbare Stellung der Armee an der Issel*; deposited at the Niedersächsisches Landesarchiv, Hanover.

49 See the Letter of 6 January 1795 from Harry Calvert to York; in Verney (ed.), *The Journals and Correspondence of General Sir Harry Calvert*, pp.421-22; the quoted passage is from p.421.

50 Gerhard Scharnhorst, 'Dislocation' (around 8 January 1795); in Kunisch (ed.), *Scharnhorst: Privat und dienstliche Schriften*, Vol.1, pp.572-73; the quoted passage is from p.573.

51 See Gerhard Scharnhorst, 'Projekt für Umgruppierung der Truppen beim Rückzug hinter den Lek' [Editor's Title] (end of December 1794); in Kunisch (ed.), *Scharnhorst: Privat und dienstliche Schriften*, Vol.1, p,552. Also see Scharnhorst's interim contingency plans (all before 10 January), along with the extensive coordination during this time between Wallmoden and Scharnhorst, and with Hammerstein, Dallwigk, and Prince Ernst August (in German), and Harcourt (in French) to prepare to implement a withdrawal behind the Leck; on pp.553-73.

52 Corporal Robert Brown, *An Impartial Journal of a Detachment from the Brigade of Foot Guards*, pp.213-15; the quoted passage is from p.213.

53 King George III to Lord William Grenville (11 January 1795); in Aspinall (ed.), *The Later Correspondence of George III*, Vol.2, p.291.

By the time the French attacked on 10 January, Wallmoden knew the British intended to evacuate their forces from the continent, while the Austrians had decided to abandon their claims in the Low Countries.[54] That would leave the Germans (the Hanoverians and Hessians), the French *émigré* troops, and the Dutch to defend Holland from French conquest.

'We are still in Holland', Scharnhorst told Klara shortly after the French attack. Without any of his usual greetings, he informed his wife that during the action on 10 January he suddenly found himself alone on the battlefield and without a horse. While not providing any details, he told Klara, 'I have experienced the most terrifying situation in the world during these days'. He was clearly upset and uneasy. In a series of some telling sentences without much coherency, he painted a picture of impending doom. 'The army is like a bunch of wild people'. 'This is a cruel war'. 'Generally, the Hanoverians have suffered the least in this war, while the English have been most unfortunate'. 'Maybe I will rest soon'. 'I have no coffee'. 'There are no people in most of the villages between the Rhine and the Waal'. 'Generally speaking, war is cruel, but a winter expedition is horrific'.[55]

When the French launched another general attack on 14 January, the coalition suffered heavy losses and Wallmoden gave the order to fall back behind the River Issel.[56] He was determined to keep what remained of his force intact for the defence of north-western Germany. While on the move with Hammerstein, Scharnhorst sent Wallmoden his analysis of a continued defence of Holland. It was pretty optimistic. He began with the current troop strengths and situation of the Hanoverians, Austrians, and British, and felt it was still possible to defend Holland provided the necessary 'arrangements' were made now to do so. 'I see no great danger in the matter', he told Wallmoden in closing his report.[57]

Even before the French attack, King George had already agreed with Wallmoden's decision, writing to Pitt on 14 January: 'I think the only step to be taken is to permit the whole remains of the army to move to the left and retire to Germany'.[58] The king implied that 'the fate' of the Dutch Republic had already been decided, and was clearly worried about 'the total annihilation of the troops' (meaning the British, Hanoverian, and Hessian forces), should they remain in Holland. He then told Pitt that the army could return to Holland if the Austrians provided an army in sufficient strength to support such an operation. If not, King George wanted his British troops home.

54 See the documentation in Hann 38 E, Nr.263: *Briefe des Majors von Löw und Hauptmanns von Berger aus London an den General von Wallmoden über politische Angelegenheiten, namentlich den Durchzug der in englischem Sold stehenden Freikorps nach England*; deposited at the Niedersächsisches Landesarchiv, Hanover.

55 Letter of 13 January 1795 to Klara; in Kunisch (ed.), *Scharnhorst: Privat und dienstliche Schriften*, Vol.1, p.577.

56 Sichart, *Geschichte der Königlich-Hannoverischen Armee*, Vol.4, pp.561-64, provides the routes of march for the columns during the retreat from the Waal to the Issel. Also see 'Disposition zum Rückzuge von der Lek hinter dem Issel' (middle of January 1795); and Scharnhorst's Letter of 13 January 1795 to Klara; both in Kunisch (ed.), *Scharnhorst: Privat und dienstliche Schriften*, Vol.1, pp.580-81. The locations of Hammerstein's corps after the retreat to the Issel can be found in 'Dislocation' (middle to the end of January 1795); on pp.574-76.

57 See Scharnhorst's Letter of 15 January 1795 to Wallmoden; in Kunisch (ed.), *Scharnhorst: Privat und dienstliche Schriften*, Vol.1, pp.578-79; the quoted passages are from p.579. This letter is also published in Klippel, *Scharnhorst*, Vol.2, p.191.

58 King George III to William Pitt (14 January 1795); in Aspinall (ed.), *The Later Correspondence of George III*, Vol.2, p.294.

Within the coalition leadership few shared Scharnhorst's confidence in the continued defence of Holland. Coalition leaders had already decided to abandon Holland; indeed, the fate of the United Provinces was sealed for the next twenty years, when the Stadtholder had abandoned Holland and fled with his family to England in January.[59] Accordingly, in his instructions to Hessian *Generallieutenant* Dallwigk, Wallmoden ordered the Hessians to round up and bring with them every piece of Dutch artillery they could find.[60] Scharnhorst had already prepared the deployment plan, 'Disposition for the Withdrawal from the Leck behind the Issel', which envisioned allied forces withdrawing in three simultaneous marches of three columns each.[61] The allies were very fortunate that Pichegru did not vigorously pursue them, permitting what remained of the shattered coalition forces to retire unmolested from the Leck to the Issel. The French were also tired and required rest and refitting.[62]

As the allies evacuated the Waal River position, coalition forces simply disintegrated as they marched across Holland to the northeast and the German frontier. This horrific march began during the bitter cold night of 14 January and ended when coalition units reached the Issel on 18 January. Scharnhorst described this complete collapse in striking detail, especially the horrors of the lonely winter march through the bleak sands and moors of the poor provinces of Gelderland and Over-Issel.[63] He repeatedly praised Hammerstein and Abercromby for their monumental efforts in finding suitable cantonments areas for their troops along the way and in sheltering them from the extreme weather.

> The cold was so severe, the exhaustion of the horses and men so great, that the battalions no longer remained together. Many people, especially a great number of English wives and children soon froze to death, and many more froze to death

59 See the exchange of letters between King George III and Lord Grenville (24-26 January 1795), discussing the arrangements in England for the Stadtholder and his family; in Aspinall (ed.), *The Later Correspondence of George III*, Vol.2, pp.296-97.

60 See Wallmoden's Letter to Dallwigk (before 15 January 1795); in Kunisch (ed.), *Scharnhorst: Privat und dienstliche Schriften*, Vol.1, p.578. Source documents for this confiscation can be found in Hann 38 E, Nr.277: *Übernahme der holländischen Artillerie in englischen Sold und Instandsetzung der Geschütze und Fuhrwerke für den Kriegsgebrauch; Kostenrechnungen darüber, 1795*; deposited at the Niedersächsisches Landesarchiv, Hanover.

61 See 'Disposition zum Rückzuge von der Lek hinter der Issel' (middle January 1795); in Kunisch (ed.), *Scharnhorst: Privat und dienstliche Schriften*, Vol.1, pp.580-81.

62 Highlights of the 1795 Campaign in Holland come from Russell F. Weigley, *The Age of Battles*, p.297. For Hanover's part, see Sichart, *Geschichte der Königlich-Hannoverischen Armee*, Vol.4, pp.328-551. British participation is analysed in Fortescue, *British Campaigns in Flanders*, pp.264-395, along with contemporary accounts by Jones, *An Historical Journal of the British Campaign on the Continent*, pp.154-83; by Anon., *An Accurate and Impartial Narrative of the War*, Vol.2, pp.105-35; and by Brown, *An Impartial Journal of a Detachment from the Brigade of Foot Guards*, pp.213-79. Hessian participation is discussed in Porbeck, *Kritische Geschichte der Operationen welche der Englisch-combinirte Armee*; and Ditfurth, *Die Hessen in den Feldzügen 1793, 1794 und 1795*, Vol.2, pp.280-527. Also see the excellent study of Demet, *'We are Accustomed to do our Duty'*, especially Chapter 6 (pp.86-102). For the French perspective, see Coutanceau, Leplus, and de la Jonquière, *La campagne de 1794 à l'armée du Nord*, Parts 1 and 2.

63 In Section V (Part 3): 'Re-Evaluating the Events of the War', Kunisch (ed.), *Scharnhorst: Privat und dienstliche Schriften*, Vol.1, pp.718-85, are a host of documents that highlight Scharnhorst's recollections and analysis of the recent conflict. See in particular, Gerhard Scharnhorst, 'Officieller Bericht von dem, was an den Rhein and der Waal, an die Lek und an der Issel bey der Englischen Armee vorgefallen ist. Von 24ten December 1794 bis den 31ten Jan. 1795' (after 31 January 1795); 'Unser Zurückzug über die Maas und über die Waal' (not after May 1795); and his Compilation of Hanoverian Casualties and their Causes (Spring 1795); pp.729-36; 736-52; and 753-55; respectively.

> on this march. Other items also froze: horses, wagons, and even cannons, and the army was in perhaps a condition never seen before now.[64]

Captain Jones recorded similar horrors in his journal:

> The suffering of the army, during their retreat, are beyond the power of words to describe, numbers dying every hour through cold and fatigue; they marched through a dreary desart [sic], where the snow drifted so strongly that it was impossible to get forward, until nature being at last overcome, and the spirits quite exhausted, without a possibility of relief, men, women, and children, who, by the darkness of the night, or through fatigue, were unable to keep up with their respective columns, and sat down to rest their weary limbs, sunk immediately to sleep, never to wake again.[65]

Calvert also wrote: 'It was a march of fearful suffering'.[66] Prince Adolphus told his father of 'continually marching', how his regiment 'is the strongest in the Corps, but I encrease [sic] daily in sick'. 'The cold we have had of late has been so very severe that one day according to the thermometer it was a degree colder than the year 40'. 'A great number of men during the march have had their hands and feet froze', Adolphus continued. 'The only consolation we have by it is that the French suffer at least as much if not more than we do'.[67] The prince told his king about the great bravery of the Hanoverians, and how thankful he was that they manned the rearguard outposts. Significantly, it was Hammerstein (accompanied by Scharnhorst) who commanded the rearguard. As Scharnhorst travelled among the German columns, he kept Hammerstein updated on their situation.[68]

In his report to Wallmoden, Scharnhorst recalled how 'fatigue and the resulting emergence of diseases increased alarmingly'.[69] Corporal Brown remembered this sickness as well: 'At this time near half the army are sick, and the other half much fatigued with hard

64 Scharnhorst, 'Officieller Bericht von dem, was an den Rhein and der Waal, an die Lek und an der Issel bey der Englischen Armee vorgefallen ist', Kunisch (ed.), *Scharnhorst: Privat und dienstliche Schriften*, Vol.1, pp.734-35; the quoted passage is from p.735. Also see a similar recollection in Anon., *A Narrative of the War by an Officer of the Guards*, Vol.2, p.121.

65 Jones, *An Historical Journal of the British Campaign on the Continent*, pp.171-72; the quoted passage is from p.171. So overwhelmed with grief was Jones that he stated he could not write anymore, so he included a copy of a letter from an officer of the guards to an unknown friend, describing in greater detail the horrors of the retreat. See pp.172-75. This letter may be the one published in Anon., *An Accurate and Impartial Narrative of the War by an Officer of the Guards*, Vol.2, pp.121-24. Another similar description can be found in Ditfurth, *Die Hessen in den Feldzügen 1793, 1794 und 1795*, Vol.2, pp.355-56. On 17 and 19 January 1795, Brown, *An Impartial Journal of a Detachment from the Brigade of Foot Guards*, pp.223-25, recalled the anguish he felt when discovering the frozen bodies of men, women, and especially children in the snow.

66 See Calvert's remarks in Verney (ed.), *The Journals and Correspondence of General Sir Harry Calvert*, p.423.

67 See the Letter of 26 January 1795 from Prince Adolphus to King George III; in Aspinall (ed.), *The Later Correspondence of George III*, Vol.2, p.297.

68 See the various correspondence Scharnhorst sent Hammerstein during this period; in Kunisch (ed.), *Scharnhorst: Privat und dienstliche Schriften*, Vol.1, pp.582-84.

69 Scharnhorst, 'Officieller Bericht von dem, was an den Rhein and der Waal, an die Lek und an der Issel bey der Englischen Armee vorgefallen ist', Kunisch (ed.), *Scharnhorst: Privat und dienstliche Schriften*, Vol.1, pp.729-36; the quoted passage is from p.734.

work. This is now the tenth day since any of us has had a night's rest or had time to undress'. Brown's description of the fate of the poor wounded and sick is particularly shocking, especially given the fact that care for the wounded and sick was supposed to be a major priority in the British army.

> The great mortality which has lately pervaded this army, added to the shameful abuse and neglect in several of the hospital departments, has made it a perfect Golgotha. Upwards of four thousand men having been buried here within the last three months.
>
> Removing the sick in wagons, without clothing sufficient to keep them warm in this rigorous season, has sent some hundreds to their eternal home; and the shameful neglect that prevails through all that department, makes our hospitals mere slaughter-houses.[70]

Jones also mourned the poor British sick.

> At this time an immense number of men were sick, from the situation of the army it was impossible to keep them with their regiments, and sending them to Rhennen hospital was generally looked upon as sealing their death warrants.

As Jones continued, he noted that the sick nearly always chose to remain with their regiments, afraid to go to the hospital, where they might be plundered by their own attendants and left to die.[71] During the retreat, the wounded and sick had to be ferried over the Waal and then dragged into the nearby houses, since angry Dutch officials refused to allow the British to establish hospitals.[72] A boat never disembarked without leaving some dead onboard. Their bodies were removed and thrown onto the riverbank.[73] For the British and German survivors of this retreat, their suffering and misery was far greater than that of the much-publicised French survivors of Napoleon's *Grande Armée* following their 1812 withdrawal from Moscow.[74]

70 Brown, *An Impartial Journal of a Detachment from the Brigade of Foot Guards*, pp.215 and 225; respectively.

71 Jones, *Historical Journal of the British Campaign on the Continent*, p.170. Also see Anon., *A Narrative of the War by an Officer of the Guards*, Vol.2, pp.119-20. Brown, *An Impartial Journal of a Detachment from the Brigade of Foot Guards*, p.207, recalled how the abuse of the sick continued, despite an order from the Duke of York to his commanders 'to pay particular attention' to the care of their sick and wounded.

72 Fortescue, *British Campaigns in Flanders*, p.391, discusses the deplorable British hospital conditions. Robert Roswell Palmer, 'Much in Little: The Dutch Revolution of 1795', *Journal of Modern History* 26:1 (March 1954), pp.15-35; noted on p. 22, 'the city of Delft refused to receive British wounded'.

73 See the scathing indictment of the British hospital system in Brown, *An Impartial Journal of a Detachment from the Brigade of Foot Guards*, pp.225-28. Brown even published the order from York for commanders at all levels to care for their sick and wounded. As Brown angrily concluded, British officers did not care about their men and completely ignored this command.

74 Lehmann, *Scharnhorst*, Vol.2, p.195, compared the allied retreat from the Waal to the Rhine in 1795 with the French retreat from Moscow in 1812, and concluded that unlike Napoleon's *Grande Armée* in 1812, Wallmoden's corps in 1795 was already on the verge of collapse before the retreat began. On Vol.2, p.364 of his study, Ditfurth, *Die Hessen in den Feldzügen 1793, 1794 und 1795*, noted the recollections of Hessian soldiers who participated in both

Without effective leadership, morale and discipline broke down among the soldiers. This was especially true with the British and the French *émigré* troops, who Scharnhorst said acted like 'the worst people in the world. Their plundering was perhaps worse than the Cossacks'. This blatant misconduct gave the coalition army a terrible reputation and drove the Dutch people into the arms of the French.[75] Calvert disagreed with Scharnhorst's assessment. In his opinion, the retreat 'testified to the admirable discipline, as well as the courage of the British'. While 'some foreign battalions in British pay' were engaged in numerous atrocities, Calvert noted that 'our own regiments maintained their discipline unshaken by reverse'.[76]

Interestingly, while Jones never mentioned any misbehaviour of the British soldier, he did recall how the Dutch 'opened their gates' to the French and 'welcomed them on all occasions'. The French overran Holland 'without the least opposition' of the local inhabitants. While never alluding to the reason why the Dutch people welcomed the French with open arms, Jones roundly condemned the Dutch people, whose 'conduct to the British was cruel and vindictive, to a degree scarcely to be credited'.

> In many instances they were so barbarous as to let them die at their doors, sooner than afford them shelter; they were greater enemies than the French, as the latter always took care of such sick or wounded as came within their power, but the inhabitants frequently murdered them, and in every instance distressed them as much as they could.[77]

Calvert wrote a similar commentary in his journal:

> The Dutch peasantry inhabiting those dreary and inhospitable provinces were enemies more cruel to our exhausted soldiers than the victorious French army who harassed and pursued them.[78]

While not condoning the conduct of local Dutch inhabitants, Brown clearly felt the British had brought this vindictiveness (as Jones described it) upon themselves.

> The Dutch and us were no great friends before, but those skulking villains [referring to British plunderers], for whom no punishment is too severe, has given them [the Dutch] more cause of hatred and discontent then ever they had before; …

campaigns and found that the retreat across Holland in 1795 was far worse than the retreat from Moscow in 1812. Also see the vivid description in Fortescue, *British Campaigns in Flanders*, pp.397-400.

75 Scharnhorst, 'Von den englischen Truppen' (not before January 1795); in Kunisch (ed.), *Scharnhorst: Privat und dienstliche Schriften*, Vol.1, pp.760-64; the quoted passages are from p.763.

76 See Calvert's conclusion in Verney (ed.), *The Journals and Correspondence of General Sir Harry Calvert*, p.423.

77 Jones, *Historical Journal of the British Campaign on the Continent*, pp.175-76.

78 See Calvert's commentary in Verney (ed.), *The Journals and Correspondence of General Sir Harry Calvert*, p.423.

For Brown, it was the bad conduct of the British soldier that had led the Dutch to acclaim with joy the French 'as their only protectors'.[79]

Scharnhorst agreed completely with Brown. 'In general, the English behave so violently. Their plundering and cruelty is often so great'.[80] Indeed, it appears that nothing was safe from them. Hessian officers guarding the quarters of *General-Major* Georg von Düring (1738-1795) had to drive British plunderers away at the point of the sword.[81] In another incident, British troops fought 'a pitched battle' with Hessian soldiers over food and shelter.[82] On 16 January, Brown recorded in his journal that Hessian troops refused shelter to the British Guards in Bickborge, where every house was already full of their infantry. They would not even permit the British to come near their fires.[83] Even Scharnhorst had his 'beautiful overcoat' stolen by the British.[84]

Scharnhorst maintained that British soldiers were completely 'useless' on outpost or guard duty. He noted that when they rode out on patrol, local inhabitants frequently fired on them. Any intelligence they brought back was questionable, since they deliberately falsified their reports to cloak their own marauding.[85] Interestingly, Calvert never mentioned any of this in his journal. Scharnhorst also believed that British officers treated war as a kind of sport and felt no moral obligation toward their men. They were constantly drunk, and 'with the exception of a few, a very few, know nothing about field warfare' [*Feldkrieg*].[86] To gratify their immeasurable thirst, English soldiers often sold their uniforms at ridiculously low prices and came back into camp the next morning nearly naked.[87] As Lieutenant Wilson recalled:

79 Brown, *An Impartial Journal of a Detachment from the Brigade of Foot Guards*, p.229. Palmer agreed, writing on p. 22 of his study, 'The Dutch Revolution of 1795', that the British army 'feebly commanded' by the Duke of York, 'behaved very badly on its retreat through the Netherlands, whereas the incoming French, under firm discipline, made a good impression'.

80 Scharnhorst, 'Von den englischen Truppen', in Kunisch (ed.), *Scharnhorst: Privat und dienstliche Schriften*, Vol.1, p.760. In his analysis, Fortescue, *British Campaigns in Flanders*, pp.397-400, wrote that the discipline of the troops in Holland had 'broken down completely'. The quoted passage is from p.397. Brown, *An Impartial Journal of a Detachment from the Brigade of Foot Guards*, p.194, noted that back on 23 September 1794, the Duke of York had to issue an order 'to put a stop to that scandalous and too prevalent practice of plundering' by British soldiers. The English Provost was even empowered 'to execute on the spot' anyone caught plundering.

81 See the recollections of Ompteda; in Hill (trans.), *A Hanoverian-English Officer*, p.76.

82 Fortescue, *British Campaigns in Flanders*, p.398. Ditfurth, *Die Hessen in den Feldzügen 1793, 1794 und 1795*, Vol.2, p.364, also mentions this fight. Remembering the altercations between English and Hessian troops, Brown, *An Impartial Journal of a Detachment from the Brigade of Foot Guards*, p.222, noted the Hessians 'are in no respects friendly to the English'.

83 Brown, *An Impartial Journal of a Detachment from the Brigade of Foot Guards*, p.222.

84 Letter of 13 January 1795 to Klara; in Kunisch (ed.), *Scharnhorst: Privat und dienstliche Schriften*, Vol.1, p.577.

85 See Gerhard Scharnhorst to letter to Hammerstein's aide, *Capitain* du Plat (12 October 1794); in Kunisch (ed.), *Scharnhorst: Privat und dienstliche Schriften*, Vol.1, pp.461-63; especially p.461 and Note 1, in which Scharnhorst acknowledged du Plat's message of 11 October 1794 that mentioned the false reporting by British patrols.

86 Scharnhorst, 'Von den englischen Truppen', Kunisch (ed.), *Scharnhorst: Privat und dienstliche Schriften*, Vol.1, p.760. Compare the scathing assessment of the British commissioning system discussed in Fortescue, *British Campaigns in Flanders*, pp.371-72, with Scharnhorst's evaluation.

87 In his analysis, Fortescue, *British Campaigns in Flanders*, pp.372-73, discusses the deplorable condition of the British soldier with respect to his clothing.

> Drunkenness was the vice of officers and men, but the men paid the penalty; and the officers who sat in judgment in the morning were too often scarcely sober from the past night's debauch.[88]

Corporal Brown also remembered how the Hessians posted sentries to prevent the local inhabitants from selling liquor to British troops.[89]

In sharp contrast to their behaviour in Holland, Scharnhorst recalled from his historical studies how under the superb German leadership of Duke Ferdinand during the Seven Years War, English soldiers were among the finest in the army. 'Their subordination in other circumstances is so great', he noted. 'You may do with them as you like'. Overall, he felt the British soldier was extremely brave, eager to attack, steady under fire, willing to sacrifice himself, usually disciplined, and almost never complaining when fatigued.[90] It was so sad, he concluded, that the noble qualities of the English warrior would soon be forgotten because of his misbehaviour during this campaign. Scharnhorst placed the reason for this misconduct squarely on the poor example set by the British officer corps.

On 28 and 29 January, elements of the British-Hanoverian-Hessian-Dutch army crossed safely over the Issel River into Germany. British forces marched toward Osnabrück, with two British infantry regiments remaining on the Issel to protect the crossing points for the German troops. As Hanoverian forces were preparing to leave their assembly areas near Lochem (Holland) and march toward Münster (Germany), Wallmoden informed Hammerstein on 24 January of his plan to reposition the German forces, while Scharnhorst on the same day told him the Commanding General had assigned ten pieces of Dutch artillery (12-pound guns) to his corps.[91]

From Lochem on 29 January 1795, Wallmoden issued a General Order to all German soldiers. 'Now that the army is at the point of treading German soil once more, I consider it necessary to remind everyone that this is our fatherland'. The Commanding General expressed his desire that every officer strongly emphasise this to their troops and set a personal example for their soldiers to emulate.

> I must mention with pain and shame for the army, the unspeakable plunder, yes robbery, and occasionally even murder and destruction of which so many, more or less, have hitherto been guilty.

88 See the recollections of Robert Wilson; in Randolph (ed.), *Life of General Sir Robert Wilson*, Vol.1, p.98. Also see the interesting article by Paul E. Kopperman, '"The Cheapest Pay": Alcohol Abuse in the Eighteenth-Century British Army', *Journal of Military History* 60:3 (July 1996), pp.445-70. Although Kopperman deals with alcohol abuse in America, the same trends were common among British soldiers in Holland as well.

89 Brown, *An Impartial Journal of a Detachment from the Brigade of Foot Guards*, p.222.

90 Scharnhorst, 'Von den englischen Truppen', Kunisch (ed.), *Scharnhorst: Privat und dienstliche Schriften*, Vol.1, pp.760-64; the quoted passage is from p.760.

91 See the Letter of 24 January 1795 from Wallmoden to Hammerstein; in Kunisch (ed.), *Scharnhorst: Privat und dienstliche Schriften*, Vol.1, pp.584-85; while Scharnhorst's Letter of 24 January 1795 to Hammerstein follows on p.585. Also see Wallmoden's thoughts about the security of his force as he withdraws into Germany; in Hann 38 E, Nr.230: *General von Wallmoden fordert das Vorrücken des an der Hunte stehenden Cordons zur Sicherung des Landes*; deposited at the Niedersächsisches Landesarchiv, Hanover.

> I can therefore, with every possible emphasis order, that henceforth, no one in the army shall be guilty of any kind of plunder, extortion, or robbery.[92]

Emphasising sound military leadership, Wallmoden stated that it was the responsibility of every battalion, regimental, and corps commander, along with their officers, to maintain good order and discipline within the ranks. Any misconduct among 'your soldiers, transporters, or laborers' will be dealt with immediately, and 'reported to the general of their corps'. Determined to avoid what had happened in Flanders and Holland, the Commanding General ended his order with the stern warning for 'all and everyone in this army' to abide by the 'Articles of War' [*Kriegsartikel*] or suffer the severest punishment.

Once behind the Issel, Scharnhorst provided Wallmoden with the 'Location' of Hanoverian forces.[93] Thinking ahead, he also submitted a contingency plan on arrangements to be made for a possible withdrawal to the Ems.[94] Around the same time, Scharnhorst informed *Capitain* du Plat of 'a crisis' in coordinating future cantonments with British and Austrian leaders. He told his friend that while Wallmoden did not want to abandon the defence of the Issel, both British and Austrian leaders appeared to want to quit the fight.[95] The Commanding General had dispatched *Major* Hardenberg to British headquarters to reassure Harcourt and to discuss with the British quartermaster their cantonment areas and logistical issues. Wallmoden wanted to make sure the British continued to supply the Hanoverians.[96] Scharnhorst then submitted a memorandum on 29 January that summarised important points from the previous campaigns for the edification of the Commanding General, and then updated him on the current situation within the coalition.[97]

As allied forces withdrew into north-western Germany, negotiations with German civil authorities in the projected areas of operation were already underway. As early as 24 January, Wallmoden had ordered his staff to begin planning the occupation and defence of all militarily significant locations along the Dutch-German border.[98] Wallmoden told his staff to focus their efforts on the County [*Grafschaft*] of Bentheim, where his forces would first

92 See 'General Befehl des Generals Grafen von Wallmoden' (29 January 1795); published in Sichart, *Geschichte der Königlich-Hannoverischen Armee*, Vol.4, pp.572-73; and in Ditfurth, *Die Hessen in den Feldzügen 1793, 1794 und 1795*, Vol.2, p.515. This order is noticeably absent in both Klippel, *Scharnhorst*; and Lehmann, *Scharnhorst*. Additionally, it is cited only in part by Ompteda; in Hill (trans.), *A Hanoverian-English Officer*, p.77.

93 See 'Dislocation' (middle to the end of January 1795); in Kunisch (ed.), *Scharnhorst: Privat und dienstliche Schriften*, Vol.1, pp.574-76.

94 See Scharnhorst's Report (end of January 1795); in Kunisch (ed.), *Scharnhorst: Privat und dienstliche Schriften*, Vol.1, pp.585-86.

95 Scharnhorst to du Plat (end of January 1795); in Kunisch (ed.), *Scharnhorst: Privat und dienstliche Schriften*, Vol.1, p.586.

96 See the documentation in Hann 38 E, Nr.278: *Verpflegungs- und Kommissariats-Angelegenheiten: Korrespondenz des Generals von Wallmoden mit dem englischen Generalleutnant Harcourt über die Verpflegung der hannoverschen Armee*; deposited at the Niedersächsisches Landesarchiv, Hanover.

97 See Scharnhorst's Memorandum of 29 January 1795; in Kunisch (ed.), *Scharnhorst: Privat und dienstliche Schriften*, Vol.1, pp.587-88.

98 See the interesting study by retired *Generalmajor* Hermann Büschleb, *Scharnhorst in Westfalen: Politik, Administration und Kommando im Schicksaljahr 1795* (Herford: E.S. Mittler & Sohn, 1979), which incorporates many source documents. As a former general staff officer, Büschleb brings a unique perspective to his analysis of Scharnhorst in Westphalia during the early months of 1795.

enter German soil. Bentheim was under the governance of the Electorate of Hanover, and Wallmoden wanted to know the distribution of the population, the size of the villages and towns (as well as the nearby farming communities), in terms of their military significance and use.[99] He then sent Hammerstein and Dallwigk their cantonment areas in Münster.[100] Wallmoden followed these orders with detailed instructions for Hammerstein and the Hanoverian forces.[101]

On the same day the Commanding General issued his general order to all German troops, he sent a letter to the Prince-Bishopric of Osnabrück. Wallmoden requested the Prince-Bishopric inspect the highways and secondary roads from Osnabrück to Rheine, Diepholz, and Lengerich, and for each township to make all necessary repairs. He also asked for the repair and maintenance of all the bridges over the Ems and the smaller streams.[102] Officials in Osnabrück took this request seriously (since the reigning Prince-Bishop was the Duke of York), and issued a notice to all cities, towns, villages, and farming communities within its jurisdiction to comply immediately with the needs of the German corps. This was an excellent example of civil-military cooperation; unfortunately, the sole exception. With French armies fast approaching the German border, many of the local petty aristocrats in this area of Germany known as Westphalia wanted no coalition presence in their lands. They erroneously believed this would keep the French out.[103]

While it is beyond the scope of this study to analyse the intricate history of Westphalia, it is important to understand that this region of Germany had suffered greatly during the Seven Years War. Vivid memories of that conflict lingered in the minds of the people, who had not yet fully recovered from the rapacious French occupation and devastation that war had brought to their communities. Geographically, Westphalia was situated between the Rhine and Weser Rivers. It was bordered on the north and northwest by the Netherlands and Hanover; on the east by Schaumburg-Lippe, Brunswick, Lippe-Detmold, Waldeck, Hanover, and Hesse-Nassau; on the south and southwest by Hesse-Nassau; and on the west by the Netherlands and the province of the Rhine. Like many of the smaller German states, much of Westphalia remained divided into areas of feudal power, with several of these lords residing far away in other parts of the Holy Roman Empire. The Catholic ecclesiastical principalities of the archbishopric of Cologne and the bishopric of Münster were two examples, both were governed by Archduke Maximilian Francis of Austria (1756-1801), a Habsburg prince and uncle of Francis II. Given the nature of the political structure of Westphalia, coordinating military operations in this region promised to be a daunting task.

99 See the source documents in Hann 38 E, Nr.255: *Kantonnierungen in der Grafschaft Bentheim, 1794-1795*; deposited at the Niedersächsisches Landesarchiv, Hanover.

100 See Wallmoden's correspondence with Hammerstein and Dallwigk (29 January 1795); in Kunisch (ed.), *Scharnhorst: Privat und dienstliche Schriften*, Vol.1, pp.588-89.

101 See Wallmoden's correspondence with Hammerstein (29-31 January 1795); in Kunisch (ed.), *Scharnhorst: Privat und dienstliche Schriften*, Vol.1, pp.590-91.

102 See Wallmoden's Letter of 29 January 1795 to the Prince-Bishopric of Osnabrück; published in Büschleb, *Scharnhorst in Westfalen*, Appendix 5/1, p.121.

103 See the discussion in Emil von Cosel, *Geschichte des preussischen Staates und Volkes under den Hohenzollernschen Fürsten: Nach den besten Quellen bearbeitet und den Gebildeten aller Stände des preussischen und deutschen Volkes* (Leipzig: Duncker und Humblot, 1869-76), Vol.5, pp.380-81.

Moving into Westphalia presented a very perplexing challenge for the Germans. From the beginning of the war, Westphalia had been a marshalling area for troops of the coalition, and the local communities were weary of the constant presence of soldiers in their homes, as well as the requisition and confiscation of their property and produce, sometimes without reimbursement. Land and people were exhausted.[104] Nevertheless, British leaders in London considered control of Westphalia as paramount for Great Britain, not only for the safety of north-western Germany, but more importantly, for their trade with the German states. During their cabinet meeting of 8 February 1795, British ministers resolved, 'the defence [sic] of Westphalia is not be abandoned, if practicable'. They recommended to King George that 'the force under General Wallmoden should not be placed in any position that will render it impracticable for them to keep up their communication with the Austrian troops'.[105] Of course, these ministers never recommended that British troops be part of that defence.

Now that war had come to Germany, Wallmoden was seeking accommodation from the recalcitrant princes and local populations, especially in Münster, where he planned to establish his headquarters. Unfortunately for the Germans, Münster was a Hapsburg possession and Austrian troops under Clairfayt were already occupying the city. Anticipating the arrival of more soldiers, Münster officials had established a 'Billeting Commission' [*Billetierungs-Commission*] to manage the quartering of men and horses. In late January they informed Wallmoden that the 2,260 homes within the city were currently housing 2,370 soldiers, while the city was having difficulty finding suitable stables for the more than 800 horses that the Austrians had brought.[106] In response, the Commanding General rejected the arguments of the Billeting Commission, informing authorities in Münster that their city had housed far more troops during the Seven Years War, and that his corps was on its way to Münster.[107] During the ensuing negotiations, Scharnhorst kept the field commanders apprised of the situation.[108] Once in Münster, he presented the Commanding General with the locations of the German units (Hanoverians and Hessians) under Wallmoden's immediate command.[109]

As Hanoverian and Hessian troops were establishing their quarters in Münster, officials in the city sent an urgent appeal to their lord, Archduke Maximilian Francis, the Imperial Elector Prince-Bishop of Cologne, to intercede on their behalf and to stop the influx of

104 Büschleb, *Scharnhorst in Westfalen*, p.31.

105 Cabinet Meeting Notes of 8 February 1795; in Aspinall (ed.), *The Later Correspondence of George III*, Vol.2, p.301.

106 See the Letter of 29 January 1795 from the President of the Münster Privy Council, Mathias von Landsberg, and Privy Councilman Christopher Münstermann to '*General en Chef* Wallmoden; in Büschleb, *Scharnhorst in Westfalen*, Appendix 6/1, p.122. The *Pro Memoria* that follows on pp.123-25, provides the data to support the arguments of the Billeting Commission.

107 Letter of 31 January 1795 from Wallmoden to the government in Münster; in Büschleb, *Scharnhorst in Westfalen*, Appendix 6/2, p.126.

108 See 'Anfrage an die kayserliche Generalität' (end of January 1795); Scharnhorst's letter to du Plat discussing the 'crisis of coordination with the British and Austrians' (end of January 1795); and a memorandum delineating the limits of Austrian support, the exhaustion of the British Army, the withdrawal of the British to the Ems, and the weakness of the Hanoverians and Hessians on the Issel (29 January 1795); in Kunisch (ed.), *Scharnhorst: Privat und dienstliche Schriften*, Vol.1, pp.585-86, 586, and 587-88; respectively.

109 Gerhard Scharnhorst, 'Dislocation der chur-hannoverischen und darmstädtschen Truppen' (February 1795); in Kunisch (ed.), *Scharnhorst: Privat und dienstliche Schriften*, Vol.1, pp.592-94.

German soldiers and horses into Münster.[110] Over the next several weeks, military and civilian leaders in this region (known as Münsterland) endeavoured to reach a suitable accommodation. Unfortunately, since there was no clear delineation of authority that either civilian or military officials possessed, and because it appears that neither desired to put in writing their respective duties and responsibilities, negotiations stalled.

Rank played a major role in dealings with both civilian and military officials in Münsterland. Wallmoden had initially appointed his aide-de-camp *Rittmeister* Ernst Idel Jobst Freiherr von Vincke (1768-1845) as his liaison officer to coordinate the requisition of food, shelter, and forage. While Vincke worked diligently to find adequate quarters and stables for the Hanoverian and Hessian troops, and to settle disputes with Austrian forces, the Commanding General soon realised Vincke simply did not possess the rank required of his task.[111] So he placed *General-Major* Georg Wilhelm Philipp von Wangenheim (1735-99) in charge of the German delegation, with *Oberstlieutenant* Johann Ludwig Hogrewe (1737-1814) handling troop billeting and Vincke food and other supplies.[112] Scharnhorst acted as their liaison with the Commanding General, continually updating Wallmoden on these activities and keeping the field commanders informed. To ease a perceived overcrowding in Münster, the Commanding General relocated a number of German soldiers to the surrounding towns, villages, and farming communities.[113]

The winter retreat from Holland had produced enormous supply problems. Provisions for both soldiers and horses – bread, meat, feed, straw, and hay – usually came from magazines located in the host country. Now that his forces were on German soil, Wallmoden focused his endeavours on improving his logistical support system, while avoiding hostility from the local population.[114] Magazines already existed in Rheine and Bentheim, and officials in Münster reluctantly agreed to establish depots in Meppen and Münster. A constant challenge came from the friction between military procurement officers and their civilian counterparts, in addition to territorial disputes with the Austrians over foraging. If payment was not immediately forthcoming, local farmers and merchants often refused to release their goods. In response, soldiers took whatever supplies they needed, in direct violation of Wallmoden's general order. This conduct came to a crisis on 11 February, when 30 Hanoverian *Jäger*

110 See the Letter of 5 February 1795 from Mayor Meiteler and the Privy Council of Münster to the Elector Prince-Bishop of Cologne; in Büschleb, *Scharnhorst in Westfalen*, Appendix 7/1, pp.128-29. Also see the Letter of 4 February 1795 from three members of the Billeting Commission to the Elector Prince Bishop of Cologne; also in Büschleb, *Scharnhorst in Westfalen*, Appendix 7/2, p.129.

111 See Scharnhorst's Concept Brief of 8 February 1795 regarding quartering disputes, which Wallmoden then sent under his name to Austrian *Feldmarschall-Lieutenant* Joseph Freiherr von Barberek Alvinczy (1735-1810); in Kunisch (ed.), *Scharnhorst: Privat und dienstliche Schriften*, Vol.1, pp.597-98.

112 Büschleb, *Scharnhorst in Westfalen*, Appendix 6/3, pp.126-27, includes a report dated 29 January 1795 from Hogrewe regarding Hanoverian troop billeting and his coordination with Austrian officials and local civilian authorities.

113 See Gerhard Scharnhorst, 'Veränderungen in der schon gegebenen Dislocation der hannövrischen Truppen' (5 February 1794); in Kunisch (ed.), *Scharnhorst: Privat und dienstliche Schriften*, Vol.1, p.595. Also see Scharnhorst's Letter of 6 February 1795 to General Hammerstein, informing him of the quartering conflicts with the Austrians (p.596); his resolution of this challenge (p.596); and his 'Separationslinie zwischen den kayserlichen und hannovrischen Truppen' (February 1795); on p.597.

114 See the documentation in Hann 38 E, Nr.290: *Verhandlungen zwischen dem Herzog von York, dem General von Wallmoden und dem englischen Staatssekretär Generalleutnant Dundas über die Verpflegung der in englischem Solde stehenden Subsidien-Truppen*; deposited at the Niedersächsisches Landesarchiv, Hanover.

slaughtered 23 deer at the animal sanctuary on the estate of Chamberlain Count Clemens August von Galen, who belonged to one of the oldest and most distinguished and influential Catholic noble families in Westphalia. Galen was in Münster at the time. After killing the deer, the Hanoverians seized some wagons, loaded the venison, and forced Galen's servants to march with them back to their cantonment area.

Outraged by this blatant violation of his order of 29 January, Wallmoden ordered those *Jäger* to be punished and to make full restitution to Chamberlain Galen.[115] A few days later he had to place the entire Hanoverian contingent on a 14-day bread ration because of the scarcity of food in Münster. Then on 28 February, he issued an order for all German troops to obtain subsistence only within their cantonment districts. Wallmoden followed this order on 8 March with a scathing letter to officials in Münster, in which he denounced their lack of support and accused them of giving preferential treatment to Austrian troops, while the native German soldiers under his command were ignored. In a veiled threat to declare martial law and confiscate whatever his troops required, Wallmoden finally gained the reluctant cooperation of the Bishopric of Münster.[116]

Care for the numerous sick and wounded soldiers of the German corps was also a top priority for Wallmoden. In January, the Austrians had established a hospital in Münster. Unfortunately, this was not sufficient for the Hanoverian and Hessian soldiers of the Coalition. Not wanting to upset the local population and authorities in Münster (who were afraid the sick and wounded would bring disease into their residential areas), Wallmoden focused his search for a suitable location for another hospital in the nearby Bishopric of Osnabrück. He was aware that the mayor of Münster and his council, after ordering local officials to cooperate with Hanoverian and Hessian military authorities, had again appealed to their Hapsburg masters in Cologne and Vienna, demanding all 'foreign' troops (meaning the Hanoverian and Hessian contingents) leave the Bishopric of Münster. In an exchange of notes between the Bishopric of Cologne and the Electorate of Hanover, it became clear to the Commanding General that the petty particularism among the various feudal lords in Westphalia threatened not only the health and welfare of his soldiers, but also the very security of this key German province that he was endeavouring to protect from French conquest.[117]

Fed up with officials and the people of Münsterland, Wallmoden decided by mid-February to transfer his headquarters to Osnabrück, and had Scharnhorst notify his subordinate commanders and the Austrians.[118] Around the same time, officials in Osnabrück had found a suitable location for a hospital in the small village of Westerkappeln, a short distance

115 See the discussion of this incident in Büschleb, *Scharnhorst in Westfalen*, p.47. What is gratifying here is the generosity of Chamberlain Galen, who gave the money he received as restitution to the poor and needy in Münster.

116 See the exchange of letters between Wallmoden and the Bishopric of Münster; cited in Büschleb, *Scharnhorst in Westfalen*, pp.48-49.

117 Büschleb, *Scharnhorst in Westfalen*, pp.44-50. The striking similarities between the situations Wallmoden and Count Wilhelm faced trying to defend their fellow Germans from French conquest is clear from the evidence Büschleb presents.

118 See the correspondence from Wallmoden to his subordinate commanders; in Kunisch (ed.), *Scharnhorst: Privat und dienstliche Schriften*, Vol.1, pp.603-13. His report to the Austrian commander follows on pp.623-25. Scharnhorst's reports to the Commanding General on the progress of the relocation, the new positions, and the associated challenges for the corps, are contained on pp.613-23 and 626-33.

northwest of Osnabrück. Dallwigk then established his headquarters at Teckleburg on 27 February. By early March 1795, German troops (Hanoverian, Brunswicker, and Hessian), along with British, Dutch, and French *émigré* contingents, occupied their new defensive positions along the Dutch-German border in and around the *Grafschaft* Bentheim.[119]

As the Austrians, British, Dutch, French *émigré* troops, Hanoverians, and Hessians were recovering and refitting from their evacuation of Holland, French forces under Pichegru were overrunning what remained of Holland. Utrecht opened its gates on 16 January; Rotterdam two days later. French troops marched enthusiastically into Amsterdam on 20 January, and along with Dutch revolutionaries, proclaimed a Batavian Republic. All of the Dutch fortresses that had successfully resisted Louis XIV more than a century earlier during the Franco-Dutch War of 1672-78 were now captured intact. Elsewhere, a French cavalry detachment conducting routine reconnaissance found the Dutch fleet icebound on the Texel. Crossing the frozen Zuyder Zee, the French captured the entire fleet of 15 ships of the line and 30 smaller vessels.[120] Holland now became a satellite of France and her active military ally.

Looking back over the previous two years, it was clear to *Major* Gerhard Scharnhorst that from the beginning of the War of the First Coalition, German soldiers in support of the coalition had fought well and bravely, often against overwhelming odds. The failure of the campaigns in Flanders and Holland owed more to disunity among the Allies (who never had any common objective), extremely poor political and military leadership at the highest levels, and the muddled and unrealistic policies of the Austrian and British governments, than to any shortcomings of the German troops on the ground.

119 Sichart, *Geschichte der Königlich-Hannoverischen Armee*, Vol.4, pp.584-88, provides the location of the Hanoverian, Brunswicker, Hessian, and British positions in and around Bentheim. Also see Demet, *'We are Accustomed to do our Duty'*, p.105.

120 Interestingly, when the British had landed at Hellevoetsluis in March 1793, they found 'several ships of war, seven of them carrying 74 guns each', just sitting there without crews, because Dutch officials 'could not procure sailors to man them'. See the recollections in Anon., *An Accurate and Impartial Narrative of the War by an Officer of the Guards*, Vol.1, p.7 and Note. Palmer, 'The Dutch Revolution of 1795', p.16, mentioned the rapid decline of the Dutch fleet after 1787, when the Prussians invaded Holland and forcibly restored the Prince of Orange. Since then, many Dutch seamen refused to serve the Stadtholder.

11

Protecting Westphalia

Scharnhorst was glad to be back in Germany. He was hoping that this war would soon be over so he could go home to his family. While traveling to Münster in early February 1795, he took time to update his beloved Klara on the strategic situation. 'This I now know, that it is possible that the enemy in a future operation may penetrate to the Weser, but it is not likely he will reach Hanover'. He assured her that she and their children would be safe in Hanover. Then he continued, 'So far, I am quite healthy, despite all of the colds, all of the exertions, all of the annoyances during the recent course of events. Some rest awaits me in Münster'. Scharnhorst followed this with news that Trew and the greater part of the Hanoverian artillery were safely home.[1] Unfortunately, he would not be coming home anytime soon. Once again, 'an avowed ignorant and completely useless man here is being sent home', he told Klara, while he remained at headquarters to do most of the staff work. 'I cannot get away', he wrote before bidding 'Adieu' to Klara and their children.[2]

A week earlier on 3 February 1795, Wallmoden had informed the Duke of York, 'Your army is destroyed'. In polite but sober terms that echoed Scharnhorst's assessment of the English officer corps, the Commanding General told the Duke:

> The officers, their carriages, and a large train are safe, but the men are destroyed. The army has now no more than six thousand fighting men, but it has all of the drawbacks of thirty-three battalions, and consumes a vast quantity of forage.[3]

Wallmoden made it clear to York that he felt British officers cared only about themselves and their comforts, and not about the men under their charge – men who died by the hundreds from disease, sickness, exposure, and starvation. A British officer's horse meant more to him than did a soldier's life. As one later English historian wrote: 'A more terrible reproach

1 Gerhard Scharnhorst to his wife Klara (before 9 February 1795); published in Kunisch (ed.), *Scharnhorst: Privat und dienstliche Schriften*, Vol.1, pp. 598-99; the quoted passages are from p.598.

2 Scharnhorst to his wife Klara (before 9 February 1795); in Kunisch (ed.), *Scharnhorst: Privat und dienstliche Schriften*, Vol.1, p.599. Scharnhorst was referring to *Major* Ernst Joachim Gottlieb von Wenckstern (1753-1821). See Note 1 on p.599.

3 Johann Ludwig, *Reichsgraf* von Wallmoden-Gimborn to York (3 February 1795); deposited at The National Archives, London, and listed as War Office (WO) Record 1/172, pp.219-26; the quoted passage is from p.222. Selected parts of this letter are published in Sir John W. Fortescue, *British Campaigns in Flanders*, pp.399-400.

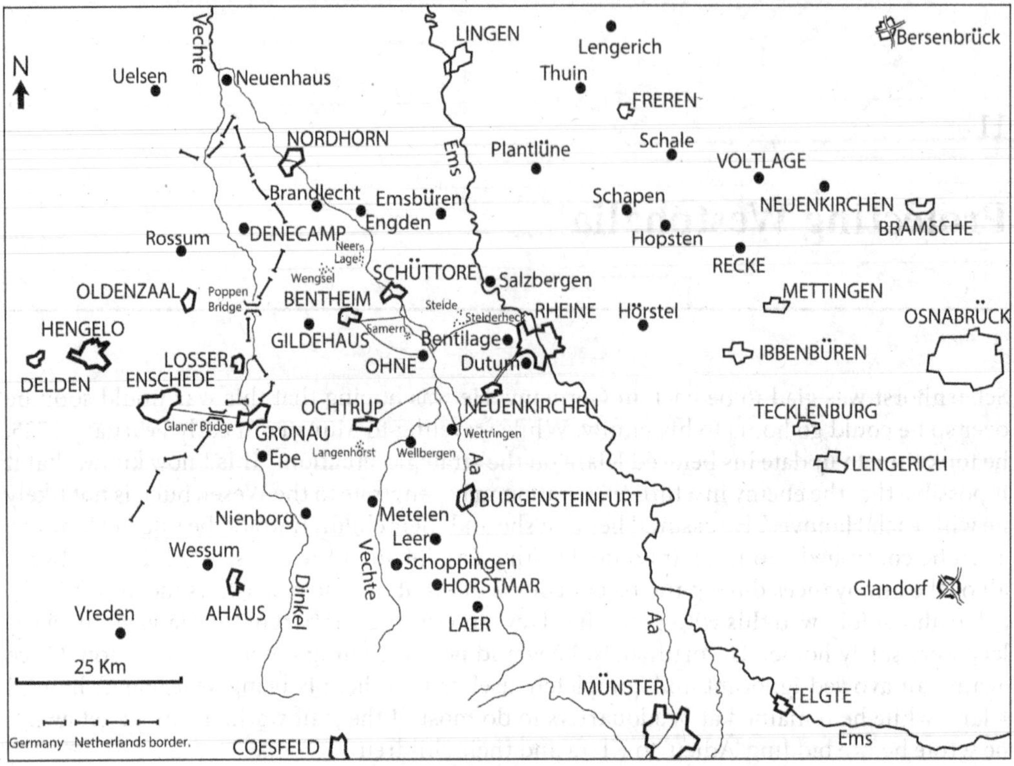

Map 11 Westphalia, February to March 1795.

was never yet levelled against any force', than the commentary with which Wallmoden had politely chastised the noble Duke of York and his officers.[4]

Once in Münster Scharnhorst told Klara, 'Your letters constantly cheer me up'. He had just received several of them and had read all from the past month and was anxious to see his family now that he was back in Germany. Other officers were home on leave, but because he had made himself virtually indispensable to the Commanding General, the possibility of any home leave for Scharnhorst was remote.[5] So he made plans for his family to visit him, but then demurred, realising that such a long journey would be extremely difficult and dangerous for Klara, given her pregnancy, the cold weather, and the terrible road conditions, not to mention any marauders. In any case, he was still hoping his family would find a way to come and see him. Changing topics, he told his wife, 'The entire army now longs for nothing but peace'. While prospects for peace were pretty good, he noted that until that happens, uncertainly will still reign. After a few other thoughts, he closed his letter without the usual 'Adieu' to Klara.[6]

4 See the commentary by Fortescue in *British Campaigns in Flanders*, p.400.

5 Klippel, *Scharnhorst*, Vol.2, pp.163-206, does a good job characterising Scharnhorst's outstanding performance of duty during this stressful period. Also see the commentary in Lehmann, *Scharnhorst*, Vol.1, pp.168-202.

6 Gerhard Scharnhorst to Klara Scharnhorst (9 February 1795); in Kunisch (ed.), *Scharnhorst: Privat und dienstliche Schriften*, Vol.1, pp.599-601; the quoted passages are from p.599.

From Münster Scharnhorst wrote to his friend Mechlenburg, updating him on the retreat from Holland and the horrors of a winter war.[7] He began by commenting on the relentless French pursuit that never allowed coalition forces any peace. He promised to send Mechlenburg his journal, which contained his detailed analysis of the retreat.[8] Continuing with his commentary on the campaign, he noted, 'This is a cruel war'. The winter weather was 'just as fierce as in 1788' (when Prussia had sent troops into Holland to crush the Dutch revolt and restore the Stadtholder) and 'two degrees colder than in 1740' (during the War of the Austrian Succession).[9] In an interesting comparison, Scharnhorst noted how a summer campaign is mostly destructive physically, while a winter war causes such 'immeasurable misery' in both a physical and psychological sense.[10] To demonstrate his point, he told his Danish friend about the enormous privations of the soldiers – the lack of food, shelter, and clothing, comparing the Dutch countryside to a barren wasteland without sufficient resources for its own people, let alone so many foreign troops. He described how 'diseases of all kinds' ravaged the sick and wounded, and how difficult it was to care for and transport these soldiers. Scharnhorst ended his letter by telling Mechlenburg that the present war, because of the extreme cold weather, the massive privations, and the numerous diseases, 'belongs to the greatest sufferings the human race has ever endured'.[11]

Meanwhile, petty particularism threatened the defence of the German Fatherland. This was Wallmoden's conclusion as he assessed the military situation in early February 1795. His Hanoverian and Hessian forces were positioned in the centre of the coalition defence. To his north (the right flank) were the Prussians, who were secretly negotiating with France for an end of hostilities. Also to his north were the British, who had withdrawn most of their troops from the front, with eyes set on embarkation and not further fighting. To his south (his left flank) were the Austrians, who had no desire to cooperate with the Germans and would later prove unreliable.[12] Dutch and French *émigré* forces were intermingled with the Germans and British. In his 'General Disposition' report, Scharnhorst told Wallmoden 'the enemy has three points from Leer to Rheine, from which he can advance'. He then recommended the English defend the 'Leer on the right bank of the Ems' and 'the area around Lingen', while the Hanoverians and Hessians would establish their defence centred on Rheine.[13]

7 Gerhard Scharnhorst to Ezechias Gustav von Mechlenburg (9 February 1795); in Kunisch (ed.), *Scharnhorst: Privat und dienstliche Schriften*, Vol.1, pp.601-02.

8 See Gerhard Scharnhorst, 'Unser Zurückzug über die Maas und über die Waal' (not after May 1795); in Kunisch (ed.), *Scharnhorst: Privat und dienstliche Schriften*, Vol.1, pp.736-52. The editor of Scharnhorst's Papers believes this may be the manuscript Scharnhorst mentioned in his letter to Mechlenburg. See Note 2 on p.601.

9 According to the compilers of Scharnhorst's Papers, the weather data Scharnhorst cited to Mechlenburg was remarkably like the 11 January 1795 journal entry of Hanoverian field guide Karl Rummel. See Note 3; in Kunisch (ed.), *Scharnhorst: Privat und dienstliche Schriften*, Vol.1, p.601. Since Rummel worked for Scharnhorst, the latter most likely included Rummel's data in his letter to Mechlenburg.

10 Again, Scharnhorst's comparison is virtually identical to Rummel's journal entry. See Kunisch (ed.), *Scharnhorst: Privat und dienstliche Schriften*, Vol.1, p.601.

11 Letter of 9 February 1795 to Mechlenburg; in Kunisch (ed.), *Scharnhorst: Privat und dienstliche Schriften*, Vol.1, p.602.

12 For a good perspective of the situation Wallmoden faced at this time, see Demet, *'We are Accustomed to do our Duty'*; especially Chapter 7 (pp.103-16).

13 See 'Allgemeine Disposition' (February/March 1795); in Kunisch (ed.), *Scharnhorst: Privat und dienstliche Schriften*, Vol.1, pp.604-05; the quoted passages are from p.604.

On 11 February, a discouraged Harcourt complained to the Duke of York that Wallmoden was playing 'German politicks [sic]', showing an 'over-eagerness' to acquiesce to Prussian policy. Harcourt also noted how Wallmoden had placed his German troops in better cantonments with a shorter line of defence, while British soldiers were left exposed along an extended front.[14] Of course, Harcourt may not have known that British positions around Leer were those selected beforehand by his own government, because they were nearest to the proposed ports of embarkation. Meanwhile, King George had promoted York to field marshal on 10 February.[15] Then on 13 February, Prince Adolphus wrote to his father, exploring the possibility of a reassignment.[16] With his older brother recalled to England, Prince Adolphus appears to have wanted to return home, as well.

Sensing the French were likely to attack his location (given the defeatist politics of coalition leaders), and realising he had insufficient troops to defend his sector, Wallmoden requested reinforcements. From London, Freytag was quick to inform the king that Hanover could raise 6,000 men and have them 'prepared to begin their march towards Holland in four weeks'. A perceptive King George had serious doubts about this dubious proposal.[17] Elsewhere, Duke Karl of Brunswick had anticipated the need for more troops before the allies had evacuated Holland.[18] French troops along the north-western German border with Holland posed a clear threat to Prussian interests, and so in December he had alerted his duchy to ready a contingent for movement to Westphalia.

Defending Westphalia was a major priority for King George III. British officials had been in Berlin negotiating with Prussian officials, seeking to gain support for the English and German troops in Westphalia.[19] Their attempts proved fruitless. Then remembering Pitt's earlier suggestion that Duke Karl of Brunswick be offered supreme command of coalition forces in Holland, King George now recommended the same for Westphalia.[20] Unfortunately, the Duke of Brunswick was tired of a war he viewed as unnecessary. Instead, he had already decided to send soldiers from his duchy to help protect the German frontier in Westphalia.

Answering Wallmoden's call were some 2,000 troops from Braunschweig-Wolfenbüttel. *Capitains* Unger and Fleischer presented their plan to Duke Karl on 1 January 1795, which was designed 'to regulate the deployment march of your troops from Brunswick to the

14 William Harcourt to York (11 February 1795); in War Office (WO) Record 1/172, pp.237-44; and quoted in Demet, *'We are Accustomed to do our Duty'*, p.103.

15 Correspondence pertaining to York's promotion to field marshal can be found in King George's command to Secretary of War William Windham (10 February 1795); in Aspinall (ed.), *The Later Correspondence of George III*, Vol.2, p.303.

16 See the Letter of 13 February 1795 from Prince Adolphus to King George III; in Aspinall (ed.), *The Later Correspondence of George III*, Vol.2, p.304.

17 See King George III to William Pitt (February 1795); in Aspinall (ed.), *The Later Correspondence of George III*, Vol.2, p.300.

18 See the Duke of Brunswick's thoughts in Hann 38 E, Nr.230: *Anträge des Herzogs von Braunschweig wegen Sicherung der Unterems*; deposited at the Niedersächsisches Landesarchiv, Hanover.

19 See the correspondence between King George III and William Pitt (2-3 March 1795), which summaries these talks; in Aspinall (ed.), *The Later Correspondence of George III*, Vol.2, pp.309-10.

20 King George III to William Pitt (8 March 1795); in Aspinall (ed.), *The Later Correspondence of George III*, Vol.2, p.312.

combined English and Hanoverian army'.[21] Unger and Fleischer had originally intended to deploy two infantry divisions four weeks apart; but like most contingency plans, this one was overcome by events.[22] With the French fast approaching the German border, the urgency of the situation demanded change. On 10 February, both divisions, supported by cavalry and artillery (plus their supply trains), left Brunswick and marched to Bentheim.

Leading the two divisions of Brunswickers was *General-Major* Johann Conrad Riedesel, Freiherr zu Eisenbach (1742-1812). While a young officer, Riedesel was energetic and resourceful, serving as adjutant to Prince Xavier of Saxony during the Seven Years War. After the war he remained in Imperial service, rising to the rank of captain in 1767. He left Austrian service in 1773 to command a dragoon regiment in Brunswick. Nineteen years later he led his regiment in France during the 1792 campaign, then returned home and settled into a garrison routine.[23] When Wallmoden called for help, Riedesel was overjoyed with this assignment.

As he 'raced ahead of his troops', Riedesel was eager for action. His mission was clear: replace the English in Bentheim, establish a formidable defence there, and secure the surrounding area.[24] It took 17 days for the Brunswickers to march the 175 miles to Bentheim.[25] As they paraded through Osnabrück, Wallmoden noticed they were in good shape. Later he discovered that no provision had been made to supply or pay them. Initially, he used Hanoverian provisions to meet their needs. On 6 March he notified the Duke of York and requested the latter authorize someone else to make these arrangements, which were considerable, especially ammunition.[26]

Arriving on the evening of 24 February, Riedesel met with his English counterpart, Abercromby, who briefed him on the current situation. Without ascertaining the situation for himself, Riedesel believed the overly pessimistic report from Abercromby.[27] He soon began inundating Wallmoden's headquarters with questions he should have been able to answer himself, had he taken the time and effort to inspect his position, as his orders stated. Over the next month the constant pressure of wartime operations would prove too much for Riedesel. Sadly, the 52-year-old general was simply not in shape psychologically for the challenges ahead.

As the Brunswickers were arriving in Bentheim, the French attacked British outposts under the command of Major General William Schaw Cathcart (1755-1843) along the western bank of the Ems and drove them back. To meet this threat, Wallmoden reassigned the British to defend just the Leer and the Ems, while he concentrated his Hanoverian,

21 See the Letter of 1 January 1795 from *Capitains* H.A.E. von Unger and A.M. Fleischer to Duke Karl of Brunswick; printed in Hermann Büschleb, *Scharnhorst in Westfalen*, Appendix 12/1, pp.133-34; the quoted passage is from p.133.

22 The organisation of both divisions can be found in Büschleb, *Scharnhorst in Westfalen*, pp.134-36.

23 Biographical information on Riedesel comes from Karl Siegmar Freiherr von Galéra, *Vom Reich zum Rheinbund: Weltgeschichte des 18. Jahrhunderts in einer kleinen Residenz* (Neustadt an der Aisch: Degener & Company, 1961).

24 Büschleb, *Scharnhorst in Westfalen*, p.59.

25 For a nice description of this deployment march, see Büschleb, *Scharnhorst in Westfalen*, pp.56-59.

26 See Demet, *'We are Accustomed to do our Duty'*, p.104.

27 On p. 62 of *Scharnhorst in Westfalen*, Büschleb published exerts from *Major* Vincke's earlier report of 16 February from Bentheim that contained Abercomby's assessment of the situation.

Hessian, and Brunswicker troops around Lingen and Rheine, under the command of Dallwigk.[28] This left the Austrians to defend Münster by themselves.

The Brunswickers completed their arrival in Bentheim on 26 February and sought to occupy their positions. Unfortunately, British troops and their artillery had not completely left. 'As long as Lieutenant General Abercromby remains in Bentheim, he retains the supreme command', Wallmoden informed Riedesel on 26 February.[29] Riedesel was anxious to occupy the town, while the British were taking their time leaving it. So Wallmoden dispatched his trusted general staff assistants – *Major* Hardenberg, *Rittmeister* Vincke, and *Hauptmann* Albrecht von Estorff – to the front to obtain a current picture of the situation there. The Commanding General had added these talented officers to his staff to ease the burden Scharnhorst carried, especially after Wallmoden had dismissed other incompetent officers.[30] Vincke rode to the German locations in Bentheim and Rheine, Hardenberg to converse with the Austrians in Münster, and Estorff to the British behind the Ems. Using Scharnhorst's General Staff with Troops concept, Wallmoden sought to rely 'not only on the minds of the commanders', but also on the views of 'the officers of his General-Quartermaster Staff'. From the latter the Commanding General expected to receive 'the factual objectivity' he required 'for the real assessment of the military situation'.[31]

While at the front, Hardenberg, Vincke, and Estorff followed the guidelines Scharnhorst had developed. They were to ascertain the situation at the various locations they visited and report the state of readiness and the activities of the forces there, along with any special problems or needs these forces encountered. They were to communicate to the Commanding General the opinions and mindsets of the field commanders, what issues they discussed, any coordination required, and what support the Commanding General needed to provide them. This would provide the Commanding General with an accurate picture of his army.[32] Wallmoden then turned to General-Quartermaster-Lieutenant Scharnhorst and ordered him to travel across the entire German front and provide his overall assessment of the situation.[33] Before leaving Osnabrück, Scharnhorst wrote a brief note to Georg Ludwig

28 See Wallmoden's Letter of 25 February 1795 to Dallwigk, informing him of the changed situation and his new assignment; in Kunisch (ed.), *Scharnhorst: Privat und dienstliche Schriften*, Vol.1, pp.608-09.

29 Wallmoden to Riedsel (which Scharnhorst wrote, dated 26 February 1795) is published in Kunisch (ed.), *Scharnhorst: Privat und dienstliche Schriften*, Vol.1, p.610. Also see Büschleb, *Scharnhorst in Westfalen*, pp.59-60.

30 See the source documents on these appointments in Hann 47, I, Nr.172, III: *Zulage für den Gehilfen des Generalquartiermeisters, 1794-97*; deposited at the Niedersächsisches Landesarchiv, Hanover.

31 Büschleb, *Scharnhorst in Westfalen*, p.78. See the interesting discussion in Chapter 15 ('A Staff Works'), pp.65-68, in which Büschleb (from a former general staff officer perspective) analyses the rationale behind Scharnhorst's General Staff with Troops model.

32 Büschleb, *Scharnhorst in Westfalen*, pp.65-67. In two letters, dated 24 and 28 February 1795, to Austrian *Feldmarschall-Lieutenant* Karl *Freiherr* von Prugglach (1730-1803), who commanded Austrian forces from the Rhine to the Ems Rivers, Wallmoden used these reports to update Prugglach on the situation and to remind him of the critical importance of Austrian support should the French attack Bentheim. Both letters are found in Kunisch (ed.), *Scharnhorst: Privat und dienstliche Schriften*, Vol.1, pp.606-08 and pp.610-12; respectively.

33 See the various reports in Hann 38 E, Nr.239: *Recognoscirungs-Berichte des Rittmeisters von Vincke über das Bourtanger Moor und das linke Ufer der Ems, des Ingenieur-Leutnants Reichard über die Wege von Osnabrück nach Ippenbühren, des Ingenieur-Leutnants Kahle über die Situationen am rechten Ufer der Ems zwischen Rheine und Lingen, des Fähnrichs Vollimhauß über die Kommunikationen zwischen Osnabrück, Lingen und Meppen, Berichte des Majors Scharnhorst über die Pässe der Römerstraße zu Coevorden und Winschoten sowie seine Dispositionen und Vorschläge*

Carl Meisner, the Secretary of the Hanoverian War Chancery (in Hanover), requesting that he inform Freytag in London that Wallmoden was forming a new artillery battery from the cannons seized from the Dutch during the evacuation of Holland.[34] This battery would be attached to the Hanoverian horse artillery and manned by Dutch officers and men. Scharnhorst then rode to the front.

After completing his mission, Scharnhorst sent his report to Wallmoden. He described the cantonment areas of the German troops, the defensive sectors within the corps area, and his ideas on how to conduct a defensive fight should the French attack.[35] The German corps area was fairly large, located between Nordhorn, Osnabrück, Rheine, and Gronau.[36] Scharnhorst reported the Brunswickers, Hanoverians, and Hessians occupied strong defensive positions and should be able to repulse any French attack. He also believed that with the timely support of British and Austrian troops nearby, the German corps had sufficient strength to hold Bentheim. He then informed Wallmoden that all British forces had completed their withdrawal from Bentheim and were situated to the north, in and around Meppen and Lingen, with a few outposts along the Ems River.

After analysing the situation in Bentheim, Scharnhorst rode to Rheine, the headquarters of the reserve force and central to the defence of the German corps. In his report he discussed the critical importance of the bridges at Rheine, the various assembly areas of the reserve force, and cooperation with the Austrians in case of a French attack.[37] Included with both reports were information and concept papers he thought might be helpful to the Commanding General as he pondered the situation and selected a viable course of action.[38] These concise reports, formulated as structured analyses, are fine examples of Scharnhorst's mission analysis, which reveal his *coup d'oeil* and 'supposing' techniques. They later became models German general staff officers used to report their observations and conclusions. One analysis called for a reorganisation of the German forces into three corps, along with their assembly areas. Another was a defensive contingency plan.

Wallmoden agreed with Scharnhorst's contingency plan for the defence of Westphalia. In this study Scharnhorst noted that the first priority was the defence of the River Ems, to prevent the French from flanking the German position. 'Bentheim is without doubt the second important point'. The third priority would be the defence of the River Weser, which would protect the left flank of the German forces in a way similar to the defence of the Ems.[39] After receiving this information, the Commanding General elected to divide his

mit Bezug auf die von den Preußen eingenommenen Stellungen und sein fernerer Operationsplan für einen defensiven Feldzug (mit Zeichnungen und Skizzen), 02.1795-03.1795; deposited at the Niedersächsisches Landesarchiv, Hanover.

34 Gerhard Scharnhorst to Georg Ludwig Meisner (before 26 February 1795); in Kunisch (ed.), *Scharnhorst: Privat und dienstliche Schriften*, Vol.1, p.609.

35 See Scharnhorst's report to Wallmoden (February/March 1795); in Kunisch (ed.), *Scharnhorst: Privat und dienstliche Schriften*, Vol.1, pp.613-14.

36 A nice map of this sector can be found in Büschleb, *Scharnhorst in Westfalen*, p.164.

37 This 'Disposition' report of February/March 1795 (which appears to be part of a larger analysis) is fragmentary. It is followed by the organisation of the three brigades of the reserve force. See Kunisch (ed.), *Scharnhorst: Privat und dienstliche Schriften*, Vol.1, pp.615-17.

38 These papers can be found in Kunisch (ed.), *Scharnhorst: Privat und dienstliche Schriften*, Vol.1, pp.617-22.

39 See Gerhard Scharnhorst, 'Ueber den nächsten Feldzug, in Fall man defenciv agiren will' (March 1795); in Kunisch (ed.), *Scharnhorst: Privat und dienstliche Schriften*, Vol.1, pp.618-21.

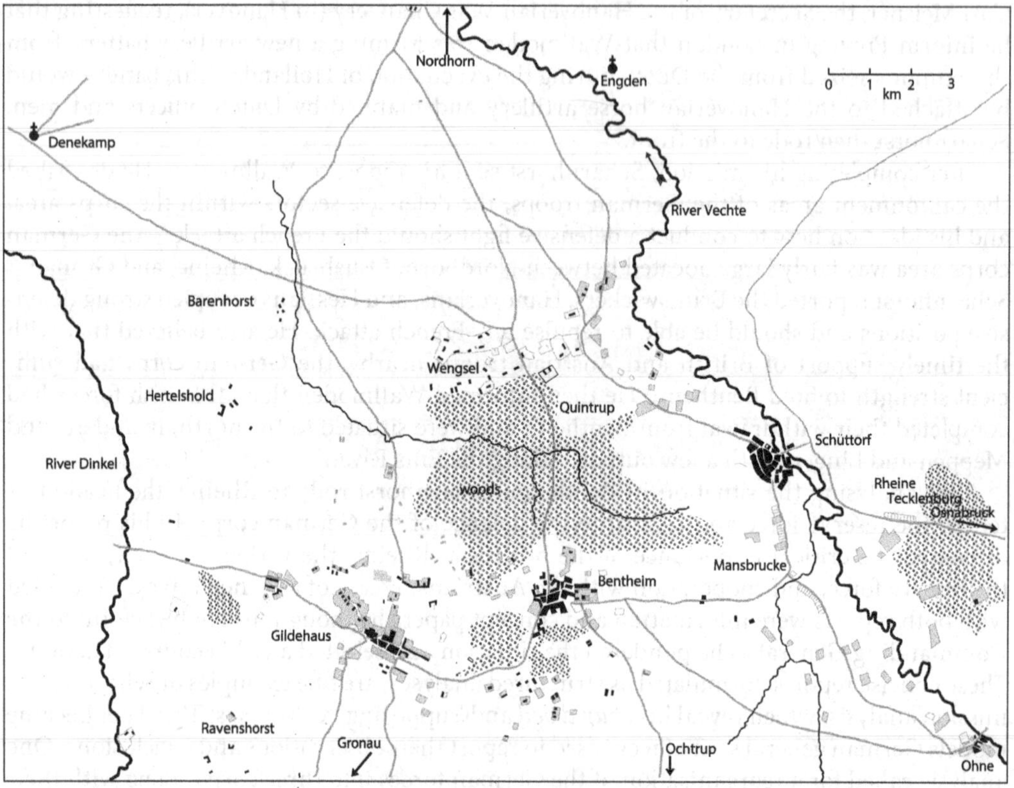

Map 12 Bentheim, March 1795.

army into three corps and reposition his forces according to Scharnhorst's concept.[40] He also contacted the Austrians, updating them on his plans and again seeking their support should the French attack.[41]

What is significant here is the evolving decentralization of command prerogatives in the German forces. This was a central feature of Scharnhorst's General Staff with Troops concept, and one which Wallmoden and his subordinate commanders wholeheartedly embraced. During the 1794 campaign in Flanders, and especially during the retreat through Holland, senior German leaders fought a desperate rearguard action against constant French pressure and came to appreciate the wisdom of the Scharnhorst's General Staff with Troops model. Now in Germany, Wallmoden's instructions to his corps commanders embodied this concept. The Commanding General began his orders with his overall assessment of

40 Wallmoden's new disposition of forces ('2t Merz 1795') can be found in Kunisch (ed.), *Scharnhorst: Privat und dienstliche Schriften*, Vol.1, pp.622-23. Demet, *'We are Accustomed to do our Duty'*, p.105, provides a detailed organisation and location of these forces.

41 Wallmoden's Letters of 2 and 3 March 1795 to Austrian *Feldmarschall-Lieutenant* Franz Freiherr von Werneck (1748-1806) are published in Kunisch (ed.), *Scharnhorst: Privat und dienstliche Schriften*, Vol.1, pp.623-24 and pp.624-25; respectively.

the situation, and then proceeded to outline the various courses of action he thought likely in case of the French attack. Then he addressed the role each commander would play in his scheme of manoeuvre. In every case, German leaders were to maintain their communications with each other and to be prepared to support each another without awaiting orders from the Commanding General should the situation change.[42]

On 3 March 1795, French forces under *Général de Division* Dominique-Joseph René Vandamme (1770-1830) launched a series of probing attacks at Gildehaus, just west of Bentheim. A few days later, Riedesel received a report that British troops had evacuated Nordhorn, while French troops were approaching from the northwest. Without confirming this information, and fearing that he would be outflanked, Riedesel ordered an immediate withdrawal of his infantry and heavy artillery from Bentheim, leaving his cavalry and light infantry to defend Gildehaus, Bentheim, and Schüttorf. He then informed Wallmoden.[43] Riedesal's sudden movement left Hanoverian forces under *General-Major* Ludwig Heinrich August von Scheither (1738-1806) at Gronau (Riedesel's left) exposed. 'The Brunswic [sic] troops abandoned Bentheim on the first advance of the enemy, and retreated to Rheine, without firing a single shot, or the enemy nearer than eight miles', Captain Jones noted.[44] In his correspondence, Riedesel assured the Commanding General that his Brunswickers would be able to retake Bentheim if necessary, provided the French did not attack in force.[45]

When news of Riedesel's action reached Scharnhorst in Rheine, he rode immediately to find the general and to assess the situation at Bentheim. Upon reaching Riedesel, Scharnhorst informed him the French were nowhere in the area, that holding Bentheim was crucial to the defence of the entire corps and urged him and his troops to return to Bentheim at once. Scharnhorst was very polite with Riedesel. Instead of telling him he had no authority to evacuate his positions without prior approval from the Commanding General (especially since the Brunswickers had not even been attacked), Scharnhorst was able to convince Riedesel how important the defence of Bentheim was to the German corps, and to persuade him to return to his previous positions.[46]

Realising he had acted prematurely and without orders, Riedesel ordered an immediate countermarch back to Bentheim. What is important here is the initial assessment of the situation at Bentheim Scharnhorst had made a few days earlier. In that report Scharnhorst had told Wallmoden that Riedesel may not be fit to command. 'From all that I learn here', he informed the Commanding General in early March, 'General von Riedesel is in no way

42 See the various correspondence between Scharnhorst and Wallmoden, and between Wallmoden and his subordinate commanders, as well as Wallmoden's letters to the Austrians describing his view of the situation and plans to counter French aggression; in Kunisch (ed.), *Scharnhorst: Privat und dienstliche Schriften*, Vol.1, pp.603-27. Büschleb analyses this unique command climate in *Scharnhorst in Westfalen*, pp.65-68.

43 See the description of these events in Büschleb, *Scharnhorst in Westfalen*, pp.75-76.

44 See the recollections of Captain Jones, *An Historical Journal of the British Campaign on the Continent*, pp.181-82.

45 Riedesel to Wallmoden (8 March 1795); cited in Büschleb, *Scharnhorst in Westfalen*, p.76.

46 Büschleb, *Scharnhorst in Westfalen*, p.76. In his analysis, Büschleb cites various parts of Riedesel's correspondence, in which Riedesel informs Wallmoden of his conversation with Scharnhorst and his subsequent decision to reoccupy the position at Bentheim. Interestingly, Jones, *An Historical Journal of the British Campaign on the Continent*, p. 182, claims it was Dallwigk who 'ordered' Riedesel back to Bentheim.

capable of commanding a post, nor possesses the determination to execute such an undertaking in an honourable way'.[47]

Over the next five days, French activity along the German corps sector increased sufficiently enough to cause concern. Both Scheither and Hessian *General-Major* Friedrich Wilhelm von Wurmb (in command of the reserve force at Rheine) requested permission to reposition their troops as necessary to accomplish their missions.[48] To gain a current picture of the situation, Wallmoden sent Scharnhorst to Bentheim to speak with the generals and get an appreciation of their points of view. After listening to the generals and discussing various options with them, and then visiting their outposts and other positions in and around Bentheim, Scharnhorst dispatched a message to the Commanding General on the evening of 8 March. The position at Bentheim was pretty weak, he told Wallmoden. He felt the 'unreliability' [*Bedenklichkeiten*] and tepidness of Riedesel (who Scharnhorst felt had lost his grasp of the situation) was the main reason.[49] Significantly, back on 26 February, when Scheither had launched a 'demonstration' to disrupt the French in this sector, Riedesel had objected.[50] Now Scharnhorst recommended that another spoiling attack be conducted immediately, even over any protests by Riedesel, in order to boast the morale and confidence of the Brunswickers.

In his morning report of 9 March, Scharnhorst recommended attacking the French. His intent was to seize the initiative, drive the enemy from German soil, and regain the east bank of the Dinkel River. As he told Wallmoden, this would convince the French the German soldier was battle worthy and determined to defend his homeland.[51] Before the Germans could execute their plan, Scharnhorst believed Riedesel had to reinforce his outposts and position at Bentheim. Under Scharnhorst's leadership, and with the support of Hanoverian and Hessian soldiers under Scheither and Wurmb, the Brunswickers were able to strengthen their defence. Working closely with Riedesel's staff, Scharnhorst took the Brunswickers by the hand and demonstrated how to conduct outpost and picket operations, and even provided them with instructions that explained in considerable detail what he had just taught them.[52] From his discussions with the Brunswickers, it was clear to Scharnhorst that Riedesel had no idea of the composition of French forces facing him, simply because he had not sent out any patrols to ascertain their locations and strengths. Instead, Riedesel appears to have believed the false reports by French liaison officers traveling through Bentheim to meet with Lieutenant General Harcourt about a prisoner exchange.[53]

47 See Scharnhorst's Letter to Wallmoden (before 8 March 1795); in Kunisch (ed.), *Scharnhorst: Privat und dienstliche Schriften*, Vol.1, pp.629-30; the quoted passage is from p.629.

48 See the correspondence between Wurmb and Wallmoden (8 March 1795); cited in Klippel, *Scharnhorst*, Vol.2, pp.195-96. Also see the discussion in Büschleb, *Scharnhorst in Westfalen*, pp.77-78.

49 Report of 8 March 1795; in Kunisch (ed.), *Scharnhorst: Privat und dienstliche Schriften*, Vol.1, pp.630-31; the quoted passage is from p.631. This report is also published in Klippel, *Scharnhorst*, Vol.2, pp.196-97.

50 Büschleb, *Scharnhorst in Westfalen*, p.64.

51 See Scharnhorst's Report of 9 March 1795; in Kunisch (ed.), *Scharnhorst: Privat und dienstliche Schriften*, Vol.1, pp.632-33.

52 Gerhard Scharnhorst, 'Verabredung des Vorhaltens der vershiedenen [sic] Posten des Corps zu Bentheim' (9 March 1795); in Kunisch (ed.), *Scharnhorst: Privat und dienstliche Schriften*, Vol.1, pp.634-36. This is also published as Appendix 20/2 in Büschleb, *Scharnhorst in Westfalen*, pp.140-41.

53 See the discussion regarding Riedesel's Letters of 2, 8, and 10 March 1795 to Wallmoden about this; in Büschleb, *Scharnhorst in Westfalen*, pp.69-72.

With his day complete in Bentheim, Scharnhorst rode back to Rheine. Later that day, Riedesel wrote to Dallwigk, informing him of Scharnhorst's activities: 'General-Quartermaster Scharnhorst has been here since yesterday and examined the local position closely. By no means does he like it, especially since it is not realistically occupied'.[54] Riedesel's correspondence seems strange and tends to confirm Scharnhorst's assessment of the general's inability to command. Why would Riedesel inform Dallwigk his position was 'not realistically occupied', since he was responsible to make sure that it was?

From Rheine on the morning of 10 March, Scharnhorst wrote an optimistic, but cautionary report to the Commanding General. 'It seems a foregone conclusion', he began, 'that the enemy has strengthened himself along our right flank'. 'All other reports about his great strength against us, of his intentions, etc., cannot be trusted (although I do not want to say that the enemy is not strong in this area)'. Undoubtedly encouraged by his discussions with Scheither, Wurmb, and Dallwigk, Scharnhorst again recommended launching a spoiling attack again the French; this time with larger forces. 'An operation from Oldensal and Delden would disrupt all enemy activities, secure our position, and certainly (like every operation against enemy quarters) have a brilliant outcome'. With Austrian support 'this would and must place the enemy in a terribly embarrassing situation'. Scharnhorst then noted how easy it would be to destroy the enemy's forward magazine at Rijssen, and how such an action would 'seriously hurt him'.[55]

In Osnabrück, the Commanding General was seriously considering Scharnhorst' plan. Such a bold attack was very promising and would certainly catch the French off guard. If successful, it would greatly improve the German defensive posture and boast the morale of Wallmoden's weary troops. The day after he had received Scharnhorst's report, he wrote to York, convinced that the French were about to attack in force and penetrate his weak defence.[56] While not mentioning any offensive action against the French, Wallmoden told the Duke of York that only the heavy rains and flooding (which had made the roads impassable) had prevented the French from launching their offensive earlier.

Just as the Wallmoden was set to issue the attack order, from Münster came a message from Estorff that Prussian troops were arriving there to replace the Austrians.[57] Without ever consulting or informing Wallmoden, the Austrians had made arrangements to withdraw their forces and to have Prussian soldiers replace them and close the large gap between Ochtrup (where the Hanoverians were positioned) and Horstmar (where the Prussians planned to station a battalion in nearby Metelen). Estorff told the Commanding General that this movement was already underway and was expected to be completed by 17 March.

Angered by this report and realising that he could not count on Austrian (or Prussian) support, Wallmoden cancelled the attack. He ordered Estorff to ride immediately to Bentheim. There he was to impress upon Riedesel the critical importance of his mission to defend and hold Bentheim and Schüttorf. The Commanding General's instructions clearly

54 Riedesel to Dallwigk, 9 March 1795; cited in Klippel, *Scharnhorst*, Vol.2, pp.197-98.

55 Report of 10 March 1795; in Kunisch (ed.), *Scharnhorst: Privat und dienstliche Schriften*, Vol.1, pp.636-37. Scharnhorst's assessment can also be found in Klippel, *Scharnhorst*, Vol.2, p.198.

56 Wallmoden to York (11 March 1795); cited in Demet, *'We are Accustomed to do our Duty'*, p.105.

57 Message from *Hauptmann* Estorff (10 March 1795); cited in Büschleb, *Scharnhorst in Westfalen*, p.82.

spelled out that the Brunswickers were to hold Bentheim at all costs. Wallmoden closed his message by informing Estorff that 'Major Scharnhorst is already in Bentheim' with 'the authority and confidence of the Commanding General to act on his behalf'.[58] Although Wallmoden's delegation of command authority to Scharnhorst was not new, this document to Estorff provides written evidence of his concurrence with Scharnhorst's General Staff with Troops concept.

Unknown to Wallmoden, Scharnhorst was still in Rheine. Learning of the situational change and the Commanding General's intent, Scharnhorst rode quickly to Bentheim early on the morning of 11 March to assess the readiness of the Brunswickers there and at Schüttorf. He met with Estorff and together they discussed the situation and potential future operations. Then Scharnhorst returned to Rheine, where on the evening of 11 March he dispatched a report to Wallmoden that summarised his evaluation of the situation and noted the difficulties of defending the Bentheim position.

Scharnhorst's report of 11 March highlights his both *coup d'oeil* and quick thinking. This keen situational awareness enabled Scharnhorst to discern the operational and tactical state of affairs in Westphalia as they related to the mission of the German corps. Given what he believed to be French intentions, he applied his 'supposing' to the situation and then informed Wallmoden that without significant support from the Prussians, Bentheim was not defensible. He noted that while the castle dominating the town and the surrounding area appeared to be central to any defence, it could easily be surrounded and cut off by a French attack. He suggested the Germans establish a new defensive line at Schüttorf, behind the Vechte River.

> Schüttorf is surrounded by a high wall and moat, and secure against a coup-de-main. If the enemy takes this place [Schüttorf], we cannot expel him from this area without a great, decisive superiority. The occupation of the castle at Bentheim would therefore be of no great benefit.

Scharnhorst closed his report, noting 'eyewitnesses' had confirmed the French were approaching in large numbers.[59]

As the German corps anxiously awaited a French attack, the low morale among the troops from Brunswick, coupled with the apparent deficiencies in their leaders, highlight what Scharnhorst had written earlier in his comparative analysis of the coalition and French. This was evident in his correspondence as well. On 12 March, Riedesel sent Wallmoden yet another message complaining about the situation of his troops.[60] He told the Commanding General that his soldiers were 'so extraordinarily fatigued that they are completely insensitive and have not the slightest attention to their post'. Riedesel worried what would happen should the French attack. This seems incredible, given the fact the Brunswickers had arrived

58 See Wallmoden's 'Instruktion für den Hauptmann von Estorff' (10 March 1795); in Büschleb, *Scharnhorst in Westfalen*, Appendiz 21/1 (p. 142).

59 Scharnhorst to Wallmoden (11 March 1795); in Kunisch (ed.), *Scharnhorst: Privat und dienstliche Schriften*, Vol.1, p.637. A copy of this report is published in Büschleb, *Scharnhorst in Westfalen*, p.84. It can also be found in Klippel, *Scharnhorst*, Vol.2, p.199.

60 Message of 12 March 1795 from Riedesel to Wallmoden; cited in Büschleb, *Scharnhorst in Westfalen*, p.86.

in Bentheim just two weeks earlier and had yet to come under fire. What is evident here is the fact that Riedesel's soldiers still had no clear understanding of how to conduct outpost operations properly, even after Scharnhorst had taken them by the hand and had shown them how to set up a picquet line and conduct this crucial mission. He also had given them written, detailed guidance. Despite this training, Wallmoden had to order Hessian and Hanoverian troops to man the Brunswick outposts. Why then were these Brunswickers so fatigued and insensitive to their duties?

Years earlier in his *Military Library*, Scharnhorst had discussed the need to study war and to conduct realistic combat training during peacetime. Such rigorous study and training would accustom the leader and his men to potential wartime conditions and give them some semblance of what to do under fire. Clearly, the study of war and realistic combat training was not part of the garrison routine in Brunswick. Their participation in the fruitless campaign of 1792 in France should have opened the eyes of Riedesel and his troops to the need for realistic combat training in peacetime. Furthermore, the War of the First Coalition had been raging for nearly three years now, with plenty of articles, books, and other information available on the various tactics, techniques, and procedures of the combatants. The fact that Riedesel and his men were not ready to fight was a direct consequence of their lack of any military *Bildung*.

Ample proof of this mindset is the leisurely stroll Riedesel's soldiers took from Brunswick to Bentheim. They marched 175 miles in 17 days, with every fourth day a day of rest. The average march speed during this time was around 20 miles in five hours. Incredibly, the deployment plan called for the Brunwickers to march only six hours a day.[61] Where was the sense of urgency here? Without the proper prior education, training, and physical conditioning, the Brunswickers were totally unprepared for combat; they knew it, and this caused their low morale. Moreover, the fact that Riedesel had demonstrated in front of his own troops that he was a weak, indecisive, and ignorant commander only added to their low esteem.

From Rheine that evening Scharnhorst sent another analysis of the situation at Bentheim to the Commanding General. It began, 'General von Riedesel believes he will be attacked in the morning'.[62] Scharnhorst informed Wallmoden of the increased French activity in the area around Bentheim, how they had captured a bridge at Poppenbrücke (despite the best efforts of Hessian *Hauptmann* Adam Ludwig von Ochs to prevent this), and that French strength was growing in the area. He emphasised how the French were currently gaining ground 'through persistent, small concentrated attacks', and that such actions 'appear to be his style and intent' for the time being. Scharnhorst told the Commanding General he would ride early the next morning to Bentheim to ascertain the situation and implied he would also try to calm the growing anxiety of Riedesel.

Why Scharnhorst chose Rheine as his base of operations offers another opportunity to examine the genius of this extraordinary combat leader. Rheine was situated along the Ems

61 See the Letter of 1 January 1795 to Duke Karl of Brunswick, in which the deployment march is shown; cited in Büschleb, *Scharnhorst in Westfalen*, p.57.

62 Scharnhorst to Wallmoden (12 March 1795); in Kunisch (ed.), *Scharnhorst: Privat und dienstliche Schriften*, Vol.1, pp.638-39; the quoted passage is from p.638. This report is also published as Appendix 22/1 in Büschleb, *Scharnhorst in Westfalen*, p.143; and in Klippel, *Scharnhorst*, Vol.2, pp.199-200.

River in the centre of the German sector of responsibility.[63] The headquarters of the German reserve force was also located in Rheine. Because he had the confidence of the Commanding General and the authority to act on his behalf, Scharnhorst had placed himself in a position where he could effectively command operations should the French attack. Ever since his superb leadership at Hondschoote and Menin, and his herculean endeavours throughout the retreat from Flanders and Holland, Wallmoden, his subordinate commanders, and the German soldiers had recognised in Scharnhorst a leader who had grasped the essentials of war and who knew how to conduct successful combat operations. While the Commanding General focused his attention on the strategic and operational levels of the art of war, he entrusted command of the tactical fight to Scharnhorst. The German field commanders and soldiers understood this and followed Scharnhorst's lead implicitly.

From his own pen, Scharnhorst credited his combat ability and success to his personal and professional *Bildung* prior to and even during the present conflict. Unfortunately, much of the historical record does not specifically acknowledge Scharnhorst's controlling influence. Most official records from this period almost always credit the senior military leader present during the fight, especially if he was an aristocrat. This was the legacy of the dynastic mindset. Fortunately, other evidence and evaluations of Scharnhorst's actions in early March 1795 clearly reveal his commanding presence and sound tactical leadership during the fight for Bentheim.[64]

Early on the morning of 13 March, *General-Major* Scheither sent *Hauptmann* Estorff a series of questions for their daily tactical discussions.[65] This message clearly shows that some German leaders and general staff officers were talking among themselves and with their subordinates about various tactical options available to them. It also reveals that they had learned some valuable lessons from nearly two years of continuous combat. The questions came from Hessian *Oberst* Philip von Wurmb, who commanded the defence at Gildehaus. Wurmb initially inquired about the best use of pickets. He wanted a standard operating procedure for his men, noting how 'everyone does what he wants to do'. Scharnhorst had recognised this as well and had taken steps to write a procedure for the Brunswickers. It is not clear if Wurmb had done the same for his troops, or if he hoped to obtain a copy of the instructions Scharnhorst had written. Whatever the case, Wurmb was seeking guidance on the best techniques.

As he walked the ground around his location, Wurmb also questioned the locations of his soldiers. To ascertain the best positions to post his men, Wurmb proposed a series of 'what if' scenarios, such as what options would be available 'if the enemy attacks us at Gronau and quickly flanks the Dinkel', implying that in such a case his troops might be 'cut to pieces'. He

63 See the detail map in Büschleb, *Scharnhorst in Westfalen*, p.164, which shows the key locations in the German sector and highlights the importance of Scharnhorst's selection of Rheine.

64 For example, Carl von Clausewitz's lecture to his students at the Prussian General War School (1810-11) is a detailed analysis of German operations in Westphalia in March 1795. See 'Beyspiel einer Postirung zur Deckung der Winterquartiere der englischen Armee in Westphalen 1795', along with his 'Bermerkungen über das Beispiel', in Werner Hahlweg (ed.), *Carl von Clausewitz: Schriften-Aufsätze-Studien-Briefe:Dokumente aus dem Clausewitz, Scharnhorst- und Gneisenau-Nachlaß sowie aus öffentlichen und privaten Sammlungen* (Göttingen: Vandenhoeck & Ruprecht, 1966 and 1990), Vol.1, pp.572-83 and 495-502; respectively.

65 See the fascinating Letter of 13 March 1795 from Scheither to Estorff; printed in Büschleb, *Scharnhorst in Westfalen*, p.88.

also thought about the best direction in which he should retire if driven back. It was this kind of detailed, intellectual analysis and discussion (called 'war gaming') that Scharnhorst had learned under *General-Major* Estorff at Northeim and later advocated while an instructor at the artillery school and in his many publications. Some German commanders were applying their *coup d'oeil* and 'supposing' to the tactical situation at hand.

Scharnhorst was certainly correct in his assessment of German leadership. While Wurmb and a few others actively sought to improve their situation, most German officers simply did nothing on their own initiative, always waiting to be told what to do. Again, this was a legacy of the royal, absolutist army, in which only the prince could exercise such initiative. Yet this dynastic command model had failed repeatedly during recent combat operations. It seemed that coalition commanders at every level demonstrated an unwillingness to alter their ways, even in the face of a changing art of war. This was due in large part because nearly all commanders were noblemen or gentlemen, entitled by birth to command. Just look at the British princes, given regimental commands in their late teens or early twenties without ever having first to prove themselves worthy of such responsibility by successfully commanding a company or battalion. The fact that they were royalty was justification enough. Rarely were they ever challenged; rarely did they ever have to perform; rarely did they ever have to earn their way through life; and rarely were they ever held accountable for their failure to perform. The fact that York was promoted to field marshal after failing to accomplish his mission in Flanders and Holland is ample proof. Rank to these aristocrats was just another token of their standing in life. It was rarely earned.

Because the aristocracy controlled the military, most German officers rarely demonstrated any professional development or drive. Instead of getting out of their warm, cosy headquarters and tramping the ground in the cold and wet weather to acquaint themselves with the terrain and weather conditions under which they and their soldiers would have to fight, and then discussing their options with their subordinate leaders to ascertain the best measures they could take given the 'what if' scenarios they had developed along the way (like Scharnhorst had done at Menin and Wurmb did at Gildehaus), most German leaders wasted precious time in leisurely activities within their comfortable headquarters. Instead of developing and implementing standard operating procedures and rehearsing their troops so they would know what to do in critical situations (as Hammerstein had done for his Hanoverians, Scharnhorst had done for the Brunswickers, and Wurmb was seeking for his Hessians), and thus be able to execute their missions with confidence, most German leaders embraced a timid passivity (coming from their negligent mindset) that seriously undermined the entire mission. Instead of seizing the initiative and making things happen (as Scharnhorst had done at Hondschoote, Menin, and Boxtel), too many German leaders simply let things happen to them, continually deferring to a higher authority and choosing not to think for themselves. Only a few German leaders showed any genuine initiative and responsibility during the War of the First Coalition.

Scharnhorst had a praiseworthy solution for this lack of leadership. It was similar to his recommendation a few months earlier, when he sought to move British and German troops out of their warm camps in the rear closer to the front, where they could react quickly to any French attack. Now, in his report of 12 March to the Commanding General, he proposed reorganising the German forces (Hanoverian, Hessian, and Brunswick) into fewer but stronger formations, amalgamating the weaker commands under stronger leadership, and eliminating incompetent commanders. He also advocated the removal of all 'luxuries' German officers had brought with them on campaign. He told Wallmoden: 'All those not under arms, all wives, all heavy baggage, all commander suites, and all other officers belong in the depot'.[66] By forcing German officers to share the misery and depravation of their men, Scharnhorst endeavoured to instil some sense of leadership and responsibility in his fellow officers. His solution was unfortunately totally inconsistent with the dynastic politics of the German aristocracy. While it was a viable solution, and one Wallmoden seriously considered implementing, it was quickly overcome by events. The next day, the French attacked.

When the French launched their offensive on the morning of 13 March, the result was predictable. Vandamme sent three columns across the Dinkel and attacked Gronau, Gildehaus-Bentheim, and Schüttorf simultaneously to fix the German forces there. The fourth and strongest column came from Nordhorn south-eastward through Engden, then along the right bank of the Vechte, and endeavoured to flank the German position east of Schüttorf, penetrate the rear of the German defences between Ohne and Rheine, and cut off the retreat of the Hanoverian, Hessians, and Brunswickers. If successful, the French would effectively envelop and destroy Wallmoden's entire corps.[67]

Scharnhorst's assessment of French objectives was correct. At Gronau, French artillery fired a massive barrage and then launched a frontal assault to fix Scheither so he was unable to support the defence at Gildehaus and Bentheim. To the German left, the remaining Austrians at Metelen offered no support. At Gildehaus, the Hessians were successfully defending their position under the sound leadership of Wurmb and his junior officers. As time passed, Wurmb was becoming increasingly anxious, concerned with what was happening in his rear at Bentheim, where the uncertainty of combat appears to have crippled Riedesel. Indeed, Riedesel had concluded that his position was untenable and ordered his men to withdraw, apparently without informing Wurmb. Around this time, Scharnhorst had just arrived at Schüttorf (which he had told Wallmoden was key to the defence of the sector) and there encountered three battalions of French infantry and four squadrons of cavalry attacking the town. By mid-afternoon, French forces had seized Gronau, Gildehaus, Bentheim, and Schüttorf. The whole of the German corps was in retreat. Now Scharnhorst and Estorff, the Commanding General's 'two stalwart officers', endeavoured to establish a new line of defence that anticipated the main French objective of Rheine.[68]

As German infantry, cavalry, and artillery units were retreating from Gronau, Gildehaus, Bentheim, and Schüttorf, French cavalry pursued them mercilessly. South of Schüttorf, they caught the Hanoverian 5. Dragoner Regiment moving westward to protect the withdrawal of its fellow Germans. Taking the Hanoverians in the flank, the French severely mauled the dragoons, but were unable to defeat them. The Hanoverians then launched several of

66 Report of 12 March 1795; in Kunisch (ed.), *Scharnhorst: Privat und dienstliche Schriften*, Vol.1, pp.638-39.

67 See 'Das Gefecht bei Bentheim am 13. März 1795', in Sichart, *Geschichte der Königlich-Hannoverischen Armee*, Vol.4, pp.588-600. Also see Ditfurth, *Die Hessen in den Feldzügen 1793, 1794 und 1795*, Vol.2, pp.406-14. For some unknown reason, the French seemed to have neglected this action in their histories. Only a passing mention is cited in most first-hand and later accounts.

68 See Scharnhorst's Report of 13 March 1795 to Wallmoden; in Kunisch (ed.), *Scharnhorst: Privat und dienstliche Schriften*, Vol.1, p.639. A facsimile of this report is published in Büschleb, *Scharnhorst in Westfalen*, p.93. The quoted passage is from Büschleb, *Scharnhorst in Westfalen*, p.78.

counterattacks and drove the French away. Witnessing this action was Estorff, who praised the skill and bravery of his fellow Hanoverians, led by *Major* Carl von Reitzenstein and other junior officers. This very positive report was the highlight of the day for the German corps.[69]

Scharnhorst had arrived near the end of this engagement and also noted it in his report of 14 March to the Commanding General. 'The situation is bad and stabilization largely insignificant', he informed Wallmoden. The Austrians had failed to provide the critical diversion Wallmoden had requested. Nevertheless, the fortress at Bentheim remained in coalition hands. Rheine was also secure, as were the outposts protecting it. Scharnhorst promised to provide a more detailed evaluation orally to the Commanding General when time permitted.[70] Losses on the German side were surprisingly light: three officers and 11 soldiers killed in action; five officers and 70 soldiers wounded in action; 10 officers and 119 soldiers taken prisoner.[71] Not a single senior German officer was on the casualty list.[72]

From Rheine on 14 March, Scharnhorst advocated launching an immediate counterattack before the French could consolidate their positions.[73] This plan was similar to the one he had suggested four days earlier. While the Austrians conducted a diversion on the French right, the German corps would attack the French at Gronau, Bentheim, Gildehaus, and Nordhorn. As talks with the Austrians commenced, German leaders began discussing the merits of Scharnhorst's plan. Elsewhere, behind French lines, coalition soldiers still held the castle at Bentheim. Led by *Lieutenant* du Plat, coalition defenders defeated every French assault and rejected all of Vandamme's demands to surrender, most likely for the same reason Hammerstein had rejected Moreau's terms at Menin. *Lieutenant* du Plat wanted to ensure the safety of the French *émigré* troops under his command.[74] Significantly, with this strongpoint in his rear, Vandamme failed to accomplish his mission of cutting off the retreat of the Germans behind the Rivers Vechte and Ems.

Amazed at the tenacity of this castle defence (especially given the ease at which the French had taken their other objectives), Vandamme offered du Plat terms of 'honourable withdrawal' instead of surrender. This meant the garrison could march out under arms, with colours flying, and bringing with it all its baggage and property. Coalition soldiers (including the French *émigré* troops) would receive full freedom of movement, meaning they could re-join their units and continue to fight against the French. There would be no prison and no parole period for the German troops, and no execution for the French *émigré* troops.[75] After consulting with his fellow officers, du Plat agreed to Vandamme's terms. On the afternoon of 14 March, the coalition garrison marched out of the fortress with full

69 See the Report of *Hauptmann* von Estorff (14 March 1795); exerted in Büschleb, *Scharnhorst in Westfalen*, p.92.

70 Scharnhorst to Wallmoden (14 March 1794); in Kunisch (ed.), *Scharnhorst: Privat und dienstliche Schriften*, Vol.1, pp.639-40; the quoted passage is from p.640.

71 Sichart, *Geschichte der Königlich-Hannoverischen Armee*, Vol.4, p.596.

72 While not listed as an official casualty, *General-Major* Scheither had become ill during the withdrawal from Gronau and Hessian *Oberst* von Düring assumed his command.

73 See Gerhard Scharnhorst, 'Project zum Angrif der feindlichen Vorposten an der Dinkel und Vechte, den 14ten Merz' (before 14 March 1795); in Kunisch (ed.), *Scharnhorst: Privat und dienstliche Schriften*, Vol.1, pp.633-34.

74 See 'Die Vertheidigung des Schlosses zu Bentheim am 13. und 14. März 1795', in Sichart, *Geschichte der Königlich-Hannoverischen Armee*, Vol.4, pp.600-04.

75 See the discussion in Büschleb, *Scharnhorst in Westfalen*, p.97.

military honours, passed French soldiers anxious to plunder what was left in the castle, and headed toward their lines at Ohne. The French even provided du Plat with two wagons to transport his wounded, sick, and baggage. Like Scharnhorst's leadership at Menin, du Plat's courage and resourcefulness at Bentheim saved the German corps from possible annihilation and became part of Hanoverian military lore.[76]

Any hope of launching a counterattack against the French ended on the evening of 14 March, when Scharnhorst's plan was overcome by other events. The situation for the German corps was changing considerably. The Austrians had begun their movement toward Mainz, while Prussian units were arriving in force in replace them. As the Prussians occupied their new positions, they also expanded their zone of control northward in the vicinity of Ochtrup, where the Hessians and Hanoverians had been. Ochtrup was directly along the right flank of the French line, and the realisation of Prussian troops on their exposed flank may have given the French pause.

In Rheine that evening, Scharnhorst and Estorff met with the generals to discuss future courses of action.[77] Dallwigk opened the discussion by briefing the assemblage on new instructions he had received earlier that afternoon from the Commanding General.[78] Wallmoden had made it clear that the abandonment of Bentheim and Schüttorf, without much of a fight, was clearly not a glorious chapter in German military history. The Commanding General placed Dallwigk in command of all German forces west of the Ems River. Their mission was to defend the Ems, while establishing a chain of outposts on both sides of the Vechte. Meanwhile, Wallmoden was trying to integrate the German defence with the Prussians and Austrians.

Following this meeting Scharnhorst asked Estorff to stay with Riedesel to support the general, who Scharnhorst still felt was 'not in full possession of his faculties'.[79] Riedesel had demonstrated a lack of leadership from the moment he had arrived in Bentheim. Now Scharnhorst wanted Estorff to work closely with him and assist the Brunswickers in setting up their chain of outposts along the Vechte. This was accomplished under the watchful eyes of Wurmb and his Hessians.[80] In accordance with the instructions from the Commanding General, Riedesel and Düring withdrew elements of their commands across the Ems River at Rheine on the evening of 14 March.[81] Scharnhorst then left Rheine and rode to Osnabrück to report personally to Wallmoden.

After receiving Scharnhorst's report of the action on 13 March, Wallmoden informed King George of the recent French attack. He told the British monarch how his German corps (but not his British soldiers) had been overwhelmed and driven back. Bentheim was

76 See the discussions in Sichart, *Geschichte der Königlich-Hannoverischen Armee*, Vol.4, pp.603-04; and in Büschleb, *Scharnhorst in Westfalen*, p.97. Büschleb even notes that Vandamme's terms of 'honourable withdrawal' were later published in the 1956 Yearbook of the County of Bentheim.

77 Information in this paragraph comes mainly from Büschleb, *Scharnhorst in Westfalen*, pp.100-02; and from Ditfurth, *Die Hessen in den Feldzügen 1793, 1794 und 1795*, Vol.2, pp.414-16.

78 Wallmoden to Dallwigk (afternoon of 14 March 1794); published as Appendix 26/1 in Büschleb, *Scharnhorst in Westfalen*, p.146.

79 Büschleb, *Scharnhorst in Westfalen*, p.101.

80 This chain of outposts can be found in 'Dislocation der Vorposten unter den Commando des Oberst v. Wurmb' (14 March 1975); published as Appendix 25/1 in Büschleb, *Scharnhorst in Westfalen*, p.145.

81 Sichart, *Geschichte der Königlich-Hannoverischen Armee*, Vol.4, p.604.

lost and the 5. Dragoner Regiment had suffered 'heavy casualties'. Wallmoden indicated that the lack of Austrian and Prussian support was a major factor in the German defeat. Neither had shown any inclination to fight. Interestingly, nor had the British, but the Commanding General did not include this in his report. He did infer that without support from other coalition members, the Germans could not hold the Ems River line. Wallmoden ended his report by noting the continuing challenges the Germans faced obtaining adequate support and subsistence in the region and indicated that it was only a matter of time before they could no longer sustain themselves under the current situation.[82]

As German forces were reorganising after their defeat at Bentheim, coalition leaders decided to establish a defence along the Ems River. With the British contingent leaving the continent, the Germans (Hanoverians, Hessians, and Brunswickers) would displace the British (with the exception of some British cavalry units) and defend the Ems from Meppen north to Emden, while the Prussians would occupy the positions previously held by the Hanoverians, Hessians, Brunswickers, and Austrians, and defend the Ems from Meppen south to Münster.[83] Prussian troops would also deploy north into Lower Saxony to reinforce the German defence and to protect Prussian possessions in Ostfriesland. Scharnhorst then submitted his analysis of the situation should the French continue their advance across the Ems.

Scharnhorst advocated an offensive spirit as the best defence. 'This extension is not a defensive plan', he stated, 'and all orders must be based on an offensive operation'. He made it clear that 'the question is no longer how one defends a certain sector', but what the coalition should do if French break through and cross the Ems. As Scharnhorst pointed out, nowhere along the entire front, from Wesel to Emden, are the existing 'defensive measures strong enough to stop the enemy'. Trying to defend the entire River Ems would be disastrous, as the coalition defence of Flanders and Holland had been. The allies must take risks and 'select an assembly point for the army' where they could mass their forces and then move quickly to engage the French (once they had penetrated the defence) 'in open areas, where our troops are superior to the enemy in any battle', and where the French would be deprived of their logistical support.[84]

Undeniably, Scharnhorst's detailed analysis represented an ideal defensive-offensive concept, but it was wholly unrealistic given the physical and psychological condition of the German troops at this point in the war. Moreover, the cautious and indecisive leadership of the coalition would never have agreed to such a bold contingency. Once again, Scharnhorst's optimism was severely tempered by the reality of a cause lost in the minds of senior coalition leaders. The British wanted to go home, the Austrians were just trying to hold on to

82 *General der Cavallerie* Wallmoden to King George III (14 March 1795); published as Appendix 26/2 in Büschleb, *Scharnhorst in Westfalen*, p.147. Also see the source documents in Hann 38 E, Nr.298: *Korrespondenz des Generals von Wallmoden mit dem englischen Commission General Brook Watson, 1795*; deposited at the Niedersächsisches Landesarchiv, Hanover.

83 Sichart, *Geschichte der Königlich-Hannoverischen Armee*, Vol.4, p.605.

84 Gerhard Scharnhorst, 'Ueber die Versamlungspunkte der allirten Armee gegen den über die Ems vordringenen Feind' (middle March 1795); in Kunisch (ed.), *Scharnhorst: Privat und dienstliche Schriften*, Vol.1, pp.640-44; and published as Appendix 29/1 in Büschleb, *Scharnhorst in Westfalen*, pp.151-55. Büschleb also includes two facsimiles from this document, one of which is a sketch map of the allied positions. The quoted passages are from Kunisch (ed.), *Scharnhorst: Privat und dienstliche Schriften*, Vol.1, p.641.

their German possessions, and the Prussians sought a separate peace. Before the displacement of the German corps began, Scharnhorst had submitted the future locations of these troops to Wallmoden.[85]

From the village of Greven on 18 March, Prince Adolphus updated his father. He told King George about the hardships he and his men had suffered during the retreat from Holland, the very great 'fatigues we have undergone', and especially 'the inclemency of the weather'. In good spirits he wrote:

> I can assure your Majesty that I never can thanck [sic] you enough for having let me remain this winter with the Army, as it is the greatest comfort in the world to have shared all hardships with the men; and now they are over I would not have missed them for anything.

Prince Adolphus mentioned that his regiment was situated along the second line of the Ems River defence, but their new cantonments 'are very bad', while the roads 'are shocking, much worse even than those in Holland, which is saying a great deal'. He also noted that his regiment 'is now beginning to get very sickly' again, due mainly to 'the severity of the last campaign'.[86]

'So now I will receive a company', Scharnhorst told Klara with joy from Osnabrück on 18 March. 'Last night General Trew informed me that the pension request for Prott was finally approved'.[87] Even though his wish for a company command was about to be fulfilled, he remained frustrated that others, whose physical and mental abilities were no match for his, were being promoted, while he was not. He spent most of this letter discussing his seething resentment, something he had repeated told his wife he would not do. His repressed feelings clearly came forth.

> All the arrangements this winter, from the defence of the Waal to Münster, were made and directed, for the most part, by me. I saw every occurrence. I predicted every attack that the enemy would make. I am to blame that we stayed longer on the Waal. I used all my powers to persuade the Count [Wallmoden] to stand there, unaware, as I now know, that this would be unsuccessful. I have seen that he believed that I alone was capable of giving him good advice; that to a certain extent, he followed my counsel in everything, not just in dangerous undertakings.[88]

Scharnhorst went on to tell Klara how quickly he was able to assess a situation correctly and provide a viable solution. He explained to her that this was why he always placed himself

85 See 'Dislocation der Truppen, so am linken Ufer der Ems stehen und sum Theil dieseble passiren' (middle March 1795); published as Appendix 25/1 in Büschleb, *Scharnhorst in Westfalen*, pp.144-45. It is also published in Kunisch (ed.), *Scharnhorst: Privat und dienstliche Schriften*, Vol.1, pp.644-45. In Note a on p.644, the editor stated that this document is 'often associated with the memorandum' cited above.

86 Letter of 18 March 1795 from Prince Adolphus to King George III; in Aspinall (ed.), *The Later Correspondence of George III*, Vol.2, p.322. It is interesting that just a few weeks earlier Prince Adolphus wanted to go home.

87 Letter of 18 March 1795 to Klara; in Kunisch (ed.), *Scharnhorst: Privat und dienstliche Schriften*, Vol.1, pp.645-68; the quoted passage is from p.645.

88 Letter of 18 March 1795 to Klara; in Kunisch (ed.), *Scharnhorst: Privat und dienstliche Schriften*, Vol.1, p.646.

at the centre of events, in order to demonstrate 'my great superiority over others around me'. Even 'the Generals' followed his leadership implicitly, 'as if I commanded the corps'. Scharnhorst closed this portion of his letter by informing his wife that he was 'certain' he possessed 'the most favour and the most confidence' among the senior leadership of the German corps.[89]

'A particularly prudent and resolute officer', *Major* Gerhard Scharnhorst clearly excelled under the most trying of circumstances.[90] Unfortunately, some of his colleagues on the General Staff were clearly resentful of his success and the high regard Wallmoden had in him. In fact, they were genuinely hostile toward Scharnhorst and sought to undermine his efforts. As he continued his letter of 18 March, he told Klara, 'The situation is also dangerous from the other side. It generates envy from different places'. He believed that his jealous and perfidious colleagues on the General Staff were 'the most dangerous enemies in the entire corps'. He specifically mentioned two engineer officers – Kuntze and Hogrewe, citing how the poor execution of their duties 'exposes' the army 'to a particular sickness' that leads only 'to the greatest of all misfortune'. Unfortunately for Scharnhorst, Kuntze and Hogrewe were members of Freytag's clique and were essentially untouchable, and they knew it. The best efforts of Wallmoden to rid his staff of these pernicious men proved futile. So, Scharnhorst kept away from headquarters as much as possible to avoid the constant rancour around him and to permit Kuntze and Hogrewe to exhibit their 'worthlessness' to the Commanding General, 'who already knows this'. So intense was the animosity of these senior staff officers toward him that Scharnhorst informed his wife that he just wanted peace and quiet, 'where I am not the most blameworthy in the army'.[91]

Turning to other news, Scharnhorst told Klara that the British were on their way back to England, while Prussian soldiers would soon be arriving in Osnabrück. He felt certain with Prussian reinforcements, 'we can beat the French'. He also alluded to the impending release from French captivity of her brother Georg Scharlock. With profound humility and joy in his heart he told Klara that she was 'such a good wife' to him, and that it was 'highly probable' that soon there would be peace. With his usual longing to be home with his family, he closed this letter, bidding 'Adieu' to Klara and telling her, 'Now is certainly not the time to be corrupted by an everlasting ambition that does not lead to true inner happiness'.[92]

Obviously upsetting his wife by his lengthy, seven-page diatribe of 18 March, Scharnhorst immediately apologised to Klara in his next letter of 28 March. He mentioned reading her sorrowful letter of 20 March, and told her he never meant to upset her, and reassured her that he was well and safe, that the headquarters was scheduled to depart Osnabrück in the morning, and that he was working feverishly on some important assignments for the Commanding General: 'Some ambitious and political projects frustrate me now. A struggle

89 Klippel, *Scharnhorst*, Vol.2, pp.196-98 and 201-03 provides documentary evidence from the field commanders to the Commanding General that supports Scharnhorst's assertion. The field commanders often cited Scharnhorst's herculean efforts in support of their operations, the great confidence they had in him, and how fortunate the army was to have Scharnhorst. The quoted passages are from Scharnhorst's Letter of 18 March 1795 to Klara; in Kunisch (ed.), *Scharnhorst: Privat und dienstliche Schriften*, Vol.1, p.646.

90 See the discussion in Stübig, *Scharnhorst*, p.38.

91 Letter of 18 March 1795 to Klara; in Kunisch (ed.), *Scharnhorst: Privat und dienstliche Schriften*, Vol.1, p.647.

92 Letter of 18 March 1795 to Klara; in Kunisch (ed.), *Scharnhorst: Privat und dienstliche Schriften*, Vol.1, pp.646 and 647.

between common sense and ambition is my permanent condition, and my fate is to follow one or the other, depending on the situation'. While not elaborating on these projects, Scharnhorst implored his wife to 'be calm about the future', telling her about 'an inner strength that will not stop tormenting me until I achieve something extraordinary'. He promised Klara that when that occurs, 'a beneficial change will take place and all ambition will be satisfied'. Once again, Scharnhorst never told his wife what this 'something extraordinary' was, nor what 'beneficial change' would take place. Indeed, he had already told Klara months earlier that his ambition had been satisfied with his promotion to major and appointment to the General Staff. Now, without ever acknowledging that it was his own unquenchable ambition and thirst for advancement, his self-pity, and his refusal to accept his situation and status in life that was upsetting his wife, Scharnhorst simply closed his letter with a prayer, 'May God give my Klara peace and health'.[93]

While Scharnhorst was fighting his personal demons and upsetting his expectant wife, French forces were marching to their natural frontiers and beyond. Austria was searching for ways to maintain her possessions along the Rhine, while Prussia was financially exhausted by war and secretly negotiating with France for an end of hostilities.[94] Based on coalition plans to defend the Ems River line, Wallmoden had his General-Quartermaster-Lieutenant formulated possible redeployment locations for the English and German contingents.[95] Once the Commanding General approved this concept, Scharnhorst then provided a plan that specified the locations of each German and British cantonment area. Never willing to remain on the defensive, he again introduced his plan for offensive action, writing, 'The Corps [meaning the Germans and Austrians] occupies these newly concentrated cantonments' to stop any French attack across the Ems. 'Should this happen', he continued, soldiers from 'every nation will assemble, namely the Hessians, Hanoverians, and Austrians', to counterattack the French.[96] In addition to these measures, he established a central reserve of Hanoverians and Austrians in the vicinity of Meppen. As he clarified the mission of the force at each location, he discussed the importance of conserving troop strength and of obtaining vital subsistence. He also indicated that if possible, coalition forces should seek to retake Bentheim.

Scharnhorst followed this memorandum with an overall assessment of the new situation. He began by acknowledging Wallmoden's 'perceptive evaluation of the situation', and proceeded to highlight the pros and cons of the new cantonment areas, the logistical problems associated with this arrangement, the dangers of too long a front, the uncertainties of

93 Letter of 28 March 1795 to Klara; in Kunisch (ed.), *Scharnhorst: Privat und dienstliche Schriften*, Vol.1, pp.655-56. The editors of Scharnhorst's Papers believe Karl Linnebach, the editor of *Scharnhrosts Briefe* (Munich and Leipzig: Georg Müller, 1914; reprinted, with commentary by Heinz Stübig, Munich: Klaus Reprint, 1980), Vol. 1: *Privatbriefe*, pp.19-20, erred when he dated this letter from March 1793. The places Scharnhorst described in this letter coincide with those where he was in 1795, not in 1793. Additionally, it was far too early in 1793 (only as few days into the deployment) for him to have received two letters from Klara, to be having difficulty with his colleagues, and to be awaiting a forthcoming visit from his family – all of which are mentioned in this letter of March 1795.

94 See the discussion in Schroeder, *The Transformation of European Politics*, pp.150-57.

95 See Scharnhorst's initial options entitled, '*Vorläufig*' (March 1795); in Kunisch (ed.), *Scharnhorst: Privat und dienstliche Schriften*, Vol.1, pp.648-49.

96 Gerhard Scharnhorst, 'Project einer veränderten Position' (March 1795); in Kunisch (ed.), *Scharnhorst: Privat und dienstliche Schriften*, Vol.1, pp.649-51; the quoted passages are from p.649.

commitment by coalition members, locations where the French may attack, and the difficulties associated with launching a counteroffensive.[97] With his plan complete, Wallmoden sent Scharnhorst in early April to the port town of Leer, the north-western part of Lower Saxony, near the border of Holland. Here is where the Commanding General intended to position his northernmost force. Wallmoden also ordered the British and German contingents to evacuate their current positions and begin their movement northward into East Frisia (the coastal region in Lower Saxony). Along the way they would establish their defence of the Ems River line from Meppen to Emden.[98]

Before traveling to Leer, Scharnhorst formally requested Wallmoden reassign him to the infantry. He offered three reasons, which he explained to Klara. First, given his seniority, he believed he would probably be promoted to *Oberstlieutenant* in the infantry sooner than he would if he remained in the artillery. Secondly, he felt he would have more opportunities and definitely more job security in the infantry. In his third rationale, he said he would be rid of Trew and Braun, both of whom were once again meddling with his career prospects.[99] While he did not elaborate on his current relationship with Trew and Braun, just two weeks earlier he had told Klara he would be receiving a company command. Then, in his letter of 28 March, he told her that Braun and his wife did not care much for him, while 'the General is angry with me'.[100] Now on 2 April he told Klara he was seeking a transfer to the infantry. What he meant regarding his comments about Braun and Trew remained unclear, because he did not explain them to Klara, who clearly became upset once again after reading her husband's remarks.

Gerhard Scharnhorst's comments in many of his letters home reveal a self-absorbed man unable to control his passions when threatened by outside influences over which he had little control. Instead of accepting his current situation in life (which by now seemed to change almost on a daily basis) and seeking to master it and control his frustration (especially in his letters to Klara), Scharnhorst let this inner rage and insecurity rule his life and his relationship with his wife. In his self-indulgence, he never seemed to grasp what he was doing to his 'beloved' Klara. Only after he had upset her did he ever apologise. In the end, the evidence clearly shows Scharnhorst never mastered his destiny.

Scharnhorst believed he had more friends and benefactors in the infantry than in the artillery. The most notable was Hammerstein. All of his combat experience as a battery commander was in support of the infantry. His exceptional combat leadership in Flanders and Holland was clearly known throughout the army. As a staff officer he had coordinated the operations of Hanoverian, Hessian, and Brunswick units during some of the most difficult circumstances for the German troops. Many of his fellow officers in the infantry and cavalry were not only grateful for his splendid leadership, but also looked upon Scharnhorst

97 Gerhard Scharnhorst, '*Ueber die Situation der Corps, so an der Gränze Hollands stehen*' (March 1795); in Kunisch (ed.), *Scharnhorst: Privat und dienstliche Schriften*, Vol.1, pp.651-54; the quoted passage is from p.652. The new cantonment areas are listed in Sichart, *Geschichte der Königlich-Hannoverischen Armee*, Vol.4, pp.605-07.

98 See General Wallmoden's 'Auszufertigender Befehl' (April 1795); in Kunisch (ed.), *Scharnhorst: Privat und dienstliche Schriften*, Vol.1, pp.658-59.

99 Letter of 2 April 1795 to Klara; in Kunisch (ed.), *Scharnhorst: Privat und dienstliche Schriften*, Vol.1, p.657. In Note 3, the editor states: 'Obviously, this memorandum is lost'.

100 Letter of 28 March 1795 to Klara; in Kunisch (ed.), *Scharnhorst: Privat und dienstliche Schriften*, Vol.1, pp.655-56; the quoted passage is from p.656.

as a brother-in-arms. Only in the artillery and on the General Staff does it appear that he was not warmly welcomed. In closing his letter of 2 April to Klara, he again showed his lack of confidence (not to mention burdening his wife again) when he wrote, 'the Field Marshal' [Freytag] would most likely 'thwart' [*contrecarrirt*] his request to be reassigned to the infantry.[101]

Meanwhile, with her eyes focused on Poland, Prussia made peace with revolutionary France, signing the Treaty of Basel on 5 April 1795. This agreement completely changed the dynamics of the coalition. King George wrote to William Pitt on that day, concerned about 'Westphalia and my electorate'. The king told his prime minister that 'the recall of the British infantry and the retreat of the whole Austrian Army to the Rhine leave those Provinces entirely open to the ravages of the enemy'.[102] Again, King George wanted assurances from the Prussians that they would 'stand forth' and defend Germany. Interestingly, the king never gave any assurance that his British troops would remain in Germany to defend his electorate.[103]

From Sögen on 7 April, Scharnhorst began reporting on the situation as he rode northward. The most crucial challenge facing the coalition was subsistence. He told Wallmoden the British commissary system was not functioning at all, that its officers (with the exception of one) had no concept of how to perform their duties or their responsibilities toward their soldiers, and urged the Commanding General to appoint an 'energetic officer' (he recommended *Oberstlieutenant* von Schulte) to head 'the Inspection over Subsistence' [*die Inspection über die Subsitance*] and to serve as 'middleman' [*Mittelperson*] between the regiments, the commissaries and depots, and the local population. He also warned of conflicts with the Prussians, who were appropriating all the food, wagons, horses, and other items they could as they deployed into Lower Saxony.[104]

As supply problems continued to plague the English and German forces, Scharnhorst reported from Leer on 9 April that Hammerstein and his command had arrived and were located in and around Leer. Scheither was situated in Emden. *General-Major* Wurmb (not to be confused with *Oberst* Wurmb) was nearby at Papenburg. Because of the recent heavy rains, the roads linking these commands 'are now almost impassable', which only exacerbated the supply challenges. Scharnhorst also informed Wallmoden of his illuminating conversation with a local Prussian official, who 'knows the country well' and who had made a fortune in 'large speculations'. According to this Prussian, 'the region has a great many resources', but since no depot had been established to gather these resources, most of the food, hay, and other vital materials were lost to speculation. Scharnhorst also reported the British commissary continued to demonstrate 'great half-heartedness and carelessness in

101 Letter of 2 April 1795 to Klara; in Kunisch (ed.), *Scharnhorst: Privat und dienstliche Schriften*, Vol.1, p.657. It is highly probable that Wallmoden, knowing the outcome, never sent Scharnhorst's request to Freytag.

102 King George III to William Pitt (5 April 1795); in Aspinall (ed.), *The Later Correspondence of George III*, Vol.2, p.326.

103 In his two-part article, 'The Military and Popular Disorder in England, 1790-1801', *Journal for the Society for Army Historical Research* 61:245 (Spring 1983), pp.10-21 and 61:246 (Summer 1983), pp.96-112, Clive Emsley writes that widespread disorder throughout England during this time caused local magistrates to request regular army troops to support their efforts to maintain internal order. Naturally, these domestic affairs were far more important than the safety of Hanover.

104 Scharnhorst to Wallmoden (7 April 1795); in Kunisch (ed.), *Scharnhorst: Privat und dienstliche Schriften*, Vol.1, pp.659-60; the quoted passage is from p.660.

each account', and this, coupled with the lack of 'petty cash' [*bar Geld*] to pay for items, caused distrust among the local inhabitants, who were unwilling to give credit. With an eye trained on potential enemy action, he told the Commanding General that he believed the positions around Papenburg could 'offer no major resistance because they are too dispersed'.[105]

As the influx of soldiers into East Frisia increased, the logistical support of the German troops became acute. 'With respect to forage, the army is in a critical situation', Scharnhorst reported on 11 April. Local depots had no rations, while the impassable roads caused the regimental quartermasters to spend more than six hours daily traveling to obtain food and supplies. Often, they returned with little or nothing. Scharnhorst recommended sending engineers and portable bridges to Hammerstein and Wurmb so they could repair the road network.[106] Turning to the worsening supply problem, he told Wallmoden: 'The English Commissar Mee told me in the presence of Lieutenant Colonel von Schulte and Lieutenant Timäus he had no permission to create a stockpile, due to the high prices here'. Scharnhorst then offered a realistic remedy:

> By all means a small magazine of approximately 100,000 rations must be at established at Stikhusen or Soesta, on the right bank of the Sater-Ems River. Furthermore, the magazines at Leer and Emden must always maintain at least 40,000 to 60,000 rations, so that the troops can be provided from one or the other during a movement of several days.[107]

These depots would greatly strengthen the logistical support of Germans soldiers in the region, while not alienating local authorities, who he noted were 'clearly working against our provisioning' [*Verproviantirung*]. Three days later he informed Wallmoden that the army would exhaust its supplies in East Frisia over the next four to six weeks. He suggested moving the British cavalry to the countrywide (where more grazing was possible) and relocating all artillery horses where they could obtain better nourishment.[108] This would be Scharnhorst's last report until the end of April.

After receiving Scharnhorst's request to be reassigned to the infantry, the Commanding General concluded that his hard-working and tenacious General-Quartermaster-Lieutenant needed some rest and time away from his duties and headquarters. So, he sent Scharnhorst home to Bordenau. Once home, joy greeted the Scharnhorst family on 20 April 1795, when

105 Scharnhorst to Wallmoden (9 April 1795); in Kunisch (ed.), *Scharnhorst: Privat und dienstliche Schriften*, Vol.1, pp.661-62.

106 See some interesting documentation on the subject of transportation and logistics; in Hann 38 E, Nr.304: *Fuhrwesen im Hannoverschen für den Transport der Armee und des Kommissariats, 1795*; deposited at the Niedersächsisches Landesarchiv, Hanover.

107 Scharnhorst to Wallmoden (11 April 1795); in Kunisch (ed.), *Scharnhorst: Privat und dienstliche Schriften*, Vol.1, pp.663-64; the quoted passages are from pp.663 and 663-64.

108 Scharnhorst to Wallmoden (14 April 1795); in Kunisch (ed.), *Scharnhorst: Privat und dienstliche Schriften*, Vol.1, pp.664-65. See the important documentation on the establisment of depots; in Hann 38 E, Nr.303: *Anlegung von Magazinen in Hannover und Bremen, 1795*; deposited at the Niedersächsisches Landesarchiv, Hanover.

Klara gave birth to their second son, Friedrich Gerhard August. He was baptised a month later on 15 May.[109] After two weeks with his family, Scharnhorst returned to Leer.

On 29 April, Scharnhorst recommended that perhaps it would be prudent to redeploy the German corps in order to ease the acute supply problems in East Frisia.[110] This solution had proven successful two months earlier in Westphalia. Scharnhorst felt that something had to be done to care for the many troops, especially the Prussians arriving daily. He also informed Wallmoden of the continuing violence of the English soldier, who now directed his anger at the local German inhabitants.[111] Three weeks later on 17 May 1795, France and Prussia reached agreement on the establishment of a Demarcation Line in north-western Germany. 'Peace was again in the land'.[112]

109 Klippel, *Scharnhorst*, Vol.2, pp.213 and 215.

110 Scharnhorst to Wallmoden (29 April 1795); in Kunisch (ed.), *Scharnhorst: Privat und dienstliche Schriften*, Vol.1, pp.667-68.

111 See the documentation regarding the ongoing supply problems in Hann 38 E, Nr.290: *Verhandlungen zwischen dem Herzog von York, dem General von Wallmoden und dem englischen Staatssekretär Generalleutnant Dundas über die Verpflegung der in englischem Solde stehenden Subsidien-Truppen (u.a. aus Braunschweig und Hessen), 05.1795-10.1795*; deposited at the Niedersächsisches Landesarchiv, Hanover.

112 The quoted passage is from Lehmann, *Scharnhorst*, Vol.1, p.203.

12

Modernising the Army

Back in Bordenau, Scharnhorst enjoyed the precious time he spent with his family. He was delighted to be home with his beloved Klara and their three young children – Wilhelm (9), Juliana (6), and newborn August. Since deploying in the early spring of 1793, he had had just two weeks leave from the front. The only other occasion he had spent time with his family was in the late summer of 1794, when Klara and their children had travelled to visit him in Holland. Mindful of the tenuous political and military situation facing German forces in Westphalia, and realising Wallmoden might summon him back to duty at a moment's notice, Scharnhorst made the most of the time with his family. He also used this period to review the management of his estate. At other times he was preoccupied with his wartime experience. After correlating the extensive research that he had collected over the past two years, he began submitting concept papers to the Commanding General for modernising the Hanoverian army.

History provided Scharnhorst with the rationale he required to suggest the modernisation of the Hanoverian army. A detailed analysis of the 1793 and 1794 campaigns in Flanders and Holland demonstrated that 'Scharnhorst's brilliant breakthrough at Menin' was the sole exception to the largely unprepared and inept Hanoverians, who 'experienced little success in battle and suffered many losses'.[1] In all his initiatives Scharnhorst sought to incorporate the lessons he had learned as a battery commander and staff officer. His productivity over the next six years was staggering, as he crafted one memorandum after another detailing his concept of a military capable of meeting the challenges of the national citizen army.[2]

Organisation and intellect were the key components of Scharnhorst's modernisation endeavours. Establishing a permanent General Staff with Troops would provide the essential organisational structure to command and control the army. Creating a formal system of military *Bildung* would educate quality leaders throughout the army. Reorganising the army into divisions of combined arms would afford the framework for future combat effectiveness. Transforming the sterile, linear tactical system of the army into a robust combination of skirmishers, attack columns, and line formations would provide battlefield flexibility,

1 See the conclusions of Richard W. Fox, 'Conservative Accommodation to Revolution', p.86.

2 The entire second volume of Kunisch (ed.), *Scharnhorst: Privat und dienstliche Schriften*, carries the title *Stabschef und Reformer* (*Kurhannover 1795-1801*), is 782 pages long, and contains over 300 documents that capture Scharnhorst's extensive staff work, teaching endeavours, modernisation plans, and writing activities during this period. Individual documents are cited below.

while realistic and intensified combined arms field training would stimulate poise among the rank and file and provide opportunities for officers and non-commissioned officers to hone their leadership skills. All of this depended on a more egalitarian society where advancement was based on talent and ability, not birth and privilege. Following the theory that Count Wilhelm had endeavoured to implement in Schaumburg-Lippe and which the French Republic had put into practice, Scharnhorst endeavoured to destroy forever the elitist character of the army by introducing universal military conscription. Other proposals aimed at reorganising and re-equipping the artillery and engineers.[3]

Strengthening the leadership of the army was the first priority. Just five days after the birth of his son, Scharnhorst added substance to the framework for his General Staff with Troops concept. It was titled, 'On the Establishment and Duty of the General Staff'.[4] Most of these ideas he had already voiced to Mechlenberg and Wallmoden and had successfully tested during the previous campaigns. This document appears to be a recapitulation of those thoughts in the form of a concept outline for a much larger study. It contains a series of key words and phrases. Under the first heading, '*Establishment of the General Staff*', Scharnhorst wrote just two phrases: 'As it must be', followed by 'As it usually is'. Even though no other commentary was included, it is reasonable to assume that based on previous writings, he probably planned to introduce historical precedence as the foundation for this organisation. This was his way of demonstrating to his colleagues that what he proposed was nothing new; rather, his modernisation efforts were part of a larger continuum based on historical precedence and were necessary if the army was to meet the challenges ahead.

The second portion dealt with the duties, 'or the chores', of the general staff. Here Scharnhorst intended to discuss 'the particulars in general', which were to cover 'in a tabular design, the details of each operation, for use in the field'. This was essentially a quick reference guide for staff officers and would include important lessons and best practices learned from experience and the pages of history. This format was similar to his *Handbook for Officers* and *Military Field Pocket Book*. Scharnhorst's intent was to clarify 'the relationship' between the general staff and the army. As he concluded, 'The army must see the general staff as its housekeeper, to indicate what is not right, and to report everything to the commanding general'.

A third section was to cover topics of special importance to Scharnhorst. These included: 'esprit de corps', 'different ways of waging war', the attack, cantonments, fortresses, 'our current military organisation', 'on experience and theory', 'on turning movements', 'detailers - esprit de trifle' (here Scharnhorst meant those who constantly become bogged down in trivial details and lose sight of the larger picture), the correct use of artillery, and how to develop a professional work ethic on the general staff.[5] Again, examples from the past would illustrate these points.

3 For a concise overview of reform efforts in Hanover from 1795-1803, see Fox, 'Conservative Accommodation to Revolution', pp.85-94.

4 Gerhard Scharnhorst, 'Ueber die Einrichtung und den Dienst des Generalstabs' (25 April/2 May 1795); published in Kunisch (ed.), *Scharnhorst: Privat und dienstliche Schriften*, Vol.1, pp.665-67.

5 Scharnhorst, 'Ueber die Einrichtung und den Dienst des Generalstabs', Kunisch (ed.), *Scharnhorst: Privat und dienstliche Schriften*, Vol.1, pp.665-66.

On 2 May, Scharnhorst continued refining his General Staff with Troops design. In this paper he outlined two major themes: the general staff itself, and what he termed, 'some items relating to the leadership of the army'.[6] Leadership of the army was the responsibility of the General Staff with Troops – a corporate genius that would assist the commanding general in peacetime and on campaign. While he listed nothing under the first theme, under the second he wrote 'On General Matters', and provided several subjects he felt needed clarification. Originally, he called these 'General strategical arrangements of the army', but lined through this phrase in the draft. Under this deleted heading he listed: 'Composition of the army, its continued existence, transportation, ammunition, artillery – light troops'. 'Experience' was initially part of this list but lined through.

Next came the most significant topic – '*Awakening Esprit*'. Here Scharnhorst discussed rewards and punishments. 'In every campaign one must punish a certain number as examples'. Rewards, he continued, are to be given only to those who have performed well 'in the face of the enemy'. Then he wrote the phrase: 'Leadership against the enemy', and cited the renowned Russian *Generalissimo* Alexander Vasilyevich Suvorov (1729-1800) as a model of generalship in war. Scharnhorst also provided ways of inspiring the troops and raising the spirit of the army, such as instilling a sense of patriotism, celebrating victories, music, songs, and religion.

Remaining topics in this concept paper included a list of important combat duties of the General Staff with Troops. First was the advanced guard, which Scharnhorst noted should be organised and led 'following Hammerstein's example'. This was the only reference to previous experience he made. Entrenching outposts and logistical support chains came next, followed by establishing good defensive positions so they could not be easily flanked. Attacking the enemy was his next subject, while maintenance of the force (subsistence, pay, medical care, economic arrangements, and hospitals) came last.[7] With these thoughts on the General Staff with Troops and its role as the command and control mechanism of the army, Scharnhorst began drafting concept papers for its implementation.

In a series of memoranda written between April 1975 and October 1797, Scharnhorst gave substance to the outlines he had developed, advocating the peacetime establishment of a permanent General Staff with Troops.[8] As usual, he began with lessons from the pages of history, explaining how in earlier times the duties of the general staff had been limited to planning routes of march and quartering troops in the field. These tasks were accomplished initially by engineers and later by a quartermaster staff. As the size of armies steadily increased, and the scope of their operations extended over progressively larger geographical areas, commanding generals could no longer see their entire army in front of them, and thus found it necessary to attach officers from their personal staffs to their subordinate

6 Gerhard Scharnhorst, 'Ueber den Generalstab und über einige sich auf die Führung der Armee beziehend, allgemeine Anordungen' (2 May 1795); in Kunisch (ed.), *Scharnhorst: Privat und dienstliche Schriften*, Vol.1, pp.666-67; the quoted passages are from p.666.

7 Scharnhorst, 'Ueber den Generalstab und über einige sich auf die Führung der Armee beziehend', Kunisch (ed.), *Scharnhorst: Privat und dienstliche Schriften*, Vol.1, p.667.

8 The editors of Scharnhorst's Papers have grouped these concept papers as 'Entwürfe zur Einrichtung des Generalstabs', found in Kunisch (ed.), *Scharnhorst: Privat und dienstliche Schriften*, Vol.1, pp.681-717. Lehmann, *Scharnhorst*, Vol.1, pp.240-44, discusses these proposals, but unfortunately often quotes from several different documents simultaneously, without properly citing from which source each quote originated.

commanders to maintain effective command and control. Normally these officers were the sons, nephews, or extended family members, or even close personal confidants of the commanding general. Most had little formal training and education, or talent required for the precise planning and execution of tactical, operational, or logistical operations. Aristocratic prerogatives guaranteed that their duties, responsibilities, and authority (as well as their qualifications) were never clearly established. Those usually depended on the personalities, attitudes, and connections between the commanding general and his subordinate commanders. The notable exception to this custom was *Major* Gerhard Scharnhorst.

What Scharnhorst sought was a consolidation of the responsibilities, duties, and authority of his General Staff with Troops. He proposed that this General Staff with Troops continue assisting the commanding general in with operational planning and the tactical disposition of the army. He also suggested assigning general staff officers to the corps commanders as responsible and authoritative spokesmen of the commanding general. Moreover, he insisted that this General Staff with Troops be charged with peacetime contingency planning.[9] Scharnhorst clearly wanted to use his General Staff with Troops to destroy the nepotism and connection that had hindered the development of truly talented officers and non-commissioned officers in the Hanoverian army.[10] Reiterating what he had written in *Handbook for Officers*, he argued that far too many officers rise to positions of leadership in war who possess neither the physical strength nor the mental ability to carry out their strenuous duties.

> It is a universal fact that during the sleepless nights and chaotic lifestyle in war, the mind is being unknowingly impaired, that auspicious moments of complete consciousness seldom occur, and that with older, as opposed to younger people, a far greater indifference and bewilderment of the spirit sets in.[11]

Tired men make mistakes, and Scharnhorst felt this was especially true of older men. In several letters to Mechlenberg and Klara during the war, he had often condemned the practice of keeping so many worthless older (and mainly aristocratic) officers in the army.

Scharnhorst rejected the notion held by many in the Hanoverian army that leaders did not need specialised education and training. Continuing his prewar assault against ignorance, he argued that without *Bildung*, intellectual sterility would set in. This was especially dangerous for general staff officers. Without *Bildung*:

> A certain mechanism now takes the place of sound reasoning in the majority of individuals, and these mechanical thinkers always seem to outlive people with

9 Gerhard Scharnhorst, 'Nothwendigkeit eines Generalquartiermeisterstaabs für die hannövrischen Truppen in Friedenszeiten' (1795/1796?); and its continuation with the same title; in Kunisch (ed.), *Scharnhorst: Privat und dienstliche Schriften*, Vol.1, pp.693-94 and 694-96; respectively.

10 This is the central theme of '*Von der Einrichtung eines Generalquartiermeister-Staabs*', which is Chapter 3 of Scharnhorst's untitled memorandum on the duties of the general staff officer in war; in Kunisch (ed.), *Scharnhorst: Privat und dienstliche Schriften*, Vol.1, pp.708-16.

11 Scharnhorst, '*Von der Einrichtung eines Generalquartiermeister-Staabs*', Kunisch (ed.), *Scharnhorst: Privat und dienstliche Schriften*, Vol.1, p.716. Scharnhorst starred this portion in the original text, intending it to be part of the first section of Chapter 3.

> talent. So a certain mechanism, unperceived from above, soon disseminates itself throughout the entire corps, restricting the intellect more and more, and finally turning scholarship into a drill.[12]

A means of destroying this mechanism had to be found. Scharnhorst found his solution from his observations of the Prussian General Staff.

Following the example of Frederick the Great, Scharnhorst believed the constant rotation of talented regimental officers through the general staff would furnish the best vehicle for eliminating mental incompetence while simultaneously obtaining 'superior minds'. Although he clearly advocated a permanent general staff organisation, Scharnhorst did not believe in a permanent general staff corps. General staff personnel must be well-rounded leaders with both staff and regimental duty.

> It would be entirely different if the officers of this corps alternated with other types of troops. Through this rotation the spirit of despotism would die – such an individual would not be slavishly bound to the spectre of senior officers. His success would not be made by them, and his future success would not depend upon them.

Scharnhorst wrote that rotating officers between staff and troop duty as the Prussians did would also provide 'a great and substantial service' to the regiments, since 'a great number of well-educated officers' would be constantly returned to the line units, and this in turn would raise the quality of leadership throughout the entire army. Again, he did not subscribe to the commonly-held belief within the officer corps that regimental duty alone prepared officers for their wartime responsibilities. The General Staff with Troops would become 'to some extent a school in which many officers are educated for the army'. The General Staff with Troops would also benefit. In time of war it would be able to obtain talented officers already educated and trained in the duties of the general staff.[13]

Here is the essence of the modern general staff system – a corporate genius selected, educated, and trained along uniform lines. *Major* Gerhard Scharnhorst clearly understood the need for an operational field staff in an age of mass, citizen armies. Careers had to be opened to all classes, and especially to those officers with proven talent and ability. French military success was a direct result of the transformation of French society and the emergence of a national army. Developing leaders capable of leading a national army was his primary concern, even if this meant creating an entirely new officer corps.

Scharnhorst justified his General Staff with Troops by comparing it with the existing system in Hanover, in which connection and favouritism had created a small and isolated general staff corps: 'With a separate, standing corps, a certain nepotism and spirit of self-interest creeps in instead of a dedication to the common good'. Clearly thinking of his own experience and the useless officers with whom he had served (especially Kuntze and Hogrewe), Scharnhorst stated that the educated and talented, but independent officer

12 Scharnhorst, '*Von der Einrichtung eines Generalquartiermeister-Staabs*', Kunisch (ed.), *Scharnhorst: Privat und dienstliche Schriften*, Vol.1, pp.709-10.

13 Scharnhorst, '*Von der Einrichtung eines Generalquartiermeister-Staabs*', Kunisch (ed.), *Scharnhorst: Privat und dienstliche Schriften*, Vol.1, pp.714, 711, and 715.

sees 'his career is limited and is morally certain that he cannot earn extraordinary advantages through personal distinction, nor can he be reduced by the average performance of his duty'.

> Therefore, his activity directs itself in a natural way toward things that promise him some side advantages. He soon sees his comrades doing this, too. So the conduct of one justifies that in others; and thus, little by little begins a spirit of self-interest that is always closely connected with narrow-mindedness.
>
> Nepotism brings along with it a kind of creation that completely paralyzes the small surviving nucleus of military spirit.
>
> But where a great deal depends on harmonious relationships, there rivalry is suppressed.

Unfortunately, in the Hanoverian army, harmonious relationships depended more on family ties and friendships, and not on any professional standard of performance. The result was obvious to Scharnhorst. As he so aptly described it:

> A small isolated corps resembles a small pool of stagnant water, which never has the characteristics of a great flowing river, and in the long run almost entirely loses its initial good quality.

Only by creating 'an entirely different class of officers' in the Hanoverian army, and especially within its general staff, could the evils of custom and privilege, connection and favouritism, be destroyed.[14]

These comments clearly indicate that Gerhard Scharnhorst wanted to replace the Hanoverian aristocracy of birth with an aristocracy of education. He understood the need for an effective general staff system in the age of mass, citizen armies. Senior leadership in the army had to be opened to all classes, and especially to those officers who demonstrate superior talent and ability. Interestingly, these papers also reveal a great deal about Scharnhorst himself. An extremely ambitious and highly talented officer, he was certainly relating his innermost feelings after being repeatedly slighted in favour of his well-connected noble and commoner associates. Fortunately, these emotions did not affect his sound judgment and clear understanding of the challenges facing the Hanoverian army.

In all his recommendations Scharnhorst identified three key elements in his program of military *Bildung*: training, education, and leadership. Training would lay the foundation of all soldierly skills, knowledge, and procedure, and would be grounded upon an objective and critical study of history to ensure realism. 'Nothing is more dangerous here than using personal experience without consideration for that experience which military history teaches us'. This was so important to Scharnhorst. Knowledge alone was not sufficient.

14 Scharnhorst, '*Von der Einrichtung eines Generalquartiermeister-Staabs*', Kunisch (ed.), *Scharnhorst: Privat und dienstliche Schriften*, Vol.1, pp.711 and 712.

> I have often seen how pathetic those officers are who draw their advice from their own observed data, how indecisive and timid they are to accomplish anything that the nature of the circumstances demands, but which has not occurred in their career. They make the general to whom they are attached uneasy by the recollection of a hundred possible but not probable disasters. They probably never risk a bold idea, since no similar situation crowned with success in the past gives them the necessary self-confidence.[15]

Without the ability to discern and then apply their experience, officers would be utterly useless in combat.

Scharnhorst hoped to develop wisdom through education. Education would clarify the officer's experience and prepare him to think and respond intelligently and resourcefully under complex and uncertain circumstances. As he stated:

> If the officer of the General-Quartermaster Staff has received a good military *Bildung* in peacetime, then in war he will be useful in all endeavours in less time. But without a good *Bildung* in peacetime, an officer of the General-Quartermaster Staff will never perform anything very well in war.[16]

Skilful synthesis of training and education would develop sound leadership and promote realism and intellectual independence, avoiding the tendency of earlier military institutions of solely conveying facts and drilling officers in a particular theory of war. This was Scharnhorst's concept of military formation [*Bildung*]. It was central to all of his modernisation efforts.

Scharnhorst based his modernisation ideas on a clear understanding of the French Revolution and its impact on the art of war. In one of his papers, *'On the Training and Formation of an Army in Peacetime'*, he claimed the superiority of the French lay in a coherent, aggressive strategy that reflected national rather than dynastic interests.[17] It was the spirit of the French people, embodied in the nation-in-arms, which had revolutionized the art of war. The French army had been transformed. Lazy, cowardly, and inept officers had been ruthlessly weeded out. Many were executed, while others had fled the country. In their

15 See Gerhard Scharnhorst, 'Fragment on Theory and Practice', Kunisch (ed.), *Scharnhorst: Privat und dienstliche Schriften*, Vol.1, pp.716-17; the quoted passages are from pp.716 and 716-17; respectively. In their note on p.716, the editors state that this piece 'is obviously closely linked to the preceding text' [Scharnhorst's untitled paper on the duties of the general staff officer in war; cited above, pp.697-716] and is mostly likely part of 'the missing Chapter II'. This fragment is published in Stadelmann, *Scharnhorst*, pp.155-56; and is excerpted in Lehmann, *Scharnhorst*, Vol.1, p.244. The title of this piece comes from Stadelmann. In her edition *Gerhard von Scharnhorst: Ausgewählte Schariften*, pp.147-50, Ursula von Gersdorff incorrectly dates this piece from 1804, following the citation by Stadelmann, *Scharnhorst*, p.155.

16 Scharnhorst, 'Fragment on Theory and Practice', Kunisch (ed.), *Scharnhorst: Privat und dienstliche Schriften*, Vol.1, p.716.

17 Gerhard Scharnhorst, '*Ueber die Uebung and Bildung einer Armee in Friedenszeiten, 30 May 1797*', *Nachlaß Scharnhorst*, Nr. 131, Sheets 2-10; deposited at the Geheimes Staatsarchiv Preussischer Kulturbesitz, 196/VI. HA Familienarchive und Nachlässe, Berlin (Dahlem). The concept outline of this paper is published in Kunisch (ed.), *Scharnhorst: Privat und dienstliche Schriften*, Vol.2, pp.86-87. Sheets 6-10 were published as 'Scharnhorst über Führerauswahl und Führerverantwortlichkeit', *Militärwissenschaftliche Rundschau* 2 (1944), pp.117-19.

place emerged competent, effective, and enthusiastic leaders.[18] Advancement depended on merit, service, and bravery, not birth, privilege, and connection. With a capable officer corps to lead and instil confidence and a high sense of morale in the rank and file, the French were able to exercise initiative and independence on the battlefield. This enabled them to adapt quickly and resourcefully to new and unexpected situations, which in turn resulted in greater mobility, a more flexible tactical doctrine, and the unparalleled freedom, enthusiasm, and heroism of the individual soldier.[19] 'In other armies this is not possible without completely destroying all inner relationships'.[20]

The success of Scharnhorst's organisational changes depended upon an intellectual foundation to lead this national army. This meant restructuring the Electorate's educational institutions with a better and more comprehensive military *Bildung* for officers, non-commissioned officers, and soldiers. The *Bildung* of senior officers was paramount, since it was their conceit and ignorance that had produced the leisurely attitude and lack of study among the officer corps before the war, and then had caused so much needless suffering for the troops and the inevitable defeat of the Hanoverian corps during combat operations. Scharnhorst titled this paper, *On the Formation of Officers and Non-Commissioned Officers*, and in it he was unequivocal in both his language and intent.[21]

Reiterating the arguments that he had made before and during the war, Scharnhorst again advocated a comprehensive program of education for all officers and non-commissioned officers, together with better and more realistic field training for the soldier. To his great joy and satisfaction, he had seen first-hand how those young officers and non-commissioned officers who had distinguished themselves through study and hard work, skill and diligence at the artillery school were those who had been the most successful under fire. Many of these men had been his students, had fought alongside him, and were frequently mentioned in his letters home and in his reports to his superiors. Scharnhorst also noted how worthless so many noblemen were as officers, and how poorly and disgracefully many senior leaders had performed under fire. These were the individuals who had scorned *Bildung*, convinced that theoretical formation in time of peace had no practical utility in war. Scharnhorst felt the main reason why so many aristocratic officers 'can neither write nor reckon' was the customary practice of most noble families of sending their least capable sons in the military. As soon as these children become officers, 'they cease to apply themselves and, on the contrary, yield to idleness and often to debauchery'. When these individuals reach the higher ranks, 'they were incapable of performing the duties of a non-commissioned officer'.[22] Noteworthy here is the fact that Scharnhorst was not the only one to spot the bankruptcy of the German aristocracy.

18 Gerhard Scharnhorst, 'Bruchstück über das Glück der Franzosen', *Nachlaß Scharnhorst*, Nr. 117, Sheets 16-17; deposited at the Geheimes Staatsarchiv Preussischer Kulturbesitz, 196/VI. HA Familienarchive und Nachlässe, Berlin (Dahlem). This fragment is printed (in part) in Lehmann, *Scharnhorst*, Vol.1, pp.232n-33n. Interestingly, in this essay Scharnhorst refutes his earlier view that 'young, dynamic generals' were solely responsible for French success.

19 Scharnhorst, '*Ueber die Uebung and Bildung einer Armee in Friedenszeiten*', *Nachlaß Scharnhorst*, Nr. 131, Sheets 4-7.

20 Scharnhorst, '*Ueber die Uebung and Bildung einer Armee in Friedenszeiten*', Sheet 6.

21 See Gerhard Scharnhorst, '*Über die Bildung der Officiere und Unterofficiere*' (between 1795 and 1801); in Kunisch (ed.), *Scharnhorst: Privat und dienstliche Schriften*, Vol.2, pp.253-58.

22 Scharnhorst, '*Über die Bildung der Officiere und Unterofficiere*', Kunisch (ed.), *Scharnhorst: Privat und dienstliche Schriften*, Vol.2, pp.253-58; the quoted passages are from p.254.

Questioning the continued relevance of the aristocratic character of the state, its civil and military arms, became a topic of discussion among 'scholars' [*Gelehrter*] in Germany long before the French Revolution. After the defeat of coalition forces during the War of the First Coalition, this debate intensified. One of these *Aufklärer* was Johann Gottlieb Fichte (1762-1814), a major figure of German idealism at this time. Provoked by August Rehberg's *Investigations on the French Revolution* (1793), Fichte published his spirited rebuttal, *Contributions toward Correcting the Public's Judgment of the French Revolution* (1793).[23] Like many of his contemporaries, Fichte greeted the Revolution with great delight and was outraged by the increasing negative influence of anti-revolutionary publications in Germany. Directing his message at state authorities, Fichte declared: 'no aristocrat, no military person in monarchical states, no businessman in the service of a court declared against the French Revolution, should be heard in this investigation'.[24] Not only did Fichte ardently defend the principles and practices of the French revolutionaries (blaming their excessive use of force on foreign intervention), he also launched a blistering attack on the feudal institutions and the traditional privileges of the nobility in Germany, to include church officials.

Outlining a truly republican view of legitimate state authority, Fichte may have taken an example from the American people when he insisted that citizens (not subjects) were bound to obey only those laws they themselves had enacted. People also had the right to renounce their state and form their own politically sovereign associations that obligated its citizens to live in peace and harmony with each other. While he noted most German princes demonstrated good will and encouraged learning, Fichte implied this was merely a façade, and sharply denounced the greed and avarice of the aristocratic classes, blaming the tyranny of these elites for bringing about the ruin of Germany. Equally culpable for the demise of Germany since the Reformation were the people themselves, who overly exaggerated the importance of their princes and slavishly obeyed them as if the aristocracy had the right to rule.

This was the legacy of Martin Luther. While Luther had criticised the injustices of the nobility against the peasantry, he strongly believed the German people should obey their early masters, regardless of the brutality of that rule. This was God's will, proclaimed Luther. When the people revolted in what became known as the 'German Peasants' War' [*Deutscher Bauernkrieg*] of 1524-25, Luther sided with the nobility against the people. Fichte wanted to sweep away this old order, especially its religious rationale, and along with it, every vestige of German particularism, which he believed had undermined the concept of a German nation. He clearly rejected the ideas of Möser and Rehberg. Invoking Lessing and his *Education of the Human Race*, Fichte insisted that only through a national revival of *Bildung* that was both egalitarian and universal in its application, could the German *Volk* obtain and preserve their independence and liberty, as Kant and Herder had preached.[25]

Interestingly, a year before Fichte published his treatise, Scharnhorst had advocated such a universal *Bildung* in his article, 'On the Advantages and Disadvantages of the Standing

23 Johann Gottlieb Fichte, *Beitrage zur Berichtung der Urtheile des Publikums über die französischen Revolution* (Danzig: Troschel, 1793).

24 Fichte, *Beitrage zur Berichtung der Urtheile des Publikums über die französischen Revolution*, pp.15-16.

25 See the interesting discussion of Fichte in Anthony J. La Vopa, 'The Revelatory Moment: Fichte and the French Revolution', *Central European History* 22:2 (June 1989), pp.130-59.

Army'. Unlike Fichte, who believed educated people had no need for standing armies, Scharnhorst understood that Europe had not yet reached the point where standing armies were no longer necessary and focused his efforts instead on finding a manageable solution to the education of soldiers. He also suggested Lessing's *Education of the Human Race* as the model program and warned what would happen if the state failed to keep pace with the art of war.

> The art of war places at the disposal of a cultured nation the means that permit it to overcome or maintain itself against a barbaric one. Without the arts and sciences making equal strides, the great work of educating the human race, which Lessing portrays as the sure path to perfection, is probably not possible. If the art of war falls behind in one nation, then it is conquered by a barbaric one, and all progress in art and culture is lost. This was the case with Rome.[26]

Echoing his pre-war commentary on the education of the military, Scharnhorst now asked how the 'ordinary citizens' of a cultured society can look favourably upon their army when its soldiers 'lack the dexterity of a proper education and training'. 'Already a large number of people believe our military does not hold very distinctive advantages for the nation'.[27]

To raise the level of education in the Hanoverian officer corps, Scharnhorst recommended that promotion to lieutenant should come only after the candidate (usually an ensign) had served time in the ranks and had passed an examination that measured not only his practical field skills, but also his theoretical knowledge. No longer should promotion to this important rank be viewed as a rite of passage for the nobility or through wealth or connection for commoners. It was time to stop pampering aristocratic prima donnas. They had to earn their rank and privileges, just like the commoner. This would be achieved through demonstrated performance of duty (or 'merit promotion' as Trew said), which would include both theoretical and practical knowledge.

Scharnhorst was fully aware how this recommendation would be received. Indeed, he anticipated its outright condemnation and rejection, and so greatly limited its demands in order to make it more acceptable to the uneducated nobility.[28] As he so aptly put it, 'There is not much to be asked for in this examination'.[29] Only the most ignorant of candidates would have difficulty passing it, but even they would most likely succeed, since Scharnhorst placed the conduct of this evaluation under the supervision of the candidate's regimental commander or the senior garrison commander. Nevertheless, the fact that the candidate had to perform satisfactorily under the eyes of his superiors and peers meant Scharnhorst was achieving some progress towards educating the ignorant nobleman.

26 Scharnhorst, 'Ueber die Vor-und Nachtheile der stehenden Armeen', pp.234-54 and 345-80; the quoted passage is from p.369.

27 Gerhard Scharnhorst, 'Die Uebung auf den Felde ist selbst den Fähigsten hier unentbehrlich', Kunisch (ed.), *Scharnhorst: Privat und dienstliche Schriften*, Vol.2, pp.258-59; the quoted passages are from Note a on p.259.

28 See the discussion in Lehmann, *Scharnhorst*, Vol.1, pp.227-29.

29 Scharnhorst, *Über die Bildung der Officiere und Unterofficiere*; in Kunisch (ed.), *Scharnhorst: Privat und dienstliche Schriften*, Vol.2, p.255.

The examination to lieutenant would comprise both a theoretical and practical element. The examinee would begin by writing a letter about his company or regimental experience. He would also have to compose a short essay in response to a question relating to the articles of war, since Scharnhorst felt most officers had little understanding of how to conduct themselves morally or legally in war. Next the candidate would have to solve problems of geometry, tactics, artillery, and entrenchments (essential knowledge that any lieutenant of infantry or cavalry must possess). This ended the theoretical portion. Traveling to a field location, the examinee would have to conduct a series of company operations before an examination commission. These included manoeuvres prescribed in the regulations, as well as the establishment of an outpost and a line of picquets.[30] Still preoccupied with the painful experiences of war, Scharnhorst closed his argument with an emotion appeal that promotion to lieutenant must rest upon demonstrated ability and merit, not upon birth, connection, or favouritism.[31] He hoped such changes would improve the quality of junior leadership in the Hanoverian army.

Turning to the formation of the non-commissioned officer, Scharnhorst noted how critically important the non-commissioned officer is to the army.

> Without good non-commissioned officers, one cannot accustom the soldier to order and obedience. Non-commissioned officers are always with the soldiers, so they know them better than the officers, and they are the ones who, through constant corrections, impress upon them the spirit of discipline.

Stating the obvious, Scharnhorst said the non-commissioned officer is the one who trains, provides, and cares for the soldier, and 'is therefore rightly the soul of the army'.[32] Sadly, as with so many officers, he felt that due to connection and favouritism, 'many quite useless people' become non-commissioned officers. To remedy this situation, he insisted that corporals and sergeants be examined periodically by their regimental commander as they drill new recruits, and as they train their soldiers in company combat movements.

Regimental officers should be present at all times to affirm the authority of non-commissioned officers. This would greatly enhance the prestige of the corporal and sergeant. Scharnhorst also wanted to end the 'humiliating' practice of reprimanding or punishing the corporal or sergeant (for some minor infraction) in front of the troops. As he put it, this leads to 'the denigration' of the non-commissioned officer, erodes his authority in the eyes of the soldiers, lowers his self-esteem, and makes him reluctance to act forcibly when he must'. It was clear to Scharnhorst that 'a main cause of the restriction of the power to punish the soldier is the egoism of the company and regimental commanders', who wanted

30 For the requirements of this examination, see Scharnhorst, *Über die Bildung der Officiere und Unterofficiere*; in Kunisch (ed.), *Scharnhorst: Privat und dienstliche Schriften*, Vol.2, p.254. The failure to establish secure outposts and maintain a secure line of pickets was a recurring theme of Scharnhorst's criticism of coalition forces in Belgium and Holland.

31 Scharnhorst, *Über die Bildung der Officiere und Unterofficiere*; in Kunisch (ed.), *Scharnhorst: Privat und dienstliche Schriften*, Vol.2, pp.255-56.

32 Scharnhorst, *Über die Bildung der Officiere und Unterofficiere*; in Kunisch (ed.), *Scharnhorst: Privat und dienstliche Schriften*, Vol.2, p.256.

'to dictate every punishment themselves. They want to unite all authority within themselves and forget that their function is to put the officers and non-commissioned officers in charge'. Scharnhorst wanted to crush this 'egoism' by restricting the authority of petty company and regimental commanders to abuse or punish non-commissioned officers.[33] He understood that the foundation of any organisation is its people, and only by giving control to those people does the organisation create leaders. The duty of the officer was to create the environment in which his subordinates could develop their natural talents and abilities as leaders.

Economic improvements and educational opportunities were also vital for raising the prestige and performance of the non-commissioned officer. Scharnhorst advocated much better pay and privileges for non-commissioned officers, 'especially the corporal in the infantry', maintaining that many potential non-commissioned officers often refuse that rank, simply because far too much is required of the sergeant and corporal without any requisite increase in pay and benefits. 'Finally, it would be extremely beneficial to the service to establish regimental schools in writing and arithmetic for improving the non-commissioned officer corps'. Highlighting the advantages of his recommendations, Scharnhorst suggested how much better the soldier would be trained and led by educated sergeants and corporals who possessed the authority of their officers, the esteem of their fellow non-commissioned officers, and the respect of their men. He then closed this memorandum with a reference to the previous campaign, writing about the want of officers and how 'extremely important' it would be 'for the service to have non-commissioned officers who would be able to perform the duties of the officer in the event of need'.[34]

After addressing the need of educating officers and non-commissioned officers, Scharnhorst advocated more realistic and intensified combat field training for the soldier. In an interesting concept paper, '*On the Exercise of Troops in the Field*', he began with the French Armée du Nord during the 1794 and 1795 campaigns in Belgium and Holland.[35] He explained why the French were victorious.

> The mutual support of the various arms, a great regularity in the movements of the various units (even with some internal disorder), a good use of the terrain, and the special events during battle, characterized the Armée du Nord in most cases in 1794 and 1795, and in this case (why not admit it), it had an advantage over the allies.

'We saw them daily in the spring of 1794', Scharnhorst continued, exercising their tactical movements and training their soldiers on the march. Meanwhile, 'we often noticed how our officers were unable to assist one other when it came to the mutual support of the various

33 Scharnhorst, *Über die Bildung der Officiere und Unterofficiere*; in Kunisch (ed.), *Scharnhorst: Privat und dienstliche Schriften*, Vol.2, p.257.

34 Scharnhorst, *Über die Bildung der Officiere und Unterofficiere*; in Kunisch (ed.), *Scharnhorst: Privat und dienstliche Schriften*, Vol.2, pp.257-58.

35 Gerhard Scharnhorst, '*Über die Übung der Truppen im Felde*' (not before 1795); in Kunisch (ed.), *Scharnhorst: Privat und dienstliche Schriften*, Vol.2, pp.263-65.

arms, the use of the terrain, on the combinations required in special circumstances, and every arrangement necessary in battle'.[36]

According to Scharnhorst, Hammerstein's force was the sole exception in the Hanoverian army. Observing the lack of combat proficiency among his officers and men, and the appalling results it was having in battle, Hammerstein had taken immediate steps to remedy the unpreparedness of his troops.

During the campaigns of 1794 and 1795, *General-Major* Rudolf Hammerstein began training his troops while in camp and on the march. As the artillery commander of this force, Scharnhorst had obtained copies of his instructions.[37] Regrettably, as he noted, other 'senior officers, whose ignorance was soon discovered', maintained that their soldiers were in camp to rest, and that such exercises were dangerous in the face of the enemy. Scharnhorst concluded just 'the opposite was proven'. By constantly training his soldiers while on campaign, Hammerstein's troops had 'become acquainted with one another', had mastered 'the manoeuvres' which they conducted, and were both physically and mentally prepared for combat. Officers and non-commissioned officers learned how to lead troops over various types of terrain and during different weather conditions, while the soldiers learn fire and movement discipline and gained confidence. They also came to know the capabilities of different weapons and how to position artillery to support their schemes of manoeuvre. What was far more important was the fact that Hammerstein's officers, non-commissioned officers, and soldiers learned how to think and act as part of a team, 'and this knowledge brings immediate advantages, which are not achieved in times of peace'. As proof, Scharnhorst offered the experience of Frederick the Great, who exercised his troops in time of war, and this produced the great victories at Rossbach, Leuthen, and Zorndorf.[38]

As he reflected on the training Hammerstein had given to his troops during the recent campaigns, Scharnhorst jotted down some thoughts on the tactical integration of light troops. In a number of interesting pieces, he used situations (most likely drawn from recent campaigns) to illustrate how light troops and sharpshooters were to fight on various types of terrain and in different scenarios, how they were to be amalgamated with line infantry as the third rank, and how were are to be integrated with cavalry and artillery.[39] In one example he discussed the use of sharpshooters during the Battle of Hastenbeck (1757). In another he analysed the defence of a bridge, using a combined arms approach. He may have been referring to the Hessian defence of the bridge at Poppenbrücke on 12 March 1795, in

36 Scharnhorst, '*Über die Übung der Truppen im Felde*' (not before 1795); in Kunisch (ed.), *Scharnhorst: Privat und dienstliche Schriften*, Vol.2, p.263. Compare Scharnhorst's commentary with the intriguing study, *Bayonets of the Republic: Motivations and Tactics in the Army of Revolutionary France, 1791-94*, in which John A. Lynn provides a fascinating account of how the French moulded their Armée du Nord into an effective military unit.

37 See 'Instrukion Hammersteins zur Übung des Tirailleurgefechts' (30 January 1795); which can be found in *Nachlaß Scharnhorst*, Nr. 79, Sheets 5-8; deposited in the Geheimes Staatsarchiv Preussischer Kulturbesitz, 196/VI. HA Familienarchive und Nachlässe, Berlin (Dahlem). Also see Hammerstein's 'Instrukion zu Regimentsmanövern' (15 September 1795), Sheets 11-12.

38 Scharnhorst, '*Über die Übung der Truppen im Felde*', Kunisch (ed.), *Scharnhorst: Privat und dienstliche Schriften*, Vol.2, pp.263 and 264.

39 The editors of Scharnhorst Papers have grouped these memoranda under the title, 'Studien über den Einsatz von Scharfschützen', Kunisch (ed.), *Scharnhorst: Privat und dienstliche Schriften*, Vol.2, pp.604-67.

which a valiant infantry effort failed to stop the French, due to a lack of artillery and cavalry support. Scharnhorst clearly recognised the importance of light infantry and sharpshooters, and their integration with artillery and cavalry in any combined arms team.

Returning his analysis of army leadership, Scharnhorst turned his attention to the nepotism and connection that was choking the life out of the army. He had fiercely opposed favouritism before the war and had seen its catastrophic consequences on the leadership and morale of the army during the recent campaigns.[40] The plundering, mutinies, and other acts of savagery and insubordination in direct violation of the articles of war demanded accountability from the officer corps, especially among noble officers. In a series of short concept papers on military discipline, Scharnhorst touched on this very sensitive issue. He noted that during the recent campaign only enlisted soldiers faced disciplinary action for their misconduct, while their noble leaders, because of their family connections, never answered for their misdeeds. Aristocrats protected themselves from accountability.[41] Nearly all officers lived apart from their men in the field and never took the time to inspect their soldiers to gauge their morale and ascertain their needs. This was particularly true of regimental commanders and general officers. Scharnhorst noted that the excuse most officers gave for the poor discipline within the ranks was that they could no longer compel their soldiers to abide by the articles or war, since it would restrict their personal freedom. As a result, 'our entire First Grenadier Battalion revolted at Vilvorde' (a small village in Catholic Brabant). Scharnhorst emphasised the fact that neither the battalion commander, his company commanders, nor any officer was held accountable or punished.[42]

Once he had defined the challenge, Scharnhorst offered his solution. The implementation of a practical and impartial code of military justice would bring order, discipline, and stability to the army. Along with judicial reforms were stern measures to enhance accountability in the army, especially among officers and senior leaders. 'Is it possible with our way of thinking, with our depraved morality, to get back our discipline?' This was the question Scharnhorst posed in a second paper, which he titled, 'Lecture: Means of Bringing Discipline to a Regiment'.[43] As its title suggests, he intended to present his ideas in the form of a lecture in which he maintained that instilling good order and discipline was a matter of 'military breeding' [*Kriegeszucht*] that officers, non-commissioned officers, and soldiers must have, and which could be achieved only through *Bildung*. 'Without discipline, a regiment would be like a horde of savage men', he continued.[44] Only by educating officers and enlisted men to respect and obey civil and military law, especially in time of war, could

40 Some interesting data on the nepotism and connection in the Hanoverian army can be found in Hann 41, III, Nr.183: *Gemeraladjutanten und Flügeladjutanten, 1792*; deposited at the Niedersächsisches Landesarchiv, Hanover. Nearly all of the adjutants in the Hanoverian army in 1792 came from aristocratic families.

41 Scharnhorst seems to have forgotten the incident involving *Capitians* Mechlenburg and Bülow.

42 Gerhard Scharnhorst, '*Discipline*' (1795?); in Kunisch (ed.), *Scharnhorst: Privat und dienstliche Schriften*, Vol.1, pp.779-80; the quoted passage is from p.780. Also see Scharnhorst's Letter of 29 April 1793 to Klara about this incident, discussed in Chapter 7 above, as well as the interesting remarks of nobleman Ompteda, in Hill (trans.), *A Hanoverian-English Officer*, pp.32-33; also discussed in Chapter 7 above.

43 Gerhard Scharnhorst, '*Vorlesung: Mittel, ein Regiment in Disciplin zu bringen*' (1795-1801?); in Kunisch (ed.), *Scharnhorst: Privat und dienstliche Schriften*, Vol.1, pp.781-82; the quoted passages are from p.781.

44 Compare this remark to Scharnhorst's Letters of 4 (to Klara) and 5 (most likely to Jacob Mauvillon) June 1793, in which he told them that a man without *Bildung* is 'an inhuman animal'. See Chapter 7 above.

discipline be restored. Soldiers must be held accountable for their behaviour, and officers must be held responsible for not only their own conduct, but that of their soldiers as well. To ensure strict obedience to the law, Scharnhorst went as far as to demand that regimental commanders be punished for any misconduct of their men and must be made to pay out of their own pocket for any looting by their soldiers. 'One will never create the spirit of discipline' unless all 'laws and commands', regardless of the circumstances, 'even in the slightest matters, are most closely followed'.[45]

Scharnhorst clearly understood the importance of good order and discipline in the army. He began his third paper summarising the key points he had made in the previous two, reiterating the need to hold regimental commanders accountable for the actions of their officers and men. Then he cited examples from history to support his case. He pointed to the famed discipline of the Prussian army under Frederick the Great, how it had been instilled ruthlessly in time of peace, and how it had sustained the Prussians under the most trying of circumstances in war. He also cited the inspiring leadership and noble character of Austrian *Generalissimo* Ernst Gideon Freiherr von Laudon (1717-1790). Upon assuming command of Austrian forces in Bohemia, Moravia, and Silesia in 1760, Laudon immediately implemented and enforced a code of conduct that ended the insubordination and lawless behaviour that had plagued the army on campaign. An aggressive and daring commander, Laudon was one of the few generals (as Scharnhorst noted) who often frustrated the designs of Frederick the Great. Turning to the War of the First Coalition, Scharnhorst concluded his commentary by praising the Hessians, 'that small corps' of 'highly disciplined' soldiers who set a noble standard for coalition forces. The professionalism of the Hessians continually impressed Scharnhorst.[46]

For some time now Scharnhorst and Wallmoden had been exchanging ideas on ways to enhance the combat effectiveness of the army. Among the topics they discussed was the artillery.[47] In April 1795, he forwarded to Wallmoden and Trew some recommendations for strengthening the artillery. He focused solely on the horse artillery, since it had become 'an indispensable part of an army', implying that if Hanover was to keep pace with the French, it must increase its mobile artillery.[48] Using historical examples from the previous campaigns, as well as from the Seven Years War, he pointed out the many benefits of mobile artillery, its fewer losses in battle, its more daring applications in combat, and its unique ability to operate with cavalry. He noted the testimony of soldiers and generals alike, who placed 'great trust' in mobile artillery. As a result, mobile artillery has become 'very popular among all armies'. Even states like Denmark and Sweden, 'who are unable to pay their military expenditures, have nevertheless introduced horse artillery as part of their present peacetime organisations'. Comparing the speed and agility of mobile artillery with heavier artillery,

45 Scharnhorst, '*Mittel, ein Regiment in Disciplin zu bringen*', Kunisch (ed.), *Scharnhorst: Privat und dienstliche Schriften*, Vol.1, p.782.

46 Gerhard Scharnhorst, '*Disciplin*' (1795-1801?); in Kunisch (ed.), *Scharnhorst: Privat und dienstliche Schriften*, Vol.1, pp.783-85; the quoted passage is from p.784. Parts of this paper are quoted in Reinhard Höhn, *Scharnhorst: Soldat-Staatsmann-Erzieher* (Munich: Bernard & Graefe, 1981), pp.94-95.

47 See the collection of source documents on this subject in Hann 41, VIII, Nr.44: *Rapporte (Berichte) über den Bestand der Regimentsartillerie. 1795-1802*; deposited at the Niedersächsisches Landesarchiv, Hanover.

48 Gerhard Scharnhorst, 'Die reitende Artillerie betreffend' (between April 1795 and November 1796?); in Kunisch (ed.), *Scharnhorst: Privat und dienstliche Schriften*, Vol.2, pp.331-33; the quoted passage is from p.331.

Scharnhorst concluded with an important sentence: 'All movements in the presence of the enemy must almost always be done with horses'.[49]

When Scharnhorst had written to the Commanding General on 14 April 1795 advocating the strengthening of the mobile artillery, he also sent Wallmoden three additional memoranda that elaborated his concept.[50] One was a plan for strengthening the artillery; another estimated the number of horses required for this expansion; while a third totalled the number of horses and personnel require to achieve this goal.[51] Wallmoden agreed with Scharnhorst. As he was leaving Hanover for his headquarters in Diepholz, he notified Trew of some key modifications he was making to improve the performance of the Hanoverian artillery. From Hanover on 28 May 1795, Wallmoden informed his artillery chief: 'Since it would be irresponsible in the present situation to procure the horses required for the 6-pounders of the mobile artillery, I have decided to take the horses from the large reserve'.[52] Wallmoden explained that he had already given the order to procure the horses and saddles, and to have them in Drebber by 2 June. He then requested Trew move the Reserve Camp to Neustadt 'as soon as possible'. Wallmoden closed his message by telling his artillery commander that he would soon be back in Diepholz, where they could discuss this and 'some other matters of detail'.[53]

Trew was obviously upset with the changes Wallmoden was making with the Hanoverian artillery.[54] Without awaiting the concurrence of his artillery chief, the Commanding General had implemented parts of the concept plan Scharnhorst had developed.[55] Earlier, during the winter of 1793/94, Scharnhorst had recommended modernising the mobile artillery based on recent combat experience, but Trew had ignored his suggestions.[56] In the heat of battle on 20 May 1794, the guns supporting Hammerstein were too heavy and cumbersome to manoeuvre, so Hammerstein had sent an urgent request to Wallmoden to have Scharnhorst and his battery of mobile artillery attached to his command for fire support.[57] Diepenbroick had also witnessed the skill and dexterity Scharnhorst had displayed in manoeuvring his guns during the fight at Hondschoote in September 1793, and had reported

49 Scharnhorst, 'Die reitende Artillerie betreffend', Kunisch (ed.), *Scharnhorst: Privat und dienstliche Schriften*, Vol.2, pp.331-33; the quoted passages are from pp.332, 331, and 333; respectively.

50 Scharnhorst to Wallmoden (14 April 1795); in Kunisch (ed.), *Scharnhorst: Privat und dienstliche Schriften*, Vol.1, pp.664-65.

51 These papers are published in Kunisch (ed.), *Scharnhorst: Privat und dienstliche Schriften*, Vol.1, pp.671-73.

52 Wallmoden to Trew (28 May 1795); in Kunisch (ed.), *Scharnhorst: Privat und dienstliche Schriften*, Vol.1, pp.669-670; the quoted passage is from p.669. An explanatory note mentions Scharnhorst as the one who composed this message in Wallmoden's name.

53 Wallmoden to Trew (28 May 1795); in Kunisch (ed.), *Scharnhorst: Privat und dienstliche Schriften*, Vol.1, pp.670.

54 This is clear in Wallmoden's Letter of 29 May 1795 to Trew, in which he acknowledged Trew's earlier Letter of 25 May 1795; in Kunisch (ed.), *Scharnhorst: Privat und dienstliche Schriften*, Vol.1, p.670. Wallmoden's letter was also composed by Scharnhorst in the Commanding General's name.

55 See Gerhard Scharnhorst, 'Gegenwärtiger Etat der hannoverschen Artillerie'/'Zu verändernder Etat' (1795/1796?); in Kunisch (ed.), *Scharnhorst: Privat und dienstliche Schriften*, Vol.1, pp.671-72.

56 See Gerhard Scharnhorst, 'Einige Bemerkungen über den Gebrauch der Artillerie in der Campagne von 1793' (Winter 1793/94?); in Kunisch (ed.), *Scharnhorst: Privat und dienstliche Schriften*, Vol.1, pp.298-303; and Gerhard Scharnhorst, '*Reitende Artillerie*' (Winter 1793/94?); in Kunisch (ed.), *Scharnhorst: Privat und dienstliche Schriften*, Vol.1, pp.303-06. These memoranda are discussed in Chapter 7 above.

57 See Klippel, *Scharnhorst*, Vol.2, p.129; and discussed in Chapter 9 above.

this to Wallmoden. Now Scharnhorst had the Commanding General's ear, and Wallmoden (who understood the vital need of modernising the artillery) implemented some of the very ideas Scharnhorst had advocated to Trew more than a year earlier to improve the speed and agility of the mobile artillery.

In his brief letter of 29 May 1795 to Trew, Wallmoden politely informed his artillery chief that each of the four batteries of mobile artillery was to be reinforced with two six-pound cannons, which were to be taken from the four batteries of heavy artillery. Judging from the dates and content of this correspondence, it seems likely Trew had once again brushed aside Scharnhorst's suggestions, unaware that Scharnhorst had also sent his recommendations to Wallmoden. Since the Commanding General had not heard from Trew for nearly a month, he decided to accept the recommendations of his General-Quartermaster-Lieutenant and gave the order to make these changes. Now he was notifying his artillery chief of his decision.

Wallmoden was well aware of Trew's passionate resistance to any change. Although the Commanding General told his artillery chief that his decision was final, Wallmoden certainly knew of Trew's dislike for Scharnhorst and his eagerness to recommend continual improvements in the artillery. He was also aware of the artillery chief's propensity to go directly to Freytag whenever he was pressured to change or to achieve his goals. Perhaps Wallmoden sought to calm Trew's anger by informing him, 'I will discuss these and various other topics in a few days with your Highborn Excellency in Diepholz'.[58] In the end both compromised. The restructuring Scharnhorst sought became just another wartime expedient and ended three years later in 1798, when the threat of a French offensive in north-western Germany had subsided.[59]

Around this time Scharnhorst began sketching the framework for a campaign study of the war in Flanders in 1793 and 1794. He titled his work, 'History of the War in Flanders in the Year 1793 and 1794, along with some Contributions to the Art of War'.[60] He had originally intended to broaden his coverage to include the conflict in the Brabant and in Holland from 1792 to 1795, but dropped this idea, probably because he was in a rush to publish something. Based on his research notes, he planned to write this in two parts. The first would be a general overview of the campaign in 1793 and would contain critical commentaries on the 'Battle of Famars' and the 'Siege of Valenciennes', as well as three specific case studies: one on outposts; another on entrenched support positions; and a third on 'what to do if attacked'. Here he planned to analyse 'the noblest principles contained in these three cases'. The second part would complement the analysis of the first with detailed maps, tables, charts, descriptions of the terrain, and the military dispositions of the forces during each campaign. This campaign study was later published in two instalments in 1798 and 1801 in *New Military Journal*.[61]

58 Wallmoden's Letter of 29 May 1795 to Trew; in Kunisch (ed.), *Scharnhorst: Privat und dienstliche Schriften*, Vol.1, p.670.

59 See the discussion on this point in Sichart, 'Das hannoversche Observations-Corps 1796', *Geschichte der Königlich-Hannoverischen Armee*, Vol.4, pp.654-65.

60 Gerhard Scharnhorst, 'Geschichte des Kriegs in Flandern im Jahr 1793 u. 1794, nebst einige Beyträgen zu der Kriegskunst' (31 May 1795); in Kunisch (ed.), *Scharnhorst: Privat und dienstliche Schriften*, Vol.1, p.674.

61 See Gerhard Scharnhorst, 'Feldzug der verbundenen Armeen in Flanders, im Jahre 1794', *Neues militärisches Journal* 9 (1798), pp.169-369; and 'Geschichte des Feldzugs der verbundenen Armeen in Flandern, im Jahre 1794', *Neues militärisches Journal* 10 (1801), pp.134-383.

Scharnhorst wanted to include maps of the area from Bergen op Zoom to Breda and Nimwegen, and from Wesel to Leer. He planned to obtain these from the recently published atlas by Dutch cartographer Jean-Baptiste de Bouge (1757-1833).[62] He also made a note to check the cost of this edition. Beneath this notation he wrote the term 'General Staff', but did not elaborate further. Significantly, the connection between military cartography and the general staff, while not discussed in this document, becomes clear in other concept papers Scharnhorst wrote, and in his later activities as a general staff officer. For Scharnhorst, military cartography was one of the critical duties of the general staff officer.

Scharnhorst concluded his book draft with two additional items. From the keywords he used, these were issues he felt needed to be addressed. The first dealt with cantonment areas and brigade outposts, the requirement for an 'assembly point signal', and financial matters regarding weapons. The second listed 'winter quarters' and concluded with a curious phrase: 'That one could not act defensively in both'. What Scharnhorst meant is open to conjecture, but based on his experience in Holland during the winter of 1794-1795, coalition forces found themselves constantly on the defensive and under the relentless pressure of the French. As a result, allied soldiers never had time to establish adequate cantonment areas, outposts, or winter quarters. At that time Scharnhorst had recommended launching counterattacks against the French to keep them off balance and to give coalition troops time to rest and recover their strength while retreating across Holland. Unfortunately, allied leaders had neither the resolve to plan or conduct such operations, nor did they have a body of general staff officers capable of coordinating the kind of spoiling attacks Scharnhorst envisioned. Moreover, coalition soldiers were clearly in no condition, both physically and mentally, to execute such operations.

When Hanover sought to replace its losses from the 1793 campaign, the glaring inadequacies within its feudal society revealed themselves in traumatic fashion. Raising troops 'encountered massive indifference and outright hostility'.[63] Peasants fled the Electorate, some poor farmers and heads of households refused to be inducted, while those traditionally exempt from military service were drafted. When Privy Councillor Ernst Ludwig Julius von Lenthe (1744-1814), head of the Hanoverian Chancery in London, presented a plan to King George on 2 December 1793, it touched off a firestorm between the army and the *Ständestaat*. In deference to the prerogatives of the ruling elites, Lenthe called for the segregation of native conscripts from foreign mercenaries inducted into the army. It seems Lenthe may have been thinking about establishing a kind of militia force composed solely of Hanoverian levies (later known as the *Landwehr*). When the king agreed to this plan and ordered its immediate implementation, the army refused to comply. Instead, Freytag established a military commission, ostensibly to study (but actually to criticise) Lenthe's concept.[64]

When the campaign of 1794 began that spring, Lenthe's plan sat in limbo, as the army focused its efforts on fighting the French. Later that summer Minister Georg August von

62 Jean-Baptiste de Bouge, *Nouvelle carte chorographique des ci-devant Païs-Bas Autrichiens* (Brussels, 1794).

63 See the discussion on the various plans to raise troops in Fox, 'Conservative Accommodation to Revolution', pp.86-90; the quoted passage is from p.86. Sichart, *Geschichte der Königlich-Hannoverischen Armee*, Vol.4, pp.112-17, provides a good overview of the recruitment process for the various arms of the service.

64 See the discussion surrounding this proposal in Lehmann, *Scharnhorst*, Vol.1, pp.265-70.

Steinberg proposed a limited military conscription.[65] Lenthe and the estates vehemently opposed this measure, since it would restrict their traditional control over people and finances. On the other hand, the army (including Scharnhorst) favoured Steinberg's concept. Scharnhorst's main concern was maintaining the wartime strength of the field regiments. Later, around 1796, he proposed this militia serve as depot battalions for the regular army. By 1799 he preferred utilising these troops as part of the land regiments.[66]

Differences between these competing plans came to a head in 1796, when Freytag assigned Prince Ernst to consolidate the opinions of some senior army generals into a memorandum to be delivered personally to the king. Generals Mecklenburg, Diepenbroick, Hammerstein, Scheither, Cambridge, and Wallmoden signed this document on 22 December 1796, in which they clearly desired to integrate both conscripts and mercenaries into the line regiments.[67] A week later Prince Adolphus wrote to his father, explaining in detail the concerns of the army's leadership. He told King George that Lenthe's proposal would seriously undermine the '*esprit de corps*' in the army. Segregating the army into two distinct groups would not only cause 'the greatest disharmony' between them, but also among the officers and non-commissioned officers, especially those assigned to train these contingents.

> The Regimental service will also suffer very much by this new plan, for the men who have but six weeks to serve will never learn their garrison duty properly, and the officers who have also nothing to do as soon as the Bataillon [sic] is on furlow [sic], will fall into all sorts of follies from what of occupation, at least it is a wonder if they do not.

Using history, the prince reminded the king that this is precisely what had happened in 1793, when hastily trained recruits were marched off to war without the proper indoctrination and training, which led to disciplinary and morale problems, as well as to health issues during the campaign. He also stressed the critical importance of unit cohesion that comes only from the integration of all soldiers into the regiments. Prince Adolphus concluded with the 'firm conviction that your Hanoverian Infantry *Service* would be ruined by this new plan'.[68] In the end, neither plan was carried out.

Meanwhile, *Oberst* Johann Wilhelm du Plat, Commander of the 7. Infanterie Regiment and now *General-Inspektor der Infanterie*, recommended important changes in the recruiting, training, and uniform standards of the line infantryman.[69] He advocated modifying the

65 Georg August von Steinberg, *Gedanken wie vielleicht beim Frieden das Hannoversche Truppen Corps eingerichtet werden könnte* (1 September 1794); in Hann 41, III, Nr.94; deposited at the Niedersächsisches Landesarchiv, Hanover.

66 Scharnhorst's evolving views can be found in Lehmann, *Scharnhorst*, Vol.1, pp.270-75, 279-80, and 337-38.

67 See the 'Memorandum', dated 22. Dezember 1796; in Hann 41, III, Nr.98: *Endgültige Formationspläne, welche vom König aus England übersandt und in Hannover einer näheren Prüfung durch die Generäle unterzogen worden sind, 1796-1797*; deposited in the Niedersächsisches Landesarchiv, Hanover.

68 See the detailed explanation from the army point of view in the Letter of 31 December 1796 from Prince Adolphus to King George III; in Arthur Aspinall (ed.), *The Later Correspondence of George III*, Vol.2, pp.529-30.

69 Johann Wilhelm du Plat, 'Von der Ausbildung und Dressur der Rekruten' (19. März 1796), *Gutakhten du Plat*, Hann 41, III, Nr. 130; deposited at the Niedersächsisches Landesarchiv, Hanover. Documents relating to the appointment of du Plat as Inspector General of the Infantry can be found in Hann 41, III, Nr.176: *Ernennung des Generals von dem Bussche zum Inspekteur der Infanterie und degleichen des Obersten zu Plat, 1780-1800.*

infantryman's equipment to reflect actual battlefield and not parade-ground conditions. The infantryman's musket needed to be modernised, the useless sabre he carried removed, and the uniform he wore changed to protect and not to decorate the soldier. The bright red, blue, green, and white colours silhouetted the soldier on the battlefield, making him an easy target for the enemy. At the same time du Plat hoped to improve the infantryman's skill in executing the close-order movements prescribed in the 1786 Drill Manual. Unfortunately, he made no mention of updating these 10-year old regulations to meet current battlefield conditions.

Seeking to develop the light infantry in the Hanoverian army, du Plat submitted a second recommendation entitled, 'Preliminary Ideas Regarding the Formation of Riflemen in the Hanoverian Infantry'.[70] In this paper he proposed adding of one sharpshooter armed with a rifle for every 10 musketeers in the line infantry. In a battalion of 498 musketeers, this would generate nearly 50 *Schützen* or skirmishers, who would fight outside the battalion line, leading the advance, covering the retreat, and conducting patrols when necessary. Unfortunately, 50 *Schützen* would hardly affect infantry tactics, since they were too few to sustain a firefight for any length of time.[71] *Oberst* du Plat's modernisation efforts were commendable and highlighted significant weaknesses of the Hanoverian infantry. Few were implemented until 1803, when it was too late to stop a French invasion of the Electorate.[72]

Complementing du Plat's ideas were two unfinished papers in which Scharnhorst discussed the education and training of soldiers during peacetime. The first was entitled, '*On the Exercise of Troops*', and dealt with lessons he had learned in combat.[73] He believed combat presented two distinct possibilities. The first was the traditional approach in which opposing forces lined up on open terrain opposite each other and then proceeded to fight. The second was non-traditional, in which one opponent refuses to give battle on open ground and choses instead to fight on all types of terrain, with his operations being covered by skirmishers. Scharnhorst felt soldiers must be trained to fight both types of combat.

In his second draft, '*On the Formation and Exercise of Troops in Times of Peace*', Scharnhorst listed four areas he felt needed further clarification.[74] These included: 'I. *Aim* of education and training', 'II. *Description of the present formation and exercise of soldiers*', 'III. *Difficulty of introducing proper education and training in a standing army*', and 'IV. *Suggestion of a means by which a more appropriate education and training could be introduced in current armies*'. Although little substance can be found in this paper, Scharnhorst did make it clear that it was time princes and their senior commanders led by example, applied their leader-

70 Johann Wilhelm du Plat, 'Vorläufige Ideen, wegen der Formierung von Schützen bei der Hannöverschen Infanterie' (19. März 1796), *Gutakhten du Plat*, Hann 41, III, Nr. 130; deposited at the Niedersächsisches Landesarchiv, Hanover. Other documents relating to the use of sharpshooters can be found in Hann 41, III, Nr.130: *Die Einführung der Scharfschützen bei der Infanterie. Ausführung von Gefechtsformationen zur Formierung von Quarres (Quarrés). (Zeichnungen). Kommandos. Schwenkungen und Marschieren, 1796-1802.*

71 The number of musketeers in a battalion comes from the table of organisation found in Sichart, *Geschichte der Königlich-Hannoverischen Armee*, Vol.4, p.34. Also see Sichart's discussion of du Plat's proposal on p.128.

72 See the conclusions of Fox, 'Conservative Accommodation to Revolution', pp.90-91.

73 Scharnhorst, '*Ueber die Uebung der Trupen*', Kunisch (ed.), *Scharnhorst: Privat und dienstliche Schriften*, Vol.2, pp.259-61.

74 Gerhard Scharnhorst, '*Ueber die Bildung u. Uebung der Truppen in Friedenszeiten*', Kunisch (ed.), *Scharnhorst: Privat und dienstliche Schriften*, Vol.2, pp.261-62.

ship equally among all troops, and implemented a more equitable and sensible code of military justice. The days of preferential treatment for noblemen, while constantly threatening the common soldier with punishment should he fail to obey had to end. There were more positive ways of motivating soldiers.[75]

Unfortunately for Scharnhorst, Steinberg, du Plat, and others seeking to modernise the army, Hanover (like its master Great Britain) remained shackled to a static medieval corporatism 'dominated by an exclusive nobility'.[76] Even though the War of the First Coalition had exposed this inertia, officials in England and Hanover remained oblivious to it. Neither possessed a robust or representative government that demanded reform. Indeed, to implement any comprehensive reform in Hanover 'would have required important political adjustments' that would have caused 'no less than a revolution in the service'. King George clearly did not want 'to test the resistance of the Hanoverian aristocracy and the estates in the defence of their long-standing privileges'.[77] While authorities in Hanover debated the merits of his proposals, *Major* Gerhard Scharnhorst created opportunities to implement his ideas and commenced the military *Bildung* of leaders in the Hanoverian army.

75 Scharnhorst, '*Ueber die Bildung u. Uebung der Truppen in Friedenszeiten*', Kunisch (ed.), *Scharnhorst: Privat und dienstliche Schriften*, Vol.2, p.262.

76 Fox, 'Conservative Accommodation to Revolution', p.i.

77 See the important discussion on this subject in Paret, *Clausewitz and the State*, p.65.

13

With the Observation Army

On 4 June 1795, Scharnhorst travelled with Wallmoden to Hanoverian headquarters at Diepholz. Over the next six years he improved and expanded his knowledge of the daily battle rhythm and divergent personalities of a major operational headquarters. At the same time, he lamented the fact that he was unable to be home with his family. Like so many others, Scharnhorst longed for a genuine peace, not just a cessation of hostilities in north-western Germany. On 6 September 1795, he told Klara he would ask Wallmoden for some home leave. He also updated her with news about her half-brothers, Georg and August Scharlock. Georg was now assigned to the 9. Infanterie Regiment where, as Scharnhorst wrote, 'I hope he will finally become an officer'. A day earlier he had written to Hammerstein, hoping to obtain for Georg one of the officer vacancies now available in that regiment.[1] With regard to August, he was unfortunately still a prisoner of war, 'even though almost all of the other officers have returned home'. Scharnhorst informed Klara that he had been told August was doing well, 'actively learning both French and English'. He also mentioned that he had asked Trew a few days earlier about the company command Trew 'had promised me', but as usual provided no additional information. In closing he wrote: 'I am working on a project, which to my sense of honour is the most important thing I have written, if it is otherwise reasonably successful.[2] What he meant here is also unclear, since he did not elaborate further. Before biding his usual 'Adieu' to his wife, a homesick Gerhard Scharnhorst wrote: 'In a few days I will see my Klara, my dear wife and children. Don't worry, my only Klara. Peace is certain. Your Scharnhorst returns this fall to your side. When I come home, little August will already be grown up and cute'.[3] Less than a week later, his optimism about the future had changed dramatically.

While Scharnhorst, his German countrymen, and their British and Prussian allies dreamed of peace, France and Austria prepared for war.[4] West of Coblenz, *Général de*

1 Gerhard Scharnhorst to Georg Wilhelm Freiherr von Hammerstein (5 September 1795); in Kunisch (ed.), *Scharnhorst: Privat und dienstliche Schriften*, Vol.8, p.516.

2 Gerhard Scharnhorst's Letter of 6 September 1795 to Klara; in Kunisch (ed.), *Scharnhorst: Privat und dienstliche Schriften*, Vol.1, pp.677-78.

3 Letter of 6 September 1795 to Klara; in Kunisch (ed.), *Scharnhorst: Privat und dienstliche Schriften*, Vol.1, pp.677-78.

4 See the excellent analysis and wonderful discussion in Chapter 7 (pp.257-312) of Jordan R. Hayworth, 'Conquering the Natural Frontier: French Expansion to the Rhine River during the War of the First Coalition, 1792-1797' (Ph.D. Thesis, University of North Texas, 2015); later published as *Revolutionary France's War of Conquest in the Rhineland: Conquering the Natural Frontier, 1792-1797* (Cambridge: Cambridge University Press, 2019).

Division Jean Baptiste Jourdan (1762-1833) led the French Armée de Sambre-et-Meuse (about 100,000 men). Opposite Jourdan were nearly 100,000 allied soldiers under Austrian *Feldzeugmeister* Count Clairfayt. In Alsace was Pichegru's Armée de Rhin-et-Moselle (approximately 90,000 troops). East of Pichegru was Austrian *Feldmarschall* Dagobert Sigismund, Graf von Wurmser (1724-97) with 85,000 men. Both Austria and France were planning offensive operations in the fall. France struck first in September, with Jourdan invading Germany. As he marched eastward toward Frankfurt, consternation gripped the greatly outnumbered German and Prussian forces in north-western Germany.

'For the past three days', Scharnhorst told Klara on 12 September, 'we made dispositions, march routes, and God knows what else'. 'And now, thank Heaven, we learn the French are respecting the demarcation line, and that you are as safe in Bordenau as we are here'.[5] The initial anxiety Scharnhorst felt when news of the French offensive reached Diepholz brought back fears of a never-ending war that would engulf Germany. He was worried that Klara 'would be all alone' and that he would be unable to protect his family should the French invade Hanover. It was a truly awful feeling as this letter reflects. Even Scharnhorst's colleagues worried about him. As he informed his wife, 'They all said they had never seen me so depressed. But if this were the case, Hanover would be totally ruined, and God knows where the military would be'. He promised to keep her posted on the situation and informed her Trew 'is back again' and had turned his furious wrath on recently promoted *Oberstlieutenant* Braun, 'like he did with me'. It appears that Braun had taken a leisurely attitude towards his duties and responsibilities in the forward area. In Scharnhorst's mind, Braun deserved his fate, since he 'has really neglected everything'.[6]

Throughout the remainder of 1795 and into the first half of 1796, Hanoverian, Hessen, and Brunswick forces (together with British cavalry in Hoya and Oldenburg) continued to execute their cordon defence of north-western Germany, while seeking assistance from Prussia and Austria.[7] In June the German forces formed 'The Hanoverian Observation Corps' of initially 10,000 men (later reinforced by another 5,000 troops) as part of their treaty obligation.[8] That month they joined Prussia to establish a provisional 'Observation

5 Gerhard Scharnhorst to Klara Scharnhorst (12 September 1795); in Kunisch (ed.), *Scharnhorst: Privat und dienstliche Schriften*, Vol.1, pp.678-79; the quoted passage is from p.678.

6 Letter to Klara (12 September 1795); in Kunisch (ed.), *Scharnhorst: Privat und dienstliche Schriften*, Vol.1, pp.678 and 679.

7 The establishment of this cordon defence can be found in Sichart, 'Der Cordon an der unteren Hunte im März 1795', *Geschichte der Königlich-Hannoverischen Armee*, Vol.4, pp.639-51. Some interesting documents related to this can be found in Hann 38 E, Nr.260: *Diplomatische Sendung des Oberstleutnants von Schulte vom Leibgarde-Regiment an den Kurfürsten Max von Köln und in das Hauptquartier des Generals Clerfayt zu Frankfurt zur Betreibung der für die Armee wichtigen Angelegenheiten; dessen Berichte daher, 09.1795-11.1795*; deposited at the Niedersächsisches Landesarchiv, Hanover.

8 See 'Formation eines Corps hannoverschen Truppen zur Aufstellung der combinirten Observations-Armee im Jahre 1796', Sichart, *Geschichte der Königlich-Hannoverischen Armee*, Vol.4, pp.69-79; and 'Das hannoversche Observations-Corps 1796', pp.651-65. The source documents for this organisation can be found in Hann 41, I, Nr.9: *Protokolle über die Einrichtung und Mobilmachung des Hannoverschen Korps von 15.000 Mann unter Befehl des Generals der Kavallerie von Wallmoden-Gimborn, 03.1796*; and Hann 41, I, Nr.15: *Verhandlungen zwischen der Regierung und dem General Wallmoden sowie dem Herzog von Braunschweig über die vorläufig noch nicht ins Feld gestellten 5.000 Mann, 05.1796-07.1796*; deposited at the Niedersächsisches Landesarchiv, Hanover.

Army' in Westphalia and East Frisia to counter any future French ambitions in northern Germany and to enforce the stipulations of the Treaty of Basel.[9]

Commanding this coalition was Prussian Duke Karl of Brunswick. As the German liaison officer to the Prussians, Scharnhorst often travelled between Hanoverian headquarters at Diepholz and Prussian headquarters at Osnabrück. He routinely visited the field locations of the various troop contingents, assisting Wallmoden with the disposition, readiness, and logistical support of the German contingents, and coordinating the Commanding General's wishes with the field commanders. In the absence of Wallmoden, his General-Quartermaster-Lieutenant had the authority to issue instructions in his name. Having grown accustomed to Scharnhorst's methodology during the recent campaign, many of the German field commanders informed Wallmoden how truly fortunate the German forces were to have *Major* Gerhard Scharnhorst.[10]

At Prussian headquarters Scharnhorst worked with a number of his future colleagues. Among these were: Duke Karl Wilhelm Ferdinand; *Feldmarschall* Wichard Joachim Heinrich von Möllendorff (1724-1816); *General der Infanterie* Alexander Friedrich von Knobelsdorff (1723-99), *Generallieutenanten* Wilhelm René de l'Homme de Courbière (1733-1811) and Friedrich Adolf Graf von Kalkreuth (1737-1818); *Generalmajore* Levin von Geusau (1734-1808), Gebhard Leberecht von Blücher (1742-1819), and Ernst Friedrich von Rüchel (1754-1824). Others were: *Obersten* Anton Wilhelm von L'Estocq (1738-1815) and Julius August Reinhold von Grawert (1746–1821); *Oberstlieutenanten* Karl Leopold von Köckritz (1744-1821), Friedrich Wilhelm Christian von Zastrow (1752-1830), and Karl Ludwig von Lecoq (1754-1829); *Major* Karl Ludwig August Friedrich von Phull (1757-1826); and *Hauptmann* Friedrich Emil Ferdinand Heinrich Graf von Kleist (1762-1823). The most kindred spirit Scharnhorst met in Osnabrück was Heinrich Friedrich Karl, *Reichsfreiherr* von und zum Stein (1757-1831), the civilian director of the Prussian War and Domains [*Kammerdirektor*] department west of the Weser River. Stein and Scharnhorst agreed on many substantive notions of civil-military relationships, and on the nature of a free, productive society. Stein was also Wallmoden's son-in-law. All of these men would play important roles in Scharnhorst's later career in Prussian service.

It came naturally for Scharnhorst to investigate and evaluate his Prussian colleagues and their military organisation. Among his papers are a number of documents containing his

9 See 'Aufstellung einer "Combinirten Preussisch-Hannoverschen Observations-Armee" in nordwestlichen Deutschland 1796 bis 1801', Sichart, *Geschichte der Königlich-Hannoverischen Armee*, Vol.4, pp.650-667. Also see Lehmann, *Scharnhorst*, Vol.1, p.200. Source documents on the formation of this Observation Army can be found in Hann 41, I, Nr.13: *Übertragung des Oberbefehls der Observationsarmee (Beobachtungsarmee) an den Herzog Carl Wilhelm Ferdinand von Braunschweig, desgleichen Kommandos der hannoverschen Truppen an den General von Wallmoden und die darüber mit dem König, der Regierung und so weiter geführte Korrespondenz, 03.1796-05.1796*; and Hann 41, 1, Nr.16: *Korrespondenz des Feldmarschalls von Freytag mit dem Herzog von Braunschweig als kommandierenden General der Observationsarmee (Beobachtungsarmee) über Formation der hannoverschen Truppen, 05.1796-06.1796*; deposted at the Niedersächsisches Landesarchiv, Hanover.

10 For example, see the Letter of 13 August 1795 from Hessian *Generallieutenant* Dallwigk to Wallmoden, acknowledging that he has complied with the orders he had received from *Major* Scharnhorst to relocate the Hessian train; published in Klippel, *Scharnhorst*, Vol.2, p.213. Klippel included some of this correspondence as examples of the trust Wallmoden and his field commanders placed in the competence and ability of Scharnhorst. The editors of Scharnhorst's Papers published similar correspondence; in Kunisch (ed.), *Scharnhorst: Privat und dienstliche Schriften*, Vol.1, pp.395-680; and Vol.2, pp.1-404.

assessments of the Prussian army, its organisation and leadership. One fragment entitled, 'The Prussian Army in the Campaigns of 1793 and 1794', began as a glowing testimony to Duke Karl of Brunswick. Scharnhorst was clearly impressed with the career of Duke Karl who 'as a young man had already gained great fame. He executed a brilliant operation in almost every campaign'.[11] Scharnhorst also marvelled at the 'great confidence' with which Frederick the Great had placed in the 'military talents' of this 25-year-old commander, 'the prudence he demonstrated in the subjugation of the Dutch patriots in 1787', and 'the indescribable love' which he had shown toward his own subjects and others. Scharnhorst attributed these traits to 'a solicitous feeling of justice and suffering humanity' that Duke Karl Wilhelm of Brunswick possessed.[12]

Another informative paper included commentary on various 'Prussian Arrangements' established following the Peace of Basil.[13] Scharnhorst made some important observations on the Prussian General-Quartermaster Staff that coincided with his thoughts on the General Staff with Troops. In Osnabrück he noticed the Prussians had just one general staff officer – *Major* Phull, with five regimental officers attached on temporary duty to assist him. He also pointed out that whenever a Prussian column moved, an officer from the General-Quartermaster Staff accompanied it. Then he mentioned how 'mounted light troops' [*Feldjäger*] served as couriers and guides for Prussian columns and lamented, 'We have no such guides'. After examining the medical department, he learned that during the 1792 campaign in France, the Prussian hospital system was 'simply awful, because everything was improvised. Now it is good'.[14] Currently, every morning a hospital official, accompanied by several line officers, is required to visit the sick to ascertain their wellness. Scharnhorst noted that the sick totalled almost a third of the Prussian force in northern Germany.

Turning his attention to the Prussian artillery, Scharnhorst described its organisation and equipment, its ammunition allocations and logistical support. He noted the different types of batteries, the types of cannon in each, and the number of horses. Unlike the Hanoverians, he observed that the Prussians did not maintain an artillery reserve. Instead, Prussian 'batteries are divided among the brigades and remain there'. He finished this portion with a short assessment of the Prussian wartime supply system. He noted that Prussian arrangements were much like the British Commissariat in the Netherlands and (like the British Commissariat) clearly did not meet expectations. To correct these shortcomings, Prussian

11 Gerhard Scharnhorst, 'Preußische Armee im Feldzuge von 1793 und 1794' (after 1794); in Kunisch (ed.), *Scharnhorst: Privat und dienstliche Schriften*, Vol.1, pp.770-71; the quoted passages are from p.770. The editorial note states it was part of an 'earlier concept'.

12 Scharnhorst, 'Preußische Armee im Feldzuge von 1793 und 1794', Kunisch (ed.), *Scharnhorst: Privat und dienstliche Schriften*, Vol.1, p.771.

13 Gerhard Scharnhorst, 'Einrichtungen der Preußen' (not after 1796); in Kunisch (ed.), *Scharnhorst: Privat und dienstliche Schriften*, Vol.1, pp.771-73.

14 Scharnhorst, 'Einrichtungen der Preußen', Kunisch (ed.), *Scharnhorst: Privat und dienstliche Schriften*, Vol.1, p.771. Also see the scathing indictment of the Prussian hospital at Grandpré, France; in Johann Wolfgang Goethe, 'Kampagne in Frankreich 1792', *Goethe Werke*, Herausgegeben im Auftrage der Großherzogin Sophie von Sachen, Band 33 (Weimar: Hermann Böhlaus, 1898), pp.76-77.

leaders had authorized small unit commanders to improvise as necessary, providing cash subsidies for local purchase.[15]

Scharnhorst ended his paper on Prussian institutions with some interesting titbits of information he had gathered about Tempelhof and his actions during the campaign in France and along the Rhine. He began with two telling sentences: 'Tempelhof's mortars had no effect before Verdun. The cannonade at Valmy was a mess, where no one knew what to do'. Both actions infuriated the Duke of Brunswick who, upon his return from France, ordered Tempelhof and his artillery to assemble at Erlangen, where he admonished them for their failure in France. The Duke informed Tempelhof of his desire 'to act aggressively on the left bank of the Rhine' should the French pursue. According to eyewitness testimony, 'Tempelhof laughed aloud'. Upon hearing this, Prussian King Friedrich Wilhelm II believed his artillery chief 'had lost his mind'. Scharnhorst explained that contrary to the king's diagnosis, 'Tempelhof was concerned'. He was a seasoned artilleryman and clearly understood the role of the artillery was to support the manoeuvre plan of the infantry or cavalry commander. Tempelhof may have thought that Brunswick's plan to act aggressively was unsupportable and may have concluded that the Duke was merely intent on regaining his reputation, since he certainly did not act as aggressively as he could have in 1792 (most likely because he did not agree with the decision to invade France in order to restore Louis XVI). In any case, Scharnhorst wrote that during Prussian operations along the Rhine, 'the Duke complained about Tempelhof, about his failure, his mortars, etc'. Fed up with the constant disputes with his artillery chief over the proper employment of the artillery, the Duke of Brunswick 'had Tempelhof arrested' and returned to Berlin.[16]

The next three topics Scharnhorst addressed were the Prussian General-Quartermaster Staff, the Adjutancy, and the Engineer and Mining Corps. This fragment appears to have been part of a larger study, since the section dealing with the General-Quartermaster Staff began with 'II'. What came before is unknown. Scharnhorst began by discussing the current organisation of the entire Prussian General Staff, which consisted of just 18 officers: two with the rank of *Oberst* (one was the General-Quartermaster; the other the General-Quartermaster-Lieutenant), four with the rank of *Oberstlieutenant* and four with the rank of *Major* (all served as Quartermasters), and eight other Quartermasters (no rank was listed). 'Six of these officers were with the army when it marched into Westphalia in 1794'. Scharnhorst noted that under Frederick, 'the quartermaster staff was not as large and did not have the present formal establishment'. Then he touched on the most significant feature of the Prussian General Staff. 'Officers of the Quartermaster Staff are for the most part taken from the field regiments, and subsequently return to the same'.[17] This was a crucial dynamic of his own concept of the General Staff with Troops, which was intrinsically coupled with the field army or troops. An isolated, bureaucratic, and separate general staff corps was clearly repugnant to him and he seemed delighted with the Prussian model.

15 Scharnhorst, 'Einrichtungen der Preuβen', Kunisch (ed.), *Scharnhorst: Privat und dienstliche Schriften*, Vol.1, pp.772 and 773.

16 Scharnhorst, 'Einrichtungen der Preuβen', Kunisch (ed.), *Scharnhorst: Privat und dienstliche Schriften*, Vol.1, pp.772-73.

17 See Gerhard Scharnhorst, 'Notes' (not after 1797); in Kunisch (ed.), *Scharnhorst: Privat und dienstliche Schriften*, Vol.1, pp.773-74; the quoted passages are from p.773.

He also wondered why some believed the Prussians 'have a separate corps, which has its own budget and its own augmentation?'[18] Scharnhorst closed his assessment of the general staff by reiterating how the Prussians used mounted light troops as field guides and couriers. Clearly, this also impressed him.

Scharnhorst briefly described the Prussian Adjutancy and the Engineers in the third and fourth parts of this segment. The former included the general adjutants, the aides, and the personal adjutants of the commanding general. He observed how Möllendorff had an entourage that included four adjutants (majors and captains), three aides (one from the infantry and two from the cavalry), and two brigade majors – for a total of nine officers to address his personal and professional needs. He then turned his attention to the engineers, noting that only 12 engineer officers had accompanied the Army of the Rhine during the campaign of 1794. In both of these sections Scharnhorst stated just the facts as he knew them and made no commentary on the large number of adjutants serving Möllendorff, nor on the comparatively few engineers with the army on campaign. This was odd, given his propensity to analyse information as he acquired it, and to compare and contrast various organisational aspects of the Prussian army. In any case, he noted that engineer *Oberst* Heinrich von der Lahr (1734-1816) had conducted the siege of Mainz. He was Chief of the Prussian 'Mining Corps' [*Minuerkorps*]. Scharnhorst then concluded his examination with some illuminating remarks: 'The Prussians have no real pioneers and sappers. The miners perform the duties of the pioneers and sappers'.[19] The title of a proposed fifth section, 'The Operations of the Army', was lined through. Nothing followed.

Scharnhorst ended his assessment of the Prussian army with a variety of topics, beginning with the artillery regiment. He noted it is 'just like ours'. He listed the types of ammunition the Prussian artillery used, its allocations, the transportation of ammunition, the number of horses per battery, and other details of interest to an artilleryman, such as Prussian gun crews have 'no carpenters', but are given two axes per gun crew. He then concluded with a significant historical fact: 'That the Prussians have so few canister rounds lies in the offensive system of the previous king'.[20] This was Frederick the Great, who preferred mobility over fire power. As a result, the Prussians suffered enormous casualties. Although Frederick later modernised his artillery, he failed to learn the value of canister fire.[21] The rest of Scharnhorst's analysis contained various topics in which he provided some interesting commentary, such as 'the lack of theory among [Prussian] officers', that Prussian infantry 'fought in two lines in these wars, but are now back to three lines', that Prussian '*Jäger* are good for nothing' [*Jäger taugen nichts*], and that 'engineer geographers' are customarily assigned 'as students to the General Staff', serving under the General-Quartermaster. This last comment he took to heart, as he later employed Hanoverian engineer officers as map makers. He also mentioned the Prussians had used French maps dating from 1740 and 1775

18 Scharnhorst, 'Notes' (not after 1797); in Kunisch (ed.), *Scharnhorst: Privat und dienstliche Schriften*, Vol.1, p.773.

19 Scharnhorst's discussion on the Prussian Adjutancy and Engineers can be found in his 'Notes' (not after 1797); in Kunisch (ed.), *Scharnhorst: Privat und dienstliche Schriften*, Vol.1, p.774.

20 Gerhard Scharnhorst, 'Notes' (not after 1797?); in Kunisch (ed.), *Scharnhorst: Privat und dienstliche Schriften*, Vol.1, pp.774-77; the quoted passages are from pp.774, 775, and 776; respectively.

21 Frederick's acknowledgement of the increasing importance of artillery can be found in Luvaas (trans. and ed.), *Frederick the Great and the Art of War*, pp.84-85, 93-94, and especially 159-63.

during the previous campaigns in Flanders (information Phull had given him). As usual, Scharnhorst included some historical discussion on combat actions during the previous campaigns. In the vignette with this paper he covered the fight for Vicoigne (8 May 1793), in which Prince Coburg defeated the French Armée du Nord, commanded by *Général de Division* Auguste Marie Henri Picot de Dampierre (1756-93). Scharnhorst focused his analysis on the role artillery played in stopping the French attack.[22]

In all of these fragmentary papers, Scharnhorst initially presented information on the current organisation and functions of the Prussian army, and then shifted his focus to a commentary on the recent war. His last set of notes contained a topical outline for what appears to be a doctrinal manual that summarised what he had learned from the Prussians. He originally titled this draft, 'A Safe and General Means', and intended to explain how to conduct an attack with an army. He provided three courses of action: (1) if the army is acting defensively; (2) if the enemy acts defensively; and (3) if one is unsure whether the enemy is acting defensively. Obviously not comfortable with this approach, he deleted this portion and substituted *On Positions and Battles* as his new heading. Under *General Rules* he listed seven topics: 'Position', 'The Security of an Army Encamped', 'Secure Camps', 'Stratagems', 'The Attack', 'Defensive Measures', and 'Retreats'. Under the section *Cantonments and Winter Quarters* he wrote: 'Security', 'Assembly', 'Position', and 'Behavior in Such Cases'.[23] Nothing more followed in this note. Once again, identical topical areas appear in other drafts and clearly indicate the winter war in Holland had a profound influence on Scharnhorst's thinking.

Perhaps the most significant topic Scharnhorst discussed dealt with hospitals. He was clearly upset with how the wounded and the sick had been treated during the war, as his emotions in this paper suggest. He began by emphasising that every hospital must have five departments. The first was for patients with contagious diseases, while the second was for those without any contagious diseases. The third was for those troops with diseases that have not yet been identified. The fourth was for convalescing soldiers, while the fifth was for the wounded. What follows is his analysis. 'The use of churches for housing the sick is shameful', Scharnhorst maintained:

> Should not the defenders of all property and goods – even civil liberties – be given some houses to preserve their lives?
>
> The soldier, who is ten times more likely to suffer misfortune than other men, who gains nothing in the sacrifice of his life, should he not have even a free roof when in extreme misery, when he has a sickness in which he sacrificed himself for others?

Referring to how the sick and wounded had been robbed and abused by their own attendants, Scharnhorst made a significant statement that clearly testified to his beliefs: if 'soldiers are still regarded as the guardian of the prince', should they not be treated with the same

22 Scharnhorst, 'Notes' (not after 1797?); in Kunisch (ed.), *Scharnhorst: Privat und dienstliche Schriften*, Vol.1, pp.775 and 776.

23 Gerhard Scharnhorst, 'Notes,' Kunisch (ed.), *Scharnhorst: Privat und dienstliche Schriften*, Vol.1, pp.777-78; the quoted passages are from p.778.

dignity and respect accorded to the prince? 'If this is not the case', he concluded, 'then the other must not be either'.[24]

The Prussian army certainly impressed *Major* Gerhard Scharnhorst. Unlike Hanover, Prussia had a fine military organisation and tradition. He had studied the wars of Frederick the Great and had concluded that Prussia was the one state that could beat the French. From Osnabrück back on 18 March, he had witnessed the Prussians marching into Westphalia to support the German defence. Exhilarated, he told Klara that the arrival of Prussian troops meant an end to French aggression, and to the 'distress' he had been suffering since the retreat from Flanders in 1794. Now 'we can beat the French', he proclaimed confidently to his wife, 'if the Prussians want to, and provided we do not make stupid mistakes'.[25]

Meanwhile, as soon as fears of a French invasion of northern Germany subsided, forces of the Hanover Observation Corps came off alert and returned to their routines. Unwilling to wait for Hanover to implement his plans for restructuring and educating the army, Scharnhorst began introducing his modernisation ideas as opportunities presented themselves. As the General-Quartermaster-Lieutenant, he put into practice the lessons he had learned from the previous campaigns. With Wallmoden's permission, he began training his General Staff with Troops. He issued staff officers a quick reference guide 'in a tabular design' that summarised their duties; the same duties he had recommended earlier.[26] As training progressed he updated his reference guide based on the practical experience gained.[27] He then informed Wallmoden that the best work an army accomplishes in peacetime is the work general staff officers perform through study, practical application of their procedures, and field training exercises.[28] He also suggested that a general staff officer direct wartime intelligence operations, especially the use of spies.[29]

Among Scharnhorst's first priorities was the training of field guides and the mapping of the Hanoverian operational area.[30] In the very first section of his memorandum on the wartime duties of the general staff officer, he wrote:

> No one would ever believe that we campaigned for 1.5 years in the area around Moucron, Menin, Werick and Courtrai without having a map of the area, and in this time our four battalions fought more than ten actions without precise

24 Scharnhorst, 'Notes', Kunisch (ed.), *Scharnhorst: Privat und dienstliche Schriften*, Vol.1, p.778.

25 See Gerhard Scharnhorst's Letter of 18 March 1795 to Klara; in Kunisch (ed.), *Scharnhorst: Privat und dienstliche Schriften*, Vol.1, pp.645-48; the quoted passages are from p.646.

26 See Gerhard Scharnhorst, 'Ueber die Einrichtung und den Dienst des Generalstabs' (25 April/2 May 1795); in Kunisch (ed.), *Scharnhorst: Privat und dienstliche Schriften*, Vol.1, pp.665-67.

27 See Gerhard Scharnhorst, 'Nothwendigkeit eines Generalquartiermeisterstaabs für die hannövrischen Truppen in Friedenszeiten' (1795/1796); and its continuation with the same title; in Kunisch (ed.), *Scharnhorst: Privat und dienstliche Schriften*, Vol.1, pp.692-94 and 694-96; respectively.

28 Gerhard Scharnhorst, 'Entwurf eines Generalstabs für das hannövrische Corps in Friedenszeiten' (1795/1796); in Kunisch (ed.), *Scharnhorst: Privat und dienstliche Schriften*, Vol.1, p.692.

29 Gerhard Scharnhorst, 'Zu der Abhandlung über die Einrichtung und den Dienst des Generalstabs gehört noch' (not before 1795), in Kunisch (ed.), *Scharnhorst: Privat und dienstliche Schriften*, Vol.1, pp.696-97.

30 On the training of field guides, see the documentation in Hann 41, I, Nr.41: *Übungen mit den Feldguiden. Instruktion für die Feldguiden*; deposited at the Niedersächsisches Landesarchiv, Hanover.

> knowledge of the terrain, even though two engineer officers could have mapped it in five to six days.[31]

Significantly, it was precisely this lack of competent engineers on the general staff that concerned the Commanding General. Wallmoden remembered just how inadequate Kuntze and Hogrewe had been. After observing how Scharnhorst was seeking to correct this deficiency, the Commanding General had in the fall of 1795 requested his General-Quartermaster-Lieutenant present him with two courses of action for a reorganisation of the general staff, one of which was to include a discussion on the employment of engineers on that staff.[32]

In his initial response Scharnhorst noted Wallmoden's specification that engineer officers be assigned to the General Staff on a temporary basis as needed.[33] Then he discussed the many requirements where engineers would be helpful, such as mapping the area of operations and routes of march, assisting with reconnaissance missions, clearing mines, leading columns, and other tradition engineer missions.[34] Next, he advocated the establishment of an institution specifically designed to prepare selected personnel for general staff duty.[35] Graduates of this school would be assigned temporarily to the General Staff with Troops for additional training and leader development. An examination that tested both theoretical and practical knowledge would determine those who would become part of a general staff corps that rotated between general staff and troop duty. These men would then be systematically educated and trained in a common doctrine and set of procedures and groomed for senior command and staff assignments. For Scharnhorst, education must become the hallmark of the military leader, not just the social polish required to enter court life.[36]

Wallmoden gave his endorsement to Scharnhorst's idea of a general staff corps that rotated between general staff and troop duty.[37] He was well aware that the General Staff under Freytag had become a sanctuary for many useless engineer officers. Scharnhorst

31 See Gerhard Scharnhorst, '§ I. Geographische Berichte und militairische Situations-Risse', '*Von dem Dienst der Officiere des Generalquartiermeister-Staabes im Kriege*' (between April 1795 and October 1797); in Kunisch (ed.), *Scharnhorst: Privat und dienstliche Schriften*, Vol.1, pp.698-700; the quoted passage is from p.700.

32 Scharnhorst's acknowledgement of this assignment and his brief initial response can be found in his letter to Wallmoden (after the summer of 1795); in Kunisch (ed.), *Scharnhorst: Privat und dienstliche Schriften*, Vol.1, pp.679-80.

33 Letter to Wallmoden (after the summer of 1795); in Kunisch (ed.), *Scharnhorst: Privat und dienstliche Schriften*, Vol.1, p.679.

34 For example, some earlier reconnaissance reports from three engineer officers Scharnhorst had employed during the defence of Westphalia can be found in Hann 38 E, Nr.239: *Recognoscirungs-Berichte des Ingenieur-Leutnants Reichard über die Wege von Osnabrück nach Ippenbühren, des Ingenieur-Leutnants Kahle über die Situationen am rechten Ufer der Ems zwischen Rheine und Lingen, des Fähnrichs Vollimhauß über die Kommunikationen zwischen Osnabrück, Lingen und Meppen (mit Zeichnungen und Skizzen), 02.1795-03.1795*; deposited at Niedersächsisches Landesarchiv, Hanover. This folder contains some beautiful maps and drawings.

35 An undated fragment written around 1795 on the 'formation' [*Ausbildung*] of the general staff officer and his usefulness for the army can be found in Kunisch (ed.), *Scharnhorst: Privat und dienstliche Schriften*, Vol.1, p.697.

36 See Gerhard Scharnhorst, 'Ohne Bildung der Officiere in der Kriegskunst, kann der Staat keine gutte Anführung von seiner Armee erwarten' (around 1801); in Kunisch (ed.), *Scharnhorst: Privat und dienstliche Schriften*, Vol.3, pp.300-18, for his polished thoughts on military education.

37 Source documents relating to this concept can be found in Hann 41, I, Nr.10: *Vorschläge und Entwürfe zur Formation des Generalstabes, 1796*; deposited at the Niedersächsisches Landesarchiv, Hanover.

stated that under his plan, four engineer officers would be required, 'so long as they become actual [*wirklich*] captains in the engineer corps'. On second thought he wrote:

> Perhaps, given a slightly different situation, one could take six officers from this corps. This would be even more useful, since it could easily be done now, with the whole establishment of a General Staff, in which the formation [*Bildung*] of a good number of young people is by far the main issue. If we achieve only this purpose, we can soon help ourselves in war.

Once again, Scharnhorst emphasised the primacy of a military *Bildung* for young leaders.

Remembering his unfortunate experience with Kuntze and Hogrewe, Scharnhorst suggested that it might be 'advantageous' to select 'eight of the most capable non-commissioned officers', four from each of the two engineer companies (incidentally commanded by Kuntze and Hogrewe), 'free them from all guard duty', and then 'train them systemically on how to draw and record on the General Staff'. He also noted that while these non-commissioned officers would initially be needed at headquarters to draw and record, they could conduct other wartime missions, such as reconnaissance and leading columns. If there was a lack of miners or sappers, they could perform those tasks as well.[38]

Scharnhorst completed his assessment with a proposal that later became standard practice and a distinguishing hallmark of leadership in the Prussian and German armies of the nineteenth and twentieth centuries. Recalling how Count Wilhelm had commissioned officers only after their outstanding performance as enlisted soldiers, Scharnhorst suggested using competent non-commissioned officers to perform the duties of an officer, instead of commissioning useless officers. 'They would perform great services in war', he maintained. 'In this work they would do all that an officer does, cost little, and willingly submit to all work'.[39] Interestingly, in his memoranda on discipline and on the formation of non-commissioned officers, he had mentioned that it might be a good idea to commission officers only after they had served successfully in the ranks. While this practice was certainly not new or unique, it appears Scharnhorst was perhaps among the first to recommend its formal institutionalisation. Indeed, because of their proven service, two of his former assistants at the artillery school – *Feuerwerker* Heinrich Ludolph Hugo and *Feuerwerker* Cuno Josua Rehwinkel, were subsequently commissioned and distinguished themselves in combat. Scharnhorst would later recommend other outstanding non-commissioned officers for promotion to officer rank.

In his formal response to Wallmoden, Scharnhorst noted that when the Hanoverians had marched off to war in 1793, only eight engineer officers had accompanied the corps.[40] 'Seldom was this number of officers sufficient'. A year later, 13 more engineers had to be added to the General Staff. Reiterating some of the themes he had covered in his earlier

38 Letter to Wallmoden (after the summer of 1795); in Kunisch (ed.), *Scharnhorst: Privat und dienstliche Schriften*, Vol.1, pp.679-80.

39 Letter to Wallmoden (after the summer of 1795); in Kunisch (ed.), *Scharnhorst: Privat und dienstliche Schriften*, Vol.1, p.680.

40 Gerhard Scharnhorst, '*Ingenieur Officiere, welche zugleich zum Generalstabe zu gebrauchen sind*' (May 1796?); in Kunisch (ed.), *Scharnhorst: Privat und dienstliche Schriften*, Vol.2, pp.7-8; the quoted passages are from p.7.

letter, Scharnhorst informed Wallmoden that there was always a need for engineers at headquarters 'to handle unexpected situations' and to be detached to the field units to assist them in the establishment of outposts and the construction of field works and entrenchments. In this memorandum he named four engineer lieutenants and two engineer ensigns who should be assigned temporarily to the General Staff. Two of these lieutenants (Schäffer and Richard) had served with him during the retreat through Holland. A third was the son of Kuntze.

A critical task of Scharnhorst's General Staff with Troops was mapping the area of operations. As the Hanoverian corps established its new positions and depots within the sector assigned to it, Scharnhorst prepared to survey and map the corps area of operations. He assigned this mission to his two stalwart engineers, *Lieutenant* Georg Friedrich Schäffer (died 1813) and *Lieutenant* Anton Heinrich Richard (1769?-1809). In his recommendation on engineer support to the general staff, Scharnhorst had told the Commanding General that Schäffer and Richard 'were the most useful' of all the engineers in the entire army.[41] To guide Schäffer and Richard, Scharnhorst provided them with precise instructions on how they were to construct a military map.

The minute geographical and topographical detail Scharnhorst sought in a military map was striking. Not only were Schäffer and Richard to highlight all the principal cities, towns, villages, and smaller communities, but also the major structures, monasteries, noble estates, and other dwellings within these locations. This even included 'the number of chimneys and stables for horses'. Names of all locations were to be 'correctly written'. Road networks, rivers and streams, and other water obstacles, as well as all distinguishing features were to be reconnoitred and noted. Schäffer and Richard were then to confer with local officials to insure all their data was correct. Scharnhorst even provided a colour scheme for his two engineers. He told them 'Rivers and streams are to be displayed in blue, and cities and villages in red'. Mountains ranges were to be drawn and shaded in black to give a three-dimensional effect, and then classified using red roman numerals. 'The highest is represented by the Roman I, the middle by the Roman II, the lowest by the Roman III'. Green was to be used for wooded areas, with '10 to 20 trees' drawn to indicate a dense forest. Judging by the specific geographical and topographical features he demanded in a military map, Scharnhorst wanted to provide leaders with a map that visually displayed the *coup d'oeil* so essential for the combat leader.[42] Thus, when the leader looked at such a map, he could instantly ascertain the salient features of his area of operations and then, using 'supposing', would determine where to place his infantry, cavalry, artillery, and support units to obtain their maximum effectiveness. This later became a standard in the Prussian and later German armies.

While the map provided a visual representation of an area of operations, Scharnhorst also demanded a detailed written description. One of the finest examples of what he envisioned is entitled, '*Military Description of the Weser-Leine-Innerste and Diemelle Area*'. This treatise

41 Scharnhorst, '*Ingenieur Officiere, welche zugleich zum Generalstabe zu gebrauchen sind*', Kunisch (ed.), *Scharnhorst: Privat und dienstliche Schriften*, Vol.2, p.7. Interestingly, the contents description of Hann 38 E, Nr.239: *Recognoscirungs-Berichte*, incorrectly uses the German name 'Reichard' to cite *Lieutenant* Richard.

42 See Scharnhorst's 'Map-Making Instructions' in Kunisch (ed.), *Scharnhorst: Privat und dienstliche Schriften*, Vol.2, pp.193-96; the quoted passages are from pp.194 and 196.

provides in excruciating detail a dissection of the four major rivers within the corps sector, along with all their tributaries and smaller streams. Included in this 17-page paper was an in-depth analysis of the rivers themselves, the structure of their banks, the bridges that cross over them, the towns they run through, and the road networks leading to each river, as well as all of the major geographical and key topographical features that intersect these rivers. Whenever practical, Scharnhorst noted any military implications associated with the terrain. For example, he mentioned how the mountain range known as the *Reinhardswald*, 'between the Weser and Diemel, with its road network, is well represented in the map of the Battle of Wilhelmsthal'.[43] Scharnhorst never missed an opportunity to introduce military history into his work.

As Schäffer and Richard were engaged in mapping the corps area of operations, Scharnhorst began training field guides using his 'Instructions for Field Guides', an unfinished manual that he was developing, testing, and using simultaneously.[44] Traveling through the Observation Corps area of operations, Scharnhorst taught selected guides how to identify the best routes of march, how to conduct a detailed route reconnaissance, how to write complete and accurate reconnaissance reports, how to recognise and use the salient features of terrain, how to lead a column of troops, and a host of other associated tasks. He even provided examples and templates for these guides. One template was entitled, '*Report on the Route Reconnaissance from Rethen via Hanover to Misburg, provided by Guide N. N.*' This sample contained the distances from place to place, the width of the roads, the time it took to travel from town to town, and a detailed commentary on the conditions of the roads and bridges, such as how many infantrymen or cavalrymen could march side-by-side, how much weight a bridge could sustain, dangerous conditions along the way, and possible alternative routes.[45] This was the kind of meticulous staff work *Major* Gerhard Scharnhorst demanded from his subordinates, and had himself given to Wallmoden and his Hanoverian, Hessian, and Brunswick field commanders during the retreat from Belgium through Holland into Germany, and in Westphalia in 1794 and 1795.

Elsewhere, Scharnhorst took time during the summer of 1796 to return to the artillery school. There he presented lectures and taught what he had learned from his wartime experience to promising non-commissioned officers and their gun crews. Classroom instruction in geometry and arithmetic took place Monday through Thursday mornings, from six to noon. Scharnhorst taught 'artillery' from 10 to 12. Afternoons were spent in 'laboratories', in which students had the opportunity to put into practice the theory they had studied in the morning.[46]

43 Scharnhorst, '*Militärische Beschreibung der Gegend an der Weser-Leine-Immerste und Diemel*', in Kunisch (ed.), *Scharnhorst: Privat und dienstliche Schriften*, Vol.2, pp.197-207; the quoted passage is from p.204. The Battle of Wilhelmsthal (24 June 1762) was one of his favourite actions, since it was a fine example of how a coalition force of British, Prussian, Hanover, Brunswick, and Hessian troops under the able command of Duke Ferdinand of Brunswick outmanoeuvred and defeated a French threat to Hanover during the Seven Years War.

44 Gerhard Scharnhorst, 'Instruction für die Feld-Guiden' (1796/1801?); in Kunisch (ed.), *Scharnhorst: Privat und dienstliche Schriften*, Vol.2, pp.181-92. Excerpts of this pamphlet are published in Klippel, *Scharnhorst*, Vol.2, pp.227-28.

45 This sample report is contained in Section 9 of Scharnhorst's 'Instruction für die Feld-Guiden', in Kunisch (ed.), *Scharnhorst: Privat und dienstliche Schriften*, Vol.2, pp.184-86.

46 See Gerhard Scharnhorst, 'Unterrichts-Stunden für die Unterofficiere und Bombardiere im Summer 1796', in Klippel, *Scharnhorst*, Vol.2, p.218.

Another major priority for Scharnhorst was preparing contingency plans for the Observation Corps. Using his position as General-Quartermaster-Lieutenant to continue his wartime practice, Scharnhorst expanded his scope and responsibility to include Prussian forces and began providing possible solutions to French operations against the entire Coalition Observation Army. One of the earliest was his 'Memorandum Concerning the Operations Plan of the Westphalian Army in 1796', and examined a possible French offensive against north-western Germany.[47] What is significant about this plan was Scharnhorst's insistence that the Observation Army could not fight a purely defensive action; it must be prepared to launch a counterstrike against the French. Significantly, Scharnhorst was not content just to drive the French back and restore the situation. Instead, he advocated an advance across the border where the Observation Army could attack the French in their locations in Holland. He also envisioned retaking Bentheim. In this plan he discussed the various courses of action the army could take, their possible military and political implications, and the challenges and risks associated with each.

In mid-July 1796, Scharnhorst provided three supplemental reports that highlighted key considerations associated with his initial operational plan. All three dealt with defensive preparations the Coalition should take in preparation for any French incursion into northern Germany. The first was titled, '*On the Type of Fortifications at Bremen on the Left Bank of the Weser*', while the second was '*On the Protection and Defence of Bremen*', and the third, '*On the Defence of the Weser between Hameln and Bremen*'.[48] That October, at the request of the Coalition Commander-in-Chief, Scharnhorst provided Duke Karl of Brunswick with a plan for the concentration of the Observation Army for a possible offensive campaign against the French.[49] Significantly, the concept contained in this plan was virtually identical to the one he had proposed more than a year earlier in March 1795. Both were predicated on the idea that the best defence is a good offense.

Around this time Scharnhorst finished reading French Citizen Pierre David's *Chronological History of the Operations of the Army of the North* (1796) and decided that David's partisan commentary required a firm rebuttal. When ordering this book, Scharnhorst told Christian Helwing: 'This is the title of a work which is most important to me, for which I would give

47 Gerhard Scharnhorst, 'Memoir, den Operations-Plan der westphälischen Armee im Jahr 1796 betreffend' (1796); in Kunisch (ed.), *Scharnhorst: Privat und dienstliche Schriften,* Vol.2, pp.14-20. This document can also be found in Klippel, *Scharnhorst,* Vol.2, pp.252-58. Other documents which Klippel cites can be found in Hann 41 I, Nr.12 and Nr.14: *Operationsplan der sogenannten Westphälischen Armee, Projekt des Majors Scharnhorst mit Planskizze, 1796*; deposited at the Niedersächsisches Landesarchiv, Hanover.

48 Gerhard Scharnhorst, '*Ueber dei Beschaffenheit der Festungs Werke von Bremen am linken Ufer der Wesel*' (18 July 1796); '*Ueber die Dekung und Vertheidigung von Bremen*' (July 1796); and 'Ueber die Vertheidigung der Weser Zwischen Hameln und Bremen' (July 1796); in Kunisch (ed.), *Scharnhorst: Privat und dienstliche Schriften,* Vol.2, pp.20-23; 23-25; and 26-27; respectively. All three reports can be found in Klippel, *Scharnhorst,* Vol.2, pp.220-26.

49 Gerhard Scharnhorst, *Ueber die Versammlung der Demarkations-Armee 1796* (October 1796); in Kunisch (ed.), *Scharnhorst: Privat und dienstliche Schriften,* Vol.2, pp.38-39. Documents relating to this relocation can be found in Hann 41, I, Nr.11: *Dislokation (räumliche Truppenverteilung) der Truppen an der Weser und Hunte, 1796*; Hann 41, I, Nr. 21: *Korrespondenz mit den verschiedenen zum Marsch bestimmten Generälen und den vorgesehenen Regimentern, 08.1796-11.1796*; Hann 41, I, Nr.22: *Kommunikationen des Feldmarschalls von Freytag mit dem General Wallmoden über die im Felde stehenden Truppen, 08.1796-10.1796*; and Hann 41, I, Nr.23: *Marschsachen, 09,1796-10,1796*; deposited at the Niedersächsisches Landesarchiv, Hanover.

everything in the world if I could obtain it'.[50] In his critique of David's work, Scharnhorst told Wallmoden:

> It is full of inaccuracies, and to a large extent detrimental to the troops and commanding generals. I believe that now is the time to publish a true story of this campaign, to disprove the falsehoods which have been circulated so far, but have been, in a certain way, only casually disproved in anecdotal accounts. It is therefore necessary that such a history should be documented, if it is to inspire confidence and faith and has an intrinsic value.[51]

He then requested a number of key documents (orders, dispositions of forces, correspondence, war diaries, etc.) from Wallmoden and his adjutant *Oberstlieutenant* Löw von Steinfurt to complete his research for this project. Ten days later he wrote to Hammerstein, informing him of his intent and requesting copies of the war diaries Hammerstein had in his possession.[52]

As Scharnhorst was compiling the documentation for his study, he was also spending considerable time and effort on the logistical requirements of the Observation Corps. In his letter of 10 November 1796 to the Commanding General, he informed Wallmoden: 'I have carefully examined the selection of the columns and camps which the engineer officers and guides have undertaken in carrying out the task assigned to them'.[53] He then told the Commanding General that he had personally toured most of the cantonment areas and would provide him with a detailed report when his inspection of the entire area of operations was complete.

From the establishment of the Hanoverian Observation Corps and the Allied Observation Army, *Major* Gerhard Scharnhorst was actively involved in a host of various projects pertaining to the operations of the Observation Army and modernising the Hanoverian army. While not the senior general staff officer at Hanoverian headquarters, he assumed the leadership of its General Staff with the approval of the Commanding General. Wallmoden was continually impressed with the energy and drive of his General-Quartermaster-Lieutenant. It seemed as though Scharnhorst never slept. He was constantly on the move, coordinating the needs of the German forces with those of the Prussians. He was developing contingency plans for the Observation Army, implementing his vision for a 'General Staff with Troops', training engineers and sergeants in the duties and responsibilities of cartographers and field guides, keeping abreast with the latest historical publications, and dreaming about being home with his family.[54] *Major* Gerhard Scharnhorst was about to accomplish that extraordinary achievement he had repeatedly told Klara he would attain.

50 See Gerhard Scharnhorst's Letter of 28 October 1796 to Christian Dietrich Helwing; in Kunisch (ed.), *Scharnhorst: Privat und dienstliche Schriften*, Vol.2, pp.40-41; the quoted passage is from p.40.

51 Scharnhorst to Wallmoden (10 November 1796); in Kunisch (ed.), *Scharnhorst: Privat und dienstliche Schriften*, Vol.2, pp.52-53; the quoted passage is from p.52.

52 Scharnhorst to Hammerstein (20 November 1796); in Kunisch (ed.), *Scharnhorst: Privat und dienstliche Schriften*, Vol.2, p.55.

53 Scharnhorst to Wallmoden (10 November 1796); in Kunisch (ed.), *Scharnhorst: Privat und dienstliche Schriften*, Vol.2, p.52.

54 Documentation on Scharnhorst's activities during this period can be found in Hann 41, I, Nr.26: *Verschiedene Nachrichten, besonders Privatkorrespondenzen unter anderem des Majors Scharnhorst über die damalige Lage des Kurfürstentums Hannover, 1796-1797*; deposited at the Niedersächsisches Landesarchiv, Hanover.

14

General-Quartermaster-Lieutenant

General der Cavallerie Johann Ludwig, *Reichsgraf* von Wallmoden-Gimborn was truly impressed and profoundly grateful to *Major* Gerhard Scharnhorst for his extraordinary performance of duty. During the two years since Wallmoden had requested that King George promote Scharnhorst and appoint him to the special post of General-Quartermaster-Aide, the Commanding General had witnessed his trustworthy subordinate almost singlehandedly hold the army together during the disastrous retreat from Flanders through Holland and during the combat in Westphalia. Due to the incapacity of Kuntze, Scharnhorst had assumed the duties of General-Quartermaster-Lieutenant during those years. On 24 June 1796, Wallmoden once again showed his appreciation to Scharnhorst when he had King George appoint him to the prestigious post of General-Quartermaster-Lieutenant of the Hanoverian Observation Corps (and *de facto* General-Quartermaster of the entire Hanoverian army).[1] *Major* Gerhard Scharnhorst was now the senior general staff officer in the Hanoverian army. Significantly, his appointment highlighted the great schisms within the Hanoverian army and came about only after an intense and bitter disagreement between Wallmoden and Freytag.

When the German forces established the Hanoverian Observation Corps in June 1796, its table of organisation listed just one General-Quartermaster-Lieutenant.[2] Interestingly, no General-Quartermaster was appointed. With the death of Estorff in January 1796, Freytag named Kuntze as the General-Quartermaster (citing his seniority). Freytag never consulted Wallmoden, who immediately rejected Kuntze. The field marshal then placed Kuntze in command of the Engineer Corps.[3] Shortly afterwards, Hogrewe wrote to Freytag on 23 March, seeking the General-Quartermaster-Lieutenant post. Freytag readily agreed with Hogrewe's request. It appears that Freytag was using the General-Quartermaster-Lieutenant post as a means of rewarding two of his loyal favourites. Freytag wanted to provide both Hogrewe and Kuntze with salary increases but could not do so legally based

1 Documents relating to this appointment can be found in Hann 41, III, Nr.187: *Ernennung des Majors Scharnhorst zum Oberstleutnant und Generalquartiermeister. (Namenslisten von Oberstleutnants, Majoren und Kapitänen beziehungsweise Rittmeistern), 1796-1797*; deposited at the Niedersächsisches Landesarchiv, Hanover, and cited by Klippel below.

2 See Sichart, *Geschichte der Königlich-Hannoverischen Armee*, Vol.4, p.70. The position is listed as '1 Major, General-Quartermaster-Lieutenant'.

3 Klippel, *Scharnhorst*, Vol.2, p.235.

on their respective ranks. The General-Quartermaster-Lieutenant post was the ideal solution, since it came with a substantial salary supplement. Freytag informed the Hanoverian Chancery in London on 7 May of his decision.[4]

Freytag's communication of 7 May 1796 reveals a great deal about the Hanoverian officer corps. Professional qualifications clearly never played a role in Freytag's decision-making process. His sole intent was to reward members of his inner circle. When Wallmoden rejected Kuntze (based on his physical inability to perform his duties during the previous campaigns), Freytag gave him command of the Engineers, falsely telling King George that Kuntze could not occupy both the General-Quartermaster post and be Chief of the Engineer Corps at the same time. Interestingly, the late Estorff had served simultaneously as the General-Quartermaster and Inspector-General of the Cavalry.[5]

By his own admission, the field marshal told the king he was 'anxious to propose another person' and quickly chose Hogrewe after receiving the latter's request. Freytag justified his choice, telling King George that Hogrewe 'has rendered himself meritorious beyond his usual service, and has shown much diligence in teaching the royal princes'. Freytag was referring to when the Duke of York was in Hanover in the 1780s and *Capitain* Hogrewe had taught him geometry and trigonometry, and how to draw maps.[6] During the campaigns of 1793 and 1794, *Major* Hogrewe was a member of York's staff.[7]

Freytag revealed his true intent in his next sentence. He told the king that while on campaign, Hogrewe had been paid the salary of a major, even though he should have been paid the salary of a captain, his true rank. Now that active campaigning was over and Hogrewe was back in Hanover, he was receiving the pay of an actual [*wirklich*] captain. Freytag wanted to provide Hogrewe with a salary increase and informed King George that appointing him as General-Quartermaster-Lieutenant 'would not only reward and compensate him', but would also serve the army well.[8] In Freytag's mind, Hogrewe's desires came first; the needs of the army were never in question.

Freytag's letter clearly shows the degree of favouritism that existed in the Hanoverian army. During the War of the First Coalition, Freytag disregarded regulations and had Hogrewe paid the salary of a major. At the same time, Trew followed regulations implicitly and had Scharnhorst paid the salary of a lieutenant. The fact that Trew did not care for Scharnhorst may certainly have played a role here, even though Trew always said he had to abide by army regulations. Now that campaigning was over for Hogrewe and he in Hanover, Freytag could not justify paying him the salary of a major, and so looked for other means to assist Hogrewe. Meanwhile, Scharnhorst was a *Titular-Major* still actively involved in operations but was being paid the salary of a captain. Scharnhorst may have been aware of Freytag's nepotism, as his letter to the Prussian liaison officer at Hanoverian headquarters

4 See Freytag's Letter of 7 May 1796 to the Hanoverian Chancery in London; in Klippel, *Scharnhorst*, Vol.2, pp.235-36.

5 See Sichart, *Geschichte der Königlich-Hannoverischen Armee*, Vol.4, p.12 (1789) and p.55 (1795). In both years, Kuntze is listed as General-Quartermaster-Lieutenant. In 1795, Scharnhorst is also listed as a General-Quartermaster-Lieutenant. This is why Scharnhorst is often cited in official documents as the 'Second Aide to the General-Quartermaster', while Kuntze is considered the First Aide.

6 See the discussion of York's education in Hanover; in Derek Winterbottom, *The Grand Old Duke of York*, p.14.

7 Demet, *'We are Accustomed to do our Duty'*, p.135.

8 Klippel, *Scharnhorst*, Vol.2, pp.235-36; the quoted passages are from p.235.

suggests.[9] This was just another of the many sources of frustration that continually beset Gerhard Scharnhorst.

King George recommended prudence. In his letter of 24 May, the king suggested Freytag consult the commanding general, reminding him that Wallmoden was the one to decide who became his General-Quartermaster-Lieutenant. As the king told the field marshal:

> Due to the many and close relationships in which the General-Quartermaster-Lieutenant has with the Commanding General, we consider it fair and necessary that this post be filled by a person who our General of Cavalry von Wallmoden Gimborn finds acceptable in every respect.[10]

Significantly, Wallmoden was well aware of the Freytag's schemes. Even before Freytag had written to London in early May, the Commanding General had requested Scharnhorst provide him the exact date of his appointment as Major and General-Quartermaster-Aide, and to provide copies of these official transcripts. From Hanover on 10 April, Scharnhorst responded to Wallmoden's request. In his closing sentence he told the Commanding General that his appointment as General-Quartermaster-Aide was 'for me alone and set up as a patent'.[11]

Not surprisingly, Wallmoden selected *Titular-Major* Scharnhorst as his General-Quartermaster-Lieutenant. On 30 May he notified Privy Councilor Lenthe in London of his decision.[12] Two days later the Commanding General informed the field marshal. Wallmoden told Freytag that Scharnhorst was his choice, referring to 'the honour, which the king kindly conferred upon me'. He then used the field marshal's own words and rationale, stating that because Kuntze could not serve as the General-Quartermaster-Lieutenant and command the Engineer Corps at the same time, and because Scharnhorst had served for two years as the 'Second Aide to the General-Quartermaster', his seniority made him the logical choice. Wallmoden never mentioned Hogrewe, but closed his letter indicating he was aware of Freytag's duplicitous purpose: 'From the point of view of salary, it seems to me to be an allowance based on other circumstances, which has absolutely nothing to do with the duty of a First or Second Aide to the General-Quartermaster'.[13] When Freytag realised he would not be able to achieve his goal of rewarding his favourites using the General-Quartermaster-Lieutenant post, he sought another approach.

On 4 June 1796, Freytag wrote to King George, once again misleading the king regarding his knowledge of and involvement in the selection of the General-Quartermaster-Lieutenant. 'I have in modesty', he began his letter, 'consulted with the General of Cavalry Count von Wallmoden Gimborn', asking his 'forgiveness' because 'it was not yet known to me' that the Commanding General 'intended the Titular Major (von) Scharnhorst of the artillery'

9 See Gerhard Scharnhorst's Letter of 15 February 1797 to Karl von Lecoq; in Kunisch (ed.), *Scharnhorst: Privat und dienstliche Schriften*, Vol.2, pp.69-71.

10 King George III to *Feldmarschall* Wilhelm von Freytag (24 May 1796); in Klippel, *Scharnhorst*, Vol.2, p.236.

11 Scharnhorst to Wallmoden (10 April 1796); in Kunisch (ed.), *Scharnhorst: Privat und dienstliche Schriften*, Vol.2, p.6. This correspondence is also cited in Klippel, *Scharnhorst*, Vol.2, pp.235-36.

12 Klippel, *Scharnhorst*, Vol.2, p.237. Lenthe had succeeded Alvensleben in 1795.

13 Wallmoden's Letter of 1 June 1796 to Freytag is published in Klippel, *Scharnhorst*, Vol.2, p.237.

as General-Quartermaster-Lieutenant. Freytag continued by saying, 'this Scharnhorst was already in 1794, the 2nd Aide of the General-Quartermaster, at a time when I did not know of or had command influence over his advancement'.[14]

What a blatant lie! How could Freytag not know of Scharnhorst's appointment as Second Aide to the General-Quartermaster? The fact is that Freytag was intimately involved trying to prevent Scharnhorst's appointment as Second Aide to the General-Quartermaster, especially when the king wanted to know from Wallmoden if Kuntze should be send home.[15] Because the General-Quartermaster-Lieutenant position was 'now out of the question', Freytag requested the king 'consider' granting both Kuntze and Hogrewe the salary supplements he had originally intended for them using the General-Quartermaster-Lieutenant post. On 24 June, King George granted both Kuntze and Hogrewe their salary supplements. More importantly, the king recognised Freytag's duplicity here, specifically telling the field marshal that these stipends were to be considered 'not as the salary of a General-Quartermaster-Aide, but only as a supplement' to their salary as captains.[16]

Unknown to Scharnhorst at the time, and in direct defiance of his king, Freytag had Hogrewe paid the special allowance that came with the General-Quartermaster-Lieutenant position.[17] When news of this reached Wallmoden, he rushed to Scharnhorst's aid, reminding Freytag that King George himself had appointed Scharnhorst as the General-Quartermaster-Lieutenant. He then demanded that the special allowance for that position be paid to Scharnhorst. Although the documentary evidence is sketchy here, it does not appear that Wallmoden had knowledge of the king's admonition to Freytag not to use the salary supplement of the General-Quartermaster-Lieutenant to reward his favourites. Freytag must have known this, for in his response to Wallmoden, he told the Commanding General that what King George had done in 1794 when he had 'created' the Second Aide to the General-Quartermaster was a personal favour to Wallmoden. Both the position and rank were temporary wartime expedients. In direct contradiction to what he had told King George, Freytag informed Wallmoden he had never agreed to this special arrangement for Scharnhorst, reminding the Commanding General that he, Freytag, (and not Wallmoden) administered Hanoverian military affairs and could have the stipend paid to whomever he pleased.[18]

14 Freytag to George III (4 June 1796); in Klippel, *Scharnhorst*, Vol.2, p.238.

15 See the testimony of Wallmoden's *Adjudant* Georg Carl Löw von und zu Steinfurt to the Commanding General (November 1796?); cited in Klippel, *Scharnhorst*, Vol.2, pp.242-43.

16 George III to Freytag (24 June 1796); in Klippel, *Scharnhorst*, Vol.2, pp.238-39.

17 On the organisational chart of the Hanoverian Observation Corps in 1796, only Scharnhorst is listed as the General-Quartermaster-Lieutenant. See Sichart, 'Das hannoversche Observations-Corps 1796', *Geschichte der Königlich-Hannoverischen Armee*, Vol.4, p.652.

18 See the significant summary of these events by Wallmoden's *Adjudant* Georg Carl Löw von und zu Steinfurt to Wallmoden (November 1796?); cited in Klippel, *Scharnhorst*, Vol.2, pp.242-43. Some of the source documents can be found among Wallmoden's personal papers; in Hann 38 E: *Dienstregistratur des Feldmarschalls Grafen von Wallmoden-Gimborn über den französischen Krieg, 1792-1803*; as well as in the files of Freytag's administration of army affairs; in Hann 41, III, Nr.185: *Wiederübernahme des Kommandos im Lande von seiten des Feldmarschalls von Freytag, 1794*; deposited at the Niedersächsisches Landesarchiv, Hanover.

When Scharnhorst learned of this injustice, it must have reminded him of the treatment he had endured under Trew.[19] So he wrote to the Wallmoden on 10 November, requesting permission to contact Freytag directly. The end of his letter to the Commanding General is telling: 'I am afraid that when the field marshal promises someone, he does not even think of me'.[20] It seems that when competitive desires arose among officers in the Hanoverian army, senior officials like Trew and Freytag automatically singled out outsiders like Scharnhorst as the target of their collective fears, rather than establishing written standards clarifying professional qualifications for rank and position.[21] This was the mechanism the Hanoverian elites used to maintain order in their feudal society. Having written standards might have eased tensions among officers and their competitive desires but would have undermined connection and the use of favouritism associated with the ways of the ruling elites. The exchange of letters between Scharnhorst and Freytag certainly confirms this.

Scharnhorst's letter of 17 November 1796 to Freytag reveals the character of the General-Quartermaster-Lieutenant. Scharnhorst began by noting how he had always served the king diligently and faithfully as the Second Aide to the General-Quartermaster, 'since the beginning of the second campaign'. Due to his professional qualifications and performance of duty, he felt he was entitled to the special allowance of the General-Quartermaster-Lieutenant. He pointed out to Freytag that this salary supplement would go a long way to meet the numerous expenses he was incurring daily, 'traveling' throughout the Hanoverian area of operation, accomplishing his official and 'far-flung duties' as the General-Quartermaster-Lieutenant, 'and acquiring maps and books'. He ended his letter by noting, 'I would have long since taken the liberty' to obtain this allowance had he known it existed, and had he not been away from headquarters performing his official duties.[22]

Freytag answered Scharnhorst on 21 November. His response also reveals a great deal about his character. Freytag never acknowledged Scharnhorst, only that he had received a letter from 'the Major' with 'his mentioned expectation'. The field marshal informed 'the Major' that the special allowance he was seeking was not some 'fixed sum' [*Fixum*] that comes automatically with the General-Quartermaster-Lieutenant post; rather, it was 'a personal extraordinary honorarium' [*ein persönliches Extraordinarium*] given to deserving officers. In Freytag's mind, 'the Major' had done nothing worthy or deserving of this honour.[23] Yet, Kuntze had received this special allowance when he was the General-Quartermaster-Lieutenant, even though he had been unable to perform his duties adequately throughout most of the war. Indeed, it was not an honorarium for deserving officers as Freytag wrote; it automatically came with the position, as Wallmoden had told the field marshal. Hogrewe

19 Scharnhorst never did get the company command Trew had promised him.

20 Scharnhorst to Wallmoden (10 November 1796); in Klippel, *Scharnhorst*, Vol.2, p.239. The complete letter is published in Kunisch (ed.), *Scharnhorst: Privat und dienstliche Schriften*, Vol.2, pp.52-53: the quoted passage is from p.53.

21 On this mentality, see the interesting discussion in Chapter 2 (pp.12-23) of Yvonne Freccero (trans.), René Girard, *The Scapegoat* (Baltimore: The Johns Hopkins University Press, 1989). Girard suggests that all social arrangements are characterized by scapegoating and oppression. This was certainly true in Scharnhorst's life.

22 See Gerhard Scharnhorst to Wilhelm von Freytag (17 November 1796); in Kunisch (ed.), *Scharnhorst: Privat und dienstliche Schriften*, Vol.2, pp.53-54: the quoted passages are from p.54. The General-Quartermaster-Lieutenant stipend was intended for the expenses Scharnhorst was incurring.

23 Freytag's Letter of 21 November 1796 to Scharnhorst can be found in Klippel, *Scharnhorst*, Vol.2, p.240.

was not the General-Quartermaster-Lieutenant. He was back home receiving the salary supplement King George had provided to his captain's pay, plus whatever income he made from his company command.[24] Why then did he need the special allowance of the General-Quartermaster-Lieutenant?

In an attempt to circumvent Freytag, Wallmoden appealed directly to King George. Wallmoden knew the allowance of the General-Quartermaster- Lieutenant position was established 'by law'.[25] It looks as though Freytag clearly believed he was above the law. He no doubt used his relationship with the king to do basically whatever he wished. In this case it also appears Lenthe intervened to frustrate Wallmoden's plan; for the Commanding General's letter most likely never reached the king. Instead, Lenthe and Freytag crafted a clever reply that clearly failed to address Wallmoden's concerns, but placed Scharnhorst's career in jeopardy.

On 11 November 1796, Freytag and Lenthe had King George formally appoint Scharnhorst to the Hanoverian General Staff. He was no longer assigned to the artillery regiment.[26] Then on 22 November, Freytag notified Wallmoden that Scharnhorst would receive the salary, ration allowance, and other benefits equivalent to a major of cavalry.[27] The Commanding General then informed his General-Quartermaster-Lieutenant, who was overjoyed. Scharnhorst thanked Freytag in a letter of 28 November, telling the field marshal that he was grateful to the king for this appointment and would 'live up to the trust given to me by his Royal Highness'.[28] The next day he wrote to Hammerstein to tell him the good news, especially his new salary and benefits. 'For as long as I live', Scharnhorst told Hammerstein, 'I will never forget the gratitude which I am indebted to you'.[29] Judging from the remarks Scharnhorst made to Hammerstein, it appears that the general may have also intervened on his behalf.

From London, *Oberstlieutenant* Georg Carl Löw von und zu Steinfurt (1750-1811) wrote to Walmoden about the discussions within the Hanoverian Chancery regarding Scharnhorst and his appointment as General-Quartermaster-Lieutenant. Löw's insights are truly significant and reveal much about the nepotism and connection that plagued the Hanoverian military. He informed the Commanding General that he was 'very much connected to the circumstances surrounding the advancement of Major Scharnhorst to the General-Quartermaster'. He noted 'how much the Field Marshal [Freytag] has disliked him' [Scharnhorst], and 'how much he [Freytag] was against his first advancement' [in 1794]. Löw told Wallmoden that those 'nearest to the field marshal' never expected the Commanding

24 *Titular-Major* Hogrewe was 'Chef der Pontonnier-und Pionier-Compagnie'. See Sichart, *Geschichte der Königlich-Hannoverischen Armee*, Vol.4, p.19. The same listing shows *Titular-Major* Kuntze as 'Chef der Mineur-und Sappeur-Compagnie'. These were the two engineer companies Scharnhorst had mentioned to Wallmoden in his discussion of engineers on the General Staff.

25 See Lehmann, *Scharnhorst*, Vol.1, p.285. Sadly, this is all Lehmann writes about this significant controversy.

26 Information on Scharnhorst's permanent assignment to the Hanoverian General Staff can be found in Klippel, *Scharnhorst*, Vol.2, p.240 (Note).

27 Freytag to Wallmoden (22 November 1796); in Klippel, *Scharnhorst*, Vol.2, p.241.

28 Scharnhorst to Freytag (28 November 1796); in Klippel, *Scharnhorst*, Vol.2, p.242. This letter can also be found in Kunisch (ed.), *Scharnhorst: Privat und dienstliche Schriften*, Vol.2, pp.55-56: the quoted passage is from p.56.

29 Scharnhorst to Hammerstein (29 November 1796); in Kunisch (ed.), *Scharnhorst: Privat und dienstliche Schriften*, Vol.2, p.56.

General to recommend Scharnhorst to succeed Estorff, and related how Lenthe and other courtiers 'expressed their astonishment' that Wallmoden would not simply acquiesce to Freytag when he had tried to appoint Kuntze and then Hogrewe to that post, even after Wallmoden (having seen first-hand their poor performance during the recent campaigns) had made his rationale clear to Freytag. Löw agreed completely with Wallmoden's assessment, stating that both 'Kuntze and Hogrewe were quite ineffective and useless'.[30] According to Löw, it was the tenacity and persistence of the Commanding General that had gained for *Major* Scharnhorst the prestigious post of General-Quartermaster-Lieutenant.[31] Since the position of General-Quartermaster remained vacant, *Major* Gerhard Scharnhorst was now the senior general staff officer in the Hanoverian army.

In his letter to Wallmoden, Löw von Steinfurt also commended on the educational reforms Scharnhorst had recommended to the Commanding General. He agreed completely with Scharnhorst's demand that soldiers be educated and trained for war during times of peace. Löw also believed that 'a faulty mentality' had engendered the pre-war 'ridicule and enmity' toward those who studied their profession. He asked Wallmoden 'to make it an honour to speak of future war, to present it as much as possible to our young soldiers', impressing upon them the 'highly probable possibility' that in the future, war was 'almost certain to engulf us'. In closing, Löw von Steinfurt recommended what Scharnhorst had long advocated: 'This formation [*Bildung*] for future war can and must be the primary mission of the General-Quartermaster, and its daily and incessant occupation'.[32] Scharnhorst could not have said this any better.

Another bright moment greeted the Scharnhorst family on 29 December 1796, when Klara gave birth to her fifth child, a daughter they named Anna Sophie Emilie. Interestingly, shortly after the birth of August 20 months earlier, Scharnhorst had ordered a copy of the recently published book, *On Virginity, Marriage, and Sexual Intercourse* (1794), one of the Enlightenment works on sexuality by the Berlin pharmacist and publisher Christian Gottlieb Flittner (1770-1828).[33] Scharnhorst never revealed why he wanted this book. Perhaps he and Klara sought to educate themselves on natural family planning.

As Scharnhorst reflected on the past year, recent dealings with Hanoverian officials may have turned his thinking to what Rousseau had written about the evils of a society based on class and privilege, and how the nobility relied on oppression and exclusion to uphold its own status. He may have remembered how he had expressed similar thoughts to Klara during the campaigns. Scharnhorst clearly possessed more natural talent and ability, along with a far greater acuity of mind, than did most of his aristocratic colleagues. Why Trew, Freytag, and Lenthe disliked him so much was unclear. Why they refused to acknowledge his creative work and faithful service to Hanover is also unknown. Clearly

30 Löw von Steinfurt to Wallmoden (November 1796?); cited in Klippel, *Scharnhorst*, Vol.2, pp.242-43. Scharnhorst had also noted the uselessness of Kuntze and Hogrewe in several of his letters to Klara.

31 For example, see the forceful Letter of 30 May 1796 from Wallmoden to Lenthe, stating clearly that Scharnhorst was his choice for General-Quartermaster-Lieutenant; in Hann 41, III, Nr.187: *Ernennung des Majors Scharnhorst zum Oberstleutnant und Generalquartiermeister, 1796-1797*, Sheets 30-31; deposited at the Niedersächsisches Landesarchiv, Hanover; and only mentioned in passing in Klippel, *Scharnhorst*, Vol.2, p.237.

32 Löw von Steinfurt to Wallmoden (November 1796?); cited in Klippel, *Scharnhorst*, Vol.2, p.243.

33 Gerhard Scharnhorst to Christian Dietrich Helwing (30 July 1795); in Kunisch (ed.), *Scharnhorst: Privat und dienstliche Schriften*, Vol.8, p.514.

for Rousseau, and perhaps even for Scharnhorst, society was upside down, with aristocratic fools at the top and truly great men at the bottom. As 1796 ended, Rousseau's assessment of society weighed heavily on the mind and heart of *Major* Gerhard Scharnhorst. Then, unexpectantly in mid-January 1797, King Friedrich Wilhelm II invited him to join the Prussian army.

For the previous 18 months, Scharnhorst had had almost daily contact with the Prussian contingent in Westphalia. His superb military abilities, coupled with his professional demeanour, had so impressed Duke Karl of Brunswick (as well as other Prussian officials in Westphalia) that he notified the Prussian king that Scharnhorst would be a good acquisition for Prussia. After Prussian officials in Berlin had evaluated Scharnhorst's service record and future potential, *Oberst* Friedrich von Zastrow (the king's *Adjudant-General*) notified *Oberstlieutenant* Karl von Lecoq (Quartermaster General to the Duke of Brunswick) on 7 January 1797, authorising him to offer Scharnhorst a position in the Prussian army as a major of artillery, but with a substantial salary increase.[34]

At that time Lecoq served as the Prussian liaison officer to the Hanoverian contingent. In this capacity he had worked closely with Scharnhorst during the past year and a half. The two had become very good friends, as the informality of their correspondence confirms. Lecoq informed his colleague that Prussia was expanding its artillery and offered Scharnhorst an opportunity to be part of that reorganisation. He told Scharnhorst:

> As a major, you enter into a career which gives you the most wonderful prospect at your age, as all our officers are old, and I see for you the almost infallible hope of becoming the chief of the entire artillery corps. In 15 years you will be assured of a regiment.

Lecoq also told Scharnhorst that Prussia's offer included command of a company, which 'is extremely profitable' (especially in the artillery), with an estimated annual income of 3,000 Reichsthaler. Scharnhorst would be assigned to the newly formed 4. Artillerie Regiment in Königsberg. In closing, Lecoq asked for a response by 26 or 27 January.[35]

What an offer! Prussia promised Scharnhorst everything he desired from Hanover but had been denied. Taken completely by surprise, he initially wanted to accept Prussia's invitation but then hesitated. Lecoq wrote to him on 29 and 30 January requesting an answer.[36] 'It is very difficult for me to write to you now', Scharnhorst informed Lecoq on 1 February, 'since I cannot make a decision on the offer which you, invaluable friend, have presented to me'. He told Lecoq that while he believed the Prussian army to be the finest 'in all of Europe' and that he 'would be a most zealous soldier in your service', he was torn between his loyalty and obligations to Hanover and his intense desire and ambition to rise to the highest ranks

34 Friedrich von Zastrow to Karl von Lecoq (7 January 1797); cited in Lehmann, *Scharnhorst*, Vol.1, p.284.

35 Karl von Lecoq to Gerhard Scharnhorst (18 January 1797); *Nachlaß Scharnhorst*, Nr. 25, Sheet 7; deposited at the Geheimes Staatsarchiv Preussischer Kulturbesitz, 196/VI. HA Familienarchive und Nachlässe, Berlin (Dahlem). Excerpts of this letter are published in Klippel, *Scharnhorst*, Vol.2, pp.268-69.

36 Lecoq to Scharnhorst (29 and 30 January 1797); *Nachlaß Scharnhorst*, Nr. 25, Sheets 8 (29 January) and 9 (30 January).

of the service.[37] Although he did not state the obvious to Lecoq, Scharnhorst wanted time to speak with Wallmoden and to ascertain his future in Hanover.

Lecoq answered his friend on 2 February. He regretted Scharnhorst's apparent refusal but acknowledged that he could not 'oppose' the rationale Scharnhorst provided.[38] Realising Lecoq had completely misinterpreted his initial response, Scharnhorst wrote a lengthy letter on 15 February, explaining to Lecoq in some detail his delicate situation in Hanover and what had just transpired. 'I was exceedingly embarrassed by the proposal you were making to me'. On the one hand, he wrote, 'I would have liked to have accepted it, while on the other I saw the obstacles which hindered my desire'. Then Scharnhorst related his situation, beginning with his promotion to titular major in 1794 (while being paid the salary of an infantry captain), then his selection as General-Quartermaster-Lieutenant, whose stipend 'was given to an engineer officer'. 'They gave me nothing of the substantial 1000 Reichsthaler allowance which he [Estorff] had received annually; instead, a major's salary was paid to me'.[39] For this, Freytag had told him, he should to be grateful.

After accepting his promotion and salary increase, but before receiving Friedrich Wilhelm's offer, Scharnhorst had petitioned King George, seeking restitution for the injustices he had suffered under Trew and Freytag.[40] As he told Lecoq on 15 February: 'When I received your letter, in which you indicated to me your intention of bringing me to Berlin, I repeated my petition, to which I still have no definitive answer'. In that petition to his king, Scharnhorst had asked for two things. First, he wanted 'the prospect of a regiment' and second, 'the extraordinary income of a company command'.[41] In short, he desired what other officers in the Hanoverian army were receiving. As he told Lecoq: 'If this is not granted to me, I believe that I can leave Hanoverian service without the reproach of ingratitude. I will learn about this in 3 to 4 weeks'. Scharnhorst requested his friend and the Prussians to be patient, that his 'dislike' for his current situation and the possibility that nothing will change will lead him to make his decision. 'In a few weeks I will probably ask you to bring me as an artillery major into the expansion of the Prussian army'.[42]

Instead of a few weeks, officials in Hanover and London took nearly six months to respond to Scharnhorst's petition. They hoped Prussia would withdraw its offer, while they continued to deny him the desires of his heart and the fruits of his labour. Freytag and Lenthe had conspired to prevent him from obtaining the lawful financial benefits associated

37 Scharnhorst to Lecoq (1 February 1797); published in Kunisch (ed.), *Scharnhorst: Privat und dienstliche Schriften*, Vol.2, pp.68-69; the quoted passage is from p.68. A similar copy of this letter can be found in Vol.8, pp.518-19.

38 Lecoq to Scharnhorst (2 February 1797); *Nachlaß Scharnhorst*, Nr. 25, Sheet 10.

39 Scharnhorst to Lecoq (15 February 1797); published in Kunisch (ed.), *Scharnhorst: Privat und dienstliche Schriften*, Vol.2, pp.69-71; the quoted passages are from p.70.

40 Once again, neither Klippel nor Lehmann mention this petition. We learn of it from Scharnhorst's correspondence with Lecoq, which is also not mentioned by either Klippel or Lehmann.

41 Scharnhorst to Lecoq (15 February 1797); in Kunisch (ed.), *Scharnhorst: Privat und dienstliche Schriften*, Vol.2, pp.69-71.

42 Scharnhorst to Lecoq (15 February 1797); in Kunisch (ed.), *Scharnhorst: Privat und dienstliche Schriften*, Vol.2, p.71. Significantly, two days later on 17 February 1797, Lecoq told Scharnhorst that even when the expansion of the Prussian artillery was complete, a company command would still be available for him. See *Nachlaß Scharnhorst*, Nr. 25, Sheet 11.

with the General-Quartermaster-Lieutenant post. Now they were determined to prevent his petition of redress from reaching the king. They justified their actions to King George by insinuating Scharnhorst was not one of their own. He was not a nobleman and was thus not deserving the right of a company or regimental command, or any other senior military position within the Hanoverian army. But they never considered the ferocity with which Scharnhorst fought back, demanding his rights under law and requesting the king acknowledge these rights.

Initially, Wallmoden wholeheartedly supported Scharnhorst in this fight. The Commanding General spent considerable time with his General-Quartermaster-Lieutenant fashioning an appropriate response to the king. During this lengthy process that took seven weeks, Wallmoden realised that Scharnhorst would never be satisfied until he received the full compensation owed to him. Sensing the impatience and increasing animosity of Freytag and Lenthe (especially whenever Scharnhorst mentioned Hanoverian military law and custom to justify his rights and privileges, and by association accused Lenthe and Freytag of misconduct), Wallmoden advised his General-Quartermaster-Lieutenant to take whatever the king offered, fearful that Scharnhorst might be court-martialled for insubordination for challenging the unlawful, arbitrary, and petty prerogatives of a hateful and vindictive old field marshal; or worse, for desertion should he leave Hanover for Prussia.[43] Eventually, Scharnhorst politely declined Prussia's overture when King George promoted him to *Oberstlieutenant* and provided a modest salary increase.

A careful analysis of these events reveals the truly unfortunate situation in which Scharnhorst found himself when Prussia offered him the opportunity of a lifetime. It also sheds light on the least noble aspects of the Hanoverian army, its customs and traditions, and its ignoble leadership. Upon receipt of Prussia's invitation, Scharnhorst notified his chief, seeking Wallmoden's advice. In his heart he wanted to join the Prussian army; but as he informed Lecoq, he felt truly grateful and obligated to Wallmoden for all that the Commanding General had done for him. Scharnhorst clearly did not want Wallmoden to think he was 'ungrateful' should he readily accept Prussia's offer. He also wanted time to see how Hanoverian officials would respond. For their part, Freytag and Lenthe realised Hanover could never match the proposition Prussia had made to Scharnhorst without compromising their own class privileges and prerogatives. While both connived to give him what little they could, Wallmoden endeavoured to improve the social and financial standing of his diligent and trustworthy subordinate.

Writing to Freytag on 17 March 1797, Wallmoden requested the status of Scharnhorst's earlier petition and then made known Prussia's 'unexpected' offer, which had placed Scharnhorst in an awkward situation. Wallmoden informed Freytag that Scharnhorst had turned down 'a very generous offer' from Denmark two years earlier in 1795. At that time, he had felt there was really no future in Danish service. Now concerned Prussia's invitation 'literally is as advantageous as presented', Wallmoden told Freytag: 'No less than

43 This lengthy process can be followied in the collection of documents in Hann 41: *Akten des Generalkommandos mit den Militär-Akten der Londoner Kanzlei. 18.-19. Jahrhundert*; deposited at the Niedersächsisches Landesarchiv, Hanover. A sampling of these documents, which enables the reader to obtain a pretty clear picture of what transpired, is published in Klippel, *Scharnhorst*, Vol.2, pp.269-85. Unfortunately, Klippel is very selective with the evidence he provides and what he leaves out.

General Tempelhof himself has vouched for Major Scharnhorst'. Even more significant was Scharnhorst's outstanding service to Hanover. As the Commanding General told the field marshal, 'I cannot but regard it as a great loss to our service should Major Scharnhorst not be retained'. Referring to Scharnhorst's earlier petition to be reinstated in the artillery, Wallmoden added, 'I know of no one who is as qualified as he is', and made it clear to Freytag that 'there is no reason why the General-Quartermaster post cannot be filled by an officer of the artillery regiment'. The tone of Wallmoden's polite but terse memorandum suggests that here was an ideal opportunity for Freytag to correct the wrongs he had done to Scharnhorst when he had denied him the stipend paid to the General-Quartermaster-Lieutenant and had removed him from the artillery regiment.[44]

Clearly understanding the inference Wallmoden had made in his memorandum, Freytag replied on 22 March, informing the Commanding General that he was well aware of how Scharnhorst, 'who some time ago, in a general and undefined manner, sought to improve his present position and his future prospects'. The field marshal now claimed Scharnhorst was using the Prussian invitation as leverage, implying the General-Quartermaster-Lieutenant was acting improperly by blackmailing Hanover. Freytag also said he would forward Scharnhorst's new petition (along with the Commanding General's recommendations) to the king, who would be the determining official. Then, in a flippant and dishonest manner, Freytag wrote: 'Besides, I still note that the principal intention of Major Scharnhorst to remain in the artillery has been completely unknown to me; and that the occupation of previous vacancies had already been proposed to London'. This flagrant lie clearly contradicted the opening sentence of this letter, in which Freytag had told Wallmoden: 'I am very well acquainted with the request of Major Scharnhorst ... to be reinstated in the artillery regiment'.[45]

When Scharnhorst had sent Freytag his initial petition to be reinstated in the artillery regiment, he did so to preserve his career opportunities. This was clear to Freytag, even though he told Wallmoden otherwise. Scharnhorst had realised the precarious position he was in as the General-Quartermaster-Lieutenant. The Hanoverian General Staff had no career path for its officers. In the past it had been used to reward favourites. Under Wallmoden, Scharnhorst was transforming the General Staff into the command and control element of the Hanoverian army. When he was appointed as General-Quartermaster-Lieutenant, Scharnhorst had been quietly removed from the rolls of the artillery regiment, a move unprecedented in the Hanoverian army. Only later did he realise he had no branch of the service in which he could be promoted or obtain command of a company or a regiment. This was a first, since no engineer, cavalry, or infantry officer had ever been removed from their respective regiment when assigned to the General Staff. Only *Major* Gerhard Scharnhorst was without a regimental affiliation. Indeed, Wallmoden had emphasised this in his memorandum to Freytag.

When Scharnhorst discovered he had no regimental affiliation, and thus no prospect of advancement, he immediately contacted Wallmoden seeking his assistance. He had initially requested reinstatement in the artillery regiment, which the Commanding General had

44 Wallmoden to Freytag (17 March 1797); excerpted in Klippel, *Scharnhorst*, Vol.2, pp.269-71.

45 Freytag to Wallmoden (22 March 1797); published in Klippel, *Scharnhorst*, Vol.2, pp.271-72.

forwarded to Freytag weeks before Lecoq had contacted him with Prussia's offer. Freytag pretended to empathise with Scharnhorst, informing Wallmoden that he was unaware of Scharnhorst's predicament or his desire to return to the artillery, but would look into the matter. This was clearly not true. As head of the Hanoverian army, Freytag was aware of this, since he was the approving authority. Nevertheless, he told Wallmoden that he wished he had known of Scharnhorst's desire earlier (another lie), but now it was too late, since there were no longer any vacancies in the artillery.[46] What Freytag really meant was that there were no vacancies for Scharnhorst in the artillery.

In his report to King George on 1 April 1797, Freytag misled the king as well, telling him 'the General-Quartermaster position alone is at issue'. Then he informed the king that he could not deny knowing about 'another subject' (Scharnhorst's request to be reassigned to the artillery) sent to him, but this had already been settled. Again, this was simply not true at the time.[47] Knowing that Scharnhorst's petition to be reinstated in the artillery might expose his actions as criminal, Freytag sought assistance from Lenthe. They wanted the king to focus solely on the General-Quartermaster-Lieutenant position, and not on Scharnhorst's petition to be reinstated in the artillery regiment and compensated for the monies own to him by law. They advised King George accordingly, and is evident in the king's royal decree on 18 April 1797:

> With great pleasure we have seen that Major Scharnhorst, in spite of the very advantageous offer he has received from the Royal Prussian service, has nevertheless shown himself to have remained grateful to us and his affection for his fatherland and our service, even if he remains wanting with a lower income.

Then the king noted in passing that 'inasmuch as reinstatement in the artillery regiment, from which he came out of, is not feasible', Scharnhorst certainly deserved some compensation for remaining loyal to Hanover. As the king wrote:

> We are therefore inclined, both for this cause and for the skill and professional zeal demonstrated by the mentioned major, to give him an improvement and extraordinary grace … a monthly allowance of 45 Reichsthaler to his present salary for only him and without any consenting consequence, and furthermore, graciously to promote him to the rank of lieutenant colonel.

King George closed his decree by suggesting to Scharnhorst that this award and promotion should convince him not to accept Prussia's offer.[48] Once again, like his appointment as the Second Aide to the General-Quartermaster, this compensation was for Scharnhorst alone, and thus outside the normal procedures of the Hanoverian army.

Freytag notified Wallmoden on 6 May that he was in receipt of the king's decree. 'I am obliged', he told the Commanding General, 'to give an obedient reply to Major Scharnhorst,

46 Freytag to Wallmoden (22 March 1797); published in Klippel, *Scharnhorst*, Vol.2, p.271.

47 See Freytag's Report to King George III (1 April 1797); published in Klippel, *Scharnhorst*, Vol.2, p.272.

48 The Royal Decree of 18 April 1797 is published in Klippel, *Scharnhorst*, Vol.2, pp.272-73.

and since he has spoken against me, I would like your opinion on this matter'.[49] The Commanding General answered Freytag the next day, suggesting the field marshal permit him to inform Scharnhorst. Freytag agreed and requested Wallmoden send Scharnhorst's response directly back to him for transmittal to London.[50] When Scharnhorst received the king's decree, he was clearly upset and disappointed that his petition had been ignored and none of his expectations met. Over the next seven weeks, from 9 May to 29 June 1797, he and Wallmoden fashioned an appropriate response to the king.[51]

Meanwhile, Freytag wrote to the Commanding General on 16 May, requesting Scharnhorst's response 'soon'. He told Wallmoden that it was 'anticipated in London' and he feared 'a misinterpretation' may arise from any further delay.[52] Once again, Freytag's own words reveal his duplicity in these dealings. When he notified Lenthe the next day that he had not received Scharnhorst's response, he closed his letter wondering 'if His Royal Majesty would ask about the matter'. Freytag was obviously concerned that further delay might expose his deliberate and unlawful actions. He wanted the matter closed now. Two weeks later he told Lenthe he still had not received anything from Scharnhorst, nor had he heard from Wallmoden.[53]

On 29 June 1797, Wallmoden sent his General-Quartermaster-Lieutenant's response to the field marshal for transmittal to the king. In his letter Wallmoden apologised for the delay, admitting that it was his and not Scharnhorst's fault. Wallmoden told Freytag that he wanted to make sure King George clearly understood all of the many ramifications associated with Scharnhorst's unique situation.[54] The Commanding General understood the importance of Scharnhorst's petition to the king and deliberately required him to rewrite his response until it remained free of any emotion, and thus could not be misinterpreted by King George, Freytag, Lenthe, or any other courtier.

What truly perplexed the ambitious Scharnhorst was the lack of future career possibilities for him in the Hanoverian army. As he told Wallmoden, 'the General-Quartermaster-Staff has no career determined by regulations'. Scharnhorst had thus reached the pinnacle of his career. With no regimental affiliation, further promotion and command was unlikely. 'This condition', he continued:

> [I]n which I am excluded from the advantages that every other officer has, and which is inconsistent with the noble desires and ambitions of every officer, troubles me, and brings me to request that I be able to put myself in a position in which other officers of the General Staff stand.[55]

49 Freytag to Wallmoden (6 May 1797); in Klippel, *Scharnhorst*, Vol.2, p.273.

50 The exchange of letters between Freytag and Wallmoden (7-9 May 1797) can be found in Klippel, *Scharnhorst*, Vol.2, pp.273-74.

51 Fragments from the documentation reveal the intense deliberations between Scharnhorst and Wallmoden about a reasonable response to the king's offer; and can be found in Kunisch (ed.), *Scharnhorst: Privat und dienstliche Schriften*, Vol.2, pp.76-85.

52 Freytag to Wallmoden (16 May 1797); in Klippel, *Scharnhorst*, Vol.2, p.275.

53 Freytag's Letters of 17 and 31 May 1797 to Lenthe can be found in Klippel, *Scharnhorst*, Vol.2, pp.275-76.

54 Wallmoden to Freytag (29 June 1797); in Klippel, *Scharnhorst*, Vol.2, pp.281-82.

55 Scharnhorst to Wallmoden (between 9 May and 29 June 1797); in Kunisch (ed.), *Scharnhorst: Privat und dienstliche Schriften*, Vol.2, pp.76-79; the quoted passage is from p.77.

Scharnhorst made a very significant point here. Why was he being treated differently from other officers in the Hanoverian army?

Why had Gerhard Scharnhorst been removed from the artillery regiment? While the reason remains unclear from the available documents, it is not inconceivable to conclude that Trew had perhaps played a role in this effort. Even Wallmoden had questioned this action when he told Freytag there was no precedent in army regulations for Scharnhorst to have been denied a regimental affiliation. Every officer in the Hanoverian army had a regimental affiliation except *Major* Gerhard Scharnhorst. With no vacancies in the artillery, Scharnhorst requested assignment to his former cavalry regiment, the 8. Dragoner Regiment. He noted that the cavalry was more closely associated with the general staff than either the infantry or the artillery. Since he received the pay of a cavalry officer, and because his predecessor as General-Quartermaster (Estorff) was a cavalry officer, Scharnhorst believed his request made good sense.[56]

Following this explanation to the Commanding General, Scharnhorst presented Wallmoden with the initial draft of his petition to King George. He began by thanking the king for offering him a promotion to lieutenant colonel and an annual allowance to his salary. 'I will seek to make myself worthy of this great and undeserved grace', Scharnhorst told the king. He then asked:

> May I presuppose that my promotion brings with it all the prerogatives which our most gracious King has granted to others; and that, therefore, I shall proceed with my new seniority, receive the salary of my comrades in the same service, and one day command a regiment in the cavalry; that is, in the arm of the service in which I had first served, in which my predecessor had served, and in which I now have my salary and seniority.

Scharnhorst clearly understood that his appointment to the General Staff in 1794 and subsequent promotions were exceptions to the rule. So, he requested both be established as precedence in the Hanoverian army.

> It would be very comforting for me if, as my circumstances are new, that they were established by a most gracious decree. Without this, I would always remain in uncertainty and unrest because of the future.[57]

By requesting the king grant him (as the General-Quartermaster-Lieutenant) the same rights and privileges of other officers in the army, and by asking the king to establish this by royal decree, *Major* Gerhard Scharnhorst sought royal acknowledgement of his standing in the Hanoverian army.

Scharnhorst was clearly tired of being treated as a second-class officer. This he made known to the Commanding General when he told Wallmoden that he 'believed the

56 Scharnhorst to Wallmoden (between 9 May and 29 June 1797); in Kunisch (ed.), *Scharnhorst: Privat und dienstliche Schriften*, Vol.2, pp.77-78.

57 See Gerhard Scharnhorst, 'Entwurf des Memorials', in Kunisch (ed.), *Scharnhorst: Privat und dienstliche Schriften*, Vol.2, pp.78-79; the quoted passages are from p.78.

custom of our service' should have been extended to him when he was appointed General-Quartermaster-Lieutenant. He was certainly sick of the patronage and nepotism that characterized the Hanoverian army and which Freytag and Trew epitomised. He longed for a more equitable system. As he informed Wallmoden: 'I saw people of my age, as well as civilians and military about me, to whom this grace had been extended. *These reasons, and not the invitation to Prussian service*, made me so brazen as to seek after them'.[58] Unfortunately for Scharnhorst, he was treated with little respect by the likes of Trew, Freytag, and Lenthe. Trew had first denied him promotion and command of a company, then Freytag and Trew had him removed from the roles of the artillery regiment and refused to pay him the generous stipend associated with the General-Quartermaster-Lieutenant. Now Freytag and Lenthe convinced the king to give Scharnhorst half the annual allowance the General-Quartermaster-Lieutenant received, and then sweeten the package with a meaningless promotion to lieutenant colonel, without providing Scharnhorst with a regimental affiliation, seniority, or salary increase.

Scharnhorst's anger and frustration poured out in his discussions with Wallmoden. In one letter he questioned the rapid peacetime rise of Adolph Ludwig von Spörcken, who had died in 1794. Spörcken had been a major in the Garde Regiment in 1787, adjutant in 1788, lieutenant colonel in 1791, and a colonel and general adjutant to Freytag at the beginning of 1793. How was this possible, Scharnhorst asked? What had Spörcken accomplished to earn such rapid promotion and honours?[59] A cursorily review of Spörcken's career path reveals the answer. Spörcken was one of those well-connected Hanoverian aristocrats and courtiers in uniform, later part of Freytag's inner circle in London and known to the English royal family.[60]

Scharnhorst may have also been thinking of Count Johann Friedrich von der Decken (1769-1840). One of Scharnhorst's colleagues and friends, Decken was also a well-connected aristocrat whose family had a long record of service to Hanover. As a young infantry *Fähndrich*, Decken had been taken prisoner at Menin in 1794. Following his release in late May of 1795, he was immediately promoted to *Lieutenant* and later appointed *Adjudant* to Prince Adolphus Frederick, now a brigade commander in the Hanoverian army. By 1796, Decken was a *Capitain*. It had taken Scharnhorst 14 years to earn his captaincy; only seven for Decken. When compared to the exemplary peacetime performance and outstanding wartime record of Scharnhorst, neither Spörcken nor Decken had accomplished anything during peacetime or in combat that warranted their rapid promotions and choice assignments. The key difference was their social status and family connections. Once again, it was social standing and family connections, not professional qualifications, that made all the difference in the Hanoverian officer corps.

58 Scharnhorst to Wallmoden (Between 9 May and 29 June 1797); in Kunisch (ed.), *Scharnhorst: Privat und dienstliche Schriften*, Vol.2, p.78.

59 Scharnhorst to Wallmoden (Between 9 May and 29 June 1797); in Kunisch (ed.), *Scharnhorst: Privat und dienstliche Schriften*, Vol.2, p.79. Career data on Spörcken can be found in Note 1 (p.79).

60 Spörcken is mentioned numerous times in the correspondence of King George. See Arthur Aspinall (ed), *The Later Correspondence of George III*, Vol.2, pp.3, 8, 17, 23, 90, 136, and 300.

After refining Scharnhorst's memorandum to King George, Wallmoden forwarded it on 29 June 1797 to Freytag.[61] In his transmittal letter of 3 July to the king, Freytag wrote, 'I do not agree with the explanation of Major and General-Quartermaster Scharnhorst'. Freytag told King George it was not his fault that Scharnhorst's memorandum was so late arriving at the Court of St James.[62] It is interesting to note here that Freytag refers to Scharnhorst as 'Major', when the king had promoted him to *Oberstlieutenant* nearly three months earlier. This seems to indicate that King George had not officially promoted Scharnhorst at that time, as his correspondence to Wallmoden suggests. The king's April decree was mostly likely just a counteroffer to the one Scharnhorst had received from Prussia.

Meanwhile, on 20 June, more than a week before he had finished his petition to King George, Scharnhorst wrote to Lecoq. 'At last, I have decided to demand my release here, as soon as I have received an answer to the attached letter'. Scharnhorst knew in his heart that King George would never grant his petition and thanked Lecoq for his assistance with officials in Berlin, especially the patience the Prussians had shown to him. He requested to be stationed in Berlin, since it was closer to Bordenau than Königsberg. Berlin would also give him an excellent opportunity to 'profit from the exercises and manoeuvres there', and where 'I could perhaps be used now or at some time at the artillery school'.[63]

Then, in a surprising revelation, Scharnhorst informed Lecoq, 'I suspect they are looking for a way to keep me here'. He explained:

> I can be compelled to remain in this service for as long as it takes the soldiers of the corps to return from Westphalia, because Hanoverian service regulations do not permit dismissal in time of war, and the corps can be viewed as if it was in a state of war. I leave you, dear friend, to report this circumstance if you find it necessary.[64]

While no written evidence suggests the king's April decree was a veiled threat, it seems someone may have advised (or threatened) Scharnhorst that it would not be wise for him to leave Hanover for Prussia. Even though King George had ended his royal decree with the hope that Scharnhorst would not accept Prussia's offer and leave Hanover, it seems very plausible that some courtier may have misinterpreted the king's remarks. Scharnhorst certainly felt threatened, as his letter to Lecoq suggests.

Significantly, as they were fashioning his response to King George, Scharnhorst had asked Wallmoden to explain to him why military regulations and customs were always being used to deny him his lawful rights and privileges, as well as future opportunities to improve his situation. These same regulations were never used to support his career. Sadly, the Commanding General could not answer these questions. As Scharnhorst told Lecoq, 'he

61 The final memorandum appears to be lost or misplaced, since neither Klippel nor the editors of Scharnhorst's Papers have noted its existence or published a final version. In his analysis, Klippel, *Scharnhorst*, Vol.2, p.278, wrote that the original draft 'is completely contained in the following letter, with improvements in expression and presentation'.

62 Freytag to George III (3 July 1797); in Klippel, *Scharnhorst*, Vol.2, p.282.

63 Scharnhorst to Lecoq (20 June 1797); in Kunisch (ed.), *Scharnhorst: Privat und dienstliche Schriften*, Vol.2, pp.87-89; the quoted passages are from pp.87 and 88-89; respectively.

64 Scharnhorst to Lecoq (20 June 1797); in Kunisch (ed.), *Scharnhorst: Privat und dienstliche Schriften*, Vol.2, p.88. Interestingly, if Hanoverian regulations did not permit dismissal in time of war, why then, were *Capitains* Mecklenburg and Bülow discharged on 20 June 1794?

tried to calm me with empty words'. Realising he had missed a great opportunity, he added, 'I can tell you I am very sorry I did not leave here at once'. A few sentences later he wrote, 'We humans are often inconsistent'.[65]

From London on 1 August 1797, King George informed Freytag: 'We approve the explanation presented by Major Scharnhorst, which was included in your report of 5 July'. The king officially promoted Scharnhorst to *Oberstlieutenant* and provided him with an annual salary supplement of 550 Reichsthaler. Nowhere did he address any of Scharnhorst's concerns. Instead (knowingly or unknowingly), he supported the wishes of Lenthe and Freytag. Then the king ordered Freytag to notify Scharnhorst accordingly.[66] Freytag informed Wallmoden of the king's decision on 10 August. Scharnhorst thanked the Commanding General for his support, acknowledged receipt of the king's decree, and noted that King George had not addressed any of his concerns.[67] He was particularly disappointed that he had not received any pledge from the king regarding his status as a general staff officer or of the prospect of a company and regimental command. In yet another personal insult, eight of the 13 majors Scharnhorst passed over with his promotion to *Oberstlieutenant* still retained their seniority over him.[68]

65 Scharnhorst to Lecoq (7 September 1797); in Kunisch (ed.), *Scharnhorst: Privat und dienstliche Schriften*, Vol.2, pp.116-17; the quoted passages are from p.117.

66 George III to Freytag (1 August 1797); in Klippel, *Scharnhorst*, Vol.2, pp.282-83; the quoted passage is from p.283. Scharnhorst's 'Patent' (Certificate of Promotion) to *Oberstlieutenant* is published on p.283.

67 Scharnhorst to Wallmoden (no date); in Klippel, *Scharnhorst*, Vol.2, pp.283-85. The editors of Scharnhorst's Papers date this letter 'between 9 May and 29 June'. See Kunisch (ed.), *Scharnhorst: Privat und dienstliche Schriften*, Vol.2, pp.82-84.

68 See Lehmann, *Scharnhorst*, Vol.1, p.287. The seniority lists can be found in Hann 41, III, Nr,187: *Ernennung des Majors Scharnhorst zum Oberstleutnant und Generalquartiermeister. (Namenslisten von Oberstleutnants, Majoren und Kapitänen beziehungsweise Rittmeistern), 1796-1797*; deposited at the Niedersächsisches Landesarchiv, Hanover.

15

Scharnhorst and the French Revolution

When the Hanoverian Auxiliary Corps deployed in 1793, it was part of an alliance of royal houses of Europe against the people of revolutionary France. The awesome power of the nation in arms had so impressed Scharnhorst that when he formulated his experience in writing, this knowledge led him to focus on a people at war. He originally planned to write a comprehensive history and analysis of operations in Flanders and Holland in 1793 and 1794. Realising that this project would not be completed in the short time frame he had given his publisher, he decided to write an abbreviated version that would focus primarily on the key lessons the royal houses of Europe ought to have learned from the War of the First Coalition.

Anxious to discuss his ideas and acquire feedback before he published them, Scharnhorst renewed his friendships in Hanover and Göttingen. Among the men he may have sought out were two talented civil servants, August Rehberg and Ernst Brandes. Rehberg was a secretary of the Hanoverian Secret Committee [*Geheime Ratskollegium*].[1] Brandes served as Curator of the University of Göttingen.[2] Both were ardent opponents of the French Revolution and belonged to the 'Hanoverian Whigs', a conservative group of publicists from Göttingen that included two of Scharnhorst's former professors, August Schlözer and Ludwig Spittler.[3] Although August Rehberg and Ernst Brandes were overshadowed by more prominent political and social thinkers of their age, they were nonetheless pivotal figures in forging of a conservative German rebuttal of French revolutionary ideology.

In many respects, Rehberg was much like Scharnhorst. At a young age he possessed an insatiable thirst for knowledge. Before he turned 15, he had learned to read Greek, Latin, Italian, Spanish, French, and English. He found little inspiration from his philosophical studies at the University of Göttingen (1774-77), and so decided to educate himself. Upon leaving Göttingen in 1779, he was unable to obtain an academic position. When poet and member of 'The Göttingen Grove', Heinrich Christian Boie (1744-1806), tried to secure an appointment for Rehberg to the military secretariat, his achievements made

1 On Rehberg, see Kurt Lessing, *Rehberg und die französische Revolution* (Freiburg: Bielenfels, 1910).

2 On Brandes, see Carl Hasse, *Ernst Brandes 1758-1810* (Hildesheim: August Lax Verlag, 1973-74).

3 On Rehberg, Brandes, Schlözer, and the Hanoverian school, see Chapter 11 (pp.547-94) of Epstein, *The Genesis of German Conservatism*. Also see Frederick C. Beiser, *Enlightenment, Revolution, and Romanticism: The Genesis of Modern German Political Thought, 1790-1800* (Cambridge: Harvard University Press, 1992), pp.302-05.

him 'an uncomfortable subordinate'.[4] Rehberg was forced to earn a living as a language tutor, teaching German to Englishmen. This eventually led to his appointment in 1783 as the personal secretary of the Duke of York, who at that time was also the Prince-Bishop of Osnabrück. While in Osnabrück conducting affairs for the prince, young Rehberg impressed conservative *Aufklärer* Justus Möser, who taught him to appreciate the noble traditions of the German 'small state' [*Kleinstaat*] and urged Rehberg to channel his intellectual energies on mastering the complexities of German social and political particularism.[5] When York returned to England in 1786, he appointed Rehberg to the secretariat of the Hanoverian Secret Committee. It did not take August Rehberg long to demonstrate his considerable talents and abilities. Of course, this meant little to the landed gentry of feudal Hanover. While their noble counterparts elsewhere in Germany had recognised the talents and abilities of the middle-class and had integrated commoners into state administrations, the haughty and arrogant aristocratic officials in Hanover refused to accept the changing times. Ironically, the real threat to the Hanoverian elites came not from within, but from without.[6] Nonetheless, it did not take Rehberg long to become a prominent public official and 'one of the leading administrators of Hanover for an entire generation'.[7]

Like Gerhard Scharnhorst, August Rehberg led a simple middle-class life. As a child of the Enlightenment, he was a critical thinker, possessed a healthy scepticism of religion (he had abandoned his Protestant upbringing at an early age), and absolutely refused to be swayed by what he believed the irrationalism of romanticism. Rehberg shared the striving middle-class 'outlook' [*Gestalt*] Scharnhorst possessed, and criticised the leisurely and wasteful aristocratic way of life. Like Scharnhorst, Rehberg was constantly being set back by ignorant, jealous, and whimsical Hanoverian nobles. Oddly enough, he defended the traditional order [*Ständesstaat*], regarding it as the sure counter to despotism. This was clearly evident in his writings.[8] Furthermore, while he abhorred aristocratic exclusiveness and legal privilege, and clearly resented the fact that noblemen with lesser ability were always his superiors, Rehberg (like his mentor Justus Möser) put his faith in the ruling aristocratic elite. Unlike Scharnhorst (who emphasised the individual), Rehberg argued that the welfare of the state was paramount, and the concern of only those with a vested interest in preserving its traditions, and by only those with a specialised knowledge of its operation.[9] Rehberg maintained it was the noble feature of the *Kleinstaat* that defended the people against the two great evils of contemporary European society: radical democracy (France) and royal absolutism (Prussia).

4 See the nice discussion of Rehberg's mental abilities in Epstein, *The Genesis of German Conservatism*, p.557. In Book Three (pp.77-99) of his study, Karl Weinhold, *Heinrich Christian Boie: Beitrag zur Geschichte der deutschen Literatur im achtzehnten Jahrhundert* (Halle: Waisenhaus, 1868), provides a very interesting and at times delightful description of Hanoverian society and the suffocating environment in which Rehberg lived.

5 For a brief examination of Möser and his political and social conservatism as it relates to the German *Kleinstaat* and Rehberg, see Beiser, *Enlightenment, Revolution, and Romanticism*, pp.288-302.

6 See the important discussion on this topic in Chapter 2 (pp.38-40) of Fox, 'Conservative Accommodation to Revolution'.

7 Epstein, *The Genesis of German Conservatism*, p.549.

8 See August Wilhelm Rehberg, *Ueber das Verhältnis der Metaphysik zur Religion* (Berlin: August Mylius, 1787).

9 Rehberg, *Ueber das Verhältnis der Metaphysik zur Religion*, pp.139-41.

Imbued with similar beliefs, Ernst Brandes grew up in the university town of Göttingen, where he studied law from 1775-78. There he met August Rehberg and the two remained friends until the death of Brandes in 1810. Following his graduation, Brandes travel throughout Germany, France, and England. In London he met Edmund Burke (1729-97) and was captivated by English political theory and practice.[10] Soon after his return to Hanover, Brandes was appointed First Secretary of the Hanoverian Chancery. Like Rehberg, Brandes defended the very system that prevented him from achieving his full potential. He believed in government by hereditary caste, since noblemen were traditionally reared for public service and had centuries of experience.[11] At the same time he asked whether the nobility alone could effectively serve as the sure bulwark against despotism.[12] According to the traditional hereditary custom of the Hanoverian civil service, Ernst Brandes succeeded his father as Curator of the University of Göttingen in 1791. A prolific social and political commentator, Brandes published over 200 books, pamphlets, articles, and reviews during his lifetime.[13]

For Rehberg and Brandes, the revolution in French became a turning point in their lives. Both were initially sympathetic to the reformers in the French National Assembly. When Brandes published his *Political Reflections on the French Revolution* in 1790, he vigorously defended the Revolution and even justified its violent nature against counterrevolution.[14] Three years later he completely reversed his earlier defence in his treatise, *On Some Previous Episodes of the French Revolution, with Respect to Germany*.[15] He now claimed that there was no credible evidence of any counterrevolutionary threat that justified the extreme and totally unnecessary violence the revolutionary mobs and defence forces had employed against their own people and their property. To calm his German readers, Brandes assured them the German Fatherland was in no danger of revolution.

From the same publishing house came Rehberg's *Investigations on the French Revolution* (1793), a systematic summary of his views.[16] This work incorporated many of his previous articles (most in revised form) published in the Jena *General Literary Gazette* from 1790 to 1792. In nearly all these articles Rehberg had harshly criticised the abstract idealism of the radical revolutionaries, stressing the importance of historical continuity and tradition whenever social, cultural, and political change occurs. He also attacked the royalists who insisted France return to the days of absolute rule. Although Rehberg knew both France and Germany needed major social and political reform, it would take him a decade before

10 In his engaging study, *Enlightenment, Revolution, and Romanticism*, p.288, Beiser notes that although Burke influenced Brandes, the latter was 'anything but his disciple'.

11 See Ernst Brandes, 'Ist es den deutschen Staaten vorteilhaft, dass der Adel die ersten Staatsbedienungen besitzt?' *Berlinische Monatsschrift* 10 (1787), pp.395-439.

12 Brandes, 'Ist es den deutschen Staaten vorteilhaft, dass der Adel die ersten Staatsbedienungen besitzt?' pp.429-32.

13 On Brandes' major works, see Epstein, *The Genesis of German Conservatism*, pp.708-09.

14 Ernst Brandes, *Politische Betrachtungen über die französische Revolution* (Jena: Johann Michael Mauke, 1790).

15 Ernst Brandes, *Ueber einige bisherige Folgen der Französischen Revolution in Rücksicht auf Deutschland* (Hanover and Osnabrück: Christian Ritscher, 1793).

16 August Wilhelm Rehberg, *Untersuchungen über die Französische Revolution, nebst kritischen Nachrichten von den merkwürdigsten Schriften, welche darüber in Frankreich erschienen sind* (Hanover and Osnabrück: Christian Ritscher, 1793).

he would advocate such modernisation in Hanover.[17] By that time it was too late to save Hanover from occupation, first by Prussia, then by France.

Scharnhorst rejected the apologetic views of Rehberg and Brandes. He demanded reform now, even if that meant a radical change in the way Hanover was governed. Unlike Rehberg and Brandes who willingly accepted their subservient place in society, Scharnhorst embraced the ideals of the French Revolution – concepts of egalitarianism and rationalism that Lessing, Kant, Nicolai, Mendelssohn, Fichte, Herder, and others had years earlier demanded for German society, and which both Rehberg and Brandes had acknowledged in their works. It appears that both Rehberg and Brandes (like Schlözer and other German intellectuals) feared the unbridled power of an ignorant people more than they did ignorant aristocratic dominance. Scharnhorst, on the other hand, welcomed change and endeavoured to incorporate the ideals of egalitarianism and rationalism in his program of military reform. If the people were uneducated, he wanted to use *Bildung* (as Lessing advocated) to teach them. To clarify his own political, social, and cultural position, Gerhard Scharnhorst began to educate himself more fully on the French Revolution.

Seeking to enlighten himself on French revolutionary thought, Scharnhorst procured relevant literature on the Revolution and its impact on war and society. Among the surviving remnants of book orders that he placed during this time are works that reveal the methodical thoroughness with which he approached his subject. For Scharnhorst, this was an intellectually 'fertile time like no other'.[18] He had seen how the fire of the Revolution had produced great enthusiasm among French soldiers, and how they had used this passion to transform military operations. Now he sought to clarify and explain his views on this amazing phenomenon. His priority was to study as much of the current military literature available, especially recent memoirs, as well as other contemporary and historical works that may provide background and insight into this incredible transfiguration of warfare. In the middle of a book order he placed on 2 August 1795 are listed four foundational studies of the French Enlightenment: Montesquieu's *Spirit of the Laws* (1748), Rousseau's *Social Contract* (1762), Voltaire's *The Age of Louis XIV* (1751), and Helvetius' *Essays on the Mind* (1758). 'Undoubtedly, one has a reproduction of these works', Scharnhorst noted in his request to the Helwing Bookstore. 'I do not wish to have excellent editions of them. I wish only to have all in the French language'.[19] When Montesquieu's book did not arrive, Scharnhorst urgently asked his publisher on 9 September to order it again, adding a second book by Helvetius, *A Treatise on Man: His Intellectual Faculties and His Education* (1772).[20]

Around the same time Scharnhorst had written to his publisher, outlining a new book concept and asking if Helwing would be interested in publishing it.[21] This was a modified version of his original plan drafted two months earlier. From this brief outline (which had highlighted many issues he had already brought to the attention of Wallmoden), it became

17 See August Wilhem Rehberg, *Ueber den deutschen Adel* (Göttingen: Röwer, 1803).

18 See the interesting discussion in Stadelmann, *Scharnhorst*, p.105.

19 Gerhard Scharnhorst to Christian Dietrich Helwing (2 August 1795); in Kunisch (ed.), *Scharnhorst: Privat und dienstliche Schriften*, Vol.8, pp.514-15; the quoted passages are from p.515.

20 Stadelmann, *Scharnhorst*, pp.105-06.

21 Letter of 23 August 1795 to the Helwing Publishing House; in Kunisch (ed.), *Scharnhorst: Privat und dienstliche Schriften*, Vol.1, pp.676-77.

clear to Scharnhorst that coalition forces had been unprepared to fight the kind of war (especially a winter campaign) that the fervour of the French revolutionary armies had thrust upon them. He wanted to educate his readers on this incredible transformation of warfare. He informed Helwing that he would have the first part completed in four to five weeks. The full campaign history, which he now titled, *History of the War in Flanders and Brabant in the Year 1793 and 1794* (the title of his original draft), would encompass four to five parts, much more than he had intended back in May. True to his high academic standards, he realised that the more he researched this topic, the more pages he would need for this comprehensive campaign study to achieve its purpose. He promised to send Helwing 'the detailed plan' and his 'particular terms' soon.[22]

As he organised his thoughts for publication and awaited an answer from King George regarding his situation in Hanoverian service, Scharnhorst took time to tutor Prince Adolphus Frederick on large-scale military operations. Like his older brother, Adolphus had studied at Göttingen before the war. In 1793 he commanded the Garde Infanterie Regiment and was twice wounded leading his troops. A year later he was promoted to *General-Major* (he was only 20 years old at the time) and given command of an infantry brigade. After the war he began intensive military studies with Scharnhorst, since he was being groomed to succeed Wallmoden and the Commanding General wanted to make sure the prince was mentally fit for the role.[23] *Capitain* Friedrich von der Decken, the prince's adjutant, assisted Scharnhorst.

To educate Prince Adolphus on the value of historical study and how history can inform the planning and execution of military operations, Scharnhorst engaged him in the development of a detailed operational plan that had a coalition army manoeuvring between the Weser and Ems Rivers, poised to invade Holland should the French violate the Treaty of Basil and threaten north-western Germany.[24] This exercise conveniently coincided with the memorandum Scharnhorst had sent to Duke Karl of Brunswick on such a contingency and, more importantly, with a recent Prussian decision on 1 May to reinforce its garrisons along the demarcation line in Westphalia with an additional 25,000 troops. Prussia was watching closely as the French under the able direction of Carnot waged war against Austria in southern Germany and Italy. Prussia was clearly apprehensive of French ambitions in northern Germany.[25]

In response to a hypothetical French attack in north-western Germany, Scharnhorst posed the following problem to Prince Adolphus:

> The Cabinet has determined to attack Holland between Emmerich and Emden, and to conquer the provinces of the Issel wherever possible. The General [meaning

22 Letter of 23 August 1795 to the Helwing Publishing House; in Kunisch (ed.), *Scharnhorst: Privat und dienstliche Schriften*, Vol.1, p.677.

23 For a brief biographical sketch of Prince Adolphus Frederick, see Kunisch (ed.), *Scharnhorst: Privat und dienstliche Schriften*, Vol.2, p.783.

24 See Gerhard Scharnhorst, 'Ueber die Operationen einer Armee, zwischen der Weser und Ems, zum Unterricht des Prinzen Adolfs K.H. aufgesetzet' (not before 1796); in Kunisch (ed.), *Scharnhorst: Privat und dienstliche Schriften*, Vol.2, pp.223-36. Also see the interesting contingency plans in Hann 41, I, Nr.39: *Französische Angriffspläne gegen England und das Kurfürstentum Hannover, 1797*; deposited at the Niedersächsisches Landesarchiv, Hanover.

25 See the discussion in Lehmann, *Scharnhorst*, Vol.1, p.283.

Prince Adolphus] is consulted on this decision. He is asked whether the plan is feasible with the means available to bring it about.

Prince Adolphus was to plan an offensive operation against Holland with an army of 60,000 men. Scharnhorst instructed the prince to: '1. Determine the means which are required; and 2. Identify the ways in which they are to be accomplished'. The detail which Scharnhorst required Adolphus to include in his concept plan was astounding. The prince had to ascertain the personnel and logistical requirements of the army for this campaign, such as: the ratio of infantry to cavalry to artillery (and how they would be organised into combined-arms units); battle formations and ammunition requirements (especially with respect to the various types of artillery pieces); rations, their transportation and storage; the size and location of hospitals (as well as the transportation of the wounded); assembly areas for the army (to include the order of march of formations to their assembly areas); and all of the command and control measures. As a reference for the prince to use in formulating his response, Scharnhorst included a review of the Prussian, Austrian, and French artillery 'systems', and how they had been organised and had fought during the 1793 and 1794 campaigns.[26]

The timing of this contingency planning coincided ideally with Scharnhorst's plans to modernise the Hanoverian General Staff. His aim here was to teach the prince on the complexity involved in developing a detailed operational plan and then, as the commanding general, executing it. By having Prince Adolphus complete this exercise, Scharnhorst probably hoped that he would see just how difficult it would be to command an army on campaign without capable general staff officers with clearly defined duties and responsibilities. No doubt Scharnhorst wanted Prince Adolphus to avoid the catastrophic mistakes his brother had made, simply because the latter had been ill-advised by those surrounding him.

Once Prince Adolphus had completed these initial requirements, Scharnhorst then had him brief his proposed attack on Holland, not from a Coalition point of view; but rather, from a Dutch and French perspective. This forced him to exam the defensive capabilities available to the French in Holland – its rivers and flood plains, its towns and fortresses, and how these natural and man-made obstacles might hinder the execution of his offensive plan.[27] In this way Scharnhorst endeavoured to teach the prince not to force his plan on an uncooperative enemy, but instead to think through or 'wargame' possible and probable courses of action in give-and-take scenarios.

Using Scharnhorst's systematic approach to the planning and execution of military operations gave Prince Adolphus an opportunity to learn far more about the art of war and its execution in the field then most officers would ever have encountered in their careers. This was certainly obvious to Scharnhorst, who based his understanding on a comprehensive study of history and on his experience during the War of the First Coalition. He may have also been thinking of his two favourite military leaders, Raimondo Montecuccoli and

26 See Gerhard Scharnhorst, '*Erstes Beyspiel von den Entwurf eines Op[e]rationsplans*', Kunisch (ed.), *Scharnhorst: Privat und dienstliche Schriften*, Vol.2, pp.224-36, and 224 Notes b and c.

27 See Gerhard Scharnhorst, '*Hollands Festungen un. Ueberschwem[wun]gen*', Kunisch (ed.), *Scharnhorst: Privat und dienstliche Schriften*, Vol.2, pp.237-40. Originally, this section was titled, 'VIII. *Beschreibung von den anzugreifenden Theil von Holland*', and was mostly likely part in the previous operational study.

Frederick the Great, and the lessons they had learned the hard way from experience and wanted to ensure Prince Adolphus did not have to repeat such mistakes.

Following the completion of this operational planning exercise, Scharnhorst provided Prince Adolphus with several reports that summarised key lessons the prince should remember.[28] These 'teaching points' also reveal the military wisdom of Scharnhorst and the mental process he used to solve military problems. In one report he advised Prince Adolphus always to question 'the experts' to discover new truths and to shake off old prejudices. 'The authority of great men does not have to stop us from searching the institutions and regulations in the original source'. This was clearly an enlightenment approach to life. Scharnhorst was convinced that the extensive uniformity among the standing professional armies of the European monarchies in tactics and technology were strong indicators of their imperfections. To ascertain the combat readiness of an army, he told Prince Adolphus to focus on its wartime organisation, the major differences in its leadership, the *Bildung* of its leadership, and personal relationships with the common soldier.[29]

In a second report Scharnhorst suggested that the prince could often determine the intrinsic value of soldiers by the visible signs they projected. Here he was referring to their cleanliness and posture, how well they marched as a unit, their fire discipline, and their leadership. As he told Prince Adolphus, these indicators would reveal the esprit of the unit, whether it be a company, a battalion, or a regiment.[30] From his letters to his father, Adolphus understood these indicators. In his third report, Scharnhorst used military history to review for the prince possible courses of actions should an enemy attack. He told him to study intensely the *Works of Frederick the Great* and the *Mémories* of French General Antoine de Pas, the Marquis de Feuquières (1648-1711). Both were distinguished warriors and strong advocates of offensive war. Both always sought battle as a means of deciding a conflict.[31]

On the recommendation of newly promoted *Oberstlieutenant* Gerhard Scharnhorst, Prince Adolphus wrote to his father on 19 August 1797, desiring to visit the former Austrian positions along the Rhine before they disappeared. His rationale was characteristically Scharnhorst.

> Undoubtedly nothing is more instructive for an officer than when he has seen for this himself, for this branch of the military profession is not to be learned only by books but chiefly by practice, by examining oneself the positions taken by able Generals.
>
> My wish is that your Majesty would be so gracious as to allow me to make the military excursion this autumn, as I fear that the Peace with the Empire might be concluded next winter and then next year this tour would not be half so instructive and interesting, as all the retrenchments will be immediately destroyed; and it is particularly in this matter of retrenching their camps that the Austrians excell [sic].

28 Three of these 'Reports' can be found in Kunisch (ed.), *Scharnhorst: Privat und dienstliche Schriften*, Vol.2, pp.240-41, 242-43, and 243-44.

29 See Scharnhorst's first report; in Kunisch (ed.), *Scharnhorst: Privat und dienstliche Schriften*, Vol.2, pp.240-41; the quoted passage is from p.241.

30 See Scharnhorst's second report; in Kunisch (ed.), *Scharnhorst: Privat und dienstliche Schriften*, Vol.2, pp.242-43.

31 See Scharnhorst's third report; in Kunisch (ed.), *Scharnhorst: Privat und dienstliche Schriften*, Vol.2, pp.243-44.

> I spoke on this subject to Colonel Scharnhorst who told me that I could learn more in two months by making such an excursion that if he was to give me a whole year lessons in this branch.[32]

'Nothing but the desire of learning my profession has prompted me to ask you this favour [sic]', Prince Adolphus concluded his letter. Scharnhorst was clearly making good progress with the future commanding general of the Hanoverian army. Unfortunately, the king denied his son's request.[33]

While he was teaching Adolphus the higher components of the art of war, the prince's adjutant was tutoring him in mathematics and history. At one point Scharnhorst had to correct what he believed to be misleading historical conclusions Decken had drawn from the recent war against the French.[34] 'Permit me', Scharnhorst told Prince Adolphus, referring to a paper Decken had written, 'to take the opportunity to say a few words on the view that the French owed their success in this war primarily to their young generals. This view is contradicted by the history of this war itself'.

> Old soldiers achieved the first gains the French won in this war – the capture of Courtrai and Mainz, and the defence of Thornville and Lille. To a middle-aged general is owed the first victory of the Republic (that at Jemappes) and the first conquest of the Netherlands. An old man defended the fortress at Valenciennes, which delayed the Allies for 11 weeks. The Republic stood under the command of an aged man (Houchard) during the gamble at Dunkirk and Bergen, during the battle of Hondschoote, and at Werwick and Menin in September 1793. During the battle of Wattignies, middle-aged men commanded (Jourdan and in particular Carnot). Likewise, on the Rhine and at the foot of the Alps in the year 1793, the Republicans were victorious solely under the command of middle-aged men.[35]

Contrary to what Decken had told Prince Adolphus, age was clearly not the sole reason for French success.

Having refuted Decken's argument, Scharnhorst proceeded to turn the attention of Prince Adolphus to the real cause of French success. He would later examine this in greater clarify in his lengthy article, 'Basic Reasons for the French Success'. This short discourse provides a nice summary of his latter conclusions.

32 See the fascinating Letter of 19 August 1797 from Prince Adolphus to King George III; in Aspinall (ed.), *The Later Correspondence of George III*, Vol.2, pp.616-17; the quoted passages are from p.617.

33 Letter of 23 August 1797 from Prince Adolphus to King George III; in Aspinall (ed.), *The Later Correspondence of George III*, Vol.2, p.632.

34 Decken later published his conclusions as 'Sollen wir nur junge Generale haben?' *Neues Militärisches Journal* 9 (1798), pp.100-27.

35 Gerhard Scharnhorst, 'Bruchstück über das Glück der Franzosen', *Nachlaß Scharnhorst*, Nr. 117, Sheets 16-17; deposited at the Geheimes Staatsarchiv Preussischer Kulturbesitz, 196/VI. HA Familienarchive und Nachlässe, Berlin (Dahlem). This fragment is printed in Kunisch (ed.), *Scharnhorst: Privat und dienstliche Schriften*, Vol.2, pp.385-87; and (in part) in Lehmann, *Scharnhorst*, Vol.1, pp.232n-33n. The quoted passages are from Kunisch (ed.), *Scharnhorst: Privat und dienstliche Schriften*, Vol.2, pp.385 and 385-86.

> These first victories of the French were achieved against the entire Coalition, by armies still half formed and organised, during the time of the establishment of the Republic, during the time of internal disorder, during the time of a lack of all necessary things for the maintenance of life. At the same time these victories first inspired the nation with confidence in its abilities and united the people, gave the government internal authority and strength, and indeed required more energy, more sacrifice, more knowledge of human nature than the direction of the 1795 and 1796 campaigns in Italy, when the Republic was established and its armies organised, when it fought only half the Coalition, when it could therefore concentrate its forces better, when it had a great deal of new and crucial resources due to the conquest of the Netherlands and Holland, and to the peace treaties with Spain and Prussia.[36]
>
> And yet, despite this, only the Italian campaigns of General Bonaparte remain. One must admire the gallantry, the energy, and the great sense of honour and unlimited spirit with which only Bonaparte (a noteworthy son of the Revolution) exhibited.[37]

Scharnhorst believed the French owed their success to their revolutionary fervour, which had transformed French society and subsequently its military. What is truly significant here is the early indication that Scharnhorst was one of the first to recognise in Napoleon Bonaparte the qualities of a great captain.

While educating Prince Adolphus and reading the available literature on the War of the First Coalition, Scharnhorst also took time to comment on the very different picture of French success that had come from these sources. In one of these studies, *On War against the New Franks* (1795), Archduke Charles of Austria (1771-1847) presented the kind of conclusions many coalition leaders readily accepted as their standard response to their defeat.[38] A bewildered Charles began his discourse with an intriguing question: how could one army 'slightly larger in numbers, but consisting of raw, untrained troops, with mediocre cavalry or none at all', defeat a highly-trained army of well-equipped and disciplined professional soldiers, with 'excellent and numerous cavalry and artillery'?[39] Over the next 11 pages, the Archduke sought to answer his question. Instead of comparing the two armies he mentioned in his question (as Scharnhorst was accustomed to doing), Charles chose instead to highlight only Austrian failures. He blamed the laziness and timidity of Austrian generals and their defensive mindset as the main reasons for coalition failure. Charles felt Austrian leaders were too concerned with holding terrain and strongpoints and protecting their lines of communication. This led to the use of a cordon defence that failed miserably to

36 Scharnhorst, 'Bruchstück über das Glück der Franzosen', Kunisch (ed.), *Scharnhorst: Privat und dienstliche Schriften*, Vol.2, p.386.

37 Scharnhorst, 'Bruchstück über das Glück der Franzosen', Kunisch (ed.), *Scharnhorst: Privat und dienstliche Schriften*, Vol.2, p.387.

38 See Carl Erzherzog von Oesterreich. *Über den Krieg gegen die Neufranken durch einen österreichischen Offizier*; in Volume 5 of Franz X. Mancher (ed.), *Ausgewählte Schriften des Erzherzogs Carl von Österreich* (Vienna and Leipzig: Wilhelm Braumüller, 1893-94), pp.3-15.

39 Carl Erzherzog von Oesterreich. *Über den Krieg gegen die Neufranken durch einen österreichischen Offizier*, Vol.5, p.5.

contain 'the enemy'.[40] Coupled with their unwillingness to fight aggressively and offensively, Austrian generals simply 'handed the initiative over to the enemy'. Significantly, nowhere in his commentary did the Archduke ever address the French by name. It was as if they did not exist. In their place he used the term 'the enemy'. Incredibly, in the eyes of the Archduke, the French had nothing to do with the outcome of the campaign. The Austrians had defeated themselves. 'Ignorance, indolence, and egotism are to blame for our misfortune', Charles concluded.[41]

Scharnhorst rejected this simplistic and one-sided argument of the Archduke Charles. It clearly denied the truth. Unfortunately, it was the identical fallacy Scharnhorst would see repeatedly in the literature from this conflict. Such arguments were so convenient and reassuring. By focusing solely on coalition shortcomings, Archduke Charles and other apologists could simply dismiss any notion that the French had anything to do with their defeat or had taken the art of war to a higher plain. Any significant modernisation of their own social, political, and military systems was consequently unnecessary and foolish. All that was required were a few minor adjustments in the way they conducted their military operations, such as relieving incompetent or weak senior officers.

Archduke Charles sought to defend the Austrian professional standing army by comparing it to the raw, untrained troops of the French. This he never accomplished, simply because contrasting the professional standing army of the absolutist state with the citizen armies of revolutionary France would have undermined his entire argument. Interestingly, Scharnhorst felt the British had suffered from the same self-delusion following their defeat in the American Revolution. Unlike Archduke Charles, Scharnhorst noted this in his critique of the American Revolution. 'The Revolution in America proves nothing against standing armies'.[42] This was a significant insight. 'The English have no good standing armies', Scharnhorst stated in his comparative analysis of British and American forces. British generals, he pointed out, 'do not know how to lead armies, as the letters of Washington suggest'. Turning to the American effort, he stated the Americans had some very good generals in 'Washington, Lee, Arnold, and others', even though Arnold had changed sides during the war. Scharnhorst also stated how important French military support had been for the Americans. Returning to the British effort, he told his readers that they had to conduct their operations 'over the ocean, which is associated with a thousand difficulties and could never have been conducted in a vigorous manner'.[43] Comparing Scharnhorst's brief analysis of the American Revolution with Archduke Charles's examination of the campaigns of 1793 and 1794 reveals the mistake Charles made by focusing solely on one belligerent while

40 Carl Erzherzog von Oesterreich. *Über den Krieg gegen die Neufranken durch einen österreichischen Offizier,* Vol.5, p.13 (Note). Gunther E. Rothenberg, *Napoleon's Great Adversary: The Archduke Charles and the Austrian Army, 1792-1814* (Bloomington: Indiana University Press, 1982), p. 37, writes the plan of Prince Coburg in 1793 'epitomised the Austrian preoccupation with cordon deployment and fortress warfare'.

41 Carl Erzherzog von Oesterreich. *Über den Krieg gegen die Neufranken durch einen österreichischen Offizier,* Vol.5, p.15.

42 See Gerhard Scharnhorst, '*Bemerkungen über die Betrachtungen über die Kriegsk[unst]*' (not before 1797); in Kunisch (ed.), *Scharnhorst: Privat und dienstliche Schriften*, Vol.2, p.389.

43 Scharnhorst, '*Bemerkungen über die Betrachtungen über die Kriegsk[unst]*', in Kunisch (ed.), *Scharnhorst: Privat und dienstliche Schriften*, Vol.2, p.389. Scharnhorst's analysis here of British defeat in the American Revolution is virtually identical with the arguments he made in his 1792 defence of standing armies.

ignoring the other. Scharnhorst certainly understood that all sides had to be considered simultaneously if one wished to obtain accurate and objective conclusions. He then used a recent British account to highlight another ancient form of literature relevant to the study of war and which provided insights into British institutions.

From London in 1796 came a fascinating work that really intrigued Scharnhorst. It was published anonymously and entitled, *An Accurate and Impartial Narrative of the War by an Officer of the Guards*. What captivated Scharnhorst's interest was its style; it was a narrative, heroic poem.[44] 'The idea of transmitting martial events in this robe of posterity is not new. Father Homer, who is well known, had portrayed the fates of heroes who, two thousand years ago, broke their necks over the abduction of a beautiful woman.' Scharnhorst believed that through his poetry, Homer had rescued unknown warriors from the 'depths of oblivion', which then had led 'to the immortality of Achilles and Hector'.[45]

Such was the intent of the English author with his epic poem of British combat operations during the campaigns of 1793, 1794, and 1795. Referring to the author's explanatory notes and not his poetry, Scharnhorst wrote: 'He can certainly make a claim to historical merit'. Indeed, these notes provided the most fascinating account of British operations in Flanders and Holland.

> His notes (it sounds awkward to speak of notes as the text) contain a brief but rather correct survey of the most remarkable events which the English troops who have served on the continent have experienced, and his verses offer a bitter, yet unfortunately true picture of the defective constitution of the English army, which is not organised for land warfare. His explanation is particularly concerned with the ignorance and luxurious life of the officers, especially within the headquarters. Such a truth-based account makes it understandable why, notwithstanding the extraordinary courage of the troops and the good qualities of their leaders – to whom the author has done justice in several places – this army can no longer function.

Turning his attention to the idea of poetry as a means of describing martial events, Scharnhorst noted: 'The art of war is, of all events, more akin to poetry than it seems at first sight. The great King [Frederick the Great] certainly brought the art of murdering men according to the rules [of war] into delicate verses.'[46] Unfortunately, the same could not be said about the poetry of the author. Scharnhorst ended his review by chastising British historians, noting that if 'this comic poem is the only description which the English have provided of their campaigns on the continent', then there is something seriously lacking among English writers. The fact that the English public was being denied the memory of

44 See Anon., *An Accurate and Impartial Narrative of the War by an Officer of the Guards*.

45 Gerhard Scharnhorst, *Anzeige von einem englischen Heldengedichte* (after April 1797, before 1799); in Kunisch (ed.), *Scharnhorst: Privat und dienstliche Schriften*, Vol.2, pp.387-89; the quoted passage is from p.287. Portions of Scharnhorst's review are published in Stadelmann, *Scharnhorst*, p.183.

46 Scharnhorst, *Anzeige von einem englischen Heldengedichte;* in Kunisch (ed.), *Scharnhorst: Privat und dienstliche Schriften*, Vol.2, pp.388 and 387.

the valorous record of the British soldier during the War of the First Coalition certainly dismayed Scharnhorst. 'Too bad Homer's mind does not rest on all poets!'[47]

Another opportunity to analyse the French Revolutionary Wars came from Georg Heinrich von Berenhorst (1733-1814). The scion of the legendary Prussian *Feldmarschall* Leopold I, Prince of Anhalt-Dessau (1676-1747), Berenhorst entered Prussian service at 15 and participated in the Seven Years War, serving first as *Adjudant* to Prince Henry of Prussia and then to Frederick the Great. Once a very enthusiastic soldier, Berenhorst soon became so disillusioned with Frederick and his endless wars that in 1761 he requested dismissal from Prussian service. Frederick granted this a year later. Berenhorst returned to Anhalt-Dessau, where he spent the next three decades as a public official, eventually rising to become the Chamber President and Marshall to the Court. He retired from public service in 1791 and devoted the rest of his life to research and writing.[48] From Leipzig in 1796 he published anonymously the first of three volumes of his best known and influential work, *Observations on the Art of War, on Its Progress, Its Contradictions, and Its Reliability.*[49]

Berenhorst presented an interesting challenge for Scharnhorst. In his subtitle Berenhorst claimed that any 'layman with a knowledge of history' could understand his *Observations on the Art of War*. He then provided a brief survey of military history, in which he concluded the Greeks and Romans had brought the art of war to its first perfection, only to see it decline dramatically during the long centuries of the Middle Ages. Following some technological innovations, the art and now science of war began its ascent with the military reforms of Maurice of Nassau during the Dutch wars of independence. The beginnings of 'a new art' then commenced with Gustavus Adolphus during the Thirty Years War. Next came the great military organisational skills of French Minister of War François Michel Le Tellier, Marquis de Louvois (1641-1691), who under Louis XIV thoroughly reformed the French army and enabled it to achieve military hegemony in the art and science of war for the next hundred years. After the French came the Prussians, who under Frederick the Great brought the art and science of war to its nadir during the Seven Years War. In fact, throughout most of his first volume, Berenhorst denounced the artificial tactics and veneration of Frederick the Great.[50] Looking back on the history of warfare, Georg Heinrich von Berenhorst concluded 'the ancients' (the Greeks and Romans) were more 'artistic' then the moderns.[51] Notably absent in this first volume was a historical account of the recent wars of the French Revolution.

47 Scharnhorst, *Anzeige von einem englischen Heldengedichte;* in Kunisch (ed.), *Scharnhorst: Privat und dienstliche Schriften*, Vol.2, pp.387-89; the quoted passages are from pp.389 and 388; respectively.

48 On Berenhorst, see Eduard von Bülow (ed.), *Aus dem Nachlasse von Georg Heinrich von Berenhorst* (Dessau: Karl Aue, 1845/47; reprint ed.; Osnabrück: Biblio Verlag, 1978). Bülow's introduction provides a biographical sketch of Berenhorst and his works. Also see the article by Eberhard Kessel, 'Georg Heinrich von Berenhorst: Ein Anhaltinischer Theoretiker und Geschichtsschreiber der Kriegskunst am Ende des 18. Jahrhunderts', *Sachsen und Anhalt: Jahrbuch der Histroischen Kommission für Sachsen-Anhalt Halle* 9 (1933), pp.161-98.

49 Georg Heinrich von Berenhorst, *Betrachtungen über die Kriegskunst, ihre über Fortschritte, ihre Widersprüche und ihre Zuverlässigkeit (Leipzig: Gerhard Fleischer dem Jüngern, 1796, 1798, and 1799).*

50 See the interesting discussion of this in Rudolf Bahn, *Georg Heinrich von Berenhorst, der Vefasser der 'Betrachtungen über die Kriegskunst'* (Halle: Hofbuchdruckerei der Bernburgischen Zeitung, 1911).

51 Berenhorst, *Betrachtungen über die Kriegskunst*, Vol.1, pp.40-41. Berenhorst's comparison between ancient and modern warfare can be found in Chapters 1 (pp.1-18) and 5 (pp.88-114).

What disappointed Scharnhorst was Berenhorst's failure to define his terms clearly for the layman and then provide suitable examples to support his assertions. In Scharnhorst's opinion, this first volume displayed a general lack of clarity. Going through Berenhorst's book he cited page after page where the author was incorrect in his assertions.[52] He concluded that Berenhorst wove together his incoherent and often contradictory thoughts using history as his mosaic. Apparently confused by his own version of history, and especially the significant difference between the art and science of war, Berenhorst decided to use the words of renowned generals to speak for him. One was French Marshal Maurice de Saxe (1696-1750), who in his *Rêveries sur l'Art de la Guerre* (1757), wrote: 'War is a science covered with darkness. In darkness one cannot walk safely. Tradition and prejudice, the natural consequences of ignorance, are its basis. All sciences have principles and rules, war alone has none'.[53]

While Scharnhorst certainly agreed with de Saxe's assessment, he used this citation to point out the many contradictions in Berenhorst's book. At times Berenhorst claimed war was a science. At other times he wrote how chance, accident, coincidence, and the different personalities of military leaders dominated warfare.[54] Defining the art of war clearly baffled Berenhorst. In Berenhorst's defence Scharnhorst noted how difficult it is to describe the art of war adequately, and said that 'no good books have been written on this' until 1748, when another French marshal, Jacques-François de Chastenet, Marquis de Puységur (1656-1743), published his thoughts on the subject.[55] Scharnhorst wondered if Berenhorst really understood the nature of war.

Another source of irritation for Scharnhorst came whenever Berenhorst tried to disguise (through misdirection) his discussion of significant differences between the professional standing armies of the European monarchies and the citizen armies of revolutionary France. Berenhorst had originally intended to analyse the French Revolutionary Wars of 1793 and 1794 in his first volume, as well as Prussian operations in Poland in 1794. Instead, he incorporated this critique in the third volume of *Observations* (1798).[56] Then, in an effort to clarify what he had stated in his survey of military history, Berenhorst used topical areas as chapter headings throughout the remainder of Volume One to illustrate his concepts. Some of these were: 'Frederick II', 'The Marshal from Saxony', 'A War' or 'the so-called Seven Years War', 'Application and Phenomena' (included various illustrations from the Seven Years War), 'Names' (renowned military leaders, such as Turenne, Montecuccoli, and others from the Seven Years War), 'Knowledge', and 'Character'.

Using topical areas as chapter headings seems to have disoriented Berenhorst even more. For example, when mentioning how patriotic zeal could motivate troops, he cited the loyalty of Greek officers to Alexander, then changed his mind and said that this had more to do with honour than with patriotism. Scharnhorst disagreed, writing in his critique that patriotism

52 See Scharnhorst, *Bemerkungen über die Betrachtungen über die Kriegsk[unst]*; in Kunisch (ed.), *Scharnhorst: Privat und dienstliche Schriften*, Vol.2, pp.390-97, which is a list of these errors.

53 Maurice de Saxe as quoted by Berenhorst. *Betrachtungen über die Kriegskunst*, Vol.1, p.76.

54 Scharnhorst, *Bemerkungen über die Betrachtungen über die Kriegsk[unst]*; Kunisch (ed.), *Scharnhorst: Privat und dienstliche Schriften*, Vol.2, pp.395-97.

55 Scharnhorst, *Bemerkungen über die Betrachtungen über die Kriegsk[unst]*; Kunisch (ed.), *Scharnhorst: Privat und dienstliche Schriften*, Vol.2, pp.393-94. Here Scharnhorst was referring to the Marquis de Puységur's, *Art de la Guerre, par Principes et par Règles* (Paris: Charles-Antoine Jombert, 1748).

56 See the commentary in Kessel, 'Georg Heinrich von Berenhorst', p.169 (Note 34).

'occurred even among the Greeks and Romans'. Scharnhorst pointed out how patriotism was a more powerful stimulus in ancient times than in contemporary Europe.[57] Berenhorst later contradicted his earlier commentary, telling his readers how the inspired leadership of Themistocles and Caesar were excellent examples of patriotism.[58]

Judging from the content of Volume One of his *Observations*, it seemed to Scharnhorst that the primary goal of Berenhorst was to pour out his wrath on Frederick the Great. From his wartime experience, the author maintained that the King of Prussia lacked all appreciation of the military potential of patriotism, since he himself had no national consciousness.[59] Indeed, as Berenhorst pointed out, Frederick could barely speak German. Berenhorst was convinced that Frederick viewed his people as mere subjects and not citizens, looked down at his soldiers as soulless automata for his war machine, and held both in utter contempt.[60] As a result, Frederick suppressed rather than enhanced the moral forces of the Prussian people.[61] For Berenhorst, any objective analysis of Frederick would reveal that he was not the least interested in the morale of his soldiers. In defence of Frederick, Scharnhorst pointed out:

> Everyone who enters battle will be driven by force only. It does not matter whether patriotism, maintenance of life, honour, habit, obedience drives him. It is only by violence that he does what he does, only the cause of the effect is different – a circumstance which is here the same.[62]

Whereas Berenhorst chose not to compare the supposed patriotism of the citizen armies of revolutionary France with that of the professional standing armies of the European monarchies, Scharnhorst offered an interesting observation on this matter:

> Never before in the modern world had a nation represented the ideal of freedom so vividly, so charmingly, as the French. And yet, 9 out of 10 had to be driven forcefully into the army, and still had to be led into battle under penalty of death.[63]

Returning to his original discussion on the art and science of war, Berenhorst concluded that the wars of Frederick the Great contradicted 'all the rules of the art'. Indeed, the

57 Berenhorst, *Betrachtungen über die Kriegskunst*, Vol.1, p.30. For Scharnhorst's response, see *Bemerkungen über die Betrachtungen über die Kriegsk[unst]*; Kunisch (ed.), *Scharnhorst: Privat und dienstliche Schriften*, Vol.2, p.390.

58 Berenhorst, *Betrachtungen über die Kriegskunst*, Vol.1, pp.156 and 199; respectively.

59 Berenhorst, *Betrachtungen über die Kriegskunst*, Vol.1, pp.167 and 169-70.

60 Berenhorst, *Betrachtungen über die Kriegskunst*, Vol.1, pp.108-09. Interestingly, much of what Berenhorst wrote about Frederick the Great mirrors the thoughts of Lessing.

61 Berenhorst, *Betrachtungen über die Kriegskunst*, Vol.1, pp.155-56. For Berenhorst's discussion of Frederick the Great, see Chapter 7 (pp.143-64). Lessing would probably have agreed completely with Berenhorst.

62 Scharnhorst, *Bemerkungen über die Betrachtungen über die Kriegsk[unst]*; Kunisch (ed.), *Scharnhorst: Privat und dienstliche Schriften*, Vol.2, p.390.

63 Scharnhorst, *Bemerkungen über die Betrachtungen über die Kriegsk[unst]*; Kunisch (ed.), *Scharnhorst: Privat und dienstliche Schriften*, Vol.2, p.390. Scharnhorst's statement here is supported by the anonymous English account, *A Concise Narrative of all the Actions*, pp.41-43 and 59.

Prussians were victorious 'despite the art'.[64] Scharnhorst agreed in part with this assessment and added the reason why. It was simple: 'Frederick was superior to his enemies' and his 'army was the most adept in combat'.[65]

Unknown to Scharnhorst at the time were Berenhorst's thoughts when he had composed his *Observations*. They are contained in several notes Berenhorst made while writing his book. In one, 'The Main Idea of the Entire Work', the author professed the typical Enlightenment view that the art and science of war, like the other arts and sciences, advanced human understanding and thus supported human development.[66] Significantly, Berenhorst did not believe the art of war was based on rigid principles and rules, and that war could be reduced to a system. To him, war embraced the realm of uncertainty, with all its uncontrollable variables. No system however developed could possibly harness the endless modifications and emotions that occur in war.[67] Scharnhorst agreed completely with Berenhorst here and expressed similar ideas throughout his commentary.[68] Had Scharnhorst known Berenhorst's thought process in 1796, he might have noted how Berenhorst, in his quest to relate ideas to reality, confused himself and others. Years later in 1804, when all three volumes of *Observations* were in print, Scharnhorst wrote about this in his lengthy, critical review of Berenhorst in *New Military Journal*.[69] For now, he continued to instruct Prince Adolphus and composed a memorandum that focused on training the army to fight an entirely different kind of war.

As he was fashioning his response to the French Revolution, Scharnhorst drafted a memorandum on 30 May 1797, entitled, *'On the Training and Formation of an Army in Peacetime'*. In this important concept paper he planned to address 'the formation [of an army] for the little war' [*Bildung zum kleinen Kriege*], and to base his analysis on the works of French *Maréchal* Victor-François, Duc de Broglie; Frederick the Great; Raimondo Count von Montecuccoli; and Duke Ferdinand of Brunswick.[70] He probably intended this to be additional instruction for Prince Adolphus, since it appears to include further explanation of material he had already presented to the prince. Many of the topics Scharnhorst covered here had appeared earlier in his *Military Field Pocket Book* (1792). Interestingly, at the time of this memorandum,.he was in the process of updating and expanding his pre-war publications with the latest tactics, techniques, and procedures, and illustrated with examples

64 Berenhorst, *Betrachtungen über die Kriegskunst*, Vol.1, pp.66-67.

65 Scharnhorst, *Bemerkungen über die Betrachtungen über die Kriegsk[unst]*; Kunisch (ed.), *Scharnhorst: Privat und dienstliche Schriften*, Vol.2, p.397.

66 See 'Die Hauptgedanke des ganzen Werks', in Bülow (ed.), *Aus dem Nachlasse von Georg Heinrich von Berenhorst*, Vol.1, pp.5-6.

67 See 'Kurze Inhaltsanzeige, dies für die erbetenen Censoren der Handschrift bestimmt', in Bülow (ed.), *Aus dem Nachlasse von Georg Heinrich von Berenhorst*, Vol.1, pp.3-5.

68 For example, see Scharnhorst, *Bemerkungen über die Betrachtungen über die Kriegsk[unst]*; Kunisch (ed.), *Scharnhorst: Privat und dienstliche Schriften*, Vol.2, pp.391 and 393-97.

69 See Gerhard von Scharnhorst's Review of 'Georg Heinrich von Berenhorst, *Notwendige Randglossen zu den Betrachtungen über die Kriegskunst, ihre über Fortschritte, ihre Widersprüche und ihre Zuverlässigkeit. Leipzig: Fleischer, 1802', Neues militärisches Journal* 12 (1804), pp.244-58.

70 Gerhard Scharnhorst, *'Ueber die Uebung and Bildung einer Armee in Friedenszeiten, 30 May 1797', Nachlaß Scharnhorst*, Nr. 131, Sheets 2-10. The concept outline of this paper is published in Kunisch (ed.), *Scharnhorst: Privat und dienstliche Schriften*, Vol.2, pp.86-87; the quoted passage is from p.86.

taken from his recent combat experience. Once he had finished this draft, he published his penetrating analysis of French military success during the War of the First Coalition.

On the day King George promoted him to *Oberstlieutenant*, Gerhard Scharnhorst reintroduced *New Military Journal*. This time he partnered with *Capitain* Decken. This enterprise illustrates the finest ideals of the German Enlightenment. Friedrich von der Decken came from the ancient Hanoverian landed gentry, the *Uradel*; Gerhard Scharnhorst from the peasantry. They had served together at Menin and were now assigned to the General Staff. In both cases Scharnhorst was Decken's superior officer. And while their views on military service and the Wars of the French Revolution were polar opposites, they nonetheless complemented each other very well and remained friends until Scharnhorst's death during the 1813 campaign in Germany.[71]

In hopes of capturing the attention of potential readers, Scharnhorst and Decken chose as the subtitle for their new release: *Military Commentaries of our Time, in Particular the French Revolutionary War in the Year 1792 and Its Continuation*.[72] The first article was Scharnhorst's response to the French Revolution and its influence on the art of war. He titled this book-length monograph, 'Development of the General Sources of French Fortune in the Revolutionary War [hereafter cited as 'Basic Reasons for the French Success'], and Particularly in the Campaign of 1794. As an Introduction to the History of this Campaign'.[73] He apparently gave a draft copy to Wallmoden before its publication.[74]

After 200 years, Scharnhorst's incisive analysis remains 'one of the best surveys of the War of the First Coalition'.[75] His study went far beyond the realm of purely military considerations (strategic, operational, and tactical) and addressed the awesome power of a free society. In the very first sentence he concluded: 'The source of the misfortune which struck the Coalition powers in the French Revolutionary War must be strongly linked to their internal conditions and those of the French nation'. In a footnote associated with the word 'conditions', he told his readers that it 'refers here to both physical and moral conditions'.[76]

71 See the collection of letters between Scharnhorst and Decken that illustrate this connection; in Joachim Niemeyer (ed.), *Scharnhorst-Briefe an Friedrich von der Decken, 1803-1813* (Bonn: Ferdinand Dümmler, 1987). On pp.17-27, Niemeyer discusses the close friendship between Scharnhorst and Decken.

72 Interestingly, most secondary sources published during the late eighteenth century and during the nineteenth and into the twentieth centuries used the two titles *Military Commentaries* or *Military Memoirs* when citing this journal. The original title, *New Military Journal*, was rarely used, so that one could easily distinguish between those articles written prior to the War of the First Coalition, and those written afterwards.

73 Gerhard Scharnhorst, 'Entwickelung der allgemeinen Ursachen des Glücks der Franzosen in dem Revolutions-Kriege, und insbesondere in dem Feldzuge von 1794. Als Einleitung zur Geschichte dieses Feldzuges', *Neues Militärisches Journal* 8 (1797), pp.1-154. This study was later incorporated as part of von der Goltz (ed.), *Militärische Schriften von Scharnhorst*, pp.192-242; and then in Gersdorff (ed.), *Gerhard von Scharnhorst: Ausgewählte Schriften*, pp.45-110; and also in Usczeck and Gudzent (ed.), *Gerhard von Scharnhorst: Ausgewählte militärische Schriften*, pp.97-150. References below are from Gersdorff (ed.), *Gerhard von Scharnhorst: Ausgewählte Schriften*.

74 See Note 6 to Scharnhorst's Letter of 10 November 1796 to Wallmoden; in Kunisch (ed.), *Scharnhorst: Privat und dienstliche Schriften*, Vol.2, p.53.

75 Peter Paret, 'Clausewitz and the Nineteenth Century', in Michael Howard (ed.), *The Theory and Practice of War* (New York: Praeger, 1966), p.26.

76 Scharnhorst, 'Entwickelung der allgemeinen Ursachen des Glücks der Franzosen', in Gersdorff (ed.), *Scharnhorst: Ausgewählte Schriften*, p.49 and Note 1.

In his opinion, 'the struggle was indeed too unequal: one side had everything to lose, the other little'.[77]

Scharnhorst's use of psychology in analysing war and society was novel for his time. Later, in his introductory remarks to Volume Nine of *New Military Journal* he wrote:

> The psychological part of the art of war is a field that is not at all well understood… We owe this inconceivably to the fact that the principal benefit of history: the difficult and yet so useful knowledge of the human heart, which is obtained most readily by the study of events resulting from vast and far-reaching designs, is almost completely lost.[78]

Scharnhorst understood military and political leaders rarely committed their thought processes to paper for later analysis. Nevertheless, this did not dissuade him from seeking to comprehend the complex human nature of war. Understanding the human heart was for Scharnhorst a critical component when studying leadership and the art of war.

Scharnhorst clearly demonstrated the exceptional clarity of his brilliant and powerful intellect in this examination of French success and coalition failure. He was first and foremost a practical and experienced soldier, 'remarkably unaffected by the propagandists of either the old or the new orders'.[79] His purpose was to persuade princes, statesmen, scholars, and soldiers alike that the aroused citizen armies of a free people had completely eclipsed the professional standing armies of the royal monarchical institutions of Europe. As he so succinctly put it, 'The organisation of the French armies and the way they are led deserve our full attention'.[80] Without an equivalent modernisation of their own states, the princes of Europe could not hope to defeat the French. The social and political transformation of French society that had empowered the people went hand-in-hand with her military transfiguration and battlefield success. The two were inseparable.

Scharnhorst's study ranged from the political and social motives of the belligerent powers to a comparative analysis of the combat effectiveness of their battlefield tactics, techniques, and procedures. His conclusions were objective, defending neither the coalition nor the French. He began by again repudiating the excuses the allies gave for their dismal failure. His analysis here seemed to prefigure Prussia's later collapse in 1806.

> The unfortunate fate that befell the belligerent powers in the Revolutionary War cannot have its source in individual circumstances and random events. One has cause to take the trouble to get to know what happened.
>
> A campaign can end disastrously because of the impractical measures of a cabinet or general; a battle can be lost because of a small error of some subordinate commander; a fortress can fall because of treachery; but when 5 to 6 armies lose 10

77 Scharnhorst, 'Entwickelung der allgemeinen Ursachen des Glücks der Franzosen', in Gersdorff (ed.), *Scharnhorst: Ausgewählte Schriften*, p.58.

78 Gerhard Scharnhorst, 'Vorbericht', *Neues militärisches Journal* 9 (1798), pp.i-iv; the quoted passage is from p.iv.

79 Paret, 'Clausewitz and the Nineteenth Century', p.26.

80 See Gerhard Scharnhorst, 'Von den Vorzügen der Abtheilung einer Armee in Armee-Divisionen' (1801?); in Kunisch (ed.), *Scharnhorst: Privat und dienstliche Schriften*, Vol.2, pp.774-82; the quoted passage is from p.776.

> campaigns in 5 years, when many of the strongest fortresses in Europe fall without even a fight: then the reasons for failure cannot be just accidental events or isolated mistakes that originated through corruption, misunderstanding, cabal, or ignorance; rather, their source must lie in much deeper causes.

Scharnhorst felt that it was far too convenient for the princes to emphasise the randomness of their failures. This was 'a consequence of the innate short-sightedness' of people who permitted their 'passions to displace reason' and 'who always' tend to prejudge events 'before they can clearly see the necessary pretexts upon which their judgment is based'.

> The honour and the spirit of the German military, and the confidence of the standing armies already suffers from the false ideas which one makes of the events of this war. It is high time to give the public certain assumptions, which may have already hit deep roots.[81]

Scharnhorst told his readers to search in the social, political, cultural, and military organisations of the belligerents to find the real causes for French victory and coalition defeat.

What was so original about Scharnhorst's analysis was the way he captured the essence of war. Without solid military facts, accurate troop strengths, or battle dispositions, Scharnhorst was nevertheless able to draw his conclusions from his empirical observations, coupled with his thoughtful analysis of war and society gained from an objective study of history. In doing so he destroyed the existing paradigm of war. Success in war no longer depend solely on the genius of the generals and the discipline and obedience of the soldiers. The unbridled passions of the people now dominated war, and this is what clearly frightened Schlözer, Rehberg, and Brandes.

Turning to coalition ignorance of the French national character, Scharnhorst pointed out that a failure to know their enemy was one of the major reasons for the allied defeat. He found it inconceivable that coalition leaders accepted without any verification the false reports of French public opinion given to them by the *émigrés*, who led the allies to believe that the Revolution was the work of a small minority and could easily be crushed.

> The wrong intelligence, which the *émigrés* presented about the internal situation in France, and the hatred that the political parties of the Coalition states harbored for and against the Revolution, contributed to a circumstance whereby the Coalition could not properly judge the necessary means for war against the French nation, and thus they did not choose the appropriate measures in this war.
>
> From the beginning the *émigrés* had the greatest interest in misrepresenting the situation in France, as if a victory over this nation would involve few difficulties. By this means they moved the Coalition powers to war. Initially, they called for only a small force of combatants; they realised perhaps as well that if the small force

81 Scharnhorst, 'Entwickelung der allgemeinen Ursachen des Glücks der Franzosen', in Gersdorff (ed.), *Scharnhorst: Ausgewählte Schriften*, pp.49-51.

> proved to be insufficient, a larger one would have to be deployed, once the war had finally been started.
>
> They pretended (or perhaps they even believed it in part) that the French nation had been misled by a small number of men to its new Constitution; the greater number was (supposedly) for the old order and was yearning earnestly to be able to wrest itself from the tyranny of the National Convention. The *émigrés* spoke of their many ties to the French army and claimed these (many) French soldiers would come over to the ranks of the Coalition as soon as the Coalition presented itself in combat.[82]
>
> It seems at first sight incredible that such a great and important enterprise could be launched based on such partisan witnesses as were the *émigrés*.

Unfortunately, as Scharnhorst concluded, 'men follow their predilections and their passions', and the classic political blunder soon followed. On 24 July 1792, as the Prussians and Austrians prepared to invade France, Duke Karl Ferdinand of Brunswick issued his Manifesto, in which he told the French people that if they did not want to incur the wrath of the European princes, they must submit to the 'legitimate authority' of their king, Louis XVI. This immediately put an end to the bickering among the various factions in the National Assembly and united the people behind the Revolution.[83] An infuriated mob attacked the Tuileries palace on 10 August and imprisoned Louis XVI.

On the allied side Scharnhorst found no unity of effort. Many princes, including Duke Karl, as well as ministers and generals, were opposed to the war. To them it was unnecessary. Many argued that if the Revolution did not have the support of the people, as the *émigrés* claimed, then it would certainly fail. Others hated the Revolution because it threatened their interests. Still others simply hated the French. All of these jealousies and political differences created the inevitable friction that always hinders the effective operation of a coalition. Lastly, there were those who championed the rights of the individual.

> When the French Revolution began, a large number of the noblest minds were fired by the ideal of a more perfect and more beneficent government. This was especially true among young people with a generous feeling for right and for the suffering of the less fortunate class of people.
>
> Those who loved reading (that is, most of the educated people) had already grasped in their hearts the idea of a better constitution, which had long been seductively preached in novels and poems. Many of these ideas of liberty, independence, and equality had been brought into circulation by the American war.[84]

82 Scharnhorst, 'Entwickelung der allgemeinen Ursachen des Glücks der Franzosen', in Gersdorff (ed.), *Scharnhorst: Ausgewählte Schriften*, p.52.

83 Scharnhorst, 'Entwickelung der allgemeinen Ursachen des Glücks der Franzosen', in Gersdorff (ed.), *Scharnhorst: Ausgewählte Schriften*, p.53. Interestingly, in Footnote 5, Scharnhorst wrote: 'It would be the greatest injustice in the world if these false measures were imparted to the Duke of Brunswick'. Clearly, Scharnhorst was being 'politically-correct' here.

84 Scharnhorst, 'Entwickelung der allgemeinen Ursachen des Glücks der Franzosen', in Gersdorff (ed.), *Scharnhorst: Ausgewählte Schriften*, p.54.

Unfortunately, with divided counsels, the allies were no match for the French, who utilized the entire physical and moral resources of their nation. Indeed, time would demonstrate the validity of Scharnhorst's conclusion. With no unity of effort among the royal houses of Europe, the French and later Napoleon remained free to conquer one dynasty after another, until the allies finally (and once again half-heartedly) united in 1813 to turn back the tide of French aggression in Europe.

Over the next three chapters Scharnhorst highlighted the social, political, and moral differences of the belligerent societies that led to French victory and coalition defeat. He began with France and asked his readers to focus their attention on the history of France and how it had always influenced French nationalism, which in turn allowed France to marshal all her resources and use them in war. Ironically, it was the coalition that had done the most to mobilise the French people.

> The terrible position the French found themselves in, surrounded by several armies which sought (or so they believed) to enslave them and condemn them to eternal misery, inspired the soldier with courage, induced the citizen to make voluntary sacrifices, gathered supplies for the army, and attracted the civilian population to the colours.

Using some of the thoughts Lessing had expressed about the French in his writing, Scharnhorst also noted how pride in their allegedly superior civilization had fired French indignation over foreign interference in their internal affairs:

> They held themselves alone to be enlightened, wise, free, and happy – all of the other nations to be uneducated, brutal, and unfortunate. The happiness of all mankind would be lost if they did not preserve themselves against the Coalition armies. They believed themselves to be fighting not just for their own continued existence and fortune, but rather for that of all humanity.[85]

Turning to the rigor and terror Robespierre had introduced, Scharnhorst concluded (as did Brandes initially) that these atrocities ironically had a very favourable influence on the French people and their war effort.

> The cruelty with which the French nation was treated accustomed it to death and all the sacrifices which war required; it gave a greater vivacity to adjustments of all types, and through it man could carry out tasks that otherwise would have been impossible. Through it one could take bread from the hungry and send it to the army, without thereby causing popular unrest. Through it things went so far that, for a considerable period, no one consumed meat (the Republican Fast) when the army lacked it. This vivacity alone prompted the rich to sacrifice their buried treasures to the cause of the war; only thereby could they save their lives.

85 Scharnhorst, 'Entwickelung der allgemeinen Ursachen des Glücks der Franzosen', in Gersdorff (ed.), *Scharnhorst: Ausgewählte Schriften*, p.57.

Scharnhorst ended his discussion by again pointing out, 'The situation of the belligerents was very unequal'. Through trail, tribulation, and sacrifice, the French people were hardened for war and willing to fight. On the coalition side, 'an aversion to war, the greatest gentleness, vanity, and even opposition to the measures of war, came from both the nations and from the various branches of the government'.[86] As a result, two very different types of soldiers met on the battlefields of the War of the First Coalition.

French domestic innovations provided tremendous power to the state and made possible the most significant tactical innovation of the war – the *tirailleur*, or skirmisher. Scharnhorst maintained 'it is an undeniable truth' that the individual French soldier, epitomised by the *tirailleur*, 'had decided most of the engagements of this war, and that they are superior to those of the Coalition armies'. He understood that there was nothing stronger in war than the heart of a volunteer.

> They were more skilful, and one can also say, possessed a greater bravery than the Coalition armies. The soldier of the latter, who was accustomed to regular movements, to a machine-like behaviour, and not how to use the terrain (every ditch, every tree, every hill), and positioned with order and in mutual support, was subject here to the cunning, the inquisitive, and the speedy Frenchman.[87]

The light service had fostered the intelligence and independent judgment of the common soldier. Scharnhorst felt that the natural instincts of the soldier had returned to battlefield and to the conduct of war, much like he had stated in his essay on light troops and as Berenhorst had stated in his analysis of the Greeks and Romans. No longer was the French soldier a coerced, mindless robot in lock-step formation, moving and firing like a machine, and only upon order. Now he was able to think and respond freely (both individually and as part of a team) to the ever-changing conditions of the battlefield.

> The ingenious spirit of the French, the desire to exert themselves, and their great knowledge in positional and fortress warfare, makes them exquisitely suited for it. The physical ability and high intelligence of the common man enables the French *tirailleurs* to profit from all the advantages offered by the terrain and the general situation, while the phlegmatic Germans, Bohemians, and Dutch form on open ground and do nothing but what their officer orders them to do.[88]

Scharnhorst understood that the French had not invented this new tactical system; rather, it was the product of a gradual evolution of tactical doctrine that had been underway throughout Europe since the Seven Years War.

86 Scharnhorst, 'Entwickelung der allgemeinen Ursachen des Glücks der Franzosen', in Gersdorff (ed.), *Scharnhorst: Ausgewählte Schriften*, pp.66 and 67.

87 Scharnhorst, 'Entwickelung der allgemeinen Ursachen des Glücks der Franzosen', in Gersdorff (ed.), *Scharnhorst: Ausgewählte Schriften*, p.84.

88 Scharnhorst, 'Entwickelung der allgemeinen Ursachen des Glücks der Franzosen', in Gersdorff (ed.), *Scharnhorst: Ausgewählte Schriften*, p.85.

Count Wilhelm zu Schaumburg-Lippe had often experimented with the use of skirmishers, attack columns, and mobile artillery. Under the stimulus of the Revolution, the French were the first to amalgamate these innovations, taking full advantage of their awesome military power.

> The *Commission de l'organisation et du movement des armées de terré* considered these circumstances and based on them the system of always waging war in broken and covered terrain, where everything depends on the defence and attack of positions, of avoiding large battles if possible, and instead wearing out the Allied armies with skirmishes, outpost affairs, and isolated attacks in woods and ravines.
>
> Here they drew on the national character of the French. Here they drew the greatest advantage from their many fortresses and other strong positions without interfering with the ever-dubious outcome of a battle which would have discouraged the army and perhaps the whole nation. Here they were able to use their superior power in a decided manner, and to attack and strike individual positions with three to four times the strength. Here they had the opportunity to accustom their untrained troops gradually to fire, to teach them war, and to inspire confidence in them through small battles.[89]

French military superiority was the direct result of a new social and political order that sought to capitalize on its strengths and minimize its weaknesses.

Scharnhorst noted that the French soldier was 'guided solely by the honour of being a competitor', while in the coalition armies, 'bravery and dexterity are rarely, if ever, rewarded'. Rewards were always reserved for the princes and senior commanders, but never for the common soldier.[90] Scharnhorst also rejected the notion held by many allied officers that the German *Jäger* and fusilier 'had always done the work of the French *tirailleur*'.[91] This was sheer nonsense, as he noted. In the eighteenth century the *Jäger* had always played a subsidiary role within the framework of the so-called small war. For coalition officers, French victories were an aberration. For Scharnhorst, the spirit of the French Revolution, epitomised in the *tirailleur*, was the main reason for French tactical success.

In his summary of French success and coalition failure, *Oberstlieutenant* Gerhard Scharnhorst argued that the fundamental political, social, and military conditions of the belligerents clearly favoured the French Republic. The French people were united; the coalition divided. Competing national interests within the coalition led to a lack of any unity of effort against a united France. When reviewing the various campaigns, Scharnhorst cited the great distances the allied councils of war were located from each other and from the front. Before executing any operational plan, leaders in London, Berlin, Vienna, and The

89 Scharnhorst, 'Entwickelung der allgemeinen Ursachen des Glücks der Franzosen', in Gersdorff (ed.), *Scharnhorst: Ausgewählte Schriften*, pp.85-86.

90 Scharnhorst, 'Entwickelung der allgemeinen Ursachen des Glücks der Franzosen', in Gersdorff (ed.), *Scharnhorst: Ausgewählte Schriften*, pp.85 and 96; respectively.

91 Scharnhorst, 'Entwickelung der allgemeinen Ursachen des Glücks der Franzosen', in Gersdorff (ed.), *Scharnhorst: Ausgewählte Schriften*, p.109 (Footnote 22).

Hague took months of negotiations before deciding on a single course of action, and this decision was constantly being altered by the fluid situation at the front. Time and again, whenever allied leaders had decided to do something, and had communicated that decision to their field commanders, it was already overcome by events. As Scharnhorst concluded, 'If a single power conducts the war, these circumstances are quite different'.[92]

Scharnhorst maintained that the overwhelming superiority of the French revolutionary armies lay in a coherent and aggressive strategy that reflected national rather than dynastic interests.[93] He based his conclusions on his thorough understanding of the French Revolution and its impact on the art of war. It was the spirit of the French people (embodied in the nation-in-arms) that had truly revolutionized warfare. Once the people became involved in the survival of France, the French army had been completely transformed. Lazy, hesitant, and incompetent leaders had been ruthlessly weeded out. All were relieved of their commands. Some were executed, while others had fled the country. In their place young, dynamic, effective, and enthusiastic leaders emerged, so that by 1797 the French army was the best in Europe.

> The French have a great advantage in having at the head of their armies, divisions, and brigades, young active men who are eager to stand out. This is not possible in other armies without completely destroying all internal relationships. Only the republican enthusiasm and the spirit of the Revolution permit this arrangement of things.

While not directly citing the inept and cautious aristocratic leadership of coalition forces, Scharnhorst noted that:

> There is no doubt that the prudence and experience of an older general is required to be a master of the field, if the highest perfection is required. But because experience depends not on the number of campaigns, but on the spirit with which they are conducted; since the perception of wisdom in an older general is very misleading, since connection, nepotism, envy, and other passions come into play here; it is seldom found that these older men, who are appointed commanding generals, possess the experience and prudence which they presuppose.

Focusing on the leadership of the French army, Scharnhorst asserted that the French Republic did not readily appoint younger officers to lead her armies. On the contrary, only young officers who had distinguished themselves by their 'activity, insight, courage, and fatherly love' rose to command these armies. The most important qualities of a commanding

92 Scharnhorst, 'Entwickelung der allgemeinen Ursachen des Glücks der Franzosen', in Gersdorff (ed.), *Scharnhorst: Ausgewählte Schriften*, p.91.

93 See Gerhard Scharnhorst, '*Ueber die Uebung and Bildung einer Armee in Friedenszeiten*', *Nachlaß Scharnhorst*, Nr. 131, Sheets 6-10. This portion of his concept paper was later published as 'Scharnhorst über Führerauswahl und Führerverantwortlichkeit', *Militärwissenschaftliche Rundschau* 2 (1944), pp.117-19; and incorporated in Gersdorff (ed.), *Scharnhorst: Ausgewählte Schriften*, pp.111-16. Excerpts are also printed in Lehmann, Vol.1, pp.235-36. References in the text are taken from Gersdorff (ed.), *Scharnhorst: Ausgewählte Schriften*.

general, Scharnhorst stated, are his 'determination, a firm and enterprising character, and a great heróic feeling and energy. Without these qualities, in complicated circumstances, he will serve the state badly'.[94]

Scharnhorst then focused his attention on the selection of leaders and their responsibility, two concepts he had treated in earlier papers on discipline, rewards and punishments, and leader accountability. He noted how promotion in the French army depended upon competence, service, and bravery, not birth, privilege, and connection. With a capable officer and non-commissioned officer corps to instil a high morale and sense of duty in the rank and file, the French were able to exercise initiative, flexibility, and independence on the battlefield. This, in turn, enabled them to adapt quickly to new and unexpected circumstances, which resulted in greater mobility, more elastic tactics, and the unparalleled freedom, enthusiasm, and heroism of the individual soldier. How much of this was a result of the *leveé en masse* (which had permitted the French to sustain mass casualties), Scharnhorst did not say. What he did say was clear: in the coalition armies, where family connection and favouritism were paramount, tactical and operational flexibility were inconceivable. Even Frederick the Great had difficulty here. Fortunately for Prussia, he had been able to overcome these prejudices during his campaigns of the Seven Years War, when he cashiered his own brother and other worthless noblemen, even though they were 'counts and princes'.[95] This was certainly a lesson Scharnhorst wanted Prince Adolphus to learn, and why he insisted the prince study the wars of Frederick the Great.

French success in the War of the First Coalition was no aberration. *Oberstlieutenant* Gerhard Scharnhorst was among the first anywhere to see the dawn of this new era of warfare. The old European world order was over. It was broken. It was fully compromised, and its destruction was now just a matter of time. The creation of a free society in which the individual citizen-soldier stood paramount clearly captivated Scharnhorst's imagination. In the writings of Rousseau, Voltaire, Montesquieu, and Homme, Scharnhorst read what many German *Aufklärer* had sought for their own Fatherland, only to be denied by their ruling, aristocratic elites.

'Do not call attention to things which people will find out for themselves', Scharnhorst had advised Tempelhof in January 1793. 'And do not speak publicly of the injustices of the upper classes toward the lower'.[96] Scharnhorst's caution here was the result of prudence, not blind adherence to or satisfaction with existing conditions. He had approved of coalition intervention as a defensive war against any spirit of renewed French aggrandizement, but not as a crusade against the ideals of the Revolution, which he wholeheartedly supported. When composing his thoughts on the reasons for French success and considering his recent dealing with Hanoverian officials and King George III, Scharnhorst may have remembered what he had told his wife four years earlier, when he wrote, 'We are being set back in favour of the aristocrats, and yet we fight for them'.[97]

94 'Scharnhorst über Führerauswahl und Führerverantwortlichkeit', in Gersdorff (ed.), *Scharnhorst: Ausgewählte Schriften*, p.113.

95 'Scharnhorst über Führerauswahl und Führerverantwortlichkeit', in Gersdorff (ed.), *Scharnhorst: Ausgewählte Schriften*, pp.114-15.

96 Letter of 27 January 1793 to Colonel Georg von Tempelhof; in Kunisch (ed.), *Scharnhorst: Privat und dienstliche Schriften*, Vol.1, pp.102-04; the quoted passages are from p.103.

97 Letter of 1-3 June 1793 to Klara; in Kunisch (ed.), *Scharnhorst: Privat und dienstliche Schriften*, Vol.1, p.218 (3 June).

16

Defending the Electorate

With the Treaties of Leoben (17 April 1797) and Campo Formio (17 October 1797), the War of the First Coalition officially ended on continental Europe. Sadly, any lasting peace in Europe with a French Republic determined to conquer its natural frontiers was impossible. Indeed, French possession of her natural frontiers 'became an unquestionable article of faith among Frenchmen'. The long-term struggle between France and England (and Hanover by association) continued elsewhere, while the spectre of French aggression across the Rhine into Germany haunted ministers in London and Berlin.[1]

Over the next several months, senior officials of the Observation Army in north-western Germany discussed possible courses of action. Both Wallmoden and Duke Karl of Brunswick were really concerned that French ambitions in Germany would not be contained by pieces of paper. Both agreed that the Observation Army had to remain intact and operational.[2] In his letter to King George on 6 January 1798, Wallmoden sought a decision from London. He noted that springtime, 'the season convenient for some operations, rapidly approaches', and stated: 'The repeated and urgent ideas of the Duke of Brunswick are certainly not an empty precaution'.[3]

Four days earlier on 2 January, Freytag had died. While deciding on his successor, King George placed Wallmoden in command of all Hanoverian troops.[4] Meanwhile, in accordance with a plan Wallmoden and the Duke of Brunswick had agreed upon back on 3 July 1797, and which Scharnhorst had developed, the Commanding General moved his

1 See the interesting discussion in Albert Sorel, *L'Europe et la Révolution française* (Paris: Plon, 1885-1904), Vol.4, pp.469-70. The quoted passage is from the splendid study of Jordan R. Hayworth, 'Conquering the Natural Frontier, p.456; later published as *Revolution France's War of Conquest in the Rhineland*. Also see the analysis in Schroeder, *The Transformation of European Politics, 1763-1848*, pp.158-76.

2 Some interesting documentation on the situation in Hanover at this time can be found in Hann 41, Nr.26: *Verschiedene Nachrichten, bes. Privat-Correspondenzen über die dermalige Lage des Kurfürstenthums Hannover, 1796-1797*; deposited at the Niedersächsisches Landesarchiv, Hanover.

3 Johann Ludwig, *Reichsgraf* von Wallmoden-Gimborn to King George III (6 January 1798); excerpted in Klippel, *Scharnhorst*, Vol.2, pp.310-11.

4 Wallmoden's assumption of command address to the Hanoverian troops on 30 January 1798 is published in Sichart, *Geschichte der Königlich-Hannoverischen Armee*, Vol.4, pp.675-76; his actual assumption of command can be found on pp.471-73. Source documents on this transition can be found in Hann 41, III, Nr.189: *Interimskommando (vorübergehendes Kommando) nach dem Tode des Feldmarschalls von Freytag, 1798*; deposited at the Niedersächsisches Landesarchiv, Hanover.

headquarters to Hanover and began relocating Hanoverian units on 12 January. This continued throughout the winter and was completed on 10 May 1798. Nearly the entire Hanoverian corps was displaced to new locations along the Weser and Leine Rivers.[5] At the same time the Prussians relocated their forces, with some remaining on the Hase and Ems Rivers, while others marched to the Weser, where they joined the defensive line established by the Hanoverians. Still, there was no word from London.

Silence from London caused Wallmoden to repeat his original assessment of the situation to the king on 23 February, nearly seven weeks after he had initially notified London. He again expressed his agreement with the Duke of Brunswick that the Observation Army should not be strung out in a cordon defence; rather it should be 'concentrated closer together, so as not to be exposed to any surprise (from the French)'. He also pointed out France already had a strong concentration of forces along the Lahn River, in the Principality of Lippe, and along the lower Rhine. Their 'incessant movements' have given the French the ability 'to have a strong corps on the Weser in a very short time'. This would clearly endanger Hanover and especially Göttingen. Wallmoden also concurred with the Duke of Brunswick's suggestion that Prussia and England should convince Saxony to join the alliance and become part of the Observation Army.[6] Wallmoden ended his report with the important point that it would take the Saxons 'at least four weeks to assemble their forces'. In that time a strong French corps could have already occupied Göttingen.[7]

While senior officials within the Observation Army discussed probable courses of action and sought to gain approval for their actions from Berlin and London, Scharnhorst and Lecoq continued to provide them with valuable information and detailed analyses to help inform their decisions. Between 5 May and 2 November 1797, Scharnhorst had sent Wallmoden detailed contingency plans for Hanoverian forces should the French seek to occupy Hanover, Hamburg, and Bremen.[8] On 23 June he provided Wallmoden with the march distances between various assembly areas around Bremen, in Westphalia, and along the lower Weser in the vicinity of Hameln and Neustadt. These would provide a basis for the movement tables Scharnhorst would later construct.[9] On 2 July, he notified

5 Documentation on this relocation can be found in Hann 41, I, Nr.48: *Verteidigungsmaßregeln für das Herzogtum Bremen-Verden. Enthält u.a.: Verlegungsplan für die Truppen an der Hunte und Aller, 02.1797-03.1797*; and in Hann 41, I, Nr.40: *Verhandlungen über die militärische Deckung der Unterweser durch die im Lande befindlichen Truppen, 06.1797-07.1797*; deposited at the Niedersächsisches Landesarchiv, Hanover.

6 Some interesting source documentation that led to Wallmoden's analysis can be found in Hann 41, I, Nr.43: *Vorbereitungen des französischen Generals Hoche für eine Invasion in das Kurfürstentum Hannover. Nachrichten des Rittmeisters von Scheither aus Frankfurt und Wesel. Korrespondenz mit dem Herzog von Braunschweig, Landgraf von Hessen, dem preußischen Minister von Haugwitz und dem hannoverschen Kabinettsministerium. Bedarf an Munition, 1797-1798*; deposited at the Niedersächsisches Landesarchiv, Hanover.

7 See Wallmoden's Report of 23 February 1798 to King George III; published in Klippel, *Scharnhorst*, Vol.2, pp.311-12.

8 For example, see Gerhard Scharnhorst, '*Marsch-Routen für einen Theil der in Hoyashen und Osnabrükschen cantonirenden hannövrischen Truppen, wenn sie sich bey Hameln versammeln sollen*' (between 5 May and 2 November 1797); in Kunisch (ed.), *Scharnhorst: Privat und dienstliche Schriften*, Vol.2, pp.90-94. These troop movements and locations are also discussed in Sichart, *Geschichte der Königlich-Hannoverischen Armee*, Vol.4, pp.668-71.

9 See Gerhard Scharnhorst, 'Pro Memoria' (23 June 1797); in Kunisch (ed.), *Scharnhorst: Privat und dienstliche Schriften*, Vol.2, p.90.

Lecoq of his intent to conduct a reconnaissance of this probable future area of operations.[10] The next day Wallmoden received a note from the Duke of Brunswick regarding the latter's concerns over the security of his own principality of Brunswick, as well as the ports of Hamburg and Bremen. If the French seized these critical ports, England would be cut off from Germany.[11] Anticipating the Duke's concerns, Scharnhorst had already inspected these areas and had sent an interim report on 5 July to Wallmoden, who then informed the Duke about the key points Scharnhorst had made thus far on his reconnaissance.[12] In his final report, Scharnhorst noted that troop locations in north-western Germany might have to be extended in order to provide adequate coverage and protection of key strategic areas.[13] Throughout the remainder of 1797, Scharnhorst refined his staff work, continually updating Wallmoden with troop locations and routes of march as the situation became clearer.[14] By March 1798, the Duke of Brunswick and Wallmoden had decided units of the Observation Army could no longer remain in their perilous locations if they were to deter any French aggression in north-western Germany.

Meanwhile, on 4 March 1798, Lecoq wrote to Scharnhorst, anxious to obtain copies of the maps the Hanoverians were making of the area of operations.[15] The Prussians were operating blindly without maps, and Lecoq planned to publish a set under the authority of Friedrich Wilhelm III (for use by the Prussian army) and sought Scharnhorst's permission to do so.[16] A week later Scharnhorst informed Lecoq he would gladly forward copies of what maps he had on hand and would continue to assemble additional ones as they were being made and give them to Lecoq, but only if Wallmoden approved. He also offered to

10 Gerhard Scharnhorst to Karl Ludwig von Lecoq (2 July 1797); in Kunisch (ed.), *Scharnhorst: Privat und dienstliche Schriften*, Vol.2, pp.94-96.

11 The Duke's concerns of 3 July 1797 are addressed in Sichart, *Geschichte der Königlich-Hannoverischen Armee*, Vol.4, p.671.

12 Scharnhorst's interim report of 5 July 1797 to Wallmoden can be found in Kunisch (ed.), *Scharnhorst: Privat und dienstliche Schriften*, Vol.2, pp.112-13. Wallmoden's report of 'middle July 1797' to the Duke of Brunswick follows pp.113-14.

13 Gerhard Scharnhorst, 'Pro Memoria' (after 7 August 1797); in Kunisch (ed.), *Scharnhorst: Privat und dienstliche Schriften*, Vol.2, pp.114-15. Scharnhorst's detailed 'Notes' from his reconnaissance (3 to 14 July 1797) are on pp.96-112. Some source documents can be found in Hann 41, I, Nr.41: *Berichte der Feldguiden über Kolonnen-Wege und Lager im Hoyaischen und Lippischen, desgleichen bei Hameln nebst einer Relation (Bericht) des Oberstleutnants Scharnhorst. Enthält u.a.:13 Geländezeichnungen für den Raum nördlichen Hoya, 1797*; deposited at the Niedersächsisches Landesarchiv, Hanover. The drawings in this folder are exceptional.

14 For example, see Gerhard Scharnhorst, 'Pro Memoria' (29 September 1797) regarding the quartering of units; his 'Veränderungen in der Dislocation von einem Theile des hannövischen cantonirenden Corps' (10 October 1797); his 'Marsch-Routen der hannoverischen Trupen bey der Observations Armee in Westphalen' (between November 1797 and January 1798); his letter of 20 November 1797 to *Oberstlieutenant* and *Ober-Adjudant* Georg Carl Löw von und zu Steinfurt concerning the quartering of troops; his 'Marsch-Route für die Regimenter, welche von der Hunte and der Aller un Leine verlegt werden' (before 12 January 1798); and his 'Pro Memoria' (31 January 1798) on the quartering of troops – all contained in Kunisch (ed.), *Scharnhorst: Privat und dienstliche Schriften*, Vol.2, pp.118-119, 119-20; 122-28; 128-29; 129-30; and 130; respectively.

15 Karl Ludwig von Lecoq to Gerhard Scharnhorst (4 March 1798); published in Klippel, *Scharnhorst*, Vol.2, pp.312-13.

16 This work was later published as Karl Ludwig von Lecoq, *Topographische Karte in 22 Blättern, den größten Theil von Westphalen enthaltend, so wie auch das Herzogthum Westphalen und einen Theil der Hannöverschen, Braunschweigischen und Hessischen Länder, nach astronomischen und trigonometrischen Ortsbestimmungen auf Befehl Sr. Maj. Friedrich Wilhelm III., Königs von Preußen* (Berlin: Carl Zäck, 1805-12).

assist Lecoq in this endeavour. In a postscript, he added, 'For a long time I have asked you, dear friend, for two things'. These were copies of Prussian infantry and cavalry 'service and drill regulations' implemented after the Seven Years War. He told Lecoq that he already had the infantry regulations of 1750 and the cavalry ones of 1743. Details of how the Prussian infantry and cavalry trained and exercised in peace, and then how they fought in war, fascinated Scharnhorst and, as he told Lecoq, would greatly assist him in understanding the mind and methods of Frederick the Great.[17] On 21 April, he thanked general staff engineer *Fähndrich* Franz Ludwig Preuβ for his meticulous work in compiling geographical data and several of the maps Lecoq had requested.[18]

Elsewhere, Scharnhorst sent a brief note to his publisher Christian Helwing on 22 April, requesting he 'not issue the second volume of *Denkwürdigkeiten*' until the Commanding General had reviewed it and had given 'his consent to its publication'.[19] It seems the severe criticisms Scharnhorst had directed against the allied coalition in his piece on the 'Basic Reasons for the French Success' had clearly stung a few military and civilian officials in Hanover, London, and elsewhere. While the identity of these people is uncertain, they sought to stop any future public critique of their actions, even if it 'appeared in the relative obscurity of a scholarly journal'.[20] Scharnhorst's article was published in August 1797, around the time he had been promoted to *Oberstlieutenant* and given a salary increase. While the timing of both events was mere chance, suspicious officials at the Court of St James and in Hanover may have thought otherwise. In any case, Wallmoden was taking no chances.

Judging from his experience dealing with coalition leaders during the previous campaigns, the Commanding General certainly agreed with much of what his General-Quartermaster-Lieutenant had written. Significantly, it was Wallmoden who had encouraged and supported Scharnhorst in his modernisation efforts, and then had protected him against the nefarious schemes of Trew, Freytag, and Lenthe. With the death of Freytag, Wallmoden was in line to succeed him. It is highly doubtful that the Commanding General had any real concerns about his future. His ardent defence of Scharnhorst was well-known at the Court of St James and within the various cliques in the Hanoverian and Prussian armies. Furthermore, there was no one more qualified or senior to him in the Hanoverian army.

On 2 May 1798, King George III officially promoted his Commanding General to field marshal, replacing Freytag. With no suitable replacement (Prince Adolphus was apparently too young), *Feldmarschall* Johann Ludwig, *Reichsgraf* von Wallmoden-Gimborn retained command of the Hanoverian Observation Corps as well.[21] The king also promoted Hammerstein, Diepenbroick, and Trew to *General-Lieutenant*.[22] The second volume of *Denkwürdigkeiten* was published soon thereafter in 1798. Interestingly, Decken authored

17 Scharnhorst to Lecoq (11 March 1798); in Kunisch (ed.), *Scharnhorst: Privat und dienstliche Schriften*, Vol.2, pp.131-32.

18 Gerhard Scharnhorst to Franz Ludwig Preuβ (21 April 1798); in Kunisch (ed.), *Scharnhorst: Privat und dienstliche Schriften*, Vol.2, p.134.

19 Gerhard Scharnhorst to Christian Dietrich Helwing (22 April 1798); in Kunisch (ed.), *Scharnhorst: Privat und dienstliche Schriften*, Vol.8, p.519.

20 See the discussion in Paret, *Clausewitz and the State*, p.64.

21 Klippel, *Scharnhorst*, Vol.2, p.312.

22 Sichart, *Geschichte der Königlich-Hannoverischen Armee*, Vol.4, p.676.

all but two of the articles in this issue of *Military Memoirs*. Scharnhorst's sole contribution was the initial instalment of his 'Campaign of the Coalition Armies in Flanders in the Year 1794'.[23]

Not waiting for London to decide on a course of action, the Commanding General had decided on 25 April to reposition (once again) selected units of the Hanoverian corps. The first priority was the defence of the Weser River and the Electorate capital. Accordingly, *Feldmarschall* Wallmoden ordered Prince Adolphus and *General-Lieutenant* Hammerstein to deploy three battalions from their respective infantry commands to the neighbouring cities, towns, and villages to provide a better area defence around Hanover.[24] At the same time Scharnhorst recommended moving an infantry battalion and two companies closer to the Prussians along the Weser and its tributary the Aller, to close any gaps between Prussian and German forces and to facilitate a better defence of these rivers.[25]

On 2 May, Scharnhorst voiced concerns with the current challenges associated with this repositioning. He noted that as the perimeter of the Hanoverian Leibgarde Regiment was being extended, it required support from the 3. Artillerie Batterie in Neustadt. He also believed that while the proposed concentration of the 4. and 5. Grenadier Bataillons and the 14. Infanterie Regiment posed 'no difficulty', *General-Major* Bernhard von Linsingen (commanding the advanced guard) would have to inform local officials (who were beginning to file complaints) that these relocations were only a temporary expedient.[26] A month later Scharnhorst updated Wallmoden on the progress of the quartering of troops from the 3. Cavallerie Regiment and the 2. Grenadier Bataillon in the villages surrounding Bremen. He was delighted to report that all was going well 'and there has been no partisanship here'.[27]

Ever anxious to obtain maps of the operational area, Lecoq wrote to Scharnhorst on 25 and 28 April, requesting urgent delivery of these charts. Realising the Prussians were lagging behind the Hanoverians with respect to operational maps, and following Scharnhorst's example, Lecoq had received permission from the Duke of Brunswick a year earlier to assemble a group of young officers to make military maps of the key locations of Prussian forces in north-western Germany, especially Westphalia (a map of which the Prussians did not possess). Among those Lecoq chose was Karl Freiherr von Müffling (1775-1851), a lieutenant who had written a poem about the general staff officer for *Magazine of the Latest Noteworthy War Stories*, a publication designed to enhance the morale of the Prussian soldier. Müffling's piece was entitled, 'What is an Officer of the General Staff?'[28]

23 Gerhard Scharnhorst, 'Feldzug der verbundenen Armeen in Flandern, im Jahre 1794. (mit Tabellen), ' *Neues militärisches Journal* 9 (1798), pp.169-369.

24 See 'Veränderte Dislocation, in den Brigaden des Prinzen Adolf Königl. Hoheit und des Herrn General-Major von Hammerstein' (not after 25 April 1798); in Kunisch (ed.), *Scharnhorst: Privat und dienstliche Schriften*, Vol.2, p.134.

25 Gerhard Scharnhorst, 'Pro Memoria' (1798); in Kunisch (ed.), *Scharnhorst: Privat und dienstliche Schriften*, Vol.2, p.135.

26 Gerhard Scharnhorst, 'Pro Memoria' (not after 2 May 1798); in Kunisch (ed.), *Scharnhorst: Privat und dienstliche Schriften*, Vol.2, pp.146-47.

27 Gerhard Scharnhorst, 'Pro Memoria, die Bequartirung der bremschen Dörfer betreffend' (not after 5 June 1798); in Kunisch (ed.), *Scharnhorst: Privat und dienstliche Schriften*, Vol.2, pp.148-49; the quoted passage is from p.149.

28 Karl *Freiherr* von Müffliln g, 'Was ist ein Offizer des Generalstabes?' *Magazin der neuesten merkwürdigen Kriegsbegebenheiten* (Frankfurt am Main, 1793-96), compiled by *Hauptmann* August Wilhelm von Leipziger, a *General-Adjudant* of *Feldmarschall* von Möllendorff, and cited in Hans-Joachim Behr (ed.), *Karl Freiherr von*

Lecoq found Müffling's poetic mockery of the general staff officer amusing, and was anxious to meet *Lieutenant* Müffling who, interestingly enough, despised all scientific activities and clearly had no desire to work on the Prussian General Staff. Upon his arrival at Prussian headquarters in Minden, Müffling tried to convince Lecoq that he was not suited for the job. Müffling soon realised that the more he endeavoured to dissuade Lecoq, the more Lecoq wanted his services. And so Müffling resigned himself to his new duties. As he later wrote:

> This vocation gave my life a different direction, for there was nothing left for me to do but to sit behind the books, to think hard about my tasks, and to solve them as best I could. I reconnoitred roads, rivers, mountain ranges. I looked for advantageous positions and drew routes of march from one to the other.

Lecoq was so pleased with Müffling's work that he assigned him the mission of mapping the Principality of Minden. 'And so, from 5 o'clock in the morning until dark, throughout September [1797], I produced a very excellent draft copy made of glued-together chart measurements'.[29]

Later that fall Duke Karl told his General-Quartermaster he wanted to tour the battlefield around Minden and Gohfeld, where his famous uncle Duke Ferdinand had won his decisive victory over the French in 1759, which had ended the French threat to Hanover. At that time, young Duke Karl had commanded the force at Gohfeld. Lecoq gave Müffling the task of drawing a battlefield map for the Duke, who was so impressed that he chose Müffling as his guide. 'The weather was beautiful', Müffling recalled.

> The Duke was so thrilled by the memories from almost forty years, and I was very satisfied with the fact that I knew everything so well. I had been able to name all the places whose towers were seen, which was not difficult, since I had just recorded everything that could be overlooked.

'From that day on, until the end of his life', Müffling remembered, 'the Duke was my most gracious patron'.[30] For the next two years, Lecoq had Müffling survey the area along the Weser River from Minden to the port of Bremen, and westwards to Osnabrück. Müffling's propensity for cartography would later play a significant role in his military career and the development of the later Prussian General Staff.

Scharnhorst responded to Lecoq on 5 May, informing his colleague that he had just received Lecoq's letters on 3 May, and wondered why 'the Ohsen Map, the description of the area between the Weser and Innerste', (a tributary of the Leine River) was not already in Lecoq's possession. Scharnhorst told Lecoq that Wallmoden had brought it with him on 1 May, when he had met with the Duke of Brunswick to discuss the current situation. Scharnhorst also stated that he would have the map of Bückeburg copied within the next

Müffling: Offizier-Kartograph-Politiker (1775-1851). Lebenserinnerungen und kleinere Schriften (Köln/Weimar/Wien: Böhlau, 2003), p.53.

29 Behr (ed.), *Karl Freiherr von Müffling*, pp.52 and 53.

30 Behr (ed.), *Karl Freiherr von Müffling*, pp.53-53; the quoted passages are from p.54.

two weeks. In closing this portion of his letter, he reminded Lecoq about the 'gratuity' [*Douceur*] Duke Karl had promised to pay the Hanoverian engineer officers for their work making maps for the Prussians.[31]

In the second part of his letter of 5 May, Scharnhorst answered Lecoq's questions regarding the light artillery gun carriage – 'the *Falconet Carriage for the Infantry*', which Count Wilhelm had invented. For reasons not clarified in his correspondence, Lecoq was hoping Scharnhorst could procure for him a prototype of this carriage. Scharnhorst explained that this carriage had been perfected during the Count's defence of Portugal in 1762. It was light and versatile, capable of being 'moved by men in action' and designed mainly for a three-pound cannon. If the Prussians wanted to mount larger cannon on this carriage, the wheels would have to be enlarged, but could easily be adapted to the roads in Westphalia. Scharnhorst also told Lecoq that Count Wilhelm had presented a prototype to Frederick the Great and was certain the Duke of Brunswick had seen it in Berlin or Potsdam. 'Unfortunately', as Scharnhorst to Lecoq, 'since most armies are not equipped with the three-pounder, and the prejudice against it has become general, I believe that there is not much to be done in this matter'. He blamed this on the contempt most soldiers had for the artillery, since they had little inclination to study its capabilities and employment, and to discover its great advantages. He ended with an interesting thought, 'No science, my friend, is as full of prejudices as the artillery, when one excludes theology'. Before bidding 'Adieu' to his colleague, Scharnhorst added his thoughts to the discussion he and Lecoq had been having on European affairs. 'The new disturbances on the political horizon have made a deep impression upon me, though I have foreseen them with the greatest probability'. The two had been following the French invasion of Switzerland a month earlier, which had resulted in the formation of the 'Helvetic Republic'. Scharnhorst told Lecoq, 'May God grant that your good king and the Duke of Brunswick keep our lives safe, or else we are completely lost'.[32]

As the Hanoverian General-Quartermaster-Lieutenant rode across north-western Germany, he inspected the various troop locations, made critical notes of his discoveries, discussed important issues with the field commanders, and reported the results of his progress to the Commanding General. Throughout his journey Scharnhorst was continually analysing the challenges facing the Hanoverian army. The ideas he toyed with were kept in a notebook. Some of the subjects he discussed were peacetime field exercises for the entire army (not just for individual units), troop ammunition and equipment requirements, arranging the number of guns per battery depending on their calibre, wartime operations, some introductory considerations on field instruction, the challenges and requirements of practical warfare, the defence of Hanover, key positions around Hanover, principles of the art of war, combined arms operations (along with various tactical options based on the skills and abilities of the infantry, cavalry, and artillery), and the Battle of Pirmasens (1793).[33]

31 Scharnhorst to Lecoq (5 May 1798); in Kunisch (ed.), *Scharnhorst: Privat und dienstliche Schriften*, Vol.2, pp.147-48; the quoted passages are from p.147.

32 Scharnhorst to Lecoq (5 May 1798); in Kunisch (ed.), *Scharnhorst: Privat und dienstliche Schriften*, Vol.2, pp.147-48; the quoted passages are from pp.147 and 148; respectively.

33 See Gerhard Scharnhorst, 'Notebook' (1 May 1798 and later); in Kunisch (ed.), *Scharnhorst: Privat und dienstliche Schriften*, Vol.2, pp.135-45. The contents of this notebook compare favourably to the description of items Klippel

Many of these thoughts are found in his memoranda to Wallmoden, his modernisation ideas, and his publications. All were connected to his findings and concerns as he inspected the Observation Army and its area of operations, as well as his discussions with the field commanders, especially Hammerstein, Diepenbroick, Prince Adolphus, and Dallwigk.

Scharnhorst was concerned with the fighting ability of the Hanoverian army. He noted that while the deployed units were on a higher state of readiness than those back in garrison, 'The whole army must be brought to the field as often as possible, in short marches', and must be ready at any moment to engage the enemy, 'represented by a pre-staged corps', and to defeat it under various scenarios. Such force-on-force exercises were essential for the *Bildung* of officers and non-commissioned officers, and the realistic training of soldiers.

> Here one must teach the troops to manoeuvre in small wars, etc. For this you must design certain dispositions, you must use the stratagems of higher tactics, you must look for the greatest order and the strictest discipline, you must reject the mistakes made and teach the means to avoid them in the future.[34]

While each regiment might have its own operating procedures, Scharnhorst wanted soldiers trained to one common standard throughout the entire army. Once again, the *Bildung* of the soldier topped his modernisation agenda.

A critical component of any realistic combat training was logistics. Scharnhorst maintained ammunition requirements for the infantry and artillery must be consistent with their wartime expenditures. Noting that a large differential existed between ammunition loads used during peacetime training and those shot during actual combat operations, Scharnhorst inferred that all too often artillerymen and infantrymen were lazy and did not carry the necessary ammunition during peacetime exercises, and thus did not know what was really required on campaign. Once again he demanded that the leaders of these soldiers (the officers and non-commissioned officers) must to be held accountable. With the artillery this also included the number of personnel and horses per battery, depending on the gun calibre. Based on his experience, Scharnhorst calculated these statistics (personnel, ammunition, and horses) for each gun calibre, and even went as far as to suggest additional crewmen and horses, because at any time an artilleryman or a horse might be out of action. Significantly, he also believed that neither artillerymen nor infantrymen could ever have too much ammunition.[35]

Turning to another of his favourite topics, Scharnhorst expended considerable ink discussing military operations and the art of war. Many of his notes from this reconnaissance trip dealt with this extremely important subject. He even sketched the outline of a doctrinal piece he intended to write on tactics, which he began with an interesting observation.[36]

claimed Scharnhorst kept in his 'Manual in Folio'.

34 See Gerhard Scharnhorst, '*Annotations*' (1 May 1798); in Kunisch (ed.), *Scharnhorst: Privat und dienstliche Schriften*, Vol.2, pp.135-37; the quoted passage is from pp.135-36.

35 Scharnhorst, '*Annotations*' (1 May 1798); in Kunisch (ed.), *Scharnhorst: Privat und dienstliche Schriften*, Vol.2, pp.136-37.

36 Scharnhorst, '*Annotations*' (1 May 1798); in Kunisch (ed.), *Scharnhorst: Privat und dienstliche Schriften*, Vol.2, pp.137-38.

> All movements of an army, all its positions, must be initiated in such a way that the movements and positions of an army must not merely have the purpose of attacking the enemy or of stopping him by the strength of the position, but their chief purpose must be to strike him through stratagems.[37]

Scharnhorst then wrote that military operations are composed of two important parts: one was mechanical; the other strategic. The mechanical portion is taught during peacetime manoeuvres, and answers 'how an army, in different scenarios, positions itself on different terrain and fights on it', how 'it moves from one position to another, or from one camp to another', how 'it quarters itself in a variety of villages, and is united at a certain point', and how it then conducts offensive and defensive operations. 'This section has its rules derived mostly from the nature of the circumstances [*aus der Natur der Sache*], and generally is accepted as true and based on firm principles.[38]

This concluded Scharnhorst's discussion of the mechanical aspects of the art of war. The strategical portion is more intellectual. It addresses 'how it is possible to strike individual parts of the enemy with superior power, or how to achieve the end goal *without fighting*'.

> This section is wanting in our works on the art of war. Maurice de Saxe and the Great King [Frederick the Great] provided only a few fragments in their writings. However, it is to be found in the campaigns of these great men, and in those of Montecuccoli and Turenne, Duke Ferdinand and others.[39]

Once again Scharnhorst recommended the study of military history to discern the art of war. 'In no part of the art of war is it as difficult to give a few lessons as in this'.

> The terrain (so manifold in its variety) and the internal organisation of the division of an army (assembled in the simplest cases) combined with each other, already give rise to an incredible quantity of variations in the conduct of operations. However, their connection with the possible stratagems, with the reflections which have the moral influence upon the outcome of the operations, are almost infinite, and make it inconceivably difficult to choose the most advantageous among them, to arrange and initiate the individual means so that they can lead to a great purpose.[40]

Here is yet another expression of why Gerhard Scharnhorst believed that war is an art served by the sciences.

Following his discussion on the art and science of war, Scharnhorst sketched a topical outline that appears to be a template for a doctrinal manual on offensive operations. It

37 For some unknown reason Scharnhorst later deleted this passage. See Scharnhorst, '*Annotations*' (1 May 1798); in Kunisch (ed.), *Scharnhorst: Privat und dienstliche Schriften*, Vol.2, p.137 (Note d).

38 Scharnhorst, '*Annotations*' (1 May 1798); in Kunisch (ed.), *Scharnhorst: Privat und dienstliche Schriften*, Vol.2, p.137.

39 Scharnhorst, '*Annotations*' (1 May 1798); in Kunisch (ed.), *Scharnhorst: Privat und dienstliche Schriften*, Vol.2, pp.137-38; the quoted passage is from p.137. Interestingly, these notations are virtually identical to the commentary Scharnhorst wrote about Berenhorst in his other notes.

40 Scharnhorst, '*Annotations*' (1 May 1798); in Kunisch (ed.), *Scharnhorst: Privat und dienstliche Schriften*, Vol.2, p.138.

contained three parts. The first consisted of five chapters that analysed various ways to attack an enemy force. The second spent three chapters discussing flank attacks, while the third was devoted to stratagems that would achieve success in these attacks. One of these ruses Scharnhorst would later discuss in Prussia and dealt with how 'to induce the enemy to detach' his forces, and then to strike his separated units with *'superior power'*.[41]

Turning to the defence of Hanover, Scharnhorst used a sketch map to illustrate his points as he systematically analysed the defence of the Electorate. He carefully studied three courses of action the enemy could take: (1) a frontal assault; (2) an attack on the right flank; and (3) an attack on the left flank. Scharnhorst then provided what he believed to be the appropriate defensive countermeasures to defeat such attacks.[42] What is noteworthy is how he conducted this wargaming while on his travels in this area. As he inspected troop locations and collected information for his maps, he spoke with Hammerstein, Diepenbroick, and Prince Adolphus on the most appropriate way to defend the Electorate and its capital. From these discussions he formulated his analysis to Wallmoden, as the latter was repositioning units of the Hanoverian corps for the defence of Electorate. Several locations where forces under the commands of Prince Adolphus and Hammerstein were to be relocated are mentioned in this portion of Scharnhorst's notebook. It is very probable that his notations here contained the solution these leaders had developed together.

Returning to his doctrinal discussion, Scharnhorst sketched the outline of another piece, which he entitled, *Clarifications of the General Principles of the Art of War*. This study was to contain two chapters that treated infantry, cavalry, and artillery as a combined arms team, how they fight together on level ground and on various other types of terrain, and how the 'characteristics' of their different weapons systems contribute to combined arms tactics. As usual, he began with a general discussion of the three arms and made some interesting observations. When discussing cavalry, Scharnhorst lamented: 'How often cavalry withdraws from battle when commanders do not feel mobile artillery makes a difference here'. In another instance he wrote: 'Only regular, well-disciplined infantry can stand on level ground against cavalry'. Since all armies continued to deploy their infantry in linear formations, he used the Battle of Mollwitz (1741) during the War of the Austrian Succession (1740-48) to demonstrate the need for well-disciplined soldiers. He noted how the magnificent Prussian infantry, with its smooth precision firing, smashed the repeated assaults of the Austrian infantry and cavalry. He concluded that 'good infantry' is always 'the soul of the army'.[43] Interestingly,

41 See Gerhard Scharnhorst, *Entwurf dieses Abschnitts* (1 May 1798); in Kunisch (ed.), *Scharnhorst: Privat und dienstliche Schriften*, Vol.2, pp.138-39; the quoted passage is from p.139. Scharnhorst discussed this stratagem in his lectures on the 1800 French Italian campaign and Battle of Marengo, presented to the *Militärische Gesellschaft* in Berlin in 1801 and 1802. See Charles Edward White, *The Enlightened Soldier: Scharnhorst and the Militärische Gesellschaft in Berlin, 1801-1805* (Westport, Connecticut: Praeger, 1989), pp.68-70.

42 See Gerhard Scharnhorst, 'Hannover besetzt' (1 May 1798) and Gerhard Scharnhorst, *Stellungen bey Hannover* (1 May 1798); in Kunisch (ed.), *Scharnhorst: Privat und dienstliche Schriften*, Vol.2, pp.139-40. Some of the ideas expressed in this memorandum came from the discussions on a possible French invasion found in Hann 41, I, Nr.43: *Vorbereitungen des französischen Generals Hoche für eine Invasion in das Kurfürstentum Hannover, 1797-1798*; deposited at the Niedersächsisches Landesarchiv, Hanover.

43 Scharnhorst, *'Erklärungen der Allgemeinen Grundsätze der Kriegeskunst'* (1 May 1798); in Kunisch (ed.), *Scharnhorst: Privat und dienstliche Schriften*, Vol.2, pp.140-44; the quoted passages are from the same paragraph on pp.143 and 144.

Scharnhorst never mentioned skirmishers, which he had recently claimed were transforming the art of war.

Scharnhorst then summarised his earlier points in the last segment with some 'noteworthy' [*merkwürdig*] highlights from the Battle of Pirmasens. On 14 September 1793, the Prussian army under the command of Duke Karl of Brunswick defeated a French army under *Général de Division* Jean-René Moreau. Expecting an attack, Duke Karl had taken advantage of the broken ground and had placed his guns and troops in entrenched positions. 'Artillery was indeed decisive here, disrupting the columns, according to French officers'. Prussian artillery fire frustrated every French advance, engaging it on both flanks. Scharnhorst also noted that the French soon discovered the Prussians in prepared positions, at locations where they, the French, did not expect to find any resistance. As a result, French infantrymen found themselves in a deadly crossfire and fell back in confusion. Scharnhorst found it odd that the French continued to assault the entrenched Prussians without success. In his closing remarks he wrote how well-entrenched soldiers in well-fortified positions offer 'tactical advantages ... against the attacking enemy', and in many instances 'are indispensable'.[44] A hundred years later, in its study of this engagement, the Historical Section of the Prussian Great General Staff concluded:

> One sees in the French attacks at Pirmasens a picture of a transitional era. A new doctrine is struggling to emerge but is not yet understood; it causes misunderstanding and confusion everywhere and fails against a method of fighting that may be outdated but is familiar and executed with confidence.[45]

This assessment clearly captured what Gerhard Scharnhorst knew at the time but had difficulty convincing others of this emerging trend. In fact, just the opposite occurred. Pirmasens reinforced the accepted reputation of the Prussian army in the minds of its soldiers and leaders and convinced them that Prussia was quite capable of confronting the military challenges of the French Revolution.[46]

Current events were constant themes Lecoq and Scharnhorst discussed throughout 1798. In January, France began assembling an army at Dunkirk for an invasion of England. This may have been the reason British leadership was not focused on the situation in north-western Germany.[47] Then in February, French troops occupied Rome, captured the Pope, and proclaimed a Roman Republic. Two months later they overran Switzerland and proclaimed a similar republic. In July, they landed in Egypt.[48] Scharnhorst mentioned this deteriorating situation in his letter of 17 August to Lecoq, and then agreed with Lecoq's earlier assessment

44 See Gerhard Scharnhorst, '*Battle of Pyrmasens*' (1 May 1798); in Kunisch (ed.), *Scharnhorst: Privat und dienstliche Schriften*, Vol.2, pp.144-45; the quoted passages are from pp.144 and 145.

45 See Großer Generalstab, Abteilung für Kriegsgeschichte, *Pirmasens and Kaiserlautern: Eine Erinnerung an das Jahr 1793*; *Kriegsgeschichtliche Einzelschriften* 16 (Berlin: Ernst Siegfried Mittler und Sohn, 1893), p.312.

46 See the insightful chapter on the Prussian army by Dennis Showalter; in Frederick C. Schneid (ed.), *European Armies of the French Revolution, 1789-1802* (Norman: University of Oklahoma Press, 2015), pp.36-63.

47 Interesting documents on this situation can be found in Hann 41, I, Nr.39: *Französische Angriffspläne gegen England und das Kurfürstentum Hannover, 1797*; deposited at the Niedersächsisches Landesarchiv, Hanover.

48 See Schroeder, 'The Slide into Continental War', *The Transformation of European Politics*, pp.182-200.

about the absence of a German identity. Scharnhorst wrote, 'What you say about the lack of a common spirit is only too true; it characterizes our age, and especially us Germans'.

> The situation is sickening, and yet reason tells us that the monarchical states will not survive if they do not begin to see … that the claims of the French on the Rhine, the possession of Switzerland, of Rome, of Turin, etc., are either a challenge to war or a contempt for all the other European powers that leads to war. Only the English nation is still playing an honourable role in the history of our time.[49]

While nearly all of the European monarchies procrastinated, Great Britain continued the fight against Revolutionary France, inflicting a catastrophic defeat on her fleet during the Battle of the Nile on 1 August 1798.

Interestingly, in this same letter Scharnhorst answered several questions Lecoq had posed regarding the details of how the Hanoverians were making their maps. It was during this time that Lecoq had assigned Müffling the task of mapping the Principality of Minden and the County of Ravensberg using 'a trigonometric network'. Although not specifically mentioned in Lecoq's letter, it looks like the Prussians were having difficulty with their mapping procedures. As Müffling remembered, 'This [constructing a trigonometric network] required new and serious preliminary studies'.[50]

In his response to Lecoq, Scharnhorst explained, 'In our land survey no network is recorded trigonometrically'. 'The entire country is singled out individually using a Mensel [a field measuring instrument] following the instructions in Hogrewe's topographical surveys'.[51] Once this was completed, the individual sheets were put together to form a geographic map. Here Scharnhorst was referring to the method Georg Josua du Plat used from 1764 to 1786 to survey the Electorate of Hanover.[52] It took du Plat 172 map sheets (using a scale of 1:21,333) to record this survey. One final step remained.

Scharnhorst informed Lecoq that Abraham Gotthelf Kästner (1719-1800), a Professor of Mathematics at the University of Göttingen, and Georg Christoph Lichtenberg (1742-1799), placed the latitude and longitude calculations on the du Plat map after it was assembled.[53] 'For your convenience, I have drawn up a table which can be used'.[54] In other news, Scharnhorst told his friend that he intended to return to Münster that September for another

49 Scharnhorst to Lecoq (17 August 1798); in Kunisch (ed.), *Scharnhorst: Privat und dienstliche Schriften*, Vol.2, pp.150-52; the quoted passage is from p.151.

50 See Behr (ed.), *Karl Freiherr von Müffling*, p.54.

51 Scharnhorst to Lecoq (17 August 1798); in Kunisch (ed.), *Scharnhorst: Privat und dienstliche Schriften*, Vol.2, p.151. Scharnhorst is most likely referring to the standard work by Johann Ludwig Hogrewe, *Praktische Anweisung zur topographischen Vermessung eines ganzen Landes* (Hanover and Leipzig: Johann Wilhelm Schmidt, 1773). This is the Hogrewe Freytag sought to reward with the General-Quartermaster-Lieutenant post.

52 Scharnhorst to Lecoq (17 August 1798); in Kunisch (ed.), *Scharnhorst: Privat und dienstliche Schriften*, Vol.2, p.151 (Note 4).

53 Scharnhorst to Lecoq (17 August 1798); in Kunisch (ed.), *Scharnhorst: Privat und dienstliche Schriften*, Vol.2, p.151 (Note 5). In 1772, King George III had commissioned Lichtenberg to travel throughout the Electorate to determine the astronomical location of places.

54 Scharnhorst to Lecoq (17 August 1798); in Kunisch (ed.), *Scharnhorst: Privat und dienstliche Schriften*, Vol.2, p.151. Unfortunately, this table could not be located.

inspection tour. He then planned to return to Hanover via the Principality of Lippe – both major strategic areas of concern for Duke Karl of Brunswick. In closing, Scharnhorst promised to keep Lecoq up to date on his findings and to continue to send him maps as they were completed.

In the fall of 1798, Scharnhorst and Lecoq sent Duke Karl of Brunswick their assessment of the situation and recommendations on the new locations for the Observation Army.[55] Both jointly signed this document, which suggested quartering areas, routes of march to these cantonments, and an assembly point for the Observation Army at Löhne. The Hanoverian corps would be situated on the left flank, southwest of Hanover, around the towns of Herford, Gohfeld, and Vlotho (where units of Hammerstein's and Prince Adolphus' commands were located). Because the magazine at Hameln was not large enough to sustain both Hanoverian and Prussian contingents, Scharnhorst and Lecoq advised extending the Hanoverians south-eastward to the vicinity of Lemgo, in the County of Lippe.[56] Prussian and Brunswick positions would extend from the left bank of the Werre River, north northwest through Herford, as far as Bünde. Lecoq and Scharnhorst also informed Duke Karl that they had reconnoitred these areas and the various routes to them and would submit a complete report (to include maps of the routes and sketches of the camps and positions) to him, so that he could see and judge 'at a glance' [Scharnhorst's *coup d'oeil*] the defensive configuration of the Observation Army. This would help Duke Karl obtain the cooperation of local officials, specifically the necessary support and repairs of the roads and bridges.

Shortly after he and Lecoq had completed their report to Duke Karl of Brunswick, Scharnhorst sent his trustworthy lieutenants – Christian Ziehen and Georg Friedrich Schäffer – to conduct a reconnaissance of the projected Hanoverian area of operations. Scharnhorst told Ziehen 'to reconnoitre the way from Alverdissen to Blomberg' and 'to select a camp for an army between Horn and Blomberg, as near as possible to the first place [Horn], which has its front facing the Diemel'. Ziehen was to take with him the field guides Ludwig Jasper, E. Lindemann, and J.H. Rummel. Always endeavouring to learn from history, Scharnhorst also tasked Ziehen 'to record the position which Duke Ferdinand occupied between Reelkirchen and Siegfeld in 1761', during his defence of Hanover against France. Scharnhorst told Ziehen and his guides to be thorough in their work. He clearly wanted the kind of minute detail he had prescribed in his earlier instructions on reconnaissance.[57]

Turning to *Lieutenant* Schäffer, Scharnhorst ordered him to survey 'a camp for an army between 30 to 40,000 men at Hameln, on the left bank of the Weser'. Schäffer was 'to select a front facing an enemy coming from Paterborn and the Münstershen and record the region'. He was then to travel the route 'between Hameln and Alverdissen' and provide a detailed

55 Gerhard Scharnhorst and Karl Ludwig von Lecoq to Duke Karl of Brunswick, 'Protokoll' (before 10 October 1798); in Kunisch (ed.), *Scharnhorst: Privat und dienstliche Schriften*, Vol.2, pp.152-54.

56 Documentation on the utility of the Fortress Hameln can be found in Hann 41, 1, Nr.44: *Instandsetzung der Festung zu Hameln, 1797-1798*; deposited at the Niedersächsisches Landesarchiv, Hanover. Nicknamed the 'Gibraltar of the North', Hameln was the most heavily fortified town in the Electorate of Hanover.

57 Gerhard Scharnhorst, 'Instruction für den Lieutenant Ziehen von der hannövrischen Artillerie' (middle October 1798); in Kunisch (ed.), *Scharnhorst: Privat und dienstliche Schriften*, Vol.2, pp.154-55; the quoted passages are from p.154.

description of how 'troops and carts' are to traverse it 'in all seasons'. Once Schäffer had completed these tasks, Scharnhorst expected him to reconnoitre all the routes from Hameln to the other towns and villages within the corps area of operation, recording their suitability for troops and 'all kinds of carts in all seasons'. Schäffer was to pay particular attention to water ways and the ferry at Vlotho.[58]

From Hameln on 18 October, *Oberstlieutenant* Scharnhorst updated *Feldmarschall* Wallmoden on the present situation. He began by telling the Commanding General that the Duke of Brunswick 'now demands a different arrangement of quarters than those initially stipulated'. Scharnhorst sent Wallmoden a new draft entitled, 'Dislocation of the Hanoverian Corps in the Hameln Region', and asked the field marshal to approve it so he could send it to Lecoq, along with the march routes 'I am still drafting'.[59]

Scharnhorst then related a disgusting incident so prevalent in German towns during this period. Residents were renting out parcels of the fortress grounds at Hameln to soldiers, so they could enjoy some rest 'under the open sky'. *Oberst* Johann Wilhelm du Plat, Commander of the 7. Infanterie Regiment, was clearly upset with this situation and brought it to the attention of town officials. When he did not receive an appropriate response, du Plat asked Scharnhorst to inform Wallmoden and Prussian authorities. 'If Your Excellency would kindly answer this letter today', Scharnhorst wrote to the Commanding General, 'I can give your answer to Colonel von Lecoq tomorrow in Minden'.[60]

Wallmoden replied immediately to Scharnhorst, who thanked him for his quick response, which 'I received this morning at six o'clock'. He updated the field marshal on the quartering of the corps, telling the Commanding General he had 'immediately sent the draft of Hanoverian and Hessian cantonment quarters, along with the march routes', by special courier to *Oberst* Lecoq. Scharnhorst informed Wallmoden about some other issues he had raised with Lecoq, specifically the situation in Hameln and the forage problems with the cavalry and artillery. 'All of our heavy artillery is dependent on this area', he told the Commanding General.[61] He then enclosed two more reports and their accompanying tables for Wallmoden.

In one of these reports, Scharnhorst discussed the progress he, his lieutenants, and their guides had made concerning the quartering of the Hanoverian corps. He informed the field marshal that they had conducted a reconnaissance of the County of Lippe per order of Duke Karl, and had produced maps and sketches of the area, which were enclosed with this report. 'For the time being, Your Excellency, I have found in the region of Hameln, on the left bank of the Weser, several convenient camps for an army facing a front toward Blomberg'. He then discussed the advantages and disadvantages of this location and concluded that 'through the concentration of the separated positions, and with careful manoeuvring, the

58 Gerhard Scharnhorst, 'Instruction für den Lieutenant Shäfer von der hannövrischen Ingenieur Corps' (middle October 1798); in Kunisch (ed.), *Scharnhorst: Privat und dienstliche Schriften*, Vol.2, pp.155-56.

59 Scharnhorst to Wallmoden (18 October 1798); in Kunisch (ed.), *Scharnhorst: Privat und dienstliche Schriften*, Vol.2, pp.156-57; the quoted passages are from p.156.

60 Scharnhorst to Wallmoden (18 October 1798); in Kunisch (ed.), *Scharnhorst: Privat und dienstliche Schriften*, Vol.2, pp.156-57; the quoted passages are from pp.156 and 157.

61 Scharnhorst to Wallmoden (19 October 1798); in Kunisch (ed.), *Scharnhorst: Privat und dienstliche Schriften*, Vol.2, pp.156-57; the quoted passages are from p.157.

terrain might afford here some opportunity to remedy the disadvantages of overcoming an approaching enemy'.[62]

As he was reconnoitring the area around Alverdissen, Scharnhorst could not find 'any camp sites that combined the qualities of a good position'. Nevertheless, this region was strategically located and would provide a suitable cantonment area for a corps or an army. 'There is also a favourable cantonment area for an army on the high ground of Lichtenhagen and Barse', while 'The region around Horn and Blomberg contains better positions, both with respect to internal strength and external conditions'. Turning to the road network in the projected area, the General-Quartermaster-Lieutenant noted that 'from Hameln to Alverdissen, as well as from Detmold in the region of Horn', most of the roads 'are very bad' and 'very difficult' to navigate.[63] He noted that major repairs would be required to make these routes capable of sustaining heavy military traffic. Scharnhorst ended his report by recommending that he and the Commanding General examine the region together to determine the best course of action for the Hanoverian corps.

Elsewhere, in his letter of 23 October, Prince Adolphus updated King George on his recent tour of his brigade area. The prince had visited the regiments encamped 'in the neighbourhood of Diepholtz', and in the counties of Osnaburg and Münster. These were the repositioned units Wallmoden had recently ordered. 'I can assure your Majesty that I have found them all in very good order'.

> The 4 & 5th Grenadier Battalions and the two Regiments of Light Dragoons are particularly fine. The other three Grenadier Battalions I have not seen as they are quartered near Bremen, but I shall go there tomorrow for to review the two Companies of the Guards which belong to the 1st Battalion.

Prince Adolphus was particularly impressed with the how the infantry was making good progress in its training, which he said had 'come on prodigeously [sic]'.[64]

Scharnhorst's superb analysis of the projected area of operations for the combined Prussian-Hanoverian-Hessian-Brunswick Observation Army was a model staff study. The meticulous detail he put into this report was simply breath-taking. It was 28 pages long and divided into two major parts, complete with maps and sketches. It was titled, 'Concerning the Positions on the Weser and Leine, as an Answer to the Questions Submitted about Them'.[65] The first portion dealt almost exclusively with suitable defensive locations in and around Hameln on the right bank of the Weser River. In the second part Scharnhorst addressed positions and cantonment areas in the County of Lippe, at Hameln, on the left

62 See Gerhard Scharnhorst, 'Bericht an Se. Excellenz den General en Chef Grafen von Wallmoden Gimborn' (middle October 1798); in Kunisch (ed.), *Scharnhorst: Privat und dienstliche Schriften*, Vol.2, pp.158-59; the quoted passages are from p.158. This report is also published in Klippel, *Scharnhorst*, Vol., pp.259-60.

63 Scharnhorst, 'Bericht an Se. Excellenz den General en Chef Grafen von Wallmoden Gimborn', in Kunisch (ed.), *Scharnhorst: Privat und dienstliche Schriften*, Vol.2, pp.158-59; the quoted passages are from p.159.

64 Letter of 23 October 1797 from Prince Adolphus to King George III; in Aspinall (ed.), *The Later Correspondence of George III*, Vol.2, p.632.

65 See Gerhard Scharnhorst, 'Pro Memoria: Die Positionen an der Weser und Leine betreffend, als eine Antwort auf die darüber vorgelegten Anfrangen', Klippel, *Scharnhorst*, Vol.2, pp.285-308.

bank of the Weser River, as well as cantonment areas and positions in and around Hameln and Alverdissen.[66]

From the description Scharnhorst provided of these areas, it is clear that the Weser River was to be the first line of defence for the Observation Army. The Weser forms near the city of Münden by the union of the Fulda and Werra Rivers, and flows 273 miles northward through Hameln, Minden, Bremen, and Bremerhaven to the North Sea. Some 30 miles to the east, and running parallel to the Weser, is the Leine River, which begins in the Thuringian Forest southeast of Göttingen and runs north some 175 miles, through Göttingen and Hanover. It joins the Aller River north of Hanover, and then the Weser to the North Sea. This was to be the second line of defence. Judging by the tone and context of his writing, most of the areas Scharnhorst discussed were already occupied by troops of the Observation Army, and he was merely providing (as his title suggested) an in-depth analysis of those positions to answer the questions Duke Karl of Brunswick and Wallmoden had posed.[67] During the last week of 1798 (26 to 31 December), the remaining detachments of the Observation Army reached their new locations.[68]

With the Observation Army in its new positions, Scharnhorst wrote to Wallmoden on 19 January 1799, apologising for his absence. 'Because of a strained ankle', he said, 'I cannot report to Your Excellency verbally'.[69] He told the Commanding General that Lecoq had received his report and had given it to Duke Karl. Scharnhorst also suggested the Hanoverians needed to establish a 'provisions train' like the one the Prussians had, and which the Duke mistakenly believed the Hanoverians already possessed. This would enable the troops to campaign for nine days before requiring resupply. The Duke was obviously concerned that negotiations with local authorities for their support would not provide the requisite food and forage to sustain the army should hostilities with France begin again. Scharnhorst pointed out that a suitable train would require approximately 700 horses and 300 men, and recommended the Hanoverians constitute a small artillery reserve to accompany the provisions train should the troops be ordered to deploy.

As his ankle healed, Scharnhorst wrote to Lecoq on 20 January to thank him for his letters from Hanover and Minden, and to apologise for being absent from Hanover (and their meetings) for the past two weeks.[70] 'How sad is the prospect for Europe', he told his Prussian colleague, referring to events in Italy. 'Soon the French nation is master of half of Europe, and in the art of waging war, she surpasses everyone'. 'Only a united Europe, fighting with all forms of war, can survive'. Scharnhorst then mentioned the recent unrest in French-occupied countries. In Italy, a Neapolitan offensive launched from Rome and Livorno at the end of November 1798 had led to a national uprising, while in Belgium on 12

66 The second part, Gerhard Scharnhorst, 'Ueber die Positions und Lagerplätze im Lippischen und bey Hameln am linken Ufer der Weser' (before 19 January 1799), is also published in Kunisch (ed.), *Scharnhorst: Privat und dienstliche Schriften*, Vol.2, pp.159-66.

67 Sichart, *Geschichte der Königlich-Hannoverischen Armee*, Vol.4, pp.673-74, details the relocation of Hanoverian units to many of the locations Scharnhorst discussed in this paper.

68 Sichart, *Geschichte der Königlich-Hannoverischen Armee*, Vol.4, p.677.

69 Scharnhorst to Wallmoden (19 January 1799); in Kunisch (ed.), *Scharnhorst: Privat und dienstliche Schriften*, Vol.2, p.405.

70 Scharnhorst to Lecoq (20 January 1799); in Kunisch (ed.), *Scharnhorst: Privat und dienstliche Schriften*, Vol.2, pp.406-07; the quoted passages are from p.406.

October 1798, peasants had revolted against conscription. The French brutally suppressed both insurrections. Scharnhorst closed his letter by promising Lecoq to return the map of the Weser districts of the Duchy of Brunswick in early February.

Two weeks later Scharnhorst was back at headquarters, where he wrote to Lecoq on 3 February, thanking the Prussians 'in the name of Field Marshal Count von Wallmoden for this beautiful piece' (a map of 'Weser District' of Brunswick) and promising Lecoq 'to work seriously on the map of the area between Hoya and Hildesheim'. Turning again to the political map of Europe he noted, 'Here, as in other parts not yet occupied by the French, everything is in the most perfect state of tranquillity'. Unfortunately, the noble courts of Europe failed to see their forthcoming demise. Then, referring to Edward Gibbon's, *The History of the Decline and Fall of the Roman Empire* (1776-88), Scharnhorst told Lecoq:

> I think the privileged class, for the most part, in the whole of Europe; that is, in that part which is not occupied by the French; the mutual childish blindness of the courts leaves no room under these circumstances for any realisation for the sacrifices required for self-preservation. The sovereign who does not keep informed of current events by consulting books, does not understand his true situation.[71]

Scharnhorst clearly saw parallels in Gibbon's study of the events leading to the fall of Rome and the situation currently facing the noble houses of Europe.

As he pondered the worsening situation in Europe, Scharnhorst turned his attention to drafting standard operating procedures for the most critical tasks soldiers must execute in combat. With Hanoverian troops in their locations, Scharnhorst felt it was time to prepare these positions for the defence of the Electorate. His *Concept for an Entrenchment*, dated 4 February 1799, was particularly applicable. It was his attempt to standardise the construction of field fortifications and contained a detailed sketch.[72] During the campaigns of 1793 and 1794, Scharnhorst had observed a complete lack of uniformity in the way Hanoverians entrenched their positions.[73] He had begun putting his thoughts on paper in 1794, composing a series of concept papers that addressed the art of field fortifications.[74] One was *On the Art of Constructing Trenches, and on the Craftsmanship which is used in Them*.[75] He followed this with a description of the various tools (and their use) required for constructing trenches.[76] Several other interesting documents dealt with 'Covered Pits' [*Wolfsgruben*], 'General Regulations on the Application and Defence of Field Entrenchments', the rough draft of a

71 Scharnhorst to Lecoq (3 February 1799); in Kunisch (ed.), *Scharnhorst: Privat und dienstliche Schriften*, Vol.2, pp.407-08; the quoted passages are from p.408.

72 Gerhard Scharnhorst, *Entwurf zu einer Vershanzung [sic] den 4ten Febr. 1799*; in Kunisch (ed.), *Scharnhorst: Privat und dienstliche Schriften*, Vol.2, pp.408-10.

73 See Gerhard Scharnhorst, *Grundsätze der Anlegung und Vertheidigung der Schanzen und die Kunst diselben geschwind aufzuführen* (not before 1794); in Kunisch (ed.), *Scharnhorst: Privat und dienstliche Schriften*, Vol.2, p.677.

74 The editors of Scharnhorst's Papers have grouped these documents as 'Richtlinien für Verschanzungsarbeiten', in Kunisch (ed.), *Scharnhorst: Privat und dienstliche Schriften*, Vol.2, pp.668-708.

75 See Gerhard Scharnhorst, *Ueber die Art, wie die Schanzen gemacht warden, und über das Handwerkszeug, welches man bei denselben gebraucht*, in Kunisch (ed.), *Scharnhorst: Privat und dienstliche Schriften*, Vol.2, pp.670-74.

76 Gerhard Scharnhorst, *Einrichtung des Schanzzeugs*, in Kunisch (ed.), *Scharnhorst: Privat und dienstliche Schriften*, Vol.2, pp.674-75.

lesson plan for teaching field fortifications (complete with historical examples), a commentary on the entrenchments at Mainz in 1796, and several 'Profile Sketches' [*Profilskizzen*] he used to illustrate his discussions.[77] Together, these papers appear to have formed the basis of the construction of a brigade-size position on the Holzberg Ridge near Horn in Lower Saxony in 1798. These field fortifications (which included a redoubt, trenches, covered pits, and other earthworks) were designed to be an infantry brigade defensive position that would protect the brigade against an enemy cannonade and then enable it to defeat a subsequent infantry assault.[78]

Scharnhorst's *Concept for an Entrenchment* captured the vital lessons he had learned from his combat experience and from the construction of field fortifications by units of the Observation Army. Now he sought to standardise these procedures in the Hanoverian army. He envisioned an entrenchment for a brigade-size unit (like the one at Horn), supported by an artillery battery: 'Each redoubt has a face of 60 paces. Positioned here are 8 cannons to fire over the bank. The breastworks on this side are 7 feet high, and the remaining faces are 45 paces long, 6 feet high'. Each redoubt was protected by a moat, with three rows of covered pits in front, followed by a row of palisades, then another three rows of covered pits 150 paces behind the palisades. An infantry battalion would occupy each redoubt, while troops from the other three battalions of the brigade manned a series of trenches behind the redoubt.[79] Once he had completed the design of this entrenchment, Scharnhorst proceeded to discuss its construction. Under ideal conditions, it would take 5-6,000 men requisitioned from the local population and working three days to dig and build the covered pits. It would take 4,000 men working four days to construct the palisades. Interestingly, Scharnhorst did not discuss how this position would be constructed under less than ideal conditions. In any case, he stated the other smaller earthworks were to be built by the brigade infantrymen, with the artillery crews supervising them. Perhaps because he had discussed it earlier, Scharnhorst made no mention of how to construct the central position – the redoubt.[80]

As he was contemplating additional ideas, Scharnhorst wrote to his Danish friend, Mechlenburg, who (in January) had sent him the results of Danish experiments with artillery fire. This lengthy document was 73 pages long, complete with five 'Summary Tables' [*Extract Tabellen*] that compared the results of the different experiments. At the end of the treatise were nine pages that summarised the entire process. The first two pages were titled, 'Experiments' [*Versuche*], followed by the last seven pages of 'Experiment Tables' [*Tabelle*

77 See Gerhard Scharnhorst, *Wolfgruben* (after October 1794); 'Versuch eines: Allgemeinen Reglements über die Anlegung u. Vertheidigung der Feld-Verschanzungen'; *Entwurf* [of a Lesson Plan] (not before 1796); and *Fehlerhafte Einrichtung der Schanzen u. Verschanzungen unserer Zeit. Grundäatze, welche [man] bei der Anlegung mit Vertheidigung derselben beobachten muß* (after 1796); in Kunisch (ed.), *Scharnhorst: Privat und dienstliche Schriften*, Vol.2, pp.682-85, 668-70, 688-92; and 675-76; respectively. Sketches can be found on pp.685, 686, 693, and 694.

78 See Gerhard Scharnhorst, *Eine Ebene, eine Anhöhe, einen Berg oder jeden andern Posten für eine Brigade Infanterie zu verschanzen* (1798); in Kunisch (ed.), *Scharnhorst: Privat und dienstliche Schriften*, Vol.2, pp.706-08. A sketch of this position is on p.706.

79 See Gerhard Scharnhorst, *Entwurf zu einer Vershanzung [sic] den 4ten Febr. 1799*, in Kunisch (ed.), *Scharnhorst: Privat und dienstliche Schriften*, Vol.2, pp.408-10, for a detailed discussion of the dimensions of these entrenchments. The quoted passage is from p.409.

80 Scharnhorst, *Entwurf zu einer Vershanzung [sic] den 4ten Febr. 1799*, in Kunisch (ed.), *Scharnhorst: Privat und dienstliche Schriften*, Vol.2, p.410.

Versuch].[81] Mechlenburg was seeking Scharnhorst's opinion on a number of artillery-related issues the two had been discussing in their correspondence. Scharnhorst responded on 29 March, delighted to see that the Danish Artillery Chief was

> [A]s sincere and open as I had wished, especially on points where we are of different opinions… How rare is this. I have never been in this war, and even now, in such a situation that I was allowed to express my opinion about institution, exercise, or operations. People are too sensitive on this point. They point out nothing and lose their dedication.

'Whoever is as eager as you are to seek the truth', Scharnhorst told his friend, 'is a phenomenon'.[82]

In the five remaining pages Scharnhorst provided detailed commentary when answering Mechlenburg's questions. Using examples from the 1794 and 1795 campaigns, he revealed a number of seemingly insignificant issues that nevertheless played a crucial role in the combat actions of the War of the First Coalition. Once again, these issues are rarely contained in any official or unofficial histories, but clearly (as Scharnhorst noted) played a significant role in combat operations. One example was wheel size. Here Scharnhorst noted how the Prussian wheels were larger than those used by the Hanoverians, and this enabled the Prussians to carry heavier loads in their carts and wagons, and much more ammunition in their limbers. Hanoverian wheels were smaller and much lower to the ground. 'We have experienced the disadvantages of these', he told his friend. 'They [the disadvantages] are great'. Then he added, 'This matter is important; pay particular attention to it'.[83] He also noted how much more prepared for war the Prussians had been in comparison to the English and Hanoverians. Again, it was the little things that mattered, and the Prussians had paid attention to the details.

Unlike the British and Hanoverians, the Prussians had a standard operating procedure for just about every conceivable eventuality in war. This was apparently a legacy of Frederick the Great. Scharnhorst told Mechlenburg that Prussian artillerymen had a system for finding, consolidating, and storing their forage (oats, hay, and chaff) for their mounts. 'A certain way of packing the forage is quite necessary', he stated. The Prussians were also skilled at steadying their horses during combat and securing them in camp. Prussian artillerymen had detailed loading plans not only for their limbers, carriages, and wagons, but also for carrying and storing their own personal gear.

The Hanoverians had to learn much of this during the war. This was certainly the reason Scharnhorst advocated more realistic peacetime training. Fortunately, despite these major deficiencies, Hanoverian teamsters often, 'on their own initiative', were able to procure the

81 See Ezechias Gustav von Mechlenburg, 'Pro Memoria!' (19 January 1799); in *Nachlaß Scharnhorst*, Nr. 193; deposited in the Geheimes Staatsarchiv Preussischer Kulturbesitz, 196/VI. HA Familienarchive und Nachlässe, Berlin (Dahlem).

82 Gerhard Scharnhorst to Ezechias Gustav von Mechlenburg (29 March 1799); in Kunisch (ed.), *Scharnhorst: Privat und dienstliche Schriften*, Vol.2, pp.411-14; the quoted passages are from p.411.

83 Scharnhorst to Mechlenburg (29 March 1799); in Kunisch (ed.), *Scharnhorst: Privat und dienstliche Schriften*, Vol.2, p.411.

necessary supplies, tools, and equipment the gun crews required. Scharnhorst knew the army could not depend on chance or ad hoc arrangements in combat. He marvelled at the professional standards in the Prussian army. He concluded his letter by telling Mechlenburg that a little more than 40 percent percent of the horses and wagons Trew had requisitioned in 1793, when Hanover had mobilised for war, were ever delivered.[84]

On the same day he wrote to Mechlenburg, Scharnhorst sent a letter to Lecoq, wondering why he had not heard from his Prussian colleague in some time. He asked Lecoq if he was ruining his health with this 'thankless map work'.[85] 'I envy your diligence and perseverance in this enterprise', he then said, referring to the determination of the Prussians (especially the Duke of Brunswick) to get maps of the area of operations, and wondering if it really mattered, given the political situation in Europe. Knowing how much it meant to Lecoq, Scharnhorst informed him that *Lieutenant* Schäffer was putting the final touches – 'the military scale' – on the map of Hildesheim, which portrayed the area between Hanover, Hameln, Neudorf, and Ahlenfeld. He also told his Prussian colleague 'the geographical map of the Kahlenberg and the Grubenhagen is now being copied from the land survey; afterwards I also hope to get the map of Bremen and Lüneburg'. In a light-hearted tone Scharnhorst closed his discussion of map-making by telling Lecoq, 'So do not worry about filling the gap that our country is making in your big plan'.[86]

Moving to other issues, Scharnhorst enclosed his 'Instructions for Field Guides', which he told Lecoq that been implemented some time ago, and which *Lieutenant* Wilkens was currently using during his reconnaissance missions: 'Have the goodness, dear friend, and read this guide, and if something is not right in it, please note this to me, please. And send it back again to me, for I have no other transcript'.[87] Scharnhorst then informed Lecoq that he had completed his detailed study, 'History of the Seven Years War', especially 'in Westphalia and Prussia, ..., with new knowledge of the surrounding circumstances'. He also reported that he was able to finish his study of artillery, which he titled, 'On the Experiments and Experiences in the Artillery'. Data from the Danish tests were most likely included in this manuscript. Scharnhorst's next sentence was revealing. 'Works which have reference to our present affairs are embarrassing to me, I sincerely confess to you as a friend'. The lack of resolve among many German *Aufklärer* to speak out against blatant French aggression was clearly sickening to Scharnhorst.

> Believe me, if it goes on, the most zealous supporters of the existing constitutions will become the greatest friends of the present French, and they will create a condition of insensibility (and mistrust).

'Adieu', Scharnhorst told Lecoq. 'Stay my friend, as I am yours with all my soul'.[88]

84 Scharnhorst to Mechlenburg (29 March 1799); in Kunisch (ed.), *Scharnhorst: Privat und dienstliche Schriften*, Vol.2, pp.412-13; the quoted passages are from pp.412 and 413; respectively.

85 Scharnhorst to Lecoq (29 March 1799); in Kunisch (ed.), *Scharnhorst: Privat und dienstliche Schriften*, Vol.2, pp.414-15; the quoted passage is from p.414.

86 Scharnhorst to Lecoq (29 March 1799); in Kunisch (ed.), *Scharnhorst: Privat und dienstliche Schriften*, Vol.2, p.415.

87 Scharnhorst to Lecoq (29 March 1799); in Kunisch (ed.), *Scharnhorst: Privat und dienstliche Schriften*, Vol.2, p.415.

88 Scharnhorst to Lecoq (29 March 1799); in Kunisch (ed.), *Scharnhorst: Privat und dienstliche Schriften*, Vol.2, p.415.

Beginning in March 1799, Scharnhorst crafted an interesting essay that compared the political and military ways of the French Republic with those of the Roman Republic a thousand years earlier.[89] The similarities were striking.

> It seems that the raw republicanism, which reigned at the time of Robespierre, is reawakening in the French. Through this spirit the French nation is in a position to do great things. Here she follows the principles of the Romans at the time of the Republic, both with respect to morality, and in politics and the art of war.
>
> She flatters the conquered Dutch, Lombards, Genoese, and Venetians with liberty, and appears to leave them alone, as the Romans left the Greeks and other peoples. She spares the weak monarchies, Spain, Sardinia, etc. for a time, and weakens the mighty ones, one after another, just as the Romans did with the Orientals. She thus understands how this art is to put to sleep everyone by the prospect of an apparent distant existence and liberty, and to weaken a general coalition in the first source.
>
> Plutarch has already made comments on the policy of the Romans, about this conduct of every great republican state, which is only too applicable to our times.
>
> The French nation has precisely the same reason the Romans had – always to wage war!

'There is a sad future for mankind', Scharnhorst concluded.[90]

Reiterating many of the themes from his 'Basic Reasons for the French Success', but with much greater clarity and forcefulness, Scharnhorst noted in this essay some significant changes in the way in which the French now wage war. Having defended their liberty in 1792 and 1793, they then embarked on a total war of aggression, beginning in 1794. They were no longer fighting for liberty and equality, now they were engaged in a continuous war of conquest – just like the Romans had done. Like Rome, France had become a predatory state. 'This is not as ridiculous as it seems to be', Scharnhorst wrote. 'The French nation has more resources to continue the war than all of its neighbouring states'.[91] He also pointed out that the one, truly great advantage the French possessed was their state of mind.

> The spiritual culture by which this nation distinguishes itself from others, and especially in the ongoing war, brings with her the art of war, not in principles, but in the application of them, to a greater perfection than in other nations. The French nation has now waged war for seven years, and the other nations, even those who were at war with her, waged it only for two to three years, if the Austrians are excluded. Here the advantage of experience is united with those of the more cultivated mind.

While not expressly stating that he was referring to Hanover and other German states, he continued:

89 Gerhard Scharnhorst's untitled manuscript (March/November 1799) can be found in Kunisch (ed.), *Scharnhorst: Privat und dienstliche Schriften*, Vol.2, pp.763-68.

90 Scharnhorst's untitled manuscript in Kunisch (ed.), *Scharnhorst: Privat und dienstliche Schriften*, Vol.2, pp.763-74.

91 Scharnhorst's untitled manuscript in Kunisch (ed.), *Scharnhorst: Privat und dienstliche Schriften*, Vol.2, p.764.

> It is known that, in an uncultivated nation, art is not brought forward by experience, but that it makes progress with a cultivated one through the same rapid progress. This applies here with the armies as well as with the individuals of the same.
>
> The use of light troops in the French army, the use and establishment of their mobile artillery, the large-scale organisation of their armies, the manner of setting them in motion, and other institutions deserve to be imitated more by many other armies.[92]

Scharnhorst then wondered if any Austrian, German, or Prussian army could withstand the French.

Scharnhorst wrote Lecoq in late June 1799 to update him on the progress of making the maps the latter had requested. He informed his friend that he had received his three letters from Paderborn and had sent two officers – *Fähndrich* Hassebroick and *Lieutenant* Vollinghaus (along with four guides) – to survey the County of Lippe. He apologised for the delays, pointing out that 'contrary to the agreement made with him', *General-Major* Linsingen had kept *Lieutenant* Schäffer employed in Osnabrück until the Hanoverian force-on-force training exercises held that June had ended. Scharnhorst expected Schäffer to return to his mapping duties soon. Significantly, as he told his Prussian colleague, 'the terrain survey is an excellent school, a further training in applied tactics'. Scharnhorst also wrote that 'in a few days' he would be traveling with Prince Adolphus to the area around Osnabrück, where the Prince had 'defeated the troops of the Linsing Corps' during the recent corps exercises, and that they might even take 'a detour to the Archdiocese of Münster'. In his last paragraph Scharnhorst lamented how he had been trying unsuccessfully during those manoeuvres 'to bring our artillery into action… This weapon is everywhere employed improperly and is in every respect capable of a far greater perfection. I am not going to be concerned about this point – it is not easy to do something about it'.[93] Scharnhorst seemed at last to realise that modernising the Hanoverian artillery was not going to take place as he desired.[94]

During the inspection tour with Prince Adolphus, *Oberstlieutenant* Scharnhorst jotted down some random (and interesting) notes on a back of a recent letter he had received from his wife Klara. Scharnhorst insisted that one three-pound cannon (with sixty rounds) be assigned to every regimental artillery battery and two to each infantry company. He also advocated light field guns, called – 'Amusette' (with 112 rounds) – be assigned to every regimental battery. Turning to training, he noted the lack of coordinated exercises between the 8. Dragoner Regiment and its infantry support (the 4. Grenadier Battaillon), indicating that these units were supposed to train together as a combined arms team. Next, he focused on the training of light infantry, observing: 'In their exercises, light infantry must look for speedy evolutions and ease of movement; in their evolutions no principles need be observed'. Skirmishers 'must be divided into platoons led by non-commissioned officers', who must be

92 Scharnhorst's untitled manuscript in Kunisch (ed.), *Scharnhorst: Privat und dienstliche Schriften*, Vol.2, p.765.

93 Scharnhorst to Lecoq (27 June 1799); in Kunisch (ed.), *Scharnhorst: Privat und dienstliche Schriften*, Vol.2, pp.420-21; the quoted passages are from pp.420 and 221.

94 Documentation supporting Scharnhorst's conclusion can be found in Hann 41, IV, Nr.54: *Größere Übungen der Artillerieabteilungen bei Langenhagen, 1799*; deposited at the Niedersächsisches Landesarchiv, Hanover.

positioned behind the platoons to make sure they maintain their intervals and do not veer to the right or to the left. He also noted that the 10. Leichte Dragoner Regiment was 'not as fast or as precise as the 9th but was regular and without any disorder in its movements'. 'Without a doubt', Scharnhorst concluded, 'these manoeuvres were very useful'. 'They were designed in such a way that infantry, cavalry, and artillery supported each other, and the troops used the terrain'. Although he was not convinced that Prince Adolphus could 'ascertain from them whether the officers, the non-commissioned officers, and the soldiers were all systematically instructed in the little war', Scharnhorst ended this portion of his Notes writing that 'certain parts of the manoeuvres were quite good'.[95] He did not mention what parts.

In the second part of his Notes Scharnhorst sketched some ideas on offensive operations and plans of campaign. Stating the obvious, he wrote, 'Beware of unexpected attacks'. Recalling several historical examples, he reminded himself not to be lured into a false sense of security just because the army is on the offensive. The French had fallen into this trap at the Battle of Minden in 1759. Fourteen years earlier in 1745, the British and Hanoverians had discovered this fallacy when Maurice de Saxe (despite being flanked and on the verge of defeat) had concentrated his remaining forces and had driven the allies from the field at Fontenoy (11 May 1745).[96] At this point Scharnhorst turned to the 'Plan of Campaign', emphasising that it must be 'something big – a purpose which leads to the most important advantages'. Again, the lessons of history clearly demonstrated this fact.

> A man who continually walks around with small designs cannot go anywhere. Without a plan, without a desire to do great things, it is impossible to do them.
>
> Had Frederick calculated at the beginning of the Seven Years War all the degrees of probability, he would have remained just a Margrave of Brandenburg. Had Bonaparte subjected his plan of campaign in Italy to military calculus, as we read about now, he would not have conquered Italy.
>
> Had Duke Ferdinand been a slave to Puységur's principles, he would have sat in a corner of Stade [a city in Lower Saxony] until the spring and probably, in the end, would not have crossed the Rhine in 1758, etc.

Scharnhorst then ended his Notes with an interesting comment: 'But just as one expects good fortune with great plans, one must also take his measure of misfortune'.[97]

Upon his return to Hoya, General-Quartermaster-Lieutenant Scharnhorst began drafting a series of guidelines for the training and exercise of light infantry for the upcoming 1800 manoeuvres.[98] He was one of five distinguished field-grade officers Wallmoden had appointed to draft these instructions. Others included *Oberstlieutenant* Carl Christian von Linsingen (9. Leichte Dragoner Regiment), *Oberstlieutenant* Honosch Bogislaw von Dzierzanowski

95 Gerhard Scharnhorst, 'Notes' (July 1799); in Kunisch (ed.), *Scharnhorst: Privat und dienstliche Schriften*, Vol.2, pp.421-23; the three quoted passages are from pp.421, 422, and 423; respectively.

96 Scharnhorst, 'Notes' (July 1799); in Kunisch (ed.), *Scharnhorst: Privat und dienstliche Schriften*, Vol.2, p.422.

97 Scharnhorst, 'Notes' (July 1799); in Kunisch (ed.), *Scharnhorst: Privat und dienstliche Schriften*, Vol.2, p.423.

98 The editors of Scharnhorst's Papers have grouped these 14 documents under the title, 'Studien über den Einsatz von Scharfschützen', in Kunisch (ed.), *Scharnhorst: Privat und dienstliche Schriften*, Vol.2, pp.604-67.

(2. Cavallerie Regiment), *Major* Karl von Alten (Garde Infanterie Regiment) and either *Major* Friedrich Levin August von Arentsschildt (10. Leichte Dragoner Regiment) or *Major* Wilhelm Daniel von Arentsschildt (11. Infanterie Regiment).[99] The latter had commanded the 1. Jäger Compagnie in 1794. Wallmoden issued a directive entitled, 'Instruction on Several Points on the Exercise of Sharpshooters in all Infantry Regiments', in which he clearly showed his concern with the recent combat performance of the Hanoverian army.[100] He then ordered Scharnhorst and his associates to draft plans to integrate light troops into the manoeuvre training program for 1800.

Building upon his earlier thoughts on the need for light troops and their uses, Scharnhorst now advocated the amalgamation of light infantry with line infantry in the same tactical unit. The challenge he faced was getting the line infantry to accept open-order tactics. In one short study, 'Light Infantry and *Jäger* Support', he focused on small war operations. The worth of light troops was not their ability to execute precision evolutions like line infantry; rather, in the precise performance of their small war missions.[101] Much of this piece echoes Scharnhorst's earlier thoughts from his *Military Field Pocket Book* (1792), now reinforced by recent combat experience. Unlike the small detachments he had discussed in his book, in this paper he advocated formations of light infantry as large as a battalion. Their main mission was to disperse the enemy light infantry (so the enemy could not accomplish its covering mission), and then disrupt the actions of the enemy line infantry. Other traditional security and protection missions were also noted. Scharnhorst felt that a key to the success of light infantry operations was a system of good signal communications, both internally and externally with regular forces.

Scharnhorst followed this short essay with more than 45 pages that elaborated on Wallmoden's directive. It was entitled, 'Exercise and Instruction of the Sharpshooter', and was essentially a 'how-to-fight' manual that described in excruciating detail the selection, training, and exercise of light infantrymen.[102] Subject matter included: instructions for the

99 Members of this commission are cited in Note 1 to Gerhard Scharnhorst, *Einige Regeln des vermishten Gebrauches der Cavalerie Flanqueurs und Infantrie Scharfschützen in Rücksicht der mechanishen Anordnung bey den Unterrichtsmanouvern* (between May 1798 and May 1801?); in Kunisch (ed.), *Scharnhorst: Privat und dienstliche Schriften*, Vol.2, p.622. The editors state they obtained this information from Sichart, *Geschichte der Königlich-Hannoverischen Armee*, Vol.4, pp.685-86.

100 See Gerhard Scharnhorst, 'Instruction über einige Puncte der Uebung der Scharfschützen alle Infanterie Regimenter', *Nachlaß Scharnhorst*, Nr. 190, Sheets 31-34; deposited at the Geheimes Staatsarchiv Preussischer Kulturbesitz, 196/VI. HA Familienarchive und Nachlässe, Berlin (Dahlem). In the upper left-hand corner of Sheet 31 (beside the title) is a note that states, 'For the attention of Count Gimborn'.

101 Gerhard Scharnhorst, 'Unterstützung der leichten Infanterie und Jäger, ' *Nachlaß Scharnhorst*, Nr. 271, Sheets 14-16; deposited at the Geheimes Staatsarchiv Preussischer Kulturbesitz, 196/VI. HA Familienarchive und Nachlässe, Berlin (Dahlem). This essay was incorporated in Werner Hahlweg, *Preußische Reformzeit und revolutionärer Krieg, Wehrwissenschaftlichen Rundschau*, Beiheft 18 (September 1962), pp.60-61; and in Kunisch (ed.), *Scharnhorst: Privat und dienstliche Schriften*, Vol.2, pp.604-06. Sheet 14 shows that the original manuscript is titled 'Unterstützung' [Support] instead of 'Untersuchung' [Examination] as cited in Kunisch (ed.), *Scharnhorst: Privat und dienstliche Schriften*, Vol.2, p.604.

102 Gerhard Scharnhorst, '*Uebung und Unterricht der Scharfschütten*' (not before 1799, not after 1801?); in Kunisch (ed.), *Scharnhorst: Privat und dienstliche Schriften*, Vol.2, pp.606-20. Other source documents relating to this can be found in Hann 41, III, Nr.130: *Die Einführung der Scharfschützen bei der Infanterie. Ausführung von Gefechtsformationen zur Formierung von Quarres (Quarrés). (Zeichnungen). Kommandos. Schwenkungen und Marschieren, 1796-1802*; deposited at the Niedersächsisches Landesarchiv, Hanover.

training of sharpshooters (including a step-by-step approach for the loading and firing of the rifle); how to handle the rifle; how to estimate distances; how to establish a covered firing position; how to synchronize the shooter's firing and movement; opportunities against artillery and field works; force-on-force exercises; and marksmanship competitions (in which the best shooters were rewarded with prizes). Other sections dealt with the integration of light troops with line infantry units, such as: how the spirit of freedom among light troops could be a risk; how to deploy, advance, and coordinate the movements of light troops within the battalion; and how to defeat the enemy's light troops. Scharnhorst used the last chapters to highlight the operations of larger formations of light troops, in particular: how to search for and occupy broken terrain; how to coordinate artillery fire in support of light infantry operations; how light infantry protects artillery; how line infantrymen support light infantrymen; the use of separate detachments and larger units in the advance guard, rear guard, and outpost operations; and a host of other missions light troop would perform in combat.

As usual, Scharnhorst supported his ideas with historical examples. He chose three engagements: Vellinghausen (1761), Minden (1759), and Hastenbeck (1757) – all from the Seven Years War, probably because he could find nothing similar from the recent campaigns against the French.[103] All were important allied victories against France; all reinforced the need for light infantry; and all were achieved by one of his favourite leaders – Duke Ferdinand of Brunswick. In each battle light infantry was instrumental in supporting the flank of the allied army under Duke Ferdinand and defeating French attacks. Interestingly, shortly after the War of the First Coalition, Scharnhorst had drawn up a list of examples that included the actions noted above, plus three from the recent conflict – the Battles of Wervik (12 and 13 September 1793), Menin (April 1794), and Tournay (22 May 1794).[104] The first two were French victories. During the Battle of Tournay, the village of Pont à Chin changed hands four times. Scharnhorst included a sketch of this action, showing four brigades near the River Schelde. In his clarification he wrote, 'attacking skirmishers from the third rank and supported by the regimental guns'.[105] Comparing his sketch with later maps of the action reveals that these skirmishers were most likely coalition soldiers. In the end the French retreated. Interestingly, Scharnhorst noted that during the Seven Years War, the Austrians, British, and Hanoverians had experimented with using skirmishers as the third rank.

On order from Wallmoden, Scharnhorst and his associates wrote the instructions for the use of light cavalry as flank guards and their integration with dismounted light infantrymen

103 Gerhard Scharnhorst, *Beyspiel von dem Gebrauch der Scharfschützen und des 3ten Gliedes* (auf dem Terrain und in der Stellung des linken Flügels der allirten Armee in der Schlacht bey Vellinghausen 1761); *tes Beyspiel von dem Gebrauch der Scharfschützen und der Divisionen des 3ten Gliedes* auf dem Terrain und in der Stellung des linken Flügels der Allirten-Armee in der Schlacht bey Minden (1759); and *Beyspiel von dem Gebrauch der Scharfschützen und der Divisionen des 3ten Gliedes* (auf dem Terrain und in der Stellung des linken Flügels der allirten Armee in der Schlacht bey Hastenbek 1757); in Kunisch (ed.), *Scharnhorst: Privat und dienstliche Schriften*, Vol.2, pp.642-52; 654-56; and 656-71; respectively.

104 Gerhard Scharnhorst, 'Beyspiele von den Gebrauch der Scharfshützen' (not before May 1794); in Kunisch (ed.), *Scharnhorst: Privat und dienstliche Schriften*, Vol.2, p.666.

105 Scharnhorst's sketch is not included in Kunisch (ed.), *Scharnhorst: Privat und dienstliche Schriften*, but can be found in his 'Instruction über einige Puncte der Uebung der Scharfschützen alle Infanterie Regimenter', *Nachlaß Scharnhorst*, Nr. 190, Sheet 130; deposited at the Geheimes Staatsarchiv Preussischer Kulturbesitz, 196/VI. HA Familienarchive und Nachlässe, Berlin (Dahlem).

for the upcoming manoeuvres.[106] These instructions emphasised several points to correct the noticeable deficiencies from previous campaigns, and to train light troops on some crucial eventualities on future battlefields. Among the recommendations were: the positioning of cavalry as flank guards for the line infantry battalion; the organisation of an integrated advance guard of skirmishers and light cavalry; recognition commands for skirmishers and light cavalry in a movement to contact; the integration of skirmishers from several battalions into a larger formation; the manoeuvre of skirmishers and light cavalry over open and broken terrain, and through various natural and man-made obstacles; the organisation and manoeuvre of skirmishers and light cavalry flank guards in various combat situations; and the use of light infantry and light cavalry in various support roles. Significantly, many of the ideas about the employment of light troops in these instructions can be found in Count Wilhelm's 'New System of Tactics', developed 35 years earlier. Following Wallmoden's approval in 1800, Hanover and Hesse exercised their light troops at the training ground near Liebenau (in Hesse near the river Diemel), from 10 June to 3 July 1800. Light infantry and light cavalrymen operated together as skirmishers and flank guards; respectively, executing the detailed instructions Scharnhorst and his fellow officers had developed.[107]

Elsewhere in 1799, Wallmoden continued the practice he had begun since the establishment of the Observation Army four years earlier of returning selected Hanoverian units back to their garrisons for rest, home leave, and refitting, and replacing them with fresh troops.[108] He also rotated units within the Hanoverian area of operations, always endeavouring to provide sufficient quartiers and food for his men, shelter and grazing land for their horses, and to ease any burden on the local population. Beginning in April, he had his General-Quartermaster-Lieutenant develop the plans and drew up the necessary movement orders for these actions.[109] A month later a number of Hanoverian units began (temporarily) occupying positions vacated by the Prussians, as they conducted their spring manoeuvres.[110] These were the Leibgarde, the 10., 11., and 13. Infanterie Regimenten, the 2. Cavallerie Regiment, the 2. and 3. Grenadier Bataillonen, the 1. Schwere Artillerie Batterie, and two *Jäger* companies.[111] Later, Wallmoden had the 1. Cavallerie Regiment switch locations with

106 See Gerhard Scharnhorst, *Einige Regeln des vermishten Gebrauches der Cavalerie Flanqueurs und Infantrie Scharfschützen,* in Kunisch (ed.), *Scharnhorst: Privat und dienstliche Schriften*, Vol.2, pp.622-26.

107 See the organisation and discussion of these exercises in Sichart, *Geschichte der Königlich-Hannoverischen Armee*, Vol.4, pp.684-86.

108 Source documents relating to this practice can be found in Hann 41, I, Nr.29: *Zurückziehung und Beurlaubung eines Teiles der ausgerückten Truppen. Entsprechende Verhandlungen zwischen dem Ministerium und dem General von Wallmoden, 12.1796-1798*; and Hann 41, I, Nr.27: *Beurlaubungen von Soldaten zu häuslicher Arbeit, 1796*-1797; deposited at the Niedersächsisches Landesarchiv, Hanover.

109 See Gerhard Scharnhorst to Georg Carl Löw von und zu Steinfurt (beginning of April 1799); in Kunisch (ed.), *Scharnhorst: Privat und dienstliche Schriften*, Vol.2, pp.416-17, in which Scharnhorst discusses Wallmoden's concept of the operation.

110 See the agreement, dated 13 May 1799, signed by *Oberstlieutenant* Gerhard Scharnhorst (for Hanover) and *Major* von Kampz (for Prussia) regarding this arrangement; in Kunisch (ed.), *Scharnhorst: Privat und dienstliche Schriften*, Vol.2, pp.417-18.

111 Gerhard Scharnhorst, 'Einige Veränderungen in dem Quartierstande des hannövrischen bey der Observations-Armee stehenden Corps' (not after 21 May 1799); in Kunisch (ed.), *Scharnhorst: Privat und dienstliche Schriften*, Vol.2, pp.418-19. Also see his 'Pro Memoria' (before 16 June 1799) regarding the quartering assignments of the 10., 11., and 13. Infanterie Regimenten; on pp.419-20.

the 10. Infanterie Regiment. Perhaps prompted by Wallmoden, King George had asked King Friedrich Wilhelm to permit his Hanoverian troops stationed near Minden to participate with the Prussians as they exercised their formations. Unfortunately, this request came too late, as the manoeuvre plan had already been finalized and Duke Karl felt no need to modify it to include the Hanoverians. In any case, throughout 1799, Wallmoden displaced 14-and-a-half infantry battalions, 20 cavalry squadrons, and five artillery batteries.[112]

As Scharnhorst and his colleagues were fashioning the exercise plans for the Hanoverian light infantry and cavalry for the 1800 manoeuvres, the War of the Second Coalition (1798-1800) was producing considerable consternation throughout Europe. On 27 August 1799, a British force of 27,000 men under the command of the Duke of York landed at Den Helder on the tip of Holland's peninsula, south of the Texel. Three days later the Dutch Republican fleet surrendered to a British squadron. Reinforced by two Russian divisions, York commenced offensive operations to liberate Holland. At Bergen on 16 September, Franco-Batavian troops under the command of *Général de Division* Guillaume Marie-Anne Brune (1763-1815) defeated the combined Russo-British army, which could not coordinate its operations. Two weeks later on 2 October, British and Russian troops drove the French and Dutch from Bergen. Pressing his advantage, the Duke of York continued south. Along the sand dunes of Castricum on 6 October, and three days later at Beverwijk, French and Dutch forces once again defeated the British and Russians, who were having great difficulty communicating with each other. Realising that his ambitious plans to drive the French from Holland had failed, York signed the Convention of Alkmaar on 18 October 1799, which ended hostilities in the Netherlands. The British and Russians were permitted to re-embark their troops, while French and Dutch prisoners in England were returned, and the Dutch fleet remained in British hands.[113]

Scharnhorst wrote to Lecoq on 20 November 1799 about the geopolitical situation in central Europe: 'I read with great interest your letter of 20 October, my invaluable friend. I agree completely with your assessment. The British expedition was too dangerous'.[114] Both Lecoq and Scharnhorst believed the operation had great potential, but that there were just too many variables the British and Russians had not foreseen and could not master. Scharnhorst then asked what people were saying about Bonaparte's coup in Paris and its possible consequences. With Holland firmly in French control, Scharnhorst worried about the Hanseatic cities of Hamburg and Bremen, 'whose sympathies lay with France', and how northern Germany would suffer immeasurably if trade with England was cut off. He also noted the critical importance of the Rivers Elbe and Weser for the transport of goods to Hamburg and Bremen. Recalling what had happened to the economy of north-western

112 Hanoverian troops movements in 1799 are consolidated in Sichart, 'Ereignisse im Jahre 1799', *Geschichte der Königlich-Hannoverischen Armee*, Vol.4, pp.677-81. The Duke of Brunswick's response to King George's request can be found in Note 1 (pp.678-79).

113 See the interesting and informative study by Simon Schama, *Patriots and Liberators: Revolution in the Netherlands, 1780-1813* (New York: Vintage Books, 1992). Also see Limm, 'Fairly Out-Generaled and Disgracefully Beaten', pp.94-146; later published as *Walcheren to Waterloo*.

114 Scharnhorst to Lecoq, 20 November 1799; in Kunisch (ed.), *Scharnhorst: Privat und dienstliche Schriften*, Vol.2, pp.429-31; the quoted passages are from pp.429 and 430.

Germany during the Seven Years War and the French occupation, Scharnhorst maintained that the fortified city of Wesel was the key to the defence of this region.

> Certain events, which in individual cases appear to depend on circumstances, have an absolute consequence in the great chain of things. Apply this to North Germany and Wesel, and remember the history of Franche Comté, Lorraine and Strasburg.[115]

Once he had finished his commentary on current affairs, Scharnhorst updated Lecoq on the map-making progress. With a lieutenant, an ensign, and two guides working on the Lippe County map, Scharnhorst told Lecoq that 'little remains' for its completion. In closing he promised his Prussian colleague 'a definitive report' in December.[116]

115 Scharnhorst to Lecoq, 20 November 1799; in Kunisch (ed.), *Scharnhorst: Privat und dienstliche Schriften*, Vol.2, p.430. When referring to Franche Comté, Lorraine, and Strasburg, Scharnhorst was most likely reminding Lecoq of the never-ending aggression of France when it came to seizing and maintaining her natural frontiers.

116 Scharnhorst to Lecoq, 20 November 1799; in Kunisch (ed.), *Scharnhorst: Privat und dienstliche Schriften*, Vol.2, pp.430-31; the quoted passages are from pp,430 and 431.

17

Last Year in Hanoverian Service

Making maps for the Prussians was becoming a burdensome task for the small group working diligently under the direction of Scharnhorst. Before answering two letters he had just received from his Prussian colleague Lecoq regarding map making, Scharnhorst completed the orders and instructions for the Hanoverian units Wallmoden planned to relocate in 1800.[1] Turning to Lecoq's concerns, Scharnhorst sensed Duke Karl of Brunswick was not satisfied with the slow progress the Prussians were making producing maps of the Observation Army area of operations. Judging from the straightforward content and formal language of his letter of 15 March 1800, Scharnhorst was shielding Lecoq from Brunswick's displeasure, while simultaneously updating the Duke (through Lecoq) on the current mapping situation.

While addressed to Lecoq, Scharnhorst clearly intended this letter for Duke Karl.[2] In the opening paragraph he politely asked 'Your Excellency' to please remind 'the reigning Duke of Brunswick' of his obligation to pay each mapmaker his monthly stipend of 20 Reichsthaler. Scharnhorst then updated Lecoq on the progress of each mapmaker, often stating or implying that these men had other duties and obligations as well. He made this clear in his fifth paragraph:

> His Excellency Feldmarschal [sic] G. v. Walmoden would very much like to grant Fähnrich v. Reiche the required leave as soon as his regiment can spare him. I informed Fähnrich v. Reiche, as well as the commander of the regiment, with whom he has standing. Unfortunately, he [Reiche] commands the skirmishers, and his commander will be reluctant to do without him.

1 See 'Marsch-Route für 1 Bataillon des 10ten Infanterie Regiments von Saffe von Lessum nach Celle' (11 February 1800); published in Kunisch (ed.), *Scharnhorst: Privat und dienstliche Schriften*, pp.431-32. The title of this order is deceptive, since it also contains new locations and routes of march for the 10. Leichte Dragoner Regiment, the 2. [Horse] Artillerie Batterie, and the 1., 4., and 5. Grenadier Bataillonen, as well as the training location for the 3., 8., 9., and 10. Infanterie Regimenten. In their Note a, the editors provide a long list of additional instructions for other Hanoverian commands. A complete list of the Hanoverian troop dislocations in 1800 can be found in Sichart, *Geschichte der Königlich-Hannoverischen Armee*, Vol.4, pp.681-83.

2 Gerhard Scharnhorst to Karl von Lecoq (15 March 1800); in Kunisch (ed.), *Scharnhorst: Privat und dienstliche Schriften*, Vol.2, pp.434-35. In Note 1 on p.434, the editors wrote that Scharnhorst's 'formal salutations are in sharp contrast' to his 'otherwise informal friendship' with Lecoq. 'The content is, however, consistent with common duty obligations'.

Having worked with Scharnhorst over the past four years, Lecoq understood this, but the Duke of Brunswick (because of his position and authority) was unwilling to acknowledge that the Hanoverian mapmakers had duties and responsibilities to their own commands and not just to him. Scharnhorst clarified this in his last paragraph, recommending that 'Your Excellency' [meaning Brunswick] speak with Wallmoden directly should he not agree with the current assignment of Hanoverian personnel. Scharnhorst closed his letter with, 'I am, with the greatest esteem, Your Excellency's most willing servant'.[3]

As Hanoverian forces were relocating to new positions and preparing for their summer exercises, members of the Artillery Commission sent their initial report to Wallmoden. They requested permission to proceed with the rewriting of the field regulations for the regimental artillery, which were then to be tested during the upcoming summer manoeuvres.[4] A few months earlier in 1799, Wallmoden had establish this commission to update the manoeuvre regulations of the field artillery.[5] During the War of the First Coalition, Hanoverian artillery often performed in a manner unacceptable to many field commanders. Scharnhorst and Hammerstein had pointed this out to the Commanding General, who acted upon their recommendations. Members of this Commission included: *General-Lieutenant* Trew, *Oberstlieutenant* Braun, Prince Adolphus, *Oberstlieutenant* and *Ober-Adjudant* von Löw, *General der Cavalllerie* Albrecht von Estorff (who was in London most of the time), Prince Karl von Schwarzburg-Sondershausen (Commander of the 8. Infanterie Regiment), and *Oberstlieutenant* Scharnhorst.

Beginning with the assumption that their proposals for the employment of field artillery would coincide with the manoeuvre concepts of the infantry and cavalry, members told Wallmoden:

> Furthermore, we have been guided by nothing but the experience which the last campaigns have given us, and by the changes which must come about with the establishment of skirmishers and the manoeuvres of the cannons and horses.[6]

While this report contained nothing specific about the employment of field artillery, commission members sought Wallmoden's approval for Braun to translate their concepts into standards to be tested during the upcoming manoeuvres. Löw, Braun, Prince Karl, and Scharnhorst signed this document.

'After a cursory review', Scharnhorst wrote 10 days later, 'I find nothing more to add in the preparation of the exercise regulations'. Like most members, Scharnhorst was satisfied with the initial draft regulations. On the other hand, he did express concern with

3 Scharnhorst to Lecoq (15 March 1800); in Kunisch (ed.), *Scharnhorst: Privat und dienstliche Schriften*, Vol.2, p.435.

4 Report of the Artillery Commission (8 April 1800); in Kunisch (ed.), *Scharnhorst: Privat und dienstliche Schriften*, Vol.2, pp.437-38.

5 Source documents relating to the Artillery Commission can be found in Hann 41, III, Nr.149: *Protokolle der Commission Festsetzung der kunstigen Exercire der Regiments-Artillerie, 1800-1801*; deposited at the Niedersächsisches Landesarchiv, Hanover.

6 Report of the Artillery Commission (8 April 1800); in Kunisch (ed.), *Scharnhorst: Privat und dienstliche Schriften*, Vol.2, p.438.

some of the more technical details associated with the movement of guns.[7] One was the 'prolonge', a thick rope used to move guns on the battlefield without having to couple the gun to its limber. Scharnhorst wanted to make sure the prolonge was no more than 20 feet long. As he noted, 'Lengthy prolonges make manoeuvres more difficult'. Another challenge was connecting the gun to its limber, which he felt should be accomplished quicker. He suggested using the Prussian method, which 'is very good'. Unfortunately, he did not describe this technique. This led to confusion on Braun's part, and so Scharnhorst sent a letter to Braun on 25 May, hoping to clarify this for Braun. He pointed out that the Prussians had developed a way to using the prolonge to help the gun crew when coupling the gun to its limber in a fast and efficient manner, and to manoeuvre the gun without fatiguing the crew. He told Braun 'the Prussian method is not useless' (as Braun thought) and was confident Hanoverian artillerymen could adopt it without delay. He also rejected Braun's suggestion that 'further investigation' was needed.[8]

Under the watchful eye of *Feldmarschall* Wallmoden, Hanoverian forces conducted their annual manoeuvres from 10 June until 3 July 1800. These took place at the training centre of Liebenau, which is located on the left bank of the Weser River near Nieburg in Lower Saxony. This was a corps-level exercise. Commanding the advanced guard was *General-Major* Linsingen, while *General-Lieutenant* Diepenbroick led the corps. The corps was divided into four divisions (two infantry and two cavalry), with each infantry division supported by heavy artillery and each cavalry division supported by horse artillery. Light infantry and cavalry units also participated. These manoeuvres consisted of individual brigade and divisional exercises, but no mention was made of any combined arms operations. The exercises of light troops were guided by the regulations Scharnhorst and his fellow field-grade officers had written. Whether the integration of light troops with those of the line infantry took place as envisioned by the new regulations is not clear from the documentation.[9]

Following these exercises, General-Quartermaster-Lieutenant Scharnhorst sent Wallmoden his assessment of the field guides during the recent training.[10] Most likely following the example of the Prussians, Scharnhorst had taught these men how to lead columns. Of the five guides, three were 'quite useful'. Rummel was 'the one who has applied himself the most', followed by Jasper, who 'should return to the artillery regiment as a non-commissioned officer' (provided Trew approved), and then Wiepking, who assisted Scharnhorst as his scribe. Scharnhorst also recommended keeping the other two – Müller and Weissendahl: 'I must say that all the guides are very willing and eager to learn and have also applied themselves well. As far as the situation permits, they have also done a great

7 Gerhard Scharnhorst, 'P[ro]. M[emoria]'. (18 April 1800); in Kunisch (ed.), *Scharnhorst: Privat und dienstliche Schriften*, Vol.2, p.438. Source documents relating to these issues can be found in Hann 41, III, Nr.148: *Commissions-Verhandlungen über der Regiments-Artillerie, besonders Abschaffung der Kanonenzieher, 1797-1800*; deposited at the Niedersächsisches Landesarchiv, Hanover.

8 Gerhard Scharnhorst to Georg Gustav Braun (25 May 1800); in Kunisch (ed.), *Scharnhorst: Privat und dienstliche Schriften*, Vol.2, p.439.

9 See the discussion in Sichart, *Geschichte der Königlich-Hannoverischen Armee*, Vol.4, pp.684-86.

10 Gerhard Scharnhorst to Johann von Wallmoden (14 August 1800); in Kunisch (ed.), *Scharnhorst: Privat und dienstliche Schriften*, Vol.2, pp.441-42. Source documents on these reports can be found in Hann 41, I, Nr.181, II: *Bericht Scharnhorsts über Guiden an Wallmoden*; deposited at the Niedersächsisches Landesarchiv, Hanover.

deal of work; indeed, they are still at work, except the sickly Müller'.[11] In closing his report, Scharnhorst noted the uselessness of the Hanoverian pioneers. 'Your Excellency himself is aware that they have done almost nothing' for the army. Scharnhorst wondered why they had been mobilised in the first place.[12] Shortly after his evaluation of the field guides, he sent Wallmoden a recommendation to relocate two artillery batteries to the Lower Elbe. He noted the poor positioning of these batteries and indicated by his discussion of the road network and its bridges that the battery commanders had failed miserably to conduct a proper route reconnaissance to ensure the roads and bridges over which their batteries would travel were structurally sound enough to bear the load. The very next day Wallmoden sent each battery commander a letter of admonishment.[13]

Convinced that neither civilian nor military authorities in Hanover had any intention of modernising society and its armed forces, Scharnhorst reopened negotiations with Prussian officials in the late summer of 1800. King Friedrich Wilhelm III (1797-1840) responded favourably to his inquiries. The king was apprised of Scharnhorst's attempts to modernise the Hanoverian army and was cognisant of the nature of his efforts. He may have also been mindful of the need for such a program in his own army. Once again Lecoq acted as the intermediary on behalf of his monarch.[14] On 5 October, Scharnhorst sent Lecoq three letters, updating his friend on his current situation and clarifying the views he had expressed in the essays he had sent Friedrich Wilhelm in response to the king's queries.[15]

Friedrich Wilhelm III was very interested in Scharnhorst's thoughts on field artillery. When answering the king, Scharnhorst begged Lecoq, 'For God's sake, do not let the essay on regimental artillery come into the hands of the artillerymen'. While this piece had nothing to do with Scharnhorst's endeavours with the Hanoverian Artillery Commission, he told Lecoq that this monograph was 'the result of many painful hours' of reflection and was intended for the king's eyes only. Then turning to another issue, 'which is very dear to my heart', he asked Lecoq his advice on requesting that the king ennoble him. He told Lecoq that this request was not for himself; rather, he was very concerned about the future of his two sons – Wilhelm and August, should they decide to become Prussian soldiers. He felt that without the patent of nobility, they would have little chance of advancement. Scharnhorst was clearly not forthright with Lecoq here, since being ennobled would also benefit his ego, as well as further the likelihood of his own advancement and success. This

11 Scharnhorst to Wallmoden (14 August 1800); in Kunisch (ed.), *Scharnhorst: Privat und dienstliche Schriften*, Vol.2, pp.441-42; the first three quoted passages are from p.441, while the fourth is from p.442.

12 Scharnhorst to Wallmoden (14 August 1800); in Kunisch (ed.), *Scharnhorst: Privat und dienstliche Schriften*, Vol.2, p.442.

13 Scharnhorst, 'Pro memoria die Verlegung der Artillerie in das Kedingsche und Alteland betreffend' (not after 8 July 1800); in Kunisch (ed.), *Scharnhorst: Privat und dienstliche Schriften*, Vol.2, pp.440-41. Note b (p.440) mentions these letters of reprimand.

14 The course of Scharnhorst's negotiations may be followed in some detail in Linnebach (ed.), *Scharnhorsts Briefe*, Vol.1, pp.206-17. The positions of the other parties can be found in Klippel, *Scharnhorst*, Vol.2, pp.331-45. Three letters also appear in Priesdorff, *Soldatisches Führertum*, Vol.3, pp.227-28. Much of this correspondence can also be found in Kunisch (ed.), *Scharnhorst: Privat und dienstliche Schriften*.

15 Scharnhorst to Lecoq (5 October 1800); in Kunisch (ed.), *Scharnhorst: Privat und dienstliche Schriften*, Vol.2, pp.442-43, 443-44, and 444-46. The letter on pp.443-44 is a letter of transmittal, in which Scharnhorst asks Lecoq to present his essays to Friedrich Wilhelm.

becomes evident later in this correspondence when he told Lecoq he felt he should already have the status of a nobleman and should be permitted to use the 'von' before his name, since he owned a noble estate and was a voting member of the Calenberg *Landschaft*.[16]

In his third letter of 5 October, Scharnhorst reflected on the initial offer Prussia had made three years earlier and the circumstances which had kept him in Hanoverian service. Reiterating what he had told Lecoq back in 1797, Scharnhorst wrote that he 'could surely foresee' that he would have been 'denied dismissal' from Hanoverian service. 'Now that this danger, in all likelihood, is no longer to be feared', he said, 'my lowly duty as General-Quartermaster will have little value in the idleness of peace'. Scharnhorst believed that now was the time to transfer to Prussian service.[17] He noted how Friedrich Wilhelm, 'with his many excellent qualities, has paid particular attention to the profession of arms, like a connoisseur', thus making 'the Prussian service all the more desirable'.[18] He hoped the previous offer of placement with the artillery in Berlin still stood. He then spoke about his financial circumstances and requested a life-long pension for himself and half that pension for his wife and family upon his death, and especially 'until my youngest child is 25 years old'.[19] When Friedrich Wilhelm agreed to all of these requests, it clearly demonstrated the extraordinary confidence the Prussian king had in the character, intellect, and abilities of Gerhard Scharnhorst.

'Here is the King's reply', Lecoq wrote to Scharnhorst on 19 October. 'You see, dearest friend, that all your requests are met'. Scharnhorst would enter Prussian service as an *Oberstlieutenant* of artillery, stationed in Berlin, 'which gives you the reliable prospect of becoming chief of the whole artillery'. Then Lecoq advised caution.

> As for the 'von', you can assume it without hesitation. But it would be better, this is my advice, that you do not do it, but petition the king to ennoble you when you enter the service or request it after one year. Surely the king will not refuse you.[20]

Scharnhorst accepted Lecoq's sound advice and followed it implicitly; for Lecoq understood Scharnhorst needed the legitimacy of the reigning monarch of an established dynasty to ennoble him. He simply could not use the 'von' because he owned a noble estate and was a voting member of a *Landschaft*. No doubt Scharnhorst understood this and realised the Hanoverian aristocracy would never have permitted a commoner to use one of their titles no matter what he had achieved.

Interestingly, Scharnhorst's brief examination of the hereditary nobility around this time further demonstrated his sound understanding of history and his support for the ideals of

16 Scharnhorst to Lecoq (5 October 1800); in Kunisch (ed.), *Scharnhorst: Privat und dienstliche Schriften*, Vol.2, pp.442-43; the quoted passages are from p.443. In this letter Scharnhorst speaks of only one essay on regimental artillery. In the first letter of 5 October above he speaks of 'essays'.

17 Scharnhorst to Lecoq (5 October 1800); in Kunisch (ed.), *Scharnhorst: Privat und dienstliche Schriften*, Vol.2, pp.444-46; the quoted passages are from p.444.

18 Scharnhorst to Lecoq (5 October 1800); in Kunisch (ed.), *Scharnhorst: Privat und dienstliche Schriften*, Vol.2, pp.444-45.

19 Scharnhorst to Lecoq (5 October 1800); in Kunisch (ed.), *Scharnhorst: Privat und dienstliche Schriften*, Vol.2, p.445.

20 Karl von Lecoq to Gerhard Scharnhorst (19 October 1800); in *Nachlaß Scharnhorst*, Nr. 25, Sheet 42; deposited at the Geheimes Staatsarchiv Preussischer Kulturbesitz, 196/VI. HA Familienarchive und Nachlässe, Berlin (Dahlem).

the French Revolution. 'When society outgrows its political system', he wrote, 'shockwaves arise'. Noting that while there are always demands by various factions within a society, the concept of law is to see all demands as equal before the law. Unfortunately, this was never the case in feudal societies, in which possession of the land was 'fundamental to political prestige' and absolute power. Thinking philosophically, he wrote: 'But if having is preferred to being, there is a disorder. Nature has constituted being as a source of having'. Scharnhorst felt this 'inequality of demand is a disease in which the body strives for health'. Only by restoring equality among all classes could society move forward. If that came about through revolution, then so be it.[21]

On 25 October Scharnhorst sent Lecoq his 'most heartfelt gratitude' for all the latter's assistance in achieving his desires from Friedrich Wilhelm.[22] He also wrote to the Prussian king, thanking him for his generosity and telling Friedrich Wilhelm of his longing desire to serve in the Prussian army.

> From my early youth, the study of the military sciences has been my special vocation. How happy, therefore, is the prospect for me to be accepted into an army which has attained the highest degree of perfection, and in the future to be able to serve a monarch, who appreciates the art of war because he understands it, as my gracious sovereign lord.

In closing his letter to Friedrich Wilhelm, Scharnhorst requested 'the granting of nobility for me and my descendants'.[23] Then he sent another letter to Lecoq to let him know that he had written to Friedrich Wilhelm, thanking the king for accepting him into Prussian service and granting him all of his requests. He also told Lecoq that he had informed the king that he would be unable to leave Hanover until the Artillery Commission had completed its work, 'and indicated [to the king] that I should not be able to demand my release before the New Year'. Closing his letter Scharnhorst told his Prussian friend, 'I am always in your debt'.[24]

Four days after writing to Friedrich Wilhelm, Scharnhorst commented on the work of Braun. He was delighted with the amount of detail contained in Braun's study, 'On the Strength of Batteries', including his ideas for calculating the materials required for foraging, as well as the number of wagons needed for baggage and rations.[25] 'That a greater equality with other types of troops must prevail here is self-evident', he concluded, implying that the artillery needed to be placed on par with the infantry and cavalry when it comes to logistical support. Turning to the ratio of guns to howitzers, he noted that mixing guns and howitzers

21 Gerhard Scharnhorst, 'Untersuchung über den Geburtsadel', in Kunisch (ed.), *Scharnhorst: Privat und dienstliche Schriften*, Vol.2, p.769.

22 Scharnhorst to Lecoq (25 October 1800); in Kunisch (ed.), *Scharnhorst: Privat und dienstliche Schriften*, Vol.2, p.446.

23 Gerhard Scharnhorst to Friedrich Wilhelm III (25 October 1800); in in Kunisch (ed.), *Scharnhorst: Privat und dienstliche Schriften*, Vol.2, pp.447-48; the quoted passage is from p.448. Notice how Scharnhorst places 'me' before his 'descendants'.

24 Scharnhorst to Lecoq (25 October 1800); in Kunisch (ed.), *Scharnhorst: Privat und dienstliche Schriften*, Vol.2, pp.446-47; the quoted passages are from p.447.

25 Gerhard Scharnhorst, 'Promemoria: die Eingabe des H. O.L Braun *über die Stärke der Batterien* etc. betreffend' (29 October 1800); in Kunisch (ed.), *Scharnhorst: Privat und dienstliche Schriften*, Vol.2, pp.449-50.

in the same battery was not a good practice. Both pieces have distinctive capabilities and logistical requirements and must be employed to enable those advantages. Far too often howitzers were used only against troops in trenches or wooded areas, in villages and towns, or on heights; but as Scharnhorst suggested, what about using howitzers in other situations: 'at considerable distances, when one is firing blindly, when the exact distance is unknown or the precise elevation is not required'. In these cases, 'the howitzer is at least as good as the canon'.

> These circumstances have undoubtedly caused the infantry and the cavalry in all armies to be very much for howitzers, while the artillery is against them. The former may have looked too much at the moral, and the latter alone at the physical effect, without consideration of the particular circumstances.[26]

Scharnhorst also applauded Braun's experiments with various types of shells and suggested 'a most advantageous improvement would be if one introduced a concentric one'. 'Incidentally', he concluded, 'this matter is not new in artillery science. The Danish and other artillery have had concentric bombs for a long time now'.[27]

Because of his commitments in Hanover, Scharnhorst's negotiations with Prussia were kept strictly confidential. In Hanover he told no one, not even his mentor and superior Wallmoden; while in Prussia, besides Lecoq, only Friedrich Wilhelm, *Oberst* Friedrich von Zastrow, and Duke Karl of Brunswick were apprised of the situation.[28] On 3 November, Lecoq wrote to Scharnhorst, cautioning him once again about his quest to be ennobled.

> I really do not know what has been said regarding the nobility. *Oberst* von Zastrow, with whom I spoke, believed it was better to receive this distinction as a reward after some time. Now be quiet about it, and after you are in the service for a year, if you write to the king, it will be done immediately.[29]

Lecoq then provided some key advice to his friend: 'As soon as you have your dismissal, report this in a cordial letter to the King, to all the princes and generals, and especially to Generals Meerkatz and Tempelhof – do not to forget Pontanus'.[30] This seems to have satisfied Scharnhorst, who kept quiet as instructed, and then wrote to Lecoq on 20 November, delighted to have heard that Frederick William 'has been so gracious' in approving his enno-

26 Scharnhorst, 'Promemoria' (29 October 1800); in Kunisch (ed.), *Scharnhorst: Privat und dienstliche Schriften*, Vol.2, p.449.

27 Scharnhorst, 'Promemoria' (29 October 1800); in Kunisch (ed.), *Scharnhorst: Privat und dienstliche Schriften*, Vol.2, p.449. Danish experiments on concentric shot are discussed in Mechlenburg's January 1799 memorandum to Scharnhorst.

28 See the discussion of this in the Letter of 28 November 1800 from Lecoq to Scharnhorst; in *Nachlaß Scharnhorst*, Nr. 25, Sheet 45.

29 Lecoq to Scharnhorst (3 November 1800); in *Nachlaß Scharnhorst*, Nr. 25, Sheet 43.

30 Lecoq to Scharnhorst (3 November 1800); in *Nachlaß Scharnhorst*, Nr. 25, Sheet 44. *General-Lieutenant* Johann Friedrich Ludolf von Merkatz (1729-1815) was the Inspector General of Prussian Artillery. *Oberstlieutenant* Johann Christian Pontanus (1742-1813) was also an artilleryman and the artillery representative on the Prussian Supreme War Council.

blement. He also told Lecoq that his colleague *Capitain* Decken, while in Brunswick accompanying Prince Adolphus, had heard from Duke Karl that Prussia was going to increase its horse artillery at the expense of its foot artillery. These new units were to be organised into companies, and the prospect of commanding one certainly thrilled Scharnhorst. 'I cannot tell you with what longing I look forward to the time of my departure from here, however painful it will be for me'.[31]

Scharnhorst included several editions of *New Military Journal* with this letter to Lecoq. Much to his dismay, several pieces published a decade earlier contained commentary unfavourable to Prussia and her army, and Scharnhorst (as the sole editor at the time) seemed overly concerned about any possible negative interpretations. One piece dealt with his review of the military portions of *From the Prussian Monarchy under Frederick the Great* (Paris 1787), by Honouré-Gabriel-Victor de Riqueti, Count of Mirabeau (1749-1791). In his commentary Mirabeau had consulted Jakob Mauvillon, who later published his thoughts as *Military System of Prussia and Principles of the Current Tactics of the Most Advanced Troops* (London 1788). In his critique of these works, Scharnhorst had dismissed the conclusions of both Mirabeau and Mauvillon as being incorrect and bias.[32]

In another article Scharnhorst had reviewed a book authored by a former Prussian officer, Karl Friedrich von Lindenau (1742-1817). Lindenau had been dismissed from Prussian service and was a staff officer in Austrian service at the time he wrote his book. He also mentored the young and impressionable Archduke Karl, over whom he had significant influence. Lindenau's work, *On the Higher Prussian Tactics, Their Deficiencies, and Their Timeless Inconvenience, as well as a More Correct and Appropriate Method* (Leipzig 1790), was a confused tirade on linear traditions of pre-revolutionary warfare. Scharnhorst was not at all impressed with Lindenau's work.[33] A third piece Scharnhorst wrote was a study on 'Recruitment, Salary, Organisation, Instruction and Training of the Prussian Artillery'.[34] As he explained to Lecoq: 'I have never written anything detrimental to the Prussian army. On the contrary, from conviction I have always been her great admirer and eulogist'.[35] He then asked Lecoq to impress this upon Zastrow and Friedrich Wilhelm.

Believing that Lecoq had not received his letter, Scharnhorst wrote another on 23 November. He reiterated his thanks to Friedrich Wilhelm for the promise of being ennobled, and his gratitude to Lecoq for his 'friendship and kindness', especially for the latter's sound advice 'regarding my future behaviour'. 'I am very happy by the imminent change that I am experiencing', Scharnhorst continued. 'I have considered the matter a long time'. He then said he would seek his discharge from Hanoverian service 'around

31 Scharnhorst to Lecoq (20 November 1800); in Kunisch (ed.), *Scharnhorst: Privat und dienstliche Schriften*, Vol.2, pp.450-53; the quoted passages are from p.451.

32 See [Gerhard Scharnhorst:] 'Ausführlicher Auszug und Bemerkungen über den militärischen Teil des Werks: De la Monarchie prussienne sous Frédéric le Grand p. M. le Comte de Mirabeau 1788', *Neues militärisches Journal* 2 (1789), pp.31-94.

33 See [Gerhard Scharnhorst:] 'Beurtheilung der Lindenauischen Tactik, zweyter Theil', *Neues militärisches Journal* 5 (1791), pp.161-193.

34 See [Gerhard Scharnhorst:] 'Recrutirung, Besoldung, Etat, Unterricht und Uebung der Preussischen Artillerie', *Neues militärisches Journal* 4 (1790), pp.39-59.

35 Scharnhorst to Lecoq (20 November 1800); in Kunisch (ed.), *Scharnhorst: Privat und dienstliche Schriften*, Vol.2, p.452.

mid-December', and this time vowed not to permit officials in Hanover to delay his departure. 'The King [Friedrich Wilhelm] has allowed me to stay here until the end of this year', he told Lecoq. Turning to his future seniority and assignment in Prussia, he wrote, 'I am curious to know whether one knows something about my assignment'. He was hoping to be assigned to Tempelhof's regiment. Before closing he updated Lecoq on the continuing saga of mapping the area of operations. He noted little progress had been made over the past month, and now only two soldiers – *Lieutenant* Richard and *Guide* Rummel – were still busy with this project.[36] When news of his posting in Berlin arrived, Scharnhorst sent a brief letter to Lecoq, thanking him once again 'from the bottom of my heart' for the news he would be assigned to Tempelhof's 3. Artillerie Regiment. This 'has made me very happy'.[37]

Still anxious about any possible misinterpretation of his journal reviews, Scharnhorst send a memorandum to Friedrich Wilhelm in November, hoping to clarify this situation and end any misgivings of the king, his confidants, and his future colleagues in the Prussian army: 'I have never written anything detrimental to the Prussian army. From conviction I have always been her great admirer and eulogist… I was also the first to reject Lindenau's presumptuous and untrue criticism of Prussian tactics', he informed Friedrich Wilhelm. He then explained that his main purpose in publishing *New Military Journal* was to make soldiers aware of the latest literature on military affairs. Due a misfortunate oversight, some 'unfavourable remarks' were included about the Prussian artillery in the excerpts from Mirabeau's *Prussian Monarchy*. Turning to the subject of Frederick the Great, Scharnhorst told Friedrich Wilhelm about his 'new edition of the instructions of the great king to his generals', which included 'several smaller instructions and brief tactical essays' written by Frederick the Great, that he [Scharnhorst] had assembled for the late *General-Lieutenant* Estorff, 'who was an ardent collector of them, and always liked to see all of the [king's] instructions taught' to his troops.[38]

In December, the Hanoverian Artillery Commission met in seven sessions to review the results of various tests and experiments and to finalize its report to Wallmoden. With the exception Löw, all commission members were present. Scharnhorst kept the proceedings and signed the minutes of these meetings.[39] Members discussed the results of the numerous firing exercises and experiments that used different types of alloys, their hardness, cohesion, and durability. Interestingly, the Commission had asked civilian experts to assist with these alloy tests and to analyse the data. One was noted Hanoverian chemist, metallurgist, and teacher Johann Christoph Ilsemann (1727-1822). Another was renowned pharmacist Johann Friedrich Westrumb (1751-1819).[40] Braun and now *Oberstlieutenant*

36 Scharnhorst to Lecoq (23 November 1800); in Kunisch (ed.), *Scharnhorst: Privat und dienstliche Schriften*, Vol.2, pp.454-55.

37 Scharnhorst to Lecoq (after 29 November 1800); in Kunisch (ed.), *Scharnhorst: Privat und dienstliche Schriften*, Vol.2, p.457.

38 Gerhard Scharnhorst, 'Pro memoria' (November 1800); in Kunisch (ed.), *Scharnhorst: Privat und dienstliche Schriften*, Vol.2, p.456. Scharnhorst's brief transmittal letter can be found on pp.455-56.

39 See 'Sitzungsprotokolle' (12-29 December 1800); in Kunisch (ed.), *Scharnhorst: Privat und dienstliche Schriften*, Vol.2, pp.457-64.

40 See 'Protocoll von den 15ten Dec. 1800' and 'Protocoll von 16ten Dec. 1800', Kunisch (ed.), *Scharnhorst: Privat und dienstliche Schriften*, Vol.2, pp.460-61 and 461-62; respectively.

Wissel (not a commission member) oversaw these experiments. Significantly, commission members suggested metallurgical training for artillery officers, with Trew insisting officers attend Ilsemann's collegium.[41] The Commission also felt the artillery should assign officers to the Giesshaus Foundry to monitor the production of artillery material. Adding a chemist to the faculty of the artillery school was also recommended, as was procuring current technical literature. At the 19 December meeting, members adopted an interim report to be sent to Wallmoden.

On 30 December 1800, Scharnhorst requested his unconditional release from Hanoverian service. He informed Wallmoden that the lure of Prussian service was too much for him to remain in Hanover. In Prussia he would not only receive 'a considerable' salary of 3,500 Reichsthaler (much more than what Hanover was paying him), but also an annual pension of 1,000 Reichsthaler for his wife and family should anything happen to him. If both he and Klara died, their children would receive a yearly supplement of 500 Reichsthaler until the youngest child reached 25. As he told Wallmoden, how could 'a father who loves his children' turn down such an offer? He then thanked the field marshal for being 'so gracious a superior' and lamented that he 'must renounce the most agreeable personal circumstances under which I serve'.[42] He felt his peacetime service on the General Staff would be of little value to King George, implying that he had no future in Hanover. He then requested the field marshal's support with his resignation process. On 4 January 1801, he wrote to King George III, formally requesting his discharge from Hanoverian service. His letter contained just three concise sentences. He told the king he was grateful for being able to have served 24 years in the king's German service. Now, 'imperious circumstances, which I as the father of a large innocent family cannot escape', made it impossible for him to continue in Hanoverian service. He then asked for his dismissal.[43]

On 22 January Scharnhorst followed up his initial letter to Wallmoden, respectfully reminding him that time was crucial. Prussia had a few vacancies in their artillery to be filled in the spring and he needed to notify Berlin when he would be reporting for duty. He informed Wallmoden he was maintaining the strictest confidentially regarding his plans. To his knowledge only Prince Adolphus and his 'two most trusted friends', *Capitains* Decken and Ende, knew of his acceptance in Prussian service. He urgently requested the field marshal forward his request to London and King George.[44]

On 2 February Scharnhorst reassured Wallmoden his plans were being kept secret 'in the most sacred way'. Interestingly, in this letter he noted that only 'von Ende, Decken and Bok' were aware of his situation. He apologised to the Commanding General, writing, 'I am also aware that this matter is very annoying', but hoped that it would be handled expeditiously. Turning to the main purpose of his letter, he updated the field marshal on the

41 'Protocoll von den 15ten Dec. 1800', Kunisch (ed.), *Scharnhorst: Privat und dienstliche Schriften*, Vol.2, p.461.

42 Scharnhorst on Wallmoden (30 December 1800); in Kunisch (ed.), *Scharnhorst: Privat und dienstliche Schriften*, Vol.2, pp.464-65; the quoted passage is from p.465.

43 Gerhard Scharnhorst to King George III (4 January 1801); in Kunisch (ed.), *Scharnhorst: Privat und dienstliche Schriften*, Vol.2, p.466. Documents relating to Scharnhorst's transfer to Prussian service can be found in Hann 41, III, Nr.190: *Scharnhorsts Abgang und Übertritt in preußische Dienste, 1801*; deposited at the Niedersächsisches Landesarchiv, Hanover; and discussed in Lehmann, *Scharnhorst*, Vol.1, pp.285-88.

44 Scharnhorst to Wallmoden (22 January 1801); in Kunisch (ed.), *Scharnhorst: Privat und dienstliche Schriften*, Vol.2, p.466.

progress of the Artillery Commission. He was delighted to report that the Commission was finalising its report, that it had been very thorough in its 'investigation of artillery matters', and that 'nothing will be omitted here'.[45] 'Only an unpleasant discussion is still before us', he continued, 'the determination of which powder is useless!' Braun had been assigned this study but had still not completed all experiments to his satisfaction. Scharnhorst stated as soon as Trew signed all the Commission reports, he would forward them to the field marshal. In closing, he emphasised that as long as he remained in Hanoverian service, he would 'never lose sight of the duties and gratitude I owe to Your Excellency and to the state'.[46]

Anticipating his entry into Prussian service, Scharnhorst began drafting memoranda on subjects he planned to address to his Prussian colleagues. In one lengthy memo sent to Zastrow in early 1801 and titled, 'On the Introduction of a Certain Mechanism in the Leadership of Armies, Appropriate to the Present State of the Art of War', Scharnhorst discussed the critical need to educate and train senior military leaders in the art of leading soldiers in battle.[47] Restating much of what he had told Mechlenberg, Scharnhorst began with historical precedence. 'This is according to the experiences of the greatest army leaders'. Duke Ferdinand of Brunswick and Frederick the Great had 'established a permanent, always to be followed mechanism' [*setzte einen permanenten, immer zu befolgenden Mechanismus fest*]. While Ferdinand's instructions to his commanders during operations in 1762 and Frederick's famous instructions to his generals were appropriate, Scharnhorst noted that they were 'only suited to the needs of the times and were calculated only according to the individual experiences of the great man'. What was required now are similar instructions 'appropriate to the present state of the art of war and to the special needs of the army for which it is designed'.[48]

Scharnhorst described the current standing army as a 'large and very complicated machine', whose leadership 'does not have to depend in all of its parts on the constant, direct action of a single man,

> It must have a firm course of its own… The leader must only steer, communicate the inner strength to the whole, test and arrange only the inner goodness of the various motivating forces, and modify them according to the particular circumstances'.

45 Source documents of items not submitted to the Artillery Commission can be found in Hann 41, III, Nr.138: *Die Organisation der Artillerie Regiments betreffend, 1800-1801. P.M. der Commission nicht vorgelegt*; deposited at the Niedersächsisches Landesarchiv, Hanover.

46 Scharnhorst to Wallmoden (2 February 1801); in Kunisch (ed.), *Scharnhorst: Privat und dienstliche Schriften*, Vol.2, p.467.

47 Gerhard Scharnhorst, 'Ueber die Einführung eines gewiβen Mechanismus in der Führung der Armeen, den jetzigen Zustande der Kriegeskunst angemeβen' (beginning 1801); in Kunisch (ed.), *Scharnhorst: Privat und dienstliche Schriften*, Vol.2, pp.468-74. 'To H[err] v. Z[astrow]' appears just above the title. Lehmann, *Scharnhorst*, Vol.1, pp.230-31 (Note 1) writes this memorandum was addressed to Zastrow, who would soon become the king's general adjutant.

48 Scharnhorst, 'Ueber die Einführung eines gewiβen Mechanismus in der Führung der Armeen', Kunisch (ed.), *Scharnhorst: Privat und dienstliche Schriften*, Vol.2, pp.468-69; the quoted passages are from p.468.

General rules and standard operating procedures must be the foundation here, 'like the law in the bourgeois constitution'.[49] Continuing his comparison of the present standing army with a civil governmental structure, Scharnhorst maintained that the commanding general (like the prince) cannot 'oversee and govern without laws'. And like the prince, the commanding general must be unencumbered by all the daily minutia of administration and operations.

> The army commander must determine only the plan, communicate the energy for its execution, place people in the right position according to their abilities and zeal, watch over the execution of commands, give strength and life to the whole through reward and punishments.

'The army leader must be entirely free – upon his 'nod' [*Wink*] the machine must be set in motion'.[50]

Because a national army possessed more soldiers, more guns, more horses, more ammunition, more supplies, and more transportation than a dynastic force, Scharnhorst reiterated his earlier recommendations that the army be partitioned into smaller, more manageable units that combined infantry, cavalry, artillery, and supporting units.[51] To centralise the activities of these combined-arms division and corps, and to assist the commander-in-chief on campaign, he again advocated a General Staff with Troops recruited from the regiments and trained along a common doctrine.[52] With a clearly defined standard operating procedure, general staff officers would be capable of adapting quickly to the ever-changing circumstances on the battlefield.

Scharnhorst informed Zastrow the Austrians pioneered the way here. Under the direction of *Feldmarschall* Franz Moritz Count von Lacy (1725-1801), who had served for years as the head of the general staff, Austria had developed sound field procedures for virtually every conceivable eventuality in war. Scharnhorst felt this may have been why the Austrians had fought so well, even without quality leadership. They had no genius like Frederick and needed to provide clear guidance to their field commanders.[53] Synthesising again what he had described to Mechlenberg years earlier, Scharnhorst made it clear to Zastrow that the General Staff with Troops was the indispensable organisation the commanding general

49 Scharnhorst, 'Ueber die Einführung eines gewiβen Mechanismus in der Führung der Armeen', Kunisch (ed.), *Scharnhorst: Privat und dienstliche Schriften*, Vol.2, pp.469-70.

50 Scharnhorst, 'Ueber die Einführung eines gewiβen Mechanismus in der Führung der Armeen', Kunisch (ed.), *Scharnhorst: Privat und dienstliche Schriften*, Vol.2, p.470.

51 Among these recommendations are four studies: Gerhard Scharnhorst, 'Ueber die Organisation einer Armee', 'Fälle, wo Armeen in Corps vertheilt stehen' (not before 1795, not after 1801), 'Von den Vorzügen der Abteilung einer Armee in Armee-Divisionen' (1801), and 'Ueber die Stärke und Vertheilung der Artillerie bey einer in Divisionen oder Corps getheilten Armee' (between 1801 and 1802); in Kunisch (ed.), *Scharnhorst: Privat und dienstliche Schriften*, Vol.2, pp.545-46, 773, 774-82, and Vol.3, pp.233-47; respectively. Also see the discussion in Lehmann, *Scharnhorst*, Vol.1, pp.237-40.

52 See the source documents in Hann 41, III, Nr.191: *Errichtung eines General-Quartiermeister-Stabes betreffend, 1801-1802*; deposited at the Niedersächsisches Landesarchiv, Hanover.

53 Scharnhorst, 'Ueber die Einführung eines gewiβen Mechanismus in der Führung der Armeen', in Kunisch (ed.), *Scharnhorst: Privat und dienstliche Schriften*, Vol.2, p.471.

needed to command and control his army. This General Staff with Troops prepares the instructions the army needs – 'the operations plan', the establishment of positions, and the 'conduct of battles'. It also manages the daily business of the army, relieving the commanding general of these tasks. As his discussion shows, Scharnhorst clearly had his General Staff with Troops in mind, as opposed to a capital staff which Prussian already had in Potsdam.[54]

In February, Scharnhorst began keeping a notebook with his thoughts on various topics relating to the art of war. These miscellaneous (and at times random) insights and ideas he grouped into 16 categories. The major ones included: artillery, military stratagems, dimensions of the art of war, orders of battle, various ways of fighting, different divisional organisations, offensive advantages of defensive behaviour, and general thoughts on military training for war.[55] Many of these discussions included examples from his own experience or from the pages of history. He also cited various works on military affairs written by renowned soldiers. Scharnhorst indicated he was planning to write a treatise on the art of war, and it appears that the commentary in this notebook was directly related to this forthcoming study. With every topic Scharnhorst discussed, he included a section entitled, 'Art of War', in which he jotted down key thoughts or phrases for future elaboration. Here he intended to provide a detailed analysis of various stratagems, the relationship between the various branches of the service, a description of the little war, and the employment of light troops. An 'atlas of plans and maps is required for this treatise', he noted. As he was complying this study, Scharnhorst also noted that his 'intention' was 'to write a series of memoranda, in which I draw attention to the chief objects which are important in an army going to the field'.[56]

In all of his sections on military stratagems, Scharnhorst included great military leaders, such as Santa Cruz, Maurice of Saxony, and Turenne, as examples to follow, as well as decisive battles, such as Ramillies, Minden, Rossbach and Leuthen, to illustrate his points. For those interested in learning more on stratagems and their use he recommended three French studies: Gui-Alexis Lobineau, *Polyaenus's Ruses of War and Frontin's Stratagems* (Paris, 1770); Jacques-Marie Ray de Saint-Geniez, *François's Stratagems of War* (Paris, 1769); and Paul-Gédéon Joly de Maizeroy, *Treatise on Stratagems Permitted in War* (Paris, 1765).[57] Additionally, he did not pass up the opportunity to comment on current military literature, writing that Johann Wilhelm von Archenholz (1743-1812), a former Prussian captain and now editor of the journal *Minerva*, 'is wrong when he rejects the column attack at Hohenlinden'. At Hohenlinden on 3 December 1800, the French Armée du Rhin under Jean Victor Moreau (1763-1813) enveloped the column attack of the Austrians and Bavarians under Archduke John.[58] Interestingly, just a few pages later, Scharnhorst cited as the first

54 Scharnhorst, 'Ueber die Einführung eines gewiβen Mechanismus in der Führung der Armeen', in Kunisch (ed.), *Scharnhorst: Privat und dienstliche Schriften*, Vol.2, p.469.

55 Gerhard Scharnhorst, 'Aide-Mémoire Februar 1801 bis …', in Kunisch (ed.), *Scharnhorst: Privat und dienstliche Schriften*, Vol.2, pp.474-89. Material in this Notebook is consistent with the contents of his 'Manual in Folio'.

56 Scharnhorst, 'Aide-Mémoire Februar 1801 bis …', in Kunisch (ed.), *Scharnhorst: Privat und dienstliche Schriften*, Vol.2, pp.474-89; the quoted passages are from pp.479 and 482.

57 Scharnhorst, 'Aide-Mémoire Februar 1801 bis …', in Kunisch (ed.), *Scharnhorst: Privat und dienstliche Schriften*, Vol.2, p.478.

58 Scharnhorst, 'Aide-Mémoire Februar 1801 bis …', in Kunisch (ed.), *Scharnhorst: Privat und dienstliche Schriften*, Vol.2, p.476.

example of his section on 'Stratagems in the Operational Concept', the recent 'Campaign of Bonaparte before the Battle of Marengo'.[59]

By far, the largest topic Scharnhorst discussed was the artillery. As an artilleryman, he was naturally concerned with what he felt was the improper deployment of artillery as part of the combined arms team. Too often the artillery failed to provide the timely and accurate fire support the infantry and cavalry needed. Addressing this issue, Scharnhorst suggested assigning a specialist 'with great skill in judging distances' to each battery. This soldier would work closely with the battery commander and 'must be able to record and draw'. Furthermore, 'It is very important to know the distance, the exact distance. Without this there is no possibility of getting good [fire] effect'. Scharnhorst stated that this subject would require 'a separate treatise'.[60] Judging from his sketchy notes here, Scharnhorst is describing what later became known as the artillery forward observer, whose task was to direct and adjust fire for his assigned battery. He also toyed with various organisational structures, attempting to find the ideal mix of artillery to support various infantry and cavalry formations. He wrote that he would 'elaborate' on this topic in an article, and it appears he planned to compare the views of past and current theorists and practitioners. He specifically cited the French artillerists Gribeauval and L'Espinasse.[61]

Anxious to leave Hanover and frustrated that he had not heard anything about his discharge, Scharnhorst sent a note to Wallmoden on 20 February, stating the Artillery Commission would be finished its 'most important work' in the next two weeks, and pleaded with the field marshal to forward his request to London, 'if it had not already been done'.[62] He then sent a letter to Zastrow to inform him of the situation. Scharnhorst said Wallmoden would not let him leave until the Artillery Commission had finished its work. Since the Commission was working 'uninterruptedly', he hoped that it would complete its tasks 'in three weeks'.[63] Unbeknownst to Scharnhorst, the Commanding General had forwarded his request for discharge to London on 18 February. In his correspondence with King George, Wallmoden 'warmly and sincerely' endorsed Scharnhorst's request.[64] A few days later, on 24

59 Scharnhorst, 'Aide-Mémoire Februar 1801 bis …', in Kunisch (ed.), *Scharnhorst: Privat und dienstliche Schriften*, Vol.2, p.480. The Battle of Marengo (14 June 1800) would become one of Scharnhorst's favourite topics of discussion in Prussia.

60 Scharnhorst, 'Aide-Mémoire Februar 1801 bis …', in Kunisch (ed.), *Scharnhorst: Privat und dienstliche Schriften*, Vol.2, p.475.

61 Scharnhorst, 'Aide-Mémoire Februar 1801 bis …', in Kunisch (ed.), *Scharnhorst: Privat und dienstliche Schriften*, Vol.2, p.486. Scharnhorst later presented a lecture to the *Militärische Gesellschaft* in Berlin, entitled, 'On the Relationship of the Artillery with other Types of Troops'. See Gerhard Scharnhorst, 'Über das Verhältnis der Artillerie zu den übrigen Gattungen von Truppen; eine Vorlesung in der militärischen Gesellschaft, bey der Anzeige des Werks von dem französischen General L'espinasse: *Essai sur l'organisation de l'arme d'artillerie*', *Nachlass Scharnhorst*, Nr. 201; deposited at the Geheimes Staatsarchiv Preussischer Kulturbesitz, 196/VI. HA Familienarchive und Nachlässe, Berlin (Dahlem).

62 Scharnhorst to Wallmoden (20 February 1801); in Kunisch (ed.), *Scharnhorst: Privat und dienstliche Schriften*, Vol.2, p.489.

63 Gerhard Scharnhorst to Friedrich von Zastrow (after 20 February 1801); in Kunisch (ed.), *Scharnhorst: Privat und dienstliche Schriften*, Vol.2, p.491.

64 Klippel, *Scharnhorst*, Vol.2, p.335. Once again, Klippel does not publish this important letter that demonstrates Wallmoden's wholehearted endorsement of Scharnhorst's transfer into Prussian service. See Sheets 8-9 of Hann 41, III, Nr.190: *Scharnhorsts Abgang und Übertritt in preußische Dienste, 1801*; deposited at the Niedersächsisches Landesarchiv, Hanover.

February, Scharnhorst forwarded the report of the Artillery Commission to Wallmoden. He was pleased to inform the field marshal that both officers and non-commissioned officers of the artillery regiment had 'thoroughly scrutinised' the new artillery regulation and many of their suggestions were incorporated in the final draft. For example, he told the field marshal, 'The previously large, uninhabitable, artificially furnished and expensive masthead, which was very useless in the field', was removed from the artillery baggage train. For the artilleryman (like the infantryman du Plat had described), 'the useless' and 'superfluous' sword, 'worn with much discomfort', was removed from the soldier's wardrobe. Löw, Braun, Prince Karl von Schwarzburg, and Scharnhorst signed the report.[65]

Just about a month later, on 19 March, Scharnhorst wrote to Zastrow to let him know he had received the latter's letter of 3 March, and to inform him Wallmoden was not pleased with the final report of the Artillery Commission. Scharnhorst did not elaborate much here but did tell Zastrow that Wallmoden had forwarded his request for dismissal from Hanoverian service to London 'in the beginning of this year'. 'It troubles me very much to have to report obediently, that up to now I have not yet received my release from England'. Scharnhorst stated that the delay was due to 'local artillery matters', as well as to the current illness of King George. 'This is even more unpleasant to me, as my departure here has been known for about eight days'. To reassure Friedrich Wilhelm, Zastrow, and other Prussian officials, he included the letter of support Wallmoden had sent to London, and which Scharnhorst hoped would convince officials there to expedite his 'permission to leave'.[66]

The next day members of the Artillery Commission sent a memorandum to Wallmoden, addressing the latter's concerns regarding their report. Once again, it appears Trew was standing in the way of progress. Löw most likely wrote this brief, which Löw, Braun, Schwarzburg, and Scharnhorst signed. All four agreed that many of the suggestions the Commission had received from those who had read the draft regulation 'were extremely good and correct, so we did not hesitate to include them in the revised regulation'. The only dissenting view appears to have been Trew, who sharply criticised the feedback from his own officers and non-commissioned officers. So Löw, Braun, Schwarzburg, and Scharnhorst felt that it was their duty to submit the Commission's report without Trew's official consent.[67]

On 28 March, Zastrow wrote to Scharnhorst, informing him that, due to the difficulties he was having getting his dismissal, Friedrich Wilhelm was willing to delay the occupation of his post, but wished to see the Scharnhorst's release as soon as possible.[68] Once again, this letter reveals how eager and patient the Prussian leadership was to obtain the services of Gerhard Scharnhorst. On 2 April, Scharnhorst forwarded Zastrow's letter to Wallmoden, again asking his support in hastening his release from Hanoverian service.[69] Nine days later Scharnhorst sent another request to Wallmoden, reminding him of their discussion 'eight

65 Report of the Hanoverian Artillery Commission, 24 February 1801; in Kunisch (ed.), *Scharnhorst: Privat und dienstliche Schriften*, Vol.2, pp.489-90; the quoted passages are from p.490.

66 Scharnhorst to Zastrow (19 March 1801); in Kunisch (ed.), *Scharnhorst: Privat und dienstliche Schriften*, Vol.2, pp.491-92.

67 Artillery Commission Memorandum to Field Marshal Wallmoden (20 March 1801); in Kunisch (ed.), *Scharnhorst: Privat und dienstliche Schriften*, Vol.2, pp.492-95; the quoted passage is from p.493.

68 Friedrich von Zastrow to Gerhard Scharnhorst (28 March 1801); in Klippel, *Scharnhorst*, Vol.2, p.337.

69 Scharnhorst to Wallmoden (2 April 1801); in Kunisch (ed.), *Scharnhorst: Privat und dienstliche Schriften*, Vol.2, p.495.

days ago' that if no news was forthcoming from London regarding his release within a week, he would be free to report to Berlin. Scharnhorst asked to whom he should deliver his official papers and then requested permission to leave Hanover.[70]

Meanwhile, in response to Wallmoden's request that he provide an assessment of officers under his charge, and to recommend his successor, Scharnhorst responded with a 10-page report. 'It is very difficult for me', he began, to recommend 'people for the temporary takeover of my duties'. 'Even with the best pretension to be impartial', Scharnhorst believed no one person was fully qualified to accomplish his tasks.[71] Indeed, 'Scharnhorst was rightly thought to be the most knowledgeable, intelligent, and competent officer in the army'. He was clearly 'the favourite' of Wallmoden, 'who was reluctant to lose him and looked at his departure as a loss for the Hanoverian army'.[72] The field marshal most likely sought Scharnhorst's opinion to compare with his own. The General-Quartermaster-Lieutenant began with *Lieutenant* Schäffer, who would be able 'to take over the preparation of march routes', as well as 'the determination of quarters with the transfer of the troops'. He then recommended that *Fähnrich* Hagenbroik assist Schäffer, since Hagenbroik 'is familiar with the mechanics of this work and has always carried out all the tasks assigned to him'. Unfortunately, both Schäffer and Hagenbroik lacked the requisite 'knowledge of tactics and the art of warfare' to accomplish their duties without proper supervision from 'Your Excellency'. While Scharnhorst felt Hagenbroik had 'in a far greater degree' more tactical sense than did Schäffer, the former's age and 'utterly ruined health' made Hagenbroik unreliable 'and leave him little hope for the future'.[73]

Turning to those officers 'known to me', Scharnhorst stated that there 'is none who combines the indispensable knowledge of the details of artillery and engineering with the essentials of the art of war'. Here he is not being arrogant or prideful. These were the fundamental prerequisites for the general staff officer, which he had established in his writings and actual wartime conduct. Among all the field-grade and company-grade officers in the Hanoverian army, Scharnhorst had no peer. Wallmoden, Hammerstein, and Diepenbroick, as well as other senior officers knew this. Few of Scharnhorst's contemporaries had taken the time during peace to study the art and science of war as he had done, and their performance under fire had demonstrated this. Some, like Braun, had recognised their shortcomings and were trying to improve themselves. Others, like Trew, continued to deny the art of war had changed dramatically.

Responding to Wallmoden's question, Scharnhorst recommended augmenting the General-Quartermaster Staff with an additional 'two or three officers'. He strongly suggested appointing *Lieutenant* Christian Sigismund von Ziehen as the 'Second Officer' of the General-Quartermaster Staff. 'Your Excellency would find no one more fitting than *Lieutenant* Ziehen. He has a vast knowledge of the artillery, the engineering sciences, and all

70 Scharnhorst to Wallmoden (11 April 1801); in Kunisch (ed.), *Scharnhorst: Privat und dienstliche Schriften*, Vol.2, p.496.

71 Scharnhorst to Wallmoden (Spring 1801); in Kunisch (ed.), *Scharnhorst: Privat und dienstliche Schriften*, Vol.2, pp.496-98; the quoted passages are from p.496.

72 See the discussion in Klippel, *Scharnhorst*, Vol.2, p.346.

73 Scharnhorst to Wallmoden (Spring 1801); in Kunisch (ed.), *Scharnhorst: Privat und dienstliche Schriften*, Vol.2, pp.496-97; the quoted passages are from p.497.

other parts of war'. Moreover, 'he has always distinguished himself' in his daily affairs, and especially under fire at 'Pont à Chin, Apeltheren and Bentheim'.[74] As for the 'First Officer', Scharnhorst offered Wallmoden four choices: *Majore* Albrecht von Estorff (of the 9. Leichte Dragoner Regiment) and von Ende, and *Capitains* Decken and Scheiter (*Ober-Adjudant* of the Cavalry). Of the four, 'no one would be more lucid with the mechanical chores' of the general staff officer than *Major* von Estorff. Unfortunately, as Scharnhorst told Wallmoden:

> His rare activity and great service would give him very great advantages in every kind of work before every other man, had he acquired more knowledge of the art of war, and had trained his judgment more. It is not to be hoped that he will make progress in this, for he has long ceased to read, and has taken a point of view that does not seem very promising for the future.[75]

Scharnhorst felt that *Major* von Ende 'has a much more detailed assessment of military matters' than does Estorff. Additionally, Ende 'possesses a lot of his own ideas, and knows much better how to conduct himself in personal relationships'. Sadly, 'he too lacks knowledge of the actual art of war' [*der eigentlichen Kriegeskunst*]. Turning to his friend Decken, Scharnhorst wrote one brief sentence: 'Without doubt, *Capitain* von Decken has advantages over the rest when it comes to knowledge of tactics and the art of war and works with unmistakable progress'. Scharnhorst then praised *Capitain* von Scheiter, 'whose worth is invaluable'. He was 'clearly one of the most capable, brave, and zealous officers in the entire corps, and also on the General Staff'.

> But in matters where a certain mechanism is the basis, in situations where a profound judgment is required, in negotiations where an examination of all the various aspects of the military sciences is necessary, he has not the benefits which are otherwise peculiar to him.[76]

This completed Scharnhorst's assessment of possible replacements for him as the General-Quartermaster-Lieutenant.

Scharnhorst knew what the Commanding General desired in a General-Quartermaster-Lieutenant and thus placed mental fitness above all else in his evaluations. While many officers (and non-commissioned officers) might have the requisite physical and technical skills and abilities demanded by their daily routines, Scharnhorst focused on the *Bildung* of leaders, which was a life-long process. And he made it clear to others that this was what the army should be looking for when selecting leaders. Having thus completed his evaluations, he recommended Decken and Ziehen as the two officers 'most promising for the future'. He suggested retaining the services of both Schäffer and Hagenbroik in their current

74 Scharnhorst to Wallmoden (Spring 1801); in Kunisch (ed.), *Scharnhorst: Privat und dienstliche Schriften*, Vol.2, p.497. Scharnhorst would later recruit Ziehen to join him in Prussian service. Ziehen was commissioned a Prussian captain in 1804, and assumed responsibility for teaching gunnery, siege warfare, fortifications, tactics, and strategy at the Berlin Academy for Young Officers. See the discussion in Lehmann, *Scharnhorst*, Vol.1, pp.310-11.

75 Scharnhorst to Wallmoden (Spring 1801); in Kunisch (ed.), *Scharnhorst: Privat und dienstliche Schriften*, Vol.2, p.498.

76 Scharnhorst to Wallmoden (Spring 1801); in Kunisch (ed.), *Scharnhorst: Privat und dienstliche Schriften*, Vol.2, p.498.

supporting roles. He praised Hagenbroik who has, 'in many scientific discoveries, a rare and correct appraisal of the practical and useful. I have always consulted him in my military essays, and almost never without profit'.[77] Scharnhorst then focused on answering another request from Wallmoden.

In mid-April, the Hanoverian General-Quartermaster-Lieutenant sent a letter to the Commanding General clarifying the disposition of his official maps and papers. He explained that all of the Hanoverian quartering lists from the beginning of the establishment of the Observation Army are with *Oberst* Löw and in the archives of the General Staff. He stated that he had 'handed over' to now *General-Major* Kuntze the maps of the Hildesheim area and those portions of the Duchy of Brunswick situated around Hanover. He still had in his possession 'two more maps, both geometrically measured', of Bückeburg and Pyrmont, 'which I gladly surrender to General Kunze for the registry'.[78] Next, he said he had 'a collection of lists of cities and villages, with the number of their houses, from most of the provinces of Westphalia', which he said may be useful to his successor. Scharnhorst then noted 'another bundle that I have to surrender', which consisted of the reconnaissance reports from the various Observation Army areas of operation. Lastly, he mentioned that Kunze was still waiting for *Lieutenant* Preuβ to complete his maps of Ravensberg and the Diocese of Münster, for *Lieutenant* Vollinghaus to finish his map of Lippe, and for *Lieutenant* Richard to turn in his triangulations of Paterborn and parts of Brunswick and Hanover. Scharnhorst was delighted to tell Wallmoden that 'with these individual pieces, we possess a collection of situational plans and terrain descriptions from most counties surrounding the Electorate of Hanover, from this side of Holland and the Rhine'. He then took the liberty of enclosing for the Commanding General several essays dealing with current tactics and army affairs, 'as a sign of my unconditional respect and eternal gratitude'.[79]

On 20 April, Scharnhorst sent yet another letter to Wallmoden, declaring that he had no official 'memoranda, plans, and other manuscripts belonging to the General-Quartermaster Department' in his possession.[80] Included with this letter was a memorandum that listed all of the papers and maps the General-Quartermaster-Lieutenant had delivered to the General Staff archives.[81] Then he wrote: 'Since my duty here is complete, I request, Your Excellency, for the favour of sending me my discharge'. He explained that his departure from Hanover has caused him 'much pain' and indicated the sooner he was permitted to leave, the better it would be for all concerned.[82] In accordance with army protocol, he signed

77 Scharnhorst to Wallmoden (Spring 1801); in Kunisch (ed.), *Scharnhorst: Privat und dienstliche Schriften*, Vol.2, p.498.

78 Scharnhorst to Wallmoden (before 20 April 1801); in Kunisch (ed.), *Scharnhorst: Privat und dienstliche Schriften*, Vol.2, pp.499-500; the quoted passages are from p.499.

79 Scharnhorst to Wallmoden (before 20 April 1801); in Kunisch (ed.), *Scharnhorst: Privat und dienstliche Schriften*, Vol.2, p.500.

80 Scharnhorst to Wallmoden (20 April 1801); in Kunisch (ed.), *Scharnhorst: Privat und dienstliche Schriften*, Vol.2, pp.500-501; the quoted passage is from p.500.

81 Gerhard Scharnhorst, 'Verzeichniβ der zum Generalquartiermeisterstabe gehörenden Manuscripte und Zeichnungen' (20 April 1801); in Kunisch (ed.), *Scharnhorst: Privat und dienstliche Schriften*, Vol.2, pp.501-02.

82 Scharnhorst to Wallmoden (20 April 1801); in Kunisch (ed.), *Scharnhorst: Privat und dienstliche Schriften*, Vol.2, p.501.

an official 'dismissal declaration' [*Entlassungsrevers*] on 20 April, reiterating what he had told Wallmoden in his letter of the same date.[83]

Wallmoden answered Scharnhorst the next day. He informed Scharnhorst that he had forwarded the latter's request for discharge 'most obediently' to London on 18 February, 'convinced' that due to the king's ill health, 'no answer has followed'. Not willing to take any chances that Scharnhorst's request for discharge might be denied (due to suspicions in Hanover and London), Wallmoden suggested that since Scharnhorst had an intimate knowledge of Hanoverian military affairs, 'which are not generally permitted to any officer in their entire extent and in their most secret circumstances', he should write an official declaration to assuage any doubts about his future conduct.

Here is another fine example of the complete trust Wallmoden had placed in his General-Quartermaster-Lieutenant, even though Scharnhorst was a mere *Oberstlieutenant* and apparently not entitled to possess states secrets in their entirety. Now, the Commanding General outlined what Scharnhorst should say, and he willingly complied.[84] Then the field marshal forwarded Scharnhorst's declaration to London. With all requirements asked of him concerning his departure completed, Scharnhorst once again politely requested permission to leave Hanover and to notify Prussian officials accordingly, telling Wallmoden the Berlin postal rider 'will leave here on Thursday afternoon'.[85]

In early May Scharnhorst sent Wallmoden his evaluation of the field guides he had been training for the past couple of years. He began by stating that *Guide* Müller deserved 'special grace and protection. He has served so faithfully and righteously in the previous war as well as with the army of demarcation'. Unfortunately, the strain of combat and his duties with the Observation Army had finally destroyed his health, and now he was 'in the saddest physical condition in which a man could find himself'. Scharnhorst explained that gout and consumption had forced Müller to remain bed-ridden 'for almost half a year'. He requested the War Chancery provide a special pension to Müller for his services. Continuing his assessment, Scharnhorst recalled how *Guides* Jasper and Rummel 'have applied themselves with such good success serving as guides, recording and drawing'. For the past two years they had been assisting with the surveys of Lippe and Paderborn, 'like the engineer officers'. *Guides* Weichtdahl and Wiebeking 'have always been willing, faithful, and perfect in their service'. Both, Scharnhorst noted, write well, especially Wiebeking. In closing, he recommended Wallmoden appoint *Guide* Rummel to the General Staff, because his '*reliability*, *secrecy*, and *fidelity*' were above reproach. 'I have never seen anyone like him'.[86]

Later, on 3 May, Scharnhorst sent an impassioned letter to Wallmoden, politely pleading for his release from Hanoverian service. He told the field marshal that 'for five months now',

83 See Gerhard Scharnhorst, 'Entlassungsrevers' (20 April 1801); in Kunisch (ed.), *Scharnhorst: Privat und dienstliche Schriften*, Vol.2, p.502.

84 Wallmoden to Scharnhorst (21 April 1801); in Klippel, *Scharnhorst*, Vol.2, pp.341-44; the quoted passages are from p.342. Scharnhorst's official 'Entlassungsrevers' of 22 April 1801 can be found in Kunisch (ed.), *Scharnhorst: Privat und dienstliche Schriften*, Vol.2, p.503.

85 Scharnhorst to Wallmoden (22 April 1801); in Kunisch (ed.), *Scharnhorst: Privat und dienstliche Schriften*, Vol.2, pp.502-03; the quoted passage is from p.503.

86 Scharnhorst to Wallmoden (1 May 1801); in Kunisch (ed.), *Scharnhorst: Privat und dienstliche Schriften*, Vol.2, p.504. Source documents for these evaluations can be found in Hann 41, I, Nr.181, II: *Bericht Scharnhorsts über Guiden an Wallmoden*; deposited at the Niedersächsisches Landesarchiv, Hanover.

his staff position in the Prussian artillery had remained vacant, while officials in London and Hanover failed to act on his request for dismissal. Scharnhorst was truly beside himself, as he implored Wallmoden to 'let me proceed to my affairs' in Berlin. His work with the Artillery Commission was complete, there was nothing more for him to do in Hanover, and thus, he concluded, 'a long delay could have the greatest and most detrimental consequences for me'.[87]

Wallmoden answered Scharnhorst promptly the next day. He informed Scharnhorst that he had still not received any correspondence from London, and that it was 'not in his powers' to grant Scharnhorst his 'formal' release. Clearly sympathetic toward his good and faithful General-Quartermaster-Lieutenant, the Field Marshal granted Scharnhorst a 'preliminary release' from Hanoverian service and permitted him to travel to his assignment in Berlin. He informed him that as soon as his formal discharge came, he would forward it to him in Berlin.[88]

The circumstances surrounding Scharnhorst's transfer to the Prussian army clearly demonstrate the solid reputation he held. Long before entering Prussian service, Gerhard Scharnhorst 'was the best-known military writer in Germany'.[89] He was also an acknowledged authority on military education, who 'tested the facts in the light of reality and drew from them simple rules of practice'.[90] Moreover, he was an exceptional combat leader. It is difficult to believe that Hanover refused to appreciate the enlightened soldier Scharnhorst was, but a social pattern devised to meet only the needs of the high-born estate simply could not be altered without traumatic repercussions. On the other hand, a rapacious Prussia continued to attract competent and energetic men from all regions of Germany.[91] Scharnhorst in saw in Prussia the opportunity he was denied in Hanover. On 12 May 1801, he transferred to Prussian service in Berlin, where he was assigned to the 3. Artillerie Regiment. His formal discharge from Hanoverian service arrived from London on 28 May. It was dated 19 May 1801.[92]

87 Scharnhorst to Wallmoden (3 May 1801); in Kunisch (ed.), *Scharnhorst: Privat und dienstliche Schriften*, Vol.2, pp.504-05; the quoted passages are from p.505.

88 See Wallmoden's Memorandum of 4 May 1801; in Klippel, *Scharnhorst*, Vol.2, p.345.

89 Ropp, *War in the Modern World*, p.132.

90 See the recollections of Sir Julius von Hartmann; in *Major* Julius von Hartmann (ed.), *Königlich Hannoversche General Sir Julius von Hartmann*, pp.36-37; the quoted passage is from p.37.

91 See the important discussion of this point in Paret, *Clausewitz and the State*, pp.59-60.

92 Scharnhorst official discharge was signed by Lenthe, and is published in Klippel, *Scharnhorst*, Vol.2, p.345.

Epilogue

The Enlightened Soldier

Gerhard Johann David von Scharnhorst (1755-1813) lived during a time of great upheaval in Europe. The Seven Years War, followed two decades later by the Wars of the French Revolution and then Napoleon, brought untold violence and destruction to his native land. These conflicts shaped his worldview and determined the path he travelled throughout life. Scharnhorst never ceased studying the profession of arms and the transformation it brought to society and to the conduct of war.

Scharnhorst 'was not a typical soldier for his time'.[1] Born in the small village of Bordenau near Hanover, he grew up tenant farming with his father, a former non-commissioned officer in the Hanoverian cavalry. He was a lively and cheerful boy; the favourite of his simple and gentle mother. Wanting to pursue a career as a soldier, he had to wait until his father was able to secure his mother's inheritance (the noble estate in Bordenau) and with it the social and economic standing that would enable him to seek admission to the prestigious academy of Wilhelmstein in the tiny state of Schaumburg-Lippe. To pass its entrance examination, he needed to close the significant gaps in his education, and so dedicated himself to an intensive self-study program that covered spelling and grammar, mathematics, French, English, and the military sciences.

At 17 and a half (much older than the average pupil) Scharnhorst passed the entrance examination and entered the military academy of Count Friedrich Wilhelm Ernst zu Schaumburg-Lippe-Bückeburg, one of the most enlightened and eminent soldiers then living in Germany. Arriving at Wilhelmstein with a very basic and incomplete education, Scharnhorst was driven by an extraordinary ambition to succeed. As he later admitted in *Military Library*, before attending Wilhelmstein, 'I never enjoyed oral instruction in any science'.[2] Despite a schooling that was mediocre at best, Scharnhorst was endowed with an innate intelligence, industry, and resolve, and left Wilhelmstein four years later as one of its most distinguished graduates.

It was Count Wilhelm who introduced Scharnhorst to the profession of arms and to the concept of *Bildung*. A fruit of Germany's classical age, *Bildung* was the perfectibility of the individual's character and intellect through the process of education. Under the skilful

1 Michael Sikora, 'Spuren einer politischen Soldatenkariere', which is the Introduction in Kunisch (ed.), *Scharnhorst: Privat und dienstliche Schriften*, Vol.1, p.ix.

2 Scharnhorst, 'Anleitung zur Lecture und zu den Feld-Uebungen der Officiere', *Militair-Bibliothek*, Vol.1, pp.1-38; the quoted passage is from p.30.

tutelage of Count Wilhelm, Scharnhorst learned that soldiering required the leader to devote himself to formal schooling, continuous study, and practical field training. The fact that the leader is constantly interacting with people demanded that he possess a deep appreciation of human attitudes, motivations, and behaviour that only a liberal education in the arts and sciences stimulates. During his years at Wilhelmstein, Scharnhorst received a classical formation in the arts and sciences, with an extensive professional emphasis on military knowledge and skills, as well as a foundational education in mathematics, the sciences, and foreign languages.

In keeping with the spirit of the Enlightenment, Count Wilhelm emphasised the integration of professional and technical knowledge with humanistic values. He supplemented Scharnhorst's comprehensive education in the military sciences with the study of contemporary literature: the early poetry of Goethe, the poems of Klopstock, the 'Night Thoughts' of Young, the sermons of Herder, the lectures of Möser, the writings of Mendelssohn, Zimmermann, and *The Wandsbeck Messenger* by Claudius. It was this concept of *Bildung* that guided Scharnhorst's entire military career. Even more significant was the importance his mentor placed on the objective study of history to understand human relationships and to bridge the gap between theory and practice.

Scharnhorst left Wilhelmstein imbued with these Enlightenment notions of *Bildung*. Now he felt capable of acquiring information independently, of dealing with challenges scientifically, and of seeking solutions, organising findings, and checking their practical suitability to obtain new insights.[3] His superiors quickly recognised his talents and appointed him an instructor, initially at his regimental school in Northeim, then at the artillery school in Hanover. While teaching he edited three professional journals and published two books. In all these works Scharnhorst's aim was to promote the formation of leaders, which earned him the reputation of a military scholar. Throughout these 15 years Scharnhorst continued his intensive self-study under the mentorship of *General-Major* Estorff and *Oberstlieutenant* Trew, joining several learned societies and freemasonry. He was also involved in a number of scientific endeavours, the most noteworthy was his development of a micrometre telescope that, with the help of a measuring scale, permitted its user to obtain a more accurate estimation of distances for artillery gunners.[4]

An early indication of Scharnhorst's efforts to influence the *Bildung* of leader development came when he published *Military Library* in 1782. In his 'Instructions for Reading', he argued the case for military education. As a true child of his age, Scharnhorst continually endeavoured to apply his Enlightenment ideals to the profession of arms and embarked on a long journey that would lead him from the standing professional army to the nation-in-arms. This was purely an intellectual exercise at first, and his emancipation came only gradually. Significantly, he found it problematic at this time to conceive of an educated citizen passing through the gauntlet of the professional standing army. Then came the French Revolution with its *levée en masse*, and almost immediately Scharnhorst comprehended the awesome power of the nation-in-arms.

3 Scharnhorst later discussed this ability in Scharnhorst, *Handbuch der Artillerie*, Vol.1, p.9.
4 Scharnhorst described his experiments in Scharnhorst, *Handbuch für Officiere*, Vol.2, pp.3-38.

When Hanover joined the First Coalition against France in 1793, *Titular-Capitain* Gerhard Scharnhorst left the classroom for duty with the English-Hanoverian army. During several engagements in Flanders he demonstrated exceptional leadership under fire and came to realise the value of a sound, formal military education. In sharp contrast to previous ideas that all an army required in order to fight was the proper amount of order and discipline, training and drill, Scharnhorst recognised that a well-organised intellect was the essential ingredient to the profession of arms. As a true empiricist he never succumbed to lofty ideas that demanded the abolition of the standing army in favour of a so-called people's army. He had to see the worth of these new forces demonstrated in combat before he would accept them. The War of the First Coalition offered undeniable proof of the inherent weaknesses of traditional military institutions and the promising future of national armies.

For the rest of his career Gerhard Scharnhorst never ceased studying the transformation of warfare unleashed by the French Revolution. One of the first lessons he appreciated was the enormous energy of a free society. Time and again ordinary Frenchmen showed their willingness to sacrifice, fight, and die for their country. Scharnhorst reasoned that German citizens would be just as eager if all gifted men could aspire to the highest positions of leadership. This was the obvious conclusion for an enlightened soldier of humble origins. His reaction to the French Revolution and its impact on the art of war was clearly stated in a series of memoranda and articles; the most notable was his 'Basic Reasons for the French Success'. The nation-in-arms had completely altered warfare. Scharnhorst was one of a few anywhere who understood that the role of the officer must also change. The problem was to define his role in terms of a new social and political structure of society. It was during these years that there crystallized in his mind a set of specific reforms designed to meet the challenge of the nation-in-arms.

Bildung became the cornerstone of Scharnhorst's modernisation efforts. This meant realistic military training and combat readiness were essential for soldiers, while the intellectual pursuit of understanding the art of war was paramount for leaders. Only through the cultivation of the individual soldier could the army maintain a progressive response to the changing art of war. Scharnhorst advocated better education for officers and non-commissioned officers, and more realistic combat training for the soldier. He planned to teach the lessons he had learned from the new tactics, strategy, and logistics the French had used to conquer their natural frontiers, as well as Flanders, Holland, and parts of Germany and Italy. He hoped to develop a cult of objectivity within the army, instructing its leaders not to react to structured or ritual things lest they become mechanical themselves. Scharnhorst wanted them to question all received 'truths' in a disciplined fashion, responding correctly to a critical, independent analysis of the facts. He clearly recognised that good leaders are not developed if given scenarios to follow. It was here that the objective analysis of history was so important, since Scharnhorst believed that the study of the past enabled leaders to appreciate their profession and the role chance and the unknown play in combat.

Scharnhorst's program of education for victory was designed to develop leaders capable of commanding the nation-in-arms. Since he could not stop the admission of ignorant noblemen in the army, he recommended promotion to lieutenant only after the successful passage of an examination that covered both theory and practice. He also advocated abolishing nepotism, connection, and the deadwood associated with the professional standing army. At the same time, he wanted to retain the vital elements that the standing army provided the profession of arms: its discipline, sense of honour, and esprit de corps. This could only be achieved through a more equitable application of military justice for the common soldier and a system of advancement based on demonstrated talent and ability, not birth and family connection.

The challenge Scharnhorst faced was how to integrate these new leaders into the Hanoverian army and get them accepted. Somehow, he had to introduce brains into the whole structure, a different kind of standing army. His solution was the 'General Staff with Troops' [later known in Germany as the *Truppengeneralstab*]. He understood that the nobility had rarely shown any zeal for formal schooling or even private study, simply because aristocrats had everything handed to them because of their birth. They rarely had to earn anything. Furthermore, noblemen had the reserved right of command without having any real military competence. Scharnhorst would achieve his goal by educating promising officers in a general school of war. He would then select a small elite of graduates and further cultivate them in the advanced components of the art of war. Assigning them to the General Staff with Troops, he would permeate the army with enlightened men of character and intellect. They would not 'command' but would 'assist' their dilettante commanding generals. For Scharnhorst, the General Staff with Troops was to become the brain and nervous system of the army, animating its operations and providing the impulse that set the army in motion.

Throughout his endeavours to modernise the Hanoverian army, Gerhard Scharnhorst remained cautious and deliberate. He never permitted the arcane thinking of royal absolutism to diminish or to obscure the revolutionary reasoning of the nation-in-arms. This national army would have to be organised into divisions and corps that combined infantry, cavalry, artillery, and supporting units. It would then be led by the General Staff with Troops. Major changes in the infantry would transform its tactical doctrine and operational concepts from a linear system of line formations into a combination of line formations, attack columns, and skirmishers. To support the infantry attack, he sought to expand, reorganise, and modernise the artillery with better equipment and organisation. All of these measures were designed to ensure tactical flexibility on the battlefield and operational independence in the theatre of operations. Realistic and frequent combat training in times of peace and during active military operations would keep the soldier in tune with an ever-changing art of war.

In keeping with the concept of the nation-in-arms, Scharnhorst insisted that Hanover end the mercenary character of its army by introducing universal military conscription. As his mentor Count Wilhelm had done, Scharnhorst advocated no exemptions among the citizenry. To obtain victory, the soldier must once again become a warrior. He must infuse his military actions with his personal, social, and political convictions, and that was possible only if he felt himself to be a citizen of worth and not a mere subject of royal absolutism. The people themselves become a reservoir of military strength. Through this *Bildungprinzip* Scharnhorst hoped to create a new generation of leaders and soldiers who would transform the Hanoverian army with a new spirit.

The armies of revolutionary France offered conclusive proof that soldiering was no longer a craft or occupation, but a profession that demanded continuous study. It was Scharnhorst's great achievement that he not only recognised this new dimension of warfare, but also attempted to develop institutions to harness it. Convincing the ruling elites of Hanover that the role of the professional soldier would have to conform to a new social and political structure proved an arduous task. Hanover rejected his ideas without ever considering their merit. Such 'Jacobin' sentiments were totally alien and unacceptable. Sensing he had no future in the Electorate of Hanover, Gerhard Scharnhorst accepted an appointment in the Prussian army in the spring in 1801. There he hoped to implement the modernisation ideas he had developed and refined in Hanover.

Bibliography

A Note on Sources

Gerhard Scharnhorst was a prolific writer who published much during his 23 years of military service in Hanover. His papers, lectures, articles, and books deal almost exclusively with military affairs, and like his modernisation ideas, reflect his constant search to understand the complexity of warfare. As a true empiricist, he never stopped testing the results of his research and study against the record of history, expanding and recasting his solutions until he achieved the best practical application. Scharnhorst was never the prophet nor theoretician, but rather the meticulous explorer, developer, and perfecter of ideas and methods.

Among the personal papers of German officers that survived the Second World War are those of Gerhard von Scharnhorst. They were captured at the end of the war, brought to the United States, where the National Archives microfilmed them on 12 rolls before returning them to the Federal Republic of Germany in 1954. Today they can be found in the Gehimes Staatsarchiv Preuβischer Kulturbesitz, 196/VI. HA Familienarchive und Nachlässe, Berlin (Dahlem). Most of his reports, memoranda, instructions, and modernisation proposals during his service in Hanover are located in the Niedersächsisches Landesarchiv in Hanover. Many are published in the first two volumes of Georg Heinrich Klippel, *Das Leben des Generals von Scharnhorst* (1869/71). Comparing Klippel's text with the original documents reveals some minor inaccuracies, but on the whole his work is reliable. Other source material can be found in Scharnhorst's *Gutakten* (Estate Papers) in Bordenau. The Bundesarchiv in Koblenz also contains some valuable documents relating to this study. Important transcripts that Rudolf Stadelmann prepared for his study of Scharnhorst proved extremely useful, as did the research notes of historians Gerhard Ritter and Hans Rothfels. All of the archivists were very hospitable, considerate, and helpful to this researcher.

Until 2002, only a very small portion of Scharnhorst's voluminous papers had been published. His candid observations and reflections, together with his occasional doubts, fears, and hopes are mirrored in his private letters, which Karl Linnebach edited in 1914 under the title *Scharnhorsts Briefe*. The First World War and Linnebach's death prevented the completion of a planned second volume of his official correspondence. Gerhard Oestreich undertook this project in 1935, but the Second World War destroyed his only manuscript. Fortunately, Oestreich's corrections to Linnebach's edition survived the war; and in 1980, Heinz Stübig published them in a reprinted edition of Linnebach's book. Excerpts from Scharnhorst's Papers can be found in *Militärische Schriften von Scharnhorst* (1888), edited by Colmar von der Goltz; *Scharnhorst, der Schöpfer der Volksbewaffung. Schriften von und über Scharnhorst* (1953), edited by Gerhard Thiele; *Gerhard von Scharnhorst: Ausgewählte Schriften* (1983), edited by Ursula von Gersdorff; and *Gerhard von Scharnhorst: Ausgewählte militärische Schriften* (1986), edited by Hansjürgen Usczeck and Christa Gudzent. Other selections from his *Nachlaß* were published in *Historische Zeitschrift* (1887); *Österreichische Militärische Zeitschrift* (1903); *Militärwissenschaftliche Rundschau* (1944 and 1962), and *Jahrbuch für die Geschichte Mittel-und Ostdeutschlands* (1962). Peter Paret published three of Scharnhorst's tactical essays in *Yorck and the Era of Prussian Reform* (1966), while Ursula von Gersdorff edited his short treatise on military history in *Bibliotheca Rerum Militarium* (Band 44). She also provided a brief historical overview of his papers.

While conducting research at the Prussian Archives in the early 1980s, officials there informed me that Walther Hubatsch was planning to direct the editing and publication of Scharnhorst's Papers (*Nachlaß Scharnhorst*). Unfortunately, his death in December 1984 ended this project. A decade later, a joint venture between German academia, the Gehimes Staatsarchiv Preußischer Kulturbesitz in Berlin, the Militärgeschlichtliche Forschungsamt in Potsdam, and the Bohlau Publishing House in Cologne, began collecting, editing, and organising the papers of Gerhard Scharnhorst. Historians Johannes Kunisch (Cologne), Michael Sikora (Münster), and Tilman Stieve (Aachen) headed this endeavour. Bohlau published the first volume in 2002, with the eighth and final volume appearing in 2014.

Published under the title, *Gerhard von Scharnhorst: Privat und dienstliche Schriften*, these eight volumes contain the most comprehensive collection of Scharnhorst's papers. All eight books are magnificent in their breath, depth, and presentation. This study used Volume 1: *Kurhannover bis 1795: Schüler, Lehrer, Kriegsteilnehmer* (2002); Volume 2: *Kurhannover 1795-1801: Stabschef und Reformer* (2003); Volume 3: *Preußsen 1801-1804: Lehrer, Artillerist, Wegbereiter* (2005); and Part II: 'Nachträge und Ergänzungen' (Supplements and Completions) of Volume 8: *Preußen 1813: Tragischer Vollender* (2014). Each book contains an extremely interesting and vital introduction which places that particular volume of Scharnhorst's papers in the context of his life and career at that time. In the opening sentence of his first remarks in Volume One, Michael Sikora wrote, 'Gerhard von Scharnhorst was not a typical soldier for his time'.[1] This statement clearly captured the essence of Scharnhorst and set the stage for the fascinating documents that follow in all eight volumes.

Turning to the volumes themselves, each book follows a specific pattern. A forward and introduction acquaint the reader to that volume, its purpose and arrangement. Next is a list of abbreviations used in the documents themselves. A bibliography of the most significant German and English works of that period of Scharnhorst's life and career follows. Then come the documents arranged in a chronological order, supplemented with some very helpful annotations. At the end of each book are informative appendices that contain biographies of the key people who helped to shape Scharnhorst's life and career, a glossary of military and civilian terms from the times, to include ranks and titles, and (most useful), translations of the often 'confusing German mutations' of French military terminology of the period 'that cannot be found in most German/English dictionaries'.[2] Following the

1 Sikora, 'Einleitung: Spuren einer politischen Soldatenkarriere', in Kunisch (ed.), *Scharnhorst: Privat und dienstliche Schriften*, Vol.1, pp.ix-xxx; the quoted passage is from p.ix.

2 See Michael V. Leggiere's splendid review of Vol.1 of *Gerhard von Scharnhorst: Private und Dienstliche Schriften*; in *The Journal of Military History* 67:4 (2003), pp.1284-1285; the quoted passages are from p. 284.

appendixes are two indexes with a detailed glossary of people important to this era, their dates of birth and death, and career highlights. Then comes an index of towns, cities, countries, and geographical locations. Completing each volume is a register of all of the documents, listed by type, with their dates, addressees, titles, and page numbers. Volumes 1 and 2 contain nearly 800 documents, spanning almost 1,600 pages.

Among Scharnhorst's several biographers, Max Lehmann remains the most influential. His masterful study, *Scharnhorst* (1886/87), is considered the authoritative German account of the Hanoverian's life. His conclusion that Gerhard Scharnhorst was the mediator between eighteenth and nineteenth century warfare, between the old and the new, has become the standard interpretation of Scharnhorst. Unfortunately, Lehmann's scholarship presupposes an intimate knowledge of his subject. Without informing the reader, Lehmann often groups excerpts from several different sources together, giving the impression that they come from the same document. Most of the time these amalgamations do not distort what Scharnhorst intended to say. At other times, Lehmann changes words, word order, and punctuation in order to fit his citations smoothly into the text. Again, this does not alter the concept Scharnhorst had in mind. When Lehmann cites such a passage, he usually chooses the source that best conveys the central theme of his text. This methodology really frustrates the student who wants to examine in greater detail all of the sources Lehmann uses (not just those he cites), and to verify his thought-provoking conclusions.

Several other biographers of Scharnhorst deserve mention. A native of Hanover and a state employee, Georg Heinrich Klippel, *Das Leben des Generals von Scharnhorst* (1869/71), was the first extensive study of Scharnhorst. This narrative work offers few interpretations but does incorporate a great quantity of primary source material. Klippel develops Scharnhorst's life around the source documents, allowing the reader to analyze the original texts more objectively. Unfortunately, Klippel was highly selective with the sources he chose to exclude from his treatise. Not a single letter Scharnhorst wrote home to his wife Klara during the War of the First Coalition appears in Klippel's work. Perhaps he desired to present only the more positive aspects of Scharnhorst's life and military career in Hanover. As a state employee, Klippel may not have had the liberty to express Scharnhorst's candid thoughts openly.

Das Leben des Generals von Scharnhorst greatly distorted the truth. It portrayed Scharnhorst as a highly talented and diligent officer content with serving the caste-ridden Electorate of Hanover and willingly accepting his subservient place in that society and the lack of opportunities open to him. By relying solely on Klippel's interpretation, the reader would never know there was a great divide within both the civil and military societies of Hanover, and just how deeply Scharnhorst despised the ways of the ruling elites. In the first two chapters of his second volume, which examined the 1793, 1794, and 1795 campaigns in Flanders, Holland, and Germany, Klippel rarely mentioned Scharnhorst at all, his daily routine, or the wealth of information contained in his very candid letters to his wife Klara. Instead of building his study around Scharnhorst (the subject of his biography), Klippel offered a pretty general synopsis of the campaign, often citing verbatim from the narrative anonymous history, *Uebersicht der Campagne, der Königlich Chur-Hannöverschen Truppen in Flandern, vom Jahre 1793* (1794). This methodology led one early English reviewer to make a number of incorrect assumptions and conclusions about Scharnhorst, his situation in Hanover, and why he left Hanover for Prussia.[3] Why Professor Klippel failed to include even one of Scharnhorst's numerous letters to Klara that revealed his true feelings remains a mystery. Fifteen years later, Prussian historian Max Lehmann, who studied the same documents Klippel did, wrote a much more honest appraisal of Scharnhorst, his activities and convictions during the War of the First Coalition. With the exception of Linnebach's publication of Scharnhorst's private letters, no other important study of Scharnhorst appeared until after the Second World War.

Seven years after the Second World War, Hans Rothfels published *Scharnhorst: Schicksal und geistige Welt. Ein Fragment* (1952), written by his late colleague Rudolf Stadelmann. As its titles suggests, this is a brief (but brilliant) interpretation that endeavoured to comprehend Scharnhorst, his social, cultural, political, and intellectual antecedents, his surroundings, his experiences, and the way in which they influenced and often determined his understanding of war and his later modernisation concepts. Stadelmann divided his study into two major parts: Scharnhorst's 'destiny' [*Schicksal*] and his 'intellectual world' [*geistige Welt*]. Although Scharnhorst had shown exceptional leadership during the War of the First Coalition and later during the Napoleonic wars, Stadelmann correctly concluded internal social forces in Hanover and Prussia prevented him from achieving lasting fame as a great military leader. Significantly, Scharnhorst stated this clearly in a number of his letters to his wife and daughter. Yet neither Klippel nor Lehmann fully enunciated this interpretation in their biographies of Scharnhorst.

Another major contribution Stadelmann made lies in the second part of his work on the spiritual forces affecting Scharnhorst. Here Stadelmann demonstrated conclusively how the rationalism and humanism of the German Enlightenment, epitomized by Scharnhorst's mentors, Count Friedrich Wilhelm zu Schaumburg-Lippe and *General-Major* Emmerich Otto von Estorff, began molding his intellectual development at an early age, which then continued throughout the remainder of his life. The concept of 'formation' [*Bildung*], with its emphasis on empirical explanation, professional mastery, and continuous education and training, was for Gerhard Scharnhorst the intrinsic component of the German Enlightenment, and that which enabled him to become a great soldier, leader, thinker, writer, and organiser.

Reinhard Höhn and his studies of Scharnhorst also deserve mention. His first book, *Revolution-Heer-Kriegsbild* (1944), attempted to relate the history of military ideas from the end of the Seven Years War through the transformation of war introduced by the French Revolution and Napoleon. Most copies of this book were destroyed during an Allied air raid. After the war Höhn published a much shorter version under the title, *Scharnhorsts Vermächtnis* (1952), then a second edition of the same retitled, *Scharnhorst: Soldat-Staatsmann-Erzieher* (1981). The evolution of these titles reveals the maturity of Reinhard Höhn's thoughts on Scharnhorst.

Adopting the main thesis of Lehmann, Höhn strived to show Gerhard Scharnhorst was among the first in Germany to see the dawn of a new era of warfare and to bridge the gap between 18th and 19th Century warfare. Unlike Lehmann, Höhn's treatment of sources

3 See 'Art. I. – *Das Leben des Generals Von Scharnhorst.* Von G.H. Klippel. Leipsic: 1870', *The Edinburgh Review* 286 (October 1874), pp.287-321.

is perplexing. Höhn tried to append Nazi ideology to Scharnhorst's ideas, but ended up contradicting much of what Scharnhorst cherished. Scharnhorst would never have agreed with Höhn's notions on ending the sovereignty of the individual and subjecting him to the worship of the state. For Scharnhorst, this was just another form of slavery. What makes reading Reinhard Höhn both difficult and (at the same time) extremely enjoyable is following his attempts to conform Scharnhorst to his own confusing ideas on the centrality of the state, war, and revolution (as the title of his first book states). Höhn incorporates a great deal of archival material (much of which he claims was destroyed during the Second World War), and while all three of his works are challenging to digest, they are wonderful mosaics of extensively quoted passages (many from those lost documents) placed within a disjoined and confused portrayal of German military literature of the period. Nevertheless, Reinhard Höhn provides many thought-provoking ideas.

In 1972, Hansjürgen Usczeck published *Scharnhorst: Theoretiker-Reformer-Patriot. Sein Werk und seine Wirkung in seiner und für unsere Zeit.* An officer in the National People's Army (NPA) [*Nationale Volksarmee* – NVA] of East Germany, Usczeck fashioned his study around the three themes of his subtitle, *Theorist-Reformer-Patriot.* Usczeck believed Scharnhorst was 'the most important German military theorist on the eve of the 19th Century'. Scharnhorst was the one who developed the first prototype of modern civil-military relationships. Due to Usczeck's careful analysis of the sources, many of which he published 12 years later as *Gerhard von Scharnhorst: Ausgewählte militärische Schriften*, this narrative is very informative and contains important new insights about Scharnhorst. Unfortunately, like Reinhard Höhn, who tried to wrap Nazi ideology around Scharnhorst, Hansjürgen Usczeck sought, in the last part of his work, to use Scharnhorst to promote Marxism. Fortunately, this portion can be detached and viewed independently from the rest of Usczeck's study and may indicate Usczeck found a way to be politically correct while not distorting the theorist, reformer, and patriot Scharnhorst.

In his 2009 anthology, *Gerhard von Scharnhorst - preussischer General und Heeresreformer*, renowned German historian Heinz Stübig noted that no modern, scientific study of Scharnhorst has appeared since the 1888 publication of Lehmann's biography.[4] Professor Stübig also suggested that his earlier book, *Scharnhorst: Die Reform des preußischen Heeres* (1988) could serve as an outline for such a biography. Hopefully, the present work will attempt to satisfy the need for a more comprehensive study of Gerhard von Scharnhorst.

Archival Sources

Berlin (Dalhem). Gehimes Staatsarchiv Preußischer Kulturbesitz, VI. HA Familienarchive und Nachlässe

Nachlaß Boyen (Rep 146)

Nachlaß Stein (Rep 154)

Nachlaß Gneisenau (Rep 190)

4 Heinz Stübig, *Gerhard von Scharnhorst: preußischer General und Heeresreformer. Studien zu seiner Biographie und Rezeption* (Berlin: LIT Verlag, 2009), p.1.

Nachlaß Scharnhorst (Rep 196)

Hanover. Niedersächsisches Landesarchiv

Hann 38 E: *Dienstregistratur des Feldmarschalls Grafen von Wallmoden-Gimborn über den französischen Krieg, 1792-1803*

Nr.20: *Etat, Formation und Abmarsch eines kurhannoverschen Auxiliar-Korps von 12.000 Mann*

Nr.30: *Verzeichnis des gesamten Generalstabes und Besetzung der Offiziersstellen bei den Regimentern; Etats der Kavallerie und Infanterie; Instruktionen für den Generalstabsquartiermeister und Generalwagenmeister; Adjutanten der königlichen Prinzen; Besetzung der Feldhospital-Stellen, 02.1793-03.1793*

Nr.35: *Aushebung der Rekruten im Lande und Abgabe derselben an die marschierdenden Regimenter*

Nr.49: *Grundsätze über Avancement der Offiziere im Felde und bei den im Lande sich befindenden Regimentern, 1793-1794*

Nr.78: *Schlacht bei Famars am 23. Mai 1793: Berichte über die Schlacht nebst einem Rapport vom Sturm der kaiserlichen Truppen auf Le Quesnoy im Rücken der englisch-hannoverschen Armee, Bericht des Feldmarschalls von Freytag an den König, 05.1793-06.1793*

Nr.92: *Affäre bei Hondscooten: Pläne und Dislokationen; Ordres des Herzogs von York, 09.1793*

Nr.93: *Affäre bei Hondscooten: Listen der von 5. bis 8. September 1793 Gefallenen, Verwundeten und Gefangenen (unvollständig), 09.1793*

Nr.94: *Affäre bei Hondscooten: Meldungen nach der Affäre vom 8. bis 16. September 1793, 09.1793*

Nr.95: *Affäre bei Hondscooten: Briefe des Königs an den Feldmarschall von Freytag über seine und des Prinzen Adolph Verwundung in der Affäre, 09.1793*

Nr.139: *Winterquartiere 1793/1794: Verhandlungen mit dem Magistrat zu Brügge wegen des dahin zu legenden Hauptquartiers, Hospitals usw., 11.1793-12.1793*

Nr.164: *Menin: Rapporte des Generals von Hammerstein aus Menin an den General von Wallmoden zu Courtray vom 27.3 und 30.4.1794 über verschiedene die Festung und deren Außenwerke betreffende Angelegenheiten, Ausgang der Belagerung. Affäre bei Ten Brielle (6.4.1794), 03.1794-04.1794*

Nr.168: *Menin: Rapporte des in englischem Sold stehenden französischen Ingenieur-Capitains Chevalier de St.Paul über die Armierung und Befestigung von Menin. Dispositionen des Capitains Scharnhorst für einen etwaigen feindlichen Angriff. Pläne von Menin und Werwicq. Korrespondenz mit dem Herzog von York und General Clerfayt, 03.1794-04.1794*

Nr.180: *Berichte von Spionen und Kundschaftern über die feindliche Armee, 05.1794-06.1794*

Nr.189: *Besetzung und Verteidigung der Festung Nieuport unter General von Diepenbroick*

Nr.190: *Englisch-hannoversche Armee während der Monate Juli und August, Korrespondenz des Herzogs von York mit General von Wallmoden, Rapporte und Berichte des Generals von Hammerstein als Kommandant sämtlicher Vorosten, Recogniscierungsberichte des Hauptmanns Scharnhorst. Marschdispositionen,*

Stellung der Vorposten an der Dommel, Lager bei Dongen, Bericht von der Festung Willemstadt, Fort Klunder und Breda, Marschordre für die Armee des Herzogs von York. Enthält: u.a. Situationsskizze Menin-Courtray-Tournay; Zeichnung der Position der Armee bei Breda; Skizzen der verschiedenen Lager; Plan von dem Lager vor Breda, 07.1794-08.1794

Nr.193: *Bericht des Generals von Hammerstein über die Vorpostengefechte bei Boxtel und Strybeck am 14. und 15. Sept.1794. Bedeutender Verlust des hessischen Korps, 1794*

Nr.198: *Verteidigungslinie an der Maas und Waal*

Nr.203: *Verteidigungslinie an der Maas und Waal: Verschiedene auf die obige Stellung der Truppen sich beziehende, unwichtige Meldungen, 12.1794*

Nr.230: *Verhandlungen zwischen General von Wallmoden und Feldmarschall von Freytag in Hannover über die kritische und unhaltbare Stellung der Armee an der Issel, General von Wallmoden fordert das Vorrücken des an der Hunte stehenden Cordons zur Sicherung des Landes, Anträge des Herzogs von Braunschweig wegen Sicherung der Unterems, 01.1795-03.1795*

Nr.239: *Recognoscirungs-Berichte des Rittmeisters von Vincke über das Bourtanger Moor und das linke Ufer der Ems, des Ingenieur-Leutnants Reichard über die Wege von Osnabrück nach Ippenbühren, des Ingenieur-Leutnants Kahle über die Situationen am rechten Ufer der Ems zwischen Rheine und Lingen, des Fähnrichs Vollimhauß über die Kommunikationen zwischen Osnabrück, Lingen und Meppen, Berichte des Majors Scharnhorst über die Pässe der Römerstraße zu Coevorden und Winschoten sowie seine Dispositionen und Vorschläge mit Bezug auf die von den Preußen eingenommenen Stellungen und sein fernerer Operationsplan für einen defensiven Feldzug (mit Zeichnungen und Skizzen), 02.1795-03.1795*

Nr.255: *Kantonnierungen in der Grafschaft Bentheim, 1794-1795*

Nr.260: *Diplomatische Sendung des Oberstleutnants von Schulte vom Leibgarde-Regiment an den Kurfürsten Max von Köln und in das Hauptquartier des Generals Clerfayt zu Frankfurt zur Betreibung der für die Armee wichtigen Angelegenheiten; dessen Berichte daher, 09.1795-11.1795*

Nr.263: *Briefe des Majors von Löw und Hauptmanns von Berger aus London an den General von Wallmoden über politische Angelegenheiten, namentlich den Durchzug der in englischem Sold stehenden Freikorps nach England, 05.1795-06.1795*

Nr.277: *Übernahme der holländischen Artillerie in englischen Sold und Instandsetzung der Geschütze und Fuhrwerke für den Kriegsgebrauch; Kostenrechnungen darüber, 1795*

Nr.278: *Verpflegungs- und Kommissariats-Angelegenheiten: Korrespondenz des Generals von Wallmoden mit dem englischen Generalleutnant Harcourt über die Verpflegung der hannoverschen Armee, 02.1795-04.1795*

Nr.290: *Verhandlungen zwischen dem Herzog von York, dem General von Wallmoden und dem englischen Staatssekretär Generalleutnant Dundas über die Verpflegung der in englischem Solde stehenden Subsidien-Truppen (u.a. aus Braunschweig und Hessen), 05.1795-10.1795*

Nr.291/1: *Korrespondenz des Generals von Wallmoden mit dem englischen Generalkommissar Mr. le Mesurier über Verpflegungssachen der hannoverschen und der übrigen englischen Subsidientruppen*

Nr.291/2: *Korrespondenz des Generals von Wallmoden mit dem englischen Generalkommissar Mr. le Mesurier über Verpflegungssachen der hannoverschen und der übrigen englischen Subsidientruppen*

Nr.295: *Berichte des Generals von Wallmoden an den Herzog von York über die vom englischen Kommissariat beschafften Rationen und Portionen im Feldzuge von 1793*

Nr.297: *Korrespondenz des Generals von Wallmoden mit dem englischen Commission General Brook Watson, 1794*

Nr.298: *Korrespondenz des Generals von Wallmoden mit dem englischen Commission General Brook Watson, 1795*

Nr.303: *Anlegung von Magazinen in Hannover und Bremen, 1795*

Nr.304: *Fuhrwesen im Hannoverschen für den Transport der Armee und des Kommissariats, 1795*

Hann 41: *Akten des Generalkommandos mit den Mililtär-Akten der Londoner Kanzlei. 18.-19. Jahrhundert*

Nr.26: *Verschiedene Nachrichten, bes. Privat-Correspondenzen über die dermalige Lage des Kurfürstenthums Hannover, 1796-1797*

Nr.41: *Berichte der Feldguiden über Colonnen-Wege und Lager im Hoyaischen und Lippischen, desgl. Hameln nebst einer Relation des Oberstl. Scharnhorst. Übungen mit den Feldguiden, 1796*

Hann 41: *Kombinierte Observationsarmee (Beobachtungsarmee) im nördlichen Deutschland unter Oberbefehl des Herzogs von Braunschweig*

I, Nr.6: *Dienstverpflichtungen der königlichen Hoheiten, der Prinzen Eduard, Ernst, Adolph als Obersten in der Armee, 1787-1793*

I, Nr.7: *Verschiedene Aktenstücke, die Militärdienstzeit des Prinzen Ernst August betreffend (aus dem Nachlass des Generals von Linsingen), 1791-1797*

I, Nr.9: *Protokolle über die Einrichtung und Mobilmachung des Hannoverschen Korps von 15.000 Mann unter Befehl des Generals der Kavallerie von Wallmoden-Gimborn, 03.1796*

I, Nr.10: *Vorschläge und Entwürfe zur Formation des Generalstabes, 1796*

I, Nr.11: *Dislokation (räumliche Truppenverteilung) der Truppen an der Weser und Hunte, 1796*

I, Nr.12: *Operationsplan der sogenannten Westphälischen Armee, Projekt des Majors Scharnhorst mit Planskizze, 1796*

I, Nr.13: *Übertragung des Oberbefehls der Observationsarmee (Beobachtungsarmee) an den Herzog Carl Wilhelm Ferdinand von Braunschweig, desgleichen Kommandos der hannoverschen Truppen an den General von Wallmoden und die darüber mit dem König, der Regierung und so weiter geführte Korrespondenz, 03.1796-05.1796*

I, Nr.14: *Operationsplan der sogenannten Westphälischen Armee, Projekt des Majors Scharnhorst mit Planskizze, 1796*

I, Nr.15: *Verhandlungen zwischen der Regierung und dem General Wallmoden sowie dem Herzog von Braunschweig über die vorläufig noch nicht ins Feld gestellten 5.000 Mann, 05.1796-07.1796*

I, Nr.16: *Korrespondenz des Feldmarschalls von Freytag mit dem Herzog von Braunschweig als kommandierenden General der Observationsarmee (Beobachtungsarmee) über Formation der hannoverschen Truppen, 05.1796-06.1796*

I, Nr. 21: *Korrespondenz mit den verschiedenen zum Marsch bestimmten Generälen und den vorgesehenen Regimentern, 08.1796-11.1796*
I, Nr.22: *Kommunikationen des Feldmarschalls von Freytag mit dem General Wallmoden über die im Felde stehenden Truppen, 08.1796-10.1796*
I, Nr.23: *Marschsachen, 09,1796-10,1796*
I, Nr.24: *Berichte des Oberstleutnants von Löw an den General von Wallmoden während der zeitlichen Abwesenheit des letzteren von der Armee, 10.1796-11.1796*
I, Nr.25: *Formation des ausmarschierenden Korps hannoverscher Truppen von 15.000, eventuell 100.000 Mann, 1796*
I, Nr.26: *Verschiedene Nachrichten, besonders Privatkorrespondenzen unter anderem des Majors Scharnhorst über die damalige Lage des Kurfürstentums Hannover, 1796-1797*
I, Nr.27: *Beurlaubungen von Soldaten zu häuslicher Arbeit, 1796-1797*
I, Nr.29: *Zurückziehung und Beurlaubung eines Teiles der ausgerückten Truppen. Entsprechende Verhandlungen zwischen dem Ministerium und dem General von Wallmoden, 12.1796-1798*
I, Nr.30: *Zollfreiheit der zum Bedürfnis dere Observationsarmee (Beobachtungsarmee) dienenden Provisionen, 1796-1798*
I, Nr.39: *Französische Angriffspläne gegen England und das Kurfürstentum Hannover, 1797*
I, Nr.40: *Verhandlungen über die militärische Deckung der Unterweser durch die im Lande befindlichen Truppen, 06.1797-07.1797*
I, Nr.41: *Berichte der Feldguiden über Kolonnen-Wege und Lager im Hoyaischen und Lippischen, desgleichen bei Hameln nebst einer Relation (Bericht) des Oberstleutnants Scharnhorst. Übungen mit den Feldguiden. - Instruktion für die Feldguiden. Enthält u.a.: 13 Geländezeichnungen für den Raum nördlichen Hoya, 1797*
I, Nr.43: *Vorbereitungen des französischen Generals Hoche für eine Invasion in das Kurfürstentum Hannover. Nachrichten des Rittmeisters von Scheither aus Frankfurt und Wesel. Korrespondenz mit dem Herzog von Braunschweig, Landgraf von Hessen, dem preußischen Minister von Haugwitz und dem hannoverschen Kabinettsministerium. Bedarf an Munition, 1797-1798*
I, Nr.44: *Instandsetzung der Festung zu Hameln, 1797-1798*
I, Nr.48: *Verteidigungsmaßregeln für das Herzogtum Bremen-Verden. Enthält u.a.: Verlegungsplan für die Truppen an der Hunte und Aller, 02.1797-03.1797*
I, Nr.181, I: *Marsch Routen, 08.03.1801*
I, Nr.181, II: *Bericht Scharnhorsts über Guiden an Wallmoden*

Hann 41: *Organisation der Armee*
III, Nr.66: *Die Unterweisung der Bombardiere (Artillerieunteroffizier) und Kadetten. Die Verteilung der Bombardierungskompanien und ihrer Offiziere. Promemorien des Generalleutnants Braun und des Majors von Trew zu Harburg, 1779-1781*
III, Nr. 67: *Unterhaltung und Ordonnanz der Regimentsartillerie im Frieden und im Felde. Aufwand für die jährlichen Übungen, 1780-1784*
III, Nr.94: *Gedanken wie vielleicht beim Frieden das Hannoversche Truppen Corps eingerichtet werden könnte, 1. September 1794*

III, Nr.98: *Endgültige Formationspläne, welche vom König aus England übersandt und in Hannover einer näheren Prüfung durch die Generäle unterzogen worden sind, 1796-1797*

III, Nr.130: *Die Einführung der Scharfschützen bei der Infanterie. - Ausführung von Gefechtsformationen zur Formierung von Quarres (Quarrés). (Zeichnungen). Kommandos. Schwenkungen und Marschieren, 1796-1802*

III, Nr.138: *Die Organisation der Artillerie Regiments betreffend, 1800-1801. P.M. der Commission nicht vorgelegt*

III, Nr.148: *Commissions-Verhandlungen über der Regiments-Artillerie, besonders Abschaffung der Kanonenzieher, 1797-1800*

III, Nr.149: *Protokolle der Commission Festsetzung der kunstigen Exercire der Regiments-Artillerie, 1800-1801*

III, Nr.176: *Ernennung des Generals von dem Bussche zum Inspekteur der Infanterie und degleichen des Obersten zu Plat, 1780-1800*

III, Nr.178: *Ernennung des Prinzen Adolph zum Inspekteur der Kavallerie und Infanterie, 1801*

III, Nr.179: *Ableben des Feldmarschalls von Hardenberg und Übertragung des Armeekommandos an den General der Infanterie von Reden, 1781*

III, Nr.180: *Ernennung des Generals von Reden zum Feldmarschall und Bestimmungen wegen des vom General von Freytag zu führenden Kavalleriekommandos, 1781-1788*

III, Nr.182: *Aide-General-Quartiermeister. Rittmeister Vogelstand, Rittmeister von Estorff, Oberstleutnant Kuntze, 1787-1792*

III, Nr.183: *Gemeraladjutanten und Flügeladjutanten, 1792*

III, Nr.185: *Wiederübernahme des Kommandos im Lande von seiten des Feldmarschalls von Freytag, 1794*

III, Nr.186: *Ernennung des Capitäns Scharnhorst von der Artillerie zum Major und Aide-Generalquartiermeister, 1794*

III, Nr.187: *Ernennung des Majors Scharnhorst zum Oberstleutnant und Generalquartiermeister. (Namenslisten von Oberstleutnants, Majoren und Kapitänen beziehungsweise Rittmeistern), 1796-1797*

III, Nr.188: *Ableben des Feldmarschalls von Freytag und dessen stille Beerdigung. Übertragung seines Kommandos an den General der Kavallerie von Wallmoden-Gimborn. Ernennung des letzteren zum Feldmarschall, 1797-1798*

III, Nr.189: *Interimskommando (vorübergehendes Kommando) nach dem Tode des Feldmarschalls von Freytag, 1798*

III, Nr.190: *Scharnhorsts Abgang und Übertritt in preußische Dienste, 1801*

III, Nr.191: *Errichtung eines General-Quartiermeister-Stabes betreffend, 1801-1802*

III, Nr.192: *Enthebung des Feldmarschalls von Reden vom Armeekommando und Übertragung desselben an den General von Freytag (1792), Avancement (Beförderung) des letzteren zum Feldmarschall (1793), Ableben des Feldmarschalls von Reden (1801)*

Hann 41: *Exercice (Übungen), Campements (Feldlager), Manöver, Musterung der Truppen. Exercier-, Dienst- und Lagerreglements (Regelungen)*

IV, Nr.50: *Artillerieexerzierreglement vom Jahre 1782. Enthält u.a.: 3 Tabellen mit 14 Aufstellungsplänen am Geschütz und Lafette*

IV, Nr.51: *Größere Übungen der Artillerie und Ingenieure im Lager zur Garkenburg im Jahre 1789. Enthält u.a.: farbige Zeichnung, Polygon zum Exercice (Übung) der Artillerie (Zeichner: Stückjunker Dankwerth) 1785*

IV, Nr.52: *Größere Übungen der Artillerie und Ingenieure im Lager auf der Garkenburg bei Wülfel. Enthält u.a.: handgeschriebenes kleines Buch: 'Disposition eines Manövers mit einer Brigade von 16 Stück 3 pfündige Kanonen, in 4 Divisionen geteilt'*

IV, Nr.53: *Verabfolgung neuer Regimentskanonen an die Infanterieregimenter und Untersuchung der alten Kanonen, 1789-1797*

IV, Nr.54: *Größere Übungen der Artillerieabteilungen bei Langenhagen, 1799*

IV, Nr.75: *3 farbige Zeichnungen Scharnhorsts für das Manöver im Raume Herberg-Oder, 1799*

Hann 41: *Durchmärsche*

V, Nr.10: *Verhandlung der Regierung zu Hannover mit dem Feldmarschall von Freytag wegen des Durchmarsches der hessischen Truppen im Allgemeinen. Korrespondenz mit dem die englische Werbung leitenden Obersten Faucitt, 01.1776*

V, Nr.13: *Rapporte (Berichte) des Hauptmanns Niemeyer über die Durchführung der ersten Kolonne hessischer Truppen, bestehend aus dem Grenadieerbataillon von Block, dem Regiment von Mirbach, dem Regiment von Donop und dem Regiment Erbprinz, 03.1776*

V, Nr.15: *Korrespondenz des Generalquartiermeisters von Estorff mit den hessischen Generalleutnants von Gohr und von Heister nebst einem Gesamtetat (Gesamthaushalt) der hessischen an England überlassenen Truppen, 01.1776-03.1776*

V, Nr.17: *Verhandlungen mit den verschiedenen Ämtern und Gerichten über den Durchmarsch und die Verpflegung der hessischen Truppen, 02.1776-03.1776*

V, Nr.18: *Korrespondenz des Generalquartiermeisters von Estorff mit dem Amtmann Hintze zu Lilienthal über die Bequartierung im Bremenschen, 02.1776-03.1776*

V, Nr.26: *Marschrouten der hessischen Truppen durch das Kurfürstentum Hannover, darin auch solche, die bereits 1756 für das Bremensche entworfen sind (ohne Datum)*

V, Nr.31: *Rapporte (Berichte) von den als Marschkommissäre bestellten Hauptleuten Niemeyer und von Wangenheim über die Führung der Truppen bis zu ihrer Einschiffung in Ritzebüttel, 05.1776-06.1776*

Hann 41: *Artillerieregiment und Ingenieurskorps*

VIII, Nr.19: *Verlegung der Stückgießerei von Celle nach Hannover. Erbauung der Artillerie-Schuppen vor dem Calenberger Tore und des Gießhauses am Steintore, 1775-1796*

VIII, Nr.21: *Verhandlungen zwischen dem König Georg III. und der Kriegskanzlei wegen Artilleriesachen, 1775-1802*

VIII, Nr.22: *Avancementsbewilligungen (Beförderungsbewilligungen), Dimissionsbewilligungen und Urlaubsbewilligungen. Berücksichtigung junger Edelleute und anderer Männer von gutem Herkommen bei den Avancementsvorschlägen (Beförderungsvorschlägen); Ableben des Generalleutnants Braun, dessen Testament in Bezug auf seine Verlassenschaft an Büchern, Instrumenten und so weiter; Verleihung des Artillerieregiments an den Obersten von Trew, 1776-1784*

VIII, Nr.33/1: *Entwürfe und Pläne zur Einrichtung einer Artillerieschule und Ingenieurschule Vakanthaltung der Chefstelle beim Artillerieregiment , 1781-1793*

VIII, Nr.33/2: *Entwürfe und Pläne zur Einrichtung einer Artillerieschule und Ingenieurschule Vakanthaltung der Chefstelle beim Artillerieregiment, 1781-1793*
VIII, Nr.41: *Verlustlisten der Regimentsartillerie, 1793-1795*
VIII, Nr.42: *Dienstsachen der im Felde gestandenen Artilleriekompanien, 1793-1802*
VIII, Nr.43: *Formation der Artillerie zum Ausmarsch. Bewaffnung und Verstärkung derselben. Gehaltsverbesserungen der reitenden Artillerie, 1794-1796*
VIII, Nr.44: *Rapporte (Berichte) über den Bestand der Regimentsartillerie. 1795-1802*
Hann 41: *Ausbildung, Militärschulen*
XXVI, Nr.7: *Regimentsberichte über die seit dem Jahre 1780 als Offiziere angestellten Hofpagen, 1788*
XXVI, Nr. 8: *Das für Offiziere von dem Artillerieleutnant Scharnhorst entworfene Handbuch zum Unterricht der Kanoniere und Unteroffiziere: 'Einleitung in die Kriegs-Wissenschaft' mit Zeichnung: Kugelbahn und Visierlinie, 1788*
XXVI, Nr. 9: *Erweiterung der Artillerieschule und Ingenieurschule zum Besten der Kavallerieoffiziere und Infanterieoffiziere. Instruktion für die Direktoren der Schule, 1788-1799*
XXVI, Nr.14: *Die Bibliothek der Schule und ihre Ausgaben. Bergung der Bücher und Instrumente im Jahre 1795*
XXVI, Nr.15: *Verzeichnis sämtlicher Bücher, mathematischen Instrumente, Modelle und Armaturstücke (Bewaffnung) der Artillerie-Schule Hannover, 1789*
Hann 41: *Gutakhten du Plat*
Hann 47: *Akten der Kriegskanzlei. 1610-1831*
I, Nr.172, III: *Zulage für den Gehilfen des Generalquartiermeisters, 1794-97*
Hann 91: *Gutakten Kuntze*

Koblenz. Bundesarchiv
Nachlaß Ritter
Nachlaß Rothfels
Nachlaß Stadelmann
London. The National Archives of the United Kingdom
War Office (WO) Record 1/172

Scharnhorst: Published Works

Bibliothek für Officiere, 4 vols (Göttingen: Johann Christian Dieterich, 1785).

Die Vertheidigung der Stadt Menin und die Selbstbefreiung der Garnison unter dem Generalmajor v. Hammerstein (Hanover: Helwing, 1856).

Die Vertheidigung der Stadt Menin und die Selbstbefreiung der Garnison unter dem Generalmajor v. Hammerstein. Kriegsgeschichtliche Bücherei, Band 11 (Berlin: Junker and Dunnhaupt, 1936).

Geschichte der Belagerung von Gibraltar, vom Anfange derselben im Jahre 1779 bis zur Beendigung durch den Friedensschluß (Hanover: Gebrüdern Helwing, 1782).

Handbuch für Officiere in den anwendbarne Theilen der Kriegswissenschaften, 3 vols (Hanover: Gebrüdern Helwing, 1789-90).

Militair Bibliothek, 4 vols (Hanover: Gebrüdern Helwing, 1782-84).

'Militärische Gedankensplitter aus vergangener Zeit', *Österreichische Militärische Zeitschrift* 44 (1903:), pp.25-26.

Militärisches Taschenbuch, zum Gebrauch im Felde (Hanover: Gebrüdern Helwing, 1794).

Military Field Pocket Book. Translated and Edited by Hofmann and Haverfield (London: Vogel and Schulze, 1811).

'Nachricht von der Einrichtung, dem Fortgang, und sich zeigenden Nutzen der, beim 8ten Hannoverischen Cavallerie Reglment von Estorff Dragoner, etablirten KriegsSchule', *Stats-Anzeigen* 8:32 (1785). pp.465-75.

'Nachricht von einer zu Hannover errichteten KriegsSchule', *Stats-Anzeigen* 8 (1785), pp.316-17.

Neues militärisches Journal. 13 vols (Hanover: Gebrüdern Helwing, 1788-93 and 1797-1805). (The last five volumes carried the subtitle *Militärische Denkwürdigkeiten unserer Zeiten, insbesondere des französischen Revolutionskrieges im Jahr 1793 u.s.f.*)

'Ausführlicher Auszug und Bermerkungen über den militärischen Theil des Werks: De la Monarchie prussienne sous Frédéric le grand. p. M. le Comte de Mirabeau 1788', 2 (1789), pp.31-94.

'Belagerund von Gibralter, größten theils aus dem englischen Werke: A History of the late Siege of Gibralter etc. (By John Drinkwater Captain etc. London 1786) gezogen', 2 (1789), pp.217-84.

'Beschreibung der Vestungswerke der Stadt Maynz, und die Belagerung derselben im Jahre 1689', 7 (1793), pp.222-30.

'Charakterzüge und Anecdoten von dem verstorbenen Grafen Wilhelm von Schaumburg-Bückeburg', 1 (1788), pp.123-27.

'Die Vertheidigung der Stadt Menin und die Selbstbefreiung der Garnison unter dem Königlich Großbrittannisch-Chur-Hannöverschen General-Major von Hammerstein, im April 1794', 11 (1803), pp.173-320n.

'Dispositionen der Vertheidigung und des Angriffs der Infanterie-Posten, Feldwaschen und Vorposten eines Lagers', 2 (1789), pp.101-07.

'Ein Beytrag zur Geschichte der Tactik. Auszug aus: *Verordnung, wie des Durchlauchtigsten Fürsten und H.H. Johann Friederichs, Herzogen zu Braunschweig und Lüneburg Infanterie zu üben und zu unterweisen*', 6 (1792), pp.230-33.

'Ein Mittel, wodurch man die Officiere zu militärischen Arbeiten ausmuntern und ihre weitere Ausbildung bewirken kann', 6 (1792), pp.199-203.

'Einige Bemerkungen über die Schlacht bey Hastenbeck und einige Erläuterungen der gegebenen Relationen', 1 (1788), pp.237-56.

'Einige zuverläßige Nachrichten von der Preussischen Artillerie, im Jahr 1784', 4 (1790), pp.39-59.

'Einrichtung und Gebrauch des Micrometer-Fernrohrs des Herrn Carochez', 4 (1790), pp.297-300.

'Entwickelung der allgemeinen Ursachen des Glücks der Franzosen in dem Revolutions-Kriege, und insbesondere in dem Feldzuge von 1794. Als Einleitung zur Geschichte dieses Feldzuges', 8 (1797), pp.1-154.

'Feldzug der verbundenen Armee in Flandern, im Jahre 1794', 9 (1798), pp.169-369.

'Geschichte der Belagerung von Gibralter, von dem Ausfall bis zu Aufhebung der Belagerund, als eine Fortsetzung des Anfangs dieser Geschichte in 5ten Stück', 3 (1789), pp.60-137.
'Geschichte des Feldzugs der verbundenen Armeen in Flandern, im Jahre 1794', 10 (1801), pp.134-343.
'Nachricht von dem Exercier-Lager des Königl. Groβbritanischen und Churfürstlichen Hannöverischen Artillerie-Regiments, ohnweit Hannover vom 1sten bis 21sten September 1789', 3 (1789), pp.179-83.
'Nachricht von den Landkarten des jetzigen Kriegestheater', 7 (1793), pp.101-08.
'Nachrichten von den Preuβsichen, Oestereichischen und einigen andern Armeen', 1 (1788), pp.39-72; and 'Fortsetzung der nachrichten von der Preuβischen, Oestereichischen und einigen andern Armeen', 2 (1780), pp.162-200.
'Neue Tactik, welche der verstorbene regierende Graf Wilhelm von Schaumburg-Bückeburg bey seinen Truppen eingeführt', 1 (1788), pp.1-38; and 'Fortsetzung der neuen Tactik des verstorbenen regierende Grafen Wilhelm von Schaumburg-Lippe', 2 (1788), pp.131-61.
'Prüfung des Werks: *Ueber die höhere Preussische Taktik, deren Mangel und zeitherigen Unzweckmäβigkeit, nebst einer dagegen vorgetragenen richtigen und zweckmäβigern Methode*', 3 (1790), pp.230-65.
'Recension: Anmerkung zu der Schrift des Herrn Lindenau, *über die höhere preussischen Tactik und ihre zeitherige Unrichtigkeit und Unzweckmäβigkeit*', 4 (1790), pp.262-67.
'Recension: Ausführlicher Auszug und Bemerkungen über den militärischen Teil des Werks: *De la Monarchie prussienne sous Frédéric le Grand* p. M. Le Comte de Mirabeau 1788', 2 (1789), pp.31-94.
'Recension: Beurtheilung der Lindenauischen Tactik, zweyter Theil', 5 (1791), pp.161-193.
'Recension: *Geschichte des siebenjährigen Krieges in Deutschland zwischen dem Könige von Preussen und der Kaiserinn-Königin mit ihrem Allirten, als eine Fortsetzung des Geschichte der General Lloyd*, von G.F. von Tempelhof Königl. Preussischer Obristlieutenant, 4r Theil, welcher dem Feldzug von 1760 enthält', 4 (1790), pp.147-61.
'Recrutirung, Besoldung, Etat, Unterricht und Uebung der Preussischen Artillerie', 4 (1790), pp.39-59.
'Relation der Schlacht bey Hastenbeck von französischer Seite; ein Schreiben eines französischen Officiers. Aus einem französischen Manuscript übersetzt', 1 (1788), pp.220-36.
'Relation von der Bataille bey Dettingen im Jahr 1743. Von einem Augenzeugen', 4 (1790), pp.315-25.
'Relation von der Schlacht bei Hastenbeck und den Bewegungen der Französischen und Alliirten Armée von 16ten bis incl. den 26sten July 1787, von einem Augenzeugen. Aus einer Französischen Handschrift übersetzt', 1 (1788), pp.201-19.
'Stärke innerer Zustand und Kriegstheater der verbundenen Armeen in den Niederlanden, im Jahre 1794', 8 (1797), pp.274-326.
'Ueber den jetzigen Krieg und das jetzigen Kriegstheater', 7 (1793), pp.52-78.
'Ueber den Krieg mit den Türken', 4 (1790), pp.130-46.
'Ueber die Berichte von den vorfallen des französischen Revolutions-Krieges und den Nutzen der Bekanntmachung eines richtigen Tagsbuches der Operationen der Armeen', 8 (1797), pp.253-73.
'Ueber die Veränderung und Einrichtung des Schwedischen Kriegeswesens durch Gustav Adolph', 9 (1798), pp.1-61.

'Ueber die Vor-und Nachteile der stehenden Armeen', 6 (1792), pp.234-54 and 345-80.

'Verhalten eines Officiers, welcher im Felde mit 30 bis 40 Pferden von dem Corps oder Regimente, bey welchem er dienet, auf 1 bis 2 oder wol mehrrere Student entfernt voraus commandirt wird', 7 (1793), pp.231-76.

'Vorbericht', 9 (1798), pp.i-iv.

'Verfertigung der Faschinen, Schanz-Körbe und Horden und Anwendung derselben', 4 (1790), pp.60-89.

'Winterquartiere der verbundenen Armee zwischen Luxemburg und der See, im Anfange des Jahrs 1794', 8 (1797), pp.327-89.

'Woraus kann man den Fortgagn, den eine Armee in diesem oder jenem Zweige der Kriegeskunst macht, am sichersten abnehmen?' 6 (1792), pp.182-88.

'Scharnhorst über Führerauswahl und Führerverantwortlichkeit', *Militärwissenschaftliche Rundschau* 2 (1944), pp.117-19.

Unterricht des Königs von Preußen an die Generale seiner Armee (Hanover: Gebrüdern Helwing, 1794).

Verzeichniß von größenteils in die mathematische und Militär-Wissenschaften einschlagenden Bücher der Artillerie-Bibliothek (Hanover, 1783).

'Von den Militär-Anstalten des verstorbenen regierenden Grafen von Schaumburg-Lippe Königl. Portugisischen Generalissimi &c'., *Briefwechsel meist historischen und politischen Inhalts* 10:56 (1782), pp.93-101.

Scharnhorst: Collected Works

Bundesministerium der Verteidigung (ed.), *Scharnhorst: Ausgewählte Briefe und Schriften,* in *Schriftenreihe Innere Führung,* Beiheft 3:85 (1985).

Gersdorff, Ursula von (ed.), *Nutzen der militärischen Geschichte: Ursach ihres Mangels, Ein Fragment aus dem Scharnhorst-Nachlass,* in *Bibliotheca Rerum Militarium* (Band 44), (Osnabrück: Biblio-Verlag, 1973).

Gersdorff, Ursula von (ed.), *Scharnhorst:Ausgewählte Schriften,* in *Bibliotheca Rerum Militarium* (Band 49), (Osnabrück: Biblio-Verlag, 1983).

Goltz, Colmar von der (ed.), *Militärische Schriften von Scharnhorst* (Berlin: F. Schneider, 1881).

Kunisch, Johannes, (ed.; arranged by Michael Sikora and Tilman Stieve), *Gerhard von Scharnhorst: Privat und dienstliche Schriften,* 8 vols (Köln/Weimar/Wien: Veroffenlichungen aus dem Archiven Preuβischer Kulturbesitz, 2002-15).

Linnebach, Karl (ed.), *Scharnhorsts Briefe,* Vol.1: *Privatbriefe* (Munich and Leipzig: Georg Müller, 1914; reprint ed., with commentary by Heinz Stübig, Munich: Klaus Reprint, 1980).

Niemeyer, Joachim (ed.), *Scharnhorst-Briefe an Friedrich von der Decken, 1803-1813* (Bonn: Ferdinand Dümmler, 1987).

Thiele, Gerhard (ed.), *Scharnhorst, der Schöpfer der Volksbewaffung. Schriften von und über Scharnhorst* (Berlin (Ost): Rutten & Loening, 1953).

Usczeck, Hansjürgen and Gudzent, Christa (ed.), *Gerhard von Scharnhorst: Ausgewählte militärische Schriften* (Berlin (Ost): Militärverlag der Deutschen Demokratischen Republik, 1986).

Other Primary Sources

Abbt, Thomas, *Vom Tode für das Vaterland* (Berlin: Friedrich Nicolai, 1761).

Alent. 'On Reconnoitring', *Essays on the Theory and Practice of the Art of War* [Chiefly Translated from the Best French and German Writers by the Editor of *The Military Mentor*], 3 vols (London: T. Gillet, 1809).

Allgemeine Literatur-Zeitung (Jena): 1788, 1789, 1794, and 1799.

Anon., *A Concise Narrative of all the Actions, in which the British Forces were engaged during the Present War on the Continent of Europe, Extracted from Private Letters of Officers on Service There* (Manchester: Sowler and Russell, 1797).

Anon., *An Accurate and Impartial Narrative of the War by an Officer of the Guards.* 2 vols (London: Cadell and Davies, 1796).

Anon., *The Present State of the British Army in Flanders, With an Authentic Account of their Retreat from before Dunkirk by a British Officer of that Army, Who was living on the 24th of September* (London: H.D. Symonds, 1793).

Anon., *Uebersicht der Campagne, der Königlich Chur-Hannöverschen Truppen in Flandern, vom Jahre 1793* (Hanover: Gebrüdern Hahn, 1794).

Aspinall, Arthur (ed.), *The Later Correspondence of George III*, 5 vols (Cambridge: Cambridge University Press, 1962-70).

Batz, August Friedrich, *Beschreibung der Hohen Karls-Schule zu Stuttgart* (Privately-Published, 1783).

Behr, Hans-Joachim (ed.), *Karl Freiherr von Müffling: Offizier-Kartograph-Politiker (1775-1851), Lebenserinnerungen und kleinere Schriften* (Köln/Weimar/Wien: Böhlau, 2003).

Bélidor, Bernard Forêt de, *Nouveau cours de mathématique à l'usage de l'artillerie et du genie* (Paris: Charles-Antoine Jombert, 1725).

Berenhorst, Georg Heinrich von, *Betrachtungen über die Kriegskunst, über ihre Fortschritte, ihre Widersprüche und ihre Zuverläßigkeit, Auch für Layen verständlich, wenn sie nur Geschichte wissen,* 3 vols (Leipzig: Gerhard Fleischer dem Jungern, 1796-99).

Berenhorst, Georg Heinrich von, *Notwendige Ranglossen zu den Brachtungen über einige Unrichtigkeiten in den Brachtungen über die Kriegskunst, über ihre Fortschritte, ihre Widersprüche und ihre Zuverläßigkeit, Auch für Layen verständlich, wenn sie nur Geschichte wissen* (Leipzig: Gerhard Fleischer dem Jungern, 1802).

Berlepsch, Friedrich Ludewig von, *Pragmatische Geschichte des landschaftlichen Finanz-und Steuerwesens der Fürstentümer Galenberg und Göttingen* (Frankfurt und Leipzig, 1799).

Beutler, Ernst (ed.), *Gedenkausgabe der Werke, Briefe und Gespräche,* 27 vols (Zürick: Artemis-Verlag, 1950-71), Vol.10: *Dichtung und Wehrheit.*

Bohr, Ehrhard (ed.), *Was ist Aufklärung? Thesen und Definitionen* (Stuttgart: Phillipp Reclam, 1974).

Bonaparte, Napoleon, 'Observations sur un project d'établissement d'une école spéciale de littérature et d'histoire au collège de France' (19 April 1807), *Correspondance de Napoleon Ier*, 32 vols (Paris: Henri Pion and J. Dumaine, 1858-70), Vol.15, pp.102-10.

Bouge, Jean-Baptiste de, *Nouvelle carte chorographique des ci-devant Païs-Bas Autrichiens.* (Brussels: J.C. Maillart, 1794).

Boyen, Hermann von, *Beiträge zur Kenntnis des Generals von Scharnhorst und seiner amtlichen Thätigkeit in den Jahre 1808-1813* (Berlin: Ferdinand Dümmler, 1833).

Brandes, Ernst, 'Ist es den deutschen Staaten vorteilhaft, dass der Adel die ersten Staatsbedienungen besitzt?' *Berlinische Monatsschrift* 10 (1787), pp.395-439.

Brandes, Ernst, *Politische Betrachtungen über die französische Revolution* (Jena: Johann Michael Mauke, 1790).

Brandes, Ernst, *Ueber einige bisherige Folgen der Französischen Revolution in Rücksicht auf Deutschland* (Hanover and Osnabrück: Christian Ritscher, 1793).

Brown, Robert, *An Impartial Journal of a Detachment from the Brigade of Foot Guards, commencing 25th February, 1793, and ending 9th May, 1795* (London: John Stockdale, 1795).

Bülow, Eduard von (ed.), *Aus dem Nachlasse von Georg Heinrich von Berenhorst*, 2 vols (Dessau: Karl Aue, 1845/ 47; reprint ed.; Osnabrück: Biblio Verlag, 1978).

Bülow, Heinrich Dietrich von, *Der Feldzug von 1800* (Berlin: Heinrich Frölich, 1801).

Carlyle, Thomas, *History of Friedrich II of Prussia, called Frederick the Great*, 8 vols (London: Chapman and Hall, 1897/98).

Cassirer, Ernst (ed.), *Immanuel Kants Werke*, 11 vols (Berlin: Bruno Cassirer, 1922/23), Vol 4: *Schriften von 1783-1788.*

Clausewitz, Carl von, 'Ueber das Leben und den Charakter von Scharnhorst', *Historisch-politische Zeitschrift* 1 (1832), pp.175-222.

Clausewitz, Carl von, *Vom Kriege* (Bonn: Ferdinand Dümmler, 1973).

David, Pierre Drapeyron de. *Histoire Chronologique des Opérations de l'Armée du Nord et de celle de Sambre et Meuse* (Paris: T. Baylis, 1796).

Decken, Johann Friedrich von der, 'Sollen wir nur junge Generale haben?' *Neues militärisches Journal* 9 (1798), pp.100-27.

Ekkard, Friedrich, *Allgemeines Register über die Göttingischen gelehrten Anzeigen von 1753 bis 1782* (Göttingen: Johann Christian Dieterich, 1784).

Estorff, Emmerich Otto August von, *Fragmente militairischer Betrachtungen über die Einrichtung des Kriegswesens in mittlern Staaten, in der Muße des Friedens angestellt* (Frankfurt und Leipzig, 1780).

Fenner, Wolfgang (ed.), *Adolph Ludwig Freiherr von Knigge, Ausgewählte Werke*, 10 vols (Hanover: Fackelträger Verlag, 1991-96).

Fichte, Johann Gottlieb. *Beitrage zur Berichtung der Urtheile des Publikums über die französischen Revolution* (Danzig: Troschel, 1793).

Forster, Michael N. (trans. and ed.), *Herder: Philosophical Writings* (Cambridge: Cambridge University Press, 2002).

Friedrich, Reinhold, *Johann Matthias Gesner: Sein Leben und sein Werk* (Roth: Genniges, 1991).

Gatterer, Johann Christoph. *Historisches Journal, von Mitgliedern des königlichen historischen Instituts zu Göttingen*, 16 vols (Göttingen: Witwe Vandenhoeck 1772–81).

Gay de Vernon, Simon François, *Mémoire sur les Opérations Militaire des Généraux en Chef Custine et Houchard, pendant les Années 1792 et 1793* (Paris: Librairie de Firmin Didot Frères, 1844).

George II. 'Edict, gegen die Preussischen und fremden Werber, vom 3./14. Decembr. 1731', *Chur-Braunschweig-Lüneburgische Landes-Ordnungen und Gesetze* (Lüneburg: Sternischen Buchdruckerei, 1742), 2 (Cap. III. Sectio I), pp.117-118.

Grimm, Gunter E. (ed.), *Gottfried August Bürger: Gedichte* (Ditzingen: Reclam, 1997).

Guthke, Karl S. (ed.), *Hallers Literaturkritik* (Tübingen: Max Niemeyer, 1970).

Hahlweg, Werner (ed.), *Schriften-Aufsätze-Studien-Briefe: Dokumente aus dem Clausewitz, Scharnhorst- und Gneisenau-Nachlaß sowie aus öffentlichen und privaten Sammlungen*, 2 vols (Göttingen: Vandenhoeck & Ruprecht, 1966 and 1990).

Harris, James, *Diaries and Correspondence of James Harris, First Earl of Malmesbury*, 3 vols (London: Richard Bentley, 1844).

Hartmann, Major Julius von (ed.), *Der Königlich Hannoversche General Sir Julius von Hartmann: Ein Lebensskizze* (Hanover: Helwing Hofbuchhandlung, 1858).

Hassell, Wilhelm L.A. von, *Das Kurfürstentum Hannover vom Basler Frieden bis zur preussischen Occupation im Jahre 1806* (Hanover: Carl Meyer, 1894).

Hewgill, Edwin (ed.), *The Field Engineer* (London: John Walter, 1789).

Hill, John (trans. and ed.), *A Hanoverian-English Officer: A Hundred Years Ago: Memoirs of Baron von Ompteda* (London: H Grevel and Company, 1892).

Hinske, Norbert (ed.), *Was ist Aufklärung? Beiträge aus der Berlinischen Monatschrift* (Darmstadt: Wissenschaftliche Buchgesellschaft, 1981).

Hogreve, Johann Ludwig. *Praktische Anweisung zur topographischen Vermessung eines ganzen Landes* (Hanover and Leipzig: Johann Wilhelm Schmidt, 1773).

Howard, Michael and Paret, Peter (trans. and ed.), *On War* (Princeton University Press, 1976).

Jones, Lewis Tobias, *An Historical Journal of the British Campaign on the Continent, in the Year 1794; with the Retreat through Holland, in the Year 1795* (Birmingham: Swinney & Hawkins, 1797).

Justi, Johann Heinrich Gottlob von. 'Ueber die von den Deisten vorgegebene Unnötigkeit der christlichen Offenbarungslehre', *Hessische Beiträge zur Gelehrsamkeit und Kunst* 2:1 (1785), pp.5-11.

Lachmann, Karl and Muncker, Franz (ed.), *Gotthold Ephraim Lessings Sämtliche Schriften*, 23 vols (Leipzig: G. J. Göschen'sche Verlagshandlung, 1886-1924).

Lecoq, Karl Ludwig von. *Topographische Karte in 22 Blättern, den größten Theil von Westphalen enthaltend, so wie auch das Herzogthum Westphalen und einen Theil der Hannöverschen, Braunschweigischen und Hessischen Länder, nach astronomischen und trigonometrischen Ortsbestimmungen auf Befehl Sr. Maj. Friedrich Wilhelm III., Königs von Preußen* (Berlin: Carl Zäck, 1805-12).

Loeper, Gustav von (ed.), 'Kampagne in Frankreich 1792', *Goethe Werke*, Band 33 (Weimar: Hermann Böhlaus, 1898).

Lessing, Gotthold Ephraim. *Briefe, die Neueste Literatur betreffend* (Berlin: Friedrich Nicolai, 1759-65).

Lloyd Henry H.E. *Continuation of the History of the Late War in Germany between the King of Prussia and the Empress of Germany and Her Allies* (London, S. Hooper, 1781).

Luvaas, Jay (trans. and ed.), *Frederick the Great on the Art of War* (New York: The Free Press, 1966).

Mancher. Franz X. (ed.), *Ausgewählte Schriften des Erzherzogs Carl von Österreich,* 6 vols (Vienna and Leipzig: Wilhelm Braumüller, 1893-94), Vol.5: *Über den Krieg gegen die Neufranken durch einen österreichischen Offizier.*

Meister, Albrecht Friedrich Ludwig, *Abhandlung von dem Kriegsunterricht und Nachricht von den königlich französischen Kriegsschulen* (Göttingen: Bossiegel, 1766).

Mendelssohn, G.B. (ed.), *Moses Mendelssohn's Gesammelte Schriften,* 7 vols (Leipzig: F.A. Brockhaus, 1843-45).

Mesurier, Havilland le, *The British Commissary* (London C. Roworth, 1801).

Michaelis, Johann David, *Raisonnement über die protestantischen Universitäten in Deutschland,* 4 vols (Frankfurt und Leipzig, 1768-76).

Müffling, Karl Freiherr von, 'Was ist ein Offizer des Generalstabes?' *Magazin der neuesten merkwürdigen Kriegsbegebenheiten,* 7 vols (Frankfurt am Main, 1793-96).

Nicolai, Ferdinand Friedrich von, *Anordnung einer allgemeinen Kriegsschule für alle Waffen* (Stuttgart: Johann Benedikt Mezler, 1781).

Nicolai, Ferdinand Friedrich von, *Versuch eines Grundrisses zur Bildung des Officiers* (Ulm: August Lebrecht Stettin, 1775).

Nisbet, H.B. (trans. and ed.), *Lessing: Philosophical and Theological Writings* (Cambridge: Cambridge University Press, 2005).

Ochwadt, Curd (ed.), *Wilhelm zu Schaumburg-Lippe: Schriften und Briefe,* 3 vols (Frankfurt am Main: Vittorio Klostermann, 1977/83).

Ompteda, [Ludwig] von, 'Hannoversche leichte Grenadiere im Feldzuge von 1793. Nach dem Tagebuche des Lieutenants von Ompteda, vom 1sten Grenadier-Bataillone', *Zeitschrift des historischen Vereins für Niedersachsen* 28 (1862), pp.292-374.

Porbeck, Heinrich Philipp Reinhard von, *Kritische Geschichte der Operationen welche der Englisch-combinirte Armee zur Vertheidigung Holland in den Jahren 1794 und 1795 ausgehürt hat,* 2 vols (Braunschweig: Friedrich Bernhard Culemann, 1802/04).

Preuss, J.D.E. (ed.), *Oeuvres de Frédéric le Grand,* 31 vols (Berlin: Rodolphe Decker, 1846-56), Vol. 30: *Oeuvres militaires de Frédéric II. Roi de Prusse.*

Pütter, Johann Stephan, *Historische Entwickelung der heutigen Staatsverfassung des Teutschen Reichs,* 3 vols (Göttingen: Wittwe Vandenhoeck, 1786-87).

Pütter, Johann Stephan, *Versuch einer akademischen Gelehrtengeschichte von der Georg-Augustus-Universität zu Göttingen,* 2 vols (Göttingen: Wittwe Vandenhoeck, 1765/88).

Puységur, Jacques F. Marquis de, *Art de la Guerre, par Principes et par Règles,* 2 vols (Paris: Charles-Antoine Jombert, 1748).

Randolph, Herbert (ed.), *Life of General Sir Robert Wilson,* 2 vols (London: John Murray, 1862).

Rehberg, August Wilhelm, *Ueber das Verhältnis der Metaphysik zur Religion* (Berlin: August Mylius, 1787).

Rehberg, August Wilhelm, *Ueber den deutschen Adel* (Göttingen: Röwer, 1803).

Rehberg, August Wilhelm, *Untersuchungen über die Französische Revolution, nebst kritischen Nachrichten von den merkwürdigsten Schriften, welche darüber in Frankreich erschienen sind*, 2 vols (Hanover and Osnabrück: Christian Ritscher, 1793).

Robertson, F.W. (ed.), *The Education of the Human Race* (London: Anthroposophical Publishing Company, 1927).

Robins, Benjamin, *New Principles of Gunnery* (London, J. Nourse, 1742).

Schlözer, August Ludwig, *Briefwechsel meist historischen und politischen Inhalts* and *Stats-Anzeigen*, 10 vols (Göttingen: Vandenhoekschen Buchhandlung, 1776-93).

Schmalz, T[heodor], 'Beschreibung der Vestung Wilhelmstein im Steinhuder Meer', *Journal von und für Deutschland* 5 (1788), pp.90-92.

Schmalz, T[heodor], *Denkwürdigkeiten des Grafen Wilhelms zu Schaumburg-Lippe* (Hanover: Helwingisches Hofbuchhandlung, 1783).

Schmidt, James (ed.), *What is Enlightenment? Eighteenth-Century Answers and Twentieth-Century Questions* (Berkeley: University of California Press, 1996).

Stützer, Christian August, 'Charakterisik des Grafen Wilhelms von Lippe-Bückeburg', *Militärischer Kalender auf das Gemein-Jahr 1805* (Berlin: Johann Friedrich Unger, 1805).

Suphan, Berhard (ed.), *Herders Sämmtliche Werke*, 33 vols (Berlin: Weidmann, 1877-1913).

Taylor, Ernest (ed.), *The Taylor Papers, Being a Record of Certain Reminiscences, Letters, and Journals in the Life of Lieut-Gen Sir Herbert Taylor* (London: Longmans, Green and Co., 1913).

Tielke, Johann Gottlieb, *Beyträge zur Kriegs-Kunst und Geschichte des Krieges von 1756-1763*, 6 vols (Freiberg: Samuel Friedrich Barthel, 1775-87).

Tielke, Johann Gottlieb, *Unterricht für die Officiers, die sich zu Feld-Ingenieurs bilden, oder doch den Feldzügen mit Nutzen beywohnen wollen* (Dresden and Leipzig: Johann Nicholaus Gerlach W. und Sohn, 1769).

Trew, Victor Lebrecht von, 'Nachricht von einer zu Hannover errichteten KriegsSchule', *Stats-Anzeigen* 8 (1785), pp.316-17.

Unterberger, Leopold Freiherr von, *Tagebuch der Belagerung und Bombardirung der französischen Festung Valenciennes, durch die Kaiserlichen Königlichen, Königlichen Englischen und Chur-Hannöverischen Truppen, im Monat Junius und Julius, des Jahres 1793* (Vienna: Carl Ferdinand Beck, 1815).

Varnhagen von Ense, Karl August. *Biographische Denkmale*, 5 vols (Berlin: Georg Reimer, 1846-48).

Veltzé, Alois (ed.), *Ausgewaehlte Schriften des Raimund Fürsten Montecuccoli*, 4 vols (Vienna: Wilhelm Braumüller, 1899-1900).

Verney, Sir Harry (ed.), *The Journals and Correspondence of General Sir Harry Calvert, Adjutant-General of the Forces under H.R.H. the Duke of York, Comprising the Campaigns in Flanders and Holland in 1793-4* (London: Hurst and Blackett, 1853).

Zeissberg, Ritter Heinrich von (ed.), *Quellen zur Geschichte der Politik Oesterreichs während der Französiscgen Revolutionskriege (1793-1797)*, 3 vols (Vienna: Wilhelm Braumüller, 1882-90).

Bibliographical Aids and Other Reference Sources

Adler, G.J, *A Dictionary of the German and English Languages* (New York: D. Appleton & Company, 1884).

Allgemeine Deutsche Biographie, 56 vols (Leipzig: Duncker & Humblot, 1875-1912).

Baumgart, Winfried, *Bücherverzeichnis zur deutschen Geschichte: Hilfsmittel-Handbücher-Quellen* (Munich: Deutscher Taschenbuch Verlag, 1982).

Behr, Hans-Joachim, 'Militärgeschichtliche Quellen im Staatsarchiv in Osnabrück', *Militärgeschichtliche Mitteilungen* 10 (1971), pp.159-45.

Bibliographie der deutschen Zeitschriftenliterature, 128 vols (Leipzig and Osnabrück: Felix Dietrich, 1896-1964).

Brockhaus, Eberhard, *Der Sprach-Brockhaus: Deutsches Bildwörterbuch für jedermann* (Wiesbaden: F.A. Brockhaus, 1954).

Deutsch, Ute, *Familienarchive und Nachlässe im Geheimen Staatsarchiv Preußischer Kulturbesitz, Ein Inventar,* Veröffenlichungen aus den Archiven Preußischer Kulturbesitz (Berlin: Selbsverlag des Geheimen Staatsarchivs PK, 2008).

Dupuy, R. Ernst and Trevor N., *Encyclopedia of Military History from 3500 B.C. to the Present* (New York: Harper and Row, 1986).

Ebers, John, *The New and Complete Dictionary of the German and English Languages composed chiefly after the German Dictionaries of Mr. Adelung and Mr. Schwan,* 3 vols (Leipzig: Breitkopf and Haertel, 1796-99).

Eger, Gustav (ed.), *Technological Dictionary in the English and German Languages* (Brunswick: Frederick Vieweg and Son, 1882).

Ekkard, Friedrich, *Allgemeines Register über die Göttingischen gelehrten Anzeigen von 1753 bis 1782* (Göttingen: Johann Christian Dieterich, 1784).

Emmett, Jim (ed.), *The British Library General Catalogue of Printed Books to 1975* (London: Clive Bingley, 1979).

Farrell, R.D., *Dictionary of German Synonyms* (Cambridge: Cambridge University Press, 1977).

Frobenius, H., *Militär-Lexikon. Handwörterbuch der Militärwissenschaften* (Berlin: Martin Oldenbourg, 1901).

Gelbke, Claus-Dieter and Kaufmann, Jens Th., 'Genealogische Übersichten über den Preußischen General und Heeresreformer Gerhard von Scharnhorst' (27. Juni 2010); deposted at the Bordenau Archives.

Genealogisches Handbuch des Adels, 86 vols (Limburg am Lahn: C.A. Starke, 1951-85).

Gieraths, Günther, *Die Kampfhandlungen der Brandenburgisch-Preussischen Armee, 1626-1807, Ein Quellenhandbuch* (Berlin: Walter de Gruyter & Co., 1964).

Griffin, Appleton P.C. (ed.), *A Catalogue of the Washington Collection in the Boston* (Boston: The Boston Athenaeum, 1897).

Haase, Carl, 'Das militärgeschichtliche Archivgut im Niedersächsischen Staatsarchiv in Hannover', *Militärgeschichtliche Mitteilungen* 5 (1969), pp.155-64.

Helmpel, Hermann and Geuss, Herbert (ed.), *Dahlmann-Weitz Quellenkunde der deutschen Geschichte,* 5 vols (Stuttgart: Anton Hiersemann, 1969-80).

Internationale Bibliographie der Zeitschriftenliteratur, 198 vols (Osnabrück: Felix Dietrich, 1964-79).

Jähns, Max. *Geschichte der Kriegswissenschaften vormehrlich in Deutschland*, 3 vols (Munich and Leipzig: R. Oldenbourg, 1889-91; reprint ed. Hildesheim: Georg Ohms, 1966).

Kirchner, Joachim (ed.), *Bibliographie der Zeitschriften des deutschen Sprachgebietes bis 1900*, 3 vols (Stuttgart: Anton Hiersemann, 1969/77).

Kloosterhuis, Jürgen (ed.), *Militär und Gesellschaft in Preußen Quellen zur Militärsozialisation 1713-1806*, 4 vols, Veröffenlichungen aus den Archiven Preußischer Kulturbesitz Arbeitsberichte. (Berlin: Selbsverlag des Geheimen Staatsarchivs PK, 2015).

Kneschke, Ernst Heinrich, *Neues allegemeines deutsches Adels-Lixicon, im Vereine mit mehreren Historikern*, 9 vols (Leipzig: Degner & Co., 1929-30).

Koerner, Bernhard (ed.), *Deutsches Geschlechterbuch. Genealogisches Handbuch Bürgerlicher Familien* (Görlitz: C.A. Starke, 1918).

Konzett, Matthais (ed.), *Encyclopedia of German Literature* (Chicago: Fitzroy Dearborn Publishers, 2000).

McMillin, Teresa S., *Guide to Hanover Military Records, 1516-1816, on Microfilm at the Family History Library* (Inverness, Illinois: Lind Street Research, 2014).

Meier-Weicker, Hans, *Handbuch zur deutschen Militärgeschichte, 1648-1939*, 6 vols (Frankfurt am Main: Bernard & Graefe, 1964-75).

Müller, Kalus, *Absolutismis und Zeitalter der französischen Revolution (1715-1815, Quellenkunde zur deutschen Geschichte der Neuzeit von 1500 bis zur Gegenwart*, Band 3 (Darmstadt: Wissenschaftliche Buchgesellschaft, 1982).

National Park Service, *Manual of Instruction for the Safe Use of Reproduction 18th Century Artillery in Historic Weapons Demonstrations*, n.d.

Neue Deutsche Biographie, 12 vols (Berlin: Dancker & Humboldt, 1952-79).

Neugebauer, Wolfgang, 'Auswahlbibliographie zur preussischen Geschichte', Appendix 2 of *Moderne Preußische Geschichte 1648-1947: Eine Anthologie*, 3 vols (Berllin: Walter de Gruyter, 1981).

Paschmann, Brigitte, 'Das militärgeschichtliche Schriftgut im Niedersächsischen Staatsarchiv in Bückeburg', *Militärgeschichtliche Mitteilungen* 9 (1971), pp.183-85.

Poten, Karl Georg Heinrich Bernhard von, *Handwörterbuch der gesamten Militärwissenschaften*, 9 vols (Bielefeld and Leipzig: Velhagen & Klasing, 1877-80).

Priesdorff, Kurt von, *Soldatisches Führertum*, 10 vols (Hamburg: Hanseat, 1936-42).

Rössler, Helmuth and Franz, Günther (ed.), *Biographisches Wörterbuch zur deutschen Geschichte*, 3 vols (Munich: Francke, 1973-75).

Schöning, Kurd Wolfgang von, *Die Generale der Chur-Brandenburgischen und Königlich Preußischen Armee von 1640-1840* (Berlin: C.G. Lüderitz, 1840).

Showalter, Dennis E., *German Military History, 1648-1982: A Critical Bibliography* (New York: Garland Publishing, 1984).

Stephen, Sir Leslie and Lee, Sir Sidney (ed.), *Dictionary of National Biography*, 22 vols (Oxford: Oxford University Press, 1921-22).

Übersicht über due Bestände des Deutschen Zentralarchives Potsdam. Schriftenreihe des Deutschen Zentralarchive Nr. 1. (Berlin (Ost): Rutten & Leoning, 1957).

Übersicht über die Bestände des Geheimen Staatsarchivs in Berlin-Dahlem, 2 vols (Berlin: G. Grote, 1966/67).

Umbreit, Hans, 'The Development of Official Military Historiography in the German Army from the Crimean War to 1945', in Robin Higham (ed.), *Official Histories: Essays and*

Bibliographies from around the World (Manhattan, KS: Kansas State University Library, 1970).
Verzeichnis der schriftlichen Nachlässe in deutsche Archiven und Bibliotheken, 2 vols, *Schriften des Bundesarchiv* 17 (Boppard am Rhein: Harold Boldt, 1969/71).
Wehler, Hans-Ulrich (ed.), *Deutscher Historiker* (Göttingen: Vandenhoeck & Ruprecht, 1971-82).
Weinberg, Gerhard L, *Guide to Captured German Documents* (Maxwell Air Force Base, AL: Air University Human Resources Research Institute, 1952).

Secondary Sources

Abellán, Mónica Blanco, 'Textbooks on Different Calculus in Eighteenth Century Europe: A Comparative Stylistic Analysis', *Journal of Data Science* 5 (2007), pp. 597-612.
Adler, Hans, and Wulf Koepke (ed.), *A Companion to the Works of Johann Gottfried Herder* (New York: Camden House, 2009).
Anon., 'Anweisung für Officiere aus dem Jahre 1768', *Militär-Wochenblatt* 84:44 (20 May 1899), pp.1173-80.
Anon., 'Art. I. – *Das Leben des Generals Von Scharnhorst.* Von G.H. Klippel. Leipsic: 1870', *The Edinburgh Review* 286 (October 1874), pp.287-321.
Anon., 'Aus Scharnhorsts erster militärischer Dienstzeit', *Militär-Wochenblatt* 101 (3 December 1887), pp.2202-2209.
Arnsberger, Walter, 'Graf Wilhelm zu Schaumburg-Lippe', *Zeitschrift des Historischen Vereins für Niedersachsen* 3 (1902), pp.331-47.
Avant, Deborah, 'From Mercenary to Citizen Armies: Explaining Change in the Practice of War', *International Organisation* 54:1 (Winter 2000), pp.41-72.
Bahn, Rudolf, *Georg Heinrich von Berenhorst, der Vefasser der 'Betrachtungen über die Kriegskunst'* (Halle: Hofbuchdruckerei der Bernburgischen Zeitung, 1911).
Bald, Detlet, 'The Impact of Tradition on the Education of the Military in Germany', *Military Affairs* 45 (October 1981), pp.109-12.
Banaschlik-Ehl, Christa, *Scharnhorsts Lehrer: Graf Wilhelm von Schaumburg-Lippe in Portugal, Studien zur Militärgachichte, Militärwissenschaft und Konfliktsforschung*, Band 3 (Osnabrück: Biblio-Verlag, 1974).
Barker, Thomas M. *The Intellectual and Battle: Raimondo Montecuccoli and the Thirty Years War* (Albany: The State University of New York Press, 1975).
Barnett, Corelli, 'The Education of Military Elites', *The Journal of Contemporary History* 2 (July 1967), pp.15-35.
Bartlett, Keith, *A Most Compete Machine: The Development of the British Army during the War with France, 1793-1815* (Staplehurst: Spellmount Publishers, 2001).
Basier, Otto, *Wehrwissenschaftliches Schriftum im 18. Jahrhundert* (Berlin: E.S. Mittler & Sohn, 1933).
Beiser, Frederick C., *Enlightenment, Revolution, and Romanticism: The Genesis of Modern German Political Thought, 1790-1800* (Cambridge: Harvard University Press, 1992).
Beiser, Frederick C., *The German Historicist Tradition* (Oxford: Oxford University Press, 2011).

Benicken, Friedrich Wilhelm von, *Scharnhorst. Preußens Helden*, Band 1 (Weimer: Wilhelm Hoffmann, 1830).

Berlepsch, Friedrich Ludewig von, *Pragmatische Geschichte des landschaftlichen Finanz-und Steuerwesens der Fürstentümer Galenberg und Göttingen* (Frankfurt und Leipzig, 1799).

Bernal, John Desmond, *Science in History*, 4 vols (Cambridge, MA: MIT Press, 1971).

Berney, Arnold. 'Reichstradition und Nationalstaatsgedanke (1789-1815)', *Historische Zeitschrift* 140 (1929), pp.57-86.

Biskup, Thomas, 'The university of Göttingen and the Personal Union, 1737-1837', in Brenden Simms and Torsten Riotte (ed.), *The Hanoverian Dimension in British History, 1714-1837* (Cambridge: Cambridge University Press, 2007).

Blanning, Thomas Charles William, *The French Revolutionary Wars, 1787-1802* (London: Arnold, 1996).

Blazek, Matthias, *Die Grafschaft Schaumburg 1647–1977: Episoden und Quellensynthese* (Stuttgart: Ibidem, 2011).

Blum, Jerome, 'The Internal Structure and Polity of the European Village Community from the Fifteenth to the Nineteenth Century', *The Journal of Modern History* 43:4 (December 1971), pp.541-76.

Bod, Rens, *A New History of the Humanities: The Search for Principles and Patterns from Antiquity to the Present* (Oxford: Oxford University Press, 2013).

Bödeker, Han Erich, 'The Concept of the Republic in Eighteenth-Century German Thought', in Jürgen Hiedeking and James A. Henretta (ed.), *Republicanism and Liberalism in America and the German State, 1750-1850* (Cambridge: Cambridge University Press, 2004).

Breisach, Ernst, *Historiography: Ancient, Medieval, and Modern* (Chicago: University of Chicago Press, 1994).

Broicher, Andreas, *Gerhard von Scharnhorst: Soldat-Reformer-Wegbereiter* (Aachen: Hedios, 2005).

Brüdermann, Stefan (ed.), *Schaumburg im Mittelalter* (Bielefeld: Verlag für Regionalgeschichte, 2014).

Brühl, Reinhard, 'Scharnhorst und die Erfahrungen der Geschichte', *Revue Internationale d'Historie Militaire* 43 (Potsdam, 1979), pp.9-23.

Bruford, Walter Horace, *Culture and Society in Classical Weimar, 1775-1806* (Cambridge: Cambridge University Press, 1962).

Bruford, Walter Horace, *The German Tradition of Self-cultivation: Bildung from Humboldt to Thomas Mann* (London: Cambridge University Press, 1975).

Buff, Walter, *Gerlach Adolph Freiherr von Münchhausen als Gründer der Universität Göttingen* (Göttingen: Dieterichschen Universitäts-Buchdruckerei, 1937).

Bultmann, Christoph, 'Herder's Biblical Studies', in Hans Adler and Wulf Koepke (ed.), *A Companion to the Works of Johann Gottfried Herder* (New York: Camden House, 2009).

Burne, Alfred H., *The Noble Duke of York: The Military Life of Frederick Duke of York and Albany* (London: Staples Press, 1949).

Büsch, Otto., *Militärsystem und Sozialleben im alten Preußen 1713-1807: Die Anfänge der sozzialen Militärisierung der preußisch-deutschen Gesellschaft* (Berlin: Walter de Gruyter, 1962).

Büschleb, Hermann, *Scharnhorst in Westfalen: Politik, Administration und Kommando im Schicksaljahr 1795* (Herford: E.S. Mittler & Sohn, 1979).

Butler, Eliza Marian, *The Tyranny of Greece Over Germany: A Study of the Influence Exercised by Greek Art and Poetry over the Great German Writers of the Eighteenth, Nineteenth and Twentieth Centuries* (Cambridge: Cambridge University Press, 1935).

Butterfield, Herbert, *Man on His Past* (Cambridge: Cambridge University Press, 1969).

Carrias, Eugène, *La Pensée militaire Allemande* (Paris: Presses Universitaires de France, 1948).

Carsten, F.L., 'Was There an Economic Decline in Germany before the Thirty Years' War?' *The English Historical Review* 71:279 (April 1956), pp.240-47.

Childs, John, *Armies and Warfare in Europe, 1648-1789* (Manchester: Manchester University Press, 1982).

Chuquet, Arthur, *Les Guerres de la Révolution,* 11 vols (Paris: Léon Chailley, 1887-96).

Citino, Robert M., 'Military Histories Old and New: A Reintroduction', *The American Historical Review* 112:4 (October 2007), pp.1070-90.

Citino, Robert M., *The German Way of War: From the Thirty Years War to the Third Reich* (Manhattan: University of Kansas Press, 2005).

Clark, Robert T. Jr., *Herder: His Life and Thought* (Berkeley: University of California Press, 1969).

Cosel, Emil von, *Geschichte des preussischen Staates und Volkes under den Hohenzollernschen Fürsten: Nach den besten Quellen bearbeitet und den Gebildeten aller Stände des preussischen und deutschen Volkes,* 8 vols (Leipzig: Duncker und Humblot, 1869-76).

Coutanceau, Michel Henri Marie; Leplus, Henri; and de la Jonquière, Clément Étienne Lucien Marie de Taffanel, *La campagne de 1794 à l'armée du Nord,* Parts 1and 2 (Paris: R. Chapelot et ce, 1903-08).

Dann, Otto, 'Herder und die Deutsche Bewegung', in Gerhard Sauder (ed.), *Johann Gottfried Herder, 1774*-1803 (Hamburg: Meiner, 1987).

Deike, Ludwig, 'Die Celler Sozietät und Landwirtschaftsgesellschaft von 1764', in Rudolf Vierhaus (ed.), *Deutsche patriotische und gemeinnützige Gesellschaften* (Munich: Klaus International Publications, 1980), pp.161-194.

Delbrück, Hans, *Geschichte der Kriegskunst im Rahman der politischen Geschichte,* 4 vols (Berlin: Georg Stilke, 1900-20).

Demet, Paul, *'We are Accustomed to do our Duty:' German Auxiliaries with the British Army 1793-95* (Warwick: Helion & Company, 2018).

Demeter, Karl, *Das deutsche Heer und seine Offiziere* (Berlin: E.S. Mittler & Sohn, 1930).

Demeter, Karl, *The German Officer-Corps in Society and State, 1650-1945* (New York: Praeger, 1965).

Demeter, Karl, *Scharnhorst und die Freimaurerei* (Hamburg: Akazien-Verlag, 1961).

Dette, Erwin, *Friedrich der Große und sein Heer* (Göttingen: Vandenhoeck & Ruprecht, 1914).

Ditfurth, Maximilian von. *Die Hessen in den Feldzügen 1793, 1794 und 1795 in Flandern, Brabant, Holland und Westphalen.* 2 vols. (Kassel: J. Bohné, 1839).

Duchhardt, Heinz and Espenhorst, Martin (ed.), *August Ludwig (von) Schlözer in Europa* (Göttingen: Vandenhoeck & Ruprecht, 2012).

Duffy, Michael, '"A Particular Service:" The British Government and the Dunkirk Expedition of 1793', *The English Historical Review* 91 (July 1976), pp.529-54.

Dupuis, Victor César Eugène, *La champagne de 1793 à l'Armée du Nord et des Ardennes, de Valenciennes à Hondschoote* (Paris: Librairie Militaire R. Chapelot et Ce, 1906).

Düring, G.W. von, *Geschichte des Schaumburg-Lippe-Bückeburgischen Karbiner-und Jäger-Korps* (Berlin, Posen, und Bromberg: Ernst Siegfried Mittler, 1828).

Dwyer, Philip G., 'Prussia and the Armed Neutrality: The Invasion of Hanover in 1801', *The International History Review* 15:4 (November 1993), pp.661-87.

Ebel, Wilhelm, *Der Göttinger Professor Johann Stephan Pütter aus Iserlohn* (Göttingen: O. Schwartz, 1975).

Eijnatten, Joris van (ed.), *Preaching, Sermon and Cultural Change in the Long Eighteenth Century* (Leiden: Koninklijke Brill, 2009).

Emsley, Clive, 'The Military and Popular Disorder in England, 1790-1801', *Journal for the Society for Army Historical Research* 61:245 (Spring 1983), pp.10-21 and 61:246 (Summer 1983), pp.96-112.

Epstein, Klaus, *The Genesis of German Conservatism* (Princeton: Princeton University Press, 1966).

Estorff, Ludwig von, 'Von der hannoverschen Armee in den Revolutionskriegen 1793-1795', *Zeitschrift des historischen Vereins für Niedersachsen* (1906), pp. 49-75.

Estorff, Ludwig von, *Scharnhorst und Wir* (Berlin and Leipzig: R. F. Koehler, 1926).

Eystrulid, Lee W., 'The Archduke Carl and the Realities of Habsburg Warfare from 1793-1814: Less Change Then You Thought', Presentation at the 2011 Meeting of the Society for Military History.

Eystrulid, Lee W., 'The Military Principles of the Archduke Carl in the Context of His Intellectual Antecedents and His Military Reality' Presentation at the 2010 Meeting of the Consortium on Revolutionary Europe, 1750-1850.

Falkmann, Rudolf, 'Wilhelm, Graf von Schaumburg-Lippe', *Allgemeine Deutsche Biographie* 43 (1898), pp.202-03.

Fiedler, Siegfried, *Scharnhorst: Geist und Tat* (Herford and Bonn: Maximilian-Verlag, 1963).

Fischer, David Hackett, *The Great Wave: Price Revolutions and the Rhythm of History* (Oxford: Oxford University Press, 1996).

Flügel, Alex, *Bürgerliche Rittergüter: sozialer Wandel und politische Reform in Kursachsen (1680 – 1844)*; in *Bürgertum: Beiträge zur europäische Gesellschaftgeschichte*, Band 16 (Göttingen: Vandenhoeck & Ruprecht, 2000).

Ford, Franklin L., 'The Revolutionary-Napoleonic Era: How Much of a Watershed?' *The American Historical Review* 69:1 (October 1963), pp.18-29.

Ford, Guy Stanton, *Hanover and Prussia 1795-1803: A Study in Neutrality* (New York: The Columbia University Press, 1903).

Fortescue, Sir John W., *British Campaigns in Flanders, 1690-1794, Being Extracts From 'A History of the British Army'* (London: Macmillan and Company, 1918).

Fox, Richard W., 'Conservative Accommodation to Revolution: Friedrich von der Decken and the Hanoverian Military Reform, 1789-1820: An Inquiry into the Role of the Military in State and Society' (Ph.D. Thesis, Yale University, 1972).

Freedman, Jeffrey, *A Poisoned Chalice* (Princeton: Princeton University Press, 2002).

Frevert, Ute, *A Nation in Barracks: Conscription, Military Service and Civil Society in Modern Germany* (New York: Berg, 2004).

Frevert, Ute, 'Die bürgerlichen Meisterdenker und das Geschlechterverhältnis: Konzepte, Erfahrungen, Visionen an der Wende vom 18. zum 19. Jahrhuntert', in Ute Frevert (ed.), *Bürgerinnen und Bürger* (Göttingen: Vandenhoeck & Ruprecht, 1988), pp.17-48.

Friedrich, Reinhold, *Johann Matthias Gesner: Sein Leben und sein Werk* (Roth: Genniges, 1991).

Fuchs, Thomas and Kandolf, Ulrich, 'Die Wehrbereichsbibliothek II und ihre Vorgängerinstitutionen', in *Die Wehrbereichsbibliothek II (Hannover)* (Hameln: Niedersächsischen Landesbibliothek, 2004), pp.169-76.

Fuller, John Frederick Charles, *A Military History of the Western World*, 3 vols (New York: Funk & Wagnalls Company, 1954-56).

Gaertner, Franz von, *Scharnhorst: Weg und Werk, Seine Bedeutung für die Gegenwart* (Munich: R. Oldenbourg, 1954).

Gagliardo, John G., *Germany Under the Old Regime, 1600-1790* (London: Taylor and Francis, 1991).

Galéra, Karl Siegmar Freiherr von, *Vom Reich zum Rheinbund: Weltgeschichte des 18. Jahrhunderts in einer kleinen Residenz* (Neustadt an der Aisch: Degener & Company, 1961).

Gat, Azar, *The Origins of Military Thought: From the Enlightenment to Clausewitz* (Oxford: The Clarendon Press, 1989).

Gay, Peter, *The Enlightenment: An Interpretation*, 2 vols (New York: W.W. Norton & Company, 1966/69).

Gierl, Martin, *Geschichte als präzisierte Wissenschaft: Johann Christoph Gatterer und die Historiographie des 18. Jahrhunderts im ganzen Umfang* (Stuttgart: Frommann Holzboob Verlag, 2012).

Gierl, Martin, 'Kommunikation, Institution und Fach: die *Allgemeine historische Bibliothek* und das *Historisches Journal* Johann Christoph Gatterers und die Entwicklung von Fachzeitschriften in der Geschichteswissenschaft', in Hölscher, Steffen and Schlitte, Sune Erik (ed.), *Kommunikation im Zeitalter der Personalunion (1714-1837): Prozesse, Praktiken, Akteure* (Göttingen: V&R Unipress, 2014), pp.155-82.

Gillispie, Charles C., 'Bernard Forêt de Bélidor', *Complete Dictionary of Scientific Biography* (Detroit: Charles Scribner's Sons, 2008).

Goerlitz, Walter, *Scharnhorst, Bedeutende Niedersächsische Lebensbilder* 1 (Hanover: Niedersächsische Landeszentrale für Heimatdienst, 1955).

Gooch, George P., *Germany and the French Revolution* (New York: Longmans, Green, and Company, 1920).

Graupenstein, Wilhelm, *Geschichte der St Johannis-Loge zur goldenen Kugel in Hamburg* (Hamburg: F. W. Wulff, 1870).

Groβer Generalstab, Abteilung für Kriegsgeschichte, *Pirmasens and Kaiserlautern: Eine Erinnerung an das Jahr 1793, Kriegsgeschichtliche Einzelschriften* 16 (Berlin: Ernst Siegfried Mittler und Sohn, 1893).

Grotefeld, Georg Friedrich, *Geschichte des Lyceums der Königlichen Residenz-Stadt Hannover während des Zeitraums von 1773 bis 1833* (Hanover: Brüder Jänecke, 1833).

Grubmüller, Klaus (ed.), *1050 Jahre Göttingen: Streiflicher auf die Göttinger Stadtgeschichte,* (Göttingen: Wallstein Verlag, 2004).

Gudmundsson, Bruce, 'The Education of the Enlightened Soldier', *Marine Corps University Journal* 9:1 (2018), pp.33-44.

Guthke, Karl S. (ed.), *Hallers Literaturkritik* (Tübingen: Max Niemeyer, 1970).

Hasse, Carl, *Ernst Brandes 1758-1810*, 2 vols (Hildesheim: August Lax Verlag, 1973-74).

Hahlweg, Werner, *Preußische Reformzeit und revolutionärer Krieg, Wehrwissenschaftlichen Rundschau*, Beiheft 18 (September 1962).

Hartmann, R., *Geschichte der Residenzstadt Hannover von den ältesten Zeiten bis auf die Gegenwart* (Hanover: Ernst Kniep, 1880).

Hauptmeyer, Carl-Hans, *Calenberg: Geschichte und Gesellschaft einer niedersächsischen Landschaft* (Hanover: Fackelträger, 1983).

Hauptmeyer, Carl-Hans, 'Die Bauernunruhen in Schaumburg-Lippe 1784-1793', *Niedersächsisches Jahrbuch für Langesgeschichte*, Band 49 (Hildesheim: August Lax,1977), pp. 149-207.

Haym, Rudolf, *Herder nach seinem Leben und seinen Werken* (Berlin: Rudolph Gaertner, 1880).

Haye, Thomas, 'Göttingens Ruhm in der Dictung des Johann Matthias Gesner (1691-1761)', in Klaus Grubmüller (ed.), *1050 Jahre Göttingen: Streiflicher auf die Göttinger Stadtgeschichte* Göttingen: Wallstein Verlag, 2004), pp.48-77.

Hayworth, Jordan R., 'Conquering the Natural Frontier: French Expansion to the Rhine River during the War of the First Coalition, 1792-1797', (Ph.D. Thesis, University of North Texas, 2015).

Hayworth, Jordan R., *Revolution France's War of Conquest in the Rhineland: Conquering the Natural Frontier, 1792-1797* (Cambridge: Cambridge University Press, 2019).

Hennies, Werner, *Die politische Theorie August Ludwig von Schlözers zwischen Aufklärung und Liberalismus* (Munich: Tuduv Studien, 1985).

Hewitson, Mark, 'Princes' Wars, Wars of the People, or Total War?: Mass Armies and the Question of a Military Revolution in Germany, 1792-1815', *War in History* 20:4 (November 2013), pp.452-90.

Hiedeking, Jürgen, and James A. Henretta (ed.; with the assistance of Peter Becker), *Republicanism and Liberalism in America and the German State, 1750-1850* (Cambridge: Cambridge University Press, 2004).

Hintzsche, Erich, 'Einige kritische Bemerkungen zur Bio- und Ergographie Albrecht von Hallers', *Gesnerus* 16 (1959), pp.1-15.

Höhn, Reinhard, *Revolution-Heer-Kriegsbild* (Darmstadt: L.C. Wittich, 1944).

Höhn, Reinhard, *Scharnhorst: Soldat-Staatsmann-Erzieher* (Munich: Bernard & Graefe, 1981).

Höhn, Reinhard, 'Scharnhorsts Gedanken zum Koalitionskrieg', *Vielvölkerheere und Koalitionskriege*, Auslandsforschung, Heft 1 (Darmstadt: C.W. Leske, 1952).

Höhn, Reinhard, *Scharnhorsts Vermächtnis* (Bonn: Athenäum Verlag, 1952).

Hofschroer, Peter, *The Hanoverian Army of the Napoleonic Wars* (London: Osprey, 1989).

Hohrath, Daniel, *Die Bildung des Offiziers in der Aufklärung: Ferdinand Friedrich von Nicolai (1730-1814) und seine Enzyklopädischen Sammlungen* (Stuttgart: Württembergische Landesbibliothek, 1990).

Hohrath, Daniel, 'Spätbarocke Kriegspraxis und aufgeklärte Kriegswissenschaften: Neue Forschungen und Perspektiven zu Krieg und Militär im 'Zeitalter der Aufklärung', *Aufklärung* 12:1: 'Die Kriegskunst im Lichte der Vernunft: Militär und Aufklärung im 18. Jahrhundert' 2 (2000), pp.5-47.

Hölscher, Steffen, and Sune Erik Schlitte (ed.), *Kommunikation im Zeitalter der Personalunion (1714-1837): Prozesse, Praktiken, Akteure*, (Göttingen: V&R Unipress, 2014).
Hornung, Klaus, *Scharnhorst: Soldat-Reformer-Staatsmann, Ein Lebens- und Zeitbild* (Gilching: Driffel-Vowinckel Verlag, 2013).
Hossbach, Friedrich, *Scharnhorst, Der Göttinger Arbeitskreis Schriftenreihe*, Heft 55 (Würzburg: Holzner-Verlag, 1955).
Howard, Michael, 'Jomini and the Classical Tradition', in Howard, Michael (ed.), *The Theory and Practice of War* (New York: Praeger, 1966).
Howard, Thomas Albert, *Protestant Theology and the Making of the Modern German University* (Oxford: Oxford University Press, 2006).
Hubatsch, Walter, *Frederick the Great of Prussia: Absolutism and Administration* (London: Thames & Hudson, 1975).
Hübinger, Erich, *Graf Wilhelm zu Schaumburg-Lippe und seine Wehr: Die Wurzeln der allgemeinen Wehrflicht in Deutschland* (Leipzig: Robert Noske, 1937).
Hughes, Daniel J., 'Abuses of German Military History', *Military Review* 66 (December 1986), pp.66-76.
Huntington, Samuel P., *The Soldier and the State: The Theory and Politics of Civil-Military Relations* (Cambridge, MA: Harvard University Press, 1956).
Ingrao, Charles, 'The Problem of "Enlightened Absolutism" and the German States', *The Journal of Modern History* 58, Supplement: Politics and Society in the Holy Roman Empire, 1500-1806 (December 1986), pp.161-80.
Ireton, Sean and Caroline Schaumann (ed.), *Heights of Reflection: Mountains in the German Imagination from the Middle Ages to the Twenty-First Century* (New York: Camden House, 2012).
Irvine, Dallas D., 'The French and Prussian Staff Systems before 1870', *Journal of the American Military Foundation* 2 (1938), pp.192-203.
Irvine, Dallas D., 'The Origins of Capital Staffs', *Journal of Modern History* 10 (1938), pp. 161-79.
Jacob, Margaret C., *The Radical Enlightenment: Pentheists, Freemasons and Republicans* (Lafayette, Louisiana: Conerstone Book Publishers, 2006).
Jany, Curt, *Geschichte der Königliche Preussische Armee*, 4 vols (Berlin: Karl Siegismund, 1929).
Jarrett, Nathaniel W., 'The Enemy of My Enemy is What, Exactly? The British Flanders Expedition of 1793 and Coalition Diplomacy' (M.A. Thesis, University of North Texas, 2013).
Kahn, David, 'The Prehistory of the General Staff', *The Journal of Military History* 71 (April 2007), pp.499-504.
Kafer, Frank A., 'Diderot's Encyclopedia: A Call to Reason or to Arms', *The Historian* 25:2 (February 1963), pp.151-71.
Kelletat, Alfred, *Der Göttinger Hain* (Stuttgart: Reclam, 1967).
Kerry, Paul E., and Matthew S. Holland (ed.), *Benjamin Franklin's Intellectual World* (Madison, NJ: Fairleigh Dickinson University Press, 2012).
Kessel, Eberhard, 'Georg Heinrich von Berenhorst: Ein Anhaltinischer Theoretiker und Geschichtsschreiber der Kriegskunst am Ende des 18. Jahrhunderts', *Sachsen und Anhalt: Jahrbuch der Histroischen Kommission für Sachsen-Anhalt Halle* 9 (1933), pp.161-98.

Kiefert, HansJoachim, 'Zur Geschichte der Militärbibliotheken in Hannover', *Hannoversche Geschichtsblätter* Neue Folge 17:4 (1963), pp.281-324.

Klein, Hans Heinrich, *Wilhelm zu Schaumburg-Lippe: Klassiker der Abschreckungstheorie und Lehrer Scharnhorsts, Studien zur Militärgeschichte, Militärwissenschaft und Konfliksforschung*, Band 28 (Osnabrück: Biblio Verlag, 1982).

Kelletat, Alfred, *Der Göttinger Hain* (Stuttgart: Reclam, 1967).

Kessel, Eberhard, 'Die Wandlung der Kriegskunst im Zeitalter der französischen Revolution', *Historische Zeitschrift* 148 (1933), pp.248-76.

Kiley, Kevin F., *Artillery of the Napoleonic Wars: Field Artillery, 1792-1815* (Yorkshire: Frontline Books, 2015).

Klippel, Georg Heinrich, *Das Lebens des General von Scharnhorst*, 3 vols (Leipzig: F.A. Brockhaus, 1869/71).

Kohn, Hans, 'Romanticism and the Rise of German Nationalism', *Review of Politics* 12 (1950), pp.443-72.

Kohn, Hans, 'The Eve of German Nationalism, 1789-1812', *Journal of the History of Ideas* 12 (1951), pp.256-84.

Kopperman, Paul E., '"The Cheapest Pay": Alcohol Abuse in the Eighteenth-Century British Army', *Journal of Military History* 60:3 (July 1996), pp.445-70.

Koselleck, Reinhard, *Critique and Crises: Enlightenment and the Pathogenesis of Modern Society* (Cambridge, MA: MIT Press, 1988).

Kraul, Margret, 'Bildung und Bürgerlichkeit', in Kocka, Jurgen (ed.), *Bürgertum im 19. Jahrhundert: Deutschland im europäishcen Vergleich*, 3 vols (Munich: Deutscher Taschenbuch Verlag, 1988), Vol.3, pp.45-73.

Kraus, Hans-Christof, *Theodor Anton Heinrich Schmalz (1760-1831): Jurisprudenz, Universitätspolitik und Publizistik im Spannungsfeld von Revolution und Restauration* (Frankfurt am Main: Vittorio Klostermann Verlag, 1999).

Krieger, Leonard, *The German Idea of Freedom: History of a Political Tradition* (Chicago: University of Chicago, 1972).

Krüger, Gerhard, *... gründeten aus unsere Freiheit: Spätaufklärung, Freimaurerei, preussisch-deutsche Reform, der Kampf Theodor von Schöns gegen die Reaktion* (Hamburg: Bauhütten Verlag, 1978).

Kunisch, Johannes, 'Das 'Puppenwerk' der Stehenden Heere: Ein Beitrag zur Neueinschätzung von Soldatenstand und Krieg in der Spätaufklärung', *Zeitschrift für Historische Forschung* 17:1 (1990), pp.49-83.

Kunisch, Johannes, 'Friedensidee und Kriegshandwerk im Zeitalter der Aufklärung', *Der Staat* 27:4 (1988), pp.547-568.

Kyte, George W., 'Frederick the Great and the Development of the Prussian Army', *The Historian* 5:1 (Autumn 1942), pp.24-32.

Lauer, Reinhard (ed.), *Philologie in Göttingen: Sprach- und Literaturwissenschaft an der Georgia Augusta*, (Göttingen: Vandenhoeck und Ruprecht, 2001).

La Vopa, Anthony J., 'Conceiving a Public: Ideas and Society in Eighteenth-Century Europe', *Journal of Modern History* 64 (March 1992), pp.79-116.

La Vopa, Anthony J., 'Herder's *Publikum*: Language, Print, and Sociability in Eighteenth-Century Germany', *Eighteenth-Century Studies* 29:1 (1995), pp.5-24.

La Vopa, Anthony J., 'The Revelatory Moment: Fichte and the French Revolution', *Central European History* 22:2 (June 1989), pp.130-59.

Legaspi, Michael C., *The Death of Scripture and the Rise of Biblical Studies* (Oxford: Oxford University Press, 2010).

Leggiere, Michael V., *Blücher: Scourge of Napoleon* (Norman, OK: University of Oklahoma Press, 2014).

Leggiere, Michael V., Review of Vol.1 of *Gerhard von Scharnhorst, Private und Dienstliche Schriften, The Journal of Military History* 67:4 (2003), pp.1284-1285.

Lehmann, Max, *Scharnhorst,* 2 vols (Leipzig: S. Hirzel, 1886/87).

Lehmann, Max, 'Scharnhorsts Kampf für die stehenden Heere', *Historische Zeitschrift* 116 (1922), pp.254-89.

Lessing, Kurt, *Rehberg und die französische Revolution* (Freiburg: Bielenfels, 1910).

Levinger, Matthew, *Enlightened Nationalism: The Transformation of Prussian Political Culture, 1806-1848* (Oxford: Oxford University Press, 2000).

Limm, Andrew Robert, 'Fairly Out-Generaled and Disgracefully Beaten: The British Army in the Low Countries, 1793-1814', (Ph.D. Thesis, University of Birmingham, 2015).

Limm, Andrew Robert, *Walcheren to Waterloo: The British Army in the Low Countries during the French Revolutionary and Napoleonic Wars 1793-1815* (South Yorkshire: Pen & Sword Military, 2018).

Lundgreen, Peter, *Sozial-und Kulturgeschichte des Bürgertums* (Göttingen: Vandenhoeck & Ruprecht, 2000).

Lynn, John A., *Bayonets of the Republic: Motivations and Tactics in the Army of Revolutionary France, 1791-94* (Chicago and Urbana: University of Illinois Press, 1984).

Lynn, John A., 'The Treatment of Military Subjects in Diderot's *Encyclopédie*', *Journal of Military History* 65:1 (January 2001), pp.131-65.

Maack, Walter, *Die Geschichte der Grafschaft Schaumburg* (Rinteln: Bösendahl, 1986).

Maehl, William H., *Germany in Western Civilization* (University, AL: University of Alabama Press, 1977).

Matzke, Heike, 'Die Bibliothek des Grafen Wilhelm zu Schaumburg-Lippe (1724-1777): Annäherung an die Persönlichkeit eines Landesherren des 18. Jahrhunderts durch die Rekonstrucktion seiner Büchersammlungen', Diplomarbeit im Studiengang Bibliothekswesen an der Fachhochschule Hannover-Wunstorf, 2003.

McClelland, Charles E., *State, Society, and University in Germany, 1700-1914* (Cambridge: Cambridge University Press, 1980).

Mears, John A., 'Count Raimondo Montecuccoli: Servant of a Dynasty', *The Historian* 32 (1970), pp.392-409.

Meinecke, Friedrich, *Historicism: The Rise of a New Historical Outlook* (New York: Herder and Herder, 1972).

Meinecke, Friedrich, *The Age of German Liberation, 1795-1815* (Berkeley: University of California Press, 1977).

Melton, James Van Horn, 'From Enlightenment to Revolution: Hertzberg, Schlözer, and the Problem of Depostism in the late Aufklärung', *Central European History* 12:2 (June 1979). pp.103-23.

Melton, James Van Horn, *The Rise of the Public in Enlightenment Europe* (Cambridge: Cambridge University Press, 2001).

Moeller, Bernd, 'Johann Lorenz von Mosheim und die Gründung der Göttinger Universität', in Moeller, Bernd (ed.), *Theologie in Göttingen: Eine Vorlesungsreihe* (Göttingen: Vandenhoeck & Ruprecht, 1987), pp.9-40.

Mohr, Thorsten, 'Johann Beckmann: Leben, Werk, Wirkung', (M.A. Thesis, Universität Karisruhe (TH): Institut für neuere und neueste Geschichte, 2004).

Nef, John U., *War and Human Progress: An Essay on the Rise of Industrial Civilization* (New York: W.W. Norton & Company, 1963).

Niemeyer, Joachim and Georg Ortenburg, *Die Hannoversche Armee 1780-1803,* Teil 2: *Das 'Grmundener Prachtwerk'* (Beckum: Bernh. Vogel, 1981).

Ochwadt, Curd, *Wilhelmstein und Wilhelmsteiner Feld: Vom Werk des Grafen Wilhelm zu Schaumburg-Lippe (1724-1777)* (Hanover: Charis Verlag, 1978).

Ochwadt, Curd, *Voltaire und die Grafen zu Schaumburg-Lippe* (Bremen and Wolfenbüttel: Jacobi Verlag, 1977).

Oliveira, Agamenon Rodrigues Eufrásio. 'Lazare Carnot and the Birth of Machines Science', in Pisano, Raffaele (ed.), *A Bridge Between Conceptual Frameworks: Sciences, Society and Technology Studies* (London: Springer, 2015), pp.367-83.

Opitz, Eckhard, *Gerhard von Scharnhorst: Vom Wesen und Wirken der preußischen Heeresreform - Ein Tagungsband* (Bremen: Edition Temmen, 1998).

Oppermann, Heinrich Albert, *Die Göttinger gelehrten Anzeigen während einer hundertjährigen Wirksamkeit für Philosophie, schöne Literatur, Politik und Geschichte* (Hanover: C.F. Kius, 1844).

Overhoff, Jürgen, 'Benjamin Franklin, Student of the Holy Roman Empire: His Summer Journey to Germany in 1766 and His Interest in the Empire's Federal Constitution', *German Studies Review* 34:2 (May 2011), pp.277-86.

Palmer, Robert R., 'Frederick the Great, Guibert, Bülow: From Dynasty to National War', in Edward Mead Earle (ed.), *Makers of Modern Strategy: Military Thought from Machiavelli to Hitler* (Princeton: Princeton University Press, 1971).

Palmer, Robert R., 'Much in Little: The Dutch Revolution of 1795', *Journal of Modern History* 26:1 (March 1954), pp.15-35.

Paret, Peter, 'Clausewitz and the Nineteenth Century', in Michael Howard (ed.), *The Theory and Practice of War* (New York: Praeger, 1966).

Paret, Peter, *Clausewitz and the State* (Oxford: Clarendon Press, 1976).

Paret, Peter, 'Hans Delbrück on Military Critics and Military Historians', *Military Affairs* 30 (1966), pp.148-52.

Paret, Peter, *Yorck and the Era of Prussian Reform, 1807-1815* (Princeton: Princeton University Press, 1966).

Peters, Martin, *Altes Reich und Europa: Der Historiker, Statistiker und Publizist August Ludwig (v.) Schlözer (1735-1809)* (Münster: LIT Verlag, 2005).

Piirimäe, Eva, 'Dying for the Fatherland: Thomas Abbt's Theory of Aesthetic Patriotism', *History of European Ideas* 35:2 (2009), pp.194-208.

Poten, Karl Georg Heinrich Bernhard von, 'Die Generale der Königlich Hannoverischen Armee und ihrer Stammtruppen', *Beihefte zum Militär-Wochenblatt* (1903), pp.243-334.

Poten, Karl Georg Heinrich Bernhard von, 'Estorff, Emmerich Otto August von', *Allgemeine Deutsche Biographie* 48 (1904), pp.434-35.

Poten, Karl Georg Heinrich Bernhard von, 'Freytag, Heinrich Wilhelm von', *Allgemeine Deutsche Biographie* 7 (1878), pp.374-76.

Poten, Karl Georg Heinrich Bernhard von, 'Hammerstein, Freiherr Rudolf von', *Allgemeine Deutsche Biographie* 10 (1879), pp.492-93.

Poten, Karl Georg Heinrich Bernhard von, 'Nicolai, Ferdinand Friedrich von, *Allgemeine Deutsche Biographie* 23 (1886), pp.579-80.

Poten, Karl Georg Heinrich Bernhard von, 'Scharnhorst, Gerhard Johann David von', *Allgemeine Deutsche Biographie* 30 (1890), pp.588-97.

Poten, Karl Georg Heinrich Bernhard von, 'Tempelhof, Georg Friedrich von', *Allgemeine Deutsche Biographie* 37 (1894), pp.561-62.

Poten, Karl Georg Heinrich Bernhard von, *Geschichte des Militär-Erziehungs-und Bildungswesen in den Landen deutscher Zunge* 2: *Hannover, Hessen-Cassel, Hessen-Darmstadt, Hessen-Hanau, Mecklenburg-Schwerin, Münster, Nassau, Oldenburg, Monumenta Germaniae Paedagogica* Band 17 (Berlin: A. Hofmann, 1891).

Poten, Karl Georg Heinrich Bernhard von, *Geschichte des Militär-Erziehungs-und Bildungswesens in den Landen deutscher Zunge 4: Preussen, Monumenta Germaniae Paedogogica*, Band 17 (Berlin: A. Hofmann, 1896).

Poten, Karl Georg Heinrich Bernhard von, *Geschichte des Militär-Erziehungs-und Bildungswesen in den Landen deutscher Zunge* 5: *Sachsen, Schaumburg-Lippe, Schleswig-Holstein, Schweiz, Königreich Westfalen, Württemberg, Monumenta Germaniae Paedagogica*, Band 17 (Berlin: A. Hofmann, 1897).

Quarthal, Franz, 'Die Hohe Carlsschule', in Christoph Jamme and Otto Pöggeler (ed.), '*O Fürstin der Heimath! Glükliches Stutgard' Politik, Kultur und Gesellschaft im deutschen Südwesten um 1800* (Stuttgart: Klett-Cotta, 1988), pp.35-54.

Quimby, Robert S., *The Background of Napoleonic Warfare: The Theory of Military Tactics in Eighteenth-Century France* (New York: Columbia University Press, 1957; reprint ed., New York: AMS Press, 1968).

Rabb, Theodore R., 'The Effects of the Thirty Years' War on the German Economy', *The Journal of Modern History* 34:1 (March 1962), pp.40-51.

Radbruch, Hans Eberhard, 'From Scharnhorst to Schmidt: The System of Education and Training in the German Bundeswehr', *Armed Forces and Society* 5 (Summer 1979), pp.606-25.

Redekop, Benjamin W., *Enlightenment and Community: Lessing, Abbt, Herder, and the Quest for a German Public* (Montreal: McGill-Queens University Press, 2000).

Redekop, Benjamin W., 'Language, Literature, and the *Publikum*: Herder's Quest for Organic Enlightenment', *History of European Ideas* 14:2 (1992), pp.235-53.

Redekop, Benjamin W., 'Thomas Abbt and the Formation of an Enlightened German "Public,"' *Journal of the History of Ideas* 58:1 (1997), pp.81-103.

Redlich, Fritz, *The German Military Enterpriser and His Work Force: A Study of European Economic and Social History*, 2 vols (Wiesbaden: Franz Steiner, 1964/65).

Reid, Stuart, *The Battle of Minden 1759: The Impossible Victory of the Seven Years War* (Croydon, England: Frontline Books, 2016).

Reill, Peter Hanns, 'Johann Christoph Gatterer', in Hans-Ulrich Wehler (ed.), *Deutscher Historiker*, 9 vols (Göttingen: Vandenhoeck & Ruprecht, 1971-82), 6 (1980), pp.7-22.

Reill, Peter Hanns, 'Ludwig Timotheus Spittler', in Hans-Ulrich Wehler (ed.), *Deutscher Historiker,* 9 vols (Göttingen: Vandenhoeck & Ruprecht, 1971-82), 9 (1982), pp.42-60.

Reill, Peter Hanns, *The German Enlightenment and the Rise of Historicism* (Berkeley: University of California Press, 1975).

Riotte, Torsten, 'George III and Hanover', in Brenden Simms and Torsten Riotte (ed.), *The Hanoverian Dimension in British History, 1714-1837* (Cambridge: Cambridge University Press, 2007), pp.58-85.

Ritter, Gerhard, *Frederick the Great: A Historical Profile* (Berkeley: University of California Press, 1974).

Ritter, Gerhard, *The Sword and the Scepter: The Problem of Militarism in Germany, Vol.1: The Prussian Tradition, 1740-1890* (Coral Gables, FL: University of Miami Press, 1969-73).

Roe, Shirley A., *The Natural Philosophy of Albrecht von Haller* (New York: Arno Press, 1981).

Rössler, Emil F., *Die Gründung der Universität Göttingen: Eine Sammlung Bisher Ungedruckter Entwürfe, Berichte und Briefe* (Göttingen: Verlag von Vandenhoeck und Ruprecht, 1855).

Ropp, Theodore, *War in the Modern World*, New, Revised Edition, with a new Introduction by Alex Roland (Baltimore: The Johns Hopkins University Press, 2000).

Rosenberg, Hans, *Bureaucracy, Aristocracy, and Autocracy: The Prussian Experience, 1660-1815* (Boston: Beacon Press, 1968).

Rosinski, Herbert, *The German Army* (Washington, DC: The Infantry Journal, 1944).

Rosinski, Herbert, 'Scharnhorst to Schlieffen: The Rise and Decline of German Military Thought', *Naval War College Review* 29 (Summer 1976), pp.83-103.

Rothenberg, Gunther, 'Maurice of Nassau, Gustavus Adolphus, Raimondo Montecuccoli, and the "Military Revolution" of the Seventeenth Century', in Peter Paret (ed.), *Makers of Modern Strategy: from Machiavelli to the Nuclear Age* (Princeton: Princeton University Press, 1986).

Rothenberg, Gunther, *Napoleon's Great Adversary: The Archduke Charles and the Austrian Army, 1792-1814* (Bloomington: Indiana University Press,1982).

Sandrone, Stefano, *Brain Renaissance: From Vesalius to Contemporary Neuroscience* (Oxford University Press, 2015).

Schama, Simon, *Patriots and Liberators: Revolution in the Netherlands, 1780-1813* (New York: Vintage Books, 1992).

Schaumann, Caroline, 'From Meadows to Mountaintops: Albrecht von Haller's *Die Alpen*', in Sean Ireton and Caroline Schaumann (ed.), *Heights of Reflection: Mountains in the German Imagination from the Middle Ages to the Twenty-First Century* (New York: Camden House, 2012).

Schiebinger, Londa, *The Mind Has No Sex? Women in the Origins of Modern Science* (Harvard: Harvard University Press, 1989).

Schmidt, James, 'The Question of Enlightenment: Kant, Mendelssohn, and the *Mittwochgesellschaft*', *Journal of the History of Ideas* 50:2 (Apr-Jun 1989), pp.269-91.

Schindel, Ulrich, 'Die Anfänge der Klassischen Philologie in Göttingen', in Reinhard Lauer (ed.), *Philologie in Göttingen: Sprach- und Literaturwissenschaft an der Georgia Augusta* (Göttingen: Vandenhoeck und Ruprecht, 2001).

Schnabel, Franz, *Deutsche Geschichte im 19. Jahrhundert,* 4 vols (Freiburg im Breisgau: Herder & Co., 1947).

Schroeder, Paul W., *The Transformation of European Politics, 1763-1848* (Oxford: The Clarendon Press, 1994).

Schulz, Oliver, 'Die Vorstellungen des Grafen Wilhelm von Schaumburg-Lippe von Rekrutierung, Ausbildung und gesellschaftlicher Rolle militärischer Eliten und ihre Umsetzung in der Militärschule auf der Festung Wilhelmstein', in Gundula Gahlen and Carmen Winkel (ed.), *Militär und Gesellschaft in der Frühen Neuzeit: Themenheft Militärische Eliten in der Frühen Neuzeit* (Potsdam: Universitätsverlag Potsdam, 2010).

Schumacher, Edgar, 'Scharnhorst', *Wissen und Wehr* 3 (1935), pp.132-47.

Schwartzwald, Jack L., *The Rise of the Nation-State in Europe: Absolutism, Enlightenment and Revolution, 1603-1815* (Jefferson, North Carolina: McFarland & Company, 2017).

Schweder, O.F., *Scharnhorsts Leben* (Berlin: E.S. Mittler und Sohn, 1865).

Scott, Samuel F., 'The Regeneration of the Line Army during the French Revolution', *The Journal of Modern History* 42:3 (September 1970), pp.307-330.

Selle, Götz von, *Die Georg-August Universität zu Göttingen 1737-1937* (Göttingen: Vandenhoeck and Ruprecht, 1937).

Sensberg, Patrick Ernst, 'Johann Stephan Pütter aus Iserlohn', in Patrick Ernst Sensberg (ed.), *Die grossen Juristen des Sauerlandes: 22 Biographien herausragender Rechtsgelehrter* (Arnsberg: F.W. Becker, 2002).

Showalter, Dennis E., 'The Prussian Army', in Frederick C. Schneid (ed.), *European Armies of the French Revolution, 1789-1802.* (Norman: University of Oklahoma Press, 2015).

Showalter, Dennis E., *The Wars of Frederick the Great* (London and New York: The Longman Group, 1996).

Sichart, Louis von, *Geschichte der Königlich-Hannoverischen Armee*, 5 vols (Hanover: Hahn Hofbuchhandlung, 1866-71).

Siegrist, Christoph, *Albrecht von Haller* (Stuttgart: J.B. Metzler and Carl Ernst Poeschel, 1967).

Sikora, Michael, 'Scharnhorst und die militärische Revolution', in Johannes Kunisch and Herfried Münkler (ed.), *Die Wiedergeburt des Krieges aus dem Geist der Revolution* (Berlin: Duncker & Humblot, 1999).

Sikora, Michael, ' "Ueber die Veredlung des Soldaten": Positionsbestimmungen zwischen Militär und Aufklärung', *Aufklärung*, 12:1: 'Die Kriegskunst im Lichte der Vernunft: Militär und Aufklärung im 18. Jahrhundert' 1 (1999), pp.25-50.

Simms, Brendan and Torsten Riotte (ed.), *The Hanoverian Dimension in British History, 1714-1837* (Cambridge: Cambridge University Press, 2007).

Skrine, Peter, 'Albrecht von Haller 1708-1777', in Matthais Konzett (ed.), *Encyclopedia of German Literature* (Chicago: Fitzroy Dearborn Publishers, 2000).

Sonntag, Otto, 'Albrecht von Haller on Academics and the Advancement of Science: The Case of Göttingen', *Annals of Science* 32 (1975), pp.379-91.

Sorel, Albert, *L'Europe et la Révolution français,* 8 vols (Paris: Plon, 1885-1904).

Speelman, Patrick J., *Henry Lloyd and the Military Enlightenment of Eighteenth-Century Europe* (Wesport, CT: Greenwood Press, 2002).

Speelman, Patrick J., 'Lippe, Field Marshal Friedrich Wilhelm Ernst, Graf zu Schaumburg (1724-1777)', in Daniel Coetzee and Lee W. Eysturlid (ed.), *Philosophers of War: The Evolution of History's Greatest Military Thinkers* (Santa Barbara: Praeger, 2013).

Srbik, Heinrich Ritter von, *Geist und Geschichte vom deutschen Humanismus bis zur Gegenwart,* 2 vols (Munich: F. Bruckmann, 1950/51).

Ssymank, Paul, *Die Geschichte der Freimaurerei in Göttingen: 1744 bis 1935* (Göttingen, 1935).

Stackelberg, Jürgen von, *Zur geistigen Situation der Zeit der Göttinger Universitätsgründung 1737: Eine Vortragsreihe* (Göttingen: Vandenhoeck and Ruprecht, 1988).

Stadelmann, Rudolf, *Scharnhorst: Schicksal und geistige Welt. Ein Fragment* (Wiesbaden: Limes Verlag, 1952).

Stadelmann, Rudolf, 'Scharnhorst und die Revolution seiner Zeit', *Das Innere Reich* 5 (April-September 1938), pp.44-65.

Stavenhagen, W., 'Die geschichtliche Entwickelung des preussischen Militär-Kartenwesens', *Geographische Zeitschrift* 6:8 (1900), pp.435-449 and 480.

Stroup, John, *The Struggle for Identity in the Clerical Estate: Northwest German Protestant Opposition to Absolutist Policy in the Eighteenth Century* (Leiden: E.J. Brill, 1984).

Stübig, Heinz, *Gerhard von Scharnhorst: preußischer General und Heeresreformer, Studien zu seiner Biographie und Rezeption* (Berlin: LIT Verlag, 2009).

Stübig, Heinz, *Scharnhorst: Die Reform des preußischen Heeres, Persönlichkeit und Geschichte*, Band 131 (Göttingen: Muster-Schmidt Verlag, 1988).

Thiebault, John, *German Villages in Crisis: Rural Life in Hesse-Kassel and the Thirty Years' War, 1580-1720* (New Jersey: Humanities Press International, 1995).

Tiemann, Herman, *Geschichte der Festung Wilhelmstein im Steinhuder Meer* (Stadthagen: Verlag von Heinrich Heine, 1907).

Toellner, Richard, *Albrecht von Haller: Über die Einheit im Denken des letzten Universalgelehrten* (Wiesbaden: F. Steiner, 1971).

Umbach, Maiken, *Federalism and Enlightenment in Germany, 1740-1806* (London: The Hambledon Press, 2000).

Upton, Anthony F., *Charles XI and Swedish Absolutism* (Cambridge: Cambridge University Press, 1998).

Usczeck, Hansjürge,. *Scharnhorst: Theoretiker-Reformer-Patriot* (Berlin (Ost): Militärverlag der Deutschen Demokratischen Republik, 1974).

Usener, Hermann Karl, *Aus der Porträte-Sammlung der Familie Scharnhorst: Anlässlich der Hunderjahrfeier des Regiments von Scharnhorst* (Hanover: Georg Alpers, 1903).

Vagts, Alfred, *A History of Militarism: Civilian and Military* (New York: The Free Press, 1959).

Vermeulen, Han F., *Before Boas: The Genesis of Ethnography and Ethnology in the German Enlightenment* (Omaha: University of Nebraska Press, 2015).

Vierhaus, Rudolf, 'Die Universität Göttingen und die Anfänge der modernen Geschichtswissenschaft im 18. Jahrhundert', in Hartmut Boochmann and Hermann Vellenreuter (ed.), *Geschichtswissenschaft in Göttingen: eine Vorlesungsreihe* (Göttingen: Vandenhoeck & Ruprecht, 1987).

Vierhaus, Rudolf, *Germany in the Age of Absolutism* (Cambridge: Cambridge University Press, 1988).

Wagner, Heinrich, *Geschichte der Hohen Carls-Schule*, 3 vols (Würzburg: C. Etlinger, 1856-58).

Walker, Mack, *German Home Towns: Community, State, and General Estate, 1648-1871* (Ithaca: Cornell University Press, 1998).

Ward, Adolphus William, *Great Britain and Hanover: Some Aspects of the Personal Union* (Oxford: Clarendon Press, 1899).

Watkins, John, *A Biographical Memoir of his late Royal Highness Frederick, Duke of York and Albany; Commander-in-Chief of the Forces of Great Britain, etc. etc. etc.* (London: Henry Fisher, Son, and Co., 1827).

Watson, Peter, *The German Genius: Europe's Third Renaissance, the Second Scientific Revolution, and the Twentieth Century* (New York: Harper Perennial, 2010).

Weigley, Russell F., *The Age of Battles: The Quest for Decisive Warfare from Breitenfeld to Waterloo* (Bloomington: Indiana University Press, 1991).

Weinhold, Karl, *Heinrich Christian Boie: Beitrag zur Geschichte der deutschen Literatur im achtzehnten Jahrhundert* (Halle: Waisenhaus, 1868).

Weissenbach, Strack von, *Regierender Graf Wilhelm zu Schaumburg-Lippe, bezüglich seiner Leistungen als Artillerist, insbesondere im siebenjährigen Kriege: Als Erinnerungsgabe in Kurzen Umrissen zusammengestellt von Strack von Weissenbach* (Ludwigsburg: Greiner & Ungeheuer, 1884).

Wenck, Waldemar, *Deutschland vor hundert Jahren*, 2 vols (Leipzig: Friedrich Wilhelm Grunow, 1887/90).

Wesendonck, Hermann, *Die Begründung der neueren deutschen Geschichtsschreibung durch Gatterer und Schlözer* (Leipzig: Johann Wilhelm Krüger, 1876).

Whaley, Joachim, 'The Protestant Enlightenment in Germany', in Roy Porter and Mikulas Teich (ed.), *The Enlightenment in the National Context* (Cambridge: Cambridge University Press, 1981).

White, Charles Edward, 'Scharnhorst's Mentor: Count Wilhelm zu Schaumburg-Lippe and the Origins of the Modern National Army', *War in History* 24:3 (July 2017), pp.258-85.

White, Charles Edward, 'Setting the Record Straight: Scharnhorst and the Origins of the Nineteenth Century Prussian General Staff', *War in History* (Forthcoming).

White, Charles Edward, *The Enlightened Soldier: Scharnhorst and the Militärische Gesellschaft in Berlin, 1801-1805*. New York: Praeger, 1989.

Willnat, Elisabeth. *Johann Christian Dieterich: ein Verlagsbuchhändler und Drucker in der Zeit der Aufklärung* (Frankfurt am Main: Buchhändler-Vereinigung, 1993).

Wilson, Peter H., *Absolutism in Central Europe* (London: Routledge, 2000).

Wilson, Peter H., 'The German "Soldier Trade" of the Seventeenth and Eighteenth Centuries: A Reassessment', *The International History Review*, 18:4 (November 1996), pp.757-92.

Wilson, Peter H., 'The Politics of Military Recruitment in Eighteenth-Century Germany', *The English Historical Review*, 117:472 (June 2002), pp.536-68.

Wilson, Peter H., *The Thirty Years War: Europe's Tragedy* (Cambridge: Harvard University Press, 2009).

Wilson, Peter H., *War, State and Society in Württemberg, 1677-1793* (Cambridge: Cambridge University Press, 1995).

Willnat, Elisabeth, *Johann Christian Dieterich: ein Verlagsbuchhändler und Drucker in der Zeit der Aufklärung* (Frankfurt am Main: Buchhändler-Vereinigung, 1993).

Winterbottom, Derek, *The Grant Old Duke of York: A Life of Prince Frederick, Duke of York and Albany, 1763-1827* (South Yorkshire: Pen & Sword Military, 2016).

Wishon, Mark, *German Forces and the British Army: Interactions and Perceptions, 1742-1815* (New York: Palgrave Macmillan, 2013).

Wiswall, Dorothy R., *A Companion of Selected Poetic and Scientific Works of Albrecht von Haller* (Bern: Lang, 1981).

Witzleben, August von, *Prinz Friedrich Josias von Coburg-Saalfeld, Herzog zu Sachsen*, 3 vols (Berlin, R. Decker, 1859).

Wolf, Arndt, *Zur Geschichte der Freimaurerei: Die Freimaurerlogen in Göttingen* (Göttingen: Bürger-Archiv, 1997).

Wollstein, Günter, 'Scharnhorst und die französische Revolution', *Historische Zeitschrift* 227 (1978), pp.325-52.

Index

From Reason to Revolution series – Warfare 1721-1815

http://www.helion.co.uk/published-by-helion/reason-to-revolution-1721-1815.html

The 'From Reason to Revolution' series covers the period of military history 1721–1815, an era in which fortress-based strategy and linear battles gave way to the nation-in-arms and the beginnings of total war.

This era saw the evolution and growth of light troops of all arms, and of increasingly flexible command systems to cope with the growing armies fielded by nations able to mobilise far greater proportions of their manpower than ever before. Many of these developments were fired by the great political upheavals of the era, with revolutions in America and France bringing about social change which in turn fed back into the military sphere as whole nations readied themselves for war. Only in the closing years of the period, as the reactionary powers began to regain the upper hand, did a military synthesis of the best of the old and the new become possible.

The series will examine the military and naval history of the period in a greater degree of detail than has hitherto been attempted, and has a very wide brief, with the intention of covering all aspects from the battles, campaigns, logistics, and tactics, to the personalities, armies, uniforms, and equipment.

Submissions

The publishers would be pleased to receive submissions for this series. Please contact series editor Andrew Bamford via email (andrewbamford18@gmail.com), or in writing to Helion & Company Limited, Unit 8 Amherst Business Centre, Budbrooke Road, Warwick, CV34 5WE

Titles

No 1 *Lobositz to Leuthen. Horace St Paul and the Campaigns of the Austrian Army in the Seven Years War 1756-57* Translated with additional materials by Neil Cogswell (ISBN 978-1-911096-67-2)

No 2 *Glories to Useless Heroism. The Seven Years War in North America from the French journals of Comte Maurés de Malartic, 1755-1760* William Raffle (ISBN 978-1-1911512-19-6)

No 3 *Reminiscences 1808-1815 Under Wellington. The Peninsular and Waterloo Memoirs of William Hay* William Hay, with notes and commentary by Andrew Bamford (ISBN 978-1-1911512-32-5)

No 4 *Far Distant Ships. The Royal Navy and the Blockade of Brest 1793-1815* Quintin Barry (ISBN 978-1-1911512-14-1)

No 5 *Godoy's Army. Spanish Regiments and Uniforms from the Estado Militar of 1800* Charles Esdaile and Alan Perry (ISBN 978-1-911512-65-3) (large-format paperback)

No 6 *On Gladsmuir Shall the Battle Be! The Battle of Prestonpans 1745* Arran Johnston (ISBN 978-1-911512-83-7)

No 7 *The French Army of the Orient 1798-1801. Napoleon's Beloved 'Egyptians'* Yves Martin (ISBN 978-1-911512-71-4)*

No 8 *The Autobiography, or Narrative of a Soldier. The Peninsular War Memoirs of William Brown of the 45th Foot* William Brown, with notes and commentary by Steve Brown (ISBN 978-1-911512-94-3)

No 9 *Recollections from the Ranks. Three Russian Soldiers' Autobiographies from the Napoleonic Wars* Translated and annotated by Darrin Boland (ISBN 978-1-912174-18-8)

No 10 *By Fire and Bayonet. Grey's West Indies Campaign of 1794* Steve Brown (ISBN 978-1-911512-60-8)

No 11 *Olmütz to Torgau. Horace St Paul and the Campaigns of the Austrian Army in the Seven Years War 1758-60* Translated with additional materials by Neil Cogswell (ISBN 978-1-911512-72-1)

No 12 *Murat's Army. The Army of the Kingdom of Naples 1806-1815* Digby Smith (ISBN 978-1-912390-09-0)

No 13 *The Veteran or 40 Years' Service in the British Army. The Scurrilous Recollections of Paymaster John Harley 47th Foot – 1798-1838* John Harley, with notes and commentary by Gareth Glover (ISBN 978-1-912390-25-0)

No 14 *Narrative of the Eventful Life of Thomas Jackson. Militiaman and Coldstream Sergeant, 1803-15* Thomas Jackson, with notes and commentary by Eamonn O'Keeffe (ISBN 978-1-912390-12-0)

No 15 *For Orange and the States! The Army of the Dutch Republic 1713-1772. Part I: Infantry* Marc Geerdinck-Schaftenaar (ISBN 978-1-911512-15-8)*

No.16 *'Men who are Determined to be Free': The American Assault on Stony Point 15 July 1779* David Bonk (ISBN 978-1-912174-84-3)*

No 17 *Next to Wellington. General Sir George Murray. The Story of a Scottish Soldier and Statesman, Wellington's Quartermaster General* John Harding-Edgar (ISBN 978-1-912390-13-7)

No 18 *Between Scylla and Charybdis: The Army of Friedrich August II of Saxony, 1733-1763. Part I: Staff and Cavalry* Marco Pagan (ISBN 978-1-912174-89-8)*

No 19 *The Secret Expedition: The Anglo-Russian Invasion of Holland 1799* Geert van Uythoven (ISBN 978-1-912390-20-5)

No 20 *'We Are Accustomed to do our Duty' German Auxiliaries with the British Army 1793-95* Paul Demet (ISBN 978-1-912174-96-6)

No 21 *With the Guards in Flanders. The Diary of Captain Roger Morris 1793-95* Peter Harington (ISBN 978-1-911628-15-6)

No 22 *The British Army in Egypt 1801. An Underrated Army Comes of Age* Carole Divall (ISBN 978-1-911628-17-0)*

No 23 *Better is the Proud Plaid. The Clothing, Weapons, and Accoutrements of the Jacobites in 1745* Jenn Scott (ISBN 978-1-911628-16-3)*

No 24 *The Lilies and the Thistle. French Troops in the Jacobite '45* Andrew Bamford (ISBN 978-1-911628-17-0)*

No 25 *A Light Infantryman With Wellington* Gareth Glover (ed.) (ISBN 978-1-911628-10-1)

No 26 *Swiss Regiments in the Service of France 1798-1815. Uniforms, Organisation, Campaigns* Stephen Ede-Borrett (ISBN 978-1-911628-12-5)*

No 27 *For Orange and the States! The Army of the Dutch Republic 1713-1772. Part II: Cavalry and Specialist Troops* Marc Geerdinck-Schaftenaar (ISBN 978-1-911628-13-2)*

No 28 *Fashioning Regulation, Regulating Fashion. Uniforms and Dress of the British Army 1800-1815 Volume I* Ben Townsend (ISBN 978-1-911628-09-5)

No 29 *Riflemen. The History of the 5th Battalion 60th (Royal American) Regiment, 1797-1818* Robert Griffith (ISBN 978-1-911628-46-0)

No 30 *The Key to Lisbon. The Third French Invasion of Portugal, 1810-11* Kenton White (ISBN 978-1-911628-52-1)

No 31 *Command and Leadership. Proceedings of the 2018 Helion & Company 'From Reason to Revolution' Conference* Andrew Bamford (ed.) (ISBN 978-1-911628-53-8)

No 32 *Waterloo After the Glory. Hospital Sketches and Reports on the Wounded After the Battle* Michael Crumplin and Gareth Glover (ISBN 978-1-911628-48-4)

No 33 *Fluxes, Fevers, and Fighting Men. War and Disease in Ancien Regime Europe 1648-1789* Pádraig Lenihan (ISBN 978-1-911628-51-4)

No 34 *'They Were Good Soldiers'. African-Americans Serving in the Continental Army, 1775-1783* John U. Rees (ISBN 978-1-911628-54-5)*

No 35 *A Redcoat in America. The Diaries of Lieutenant William Bamford, 1757-1765 and 1776* Edited and Annotated by John B. Hattendorf (ISBN 978-1-911628-47-7)

No 36 *Between Scylla and Charybdis: The Army of Friedrich August II of Saxony, 1733-1763. Part II: Infantry and Artillery* Marco Pagan (ISBN 978-1-911628-08-8)*

No 37 *Québec Under Siege: French Eye-Witness Accounts from the Campaign of 1759* Translated and Annotated by Charles A. Mayhood (ISBN 978-1-912866-73-1)

No 38 *King George's Hangman: Henry Hawley and the Battle of Falkirk 1746* Jonathan D. Oates (ISBN 978-1-912866-64-9)

No 39 *Zweybruken in Command: The Reichsarmee in the Campaign of 1758* Translated with additional materials by Neil Cogswell (ISBN 978-1-911628-55-2)*

No 40 *So Bloody a Day: The 16th Light Dragoons in the Waterloo Campaign* David J. Blackmore (ISBN 978-1-912866-66-3)

No 41 *Northern Tars in Southern Waters: The Russian Fleet in the Mediterranean 1806-1810* Vladimir Bogdanovich Bronevskiy, translated and annotated by Darrin Boland (ISBN 978-1-912866-71-7)

No 42 *Royal Navy Officers of the Seven Years War: A Biographical Dictionary of Commissioned Officers 1748-1763* Cy Harrison (ISBN 978-1-912866-68-7)

No 43 *All at Sea. Naval Support for the British Army During the American Revolutionary War* John Dillon (ISBN 978-1-912866-67-0)

No 44 *Glory is Fleeting. New Scholarship on the Napoleonic Wars* Andrew Bamford (ed.) (ISBN 978-1-912866-69-4)

No 45 *Fashioning Regulation, Regulating Fashion. Uniforms and Dress of the British Army 1800-1815 Volume II* Ben Townsend (ISBN 978-1-911628-45-3)

No 46 *Revenge in the Name of Honour. The Royal Navy's Quest for Vengeance in the Single Ship Actions of the War of 1812* Nicholas James Kaizer (ISBN 978-1-912866-72-4)*

No 47 *They Fought With Extraordinary Bravery. The III German (Saxon) Army Corps in the Southern Netherlands 1814* Geert van Uythoven (ISBN 978-1-912866-65-6)*

No 48 *The Danish Army of the Napoleonic Wars 1807-1814, Organisation, Uniforms & Equipment: Volume 1: High Command, Line and Light Infantry* David Wilson (ISBN 978-1-913118-91-4) (large-format paperback)

No 49 *Neither Up Nor Down: The British Army and the Flanders Campaign 1793-1895* Phillip Ball (ISBN 978-1-913118-90-7)

No 50 *Guerra Fantastica: The Portuguese Army and the Seven Years War* António Barrento (ISBN 978-1-911628-11-8)*

No 51 *From Across the Sea: North Americans in Nelson's Navy* Sean M. Heuvel and John A. Rodgaard (eds) (ISBN 978-1-913118-92-1)

No 52 *Rebellious Scots to Crush: The Military Response to the Jacobite '45* Andrew Bamford (ed.) (ISBN 978-1-912866-74-8)

No 53 *The Army of George II 1727-1760: The Soldiers who Forged an Empire* Peter Brown (ISBN 978-1-913118-96-9)*

No 54 *Wellington at Bay: The Battle of Villamuriel, 25 October 1812* Garry David Wills (ISBN 978-1-913118-95-2)*

No 55 *Life in the Red Coat: The British Soldier 1721-1815. Proceedings of the 2019 Helion & Company 'From Reason to Revolution' Conference* Andrew Bamford (ed.) (ISBN 978-1-913118-94-5)

No 56 *Wellington's Favourite Engineer. John Burgoyne: Operations, Engineering, and the Making of a Field Marshal* Mark S. Thompson (ISBN 978-1-913118-93-8)

No 57 *Scharnhorst: The Formative Years, 1755-1801* Charles Edward White (ISBN 978-1-913118-99-0)

No 58 *At the Point of the Bayonet: The Peninsular War Battles of Arroyomolinos and Almaraz 1811-1812* Robert Griffith (ISBN 978-1-913336-52-3)*

* indicates 'Falconet' format paperbacks, page size 248mm × 180 mm, with high visual content including colour plates; other titles are monographs unless otherwise noted.